Exploring the Humanities

CREATIVITY AND CULTURE IN THE WEST

VOLUME 1

Exploring the Humanities

CREATIVITY AND CULTURE IN THE WEST

VOLUME 1

Laurie Schneider Adams

John Jay College, City University of New York

PEARSON
Prentice Hall

Upper Saddle River, N.J. 07458

Library of Congress Cataloging-in-Publication Data

Adams, Laurie.
   Exploring the humanities : creativity and culture in the West / Laurie Schneider Adams.
      p. cm.
   Includes bibliographical references and index.
   ISBN 0–13–049095–4 (vol. 1)—ISBN 0–13–049087–3 (vol. 2)—ISBN 0–13–049091–1
(combined vol.)
   1. Civilization, Western—History—Textbooks. I. Title.

CB245.A324 2006
909'.09821—dc22

2005043156

Editor in Chief: Sarah Touborg
Acquisitions Editor: Amber Mackey
Editorial Assistant: Keri Molinari
Director of Marketing: Heather Shelstad
Manufacturing Buyer: Ben Smith
Creative Design Director: Leslie Osher
Interior Designer: Wanda Espana

Credits and acknowledgments of material borrowed from other sources and reproduced, with permission, in this textbook appear on pages 398–400.

Published 2006 by Pearson Education, Inc., Upper Saddle River, New Jersey, 07458. Pearson Prentice Hall.
All rights reserved. Printed in Hong Kong. This publication is protected by Copyright and permission should be obtained from the publisher prior to any prohibited reproduction, storage in a retrieval system, or transmission in any form or by any means, electronic, mechanical, photocopying, recording, or likewise. For information regarding permission(s), write to: Rights and Permissions Department.

Pearson Prentice Hall™ is a trademark of Pearson Education, Inc.
Pearson® is a registered trademark of Pearson plc.
Prentice Hall® is a registered trademark of Pearson Education, Inc.

Pearson Education Ltd.
Pearson Education Australia PTY, Ltd.
Pearson Education Singapore, Pte. Ltd.
Pearson Education North Asia Ltd.

Pearson Education, Canada, Ltd.
Pearson Educación de Mexico, S.A. de C.V
Pearson Education–Japan
Pearson Education Malaysia, Pte. Ltd.

This book was designed and produced by Laurence King Publishing Ltd., London

Every effort has been made to contact the copyright holders, but should there be any errors or omissions, Laurence King Publishing Ltd. would be pleased to insert the appropriate acknowledgment in any subsequent printing of this publication.

Commissioning Editor: Melanie White
Editor: Ursula Payne
Copy Editor: Lydia Darbyshire
Picture Researcher: Fiona Kinnear
Layout and Cover Design: Newton Harris Design Partnership, Suffolk
Map Editor: Ailsa Heritage
Maps: Advanced Illustration, Cheshire
Literary Permissions: Nick Wetton
Keyboarding: Marie Doherty

Front Cover: Two figures of Block VI, from the east Parthenon frieze, *c.* 442–438 B.C. Marble, 3 ft. 5¾ in. (1.06 m) high. Acropolis Museum, Athens. Photo © Craig and Marie Mauzy, Athens. mauzy@otenet.gr

Frontispiece: Second Style Roman painting, from the villa at Oplontis, Italy, 1st century B.C. Fresco. Photo © Fotografica Foglia, Naples.

10 9 8 7 6 5 4 3 2 1
ISBN 0–13–049095–4

Contents

Chapter 4: The Aegean World

Chapter 5: The Emergence of Historical Greece

Chapter 6: Ancient Greece: Classical to Hellenistic

Chapter 7: Ancient Rome

Chapter 8: Pagan Cults, Judaism, and the Rise of Christianity

Chapter 9: The Byzantine Empire and the Development of Islam

Chapter 10: The Early Middle Ages and the Development of Romanesque: 565–1150

Chapter 11: The Development and Expansion of Gothic: 1150–1300

Chapter 14: The High Renaissance in Italy and Early Mannerism

Maps

Music Listening Selections

Preface

What are the humanities? Why are they important? And why do we study them? These are significant questions for students at the beginning of the twenty-first century. The humanities, as the term implies, are about what is uniquely human—our art, literature, science, and civilization. We study the humanities because they teach us about our own history. What we learn from our great successes as well as from our colossal failures helps us to confront the tensions of everyday life and gives us insight into ways of shaping our future. In an age of increasing globalization, it is essential that we understand the history of our own civilization and its creative products. Only with that as a foundation does it become possible to gain meaningful insight into other cultures.

In order to provide the most coherent, straightforward, and accessible approach for students, I have organized *Exploring the Humanities: Creativity and Culture in the West* chronologically from prehistory to the present. In the first chapter I cover cave paintings, sculpture, and architecture of prehistory and discuss ideas that shaped our earliest civilizations. The next chapter, the Ancient Near East, is of particular interest because it is there that the earliest evidence of a writing system has been found. It is also there that a number of other "firsts," including cities, evolved. Since it is also important to understand the immediate past, and the recent impact of globalization, the last four chapters contain extended coverage of the twentieth century and the early twenty-first century. While the focus of the text is the West, I believe it is useful to provide students with snapshots of non-Western developments at appropriate points in the historical narrative. These appear in boxes entitled Thematic Parallels and Cross-cultural Influences. The last several chapters of the book also consider works of art and architecture, literature, and film from around the globe.

Exploring the Humanities covers traditional areas of cultural study—painting, sculpture, architecture, music, drama, literature, and history—as well as less frequently featured disciplines such as philosophy and psychology, religion and myth, science and medicine, photography, film, and dance. In all these areas, I explore the humanities as expressions of their time and place.

In my view, it is only by exploring the context of a work of art, a piece of music, an invention or a discovery, that one can understand the dynamic and creative role of the humanities in a civilization. In addition, the humanities are interdisciplinary; they are connected to each other and to society as a whole.

In each chapter of *Exploring the Humanities* I begin with a discussion of historical background and then proceed to discuss key disciplines with particular emphasis on art and literature. Each discipline and each work is presented in the context of its historical period. *Exploring the Humanities* covers significant works by major artists, philosophers, writers, and composers, as well as works by important but lesser-known figures. Later chapters also explore modern media such as photography and film, and genres such as children's literature, detective fiction, and rock music. To appeal to the visual culture of today's students, I have selected over 450 color and 200 black and white illustrations, which are analyzed throughout the text. The illustrations reinforce the narrative and reflect aspects of cultural and artistic development. Descriptive captions accompanying many of the images provide additional information about their style, content, and cultural significance. In the literature sections, I have included short excerpts from key works of poetry, prose, and theater to illustrate the author's style and point of view.

Exploring the Humanities is intended to engage students in the relevance of the humanities in today's world. To this end, the book includes in-text pedagogy—such as timelines, maps, and feature boxes—as well as linking with a range of different resources produced by the publisher. These features, together with diagrams and reproductions of major works of art and architecture, make this a user-friendly survey of the Western humanities and one that, I hope, will remind students of their own participation in the creative aspects of their lives and of their cultural history.

Laurie Schneider Adams
May 2005

Acknowledgments

Author's Acknowledgments

A number of scholars have been extremely helpful in lending their expertise to parts of this text. Oscar Muscarella (at the Metropolitan Museum of Art) reviewed the Ancient Near East chapter and Larissa Bonfante (Professor of Classics at New York University) reviewed and sections on Etruscan and Roman art; Kara Hattersley-Smith checked the Byzantine chapter, Carol Lewine (emerita, Queens College, CUNY) read the medieval chapters. Norman Harrington (emeritus, Brooklyn College, CUNY) reviewed sections on medieval literature. Mary Wiseman (emerita, Brooklyn College, CUNY, and the Graduate Center) and Professor Mark Zucker (Louisiana State University) stood ready to answer queries on philosophy and the Renaissance, respectively. I am grateful to Peter Manuel (Professor of Music, John Jay College, CUNY, and the Graduate Center), Jenny Doctor (University of York), and Ursula Sadie Payne, who devoted a great deal of time to improving the sections on music.

I would like to thank all those at Laurence King Publishing Ltd. who were involved in this project for their creative approach to the text and their tireless work. Lee Greenfield supported the project from its inception; Melanie White's valuable input and patient persistence improved the text at all stages of its development; Ursula Sadie Payne efficiently managed the text from manuscript to completion; Lydia Darbyshire copyedited with great skill; Sue Bolsom and Fiona Kinnear did a wonderful job of picture research; and Nick Newton and Randell Harris did excellent work in laying out the book.

At Prentice Hall, Bud Therien, Sarah Touborg, and Amber Mackey encouraged the project from the beginning, and I am also grateful to the development editors Harriett Prentiss and Margaret Manos, who helped organize the text.

Publishers' Acknowledgments
* Advisers
The publishers would like to acknowledge the following academics who advised on the text: Barbara Kramer (Santa Fe Community College) for her extensive reviewing of the manuscript and her significant contribution to the Key Topics, Key Questions, and Defining Moment boxes; Judith Stanford for her valuable input on literature; Peter Manuel (John Jay College, CUNY, and the Graduate Center) for his advice on music; Peter Brand (University of Memphis); Henry E. Chambers (California State University, Sacramento); Jessica A. Coope (University of Nebraska-Lincoln); Paul B. Harvey, Jr. (Pennsylvania State University); Linda Mitchell (Alfred University); Cybelle Shattuck (Kalamazoo College); Larissa Taylor (Colby College).

* Reviewers
The publishers would also like to thank all those who reviewed the manuscript:
Michael Berberich (Galveston College)
Arnold Bradford (Northern Virginia Community College)
Sarah Breckenridge (Community College at Aurora)
Daniel J. Brooks (Aquinas College)
Ken Bugajski (Rogers State University)
Charles Carroll (Lake City Community College)
Judith Cortelloni (Lincoln College)
Anthony F. Crisafi (University of Central Florida)
Eugene Crook (Florida State University)
Cynthia Donahue (Brevard Community College)
Frank Felsenstein (Ball State University)
Samuel Garren (North Carolina A. & T. State University)
Sharon Gorman (University of the Ozarks)
J. Keith Green (East Tennessee University)
Blue Greenberg (Meredith College)
Craig Hanson (Muskingum College)
Robin Hardee (South Florida Community College)
Viktoria Hertling (University of Nevada Reno)
Bobby Hom (Santa Fe Community College)
Cheryl Hughes (Tulsa Community College)
Sandi Landis (St. Johns River Community College)
David Linebarger (Northeastern State University)
Debra Ann Maukonen (University of Central Florida)
Merritt Moseley (University of North Carolina, Asheville)
Greg Peterson (Rogers State University)
Joyce Porter (Moraine Valley Community College)
Jason Swedene (Lake Superior State University)
Mary Tripp (University of Central Florida)
Margaret Urie (University of Nevada, Reno)
Joel Zimbelman (California State University, Chico)

To Know the Humanities is to Love the Humanities

Welcome to
EXPLORING THE HUMANITIES:
CREATIVITY AND CULTURE IN THE WEST,
Teaching and Learning Classroom Edition (T. L. C.)

Professors . . .

Do your students come to class having read—and thought about—the text material?

Do they leave the course inspired to love the humanities the way you do?

Now they will.

Prentice Hall proudly presents: *Exploring the Humanities: Creativity and Culture in the West, Teaching and Learning Classroom Edition* (T. L. C.) by Laurie Schneider Adams. This T. L. C. Edition will ignite students' passion to know more and think more about the importance of the humanities. This highly visual T. L. C. Edition begins with a simple premise: students will not learn what they have not read. *Exploring the Humanities* was designed especially to engage students to read the text and help them study smarter and perform better in class.

Pique students' curiosity to *read* the text

This T. L. C. Edition invites students into the text with Laurie Schneider Adams' accessible writing style that is clear and easy-to-read. Important works are explored in depth and in context, rather than presenting students with an overwhelming list of details. The book's stunning visual appeal captures student interest with beautiful, full-color reproductions illustrating the text discussion, full-color maps, and illustrated timelines. In addition, the text includes an array of pedagogical features designed to make the material accessible to students, including four kinds of boxed features that appear throughout the book:

Thematic Parallels help students compare cultures and art from around the world. These boxes consider universal themes, such as kingship, pilgrimage, notions of outer space, methods of spreading news, the persistence of the Classical tradition, and "heartthrobs" throughout history.

Cross-cultural Influences focus on areas of historical contact and artistic influence between cultures of the same time period. We discuss, for example, the impact of Greek Hellenistic style on Gandharan art from the first century B.C. to the first century A.D. Similarly, we consider the influence of Japanese woodblock prints of the Edo period on European and American Impressionists and Post-Impressionists in the nineteenth century.

Society and Culture These boxes, which appear throughout the text, elaborate further on a key person, event, or idea, providing more social and cultural background. Topics are of high interest to students and include daily life, medicine and science, technology, religion and myth, and the impact of certain individuals on history.

Defining Moments highlight an exciting turning point that has significantly influenced Western culture, whether a historical event, a scientific discovery, or an artistic innovation. A Critical Question is included at the end of each box to encourage further discussion.

Engage students to *think* about what they are reading

This T. L. C. Edition has more learning tools for students than any other humanities book, aimed at helping students understand, process, and appreciate what they are reading.

- A **Starter Kit** gives students a brief overview of the basic principles and terms they will need to know while beginning their study of the visual arts, music, literature, history, and philosophy.

- **Chapter Openers** Each chapter opens with a two-page spread, which has been carefully designed to draw students' attention and prepare them to engage with the material they are about to read. *Striking images* from the chapter capture the imagination, and a *brief introduction* to the key points of the period gets students oriented. A compelling *quotation* that embodies a main theme appears in the opener and is discussed at the end of the introduction. In addition, *Key Topics* are presented to prepare students to pay attention to the most important concepts of the chapter.

- **Timelines** Following each chapter opener is a full-page illustrated timeline designed to reinforce visually the chronology of the period and highlight key historical events, scientific discoveries, and works of art.

- **Maps** Throughout the book, colorful maps provide readers with a sense of geography. Several of the maps are thematic, indicating migrations of cultural groups, trade routes, and art centers.

- **End-of-chapter Study Tools** A consistent set of study tools is found at the end of every chapter.
  Key Terms, printed in bold type in the main text, are explained on first mention and are defined again in the glossary at the end of the chapter.
  Key Questions are included at the end of each chapter to help students focus on and review issues central to the period under discussion.
  Suggested Reading includes an annotated bibliography relevant to each chapter.
  Suggested Films have been selected to bring an era to life and also to reflect film history. Some films are based on literary works or on the lives of key figures.

Empower Students to *do* more than just read
Teaching and Learning Resources for Students and Faculty
This T. L. C. Edition comes with a state-of-the-art package of multimedia and print resources.

Online Resources for Students and Faculty

 OneKey

OneKey is a free, all-inclusive online resource giving you the best teaching and learning resources all in one place. OneKey is all your students need for out-of-class work conveniently organized by chapter to reinforce and apply what they have learned in class and from the text. OneKey is all you need to plan and administer your course. All your instructor resources are in one place to maximize your effectiveness and minimize your time and effort. For details, please visit www.prenhall.com/onekey.

Companion Website at www.prenhall.com/adams

This site features unique study and support tools for every chapter of *Exploring the Humanities* (such as chapter objectives and useful links). Multiple choice and short answer quizzes provide instant scoring and feedback to promote self-study. Students can also e-mail essay responses and graded quizzes directly to their instructor.

Student Resources

- *Music for the Humanities* **CD**
  This music CD is bound into each copy of the text and the Music Listening Selections are cited and discussed in the main text.

- **Anthology of Readings, Volumes I and II**
  Each chapter of *Exploring the Humanities* contains references to primary sources discussed in the text, which have been compiled into a two-volume anthology. Instructors also have the option of customizing their own anthology through the Penguin Custom Editions program. This allows them to select only the readings they need from an archive of more than 1700 readings excerpted primarily from the Penguin Classics™. Visit www.pecustomeditions.com for more information on Penguin Custom Editions: The Western World. Contact your local Prentice Hall sales representative for ordering information.

- **Prentice Hall and Penguin Bundle Program**
  Prentice Hall is pleased to provide adopters of *Exploring the Humanities* with an opportunity to receive significant discounts when copies of the text are bundled with Penguin titles. Contact your local Prentice Hall sales representative for details.

- **Humanities Notes: A Study Guide to Accompany *Exploring the Humanities*, Volumes I and II**
  Humanities Notes provides students with practice tests, map exercises, spaces for taking notes on the Key Topics and a place to answer Key Questions from each chapter. Free when packaged with the text.

- **The Prentice Hall *Atlas of the Humanities***
  Prentice Hall collaborates with Dorling Kindersley, the world's most innovative producer of maps and atlases. This atlas features multi-dimensional maps that include global, thematic, regional, and chronological perspectives showing political, economic, and cultural changes over time. Available at a significant discount when packaged with the text.

- **TIME Magazine Special Editions. Available for Art, World Religions, and World Politics**
  Prentice Hall and TIME Magazine are pleased to offer a way to examine today's most current and compelling issues in an exciting new way. TIME Special Editions offers the same accessible writing style, bold coverage, and photography for which TIME is known, including a selection of articles on today's most current issues in the fields. Useful for classroom discussion and research assignments. Free when packaged with the text.

-

OneSearch with Research Navigator
In addition to information on citing sources and avoiding plagiarism, this guide gives students easy access to three exclusive research databases: The New York Times Search by Subject Archive, ContentSelect Academic Journal Database, and Link Library. Free when packaged with the text.

Faculty Resources

- **Instructor's Resource Binder**
  This innovative, all-in-one resource organizes the instructor's manual, the test item file, and other resources by each chapter of *Exploring the Humanities*, all in an easy-to-access format designed to facilitate class preparation. Designed for both the novice and the seasoned professor, this invaluable guide includes resources for each chapter, such as an overview, objectives, outline, lecture and discussion ideas, and further resources. The test bank consists of multiple choice, true/false, short answer, and essay questions. Contact your local Prentice Hall sales representative for more information.

- **TestGen**
  This commercial-quality computerized test management program for Windows or Macintosh allows instructors to select test bank questions in designing their own exams. Contact your local Prentice Hall sales representative for more information.

- **Fine Art Slides**
  Slides that accompany the text are available to qualified adopters. Contact your local Prentice Hall sales representative for more information.

Starter Kit

In Latin, the word *humanitas* means "human nature" and refers to the quality that distinguishes humans from animals. Today we use the term "humanities" to encompass many educational disciplines. Even hard sciences such as physics and chemistry, and technical disciplines such as engineering, which are not usually considered "humanities," are creative products of the human mind. For the sake of clarity, however, one might divide humanities into the following broad areas of knowledge:

- **creative and expressive arts:** picture-making, sculpture, architecture, music, dance, theater, film, and literature
- **sports:** in which physical aggression and competitiveness are transformed into cultural activity. Note that for the Olympic Games in ancient Greece, all wars on Greek territory were halted so that the athletes could travel safely to the competition.
- **attempts to explain our origins and know our future:** religion and myth
- **the intellectual search for truth:** philosophy
- **the sciences:** physics, chemistry, psychology, biology, medicine, anthropology, and zoology
- **the physical study of our planet and of the cosmos:** geography and astronomy
- **the record of our past:** history and archaeology

The major disciplinary categories, however, are mainly a convenience for the purpose of discussion. We can also benefit from considering the humanities in an interdisciplinary light: it is worth noting, for example, that archaeology—the study of the past by excavating buried civilizations—is a humanist pursuit that relies on various combinations of art, science, and technology. Moreover, the major disciplines have further subdivisions that continue to evolve as the disciplines themselves evolve, and all, over time, have developed appropriate signs and symbols (see Box), rules and principles, systems of analysis, and methods of appreciation and evaluation.

Before we embark on our chronological exploration of the Western humanities, therefore, this Starter Kit introduces some of the basic principles governing the study of visual art, music, literature, history, and philosophy, and the terms used by their practitioners.

THE VISUAL ARTS

The traditional visual arts—also called the monumental arts (as opposed to craft)—are pictures, sculpture, and architecture. All are made of materials that arouse the sense of touch by creating an actual or implied **texture**. The material used in making a work of art is its **medium** (plural **media**).

TWO-DIMENSIONAL ART: PICTURES

Pictures are images that exist in two dimensions: height and width. Examples of pictures include drawings, paintings, prints, mosaics, stained glass, photographs, and films.

PICTURE SPACE   Since pictures are flat in reality, when they appear to have depth as well as height and width, the artist has created a **three-dimensional illusion**. Consider, for example, Masaccio's *Trinity* (figure **0.1**), which appears three-dimensional even though it is painted on a flat wall. Masaccio has used the system of **linear perspective** to produce the impression that a Crucifixion scene is taking place in an actual space beyond the wall. A figure of God stands on a ledge behind the Cross, making him appear farther than

0.1 Masaccio, *Trinity*, 1425–1428, Santa Maria Novella, Florence. Fresco, 21 ft. 10⅝ in. × 10 ft. 4¾ in. (6.67 × 3.17 m).

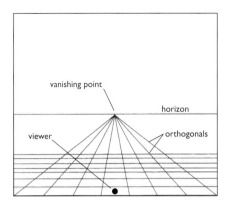

0.2 One-point perspective, according to Alberti.

Christ from the viewer. And appearing closer to us than Christ are the two figures kneeling on the illusionistic outer step. This perspective system is diagrammed in figure **0.2** and shows the grid pattern of the imaginary floor plan composed of lines parallel to the surface of the picture (the **picture plane**), the position of the viewer, and the **orthogonals** (lines perpendicular to the picture plane) that meet at the **vanishing point**, which is located on the horizon.

When artists create pictures, they organize the basic visual elements (units of design) into a **composition**. A good composition generally conveys a sense of coherence, which we read as a unified whole. This may be achieved through balance, patterning, rhythms, contrasts, and so forth.

VISUAL ELEMENTS   The main visual units are line, space, shape, color, light, and dark, all of which have expressive character. **Lines** can be horizontal (like the horizon) [——], vertical (like a soldier standing at attention) [|], diagonal (like a falling tree [/], curved (like an arc) [＼], S-shaped (like a snake) [∿]), wavy (like the ocean) [⌄⌄], or zigzagged (like a mountain range) [ＶＶＶ]. When lines enclose a **space**, they create a **shape**. Shapes can be geometric, biomorphic (life-like), open, or closed. The diagrams in figure **0.3** show regular geometric shapes (square, triangle, circle, rectangle, trapezoid), a biomorphic shape, and shapes having mass (cube, pyramid, sphere). An artist can create the illusion of a three-dimensional shape using **shadows** or **shading**. When a shape such as the cube in figure 0.3 blocks light, it casts a shadow. With the sphere in figure 0.3, we have the impression that light is coming from the right, that it is blocked by the sphere, and thus that it casts a shadow on the surface supporting it. Shading is the gradual change from

0.3 Diagrams of shapes.

flat shapes

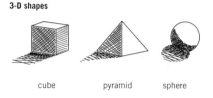

square   triangle   circle

rectangle   trapezoid   biomorphic shape

3-D shapes

cube   pyramid   sphere

light to dark, which here creates the impression that the sphere has mass. The edge of the sphere, or of any solid object, is called its **contour**.

Color is a striking element of many pictures, although some pictures, such as black and white photographs, early films, some drawings and prints, and black and white paintings do not have color. The name of a color is its **hue** (red, green, purple, etc.), and the **value** of a color is its relative darkness or lightness. Figure **0.4** illustrates a **color wheel**

showing primary, secondary, and tertiary colors. Note that the primary colors are indicated by a 1, the secondaries by a 2, and the tertiaries by a 3. A primary color is one that cannot be made by mixing two different colors. A secondary color is made by mixing two primaries, and a tertiary by mixing the primary and secondary on either side of it. Generally, the most striking contrasts are formed by juxtaposing colors opposite each other on the wheel. So, for example, a blue next to an orange is theoretically more eye-catching than a yellow next to an orange.

Primary colors on this wheel are red, yellow, and blue; they are the colors from which all the other colors of the **visible spectrum** (figure **0.5**) are derived. The spectrum itself is composed of seven colors made visible by passing white light through a prism. White light is the combination of the colors of the spectrum.

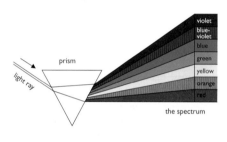

0.5 **The visible spectrum.**

0.6 Filippo Brunelleschi, *Sacrifice of Isaac*, 1401–1402. Gilt bronze, 21 × 17½ in. (53.3 × 44.4 cm). Museo Nazionale del Bargello, Florence.

THREE-DIMENSIONAL ART: SCULPTURE
In contrast to pictures, sculptures are three-dimensional and can be divided into two broad categories: *relief* and **sculpture-in-the-round** (sometimes called **freestanding**). Relief sculpture, as in Brunelleschi's *Sacrifice of Isaac* (figure **0.6**), has a background plane, just as a picture does, and the image cannot be seen from behind the background. Sculpture-in-the-round, like the *Kritios Boy* (figure **0.7**),

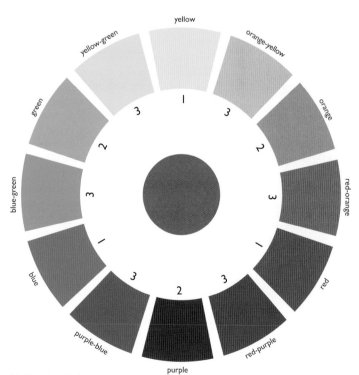

0.4 **The color wheel.**

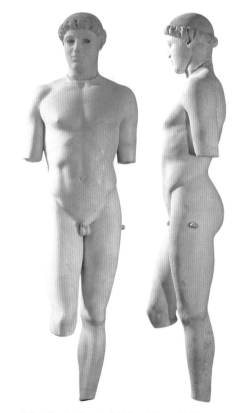

0.7 *Kritios Boy* (front and side), *c.* 480 B.C. Marble, 33⅞ in. (86 cm) high. Acropolis Museum, Athens.

can and should be seen from all sides. The traditional media of sculpture are wood, stone, and bronze, but more recent sculptures have been made of such materials as wire, cloth and stuffing, neon lights, crushed cars, and television monitors.

ARCHITECTURE

The term **architecture** refers to buildings and the practice of architecture is thought of as the most functional of the monumental arts (although paintings and sculptures can also have specific functions). Whereas we look at a picture from one viewpoint and at a sculpture-in-the-round from several viewpoints, we have to enter a building and walk through it in order to experience it fully.

A building is generally constructed with a specific idea about how it will be used and, as a consequence, there are many types of building ranging from private to public, from modest to magnificent, and from traditional to innovative. Domestic architecture can be in the form of apartment blocks or private dwellings such as individual city houses, country villas, and royal palaces; places of worship include synagogues, churches and cathedrals, temples, and mosques; museums are built to display art; bridges are constructed to span spaces; castles and forts are defensive; and in ancient Egypt, monumental pyramids were built to preserve the ruler and his belongings for the afterlife.

Buildings are designed by an **architect**, who first makes a **ground plan** indicating the placement of structural elements at ground level. In this plan of the Parthenon (figure **0.8**), the three outer lines represent the steps, the black circles show where the columns stand on the floor, the solid lines (except for the steps) indicate walls, and the spaces denote open areas—room interiors, spaces between columns, and doorways cut into the walls.

Over the course of time, architects have designed buildings according to a number of structural systems that we will encounter in this text. Figure **0.9** illustrates diagrams of some of the most frequently used systems. **Load-bearing** structures such as the ziggurats of ancient Mesopotamia had supporting walls, no windows, and no interiors. The **post-and-lintel** system consists of vertical supports holding up a horizontal, as in the Neolithic structure of Stonehenge. In ancient Rome, architects used the **round arch** for many purposes, one of which was to construct triumphal arches as passageways for victorious generals and emperors. **Pointed arches** were developed in the twelfth century and became a mainstay of Gothic cathedral architecture, whose soaring verticals are lighter and rise higher than those based on round arches. The ceiling **vaults** made by repeating round and pointed arches (**barrel vaults** and **rib vaults**, respectively) correspond to the effects of the arches themselves: barrel vaults create a sense

0.10 Louis Sullivan, Wainwright Building, St. Louis, Missouri, 1890–1891.

of heavy mass, and rib vaults create a sense of height and lightness.

In the nineteenth century, capitalizing on the advances brought about by the Industrial Revolution and with the ability to smelt steel on a large scale, architects began to use **steel-frame** skeletons for skyscrapers. To begin with, stone was used for the outer skin of the buildings, as in Louis Sullivan's Wainwright Building in St. Louis (figure **0.10**), and later, in the twentieth century, glass began to be employed for architectural exteriors.

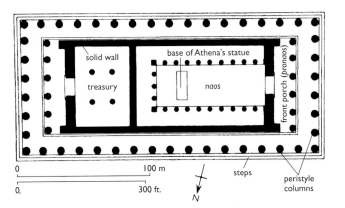

0.8 Plan of the Parthenon, Athens.

0.9 Architectural systems.

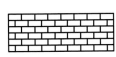
load-bearing wall

post-and-lintel

round arch

pointed arch

barrel vault

rib vault

Signs and Symbols

Signs and symbols are used in every discipline within the humanities to convey meaning, and we will examine some of the principal ones here. Our ability to think symbolically is a crucial element of being human—fundamental to what differentiates us from animals. The ability to use and read signs and symbols is thus critical to any study of the humanities.

Signs communicate a fact or a direct command and are familiar aspects of everyday life. A red rectangle on a road, for example, is a sign that we are supposed to stop. An arrow signals a one-way street, and a picture of a cigarette with a line through it means no smoking. A **symbol** stands for something besides itself and, in contrast to a sign, usually has more than a single level of meaning. In Christian art, for example, when the Virgin Mary is depicted as unnaturally large, she symbolizes the church building. The circle symbolizes the universal and never-ending character of the Church, and light inside a church symbolizes the presence of God.

In music, we use signs to denote pitch, the length of notes, rests between notes, clefs, key and time signatures, and chords (see figures 0.12 and 0.14). In some musical compositions, the sounds produced convey symbolic meaning. For example, a rising scale can symbolize ascent into heaven and a falling scale can symbolize descent into hell. Sounds can also symbolize moods—hence the Greek musical **modes**, such as the Lydian plaintive and the Mixolydian elegiac.

In literature the elements of **punctuation** are signs that are essential to our ability to read and understand. We use quotation marks (". . .") to indicate that someone is speaking, commas (,) to indicate pauses, and periods (.) to indicate the ends of sentences. There are also literary symbols created by the author's use of words, which generally include an image or comparison of some kind. In a **simile**, we use the word *like* or *as* to make a comparison—if we say that someone is "as fit as a fiddle" we mean that he or she is as taut as a violin string and thus in perfect physical condition. In **metaphor** we create a comparison without using either *like* or *as*—we may say that parks "*are* the lungs of a city." This is not literally true, but it is true in the sense that parks introduce fresh air into an urban landscape. Another device available to an author is **personification**, when something that is not a person is likened to a person. Thus when we say that "Justice is blind," we are portraying the idea of justice as a blind person (usually a woman), who is impartial. That is, she is not swayed by what she sees but, rather, bases her decisions purely on objective facts.

In visual art, especially Christian art, there are an enormous number of signs and symbols and they are essential to an understanding of the meaning of a work. The saints, for example, can be identified by specific elements such as the keys of St. Peter, the knife and flayed skin of St. Bartholomew, and the lamb of John the Baptist. A scallop shell can denote pilgrimage and resurrection, a halo signals the divine nature of a holy person, and a vine can allude to the wine of the Eucharist. In ancient Greek and Roman art, the gods also have attributes that are signs and symbols of their identity. Thus, for example, Zeus and Jupiter wield a thunderbolt as a sign of their power; Aphrodite and Venus are often accompanied by rabbits to show their association with fertility; and Hera and Juno wear a veil as goddesses of marriage.

As in dreams, the imagery of art can be interpreted in multiple ways and on multiple levels. To take a single, well-known picture, consider Leonardo da Vinci's *Mona Lisa* (figure **0.11**). We know very little about this painting, despite its fame, so it lends itself to many different readings.

One interpretation of the *Mona Lisa* is based on our knowledge of Leonardo's own writing, in which he said that the human body is a metaphor for the earth. He wrote that the soil is flesh, the waterways are blood, and the rocks are bones. Taking this metaphor, we can read Mona Lisa herself as a symbol of the earth, a kind of mythical mother earth-goddess derived from antiquity. Then we might note that her form is indeed an echo of the background mountains, that her transparent veil is similar to the mists enveloping the rocks, that the folds of her sleeves repeat the movement of the spiral road, and that the aqueduct on the right flows into the fold over her left shoulder. Formally and symbolically, therefore, Mona Lisa *is* the world; and she is as imposing and incomprehensible as the world.

In the nineteenth century, the critic Walter Pater described Mona Lisa as timeless, older even than the rocks among which she sits. Pater also found her sinister and menacing, which is a far cry from the analysis of the twentieth-century physician who asserted that she smiles contentedly because she is pregnant. According to Freud—perhaps the most famous interpreter of dreams and their symbols—Mona Lisa's smile is a trace of the smile of the artist's mother, which Leonardo recalled from his childhood and refound in the expression of his sitter.

0.11 Leonardo da Vinci, *Mona Lisa*, *c.* 1503–1515. Oil on wood, 30¼ × 21 in. (76.7 × 53.3 cm). Louvre, Paris.

MUSIC

In societies that have no writing systems, there is no musical notation and music is transmitted orally. In literate societies, however, there are different kinds of musical notation. But there are generally two essential pieces of information communicated by the written notation, namely the note itself (its **pitch**, or highness/lowness) and the length of that note.

Musical notation in the West was rare before the Middle Ages. Today, Western music is written on **staffs** of five parallel horizontal lines (figure **0.12**). Each line and space represents the location of a **note**, which denotes a sung or played sound. The physical appearance of each note indicates its length: a whole note [𝅝], half-note [𝅗𝅥], quarter-note [𝅘𝅥], eighth-note [𝅘𝅥𝅮], sixteenth note [𝅘𝅥𝅯], thirty-second note [𝅘𝅥𝅰]. The lengths of silences between notes are indicated by one of several different **rest** signs [𝄻, 𝄼, 𝄽, 𝄾, 𝄿, 𝅀]. There are twelve pitches, or **semitones** (the smallest interval commonly used in Western music): the seven notes **A**, **B**, **C**, **D**, **E**, **F**, and **G**, plus five **sharps** and **flats**. An **octave** is the name given to the interval between two notes of the same name, twelve semitones apart: A to A, B flat to B flat, and so on (figure **0.13**). The sharp sign [♯] indicates that a note is raised by a semitone; the flat sign [♭] indicates that a note is lowered a by semitone.

Many instruments have notation written on a single staff. However, in notation for the piano there are two staffs, one for the left hand and one for the right hand. Figure **0.14** shows a notation of the beginning of "Happy Birthday" for the piano. At the beginning of each staff (at the far left) the **bass clef** sign [𝄢] denotes the pitch played with the left hand. The **treble clef** [𝄞] denotes a higher pitch and is played on the piano with the right hand. The sharps or flats that must be played appear after the clef and are known, collectively, as the **key signature**. Figures on the staff (known as the **time signature**) indicate meter and rhythm.

Together, these written elements make up the **score**, or the music-copy for one or more performers. But there are other elements in music beside these written signs and symbols. A **melody**, for example, is a sequence of notes with a recognizable form, or tune. To create **harmony**, a musician combines tones into **chords** (two or more notes played simultaneously). **Rhythm** refers to meter or pulse, creating a pattern of sounds. The **theme** is the musical idea on which a composition is based—it will often have an identifiable melody. In **monophony**, such as the medieval Gregorian chant, there is a single line of melody with no accompaniment. In **polyphony**, which developed later, two or more lines of melody are combined.

Music can be sung, in which case the voice is the instrument. But many other instruments have been developed since the dawn of human history, and today these tend to be grouped into families: **strings**, either bowed like the violin, viola, cello, and double bass, or plucked like the lyre, harp, and guitar; **keyboards** including the piano and harpsichord; **wind** instruments, which may be further subdivided into **woodwind** (the recorder and flute, and instruments played with a reed, including the oboe, bassoon, clarinet, and saxophone), **brass** instruments (including horn, trumpet, and trombone), and the **organ** (which differs from other wind instruments in that the air required to produce the sound is supplied by an external source rather than by the performer); and **percussion**, or instruments—both tuned and untuned—that are sounded by being struck or shaken (drums, xylophone, cymbals, and bells). In addition to these traditional families, almost any sound can now be reproduced by **electronic** means using a synthesizer. Nevertheless, each instrument makes a distinctive sound and creates its own musical **tone color** (or timbre).

Different genres of music use different combinations of instruments or groups of instruments. A **song** (of which there are many different varieties) may be sung by a single voice or by a group of voices (a **choir**). Musical works for **orchestra** can assume a number of forms, but the **symphony**—an extended work played by a large group of instruments for a large audience—is on the grandest scale, involving the largest number of players. Usually symphonies are divided into **movements** (sections of a specific musical character). A **concerto** is a musical performance by one or more solo instruments accompanied by an orchestra, and **chamber music** was originally conceived, as its name suggests, for a small number of players performing in a private room (chamber). **Opera**, which developed in the seventeenth century, is drama set to music. Among the many genres of popular music that have developed since the beginning of the twentieth century are ragtime, blues, jazz, rock (of several varieties), and rap.

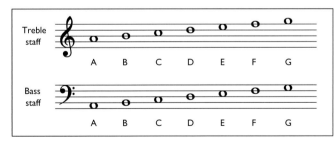

0.12 Music staffs.

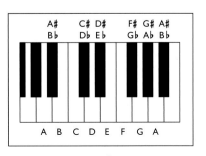

0.13 Octave shown on the piano.

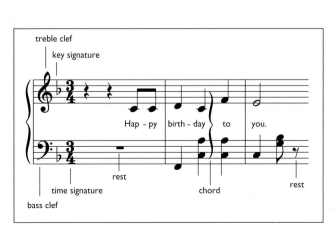

0.14 First bars of "Happy Birthday."

LITERATURE

Literature is a verbal form of expression and its medium is language. The simple building blocks of language are words and sentences. To understand how language works it can be broken down into **parts of speech** (nouns, verbs, adverbs, adjectives, conjunctions, and articles), which are the components of **grammar**, and their arrangement and structure is their **syntax**. Grammar and syntax form the character and structure of sentences and follow certain rules. Literature, however, amounts to far more than mere communication: it is a creative expression of human thought that elevates these building blocks into an art form. Literature can be broadly divided into **prose** and **poetry**. Whereas prose tends to resemble everyday speech and to extend a narrative through time, poets tend to structure their words according to an established rhythm and meter.

POETRY

Poetic lines traditionally **rhyme**, that is, their final sounds (or spellings) are similar—though they do not have to be identical. Consider, for example, the first five lines of Samuel Taylor Coleridge's "Kubla Khan":

> In Xanadu did Kubla Khan
> A stately pleasure-dome decree:
> Where Alph, the sacred river, ran
> Through caverns measureless to man
> Down to a sunless sea.

"Khan" rhymes with "ran" and "man," and "decree" rhymes with "sea." This rhyme scheme is diagrammed as ABAAB: A (Khan), B (decree), A (ran), A (man), B (sea).

Genres of poetry include **narratives** (which tell a story), **lyric** poems (which are usually brief, melodic, and imbued with emotion and imagination), **epic**, and **nonsense** poems. An epic poem is a long narrative on a grand scale, usually dealing with universal themes, gods, legends, and heroes. The earliest Western epics—the Sumerian *Epic of Gilgamesh* and the Homeric *Iliad* and *Odyssey*—were first transmitted orally and only later written down. On the other hand, Milton wrote down his epic *Paradise Lost* as he was creating it in seventeenth-century England. In nonsense poetry, authors create original word forms and syntactical constructs that do not appear to make rational sense. A famous example of nonsense is Lewis Carroll's "Jabberwocky":

> 'Twas brillig, and the slithy toves
> Did gyre and grimble in the wabe;
> All mimsy were the borogoves,
> And the mome raths outgrabe.

More recently, poets have written **free verse**, which does not necessarily use regular lines and meter, or rhyme. Nevertheless, even free verse tends to maintain an economy of form and density of meaning that distinguishes it from prose. Derek Walcott's Caribbean epic, *Omeros*, uses structured lines but not rhyme:

> Ma Kilman had the oldest bar in the village.
> Its gingerbread balcony had mustard gables
> with green trim round the eaves, the paint
> wrinkled with age.
>
> (II, 1–3)

PROSE

Within the category of prose, a further broad literary distinction can be made between **fiction** and **non-fiction**, the former being an invented narrative and the latter an account of something that actually happened. When we read a **novel** we are reading fiction, and when we read the newspaper we are reading nonfiction. History (see below), biography, and autobiography are also examples of nonfiction, whereas mystery stories and fairytales, like novels, are fiction. The **essay** (from the French word *essayer*, meaning "to try") was invented in sixteenth-century France by Montaigne. It is an author's attempt to consider an issue in depth and from a particular **point of view**, that is, a means of focusing the reader in a particular direction. (The equivalent in a painting would be the use of perspective, which directs the viewer's eye to one or more specific points on the picture plane.)

When a work of literature is written in the **first person**, the point of view is that of a narrator (the *I*). A **third-person** viewpoint is narrated by an individual (*he*, *she*, or *it*); if the story is told by more than one narrator, the viewpoint is composed of *they*. In **epistolary** writing, a story unfolds and character is revealed through letters ("epistle," from the Latin word *epistola*, meaning "a written communication," is another term for a letter). And in **stream of consciousness** a story is told through the inner thoughts of the characters, often with no formal structure or external dialogue.

THEATER

Theater is a branch of literature in which the text is a **play** (either in prose or poetic form) performed on a stage before an audience. Unlike a novel, in which the setting of the action is described in words, a play relies on a **backdrop**—either a natural one if it is outdoors, or a painted and constructed **set**. It is also possible for a play to have no constructed set and a narrator might introduce the story and its characters, thus "setting the stage" verbally rather than visually. The formal structure of a play is **dramatic**—involving conflict and contrast—rather than being an extended narrative like a novel (although novels often have dramatic elements). Both plays and novels revolve around a **plot**, which is the unfolding of events.

Plays, like novels, convey a point of view and are driven by the nature, motivations, and behavior of the characters. Whereas novels are generally divided into chapters, plays are broken down into acts and scenes, with stage directions provided by the playwright. But in a play, the written text is interpreted for the audience through the **actors** and their **director**. The hero, or main character, is called the **protagonist**. In plays, as in other literary forms, there are certain standard genres and techniques. In **tragedy**, a hero falls because of some character flaw, whereas in **comedy** the outcome is usually a happy one, dialogue is generally humorous, and the tone lighthearted.

HISTORY

History writing, like oral history, reflects the need to organize, explain, and justify human decisions. Two great historians of ancient Greece were Herodotus (called the "Father of History") and Thucydides. Herodotus set out to preserve the past by writing about it and also to understand why the Greeks and foreigners (especially Persians) went to war against each other. Thucydides wrote the history of the Peloponnesian War (between Athens and Sparta) in the belief that it would be the greatest conflict yet played out on the world stage.

Historians use **primary sources** and **secondary sources** to construct a narrative of the "facts" as they perceive them. Primary sources consist of documentary evidence—actual records that have survived from the past—and also such things as photographs, household objects, and clothing. Secondary sources are accounts written after the event. Historians select their "facts" in order to present a thesis explaining the events they describe. But in any process of selecting "facts" the personal point of view of the historian comes into play. **Historiography** is the study of history and historians. It demonstrates that there is no such thing as "objective" history, since historians are affected by their own cultural context, which colors their interpretation.

History can be subdivided into political history, social history, biography, and even autobiography.

PHILOSOPHY

The Greek philosopher Aristotle said that all human beings by nature desire to know. Philosophy (literally "love of wisdom") deals with people's place in the world, the nature of reality and truth, and the meaning of life.

In contrast to science, philosophy is not primarily driven by a search for factual knowledge. Rather, it tends to examine in a methodical, logical way what is already known and experienced by any ordinary person. Logic is one of its key tools and some philosophical arguments can be expressed in a purely abstract logical form (using "formal logic"). More commonly, however, philosophical arguments are presented discursively.

In the Western tradition, key schools of philosophical thought include scholasticism, rationalism, empiricism, idealism, and materialism. Today, Western philosophy tends to be divided into two distinct, but loosely defined, approaches: Anglo-American or analytical philosophy models itself on mathematics and logic, and demands intellectual rigor. It also focuses on the meaning and use of language and words. Continental philosophy, on the other hand, covers a range of different theories and strives to systematize the world and human experience. Primary examples are phenomenology, existentialism, and structuralism.

Within any of the more broadly defined schools cited above, there are many specialist areas of interest: metaphysics (theories of reality); epistemology (theories of knowledge); ontology (theories of being); ethics (views of morality); aesthetics (the appreciation of beauty); philosophy of religion; and philosophy of science.

INTERDISCIPLINARY ASPECTS OF THE ARTS

All the expressive arts have an interdisciplinary character that is reflected in the similar terminologies denoting their form and content. Opera, for example, combines drama with music. It has a text (the **libretto**) and is performed by singers who act out the parts as they sing the words.

Dance is an art form that combines music, movement, thematic content, lighting, and staging. The notation of dance is called **choreography**, which records the composition and sequence of steps and movements. In dance, the human form moves through space, usually accompanied by music. The main genres of dance are **folk dance**, **ballet**, and **modern dance**. Folk dance, like oral literature and music, develops over time, and has a specific cultural character. Ballet is more formal, notated, and usually tells a story. Modern dance refers to developments from the early twentieth century to the present, and does not adhere to the formal rules of ballet. There is more room for innovative choreography, costumes, sets, and lighting in modern dance than in traditional dance. In all dance genres, however, the formal elements that apply to music and art are also used: lines, shapes, colors, lightness and darkness, patterns, balance, rhythm, and harmony.

Perhaps today's most complex interdisciplinary art form is **film**, which has a technological as well as an aesthetic aspect. As with literature, film can be used to record "reality" in which case it is known as **documentary** and has a primarily historical character. Nevertheless, it must be recognized that, as with history, no documentary can be considered entirely objective because the viewpoint of the creators influences the impression made by such a film. Among major examples of documentary film in the twentieth century are **newsreels**, shown in movie theaters from the 1930s through the 1970s.

In the realm of fiction, film encompasses numerous genres, such as action, adventure, drama, fantasy, animation, science fiction, romance, and crime. Even more so than theater and dance, the production of a film requires the participation of many different people, from lighting and sound technicians to actors, directors, editors, and producers. The text of a film is called a **screenplay** and as in dance and theater, the director tells the actors how to interpret the text and how to move and gesture. The producer (as in dance and theater) raises the money to produce the work. While many screenplays are original (specifically written for the screen), it is often the case—as with the **trilogy** (three-part work) *The Lord of the Rings*—that a well-known novel is turned into a screenplay, and that people from several different countries participate in its production. This kind of participation has contributed to the globalization of the film industry.

The modern world has witnessed increased globalization, and the proliferation of rapid means of communication has expanded the potential for interdisciplinary creativity. We see this, for example, in the sciences, when clinical results are shared via the Internet. Works of art are accessible as museums around the globe digitize their collections and put them on the Web. Films and music are easily downloaded. The easy accessibility of the Web and the speed of globalization have ushered in a new era for the humanities. The Internet itself can be seen as a cross between the written text and oral history. For, on the one hand, computers can store enormous amounts of material and preserve it for future generations. On the other hand, however, computers facilitate the constant updating of material in a way that echoes oral tradition. Whereas oral "texts" change over time, written texts change only in the ways they are interpreted.

1 Prehistory

> *In early times,*
> *When Ymir lived,*
> *Was sand, nor sea,*
>
> . . . .
>
> *One chaos all,*
> *And nowhere grass.*
>
> . . . .
>
> *Under the armpit grew,*
>
> . . . .
>
> *A girl and a boy together;*
> *Foot with foot began,*
> *Of that wise Jötun,*
> *A six-headed son.*
>
> . . . .
>
> *Of Ymir's flesh*
> *Was earth created,*
> *Of his blood the sea,*
> *Of his bones, the hills,*
> *Of his hair trees and plants,*
> *Of his skull the heavens,*
>   *And of his brows*
> *The gentle powers*
> *Formed Midgard for the sons of men;*
> *But of his brain*
> *The heavy clouds are*
> *All created.*"
>
>   (NORSE CREATION MYTH)

A *humanities text deals with human achievements. These achievements, which are the components of human culture, include the creative arts, inventions that change the course of history, significant world events, scientific discoveries, religious beliefs and myths, and philosophical ideas. In this text, we explore these expressions of human creativity mainly in Western cultures—along with a few comparative glimpses beyond the West—in the context of their time and place in history.*

Most of us are curious about where and how we and the universe began. We also wonder about our place in the world and the world's place in the universe. For millennia human cultures have constructed creation myths to answer such questions. These myths vary from culture to culture, but most attribute the idea of making the world to the creative mind of a god. According to many such myths, the world begins like a work of art—with the combination of an idea, a will, and unformed material, which is given shape and life.

The quotation at the beginning of this chapter is from an ancient Norse account of how the world began. The Nordic countries of western Europe (modern Norway, Sweden, Denmark, and, from the ninth century, Iceland) spend much of the year in darkness and snow, and their climate influenced their creation myths. Norse people conceived of an original state of primordial chaos (an abyss) and a universe created through the will of a frozen giant, Ymir, who emerged from blocks of ice.

As soon as he was formed, Ymir noticed that he was hungry. He came upon a cow, who was also made from ice, and drank her milk. The cow then licked salt from an ice block and gave birth to Buri, the Creator. Ymir fell asleep, bearing two children from his armpits and a six-headed giant from his feet. Ymir's body became the source of earth, oceans, and sky, and his children multiplied. They created generations of men and women, giants (the Jötun), and gods. The Jötun wage eternal war against the gods (offspring of Buri) and the battle continues until the final clash—Ragnarök—at the end of time. Meanwhile, the Norse universe is structured according to levels of importance, with humans inhabiting Midgard (Middle Earth).

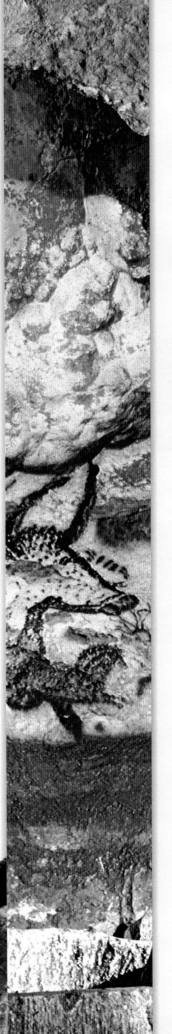

Key Topics

TIMELINE	EARLIEST ORIGINS	PALEOLITHIC ERA c. 1,500,000–c. 10,000/8000	MESOLITHIC ERA c. 10,000/8000–c. 6000/4000	NEOLITHIC ERA c. 6000/4000–c. 1500

HISTORY AND CULTURE	Early hominids,
	  7–1 million
	Homo habilis,
	  c. 2 million: stone tools
	Homo erectus,
	  c. 1.8 million
	Use of fire,
	  c. 1 million–500,000
	Archaic *Homo sapiens*,
	  c. 500,000
	Neanderthals and
	  Cro-Magnons, c. 100,000
	Food gathering, fishing
		Upper Paleolithic
		  from c. 45,000
		Hunting and gathering
			Transition from
			  hunting and
			  gathering to settled
			  communities
				Agricultural
				  communities with
				  wealth-based class
				  divisions
				Domestication of
				  animals
				Horse-drawn plows
				Trade with Near East

RELIGION AND MYTH	Ritual burial practices,
	  c. 120,000–80,000
	Ritual ornaments
		Ritual burial practices
		Gravegoods
		Ritual dancing
		Shamanism
			Ritual burial
			  practices
				Belief systems
				Ritual practices
				Ancestor worship
				Burial mounds

ART	Body decoration: Blombos
	  Cave, c. 90,000
		Chauvet cave
		  paintings,
		  c. 30,000–24,000
		Venus of Willendorf,
		  c. 25,000
		Lascaux cave
		  paintings, c. 14,000
			Pottery	Pottery
				Jewelry

ARCHITECTURE		Mammoth-bone
		  house, c. 16,000
			Settlements	Villages
				First cities: Jericho,
				  Çatal Hüyük, Ban Po
				Monumental stone
				  architecture:
				  Stonehenge,
				  c. 1800–1500
				Post-and-lintel
				  construction

MUSIC	Bone whistles and drums			Music in rituals

Although creation myths, such as this one, are devised as a way of explaining the origin of the world, they do not provide scientific information about the birth and evolution of the human race or its cultural developments. The first evidence of the use of language and the creative arts appears during the Upper Paleolithic period (the later Old Stone Age), roughly 45,000 to 10,000/8000 B.C., when people used stone tools. At some point, people told stories that evolved into literature. Music and dance accompanied religious rituals as they often do today. The earliest evidence of painting and sculpture dates to the later Old Stone Age.

Gradually, settled communities formed, with social structures based on rank. As the Paleolithic period evolved into the Middle Stone Age (Mesolithic, c. 8000–6000 B.C.) and New Stone Age (Neolithic, c. 6000–1500 B.C.) people learned to farm and, eventually, to build—first temporary shelters and, later, structures made of permanent material, such as stone. We should note, however, that these ancient dates are flexible and are continually being revised by scholars. Just as biological organisms and the elements of physics are found to be smaller and smaller as research progresses, so human history seems to reach farther and farther back in time with each new discovery. Thus, absolute dates and time periods need to be reconsidered whenever new information becomes available (see Box).

Society and Culture

The Dating System Used in this Text

Throughout the world, and even in the West, there are different systems for dating history. This text uses the traditional Western system in which B.C. stands for Before Christ, and A.D. (after the Latin words *anno domini*, meaning "in the year of our Lord") stands for After Christ. Although the exact date of Christ's birth is not certain, the term A.D. 1 is conventionally used to mean the first year after his birth and 1 B.C. to indicate the first year before his birth. There is thus no year 0. The traditional *c.*, meaning *circa* (the Latin word for "about" or "around"), is used here for approximate dates.

Readers of other texts may find that C.E. (for Common Era) or B.C.E. (for Before the Common Era) replace A.D. and B.C., respectively. While such notations may seem to be more religiously neutral, they are also less precise. In this book the more historical flavor of B.C. and A.D. has been chosen over the vaguer and chronologically ambiguous B.C.E. and C.E.

HUMAN ORIGINS: FROM MYTH TO SCIENCE

The actual origin of the human race is a vexing issue, about which there are as many myths as there are cultures, a number of scientific hypotheses, and a considerable amount of hard evidence. But, important as science is, we should not lose sight of the poetic creativity reflected in myth-making. The Norse myth is only one of many attempts to explain the mystery of creation. In our search for origins, whether it assumes a poetic or a scientific form, we differ from other living species. Both poetry and science are uniquely human expressions.

CREATION STORIES

Once the universe is created, most myths consider how people came into existence. The ancient Sumerians of southern Mesopotamia (in modern Iraq), for example, believed that people were created because the gods were aging and needed servants. The Akkadians, who lived in northern Mesopotamia, thought that the first humans were created from the blood of rebel gods. According to the Book of Genesis in the Hebrew Bible, God created the primal couple, Adam and Eve, in his own image. He made Adam from dust in the earth and Eve from one of Adam's ribs.

One Greek myth says that Prometheus formed humanity from clay. In a Native American Mohawk myth the tribe's first man was made of baked clay, hence the red color of his skin. The Hindus of India believe that people originated from the thigh of a giant, and the Maya of Mesoamerica understood the human race to have been created when the gods united their thoughts. In Norse mythology, Odin, the god of wisdom, made the first humans and gave them poetry and the secret of writing. And so on. These and other accounts of the first humans have certain elements in common. In every case, gods precede people; gods are more powerful than people; and gods have the power to create and destroy the human race.

DARWIN AND THE THEORY OF EVOLUTION

Although creation myths are the expression of a creative cultural imagination and a feature of all human societies, they are not scientific. In western Europe, it was not until the eighteenth century that naturalists (scientists and philosophers who study nature) observed similarities between certain species that suggested they were somehow linked. The naturalists then began to question the account of creation given in the Bible, in which God creates each species separately. At first, the naturalists lacked a system that would allow them to organize their knowledge according to the vast timeframe of natural history. They began by compiling encyclopedias and classifying plants and animals, and by the nineteenth century theories of the evolution of species emerged.

Modern evolutionary theory is attributed to the research of two Britons, Charles Darwin (1809–1882) and Alfred Russel Wallace (1823–1913). Both had traveled widely and observed animals in many different habitats—Wallace in the islands of Southeast Asia, and Darwin in the Galapagos Islands, as well as in other parts of the world. In 1858, Wallace published a paper arguing that humans and primates were descended from a common ancestor, and in the same year he co-authored a paper with Darwin explaining the principle of evolution. In 1859, Darwin published his famous *On the Origin of Species by Means of Natural Selection*, which was based on observations made while sailing around the world from 1831 to 1836 aboard the ship *Beagle*.

Darwin argued that each species—including humans—evolved gradually over millennia and survived according to its ability to adapt to the environment. Those that could not adapt died out. This process of **natural selection** is popularly known as the "survival of the fittest," which actually misrepresents Darwin's findings. His view of human evolution contradicted two major aspects of the Bible. One was the notion that life was created with a moral purpose, and the other that species were individually conceived and placed on earth separately rather than evolving from one another.

In 1871, Darwin published *The Descent of Man*, in which he claimed that humans were descended from lower species over a period of millions of years. This led to a new body of research aimed at locating the "missing link"—that is, the species that lies between apes and humans. Today's scientists are continuing that search, which highlights important differences between science and myth. Science continues to build information from around the globe and is open-ended, but myths originate from particular cultures and are specific to those cultures.

THE NATURE OF PREHISTORY

The earliest, and longest, era of history is referred to as **prehistory**, most of which will remain forever dimmed by the mists of time. However, because it is in our nature to search for origins, most intelligent people are curious about their personal past. This curiosity usually extends to the history of one's family, one's culture, and even one's species. Knowing how little we remember about what we did and thought only yesterday, let alone about our early childhood, we realize that information about what took place hundreds of thousands of years ago is likely to be scanty indeed.

In this text, prehistory refers to any time before the invention of writing. But prehistory is not a specific date that can be applied consistently throughout the world. Different cultures develop writing systems at different periods of their history. A civilization such as ancient Egypt in 2500 B.C. (see Chapter 3), for example, was literate long before western Europe, which had no writing until it was conquered by the Romans in the

first century B.C. And today, there are regions of the world where oral traditions persist and there are no established writing systems.

Without written records, scholars have to decipher and reconstruct prehistory from physical remains (see Box). The earliest are primarily bones, tools, and weapons. From later prehistoric periods there is evidence of burials, and, as we approach the Upper Paleolithic era, we encounter early examples of the creative arts. There are fragmentary remains of rudimentary musical instruments, decorative ornaments, small-scale statues, wall paintings, and later still, of buildings (see Box, p. 5, top).

Scholars also resort to hypotheses when shaping their theories. These hypotheses often depend on the ability to make connections between the past and modern preliterate cultures, although parallels between prehistoric cultures and contemporary societies must be drawn with caution. Nevertheless, they reflect both the continuum of human development and the fact that people have produced similar forms and ideas in very different times and places.

The term Stone Age may sound ancient, but in fact it followed millions of years during which hominids (near- or proto-humans) evolved into modern humans. This process is generally thought to have begun around 5 million years ago when pre-humans roamed East and north central Africa. Their skulls were the size of an ape's and they lived in small groups, sustaining themselves mainly by gathering edible plants and grains (see Box, p. 5, bottom).

Society and Culture

The Study of Human Prehistory

There are many categories of scientists who investigate prehistory by relying on physical, rather than written, evidence. Among these are geologists, who study the minerals of a particular region, which can provide evidence of materials available for tools, weapons, and other objects. Paleontologists analyze fossil remains, anthropologists analyze society and culture, and paleoanthropologists analyze all three. Archaeologists study artifacts such as pots, jewelry, furniture, dwellings, and weapons. Ethnographers deal with contemporary preliterate societies and sometimes make inferences from them about prehistoric cultures that no longer exist. Biologists study skeletons, and forensic scientists attempt to discover causes of death. Geneticists collect the DNA of prehistoric bones, which reinforces some traditional theories and challenges others. Additional evidence comes from the remains of human garbage (garbology), footprints, and even feces (which can offer clues to diet). Art historians study the evolution of style and artistic techniques.

Dating Prehistory

Physical evidence is dated according to a number of systems. Geologists use stratigraphy to measure layers of earth and date objects according to the layer in which they are found. Dendrochronologists determine age from tree rings, which is most useful in regions with large areas of forestation. In seriation, dating is according to stylistic changes, which evolve over time, in similar types of artifacts. Radiocarbon dating, although its accuracy is questioned, is based on the measure of carbon-14 in an organic substance. As organisms decay, the carbon-14 in them begins to decay, making it possible to determine the age of the substance. Thermoluminescence dates objects by measuring radioactive changes as electrons shift their normal positions in relation to the atom. This system is particularly accurate when used on burned materials such as flint, stones, and fired pottery.

In July 2002, in Chad in north central Africa, a skull was discovered with a small brain comparable in size to a chimpanzee brain, and human and ape-like features. Nicknamed Toumai, meaning "Hope of Life" in the local language, this find altered the prevailing view of human development, particularly the point at which the first humans branched off from the line of chimpanzees. Thought to be 6 or 7 million years old, Toumai is considered by some scientists to be the oldest known hominid, although others believe Toumai may not even be a hominid. Toumai has been given the impressive scientific designation *Sahelanthropus tchadensis*, roughly meaning "the man from Chad, in the Sahara."

An early fossil was unearthed in 1974 at Hadar, in Ethiopia. The scientific name of the fossil's genus is *Australopithecus*

Major Periods of Human Evolution

c. 5 million B.C.	evidence of pre-human fossil fragments in Africa
c. 5–3 million B.C.	*Australopithecus*
c. 2 million to *c.* 1.6 million B.C.	*Homo habilis*
c. 1.8 million to *c.* 500,000 B.C.	*Homo erectus*
c. 500,000 B.C.	Archaic *Homo sapiens*
c. 130,000–80,000 B.C.	*Homo sapiens*
c. 100,000–33,000 B.C.	Neanderthal Man
c. 40,000 B.C. to the present	*Homo sapiens sapiens*

(which existed around 5 to around 3 million years ago), but the species, *afarensis*, is named for the local Afar culture. Dr. Donald Johanson, whose team discovered the fossil, named it Lucy after the refrain of the Beatles' song "Lucy in the Sky with Diamonds," which he and his co-workers were playing as they celebrated the find. What remains of Lucy are the skull, thighbone, and lower jaw. Although it is not known if Lucy was male or female, the bones belonged to a young adult, who could walk upright (**bipedal**). "Lucy" is only one of hundreds of bipedal *Australopithecus afarensis* fossils that have been found in East and southern Africa. Today Lucy resides in an Arizona laboratory.

Homo habilis ("handy man") developed in East and southern Africa some 2 million years ago. *Homo* (meaning "man") is the genus that comprises the human species, and *habilis* designates the species that converted stones into rudimentary weapons and tools for chopping and cutting, which increased its ability to control the environment. At first it was thought that *Homo habilis*, who lived mainly by hunting and gathering, completely supplanted the hominids. But, in 1959, two British researchers, Louis and Mary Leakey, were excavating fossils in Tanzania and found that different stages of hominids could coexist. They discovered many fossils, including one they named Zinj (short for *Zinjanthropus boisei*), whose lifespan overlapped that of *Homo habilis*, but who was not yet a member of the genus *Homo*. All that survived of Zinj, who was around 1,750,000 years old, was a skull, which had to be reconstructed from many small fragments.

Homo erectus ("upright man") evolved in Africa after *Homo habilis* and is thought to have migrated into the Middle East and Asia. Evidence of this migration is suggested by the discovery in Asia in 1891 of a skull, molar, and thighbone, known as "Java Man." In 1929, a Chinese archaeologist discovered the 500,000-year-old skullcap of a *Homo erectus*. Called "Peking Man," this find came from a cave near modern Beijing. Later, more fossils of the same type were discovered around Beijing as well as in Java. In addition, a nearly complete skeleton of *Homo erectus* was found in Kenya, in Africa, in 1984.

Homo erectus, as the term indicates, walked upright, although bipedal motion is actually thought to have started by the time of *Australopithecus afarensis* at least 4.5 million years ago (see Box, p. 6). Upright posture changed the relationship of individuals to the environment, making them seem taller and giving them a wider view of their surroundings. It also freed their hands for more advanced tool-making, especially axes and chisels, and better control of their weapons.

Some time between 1 million and 500,000 years ago, *Homo erectus* had marked another monumental step in human history—the use and control of fire. With fire, people could regulate heat and cook food. Fire reduced the amount of time it took to eat, because cooked food requires less chewing.

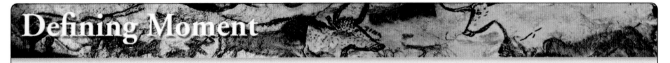

Defining Moment

Bipedalism

In the vast time span of human prehistory, there are several landmark steps that advanced the evolution of our species. Among them are the acquisition of language, the making of tools, the control of fire, and the creation of works of art. Preceding these steps, however, was the development of bipedalism—walking on two feet—which evolved over millions of years and became the defining characteristic of *Homo erectus*.

Paleoanthropologists have offered several explanations for why our ancestors adopted the consistently upright gait that differentiates us from other mammals. The prevailing view today is that bipedalism existed even earlier than *Australopithecus afarensis*, but that the pelvis, feet, and knee joints of that group were particularly suited to walking upright. Most scholars today believe that bipedalism evolved in mixed forest and open areas. These are the places where the earliest hominid fossils have been found.

Bipedalism had some important benefits. In open areas, it enabled early hominids to walk around and find food. It also allowed them to carry objects and walk at the same time, a more energy-efficient form of locomotion. Walking upright also provided better visibility and a broader sense of the environment. Bipedalism led our ancestors to use their hands in a number of new ways, including reaching for fruits on trees and carrying food back to other members of the group. Scholars have argued that females could thus leave foraging to the males and lead a more settled existence. This, in turn, allowed mothers to care more effectively for offspring, which improved their chances of survival.

Another development that followed bipedalism was the evolution of the precise opposing thumb, as compared with primates. This facilitated making tools as well as gathering food, constructing shelters, and creating works of art (figure **1.1**). The surviving evidence of art comes late in the Paleolithic period. For whatever reason prehistoric people created art, it surely required a combination of advanced symbolic thinking, an upright stance, and a developed thumb to work opposite the other four fingers.

Critical Question What do you think is the most important result of bipedalism, and why? What are some of its consequences?

1.1 *Scene of the Dead Man*, Shaft of the Dead Man, Lascaux caves, Dordogne, France, *c.* 14,000 B.C. Paint on limestone.

This developmental step, like inventions of modern household appliances, meant people had more free time to perfect other skills.

Somewhat over 500,000 years ago, an archaic form of *Homo sapiens* ("wise man") evolved in Africa and western Asia, seeming to support the view that human development began in Africa. To date, the earliest evidence for modern human behavior also comes from Africa, from preliminary finds in Blombos Cave, which is located to the east of Still Bay in a cliff overlooking the Indian Ocean. As early as around 90,000 years ago, the inhabitants of Blombos Cave, who were *Homo sapiens*, gathered seafood, ranging from shellfish to dolphins, as well as land animals. This is suggested by the oldest known bone tools with points made by a technique called pressure flaking, which was not used in Europe until 70,000 years later. So far, therefore, the Blombos people are the world's earliest known fishing community.

There is also evidence that the Blombos Cave people used ocher pigment, drilled into a fine powder, for body decoration. In addition, their organization of interior space suggests modern human behavior. The cave appears to have had a separate area for a hearth, and another for making stone and bone tools.

Overlapping the Blombos Cave group were the species of *Homo sapiens* known as Neanderthal Man and Cro-Magnon Man. The former, named for the Neander valley (in modern Germany), has so far been found in Europe and western Asia; Cro-Magnon Man was discovered in southern France. Both groups wore animal skins, but Cro-Magnons can be differentiated because they sewed clothing with bone needles and had more advanced tools than Neanderthals.

Scientists used to think that Neanderthal Man died out with the arrival of the Cro-Magnons, but in 1998 this notion was challenged by the discovery of the skeleton of a four-year-old child in the Lapedo valley, in Portugal. The child's anatomical make-up shows evidence of being a "hybrid" between Neanderthals and modern humans. The fact that the child was buried in animal skins painted with red ocher suggests ritual burial practices.

Theorists differ on the origin and lineage of *Homo sapiens.* Most agree that *Homo erectus* originated in Africa, and traveled from there to Asia and Europe. Some argue that *Homo sapiens* supplanted earlier groups in each of these areas. Others believe that the shift from *Homo erectus* to *Homo sapiens* took place in Africa alone and that it was only the latter who migrated.

In 2003, a discovery in Ethiopia provided a new link between Neanderthals and modern humans. Dated to around 160,000 years ago, this find consisted of three fossilized adult skulls and one skull belonging to a child. These skulls are longer than Neanderthal skulls, and the brain area is larger. This marked the earliest fossil evidence of modern humans and reinforced the view that *Homo sapiens* originated in Africa.

Our own species is called by some scholars *Homo sapiens sapiens* ("wise wise man") and *Homo sapiens* by others. This species appeared some 40,000 years ago and had a brain similar to ours. *Homo sapiens sapiens* traveled from Asia, through Europe, to the Americas and Australia. By 15,000 B.C., all of the earth's landmasses, except Antarctica, were inhabited by human groups (see Box).

Society and Culture

Important Developmental Steps in Early Human History

4.5 million years ago	beginning of upright gait (bipedalism)
2 million years ago	erect posture improved; brain development; beginning of stone tools
from 500,000 B.C.	rapid growth of the human brain
from 130,000 B.C.	*Homo sapiens* evolves; early language develops
from 40,000 B.C.	modern humans, with modern brains and speech function; tools assembled from different materials
from 25,000 B.C.	beginning of cave painting and small-scale sculpture
from 10,000 B.C.	bow and arrow invented; reindeer and dog domesticated
from 8000 to 4000 B.C.	sheep and goats domesticated, beginning of pottery production and farming
from 3000 B.C.	writing systems; metallurgy

WHAT MAKES US HUMAN

Certain important features distinguish the human species from other forms of life. Most of these features are aspects of symbolic thinking—the ability to think abstractly and to imagine things that are not physically present. It includes constructing language and theories, inventing new technology, telling stories, creating myths, and making art. All these activities are enriched by the use of **metaphor** (a comparison in which one thing stands for another). When we say, for example, that "the world is our oyster," we don't actually mean that the world is an oyster. We mean that we are ensconced in a comfortable space that we enjoy and can control. As a result, the saying suggests, we are bound for success and happiness. The metaphor thus creates an image that has a greater visual impact than would be conveyed by a literal description of the same idea.

SYMBOLIC THINKING

Beginning with *Homo habilis,* people made simple tools and weapons, whose uses we can usually identify. It is more difficult, however, to know what, if any, symbolic (or metaphorical) meaning may have been attached to such objects. But Stone Age ritual, such as the child burial found in Portugal, indicates symbolic thinking.

Most scholars believe that prehistoric people told stories, transmitting cultural myths orally. Thus they had a sense of **narrative sequence** (in which the events of a story follow chronologically), as well as of memory and time. Human handprints outlined with color on cave walls in different areas of the world—including western Europe, Africa, and South America—almost certainly had a ritual purpose. The prints also form repetitive, patterned images that suggest an awareness of time. Some cave paintings appear to illustrate narratives. In Spain, for example, paintings in Valtorta Gorge show humans moving from left to right and then attacking a herd of animals approaching from the opposite direction.

Another type of symbolic thinking is found in religious practices. One example is the formal burial, in which the body faces east, as if it will be reborn like the sun that rises each day. Food, tools, animal bones, and personal belongings that scholars believe were intended for the afterlife have also been found in burials. Red ocher pigment, such as that used on the child discovered in Portugal, was often sprinkled on corpses and is thought to represent blood. Since blood is a sign of life, the presence of red coloring has been interpreted as evidence of a belief in life after death.

CREATIVE ARTS

Among the most distinctly human achievements are the creative arts. Prehistoric paintings and sculptures such as those found in Europe (map **1.1,** p. 8) are sophisticated enough to

Map 1.1 Prehistoric art in Europe.

suggest that producing imagery was important, requiring both natural talent and training.

For those of us who view prehistory from a distance of thousands of years, works of art offer clues to the concerns and practices of our distant ancestors. Physical evidence of music was limited to rudimentary bone whistles and drums until the discovery of a 40,000-year-old Neanderthal bone flute. Human footprints arranged in circles preserved on cave floors have been read by some scholars as an indication of circle dancing.

The first known sculptures are Upper (Late) Paleolithic and date from around 30,000 B.C. Most represent animals or human females. The latter are usually interpreted as fertility figures, the best known being the so-called *Venus of Willendorf* (figure **1.2**). Discovered in 1908, she was named after the Roman goddess of love and beauty because the exaggeration of the breasts and pelvis suggests that the statue was associated with fertility. Carved from limestone, the *Venus* is small enough to hold in the palm of one's hand. Her small scale is typical of Paleolithic sculptures, making her easily portable and thus practical in a nomadic culture.

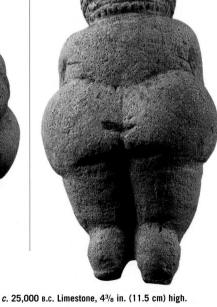

1.2 *Venus of Willendorf* (front and back), *c.* 25,000 B.C. Limestone, 4⅜ in. (11.5 cm) high. **Naturhistorisches Museum, Vienna.**

By minimizing the arms, eliminating the neck, and covering the face, the artist compresses space and conveys a sense of maternal power. The emphasis on the breasts and pelvis has led some scholars to interpret the figure as a Great Goddess. The elegant rhythms created by the curved contours and bulbous circular forms reveal a high level of artistry.

In 2000, a cave with early Upper Paleolithic incised images of animals and human females was discovered. Located south of the Dordogne region of France, the cave contained mammoths, bison, deer, horses, a rhinoceros, and a couple of geese. Figure **1.3** shows one of the human females, whose outline emphasizes her bulk and clearly delineates her breast.

The later paintings found in the caves at Lascaux, in the Dordogne itself, date to around 14,000 B.C. (figure **1.4**). They depict mainly animals—bison, deer, boar, wolves, horses, and mammoths. Occasional humans at Lascaux are represented as rudimentary stick figures, whereas the animals are **naturalistic**—that is, they resemble the appearance of the actual animals. The paintings are located hundreds of feet inside the caves, where it is thought that they might have been part of a hunting ritual. Since people did not inhabit cave interiors, it is unlikely that the paintings were purely for decoration.

Although cave paintings have been interpreted from many points of view, the most common reading is that they had a ritual, or ceremonial, meaning. The images are believed by some scholars to have been made to help hunters capture animals needed for survival. Likewise, the naturalism of the animals adds to the impression that the actual animal is captured by the image. In some places, one animal is painted over

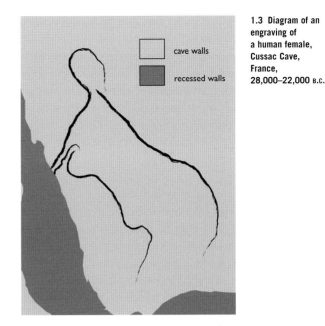

1.3 Diagram of an engraving of a human female, Cussac Cave, France, 28,000–22,000 B.C.

cave walls

recessed walls

another, suggesting that once the image was fixed to the wall it had served its function. On the other hand, some animals that were hunted are not represented, which undermines the theory that the very act of painting an animal was a symbolic capture.

1.4 **Hall of Running Bulls, Lascaux caves,** *c.* 14,000 B.C. Paint on limestone.

Whatever the explanation for the cave paintings of western Europe, they probably served a ritual purpose. Prehistoric life was not as compartmentalized as modern, technological society. As a result, art, religion, politics, and other segments of culture were more integrated than they are today. The concept of "art for art's sake," which originated in nineteenth-century France, was almost certainly not known in prehistoric cultures.

SHAMANISM

An important religious figure in most hunting and gathering societies is the **shaman**. This is an individual believed to have supernatural powers, including the ability to cure disease, foretell the future, control nature, and communicate with the animal and spiritual worlds. Shamans are associated with fire, which burns natural substances and thus has power over nature. The shaman uses fire in rituals and is believed to have an intense

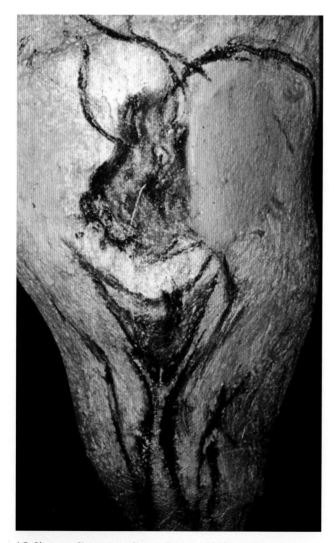

1.5 *Bison-man*, Chauvet cave, Chauvet, France, *c.* 24,000 B.C. Charcoal on a vertical section of rock.
This figure, like the Lascaux animals, is massive and naturalistically portrayed. The merger of human and animal forms reflects the transitional state of the shaman, who changes his shape and navigates between different worlds.

inner heat. This, along with trance-like states and dreams, assists in transporting the shaman to a spiritual plane of existence.

Scholars have noted that although animals and humans do not physically resemble each other, the blood of an animal is virtually indistinguishable from that of a human. For this reason, it is thought that early hunters, who depended on animals for survival, developed a kind of identification with their prey. This was expressed visually in images of the shaman. There are a number of cave paintings with figures that combine human and animal characteristics, and these are interpreted as shamans.

At Chauvet in the south of France, for example, in a recently discovered cave dated by carbon-14 to around 30,000 B.C., explorers found a composite figure with the head and upper body of a bison and the lower body and upright posture of a human (figure **1.5**). In the absence of a Paleolithic writing system, it is difficult to know the exact meaning of such images. They do, however, suggest the transformations of the shaman and the use of animal masks and animal skins in rituals (see Box, p. 13).

THE UPPER (LATE) PALEOLITHIC ERA IN WESTERN EUROPE: *c.* 45,000–*c.* 10,000/8000 B.C.

We now turn to the three main Stone Age periods in western Europe. By the Upper Paleolithic era, *Homo sapiens sapiens* (also called *Homo sapiens*) had been established on the continent. The economy and survival of this group depended on hunting and gathering. They were constantly on the move, following the seasonal migrations of animals they hunted for food. Among these were bison, deer, horses, and the now-extinct mammoth. There appears to have been a gender-based division of labor; men became hunters, and women gathered grains and plants and were guardians of the home.

The hunters and gatherers built temporary structures, such as tents, using wood, bone, and animal skins, or they found shelter at entrances to caves. In addition, they constructed more elaborate houses made of mammoth bones and skulls. Some structures dating from *c.* 16,000 B.C. have been discovered in eastern Europe and were arranged in groups of as many as ten. The mammoth bones interlocked to form walls and a roof, with large tusks creating an entrance arch. It is likely that animal hides were attached to the structure for warmth and protection. Generally, Upper Paleolithic houses had a hearth in a large central room, or several fires if additional rooms warranted them. Color found on the fragmentary remains of houses suggests that living quarters may have been decorated. The structure diagrammed in figure **1.6**, however, shows no sign of human habitation and probably served a ceremonial rather than a domestic function.

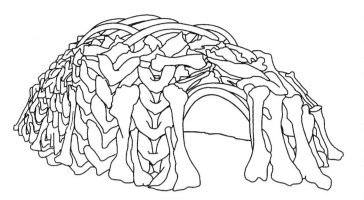

1.6 Diagram of reconstructed mammoth-bone house from Mezhirich, Ukraine, *c.* 16,000 B.C.

MESOLITHIC TO NEOLITHIC IN WESTERN EUROPE: *c.* 10,000/8000–6000/4000 B.C.

The Mesolithic period evolved in western Europe between 10,000 and 8000 B.C. With the rapid warming of the climate, glaciers receded and sea levels rose. The human population increased and migrated into northern Europe. As forests replaced the bleak plains of the Paleolithic landscape, animal populations shifted and hunters found their food supply greatly reduced. They survived by settling in groups and finding new kinds of sustenance. They wove plant fibers for fishing baskets and began to make pottery. There is evidence of early settled societies, especially along the Danube River, and of boatbuilding in the north of Europe.

The first formal human cemeteries date from the latter part of the Mesolithic period. Decorative objects, such as carved animal teeth, were found buried with the dead. This attention to burial reflects increasing social complexity, with class divisions based on wealth, as well as the idea that such objects might be needed in an afterlife. Interesting among Mesolithic developments are elaborate dog cemeteries, which suggest that dogs were valued, possibly because they could be trained to assist hunters and perform other useful tasks. The art of this period, however, is of less interest than Paleolithic and Neolithic works.

THE NEOLITHIC ERA: *c.* 6000/4000–*c.* 1500 B.C.

With the consolidation of farming communities and their expansion into settled villages, the Neolithic period began. People cultivated local staples such as grains and cereals, and used oxen to pull their plows. Other animals—cows, pigs, sheep, and goats—were domesticated and bred for food. In addition, livestock and goods were apparently imported from the Near East. Weaving and pottery

became more sophisticated and metal-working developed. The study of Neolithic villages around the world has shown evidence of ancestor worship, a preoccupation with fertility, ritual practices, belief systems, and works of art and architecture.

People who are constantly on the move do not build large-scale stone monuments. But with the evolution of agriculture, settled communities developed in Europe, following a similar pattern of settlement found throughout the world. In Jericho, in the Jordan valley, a Neolithic city dating to around 8000 B.C. was surrounded by massive stone walls and a stone tower 30 feet (9 m) high. Some 2500 years later, at Çatal Hüyük (in modern Turkey), a Neolithic city extended over 30 acres (12 ha) of land. In China, at Ban Po, near modern Xi'an, one of the best-preserved Neolithic settlements dates to around 6000 B.C. It consisted of a large central building with a hearth and smaller buildings, which were surrounded by a moat. The inhabitants of Ban Po produced pottery and burial urns, and cultivated grains.

By around 4500 B.C., copper tools were used in Europe and copper ornaments provided personal objects of decoration. The practice of self-adornment suggests the presence of status- and wealth-based class divisions, as well as the ritual use of ornamentation. A copper pot of around 4000 B.C. from the region of modern Bulgaria (figure **1.7**) is partly polished and marked with sharp incised lines. The eye design

1.7 Vessel from Hotnica, near Veliko Turnovo, Bulgaria, *c.* 4000 B.C.

1.8 Stonehenge, view of the cromlech, Salisbury Plain, Wiltshire, England,
c. **1800–1500** B.C. Diameter of circle 97 ft. (29.6 m).

suggests that the shape of the vessel was associated with human form.

In western Europe, Neolithic people used stone for burials and various types of ritual structures, which are called **megalithic**, meaning made of large stones. The most famous example of megalithic building in Europe is the **cromlech** (circle of stones) at Stonehenge (figure **1.8**).

STONEHENGE

Located on Salisbury Plain in southwestern England, Stonehenge was first chosen as a sacred site around 3000 B.C. Several stages of construction concluded with the cromlech about 1500 years later.

At first, Stonehenge was simply a circular earth mound used for burials. Later, circles of upright stones (called **menhirs**) and individual **trilithons** (in which two uprights support a horizontal stone) were added. This kind of building system is called **post-and-lintel**, the two verticals being the posts and the horizontal, the lintel. An avenue extends from the earth mound (figure **1.9**) and is marked by the Heel Stone, over

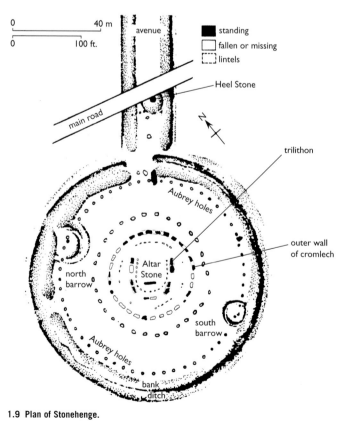

1.9 Plan of Stonehenge.

Thematic Parallels

Shamanism in Non-Western Imagery

Modern hunting and gathering societies share some of the preoccupations of Paleolithic cultures. The persistence of such societies—like the Australian Aboriginals—is a fortunate circumstance for historians, despite the caution with which comparisons must be made.

Australian Dreaming

The Aborigines of Australia have adopted the Western term *Dreaming* to designate a mythological time and place. It includes the present time and place of the Aborigine, and the balance between the human world and a greater universe populated by ancestors. Through imagery and ritual, the Aboriginal shaman contacts the spirit world of ancestors and the store of knowledge built up through time. Dreaming is the main content of rock art in Australia.

Figure **1.10** is an example from around 20,000 B.C. from Australia's Northern Territory. It depicts the Lightning Brothers and other lightning figures believed to be among the malevolent ancestors who created the universe. They stare directly out of the wall, the two Brothers in human form towering over smaller figures with serpentine bodies and human faces. Rays of light radiate from the heads. The repetition of the figures and their frontality create a series of fixed, threatening gazes.

Shamanistic Imagery in Africa

Shamanistic imagery is common among the rock paintings of the South African San, who live mainly in the Kalahari Desert. The eland—a large antelope with twisted horns—is of great importance to San hunters and appears frequently in their art.

1.11 *above* **South African human–eland composite, 19th century.**

Like the bison-man from Chauvet (see figure 1.5), figure **1.11** shows human and animal images that represent the shaman's process of transformation. The figure walks upright with a human torso and legs; but the head is that of an eland. Such works of art express the shaman's identification with the animal as well as the ability of the shaman to straddle the spiritual and the natural world.

The Anishnabe Drum

Shamanism, especially in healing and hunting rituals, plays an important role in certain Native American cultures. Various musical instruments are used by shamans, but the drum is of particular importance. Today, as in earlier cultures, the shaman's drum may be endowed with symbolic meanings related to its organic materials—wood and animal hides—which are associated with the transformations of the shaman.

It is in the nature of music that instruments are silent until taken up and played. The musician thus gives life to the instrument, and musicians, like artists and actors, seem to have magic creative powers. When played by a shaman, the drum's beat elicits ecstatic states and trances. Among the Native American Anishnabe, shaman drums are painted with images of animals, showing their interior anatomical structure. This can be seen in a late eighteenth-century drum (figure **1.12**), on which the heart and other organs are depicted in red ocher inside the outline of the animals. These images reflect the belief that shamans, in contrast to ordinary people, can see their own skeletons and have x-ray vision.

1.12 **Double-headed Anishnabe drum, late 18th century. Animal hide, wood, red ocher, diameter 18$\frac{7}{8}$ in. (48 cm). Städtisches Museum, Braunschweig, Germany.**

1.10 *Lightning Brothers and Lightning Figures*, Katherine River, Northern Territory, Australia, *c.* 20,000 B.C.

which the sun rises each year on June 21, the summer solstice. Other stones are aligned according to positions of the moon and stars as well as to eclipses and the path of Halley's Comet. These observations have led scholars to interpret Stonehenge as a monument that was used in agricultural rites to celebrate seasonal changes important in farming.

Hypotheses about the meaning of Stonehenge are numerous, but definitive conclusions remain elusive. Among the mysteries connected with the monument is the question of how the stones were transported, given that the wheel was not yet known in western Europe. The stones were brought to the site from two different quarries, probably rolled on logs. The 40-ton (42,000-kg) bluestones came from Wales, a distance of over 100 miles (160 km), and the 50-ton (50,000-kg) sarsens (made of sandstone) from 20 miles (32 km) away. The construction of Stonehenge was an enormous undertaking in terms of labor, organization, and social commitment.

As Neolithic village communities evolved into the first cities, the process of urbanization began. Early cities marked important social developments, requiring administrative centers and professional differentiation according to such occupations as artisan, merchant, soldier, religious leader, and ruler. Class systems based on rank and status, as well as profession, also evolved. Technological developments in the first cities included an increase in sophisticated tools, the use of the wheel and new modes of land transportation and boats, and the beginning of metallurgy that led from the Stone Age to the Bronze Age. In the next chapter, we consider the development of cities in the Ancient Near East.

KEY TERMS

bipedal able to walk upright on two feet.

cromlech a circle of stones, characteristic of the Neolithic period in western Europe.

megalithic a Neolithic structure made of large stones.

menhir a single upright stone.

metaphor a comparison without using "like" or "as" in which one thing stands for another.

narrative sequence a story that follows chronologically.

natural selection Darwin's theory of the survival of species best adapted to their environment.

naturalistic representing objects as they actually appear in nature.

post-and-lintel an elevation system in which two upright posts support a horizontal lintel; also called a trilithon.

prehistory a period of history before the development of writing systems.

shaman a religious figure believed to have supernatural powers, including the ability of self-transformation from human to animal.

trilithon a single post-and-lintel.

KEY QUESTIONS

1. How would we prove that Upper Paleolithic era (c. 45,000–10,000/8000 B.C.) humans were not merely on an endless quest to find the necessities of life? What other activities did they engage in?
2. What does the earliest art show about humanity's first ceremonies or rituals? What elements must be present before we can say an individual can think symbolically?
3. What is an example of one of humanity's earliest "narrative sequences"?
4. What characteristics of cave art make it "naturalistic"?

SUGGESTED READING

Barber, Elizabeth Wayland. *Women's Work: the First 20,000 Years: Women, Cloth, and Society in Early Times*. New York: W. W. Norton, 1994.
  ▶ A study of the role of women in early society.

Berlo, Janet C., and Ruth B. Phillips. *Native North American Art*. New York: Oxford University Press, 1998.
  ▶ An introduction to Native Art in North America.

Caruna, Wally. *Aboriginal Art*. London: Thames and Hudson, 1993.
▸ An introduction to the Aboriginal arts of Australia.

Casteldon, Rodney. *The Making of Stonehenge*. London: Routledge, 1993.
▸ A study of the origins of Stonehenge.

Clottes, Jean, and David Lewis-Williams. *The Shamans of Prehistory*, trans. Sophie Hawkes. New York: Harry N. Abrams, 1998.
▸ A study of the role and meaning of prehistoric shamanism.

Corbin, George. *Native Arts of North America, Africa, and the South Pacific*. New York: HarperCollins, 1988.
▸ A general introduction to the arts and customs of Native North America, Africa, and the South Pacific cultures.

Cunliffe, Barry (ed.). *The Oxford Illustrated Prehistory of Europe*. Oxford and New York: Oxford University Press, 1994.
▸ A general reference book.

Eliade, Mircea. *Shamanism*, trans. Willard R. Trask. Princeton, NJ: Princeton University Press, 1974.
▸ A study of shamanism by one of the most original scholars in the field of religious history.

——. *A History of Religious Ideas* (2 vols.). Chicago: University of Chicago Press, 1978.
▸ A survey of worldwide religious ideas, beginning with prehistory.

——. *The Forge and The Crucible*, trans. Stephen Corrin. New York and Evanston: Harper and Row, 1971.
▸ A study of the role and meaning of alchemy in different cultures.

Feder, Kenneth L. *The Past in Perspective: Introduction to Human Prehistory*. New York: Houghton Mifflin, 1996.
▸ A general overview of early human history.

Johanson, Donald, Lenora Johanson, and Blake Edgar. *Ancestors: In Search of Human Origins*. New York: Villard Books, 1994.
▸ An anthropological study of the search for human origins. Johanson's team discovered Lucy.

Onians, John (ed.). *Atlas of World Art*. London: Laurence King Publishing, and New York: Oxford University Press, 2004.
▸ A survey of world art showing the impact of geography on the development and spread of art.

Sandars, N. K. *Prehistoric Art in Europe*. New Haven, CT, and London: Yale University Press, 1995.
▸ An overview of prehistoric art in western and central Europe.

Sayers, Andrew. *Australian Art*. Oxford and New York: Oxford University Press, 2001.
▸ A survey of the arts of Australia.

Scarre, Chris. *Places in Time: Exploring Prehistoric Europe*. New York and Oxford: Oxford University Press, 1998.
▸ A study of art and culture in prehistoric Europe.

Smart, Ninian. *The World's Religions*. London: Cambridge University Press, 1998.
▸ A reference book on the nature and history of world religions.

SUGGESTED FILMS

1968   *Planet of the Apes*, dir. Franklin J. Schaffner

1970   *Beneath the Planet of the Apes*, dir. Ted Post

1973   *Battle for the Planet of the Apes*, dir. J. Lee Thompson

1981   *Quest for Fire*, dir. Jean-Jacques Arnaud

1986   *Clan of the Cave Bear*, dir. Michael Chapman

1993   *Jurassic Park*, dir. Steven Spielberg

1997   *The Lost World: Jurassic Park*, dir. Steven Spielberg

2001   *Jurassic Park III*, dir. Joe Johnston

2 The Ancient Near East

> *He ordered built the walls of Uruk of the Sheepfold, the walls of holy Eanna, stainless sanctuary. Observe its walls, whose upper hem is like bronze; behold its inner wall, which no work can equal. Touch the stone threshold, which is ancient; draw near the Eanna, dwelling-place of the goddess Ishtar, a work no king among later kings can match.*"
>
> (*The Epic of Gilgamesh*, TABLET I, COL. I, LINES 9–15)

The Ancient Near East included many civilizations located in much of what we now call the Middle East and modern Turkey (see map 2.1, p. 20). From the Neolithic period (seventh millennium B.C.), settled communities began to evolve into urban centers. Some monumental architecture has survived, along with distinctive pottery, sculptures, and fragments of painting. There are no surviving musical notations, but texts and works of art indicate that music was an important part of Ancient Near Eastern civilization.

The focus of this chapter will be Mesopotamia, which comprised most of modern Iraq, where many important advances in civilization first occurred. Literally "the land between the rivers," Mesopotamia profited from the Tigris and Euphrates rivers, and early on developed irrigation systems and improved agriculture. At some time in the late fourth millennium B.C. the earliest known writing system emerged, which for the first time in human history made record-keeping and other forms of documentation possible, including the compilation of king lists and accounts of historical events. This led to a rich literature in the Ancient Near East, where the first known epic, The Epic of Gilgamesh, was recorded.

"He" in the quotation at the beginning of the chapter is Gilgamesh, the world's earliest literary epic hero. The lines celebrate his incomparable achievement in founding the ancient city of Uruk (modern Warka, in Iraq), which was divided into three parts—the center, an orchard, and the claypits, where bricks and ceramics used in building were located. When the poet says that the "upper hem is like bronze," he is creating a metaphor associating the walls that surround the city with a skirt. He also mentions Ishtar (Inanna), the goddess who **personified** (embodied as a person) war, wisdom, and fertility, and who protected the city. And he uses the **epithet** (an identifying adjective or phrase) "Uruk of the Sheepfold" to denote the city. All such poetic devices indicate that by the time the epic was written down, a long oral tradition had already established certain literary **conventions** (accepted practices), which are still used today.

Key Topics

Cultural Developments

Urbanization

Kingship

The invention of writing

The first epic poem:
  Gilgamesh

Hammurabi's law code

Assurbanipal's library

Geography and War

The Fertile Crescent

Military campaigns of
  Assurbanipal

Humans Seek Their Place in the Cosmos

Polytheism

Zoroastrianism

TIMELINE	URUK PERIOD c. 3500–3000	EARLY DYNASTIC PERIOD c. 3000–2350	AKKADIAN PERIOD c. 2350–2100	NEO-SUMERIAN PERIOD c. 2150–1800	OLD BABYLONIAN PERIOD c. 1900–1600	ASSYRIANS c. 1300–612	NEO-BABYLONIAN PERIOD 625–539
HISTORY AND CULTURE	Development of writing Agricultural economy City-states	Gilgamesh king of Uruk	Sargon I founds Akkadian dynasty, c. 2334	Invasions from east destroy Akkadian power Gudea king of Lagash	Arabian Amorite dynasty Hammurabi king of Babylon Law code of Hammurabi, c. 1780	Assyrian Empire Assurbanipal king of Assyria Conquests in Egypt and black Africa	Nebuchad-nezzar II king of Babylon
RELIGION AND MYTH	Pantheon of gods	Elaborate temple complexes Priests and temple-workers	Naram-Sin declares himself a god				
ART			Stele of Naram-Sin, c. 2254–2210	Statue of Gudea, c. 2144–2124		Palace reliefs, 668–627	
ARCHITECTURE	Brick construction City of Uruk founded, c. 3500	Ziggurats Uruk's city wall constructed		Temple-building	Babylon built to Hammurabi's plans		Hanging Gardens of Babylon Tower of Babel
LITERATURE				The Epic of Gilgamesh, recorded late 3rd millennium		Assurbanipal founds library, 7th century	
MUSIC		Kettledrums, lyres				Stringed instruments	

THE FERTILE CRESCENT

Mesopotamia emerged from the Neolithic era around 4500 B.C., when people began smelting metals and developing metallurgy. Copper and, later, tin were imported, leading to the design of more effective tools, weapons, and vessels.

The two main cultural groups of ancient Mesopotamia roughly correspond to the north–south geographic division of the land. The first period of Sumerian culture in the south lasted from around 3800 to 2250 B.C., when the Akkadians from the north rose to power. They brought the Semitic Akkadian language, which gained primacy in the region, although Sumerian remained the literary language in the entire land for centuries.

The Tigris and Euphrates rivers provided the desert regions of Mesopotamia with an abundant source of water. The invention of the plow and the wheel, as well as irrigation, advanced agriculture and technology. The potter's wheel was used for **ceramics** (pottery), while the wagon wheel made it possible to construct carts (pulled by animals) for travel and transport. This, along with river boats, facilitated Mesopotamian trade with other cultures (map **2.1**).

URBANIZATION AND ARCHITECTURE

According to *The Epic of Gilgamesh*, the foundations of Uruk were "laid down by the seven sages" at some point in the distant past. Archaeologists generally date the founding of the city to around 3500 B.C., and the term "Uruk" also designates an archaeological period beginning at this time. Gilgamesh became Uruk's king hundreds of years later, in the Early Dynastic Period, and he is credited with the construction of the 5¾-mile (9.25-km)-long city wall. Because the poet tells us that Uruk is a sheepfold, we conclude that its economy was originally based on agriculture and farming and that its king was a metaphorical shepherd.

At the center of Uruk, Gilgamesh built the sacred sanctuary of Eanna, which contained the earliest known example of a **ziggurat**, the most characteristic form of Mesopotamian

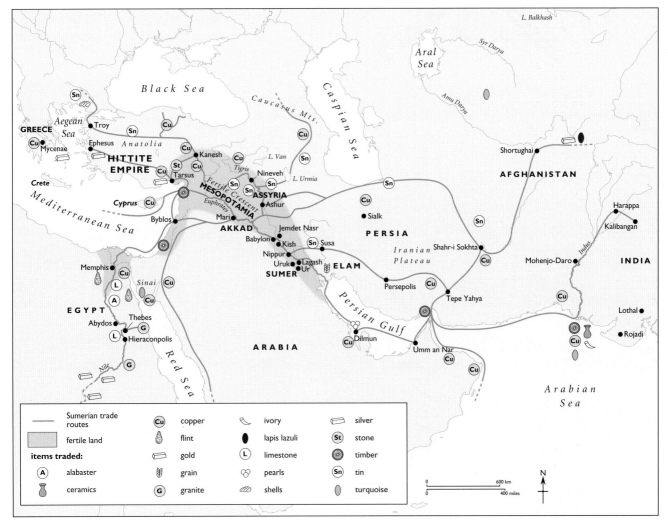

Map 2.1 Trade in the Ancient Near and Middle East.

monumental architecture (figures **2.1** and **2.2**). A ziggurat was usually part of a temple complex and supported a temple on its flat top. On the level terrain of Mesopotamia, these massive, solid structures stood out and were thought of as mountains, where the gods dwelled. By constructing a ziggurat, therefore, the Mesopotamians recognized the gods as inhabitants, patrons, and protectors of their cities (see Box).

The ziggurat at Uruk was made of brick and was over 45 feet (13.7 m) high and 150 feet (45.7 m) wide. Its four corners were oriented to the four points of the compass, reflecting its cosmic significance. At the top stood a shrine called the White Temple, possibly because of the whitewash on its outer surface (figure **2.3**). The precinct

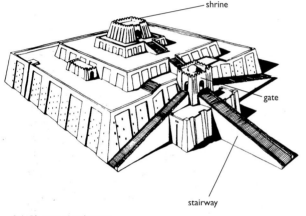

2.1 Diagram of a ziggurat.

The Mesopotamian Cosmos

The Mesopotamians conceived of the earth as a flat disk surmounted by a huge, heavenly vault. In between heaven and earth was the atmosphere, from which the celestial bodies were made. Enclosing the cosmos was an infinite, primeval sea. Death was a dreary and inevitable end to mortal life, and the spirits of the dead dwelled in an underworld. This was a region of darkness, in contrast to the radiant light emitted by gods. Mesopotamian religion was **polytheistic** (consisting of many gods) and the gods were **anthropomorphic** (human in form).

The main sky gods of Sumer were Anu and his consort, Ninhursag. Anu, Enlil (god of the air), and Enki (Akkadian Ea), god of the primeval watery abyss, formed the primary triad of deities. The sun and moon gods were Utu (Akkadian Shamash) and Nanna (Akkadian Sin), respectively; and the powerful and complex Inanna (Akkadian Ishtar) was goddess of love, war, and fertility. The pantheon ("all the gods") was ruled by a king presiding over a divine assembly that controlled fate.

Humans, according to the Mesopotamians, were created in two overlapping ways. On the one hand, they were the product of an utterance, the word of a god. The power of the word has a long history in Western thought and is reflected in a hymn to Enlil, declaring his command "far-reaching" and his word "holy." On the other hand, people were physically created like sculptures, out of clay and a god's blood. In either case, they were the gods' servants. One way in which people served the gods was by caring for their statues, which they housed (in temples), fed, and clothed.

2.2 Northeastern side of the Ziggurat at Uruk, *c.* 2255–2040 B.C. Brick, over 45 ft. (13.7 m) high and 150 ft. (45.7 m) wide.

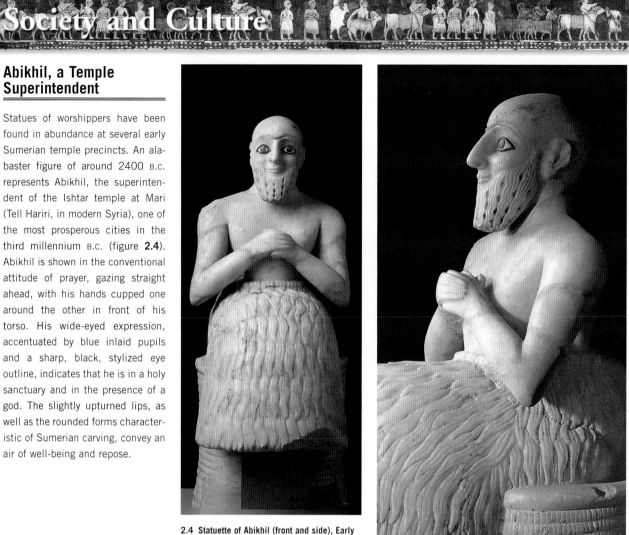

Abikhil, a Temple Superintendent

Statues of worshippers have been found in abundance at several early Sumerian temple precincts. An alabaster figure of around 2400 B.C. represents Abikhil, the superintendent of the Ishtar temple at Mari (Tell Hariri, in modern Syria), one of the most prosperous cities in the third millennium B.C. (figure **2.4**). Abikhil is shown in the conventional attitude of prayer, gazing straight ahead, with his hands cupped one around the other in front of his torso. His wide-eyed expression, accentuated by blue inlaid pupils and a sharp, black, stylized eye outline, indicates that he is in a holy sanctuary and in the presence of a god. The slightly upturned lips, as well as the rounded forms characteristic of Sumerian carving, convey an air of well-being and repose.

2.4 Statuette of Abikhil (front and side), Early Dynastic period, *c.* 2400–2300 B.C. Alabaster, 20⅝ in. (52.5 cm) high. Louvre, Paris.

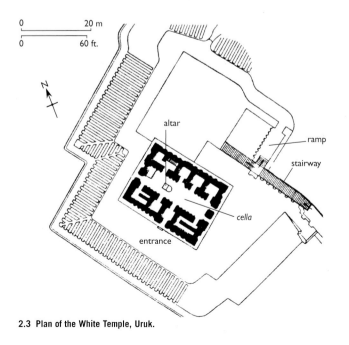

2.3 Plan of the White Temple, Uruk.

also contained two other temples, one red and the other decorated with cones inserted into the wall so that only the round ends were visible. The cones were painted and arranged with the circles forming geometric patterns of color. The layouts of interior rooms and remains found in such temples reflect the elaborate Mesopotamian belief system, sophisticated building techniques, and the presence of a class of priests and other temple-workers of considerable importance (see Box).

THE DEVELOPMENT OF WRITING

The Sumerians began to develop writing sometime before 3000 B.C., during the early Uruk period. At first they devised a system of record-keeping for administrative efficiency and identifying ownership. Soon thereafter, an important body of literature followed.

Defining Moment

Urbanization in Mesopotamia

The city of Uruk today is a vast landscape of ruins in southern Iraq. But in ancient Mesopotamia, Uruk was a city enclosed by protective walls surrounding some 2 square miles (518 ha) of houses, palaces, workshops, and temples. Urbanization started in Mesopotamia in the fourth millennium B.C. and was a defining moment in the so-called cradle of civilization.

Uruk had begun as a village like other villages; its evolution into a major city revolved around its important temple. Temples in Mesopotamia owned estates where peasants cultivated gardens and tended herds of cattle and pigs. Since Mesopotamians believed that people were created to serve and feed the gods, their towns grew up around a god's temple. By around 2500 B.C., however, military lords and kings gained political power that rivaled that of the temple priest.

Urban life offered many benefits, such as security and protection within thick walls, and prosperity through trade with other areas. New technologies, such as metallurgy, the wheeled cart, the oxen-pulled plow, and the sailboat, developed. At the same time, urban life increased the power of religious and political authorities and intensified the differences between social classes. Following urbanization, the benefits of rural life declined, and farmers became little more than slaves. In Mesopotamian cities, women exercised control

2.5 Tablet recording the delivery of bundled reeds, 2028 B.C.

over children and servants, while men controlled the entire household and participated in urban life. Merchants, as well as temple and palace workers, led a relatively comfortable existence.

The development of cuneiform writing facilitated urban life through more efficient record-keeping. Because cuneiform was difficult to learn, only the literate elite (mainly priests) could write it. This class also developed sky charts that governed planting times and kept rationing lists documenting payments for agricultural products. An example of cuneiform can be seen in figure **2.5** which was written in month twelve of the first year of the reign of Ibbi-Sin, 2028 B.C. The tablet records the delivery to a central storehouse of bales of bundled reeds, some of which were then set aside for tax payments. A cylinder seal was first rolled over the entire surface of the front and back of the tablet and then cuneiform writing was incised over the seal impressions.

Critical Question What is the function of literacy in a society?

PICTOGRAPHS, CUNEIFORM, AND THE CYLINDER SEAL

The earliest Sumerian inscriptions are **pictographic** (based on pictures)—that is, they resemble in a rudimentary way what they stand for (figure **2.6**). Pictographs were supplanted by abstract, wedge-shaped characters called **cuneiform** by modern scholars (figure **2.7**). In cuneiform script there is no longer a formal resemblance between the character and what it represents. Characters and words thus replaced the image as units of meaning.

The Sumerians invented the cylinder seal to identify ownership. This was a small stone cylinder decorated with incised images (a process called **intaglio**) that make a relief impression when rolled across a soft surface. Thousands of such seals survive, providing a rich source of Mesopotamian imagery over several millennia. The scene in figure **2.8** depicts two rams eating leaves from branches held by a bearded king or priest. The reed bundles framing the lambs may symbolize Inanna and denote fertility. The male figure wears a cap and a patterned, knee-length skirt,

2.6 Reverse side of pictographic tablet, from Jamdat Nasr, near Kish, Iraq, c. 3000 B.C. Clay, 4⅜ in. (11.1 cm) high. Ashmolean Museum, Oxford.
This illustrates an accounting record of agricultural produce, such as bread and beer, and of farm animals. We can also make out images of storage jars, bowls, stalks of wheat, and ears of grain.

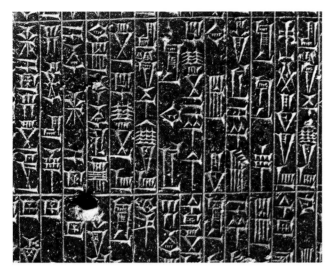

2.7 *above* **Stele of Hammurabi, detail, *c.* 1780 B.C. (see figure 2.14).**

2.8 **Seal** *right* and impression *above*, from southern Iraq, Uruk period, 4th millennium B.C. Marble and copper, 2¹⁄₂ in. (5.4 cm) high, diameter of seal 1³⁄₄ in. (4.5 cm). Vorderasiatisches Museum, State Museums, Berlin.

and his central position reflects not only his importance but also his domination of the animals. Notice that he is **frontal** (facing front) except for his profile head, which has a frontal eye. This is a convention of representation in ancient art, which shows a face from two viewpoints.

THE FIRST EPIC POEM

Ancient Mesopotamia was rich in literature, art, and music, and because so many written records survive, we know quite a lot about its cultures. It is thanks to the invention of writing that *The Epic of Gilgamesh* has been preserved. The epic was initially transmitted orally as a collection of hymns and tales about Gilgamesh shortly after his reign. It was first written down in the late third millennium B.C. in Sumerian, which is unique among all ancient languages. Later it was copied in Akkadian and Babylonian, as well as in Hittite, an Indo-European language and the name of the culture that flourished in ancient Anatolia, modern Turkey (see Box).

Society and Culture

Language Groups

Today there are 3000 different languages and many dialects in the world. A language that is no longer spoken is called a dead language, and examples include ancient Egyptian (see Chapter 3), Akkadian, Sumerian, Hittite, and Etruscan (see Chapter 7). Scholars who study languages are called linguists. They classify languages into family groups, which apparently developed from a single parent language. When groups of people sharing a common language become separated geographically, their languages continue to evolve. Eventually, the languages diverge to the point where the groups can no longer understand each other, but the languages are still related because they originally came from the same family.

The most widespread language family

that exists today is Indo-European, which is spoken by nearly 50 percent of the world's population. It is the dominant language group of Western culture and is also the basis of some major Asian languages. Scholars believe that the parent Indo-European language originated in an area north of the Black Sea, and that as groups of people migrated in different directions their languages changed. Nevertheless, many of these languages share similar words—*mother* in English, *mater* in Latin, *meter* in Greek, *mère* in French, *madre* in Spanish, and *Mutter* in German.

The earliest recorded Indo-European language was Hittite, followed by Greek and Sanskrit. Among the main subgroups of Indo-European are the Balto-Slavic languages, spoken in much of eastern Europe; Celtic (including Gaelic, spoken in Scotland

and Ireland, Welsh, spoken in Wales, and Breton, spoken in northern France); Germanic (including Dutch, English, German, and the Scandinavian languages, Danish, Norwegian, Swedish, and Icelandic); Greek; Indo-Iranian, of which Indo-Aryan and Iranian are subgroups (the Indo-Aryan languages are spoken today mainly in India and Pakistan, and the Iranian include Pashto and Persian). The Romance languages, which derive mainly from Latin, include French, Italian, Portuguese, Romanian, and Spanish.

Language groups other than Indo-European are Sino-Tibetan, which includes Chinese with its numerous dialects; Afro-Asian, which is concentrated around North Africa and the Near East and includes Arabic and Hebrew; and the Japanese and Korean group.

Returning again to the quotation at the beginning of the chapter, we can sense the author's cultural pride in Gilgamesh's accomplishments: without peer, now or in the future, the city is "a work no king . . . can match." But, in addition to giving us a view of Mesopotamian culture and mythology, *Gilgamesh* is a literary masterpiece. It is the first epic ever recorded, and it contains themes that have been addressed over the centuries and are relevant today.

The typical epic, like *Gilgamesh*, is a long poem narrating the exploits of a heroic figure on a grand scale. Encompassing mythic, religious, and social themes, epics portray larger-than-life events. The hero is usually a man of high stature, often the founder of a civilization. He suffers, undertakes perilous journeys, and, in evoking the identification of the reader, stands for all of us. Gilgamesh battles the forces of evil and searches for immortality. But in the end, he accepts the reality of death and undergoes a transformation that is both psychological and moral.

When the story opens, the city of Uruk stands as a tribute to its founder and king. Having attained this high position, Gilgamesh undertakes his journey. The first line of the epic introduces Gilgamesh in search of immortality: "The one who saw the abyss, I [the author] will make the land know."

In the course of Gilgamesh's quest, the gods create Enkidu, a double for Gilgamesh and also his opposite. Whereas Gilgamesh is a city-dweller, Enkidu inhabits the wilderness—he is covered with hair and runs with the animals. The taming of Enkidu, turning him from "the man-as-he-was-in-the beginning" (*Gilgamesh*, tablet I, col. iv, line 6) into a human, is one of the most brilliant episodes in Western literature.

Enkidu is transformed by spending six days and seven nights with a temple courtesan. His taming is a metaphor for the civilizing effects of women on men: "She made him know, the man-as-he-was, what a woman is" (tablet I, col. iv, line 19). Enkidu then ceases to "gallop as before. Yet he had knowledge, wider mind" (tablet I, col. iv, lines 28–29). In this episode, Enkidu attains sexual knowledge, which makes him human in the sense of growing up spiritually. He is no longer a carefree child, running wild without responsibility. The courtesan then prepares a meal for Enkidu, which further initiates him into civilized society, and offers to lead him to Uruk, "where Gilgamesh lives, completely powerful, and like a wild bull stands supreme, mounted above his people" (tablet I, col. iv, lines 38–39).

At this point, Gilgamesh has a dream, which he asks his mother, Ninsun, to "untie" (see Box). The dream text reads as follows:

> Last night, Mother, I saw a dream.
> > There was a star in the heavens.
> Like a shooting star of Anu it fell on me.
> > I tried to lift it; it was too much for me.
> > I tried to move it; I could not move it.

Society and Culture

Dreams and Medicine in the Ancient Near East

Dreams played an important role in the ancient world. Fragments of dream books from the Ancient Near East have been preserved, including conventional dream interpretations. These indicate that people believed dreams were sent by the gods and contained secret, enigmatic messages. Dreams thus had to be "untied." Once a dream had been interpreted, its mystery was revealed (untied). Gilgamesh's first dream described here is symbolic and alludes to the future.

The practice of medicine in the Ancient Near East was based on rituals, magic, and natural products. Two medical tablets from the last quarter of the third millennium B.C. contain fifteen prescriptions. They recommend swallowing medicinal potions and applying poultices to diseased parts of the body. Both the potions and the poultices were made by grinding up organic matter, such as herbs, fruits, or seeds, and minerals, such as salt and river bitumen. Animal products were less commonly used than plants; among these were turtle shells, wool, and water snakes. Powdered substances were mixed with liquids, such as water, milk, oil, or beer, to make the potion or poultice.

> Uruk, the land, towered over it;
> > the people swarmed around it;
> > the people pressed themselves over it;
> > the men of the city massed above it;
> > companions kissed its feet.
> I myself hugged him like a wife,
> > and I threw him down at your feet
> > so that you compared him with me.

(tablet I, col. v, lines 26–38)

The implication of this dream is that Enkidu is Gilgamesh's double. Its manifest text describes the heaven-sent origin of Enkidu, whom the gods made, and his strength. The latent content of the last three lines is the loving but competitive relationship between the men. On the one hand, Gilgamesh hugs Enkidu "like a wife," but on the other hand, he throws him before his mother. By comparing Enkidu with Gilgamesh, Ninsun cements both their sibling rivalry and their sibling bond. Enkidu is Gilgamesh's "other half"—his mirror image.

Ninsun replies:

> This means: he is a powerful companion, able to save a friend;
> his strength is great in the land.
> Like a shooting star of Anu his strength is awesome,
> whom you hug like a wife.
> He is the one who will take leave of you.
> This unties your dream.

(tablet I, col. vi, lines 1–6)

The relationship between Gilgamesh and Enkidu unfolds heroically, as was to become characteristic of later epic literature. They wrestle each other "like bulls," and they embrace like brothers. Encouraged by Shamash (god of the sun and of justice), Gilgamesh and Enkidu set out to slay the evil monster Humbaba, who guards the cedar forest inhabited by the gods. Humbaba, a kind of primordial, fearsome shadow, represents the forces of darkness. In this opposition of Shamash and Humbaba, the poet portrays another theme that became characteristic of the Western epic—the struggle between good and evil exemplified as a conflict between light and dark.

Enkidu warns Gilgamesh against undertaking the task, noting the primeval terror evoked by their quarry:

Humbaba's roar is the deluge,
his mouth is fire,
his breath is death.

(tablet II, col. v)

But for Gilgamesh this quest is a way of permanently establishing his name and his power; Enkidu agrees to accompany him. They find Humbaba near the cedar mountain, and kill him.

Ishtar is so struck by Gilgamesh's physical beauty and strength that she offers to become his lover. But he rebuffs her, noting that she is unfaithful and that her passions blow hot and cold:

You're a cooking fire that goes out in the cold,
a back door that keeps out neither wind nor storm,

. . . .

a well whose lid collapses,

. . . .

a waterskin that soaks the one who lifts it,

. . . .

a shoe that bites the owner's foot!

Which of your lovers have you loved forever?

(tablet VI, col. i)

In addition to Ishtar's inconstancy, Gilgamesh describes the power that a goddess has over a mortal, who can never be her equal. Recognizing that he would live in fear of being destroyed by her, Gilgamesh reminds Ishtar that she transformed one lover (her father's gardener) into a frog, and another (Tammuz) into a wolf, to be devoured by his own dogs.

Incensed by his rejection of her, Ishtar calls on her father, the sky god Anu, to send the great Bull of Heaven to kill Gilgamesh. When the Bull descends to Uruk, his snorting opens up vast crevasses in the earth, causing hundreds of citizens to plummet to their deaths. With Enkidu's assistance, Gilgamesh defeats the Bull, stabbing his neck like a matador. Enkidu further infuriates Ishtar by tossing a piece of the Bull's thigh at her.

The heroes celebrate their victory, but a dream announces the death of Enkidu—one of them is required to die as retribution for killing Humbaba and the Bull of Heaven. Although Enkidu's death had been foretold in the first dream, when Ninsun called Enkidu "the one who will leave you," Gilgamesh did not understand that departure meant death. Gilgamesh mourns Enkidu, as do the elders of Uruk and all of nature (echoing Enkidu's precivilized wild state). "For Enkidu," Gilgamesh cries out,

I weep like a wailing woman,
    howling bitterly.
[He was] the axe at my side, the bow at my arm,
the dagger in my belt, the shield in front of me,
my festive garment, my splendid attire . . .
An evil has risen up and robbed me.

(tablet VIII, col. ii, lines 2–5)

In other words, Enkidu is not only Gilgamesh's double, but also his protector (the axe, bow, shield, and dagger) and the source of his happiness (the festive garment and splendid attire). By using the metaphor comparing armor and clothing to Enkidu, Gilgamesh makes explicit the merged identities of the heroes. He then tears off his fine clothes and announces that he will adopt Enkidu's former life in the wild.

To commemorate his deceased companion, Gilgamesh follows the age-old custom of ordering an effigy by which to remember him. Most of the text is lost, but what survives is:

"Artisan!
Metalworker, goldsmith, engraver! Make for my friend . . ."
Then he fashioned an image of his friend, of the friend's own
    stature.
"Enkidu, of lapis lazuli is your chest, of gold your body."

(tablet I, col. ii, lines 22–23)

It appears from this fragment that the statue replicated Enkidu's actual size and appearance. The use of gold and light blue **lapis lazuli**, considered the two most precious minerals in antiquity, reflects the value that Gilgamesh placed on his poetic double.

At this point, Gilgamesh embarks on the spiritual side of his journey. Fearing death, he sets out to find eternal life and the sage Utnapishtim, the only human ever granted immortality by the gods. Gilgamesh encounters a number of obstacles along the way, including the Scorpion-people, who guard the entrance to Mashu, the mountain of the rising and setting sun. Hearing of Gilgamesh's quest, the Scorpion-man warns that no mortal has ever traveled so far. But after twelve hours of darkness, Gilgamesh reaches daylight and meets the Barmaid, "who dwells at the lip of the sea." She tells him how to find the boatman Urshanabi, who will help him over the waters of death to Utnapishtim.

Having achieved his goal, Gilgamesh tells Utnapishtim of his friendship with Enkidu and his quest for immortality. The sage replies that nothing is forever, that sleep and death are brothers, and that he will tell him "a secret of the gods." This secret turns out to be the story of the Flood, in which humanity was destroyed, and of the great ship built by Utnapishtim at the gods' command. He took on board his family, craftsmen, and every other living thing so that life would regenerate when the waters subsided. (A huge flood that inundated Mesopotamia in 2900 B.C. is thus documented before the account in the Hebrew Bible was written.) Gilgamesh finally accepts his own mortality as the fate of all people and returns to rule Uruk. He recognizes that the city walls, with their "oven-fired brickwork" and foundation laid down by the seven sages, are his legacy and his immortality.

2.9 Plaque with a musician playing a stringed instrument, from Ur III, *c.* 2300 B.C. Fired clay, approx. 4 in. (10 cm) high. Louvre, Paris.

MESOPOTAMIAN KINGSHIP AND THE ARTS

The land of Sumer was divided into city-states. Each was governed by a ruler, who presided over an assembly of important citizens. This mirrored the organization of the Mesopotamian pantheon. The earliest assemblies chose their leaders for particular missions, which were generally of a military nature. Eventually, however, a system of hereditary kingship was put in place as a way of ensuring political stability.

Kingship—its character, chronology, and succession—was the main political institution of ancient Mesopotamia. Kings grew powerful and were supported by ever larger armies. As a result, the palace began to challenge the supremacy of the temple precincts.

Although Gilgamesh is described as two-parts divine and one-part human, the Sumerian kings were not at first conceived of as gods and, as we have seen, even Gilgamesh was denied immortality. But subsequent Akkadian, Babylonian, Assyrian, and Persian rulers had a different view of kingship. Beginning around 2300 B.C., the Akkadian ruler Sargon I (ruled *c.* 2334–2279 B.C.) founded a dynasty that soon conquered Mesopotamia. His grandson, Naram-Sin (*c.* 2254–*c.* 2218), was the first ruler to decree himself a god officially.

MUSIC AND RITUAL AT THE MESOPOTAMIAN COURTS

Music was important at the Mesopotamian courts, as well as in religious festivals. This is attested by texts, images, and actual instruments that have survived. In music, as in art, the bull played a symbolic role, standing for the power of the king. Its hide was used for the kettledrum, which was a key instrument in Mesopotamian music.

2.10 Reconstructed Sumerian lyre, from Ur, 3rd millennium B.C. Wood, inlay, lapis lazuli, and gold leaf. 3 ft. 6 in. (1.06 m) high. British Museum, London.

2.11 Front of a lyre soundbox, from Ur, *c.* 2685 B.C. Shell inlay, approx. 10 in. (25.4 cm) high. University of Pennsylvania Museum, Philadelphia.

In *The Epic of Gilgamesh*, when the temple courtesan persuades Enkidu to accompany her to Uruk, she tells him that "every day there's a festival, and . . . strings and drums are played" (tablet I, col. v, lines 8–9). Her words are backed up by finds such as the **plaque** (a small, decorated slab) in figure **2.9**, which was attached to a temple wall in Ur. It shows a figure playing a hand-held stringed instrument that resembles a lyre. More elaborate Sumerian lyres were also discovered in Ur. The reconstruction in figure **2.10** was almost certainly a royal possession. The head of the bull is of gold and the beard of lapis lazuli, the same materials that Gilgamesh used for Enkidu's statue.

The bull, like the figures on the front of another lyre (figure **2.11**), combines human with animal features. It is not known if these figures represent humans dressed as animals or mythological creatures. But what they are doing is manifest—they are performing various human rituals. At the top, a hero dominates two bulls, showing both his power over the animals and his identification with them. Below, a lion and a dog carry objects associated with sacrifice: jars and animal body parts. The third scene down appears to be a concert, with a donkey playing a lyre exactly like the actual lyre from Ur. And at the bottom a goat carrying two vessels follows a scorpion-man. Although there is no documented connection between these scenes and *The Epic of Gilgamesh*, the scorpion-man resembles the description of the guardian of Mount Mashu.

NARAM-SIN AND THE IMAGERY OF CONQUEST

Whereas Gilgamesh's chief artistic achievement was architectural, Naram-Sin's legacy is a large **stele** (stone marker). In addition to a cuneiform inscription, the stele is decorated with an image in **relief** (a sculpture that is not completely carved away from its original material). Both describe a victory over Naram-Sin's enemies (figure **2.12**). The stele reflects the Akkadian interest in conquest. To this end their armies subjugated the Sumerians and other cultures and imposed the Akkadian language. Akkadian kings were worshipped as gods. Naram-Sin is thus shown as divine in his own right—he is protected by symbols of celestial deities at the top of the stele.

2.12 *right* **Victory Stele of Naram-Sin, from Susa,** *c.* **2254–2210 B.C. Pink sandstone, 6 ft. 6 in. (1.98 m) high. Louvre, Paris.**
The horned cap signifies that Naram-Sin is a god. His towering figure and formal prominence are conventions of ancient art, known as **hierarchical proportions**, in which size is equated with status. Another convention is the contrast between Naram-Sin's upward and forward march denoting success, and his defeated enemies, who fall. Similarly, the living are clothed, whereas the dead are nude.

GUDEA OF LAGASH: PIETY AND TEMPLE-BUILDING

After two hundred years of Akkadian rule, the Sumerian city-states reemerged as independent entities. Akkadian power was destroyed by invasions from the east and declined. Around 2150 B.C. a Neo-Sumerian culture gained ascendancy in Mesopotamia. This lasted about three hundred years.

The best-known early Neo-Sumerian king, Gudea (c. 2144–c. 2124), ruled Lagash (modern Telloh). His royal image depicted him as a pious builder, rather than as a ruthless conqueror, and he commissioned many temple precincts to convey his piety and his power. His relationship to the gods differed from that of the Akkadian rulers, for he was not worshipped as a god, but rather as an intermediary between the gods and his subjects. One way in which the gods communicated with Gudea was through dreams. In contrast to Gilgamesh, whose dreams foretold future events such as Enkidu's death, Gudea dreamed instructions from the gods to build their temples.

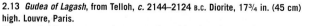

2.13 *Gudea of Lagash*, from Telloh, c. 2144–2124 B.C. Diorite, 17¾ in. (45 cm) high. Louvre, Paris.

The rounded forms, compact space, and combination of naturalism (the arm muscles) with **stylization** (forms rendered as surface patterns rather than naturalistically)—the eyebrows—are typical of Sumerian style. They recall the figure of Abikhil from the Mari temple (see figure 2.4).

The patron god of Lagash, Ningirsu, appeared in one dream, telling Gudea to build the Eninnu Temple. In Gudea's view, the fact that the temple plan in the dream was drawn on a tablet of lapis lazuli confirmed its divine origin. He then mobilized the city, performed the necessary ceremonies, imported high-quality cedar wood from Lebanon and personally oversaw the construction of the temple. Gudea himself laid the first brick of the foundation. When it was complete, the temple was known as "the House of Fifty Gods." According to a contemporary account, it rose from earth to heaven and illuminated the entire country with its radiance.

Several statues of Gudea, in which he is either seated or standing, have survived, and all show his piety. In figure **2.13** he sits on a modest throne covered with cuneiform inscriptions with his hands clasped in a conventional gesture of prayer. The **curvilinear** (having curved forms) rhythms of the Gudea statue and the sense of controlled dignity convey the king's confidence in himself and in the gods, as well as the highly developed skill of his court artists.

HAMMURABI OF BABYLON: THE LAWGIVER

The Neo-Sumerian rulers were overthrown by foreign invaders, resulting in centuries of political unrest. By around 1900/1800 B.C. a new stability was achieved under the Semitic-speaking Amorites. During this time, known as the Old Babylonian period after the capital city of Babylon, the Amorite dynasty produced King Hammurabi (ruled c. 1792–1750 B.C.), who brought about the final eclipse of Sumerian culture. He was a skilled military strategist and an effective administrator, credited with designing the grid plan of Babylon's urban streets. Above all, Hammurabi is famous for his law code (figure **2.14**), which consists of nearly three hundred statutes in fifty-one columns of Akkadian cuneiform text inscribed on a black basalt stele.

Although it was not the oldest law code of the Ancient Near East, Hammurabi's is the best preserved. It provides a clear view of the social order and legal system in second-millennium-B.C. Babylon. It also reflects the previous legal system under the Sumerians, for several of the statutes are similar.

The text opens with the claim that the gods

> named me to promote the welfare of the people, me, Hammurabi, the devout, god-fearing prince, to cause justice to prevail in the land, to destroy the wicked and the evil, that the strong might not oppress the weak, to rise like the sun over the black-headed people [the general population, most of whom had black hair], and to light up the land.

Note the repetition of the pronoun "me," calculated to emphasize the gods' choice of Hammurabi by "naming" him. His identification with Shamash is explicit in that he rises "like the sun" and "lights up the land." This metaphor, equating the ruler with the sun, falls within an age-old tradition that

has become a conventional theme of kingship throughout the world.

Hammurabi's statutes address all aspects of society, including conflicts between neighbors over water rights, marriage, violence, theft, and murder. The laws are aimed at maintaining social order in general and, more specifically, the established class system. Much of the code is based on talion law (*lex talionis*), from the Latin term meaning "like for like punishment"—"an eye for an eye" and "a tooth for a tooth." However, this applies only to people of equal rank. Penalties are harsher if offenses are committed by the lower classes against the upper classes as opposed to vice versa. So if a person knocks out the tooth of someone of equal rank, the offender's tooth is simply knocked out in kind. But if the victims are lower class, upper-class offenders are allowed to keep their teeth, as long as they pay a small fine. The same distinctions apply to the loss of an eye or a broken bone.

The laws of Hammurabi also establish a certain degree of equality in marriage. Both women and men are allowed to own property, and they have the same rights to sue for divorce. Adultery by either party is punished, but not equally: if a woman is unfaithful to her husband she can be drowned, but an unfaithful husband has only to return his wife's dowry.

The death penalty is imposed for a wide range of crimes, including helping slaves to escape, certain types of theft, murder, and failing to lock up an animal that kills someone. Lying and making false accusations are taken so seriously that failure to prove such charges results in the death of the accuser. And in a form of consumer protection legislation, Hammurabi's code condemns to death the perpetrators of poor and dangerous workmanship.

Hammurabi concludes his law code with a summation of his intentions to be, like Shamash, a "king of justice," and also a "father to the people" and a bringer of prosperity for all time. But the Old Babylonian period came to an end around 1600 B.C., when an ethnic group called the Kassites invaded. Mesopotamia became subject to foreign forces until a new stability was achieved with the rise of the Assyrians around 1300 B.C. By 900 B.C. the Assyrians had created a powerful empire. The capital city of Assur, named for its patron god, was located in the north, along the banks of the River Tigris.

2.14 Stele of Hammurabi, *c.* 1780 B.C. Black basalt, 7 ft. (2.13 m) high. **Louvre, Paris.**
The scene in the relief above Hammurabi's text shows Shamash, the sun god and god of justice, extending the ring and staff of royalty. He is seated on an architectural throne denoting a palace or temple and his feet rest on a stylized mountain (home of the gods). Shamash wears a flared robe and a horned cap of divinity. Light, alluding to his role as sun god, radiates from his shoulders. Standing before him is Hammurabi himself, whose relatively smaller size reflects his lesser importance. Scenes such as this serve a political function—they project the image of a ruler and his policies as sanctioned by the gods.

Cross-cultural Influences

Indus Valley Civilization

One of the ongoing discussions among scholars studying the Ancient Near East concerns the relationship of Mesopotamia to another ancient civilization discovered in the Indus valley, in modern Pakistan. Dating from around 2700 to *c.* 1900 B.C., this Indus valley culture overlaps Mesopotamian history from the Sumerian Early Dynastic to the Old Babylonian period.

Excavations at Mohenjo-Daro, some 140 miles (225 km) to the northeast of Karachi, have revealed a pattern of streets laid out on a grid plan. As in Uruk, Indus valley architects used brick. Some houses were equipped with bathrooms and plumbing, which suggests a highly developed culture.

The Indus valley pictorial script has not yet been deciphered, nor is the religion well understood. There is, however, evidence that the bull was prominent, which may indicate contacts with Mesopotamia. Bull motifs have been found on many Indus valley stamp seals, which differ from Mesopotamian cylinder seals in their square shape and in being made for stamping rather than rolling (figure **2.15**). In addition, unlike the Mesopotamian seals, stamp seals were carved in relief so that the impression was sunken rather than raised.

The *Bearded Man* from Mohenjo-Daro (figure **2.16**) has general parallels with Mesopotamian sculpture. Like the Sumerian statuette of Abikhil (see figure 2.4), the *Bearded Man* is frontal and his gaze is emphasized. He also combines stylization with the organic form that characterizes the statue of Gudea (see figure 2.13).

2.15 *above* **Stamp seal of a bull, from Mohenjo-Daro, *c.* 2300–1750 B.C. White steatite, 1½ in. (3.81 cm) high. National Museum, Delhi, India.**

2.16 *Bearded man from Mohenjo-Daro, c.* 2000 B.C. **Limestone, 7 in. (17.8 cm) high. National Museum, Karachi, Pakistan.**

ASSURBANIPAL: ASSYRIAN MIGHT

The last great Assyrian king, Assurbanipal (ruled *c.* 669–626 B.C.), was known for both his cultural interests and the cruelty of his armies. Tablets dating to his reign contain his description of learning the use of the bow and arrow, how to drive a chariot, and the art of writing. He also mastered "royal decorum and walked in kingly ways." Indeed, Assurbanipal's interest in intellectual achievement inspired him to found a great library containing thousands of tablets. These included letters, literature, scientific and historical documents, and mythological texts. Of his conquests in Egypt and black Africa

(see Chapter 3), Assurbanipal writes: "I made Egypt and Nubia feel my weapons bitterly and celebrated my triumph." He describes the determination with which he plundered the Egyptian city of Thebes, killing its inhabitants and looting their valuables.

The walls of Assurbanipal's palaces were lined with reliefs illustrating his ruthless pursuit of conquest. His prowess as a hunter is shown in a segment from the relief called the *Great Lion Hunt* (figure **2.17**). Like other Assyrian rulers, Assurbanipal kept gardens of lions. Because the lion was a royal symbol, the human king demonstrated his supremacy over the king of the beasts by hunting and killing him.

2.17 *Great Lion Hunt*, detail, from Assurbanipal's palace, Nineveh, 668–627 B.C. Alabaster, approx. 5 ft. (1.6 m) high. British Museum, London.
Lions and lionesses are shown dead and dying, shot through with the arrows of the king and his entourage. The naturalism of these reliefs is rendered with great skill and variety. There is both a sense of anatomical structure in the animals and a taste for surface patterning that enlivens the scene.

The skill needed for hunting lions also proved useful in war. Figure **2.18** shows a section of the palace wall relief that represents the Assyrian army storming an Elamite city (located in the southwest of modern Iran). The scene conveys the power of the Assyrians and Assurbanipal's bloodthirsty lust for war. He confirms this lust in the inscription on the upper part of the wall, where he declares that he attacked, captured, destroyed, and plundered the city, and set it on fire.

Having achieved victory, Assurbanipal reports: "With full hands and safely, I returned to Nineveh, the city where I exercise my rule." The relief in figure **2.19** shows the Assyrian conqueror relaxing after a successful military campaign. He reclines on an elaborate couch in a lush, peaceful garden. Servants fan him, and his queen, Ashur-sharrat, is seated by his feet. Both raise a cup as if to drink a toast. They are entertained by musicians at the far left playing a stringed instrument and a drum. All appear indifferent to the severed head of a defeated Elamite king hanging from a tree.

2.18 *Assurbanipal storming an Elamite city*, 668–627 B.C. Alabaster, 3 ft. 7¾ in. (1.11 m) high. British Museum, London.
Climbing a ladder in a steady advance, the Assyrians attack enemy archers positioned on the crenellated city walls. Kneeling Assyrians use their shields for protection against arrows raining down on them. Several wounded Elamites fall from the ramparts and corpses float among the fish in the river below. Here, as in the *Lion Hunt*, there is a continual interplay between arrest and movement, which is characteristic of much ancient art.

2.19 *Assurbanipal and Queen Ashur-sharrat banqueting after a victory*, 668–627 B.C. Alabaster, 4 ft. 6¾ in. (1.39 m) wide. British Museum, London.

The Assyrian Empire declined after the death of Assur-banipal and the fall of Nineveh in 612 B.C. This was followed by the brief but prosperous Neo-Babylonian period (625–539 B.C.). Under Nebuchadnezzar II (ruled 604–562 B.C.), the Hanging Gardens of Babylon (one of the Seven Wonders of the Ancient World) and the ziggurat thought to be the biblical Tower of Babel were built. But by 539 B.C. a new force had risen to power in the Near East—namely, the Persian Empire under the Achaemenid dynasty.

THE ACHAEMENIDS AND THE ROYAL PALACE AT PERSEPOLIS

Persia (modern Iran) lay to the east of Mesopotamia and had a distinctive and distinguished cultural history dating back nearly 5000 years. Cyrus the Great (ruled *c.* 559–529 B.C.) founded the Achaemenid dynasty, forming an alliance between the Persians and Medes, both of whom were Aryan-speaking. In 539 B.C., Cyrus marched into Babylon and overran most of Mesopotamia. Cyrus himself, in an inscription found on a clay cylinder, declares his power in the region: "I am Cyrus, king of

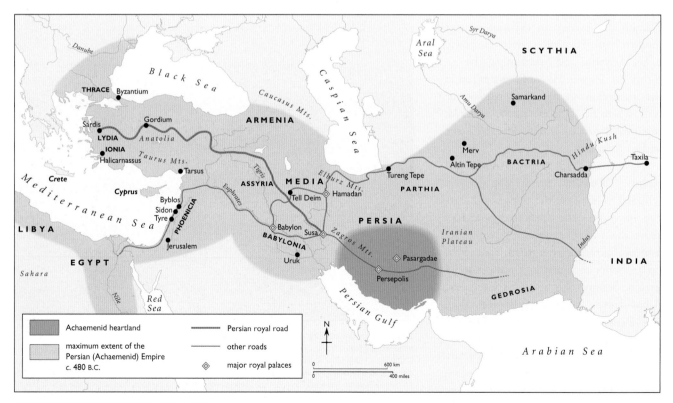

Map 2.2 The Persian (Achaemenid) Empire, *c.* **480 B.C.**

2.20 Apadana and stairway of Darius I, Persepolis, Iran *c.* 500 B.C.

the world, great king, legitimate king, king of Babylon, king of Sumer and Akkad."

During the next fifty to sixty years Cyrus's successors built up a vast empire (map **2.2**). The Achaemenid rulers constructed a number of palaces; the most important one (now in ruins) is at Persepolis (figure **2.20**). Several kings, including

Darius I (ruled 522–486 B.C.), Xerxes I (ruled 486–465 B.C.), and Artaxerxes (ruled 465–424 B.C.), contributed to the building program. The enormous audience hall (the Apadana), visible in the distance, originally had one hundred columns, each 40 feet (12.2 m) high. Figure **2.21** shows a detail of the *Procession of Medes and Persians* carved in relief on the side wall

2.21 *Procession of Medes and Persians*, detail, stairway leading to the Tripylon, Persepolis, *c.* 500 B.C.

of one of the staircases; the latter wear fluted hats. The borders of the procession are decorated with stylized plant forms. Compared with the Assyrian reliefs, which are filled with violent scenes of warfare and hunting, those decorating the Persian palaces emphasize the peaceful aftermath of conquest. As a result, there is a general air of orderly calm and a ritual, repetitive quality in the poses and gestures.

ZOROASTRIANISM: A NEW RELIGION The Achaemenid dynasty adopted a religion based on the teachings of the Persian prophet Zoroaster (first millennium B.C.), also called Zarathustra. Zoroastrianism is based on scriptures attributed to Zoroaster himself, which include poems and five *gathas* (celebratory songs). Zoroaster conceived of the universe as being in continual conflict between light and dark, or good and evil. It was up to individuals, who had free will, to decide which path they would follow. At some future time, the two forces would cease their struggle. People who chose the good would become immortal; those who chose evil would suffer. Zorastrianism was essentially a **monotheistic** religion with a single creator god, Ahura Mazda, embodying the force of light, who battled Ahriman, the force of darkness and evil.

Zoroastrians practiced marriage between close relatives, used priests in their rituals, and left their dead to be eaten by animals and birds before burial. In contrast to other Near Eastern religions, Zoroastrians did not worship in or around temples; instead, they worshipped outdoors, using fire altars. In figure **2.22** Darius I, who was a follower of Zoroaster, is enthroned before two such altars. He is elevated and larger than the other figures, which conveys his importance. The flat, open space behind the altars reinforces the impression of the king's distant, aloof character. The overall tranquility of the scene and the formality of the figures create an air of ritual.

Although Zoroastrianism was the main religion of the Achaemenid dynasty, other belief systems later developed in Persia. Among these were Manichaeism (founded by Mani in the early third century A.D.) and Mithraism, which revolved around Mithras, also a god of light. His was a mystery cult involving several stages of initiation. Both Manichaeism and Mithraism, as well as Zoroastrianism, are discussed again later in connection with early Christianity (see Chapter 8).

The dominance of the Achaemenid dynasty lasted until Persia was invaded by the Greek conqueror, Alexander the Great, in 331 B.C. (see map 6.1). The region was then taken over in turn by various cultural groups until the seventh century A.D. At that point, Muslims from Arabia converted Persia to Islam (see map 9.3).

2.22 *Darius holding an audience before two fire altars*, detail of a relief from the Persepolis treasury, *c.* 512–494 B.C. Limestone, entire relief 20 ft. (6 m) long. Archaeological Museum, Tehran, Iran.

Thematic Parallels

Kingship and "Heads" of State

The concept of kingship appears to be a feature of most cultures that become differentiated into a ruling class and a class that is ruled. In this chapter, we have seen that kingship with absolute power was an important aspect of Ancient Near Eastern cultures. Within that structure, however, there are variations in the manner in which kings are represented. Gudea of Lagash, for example, shows himself as a temple builder, whereas the conquering Naram-Sin ascends a mountain to meet the gods, and Assyrian rulers kill lions and destroy cities. In other areas of the world and in different time periods, there are related views of kingship, which are reflected in various cultural and artistic expressions. Many of these use the image of the ruler's head as a metaphor for the head of state.

The Colossal Heads of the Olmec: 1200–400 B.C.

The Olmec of Mesoamerica (map **2.3**) inhabited a region that corresponds to the Gulf Coast of modern Mexico. They developed an agricultural society with a powerful priest class ruled by

2.23 Colossal head from La Venta, Olmec culture, c. 900–500 B.C. Basalt, 7 ft. 5 in. (2.26 m) high. La Venta Park, Villahermosa, Tabasco, Mexico.

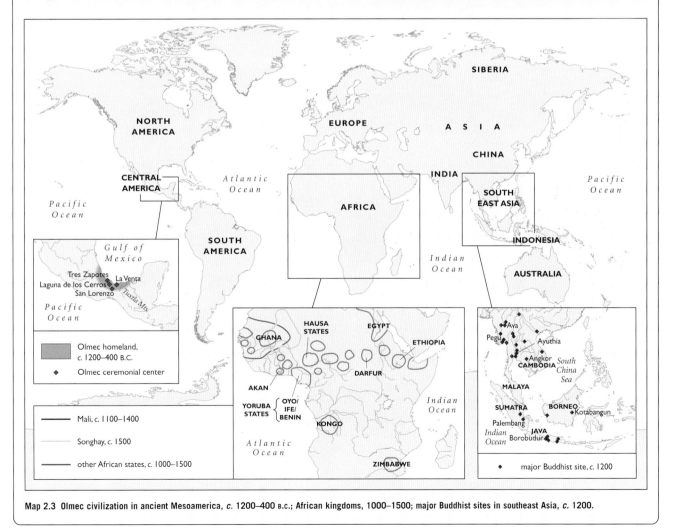

Map 2.3 Olmec civilization in ancient Mesoamerica, c. 1200–400 B.C.; African kingdoms, 1000–1500; major Buddhist sites in southeast Asia, c. 1200.

kings. The most monumental Olmec sculptures are colossal carved heads from two main ceremonial sites, San Lorenzo and La Venta (figure **2.23**). Each head weighs several tons and, like the huge monoliths at Stonehenge (see Chapter 1), had to be brought to the site from a considerable distance. The basalt quarry that produced the stone was located in the Tuxtla Mountains, 50 miles (80 km) away.

Although the Olmec left no written records, scholars have concluded that the stone heads represented kings. All are similar in style, having a flat nose, thick lips, and a fleshy, organic facial structure. A form-fitting cap, which may be a crown or a helmet, is pulled down over the head to the eyebrows. The imposing quality of the Olmec heads, their colossal size, and their significant locations convey a sense of uncanny power that reflects one ideal of kingship.

The Cambodian Devaraja: Twelfth to Thirteenth Century A.D.

King Jayavarman VII (ruled 1181–1218) reigned during a brief period of Buddhist domination in Cambodia (see map 2.3). To embody his power, he constructed the Bayon, a Buddhist temple in Angkor Thom, near Angkor Wat. Jayavarman conceived of the temple as the mythological Mount Meru, the cosmic center of the Buddhist world, and of himself as a god-king. He had images of his head embedded in the colossal towers (figure **2.24**), which reflected his identification with god and the cosmos and endowed him with absolute power over his subjects.

2.24 Towers of the Bayon Temple, Angkor Thom, Cambodia, 13th century.

Henry VIII: Sixteenth-Century England

In sixteenth-century England, Henry VIII commissioned his court artist, Hans Holbein the Younger (c. 1497–1543), to paint his portrait (figure **2.25**). Holbein shows Henry filling the picture space, so that despite the small size of the panel the king appears large. His shoulders expand sideways, creating a square torso surmounted by a frontal head. Henry assumes a regal pose and gazes authoritatively out of the picture. Accentuating his power are not only his relative size and his dominating stance, but also the elaborate costume and formal framing of his head. His head is enclosed by a hat decorated with pearls and feathers and a curved chain across his chest. He is shown both as an individual—the features are unmistakably his own—and as an image of wealth and political power.

2.25 Hans Holbein the Younger, *Henry VIII*, c. 1540. Oil on panel, 34¾ × 29½ in. (88.3 × 74.9 cm). Galleria Nazionale d'Arte Antica, Rome.

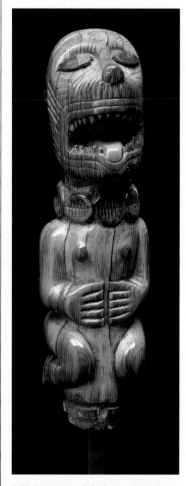

2.26 **Yombe cane finial in the shape of a combined human–leopard, from Kongo kingdom, West Africa. Ivory, 17¾ in. (19.6 cm) high. The Metropolitan Museum of Art, New York.**
The **finial** (a decorative feature at the top of an object or building) of this royal cane is made of ivory. The cowrie-shell necklace and carved bracelets are signs of the king's wealth, while his power is conveyed by inlaid eyes, a gaping mouth, and a large head. The prominent teeth are a reminder of the leopard's devouring ferocity and of the king's power over the life and death of his subjects.

Africa—the Head and the Crown: Nineteenth to Twentieth Century

The king's power is embodied in the royal imagery of tribal Africa. In the Kongo kingdom, founded around 1400 on the west coast of Africa (see map 2.3), the king's residence and burial place were located on an elevated mountaintop site. Kongo kings were associated with the leopard, king of the forest and a creature imbued with violence and power (figure **2.26**).

The elaborate beadwork of the Yoruba kingdom in Nigeria (see map 2.3) was an important part of the royal wardrobe. Figure **2.27** illustrates a beaded crown of the Yoruba type, made by artisan families working for the kings. This particular crown is highly decorative, its bright colors endowed with ritual significance. The little enclosure at the top originally contained organic materials with medicinal properties, conveying the king's power to heal. This notion is known in the western European belief in the healing power of the "king's touch."

From even this brief survey of artistic expressions of kingship, it is clear that imagery has been used in very different times and places to convey a king's divine power. Typically, a ruler's palace is elevated above the residences of his subjects. His head must remain over their heads—hence the custom of prostrating oneself, bowing, or curtseying, in the presence of royalty. To reinforce the king's high status, his head is generally large and adorned in some way, usually with a crown or other elegant headdress. In the next chapter, we consider a different type of ruler, namely, the Egyptian pharaoh, who was conceived of as the sun god on earth.

2.27 **Yoruba-style crown, from Dahomey, Republic of Benin, 19th century. Beadwork, 17¾ in. (45 cm) high. Musée de l'Homme, Paris.**

MESOPOTAMIA AND THE HEBREWS

Another important Near Eastern culture, that of the Hebrews, overlapped with some of the Mesopotamian cultures surveyed in this chapter. At this point we briefly consider their complex early history and draw some parallels with Mesopotamia. The development of Judaism is covered in greater depth in Chapter 8.

EARLY HISTORY

The Hebrews were one of many tribal groups in the Ancient Near East. During the second millennium B.C., they settled in an area that included modern Israel, on the east coast of the Mediterranean Sea, and parts of Jordan (see map 8.1). Their leader was apparently the patriarch Abraham, who is traditionally believed to have come from Ur. According to the Hebrew Bible (Old Testament), a number of Hebrews later moved to Egypt during a period of famine, and after several generations they were enslaved by the pharaohs (see Chapter 3).

Around 1250 B.C., Moses led the Hebrews out of Egypt, through the Sinai Desert, on a forty-year journey called the Exodus (the Greek term for "going out"). During the eleventh to tenth century B.C., a series of powerful kings—Saul, David, and Solomon—reigned in Israel, and under Solomon's rule the Temple was erected in Jerusalem. The Hebrews then split into two kingdoms, Israel and Judah, and fought on and off for generations with other Near Eastern cultures, including the Assyrians.

In the sixth century B.C., King Nebuchadnezzar and the Babylonians overran Israel and destroyed Solomon's Temple. The Hebrews, especially the intellectuals and the rabbis (teachers of God's law), went into exile in 586 B.C., a period known as the Babylonian Captivity. This ended in 539 B.C., when Cyrus II came to power in Persia.

The Hebrews (now referred to as the Jews) were set free to return to Jerusalem and rebuild the Temple. They dedicated the new Temple in 516 B.C. and established a **theocracy** (a government of priests or religious leaders). In the fourth century B.C., the Jews were Hellenized (underwent Greek influence) by the conquests of Alexander the Great (see Chapter 6). In A.D. 70, the Romans destroyed the rebuilt Temple along with the entire city of Jerusalem. The Jewish state thus came to an end and Israel was absorbed into the vast Roman Empire (see Chapter 7).

In the next chapter, we survey the civilization of ancient Egypt, which overlapped the cultures described in this chapter. Not only did Hebrews live in Egypt for several hundred years, but the Egyptians had constant contact with the Near East. Egyptian rulers married foreign wives, traded, and fought wars with Mesopotamia. At the same time, however, whereas the Near East was composed of different civilizations, each with its own social and political organization and distinctive styles of art and architecture, Egypt remained a separate and relatively uniform culture for thousands of years.

KEY TERMS

anthropomorphic human in form.

ceramics pottery made by firing (heating) clay.

convention an accepted practice.

cuneiform a form of writing used in Mesopotamia and consisting of wedge-shaped characters.

curvilinear having curved forms.

epithet an identifying adjective or phrase.

finial a decorative feature at the top of an object or building.

frontal facing front.

hierarchical proportion a convention in ancient art in which size is equated with status.

intaglio a process in which lines or images are incised in a surface.

lapis lazuli a semi-precious, light blue stone.

monotheism a religion whose adherents believe in a single god.

personify embody as a person.

pictographic based on pictures.

plaque a small, decorated slab.

polytheism belief in many gods.

relief a sculpture that is not completely carved away from its original material.

stele a vertical stone marker or pillar.

stylization a technique in art in which forms are rendered as surface patterns rather than naturalistically

theocracy rule by priests or other religious leaders.

ziggurat in Mesopotamia, a monumental stepped building signifying a mountain.

KEY QUESTIONS

1. Why would developing writing aid in urbanization? Which society first developed writing?
2. What characteristics of literary epics are found in *The Epic of Gilgamesh*?
3. What are two goals of the laws of Hammurabi?
4. What are two artistic devices the artist used in figure 2.22 to show Darius's two roles?
5. Which religions discussed in this chapter are monotheistic? What is the explanation given by Zoroastrianism for the presence of evil? Is this explanation used by other Mesopotamian religions?

SUGGESTED READING

Blier, Suzanne Preston. *The Royal Arts of Africa*. London: Laurence King Publishing, 1998.
  ▸ A study of royal art in Africa.

Christie, Agatha. *Murder in Mesopotamia*. London: HarperCollins, 2001.

——. *They Came to Baghdad*. London: HarperCollins, 2003.
  ▸ Archaeological mysteries set in the Middle East.

Collon, Dominique. *Near Eastern Seals*. London: British Museum Press, 1990.
  ▸ A survey of seals from the Ancient Near East with discussions of style and iconography.

Finegan, Jack. *Light from the Ancient Past* (Vol. 1). Princeton, NJ: Princeton University Press, 1974.
  ▸ A survey of Ancient Near Eastern culture and history.

Gilgamesh, trans. John Gardner and John Maier (with the assistance of Richard A. Henshaw), from the Sîn-leqi-unninni version. New York: Random House, 1984/Vintage Books, 1985.
  ▸ An English translation of the oldest surviving epic poem.

Groenewegen-Frankfort, H. A. *Arrest and Movement*. New York: Hacker Art Books, 1978.
  ▸ A study, beginning with the Ancient Near East, of how artists convey motion and stasis in their work.

Kramer, Samuel Noah. *History Begins at Sumer*. New York: Doubleday, 1959.
  ▸ A classic work on the Sumerian civilization.

——. *The Sumerians*. Chicago and London: University of Chicago Press, 1966.
  ▸ A readable survey of Sumerian arts and culture in context by a noted scholar in the field.

Muscarella, Oscar. *Bronze and Iron*. New York: Metropolitan Museum of Art, 1988.
  ▸ Bronze and Iron Age in the Ancient Near East.

——. *The Lie Became Great*. Groningen, The Netherlands: Styx Publications, 1998.
  ▸ A study of forgeries from the Ancient Near East and the problems created by the "culture" of forgery.

Oppenheim, A. Leo. *Ancient Mesopotamia*, rev. ed. Chicago and London: University of Chicago Press, 1977.
  ▸ An overview of Mesopotamian culture.

Pritchard, James B. (ed.). *The Ancient Near East* (Vol. 1). Princeton, NJ: Princeton University Press, 1973.
  ▸ The first of two volumes of a study of all aspects of Ancient Near Eastern history and culture.

SUGGESTED FILMS

1919 *The Fall of Babylon*, dir. D. W. Griffith

2001 *Murder in Mesopotamia* (television movie, based on Christie)

3 Ancient Egypt

" *Turn your face gentle upon us, Osiris!*
   Lord of the life eternal, king of the gods,
Unnumbered the names of his protean nature,
   holy his manifold visible forms,
      hidden his rites in the temples.

. . . .

God who remembers still
   down in the halls where men must speak true,
Heart of the inexpressible mystery,
      lord of regions under the earth,

. . . .

Lord of forever, first in Abydos,
   yet far off his throne in the red land of death. "

("HYMN TO OSIRIS")

One of the primary differences between ancient Mesopotamia and Egypt was Egypt's political stability. Mesopotamian cultures came and went, some growing into powerful empires while others were relatively short-lived. Egypt, however, maintained its cultural continuity for around 3000 years (roughly from 3100 B.C. until the Roman conquest in 31 B.C.). This was possible in large part because Egypt's social and political structures were more easily controlled than those of Mesopotamia.

Egypt was also more geographically isolated and unified than Mesopotamia. Located in northeast Africa, Egypt was separated from the rest of the Ancient Near East and protected by its geographical borders—the Mediterranean Sea in the north, the first cataract of the Nile in the south, desert and the Sinai Peninsula in the east, and the Sahara in the west—which made Egypt less open to foreign invasions than Mesopotamia. The country itself was united by the Nile, which, at 4160 miles (6695 km) is the longest river in the world, although less than 1000 miles (1610 km) of the Nile is in Egypt.

Egypt also had its own writing system, called "the gods' words" by Egyptians, which differed from Mesopotamian cuneiform. Egyptians used the more pictorial **hieroglyphs** (literally "sacred carvings") for official and religious texts and a simpler cursive script called **hieratic**, derived from hieroglyphs (see Box, p. 49). Because scholars can now read both hieroglyphs and hieratic, a great deal is known about ancient Egyptian culture.

As in Mesopotamia, most of the Egyptian art that has survived was made for rulers and their courts. But, because of Egypt's long period of cultural continuity, its art styles show less change over time than elsewhere in the Ancient Near East. In addition to highly skilled engineers and architects, Egypt had more local stone available than Mesopotamia, making it possible to build vast works of large-scale architecture. For the ancient Egyptians, especially the rulers, stone symbolized eternity because it lasts. In Egyptian religion, too, eternal life was of paramount importance.

Key Topics

Stability and Eternity

Myths of the afterlife

Kings as gods

Hierarchical society reflected in pyramids

Constructing Monumentality

Step pyramid at Saqqara

Pyramid complex at Giza

Monumental royal sculpture

Religion

Polytheism: gods, goddesses, demi-gods

Monotheism: Amenhotep IV becomes Akhenaton

TIMELINE	PHARAONIC RULE 3100–2469	OLD KINGDOM c. 2649–2143	MIDDLE KINGDOM c. 1991–1700	NEW KINGDOM c. 1550–1070
HISTORY AND CULTURE	Dynasties 1–2 Unification of Upper and Lower Egypt by Narmer (Menes)	Dynasties 3–6 Political and social stability Economic prosperity Trade with black Africa Hierarchical society	First Intermediate period, Dynasties 7–11 Middle Kingdom, Dynasties 12–14 Second Intermediate period, Dynasties 15–17 Hyksos introduce chariots Start of Bronze Age Famine and foreign invasion	Dynasties 18–20 Imperial expansion Amarna period, c. 1349–1336: capital moved to Amarna
RELIGION AND MYTH	Polytheism Belief in afterlife Soul consisting of *ka*, *akh*, and *ba* Pharaoh as sun god on earth	Elaborate royal burials		Brief period of monotheism under Akhenaton in the Amarna period: worship of the Aton Temples
ART	Palette of Narmer, c. 3100	Monumental royal sculpture Hierarchical scale Stylized forms Grids for sculpture and painting Hieroglyphic inscriptions Seated statue of Khafre, c. 2520 *Triad of Menkaure*, c. 2490–2472 Scribe from Saqqara	More realism in royal sculpture Cubic temple statues Coffin of Senbi, c. 2000 Senwosret-senebefny and his wife, c. 1878–1840 Head of Amenemhet III, c. 1859–1813 Jewelry	Bust of Nefretiti, c. 1349–1336 Tutankhamon's throne, c. 1336 Tutankhamon's funerary mask, c. 1327
ARCHITECTURE	Imhotep, step pyramid of King Zoser, Saqqara, c. 2630	Monumental royal architecture Pyramids at Giza, c. 2649–2100	Rock-cut tombs	Hatshepsut's building campaign at Deir-el-Bahri, c. 1473 Monumental temples Temple of Ramses II, Luxor, begun c. 1400
LITERATURE	Prayers for offerings to the dead	"Hymn to Osiris" Hymns to the Nile Hymns to the Sun Secular poetry Wisdom literature	"Tale of Sinuhe" Medical texts	*Book of the Dead*
MUSIC		Professional musicians, male and female Temple music and music at social gatherings Harp, sistrum (rattle), double-reed pipe		

The quotation at the beginning of this chapter reflects the Egyptian preoccupation with eternity. It is from a **hymn** (a song praising god) to Osiris, god of the Underworld, where those who had led a moral life were rewarded. As indicated in the hymn, the god's cult center was at Abydos, a town on the bank of the Nile in southern Egypt (see map 3.1, p. 50), but he reigned as "lord of regions under earth." When Egyptians died, their hearts were weighed against the feather of Maat (goddess of truth, justice, order, and cosmic harmony) in the Underworld: "down in the halls where men must speak true." The deceased who passed the test proceeded to the next life; those who failed were damned, and their hearts were devoured by the monster Amemet. This belief in a last judgment was inspired by the concept of **maat**, the ideal order of the universe and society—a fundamental aspect of ancient Egyptian culture.

THE NILE

E gypt is primarily desert, which makes it dependent on the Nile for water. The source of the Nile is in central Africa, from where it flows north to Memphis, divides into a delta, and empties into the Mediterranean Sea. Along the way, the Nile flows over six large cataracts—outcrops of rock formations that create rapids. The Nile was essential to ancient Egyptians' survival because its annual inundation provided fertile soil for agriculture (see Box and figure 3.1). When the Nile did not flood, vegetation was sparse and the land was beset with famine and death. Dependence on the Nile for agricultural prosperity, which was similar to the crucial role of the Tigris and Euphrates rivers in Mesopotamia, was thus a constant feature of Egyptian culture.

It was along the banks of the Nile that Paleolithic cultures in Egypt established temporary settlements, where people lived by hunting and fishing. From around 7000 to 4000 B.C., remains from more settled Neolithic communities have yielded evidence of farming, pottery, and sculpture—small statues of females might have represented fertility goddesses. Neolithic Egyptians cultivated flax, wheat, and barley, and they domesticated goats, sheep, and cattle. As in Mesopotamia, Egypt had irrigation systems and used metals. Communities became towns, and there is evidence of warfare.

Egypt traded with the Near East, especially the Levant, which had cedar, but its main trading contacts before 1900 B.C. were with Africa. The Land of Punt

Egypt and the Solar Calendar

Ancient cultures revered star gazers and makers of calendars. Mesopotamians developed star charts to predict the seasons. In Egypt, kingship embodied by the pharaoh was the foundation of life, and the calendar was crucial in supporting royal power. As divine beings, pharaohs were obliged to provide for their people and to maintain *maat* by ruling justly, celebrating daily temple rituals and presiding over major festivals, and defending Egypt against its enemies. Pharaohs had to ensure the annual inundation of the Nile to keep the land fertile, and one means of predicting this was provided by the Egyptian calendar.

The Nile flooded (figure **3.1**) between June and September, a season the Egyptians called *akhet*, the inundation. Heavy summer rains in the Ethiopian highlands swelled the tributaries and other rivers that joined to become the Nile. Ancient Egyptians recognized three seasons revolving around the inundation: one, Emergence (the growing of crops using floodwater caught in man-made canals) from June 21 to October 21; two, from October 21 to February 21; and three, Summer (harvesting crops) from February 21 to June 21.

The original pre-dynastic Egyptian calendar, which divided the year into four lunar months, proved to be inadequate. The later solar calendar, echoing Egyptian cosmology and religion, marked the beginning of the year by the appearance of the star Sirius, in the constellation of Canis Major. This constellation became visible around June 21, and was called "the going up of the goddess Sothis." The calendar had only 360 days, but at the beginning of the year, an additional five days were set aside for feasting, rituals, and celebration.

Critical Question Why do we divide time into years, months, days, hours, and seconds? What is the difference between sequential and cyclical time?

3.1 *Flooding of the Nile*, from the Sanctuary of Fortuna, Praeneste, 1st century B.C. Roman mosaic, 20 × 16 ft. (6 × 4.9 m). Archaeological Museum, Palestrina, Italy.

(somewhere to the southeast, possibly modern Somalia) was famous for its incense, and Nubia (to the south) was a source of gold, ivory, ebony wood, panther skins, ostrich eggs and feathers, and animals, such as monkeys, that were considered exotic. In addition, Nubia controlled trade routes to further south in Africa. From the late third millennium B.C., Nubia was ruled by Egypt and adopted some of its cultural and artistic traditions. At the same time, Egypt itself was influenced by black Africa and from the ninth century B.C. there were periods when Egypt was ruled by Nubia. After 1900 B.C., Egypt increased its trade with the Near East and Sinai, importing turquoise, copper, tin, bronze, and lapis lazuli.

THE PHARAOHS

The supreme Egyptian ruler, the **pharaoh**, was conceived of literally as the sun god on earth. A king list devised in the fourth century B.C. by the Egyptian priest Manetho traces the chronology of the pharaohs from 3100 B.C. to 332 B.C., when the Greek general Alexander the Great conquered Egypt (see Chapter 6). The chronology that is currently used for ancient Egypt marks the beginning of written records, by which time Egypt had formed into a unified culture along the lines of what we think of as a nation-state. The Neolithic era, which precedes this period, is termed "predynastic," because it predates the thirty **dynasties** (families of kings) in the king list. The dynasties comprise the so-called Kingdoms: Old (*c.* 2469–2143 B.C.), Middle (*c.* 1991–1700 B.C.), and New (*c.* 1550–1070 B.C.). Periods in between the Kingdoms, called Intermediate Periods, denote either decline or foreign occupation. The second and most important Intermediate Period included the Hyksos domination. Foreign rulers who spoke a Semitic language, the Hyksos probably introduced horse-drawn chariots and a new and more powerful type of bow into Egypt. Their expulsion was followed by the beginning of the New Kingdom.

Egypt's rule by pharaohs began around 3100 B.C., by which time, after a long period of warfare, Upper (south) and Lower (north) Egypt had been unified. From that time, the Egyptian pharaoh embodied the unification by his two crowns—the white crown of Upper Egypt and the red crown of Lower Egypt. These crowns are shown on the so-called Palette of Narmer (figure **3.2**), a ritual object made of slate, which was a temple dedication.

3.2 Palette of Narmer (front and back), *c.* **3100 B.C. Slate, 25 in. (63.5 cm) high. Egyptian Museum, Cairo.**

This palette resembles objects used by women for eye make-up (which was contained in the indented circle), but it is much larger and is assumed to have had a ritual purpose. The images on both sides represent the victory of a pharaoh, identified as Narmer (also called Menes), who was credited in ancient Egypt as the traditional unifier of the country. In the scene at the top, Narmer wears the tall white crown of Upper Egypt; he is about to kill a fallen enemy. The upper register of the scene at the bottom shows Narmer before a group of standard-bearers and ten dead enemies lying on the ground with their heads between their legs. Here, Narmer wears the slightly more elaborate red crown of Lower Egypt. The horned cows at the top of the palette represent Hathor, the goddess who protected the palace of the king.

Society and Culture

Principal Deities of Ancient Egypt

Amon god of Thebes (sometimes a ram), later Amon-Re

Anubis god of the dead and embalmers (depicted as a jackal)

Aten (or **Aton**) the sun-disk (worshipped by Akhenaton in the New Kingdom)

Atum early Old Kingdom creator god and sun god; later, Amon, Re, and Amon-Re

Bes protector of women in childbirth (a leonine dwarf)

Geb the earth, father of Osiris

Hapy god of the Nile and fertility (a man with heavy breasts)

Hathor protector of the palace, goddess of the sky (a horned cow)

Horus sky god and god of kingship (depicted as a falcon), son of Isis and Osiris

Isis mother goddess, guardian of coffins (in human guise), sister and wife of Osiris

Khepre rising sun, a form of Re (depicted as a scarab beetle)

Maat goddess of truth and order (depicted as a feather, or as a woman with a feather-head)

Mut Amon's wife (sometimes a vulture)

Nun the primeval ocean

Nut goddess of the sky, mother of Osiris

Osiris god of the Underworld, identical with the deceased king (depicted as the king's mummy)

Ptah crafts god (depicted as a male mummy)

Re (or **Ra**) sun god and judge, sometimes shown as a falcon, sometimes in combination with Amon as Amon-Re, or Amon-Ra; cult center at Heliopolis (the city of the sun)

Set god of disorder and violence, brother of Osiris

Sobek crocodile god of the Nile

Thoth scribal god and the inventor of writing (depicted as an ibis or a baboon)

THE PHARAOH AND THE EGYPTIAN CONCEPT OF TIME

Complicating the chronology of Manetho's king list is the fact that every pharaoh began counting time from his personal rule, so that when a new ruler ascended the throne, the date was redesignated as Year One. Each new reign was thought of as a recreation of the world and some kings referred to their first years in power as "the repeating of births." This reflected the Egyptian concept of time as cyclical and the belief that the ruler was omnipotent. Because the pharaoh was all-powerful, he and the royal family had prerogatives denied to the general population, such as making incestuous marriages for political purposes. Pharaohs had a dual human and divine nature; they were both gods and intermediaries between gods and their human subjects.

Pharaohs ruled from Memphis, halfway between the cult centers of the sun god Re at Heliopolis (literally "city of the sun") and of Amon at Thebes. (Amon became combined with Re as Amon-Re.) In addition to being identified with the sun god, whose reappearance each morning conformed to the cyclical idea of time, the pharaoh was seen as the living embodiment of other deities, such as Osiris, god of the dead, and Horus, god of kingship.

RELIGION

Egypt, like much of the ancient world, was polytheistic. Its people worshipped a myriad of gods and goddesses, demi-gods, gods in animal form, in human form, and in combined human and animal form. The gods were everywhere and controlled all aspects of life (see Box). The Egyptians composed hymns through which they prayed to the gods for help while on earth and for eternal life after death. The wish to live forever gave rise in ancient Egypt to some of the most elaborate burial practices the world has ever known.

THE OSIRIS MYTH

From around 2400 B.C. Osiris became a major figure in ancient Egyptian myth and religion. The hymn (actually a poem) quoted at the beginning of the chapter is only one of many hymns that are both a means of transmitting religious ideas and works of literature in their own right. Osiris was the son of Geb (dry land) and Nut (the sky as a reflection of the earth's primeval waters, known as Nun). The three siblings of Osiris were Set (the god of disorder) and the goddesses Nephthys and Isis (who was also his wife). Set murdered and dismembered Osiris, but Isis gathered up his bones, flesh, and organs and restored him to life.

Osiris and Isis had a son, Horus, whom Isis defended from evil. She thus evolved into a goddess devoted to mothers and their children. When Horus became an adult, he defeated Set in a battle for their father's throne in the Underworld. Horus's victory led to his role as the god of kingship; typically he is represented in art as a falcon.

There are many illustrations of Osiris as king and judge in the Underworld (figure **3.3**). This example shows Osiris enthroned inside his palace. He wears the tall white crown of Upper Egypt (the location of Abydos) and holds the crook and flail (threshing tool) of kingship. His white linen shroud identifies him with death, and his green skin denotes the rebirth of vegetation with the renewal of spring. Behind him stand his sisters, Isis and Nephthys, and before him on a lotus blossom are the four sons of Horus. Each has an identifying head: a falcon, a jackal, a baboon, and a man. Hovering over the lotus and protecting Osiris is the Horus-falcon.

3.3 *Papyrus of Hunefer: the god Thoth at the last judgment*, Thebes, 19th Dynasty, *c.* 1295–1186 B.C. Painted papyrus, 19¼ in. (39 cm) high. British Museum, London.
At the far left, the jackal-headed god Anubis carries the ankh symbol of life as he leads the dead man toward the scales where his heart is weighed against the feather of Maat. The monstrous Amemet—a composite of several animals—stands poised to devour the heart if the deceased fails the test. Anubis is shown again, adjusting the scales. Tensely awaiting the outcome, Amemet stares at the ibis-headed Thoth, who writes down the final judgment. In this case, the heart weighs the same as the feather, indicating that the man led a moral life. He is then introduced to Osiris by Horus in the guise of his father's avenger. A tribunal of squatting gods lines the top of the weighing scene, and a row of protective cobras fills the space over Osiris's throne.

The Osiris myth was of paramount importance to Egyptian culture in three respects. First, it was an example of death and rebirth and the god's role in the continual cycle of the agricultural year. Second, it reflected the fact that defenseless infants and children need the protection of their mothers. Third, it embodied the notion of Egyptian kingship through the triumph of Horus over the forces of disorder.

HYMNS TO THE NILE

Like the myth of Osiris, the Nile, with its yearly flooding that brought the earth back to life, was a metaphor of rebirth. The importance of the Nile inspired the creation of Hapy, god of the annual inundation, to whom hymns of fertility were addressed:

> Come back to Egypt, bringing your benediction of peace,
>   greening the banks of the Nile;
> Save mankind and the creatures, make life likely,
>   through the gift of all this your countryside!
> O hidden god, be it well with you! may you flourish, and return!
>   Hapy, Lord of Egypt, may you flourish, and return!

Hapy was represented as a man with pendulous, lactating breasts and a pregnant belly. His combined male/female features reflected his role as a fertility god: as a male he had generative power and as a female he provided nourishment.

In contrast to Hapy, the crocodile god, Sobek, was seen as dangerous. Sobek inhabited the Nile, but he required hymns of appeasement. Here the emphasis is not so much on fertility and plenty, but rather on primal fear:

> Hail to you, who arose from the primeval waters,
> lord of the lowlands, ruler of the desert edge,
> . . . .
> who lives on plunder,
> who goes upstream by his [own] perfection,
> who goes downstream, after hunting a multitude,
>   a [great] number.

Note that Sobek is an ever-present menace in voracious pursuit of his prey. He slithers from the desert's edge and disappears into the river. Such vivid characterization of the gods through hymns and other verse forms is typical of ancient Egyptian literature and reflects the view that all aspects of nature are physical embodiments of the gods.

HYMNS TO THE SUN

The Egyptian creator god was the sun, known as Atum in the early Old Kingdom, with his main cult city at Heliopolis, and later he was combined with Re. The journey of the sun across the sky was critical to Egyptian belief, and at night, the sun was thought to descend into the Underworld. This journey, which mirrors the cyclical notion of time, was celebrated in the New Kingdom "Hymn to the Rising Sun":

> Be praised, O Re, in your rising,
>   Atum-Horakhty!

Let your perfections be worshipped with my eyes,
 and let your sunlight come to be within my breast.
May you proceed in your own peace in the Night Barque,
 your heart rejoicing in a following breeze within the Day
  Barque.
How delightful is the crossing of the skies among the
  peaceful dead
 with all your enemies fallen!
The unwearying stars give praise to you,
 the indestructible stars adore you—
You who go to rest in the horizon of the Western Mountains,
 beautiful as the Sun each day,
  beautiful, enduring, as my Lord.

The setting of the sun and its reemergence at dawn became a model for death and rebirth. The Egyptian view that the pharaoh and the sun were equivalent appears in the following excerpt from "The Greatness of the King." By using the literary device of repetition for emphasis, the poet reinforces the parallel between god and king.

How great is the Lord of his city!
He is exalted a thousand times over; other persons are small.
How great is the Lord of his city!
He is a dyke which holds back the River, restraining its flood
 of water.
How great is the Lord of his city!
He is a cool room which lets each man sleep until dawn.
How great is the Lord of his city!
He is a rampart with walls of copper from Sinai.
How great is the Lord of his city!
He is a refuge which does not lack his helping hand.

THE EGYPTIAN VIEW OF DEATH

Believing that people continue to exist in the next world, the Egyptians attached paramount importance to the physical preservation of the dead. Figure **3.4** is a photograph of a predynastic burial. The fetal position, as in prehistoric burials (see Chapter 1), suggests that belief in the afterlife began early in human history. Reinforcing this notion are objects of daily life buried with the deceased, presumably for use after death.

From the Old Kingdom, there is evidence of efforts to prevent bodily decay by wrapping the corpse in linen. Eventually, however, the Egyptians realized that decomposition could be avoided only by removing the internal organs. Over the course of Egyptian history, this led to an elaborate, seventy-two-day process of **mummification**. Bodies were dried using natron crystals, embalmed in a covering of plaster and linen, and treated with chemicals. The organs were placed in four individual containers called **canopic jars**.

Figure **3.5** shows the mummy and case of a woman from the Late period (after the New Kingdom) who had been the consort of a priest. Both the mummy (figure **3.5a**) and the case are in the typical form of an embalmed human figure. The mummy netting is decorated with a winged scarab (dung beetle), which was a standard protective device in Egyptian burials. The image of the beetle pushing a sphere of dung symbolized both the sun-disk's daily journey across the sky and spontaneous generation and rebirth. The inside of the mummy case (figure **3.5b**) depicts the goddess of the West (the direction of death) with a falcon on her head. On the lid (figure **3.5c**), below the neck, is a falcon with a ram's head and outstretched protective wings. About halfway down the lid, the mummy itself is shown lying on a bier, and the remaining scenes depict various gods and symbols. Particularly lifelike are the wide open, staring eyes, alluding to the future life of the deceased. This complex iconography was part of an elaborate system of protective magical devices to ensure the safety of the dead person in a dangerous Underworld and his or her ultimate rebirth.

Despite all the effort that went into mummification, it was feared that the bodies still might not reach the afterlife intact. To be on the safe side, the Egyptians placed statues of the dead in their tombs as substitutes for the real person. The Egyptian

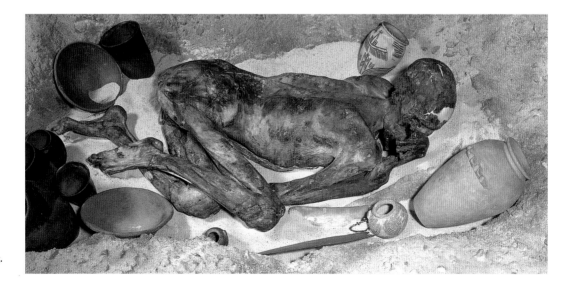

3.4 Predynastic male burial, *c.* 3300 B.C. 5 ft. 4¼ in. (1.63 m) long. British Museum, London.

3.5 (a) Mummy, and (b) and (c) Case of Nesmutaatneru, from the Temple of Hatshepsut, Deir-el-Bahri, 25th Dynasty, *c.* 760–660 B.C. Painted wood, linen, mummy net, faience, and polychrome glaze; mummy 4 ft. 11⁷⁄₁₆ in. (1.51 m) long, inner coffin 5 ft. 6⁹⁄₁₆ in. (1.69 m) long, middle coffin 6 ft. 1³⁄₄ in. (1.86 m) long. Museum of Fine Arts, Boston.

equivalent of the soul—the *ka*, a kind of double containing the life force of the deceased—could then enter the substitute and proceed to the afterlife. Offerings of food and drink were placed in tombs as sustenance for the dead and the *ka*.

The ancient Egyptian soul had two other aspects, the *akh* and the *ba*. The *akh* was overtly spiritual; it was the heavenly transfiguration of the dead into light. The *ba*, often represented as a human-headed bird, had the power of flight and could enter and exit the body at will. This image appears, for example, in a New Kingdom **vignette** (small section of decoration or literary sketch) from the *Book of the Dead*, a series of texts designed to guide the deceased on the journey to the afterlife (figure **3.6**).

3.6 *left* Funerary papyrus of the chief of the concubines of Osiris, chief of the concubines of Nebtu and Khnum, chantress of Amun, Anhai, *c.* 1300 B.C. British Museum, London.

Bird imagery appears three times in this vignette. The large falcon surmounted by a sun-disk is the sun god, Aton. He is protected by two winged eyes with ostrich-feather fans and flanked by two rows of gods. Below the falcon, three levels of worshippers include, in descending order, dancing baboons, kneeling figures of Isis and Nephthys, and two human-headed birds. These stand on platforms in the valley of a mountainous terrain and represent the *ba* of the deceased. Note the prevalence of green, denoting rebirth, which is associated with the sun god.

Society and Culture

Hieroglyphs and Egyptian Literature

Writing in Egypt began around 3100 B.C. in the form of hieroglyphs, literally "sacred carvings." These were a mixture of **ideograms** (pictorial representations of ideas) and **phonograms** (images denoting sounds). Hieroglyphs have been found on fragments of stones, pottery, and papyrus (a plant that grows along the Nile). They remained in use until the fourth century A.D.

However, it was not until 1822 that the French scholar Jean-François Champollion (1790–1832) deciphered hieroglyphs, opening up the vast body of ancient Egyptian literature to the world. He was able to translate Egyptian texts after Napoleon's army discovered the Rosetta Stone in 1799 (figure **3.7**). The stone bore three texts, one of which was in Greek and could easily be read and matched to the others: Demotic script (a simplified form of hieroglyphs) and hieroglyphs.

The earliest inscriptions are lists of offerings in tombs. These evolved into prayers for offerings to the dead and for a prosperous afterlife. Since the deceased give an account of themselves and their lives, such prayers can be seen as early examples of autobiography.

Hymns to the gods are an abundant source of Egyptian poetry, with their vivid descriptions of the pantheon and other aspects of religious beliefs in ancient Egypt. Love poems reflect the universal nature of young lovers, their devotion, passion, and even deceit. There is also wisdom literature, in which an older and wiser figure admonishes a younger one and tries to educate him or her in the ways of the world.

Most Egyptian literature is in verse, although prose stories exist as well as combinations of the two genres. The best-known example of Egyptian narrative poetry is the Middle Kingdom "Tale of Sinuhe," about a courtier who leaves Egypt to escape a palace coup. He goes to live in the Near East but at the end of his life returns to Egypt and a warm welcome from the royal family. Sinuhe describes his emotional reconciliation with the pharaoh as follows:

I found his Majesty upon the Throne of Egypt
  in the throne room all of silvered gold.
Really there, at last, before him,
  I stretched myself full length upon the floor;
But then my foolish brain turned witless in his
  presence, just as this god was offering warm welcome.
I was a man seized in the grip of darkness—
  my bird-soul flown, my limbs unstrung;
My heart, no longer was it in my body
  so that I might distinguish life from death.

The king replies:

Then said his Majesty to an attendant courtier,
  "Raise him. Let him speak with me."
And then he said, "Well, well, you have come home,
  done wandering the weary world since your departure!
I see the marks of time etched on your body;
  you have grown old.

When death must come, your rites shall not be wanting—
  your burial shall never be by bedouin tribes.
Now deprecate yourself no longer:
  you spoke no treason; your name is honored here."

The king honors his promise, and the tale ends with Sinuhe's description of his tomb and his death. This passage emphasizes Sinuhe's pleasure in having an impressive tomb and a sculpture of himself in gold. He also enjoys the material pleasures of a life that he hopes will continue after death:

There was made for me a pyramid of stone
  built in the shadow of the royal tomb.
The god's own masons hewed the blocks for it,
  and its walls were portioned out among them;
The draftsman and the painter drew in it,
  the master sculptor carved;
The overseer of workmen at the tombs
  criss-crossed the length of Egypt on account of it.
Implements and furniture were fitted in its storeroom
  and all that would be needful brought within;
Servants for my Spirit were appointed,
  a garden was laid out above,
And tended fields ran downward to the village—
  just as is ordered for a nearest Friend.
My statue was all brushed with burnished gold,
  its kilt set off with silver.

It was his Majesty who did all this for me.
  No simple man has ever had so much.
And I enjoyed the sunshine of his royal favor
  until my day of mooring dawned.

3.7 Rosetta Stone, 196 B.C. Basalt, 3 ft. 9 in. (1.14 m) high. British Museum, London.

OLD KINGDOM EGYPT: *c.* 2649–2100 B.C.

Old Kingdom Egypt was a period of continuous political and social stability and of the pharaoh's absolute power. It was also a time of relative peace and economic prosperity. The Old Kingdom pharaohs commissioned colossal works of architecture and filled them with stone statues meant to last for eternity.

THE PYRAMID COMPLEX AT GIZA

To express the desire for life after death, the ancient Egyptians evolved monumental burial structures called **pyramids** (map **3.1**). In around 2630 B.C., the first known architect to build huge stone structures, Imhotep, designed the step pyramid of King Zoser (figure **3.8**) as part of a temple complex about 30 miles (48 km) south of Cairo.

Around a hundred years later, the Old Kingdom pyramid complex at Giza was constructed and became one of the Seven Wonders of the Ancient World. Located at the edge of modern Cairo, the Giza pyramids (figure **3.9**) were made of meticulously cut blocks of limestone and capped with gold, symbolizing the sun. Thousands of people from different professions were required to build such monuments, including surveyors, engineers, masons, skilled craftsmen, and paid seasonal workers.

The three pharaohs of the Fourth Dynasty buried at Giza were Khufu (*c.* 2551–2528 B.C.), Khafre (*c.* 2520–2494 B.C.), and Menkaure (*c.* 2490–2472 B.C.). When a pharaoh died, his body was carried by boat to its funerary temple on the opposite side of the Nile. After extensive preparations for

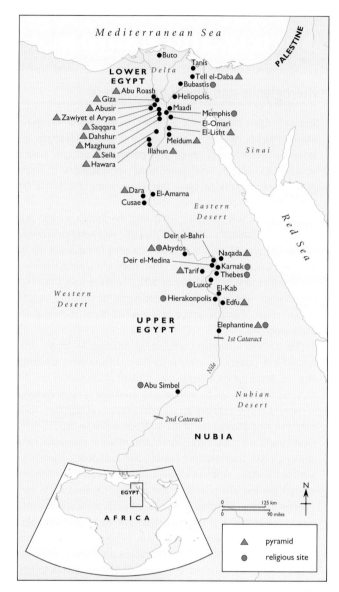

Map 3.1 Ancient Egypt.

3.8 Imhotep, Step pyramid of King Zoser, Saqqara, Egypt, *c.* 2630 B.C. Limestone, 200 ft. (61 m) high.

3.9 Pyramids of Khufu, Khafre, and Menkaure, Giza, Egypt, *c.* 2649–2100 B.C. Limestone, pyramid of Khufu approx. 480 ft. (146 m) high, base of each side 755 ft. (230 m) long.

The plan of the pyramid is a square, with each corner oriented to a cardinal point of the compass. The four triangular walls slant inward, their apexes meeting at the exact center of the square plan. The mathematical precision and architectural skill required for such buildings reflect the high level of artistic and intellectual achievement in ancient Egypt.

3.10 *left* **Diagram of a pyramid showing interior.**

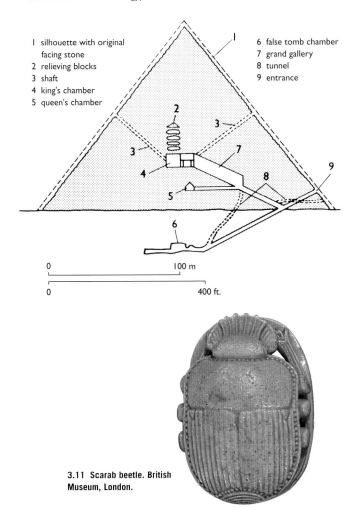

1 silhouette with original facing stone
2 relieving blocks
3 shaft
4 king's chamber
5 queen's chamber
6 false tomb chamber
7 grand gallery
8 tunnel
9 entrance

0   100 m

0   400 ft.

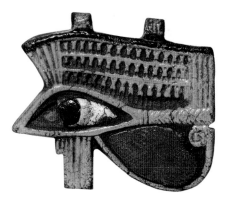

3.12 Eye of Horus. British Museum, London.

3.11 Scarab beetle. British Museum, London.

burial had been completed, the pharaoh's mummy was lowered into its coffin and placed in a chamber within the pyramid (figure **3.10**). In addition to statues and other substitutes for the deceased, offerings, texts, and numerous amulets were placed on the mummy for healing. These included the scarab (figure **3.11**) and the eye of Horus (figure **3.12**), which had been ripped out by Set in the battle for Osiris's throne and was later restored. The eye of Horus was a protection against the pervasive fear of the evil eye and came to symbolize goodness and beneficence.

3.13 Seated statue of Khafre, 4th Dynasty, *c.* 2520 B.C. Diorite, 5 ft. 6¼ in. (1.68 m) high. Egyptian Museum, Cairo.
The trapezoidal *nemes* headcloth with side flaps encloses the space around the pharaoh's head. Perched on the back of the throne is the Horus-falcon. His protective wings, enveloping Khafre's headcloth, reflect the king's literal identification with the god. Both the falcon and Khafre are rendered frontally (facing forward), emphasizing their power and foresight.

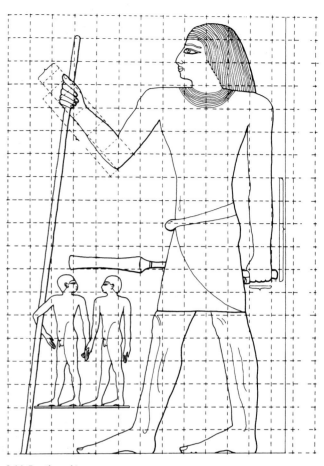

3.14 Egyptian grid.
Royal Egyptian artists followed the system of hierarchical scale used in Mesopotamia. The more important figures are thus larger than the less important ones. They are also clothed, for nudity was another sign of lesser importance and could also denote childhood.

THE SEATED STATUE OF KHAFRE AND THE EGYPTIAN PROPORTIONAL SYSTEM

In addition to monumental architecture, the Old Kingdom produced many examples of monumental sculpture. The sense of inherent power conveyed by Egyptian royal sculpture is the result of closed spaces and compact forms. This is evident in the seated statue of Khafre, found in his valley temple (figure **3.13**). Carved from a rectangular block of stone, Khafre and his throne are shown as one harmonious form. Although the feet extend forward, the stone has not been cut away behind the lower legs. Furthermore, individual features, such as the kneecaps and ceremonial beard, are rectangular. Such stylizations convey a sense of eternity, because they appear removed from the natural reality of time and space. Similarly, the use of stone for royal figures denoted the durable, long-lasting power of the kings and their immortality.

The rectangularity of Egyptian royal figures was maintained in part by the use of grids in the planning stage of a sculpture or painting. Grids could be calibrated with a figure of any size,

and they changed only slightly in the 3000-year history of ancient Egypt. Figure **3.14** shows one type of grid used by Egyptian artists. A foot is three and a half squares in length, the shoulders are six squares across, and the distance from the shoulders to the bottom of the tunic is ten squares.

Note the pose of the figure and compare it with those in the papyrus paintings described above (see figures 3.3 and 3.6). The head, arms, and legs are in **profile** (side view) whereas the shoulders and eye are frontal. This is a conceptual rather than a natural representation—that is, it depicts a mental image of the human figure rather than the way it is actually seen in three-dimensional space.

THE MENKAURE TRIAD

In the *Triad of Menkaure* (figure **3.15**), Khafre's son Menkaure occupies the conventional standing pose of royal power. Menkaure is frontal, imposing, and rigid. His left leg is extended assertively, his fists are clenched, his shoulders are squared, and his kneecaps and beard are rectangular. The king's importance

THE EGYPTIAN SCRIBE

In addition to royal figures, Egyptian artists created "professional sculptures." These identify the profession of a figure by its pose. One such type represented the **scribe**, whose job it was to write and to keep records. Literate and highly educated, he was an important member of the royal court. Figure **3.16** shows the conventional seated pose of the scribe, holding a writing instrument (usually made from reeds) in his right hand, and a papyrus roll (the writing surface) in his left. His head is slightly tilted as if he is taking dictation.

The elevated status of the scribe in Egyptian society is apparent from several texts. In one, a father, who is not very different from a modern father, urges his son Pepi to study:

And he said to Pepi:
"I have seen defeated, abject men!—
You must give yourself whole-heartedly to learning,
    discover what will save you from the drudgery of underlings.
Nothing is so valuable as education;
    it is a bridge over troubled waters."

("The Instruction for Little Pepi on His Way to School: The Satire of Trades")

A scribal student, not very different from modern students, is tired of studying. He escapes to Memphis to indulge in the distractions of city life and seek out female companionship:

Oh, I'm bound downstream on the Memphis ferry,
    like a runaway, snapping all ties,
With my bundle of old clothes over my shoulder.

3.15 *Triad of Menkaure*, 4th Dynasty, *c.* 2490–2472 B.C.
Schist, 36⅝ in. (93 cm) high. Egyptian Museum, Cairo.
Hieroglyphs are carved into the base of the statue; the hieroglyph is surrounded by a **cartouche**, the curved oval rectangle that frames the name of the king.

is shown by his greater height compared with the two goddesses flanking and protecting him. Hathor, the sky goddess at the left, carries the sun-disk between her horns. She is the protectress of the king's palace, and she holds Menkaure's hand as a gesture of support. At the right stands a *nome* (province) goddess with the symbol of her province above her head.

The women are less assertive (note the positions of the feet) and more naturalistically depicted than Menkaure. They are also more curvilinear, and their garments reveal the organic character of their bodies. This emphasis on the natural curves of the female is characteristic of royal Egyptian art.

3.16 Scribe, from Saqqara, 5th Dynasty, *c.* 2465–2323 B.C. Painted limestone, 20 in. (51 cm) high. Egyptian Museum, Cairo.
The relative naturalism of the scribe denotes his lesser status as compared with the pharaoh. The scribe has open space between the arms and the torso, the body structure is somewhat flabby, and the features are more lifelike. His expression, enlivened by the surviving paint, adds to the naturalistic impression of the figure.

I'm going down there where the living is,
  going down there to that big city,
And there I'll tell Ptah (Lord who loves justice):
  "Give me a girl tonight!"

("Oh, I'm bound downstream on the Memphis ferry")

In another poem, a disappointed teacher, echoing the sentiments of many a modern teacher, takes a dissolute scribal student to task for succumbing to the temptations of loose women and drink and for neglecting his work. The teacher describes the emptiness and emasculation of his student's lifestyle and compares his moral decline to a warped oar incapable of steering a boat:

You go about from street to street,
  and beer fumes hang wherever you have been.
Don't you know beer kills the man in you?
  It stiffens your very soul.

You are like a warped steering-oar
  that gives no help to either side!
You are a shrine without its god,
  a house with no provisions . . .

You sit there under the hussy's spell,
  soaked with perfumes and ointment,
with your wreaths of forget-me-nots round your neck.

("Rebuke Addressed to a Dissipated Scribe")

In the following, more philosophical excerpt from another example of wisdom literature (a genre in which words of wisdom are communicated), the poet extols the immortality of writers:

They [the writers] did not build pyramids in bronze
  with gravestones of iron from heaven;
They did not think to leave a patrimony made of children
  who would give their names distinction.
Rather, they formed a progeny by means of writings
  and in the books of wisdom which they left.
The papyrus roll became their lector-priest,
  the writing-board their loving son;
Books of wisdom were their pyramids,
  the reed-pen was their child, smoothed
    stone their spouse.
In this way great and small became inheritors;
  and the writer was the father of them all!

("Epilogue: The Immortality of Writers")

MUSIC IN ANCIENT EGYPT

Although no musical notations have survived from ancient Egypt, it is clear from texts, paintings, and sculptures that music was a significant aspect of Egyptian culture. Most of the hymns and love poems were read to music. Texts describe field workers and slaves singing in the fields, and the visual arts depict musicians and

3.17 Dwarf musician, 5th Dynasty, 2465–2323 B.C. Limestone with traces of paint, 4⅞ in. (12.5 cm) high. Oriental Institute, Chicago.

dancers performing at religious rites and social gatherings. Scribes learned music, and women as well as men became professional musicians. Dwarfs were also popular as musicians, especially at court (figure **3.17**).

We can see how musicians performed at temple rituals from the relief block in figure **3.18**. A man at the upper left plays the harp; below are four lively acrobats. At the lower right, three singers are designated "the choir" in the hieroglyphic inscription. At the upper right, three women play the **sistrum** (a kind of rattle), which was sacred to the goddess Hathor and used in her rites (figure **3.19**).

3.18 Musicians and dancers performing at a temple ritual, from the Chapel Rouge of Hatshepsut, block 66, Karnak, Egypt. 1473–1458 B.C.

3.20 Banqueting scene, from the tomb of Nebamun, Thebes, Egypt, 18th Dynasty, 1550–1323 B.C. Painted stucco, 25 in. (63.5 cm) high. British Museum, London.
The frontality of two of the women is a departure from Egyptian pictorial convention. Perhaps this is intended to show that musical exuberance has the power to break through strict, traditional rules.

3.19 *left* **Sistrum handle of Teti, 6th dynasty, 2323–2291 B.C. Alabaster, 10½ in. (26.5 cm) high. The Metropolitan Museum of Art, New York.**
The handle of this elegant alabaster sistrum is in the form of a papyrus stalk. Its blossom supports a building, probably a temple, surmounted by a falcon and a cobra. The inscription on the stalk praises the king and invokes the protection of Hathor.

The banqueting scene in figure **3.20** shows how music enriched life in an aristocratic home. Painted on the wall of a tomb, the scene indicates that Nebamun's comfortable earthly life will be transposed into the afterlife. Banqueters occupy the top register, with dancers and musicians represented below. Reading from left to right, we see three singers clapping, a woman playing a double-reed pipe, and two female dancers. The words of the song are recorded in the hieroglyphs between the dancers and musicians:

[Flowers of sweet] scents which Ptah sends and Geb makes
  to grow.
His beauty is in every body.
Ptah has done this with his own hands to gladden (?) his
  heart.
The pools are filled anew with water.
The earth is flooded with his love.

EGYPTIAN SOCIETY

Egyptian society was strongly hierarchical and can—very appropriately—be diagrammed as a pyramid. At the top of the universe were the gods and their realms. At the apex of human society was the pharaoh, followed by members of the royal family. Next in descending order came the aristocracy and the scribal class (the bureaucracy), which was entirely male and was administered by the king's vizier. He ran the palace, the army, and irrigation systems across the country, and supervised legal matters. The middle class included business people, builders, artists, and craftsmen. Peasants and agricultural workers were the largest segment of the population. They were assisted by slaves, who could be foreigners captured in war, debtors, or convicts.

Egypt was a male-dominated society, although women had certain important rights, and their status was determined by the same social hierarchy as the rest of the country. As early as the Old Kingdom, women were mummified and prepared for the afterlife along with men. One surviving document identifies a woman who supervised court physicians—most likely those who attended a queen mother (see Box, p. 56).

Until the Eighteenth Dynasty (*c.* sixteenth century B.C.) women could hold the title of priest at a cult site, or be high-ranking dancers and musicians. Literate woman could work in commerce and own land, but fewer women than men learned to read, and they were not permitted to work

Society and Culture

Egyptian Medicine and Dream Books

Three medical texts from the Middle Kingdom are included in the more general category of Egyptian wisdom texts. They are collections of prescriptions, whose effectiveness depended on the magic power of words and incantations. Because disease was believed to be the work of demons, magic spells were considered the best remedy. Spells were used for pregnant women, for headaches, stiffness, and as an aid to surgery, which was mainly practiced to repair injuries. For abdominal ailments, poultices were prescribed. These were made from various combinations of animal fat, blood and feces, herbs and vegetables, wine and beer, honey and ointments. From the first millennium B.C., the Eye of Horus was endowed with healing power against the evil eye.

As in Mesopotamia, dreams were believed to reveal truth. One Egyptian dream book gives the following interpretations: a dream in which a person kills a hippopotamus means that the dreamer will receive a royal meal; diving into a river means purification; looking at an ostrich means the person will suffer harm; having sex with a woman predicts mourning; feeding cattle foretells wandering the earth; and throwing wood into water means bad luck to the house.

Modern dream interpretation recognizes that there can be many layers of hidden meaning in dreams, but in the ancient world each dream image was interpreted as having a single, definitive meaning.

in the administrative bureaucracy. Most Egyptian textiles were produced by women, and in a few cases, women sold surplus textiles as a way of establishing financial independence.

Egyptian families were generally monogamous and having children was a high priority. Divorce law favored men, who could divorce a wife for infidelity or infertility. But, once divorced, both men and women were allowed to remarry. Widows were at a greater disadvantage than widowers, presumably because they were less likely to remarry. Homosexuality was frowned upon, because it interfered with fertility and reproduction.

Children and child-rearing were important features of Egyptian culture, and the high rate of infant mortality was a cause for concern. Most women breast-fed their own children, but wet nurses nourished the children of royal and upper-class families. Representations in art showing children being breast-fed are rare; but a goddess nursing a king was meant to convey the ruler's divine origins.

FEMALE PHARAOHS

Although pharaohs were normally men, when there was no male heir, a woman could become pharaoh. As such, she was accorded the same status and power as a male ruler, but had to be represented in texts and in art as a man. Of ancient Egypt's four female pharaohs, the best known was the ambitious New Kingdom queen, Hatshepsut (ruled c. 1473–1458 B.C.). She is famous for having launched a major building campaign at Deir-el-Bahri (see map 3.1, p. 50). In texts, Hatshepsut is described as her father's choice to succeed him, and to legitimize her reign further she had her mother, Queen Ahmose, depicted as the consort of the god Amon-Re in paintings and relief sculpture.

As pharaoh, Hatshepsut ruled as the senior co-ruler with her nephew, who probably led her armies. Under Hatshepsut, trade with the Land of Punt was expanded, and new administrators were appointed. It is not known how her reign ended or how she died, but her stepson, Tutmose III, eventually came to power. In order to eradicate Hatshepsut's memory after her death, Tutmose III erased her name from texts and inscriptions and destroyed her statues. He did not do so for personal reasons, but because kingship was by definition a male office and a female ruler was considered against *maat*.

Figure **3.21** shows Hatshepsut as pharaoh. Although her delicate form and facial features clearly belong to a woman, her pose and costume are those of the male pharaoh. Like him, she wears the

3.21 Hatshepsut enthroned, 18th Dynasty, c. 1473–1458 B.C. Crystalline limestone, 6 ft. 5 in. (1.96 m) high. The Metropolitan Museum of Art, New York.

royal *nemes* headcloth with a flap on either side, a necklace, and a short tunic. Her pharaonic pose is frontal, her hands rest on her lap, and there is no space between the arms and the torso or between the legs and the throne. Nevertheless, compared with the seated Khafre (see figure 3.13), which is made of very different stone, there is more open space behind the figure of Hatshepsut. The throne has no back, and the Horus-falcon is not present. This opening up of space probably reflects minor stylistic changes since the Old Kingdom. However, it is likely that it was also done in order to convey a sense of elegance in representing the female pharaoh (see Box).

Society and Culture

Egyptian Jewelry

Egyptian men and women wore elaborate make-up and many types of fine jewelry—rings, necklaces, bracelets, tiaras, and so forth. Most of what has survived belonged to royal or upper-class women and shows both the extraordinary talent of Egyptian craftsmen and the abundance of gold and precious gems. Most were found locally, some were imported or plundered from Nubia, and others, especially lapis lazuli, came by way of trade routes. The pectoral in figure **3.22**, an openwork frame in the shape of a temple, belonged to a Middle Kingdom princess. Spreading out at the top are the protective wings of the Horus-falcon; in the center below are symbols of the tomb chapel in which the pectoral was discovered and the king's cartouches. Symmetrically arranged on either side is the reigning pharaoh, who brandishes a mace to strike the small enemy kneeling before him. Behind each image of the pharaoh, an ankh with arms raises a papyrus stalk. In works such as this the complexity of Egyptian symbolism is combined with intricate workmanship and attention to detail.

3.22 Pectoral of Mereret, 12th Dynasty, *c.* 1820 B.C. Gold, lapis lazuli, carnelian, turquoise, and amethyst, 4½ in. (7.9 cm) high. Egyptian Museum, Cairo.

MIDDLE KINGDOM EGYPT: *c.* 1991–1700 B.C.

The end of the Old Kingdom was followed by the First Intermediate period, which lasted to around 1991 B.C. Civil wars destroyed prosperity and brought economic hardship. Internal unrest grew as priests, aristocrats, and local governors increased their power and threatened the iron-clad control of Old Kingdom pharaohs. The Middle Kingdom followed, beginning with the Twelfth Dynasty, and brought a resurgence of the pharaoh's power. This led to a period of artistic expansion.

SCULPTURE AND ARCHITECTURE

The problems of the First Intermediate period influenced the political atmosphere of the Middle Kingdom. Rather than projecting an image of abstract permanence as Old Kingdom images of pharaohs had, artists now showed some pharaohs with expressions of concern. This is evident, for example, in a head of Amenemhet III (figure **3.23**).

3.23 Head of Amenemhet III, *c.* 1859–1813 B.C. Obsidian, 4¾ in. (12 cm) high. Museu Calouste Gulbenkian, Lisbon.
The pharaoh wears the traditional *nemes* headcloth, but the facial expression has changed since the Old Kingdom. Amenemhet III has softer features, especially the bulging flesh around the cheeks and upper lip, which convey a more human and humane image than in Old Kingdom royal art. In addition, his eyes and mouth slant slightly downward, imparting an air of gravity, as if he is preoccupied by the weight of his office.

Another Middle Kingdom development in sculpture was a type of cubic statue meant for the interior of a temple (figure **3.24**). This shows a squatting figure with legs and/or feet projecting from the front of the block, which is covered with hieroglyphs. The arms and head emerge from the top, and the small standing figure is Senwosret-senebefny's wife. The discrepancy in their sizes is a striking example of the Egyptian hierarchical system of proportion. The power of these figures lies in their compactness, which entirely eliminates open space, and in the unusual merging of geometric with human form.

Relatively little Middle Kingdom architecture has survived. Tombs were smaller than in the Old Kingdom, and many were made of mud brick rather than stone. The most typical examples of Middle Kingdom burial architecture were rock-cut tombs, with interiors hollowed out of existing cliffs, leaving only the façades visible. Several such tombs dating from the early Twelfth Dynasty are found at Beni Hasan, about 125 miles (200 km) south of Giza (see map 3.1, p. 50).

3.25 Detail of Senbi's coffin, *c.* 2000 B.C. Painted wood, 24¾ in. (63 cm) high. Egyptian Museum, Cairo.
In its original position, the coffin faced east. Thus, the prominent eyes over the painted door permitted the deceased to look beyond the coffin toward the rising sun.

The Beni Hasan tombs resemble the forms of contemporary houses, reflecting the traditional metaphor equating the tomb with the house of the dead. A particularly impressive expression of this metaphor can be seen on the Twelfth Dynasty coffin of Senbi (figure **3.25**). Its rich decoration is characteristic of the Middle Kingdom and is derived from elements used in actual architecture.

NEW KINGDOM EGYPT: *c.* 1550–1070 B.C.

In the Middle Kingdom, Egyptian pharaohs conquered Nubia and invaded Palestine, Syria, and Phoenicia. Fierce retaliation from the Hittites (in modern Turkey) forced Egypt to a compromise, in which they agreed to share the conquered territory with them and the Assyrians. The Second Intermediate period (*c.* 1640–1550 B.C.) followed, during which Lower Egypt was invaded by the Hyksos. In the sixteenth century B.C., the Hyksos were defeated by the pharaoh Ahmose I of Thebes, and with their expulsion the New Kingdom began and with it a period of stability and architectural activity.

3.24 Block statue of Senwosret-senebefny and his wife, late 12th Dynasty, *c.* 1878–1840 B.C. Quartzite, 27 × 16½ × 19 in. (68.6 × 41.9 × 48.3 cm). Brooklyn Museum, New York.

The Hyksos invasion had alarmed Egypt and accentuated its aversion to foreigners. So that Egypt would never again be subjugated, the country went on the offensive in the Near East and Nubia, incursions that ironically increased Egypt's international contacts and made its culture more cosmopolitan. During the New Kingdom, Egypt imported ideas, words, technology, and even gods into its civilization. At the same time, through diplomacy as well as warfare, Egypt reached a peak in its influence on foreign cultures.

TEMPLES

The Egyptians called their temples "houses" or "mansions" of the gods. Temples were not open to the general public, but, as in Mesopotamia, were private residences inhabited by cult statues embodying the deities. Priests, who were called "servants of the god," functioned as household staff, feeding and clothing the statues and caring for their sacred animals.

As in the Middle Kingdom, New Kingdom temple complexes followed the typical house plan (figure **3.26**). A gateway led to an open forecourt at the front—an enclosed front yard—which *was* accessible to the public. At the center of the complex, a **hypostyle** hall containing many columns was the god's "living room" and was usually closed to the public. Beyond the hypostyle were chapels, storage rooms, and the sanctuary that housed the cult statue. Only priests and the pharaoh were allowed inside the sanctuary.

The main New Kingdom temples were either rock-cut or freestanding. The typical freestanding temple had a **pylon** façade consisting of two massive trapezoidal walls (figure **3.27**) on either side of the entrance. Flanking the entrance were two **obelisks** (tall, pointed, square pillars), and colossal statues of the pharaoh. Leading to the entrance, rows of impressive **sphinxes** (human-headed lions) created a spatial avenue. Their repetition represented the power of the pharaoh and the prosperity of Egypt under his rule.

3.26 Three-dimensional diagram of a standard New Kingdom temple.

pylon

inner sanctuary

courtyard

hypostyle hall

3.27 *below* Entrance to the Temple of Ramses II, Luxor, 1279–1213 B.C.

3.28 Festival court of Amenophis III, Temple of Ramses II, 18th Dynasty, *c.* 1390–1352 B.C. Sandstone. Luxor, Egypt.

In the festival court of Amenophis III at the Temple of Ramses II (figure **3.28**), the pharaoh presided over religious festivals. The courtyard was surrounded by a massive open wall of double columns in the form of papyrus bundles. The huge size of such temples and the columns based on vegetation forms denoted both the power of the pharaoh and the fertility produced by the Nile in flood.

The plan in figure **3.29** shows the dramatic progression from the exterior, through the open-air court, into the dimmed light and shadows of the columned hypostyle hall. The hypostyle walls were decorated with painted reliefs, and hieroglyphic carvings covered the colossal columns. Celestial imagery originally on the hypostyle ceiling reflected the view of the temple as a replica of the cosmos on earth.

The Egyptian temple was thus also designed as a model of the universe in time and space. Progressing toward the inner sanctuary, the worshipper symbolically goes back in time to original creation. According to Egyptian myth, the world

3.29 Plan of the Temple of Ramses II, begun *c.* 1400 B.C.

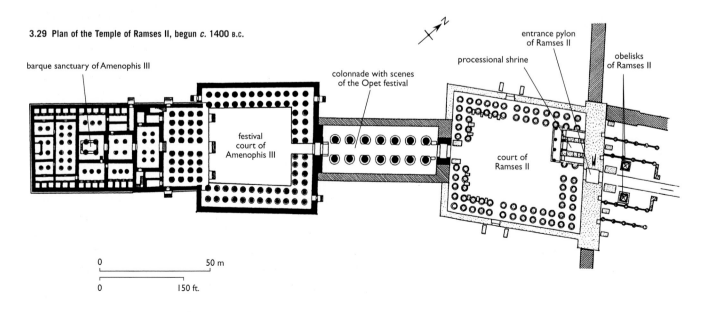

barque sanctuary of Amenophis III

colonnade with scenes of the Opet festival

processional shrine

entrance pylon of Ramses II

obelisks of Ramses II

festival court of Amenophis III

court of Ramses II

0   50 m

0   150 ft.

emerged from Nun (the primeval ocean), the waves of which were represented by undulating mudbrick walls surrounding the temple.

THE AMARNA REVOLUTION: c. 1349–1336 B.C.

Around 1352 B.C., the pharaoh Amenhotep IV (ruled 1352–1336 B.C.) ascended the throne of Egypt. Within four years, he had introduced religious beliefs that changed artistic conventions, especially in royal imagery. Amenhotep IV has been the subject of extensive, on-going research and controversy. He moved the capital north from Thebes, and south from Memphis, to Amarna (see map 3.1, p. 50), hence the name of the period. Most radical of all, Amenhotep IV challenged the established priesthood, and proclaimed Aton the one living god, which he represented as the sun-disk.

It is not known why this pharaoh changed Egyptian traditions as he did, but his ideas were not generally well received. The departure from polytheism was a short-lived, but intellectually significant, development. It is the earliest known instance of a ruler making monotheism an official religion. In honor of the Aton, Amenhotep IV changed his name to Akhenaton ("servant of the Aton").

In Akhenaton's "Hymn to the Sun," the Aton is called the one and only god and is credited with being the source of all life and the mover of the universe:

> You make Hapy, the Nile, stream through the underworld,
>   and bring him, with whatever fullness you will,
> To preserve and nourish the People
>   in the same skilled way you fashion them.
> You are Lord of each one,
>   who wearies himself in their service,
> Yet Lord of all earth, who shines for them all,
>   Sun-disk of day, Holy Light!

The most famous sculpture from the Amarna period is the limestone **bust** (showing a figure from the head to just below the shoulders) of Nefretiti, Akhenaton's principal wife (figure **3.30**). In contrast to more traditional royal sculptures, this has open space, and a long, graceful neck. Instead of the traditional headdress worn by most Egyptian queens, Nefretiti wears a tall crown, which completely covers her hair. The unusual elegance and naturalism of this bust is enhanced by the preservation of the paint. Nevertheless, the artist has also carefully indicated the presence of neck muscles and cheekbones, as well as the organic relation of forms beneath the surface of the skin.

Akhenaton and his religious beliefs were unpopular, and they led to a power struggle between priests and the pharaoh. It is not known how Akhenaton died, and when his tomb was discovered at Amarna in the nineteenth century his mummy was missing. The pharaohs who succeeded Akhenaton reinstated

3.30 Bust of Nefretiti (side and front), Amarna period, c. 1349–1336 B.C. Painted limestone, approx. 19 in. (48 cm) high. Egyptian Museum, State Museums, Berlin.

polytheism along with the traditional hierarchy of priests, and destroyed what evidence they could of Akhenaton's reign.

THE TOMB OF TUTANKHAMON

The pharaoh Tutankhamon ruled for only a short time, from about 1336 to 1327 B.C., and his name indicates that he worshipped the older Amon gods. In 1922, his tomb was discovered intact, revealing the vast wealth of the Egyptian pharaohs and their elaborate burials. Thousands of objects made of precious materials were excavated, including chariots, furniture, vases, jewels, amulets, statues, and articles of clothing (right down to the royal underwear).

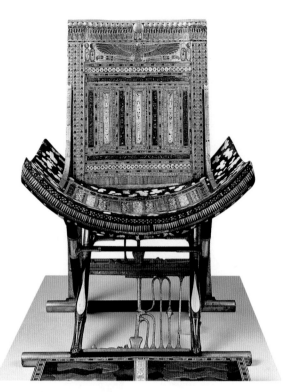

3.31 Tutankhamon's throne, *c.* 1336 B.C. Wood, gold, glass, faience, and gemstones, 3 ft. 4⅛ in. (1.02 m) high. Egyptian Museum, Cairo.

3.32 Funerary mask of Tutankhamon, *c.* 1327 B.C. Gold, lapis lazuli, glass, faience, gemstones, 21¼ in. (54 cm) high. Egyptian Museum, Cairo.

One of Tutankhamon's many thrones is illustrated in figure **3.31**. The elaborate surface decoration culminates in the conventional protective Horus-falcon flanked by cartouches on the back of the throne. Tutankhamon's gold funerary mask (figure **3.32**) retains the traditional *nemes* headcloth with a protective cobra and vulture above the forehead. Compared to representations of Akhenaton, this projects the more traditional image of the pharaoh as the embodiment of eternal royal power. Both works show how royal imagery after Akhenaton reflects a determination to eradicate the ideas and the art of the Amarna revolution.

By the end of the New Kingdom, Egypt's power was on the wane. It succumbed to Assyrian conquest in the seventh century B.C., and to Persian conquest three times (in the sixth, fifth, and fourth centuries B.C.). In 332 B.C., Alexander the Great conquered Egypt and, after his death in 323 B.C., Egypt was ruled by descendants of his Greek general Ptolemy. In 31 B.C., Egypt became part of the Roman Empire and, from the fifth century, was infiltrated by monasteries established by Coptic Christians. Some two hundred years later, as a result of Arab conquests, Egypt converted to Islam, which remains its dominant religion today.

KEY TERMS

bust a sculpture or picture showing a figure from the head to just below the shoulders.

canopic jar a container for organs removed during mummification.

cartouche a rectangle with curved ends framing the name of a king.

dynasty a family of kings.

hieratic a cursive script derived from hieroglyphs.

hieroglyphs a writing system using pictorial representations as characters.

hymn a song praising a god.

hypostyle a hall with a roof supported by rows of columns; the center columns are taller than those at the sides.

ideogram a pictorial representation of an idea.

maat the Egyptian concept of cosmic order, truth, and justice; also (when capitalized) the name of the goddess embodying those qualities.

mummification in ancient Egypt, a process taking seventy-two days in which bodies were embalmed and organs were removed.

obelisk a tall, pointed, square pillar.

pharaoh a king of ancient Egypt.

phonogram an image denoting sounds.

profile the side view of a figure or object.

pylon in ancient Egypt, a massive trapezoidal gateway.

pyramid an Egyptian tomb.

scribe in ancient Egypt, a professional record-keeper, usually a member of the court.

sistrum a type of rattle.

sphinx a human-headed lion.

vignette a small section of decoration or a literary sketch.

KEY QUESTIONS

1. Describe three measures that Egyptians took to ensure an afterlife.
2. What subjects in Egyptian society did artists treat naturalistically? What subjects did artists treat monumentally?
3. Which Egyptian leader did not follow standard religious practices? What innovations in art came about because of his leadership?
4. On what parts of a New Kingdom temple would one find hieroglyphic carvings?

SUGGESTED READING

Arnold, Dorothea. *The Royal Women of Amarna*. New York: Metropolitan Museum of Art, 1996.
▸ A study of the role of royal women during the Amarna period.

Christie, Agatha. *Death on the Nile*. London: HarperCollins, 2004.
▸ A murder mystery set in Egypt.

Faulkner, R. O. *The Ancient Egyptian Book of the Dead*. London: British Museum Press, 1989.
▸ A discussion of the texts and meanings found in the *Book of the Dead*.

Foster, John L. (trans.). *Ancient Egyptian Literature*. Austin, TX: University of Texas Press, 2001.
▸ A survey of literature in ancient Egypt.

Lichtheim, Miriam. *Ancient Egyptian Literature*, 2 vols. Berkeley and Los Angeles: University of California Press, 1975.
▸ A study of ancient Egyptian literature, with many excerpts.

Quirke, Stephen, and Jeffrey Spencer (eds.). *The British Museum Book of Ancient Egypt*. London: British Museum Press, 1992.
▸ A general survey of the arts and culture of ancient Egypt.

Redford, Donald B. *Akhenaton: The Heretic King*. Princeton, NJ: Princeton University Press, 1984.
▸ A study of Akhenaton and his religious revolution in the context of ancient Egypt.

Robins, Gay. *Women in Ancient Egypt*. Cambridge, MA: Harvard University Press, 1993.
▸ A discussion of the social role of women in ancient Eygpt and their representation in art.

Taylor, John H. *Egypt and Nubia*. London: British Museum Press, 1991.
▸ A brief study of the relationship between Egypt and Nubia.

——. *Death and the Afterlife in Ancient Egypt*. London: British Museum Press, 2001.
▸ A study of Egyptian beliefs about the afterlife and the rituals they engendered.

Waltari, Mika. *The Egyptian*. New York: G. P. Putnam's Sons, 1949, reprinted by Chicago Review Press, 2002.
▸ A recreation of the "Tale of Sinuhe."

Wilkinson, Richard H. *The Complete Temples of Ancient Egypt*. New York: Thames and Hudson, 2000.
▸ A discussion of temple architecture and the beliefs it expressed.

SUGGESTED FILMS

1932 *The Mummy*, dir. Karl Freund

1944 *The Mummy's Ghost*, dir. Reginald LeBorg

1945 *The Mummy's Curse*, dir. Leslie Goodwins

1954 *The Egyptian*, dir. Michael Curtiz

1955 *Abbot and Costello Meet the Mummy*, dir. Charles Lamont

1959 *The Mummy*, dir. Terence Fisher

1978 *Death on the Nile* (based on Christie), dir. John Guillermin

1998 *The Prince of Egypt*, dirs. Simon Wells and Steve Hickner, co-director Brenda Chapman

1999 *The Mummy*, dir. Stephen Sommers

2001 *The Mummy Returns*, dir. Stephen Sommers

4 The Aegean World

" *Zeus saw Europa the daughter of Phoenix gathering flowers in a meadow with some nymphs and fell in love with her. So he came down and changed himself into a bull and breathed from his mouth a crocus. In this way he deceived Europa, carried her off and crossed the sea to Crete, where he had intercourse with her . . . she conceived and bore three sons, Minos, Sarpedon and Rhadamanthys.* "

(HESIOD, ATTRIB., *Catalogues of Women and Eoiae* 19)

In this chapter we move northwest from Egypt, first to the island of Crete and Minoan culture and then to the Mycenaean culture that developed on the Greek mainland. These civilizations are referred to as Aegean, after the Aegean Sea (see map 4.1, p. 72). In addition, twentieth- and twenty-first-century excavations have unearthed a thriving culture, contemporary with the Minoans, on the volcanic island of Thera, north of Crete. All these Aegean cultures flourished during the Bronze Age, when people used bronze tools and weapons.

Minoan civilization lasted from around 2000 to 1200 B.C., and Crete was a seafaring culture with widespread foreign contacts. The Minoans had a high standard of living, with paved streets, stone houses, and plumbing and drainage systems. Palaces were religious centers with large bureaucratic administrations. Economically, the island was supported by agriculture and piracy, as well as by trade with Egypt, Anatolia (modern Turkey), the Middle East, and the Greek mainland. Minoans also colonized areas throughout the Aegean. Many scholars believe that the Minoans ruled through control of the sea, a system of rule known as **thalassocracy**.

In the course of its history, Crete suffered several stages of destruction. Around 1600 B.C. an earthquake devastated the island. A century or two later, sometime in the fifteenth century B.C., a volcanic eruption on Thera further damaged northern Crete (see p. 72). Then, around 1400 B.C., the Mycenaeans invaded Crete and conquered the Minoans. From this point, the Greek mainland began its rise to power, expanding westward as far as the Italian peninsula and eastward to the Middle East. The Mycenaeans took over the Minoan colonies, established additional ones of their own, and dominated the Aegean. By about 1150 B.C., Mycenaean civilization entered a period of decline known as the Dark Age.

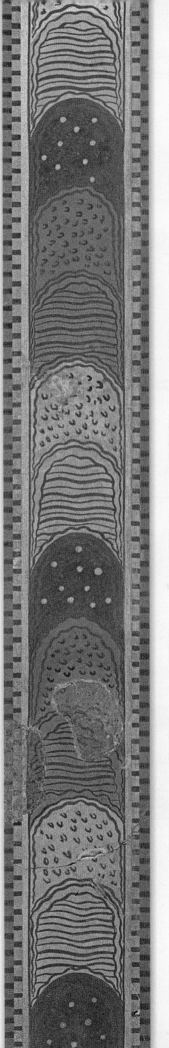

Key Topics

The Mysterious Minoans

Sacrificial rituals

Frescoes, pottery, and sculpture

Palace architecture

Linear A

The Theran Civilization

Frescoes

Plumbing and drains

The volcanic eruption

Heroic Mycenaean Myths and Legends

Warrior culture

Fortified citadels

The Trojan War

The Curse on the House of Atreus

Linear B

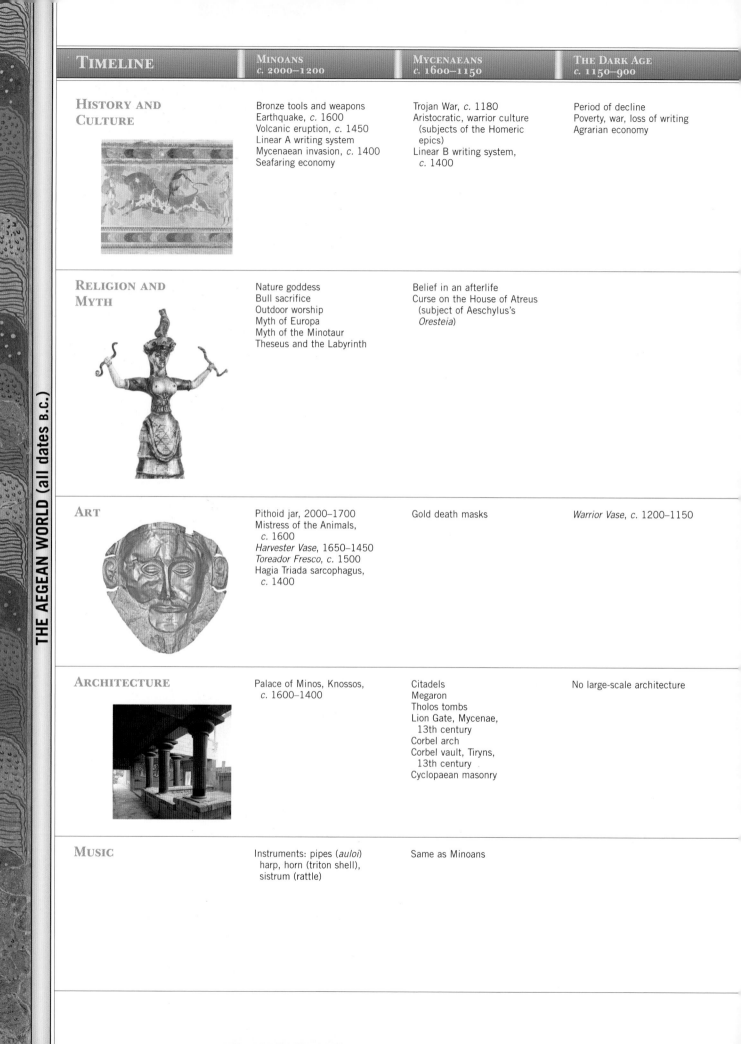

THE AEGEAN WORLD (all dates B.C.)

TIMELINE	MINOANS *c. 2000–1200*	MYCENAEANS *c. 1600–1150*	THE DARK AGE *c. 1150–900*
HISTORY AND CULTURE	Bronze tools and weapons Earthquake, *c.* 1600 Volcanic eruption, *c.* 1450 Linear A writing system Mycenaean invasion, *c.* 1400 Seafaring economy	Trojan War, *c.* 1180 Aristocratic, warrior culture (subjects of the Homeric epics) Linear B writing system, *c.* 1400	Period of decline Poverty, war, loss of writing Agrarian economy
RELIGION AND MYTH	Nature goddess Bull sacrifice Outdoor worship Myth of Europa Myth of the Minotaur Theseus and the Labyrinth	Belief in an afterlife Curse on the House of Atreus (subject of Aeschylus's *Oresteia*)	
ART	Pithoid jar, 2000–1700 Mistress of the Animals, *c.* 1600 *Harvester Vase*, 1650–1450 *Toreador Fresco*, *c.* 1500 Hagia Triada sarcophagus, *c.* 1400	Gold death masks	*Warrior Vase*, *c.* 1200–1150
ARCHITECTURE	Palace of Minos, Knossos, *c.* 1600–1400	Citadels Megaron Tholos tombs Lion Gate, Mycenae, 13th century Corbel arch Corbel vault, Tiryns, 13th century Cyclopaean masonry	No large-scale architecture
MUSIC	Instruments: pipes (*auloi*) harp, horn (triton shell), sistrum (rattle)	Same as Minoans	

*In addition to myths and legends, much of what we know of Aegean civilization comes from archaeological evidence. But some information is also provided by written scripts. Minoan writing, called **Linear A**, has not yet been deciphered, though it is known that it was used for record-keeping and religious dedications. **Linear B**, which can be read, was the Mycenaean script and an early form of Greek. The Mycenaean use of Linear B for record-keeping has provided information about the vast bureaucratic organization of Mycenaean palaces. The fact that, around 1400 B.C., Linear B appeared in Crete and elsewhere in the Aegean world reflects the extent of Mycenaean domination.*

Oral traditions and later works of Greek literature kept alive the myths and legends about the Minoan–Mycenaean era until the late nineteenth century, when archaeologists began to search for physical evidence of the truth contained in these stories. The quotation that opens this chapter is from a key Greek myth about the origins of Minoan civilization. Attributed to the late eighth-century-B.C. Greek author Hesiod, the Europa myth reflects the later Greek tradition that the Minoans came from ancient Phoenicia (roughly equivalent to the modern coastal areas of Israel and Lebanon) and that Europa herself was a Phoenician princess—in Hesiod she is the daughter of Phoenix. According to the myth, Zeus, the king of the Greek gods, disguised himself as a bull and enticed the mortal girl Europa with a sweet-smelling crocus (a sacred flower), swam with her on his back to Crete, and seduced her. Europa's three sons became rulers: Sarpedon ruled Lycia (in modern Turkey), Rhadamanthys ruled the Underworld, and Minos ruled Knossos on Crete.

WHO WERE THE MINOANS?

Legends notwithstanding, the origins of the Minoans are not known, and there is no evidence of Paleolithic culture on Crete. The island's inhabitants appear to have had links with Anatolia in the Neolithic period (*c.* 6000–3000 B.C.). The Bronze Age followed, until the eight-hundred-year Minoan civilization disappeared and faded into myth and legend. This remained the case until the early twentieth century, when the British archaeologist Sir Arthur Evans (1851–1941) excavated the site of Knossos, located a short distance inland from the north coast of Crete (see map 4.1, p. 72). The discovery of the Minoan civilization, and

4.1 Pithoid jar with fish, from the old palace, Phaistos, 2000–1700 B.C. Kamares ware. Herakleion Museum, Crete.
The jar is decorated with three orange fish (only one is visible in this view) on a dark blue background. Emerging from the fish's mouth is a cross-hatched, white design suggesting a fisherman's net. Curvilinear patterns circling the jar include waves and spirals, which, like the net, convey a sense of lively motion.

of others in the Aegean, mirrors the ongoing nature of historical research, which is continually revising perceptions of history.

Evans called the civilization on Crete "Minoan" after its legendary king, Minos. The excavations uncovered a great deal of archaeological evidence, including Linear A script, architecture, paintings, and pottery. Paintings, as well as the myth of Europa, show that the Minoans were seafarers and that the sea was crucial to the Minoan economy. Minoan artists reflected the importance of the sea in their iconography as well as in their fluid pictorial style (figure **4.1**).

The Minoans built elaborate columned palaces, which served as social, religious, and economic centers. They were also the dwelling place of the rulers. Because the sea afforded Crete natural protection from invaders, palaces were not fortified and were typically planned with a large central courtyard where people gathered. Figure **4.2** shows the sprawling, irregular plan of the palace at Knossos (see Box, p. 68). In contrast to the colossal architecture of Egypt, Minoan palaces were

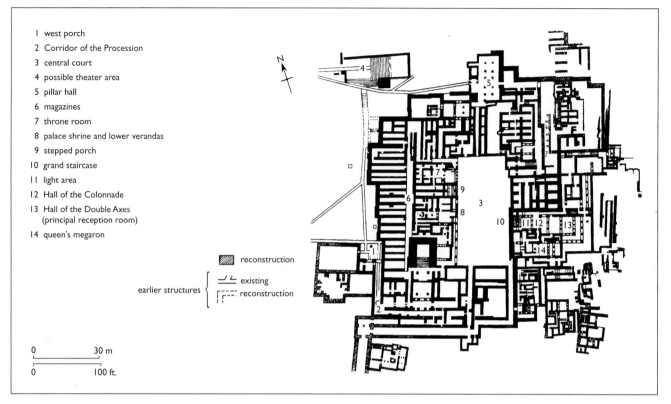

4.2 Plan of the palace of Minos, Knossos, Crete, c.1600–1400 B.C.

In the plan legend:

1 west porch
2 Corridor of the Procession
3 central court
4 possible theater area
5 pillar hall
6 magazines
7 throne room
8 palace shrine and lower verandas
9 stepped porch
10 grand staircase
11 light area
12 Hall of the Colonnade
13 Hall of the Double Axes
    (principal reception room)
14 queen's megaron

reconstruction

earlier structures { existing
                     reconstruction

0   30 m
0   100 ft.

Society and Culture

The Labyrinth in Myth

The palace at Knossos was called the labyrinth by the Greeks, because of its maze-like plan (see figure 4.2). This structure became a feature of several myths, such as the myth of the Minotaur, the tale of the wife of King Minos who fell in love with a bull. Their union produced the monstrous Minotaur, part-human, part-bull. Minos demanded from Athens an annual tribute of seven boys and seven girls, who were killed and devoured by the Minotaur—an indication that the Greeks viewed the Minoans as a powerful force in the Aegean.

The Athenian hero Theseus decided to journey to Knossos to destroy the Minotaur and end the yearly sacrifice of Athenian youths. But Theseus became lost in the maze, and he escaped only because Ariadne, the daughter of King Minos, fell in love with him. She attached the end of a long thread to the entrance of the palace, and Theseus followed it out of the maze.

human in scale and avoided **symmetry**. They were built of **ashlar** (rectangular blocks) and mud brick, and covered with a thin layer of stone and painted plaster walls. The intricate layout of the plan conforms to the different functions of its parts: long thin rooms for storage at the west, living quarters in the east, and religious rooms facing the courtyard.

The walls of the east wing stairway (figure **4.3**) were decorated with **frescoes** (water-based paint applied to damp plaster surfaces), which are now restored. Small wooden columns are unique in that the shafts taper downward, as humans do, suggesting a relationship to human form and scale. This also creates more open space and allows greater freedom of movement for the inhabitants than do the huge columns and compact spaces of Egyptian architecture, which was designed to emphasize the greatness of the gods and pharaohs.

MINOAN RELIGION

The Minoans had no separate temples, because they worshipped inside palaces, outdoors at small mountain shrines, and in caves. Little is known about Minoan religious practices, although two striking images certainly had religious significance. One of these shows a woman, a priestess or a goddess—known as the Mistress of the Animals (figure **4.4**)—dominating snakes. Her frontal pose and upraised arms convey a sense of power, and her exposed, prominent breasts suggest that she was a fertility figure. As such, she would have been associated with vegetation cults celebrating rebirth every spring. The snakes represent the underground (**chthonic**) forces of the earth. Tree-worship was also a feature of Minoan religion, and trees and their architectural equivalent—columns made of wood—could symbolize a nature goddess.

The bull motif, which is related to the myth of Europa, had a ritual purpose, although the nature and meaning of the ritual are unsure. It appears from certain images that bulls were

4.3 East wing staircase, palace of Minos, Knossos, c. 1600–1400 B.C.
Note that whereas the Egyptian columns were in the form of plants, which symbolized fertility and prosperity, the Minoan columns are abstract. They have a small, round base and a short shaft, which is consistent with the lower ceilings compared with Egypt. The Minoan **capital** consists of a round, cushionlike shape surmounted by a square block. Behind the columns, the wall is decorated with shields in the shape of figures-of-eight and the door is framed by a pattern of circles. As on the jar from Phaistos (see figure 4.1), the style is lively and curvilinear.

4.4 Mistress of the Animals, from Knossos, c. 1600 B.C. Faience, 13½ in. (34.3 cm) high. Herakleion Museum, Crete.

sacrificed with double axes (axes with two blades). In Minoan art, there are many images of bulls, some of which were associated with the double axe. Actual double axes vary in size, and many small ones have been discovered in Minoan caves and shrines. Images of the double axe were also incised on several **piers** (vertical supports) at Knossos.

A bull ritual is the subject of the most famous painting found at Knossos, the *Toreador Fresco* (figure **4.5**). It shows three slender youths somersaulting over a charging bull, a scene that has been related to the myth of the Minotaur. Notice that two of the young people are white and one is brown, indicating that there are two girls and one boy. As in

4.5 *Toreador Fresco*, from Knossos, c. 1500 B.C. 32 in. (81.3 cm) high. Herakleion Museum, Crete.
This fresco had shattered into hundreds of fragments discovered lying on a floor of the palace. Note that it has been heavily restored. The dark fragments are original and the lighter areas are modern.

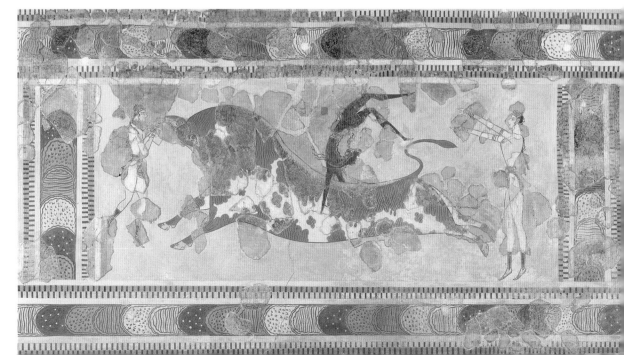

Egypt, the artistic convention of representing females with light skin and males with dark skin persisted on Crete. Similarly, the Minoans retained the conceptual representation of the profile head and frontal eye prevalent in Mesopotamian and Egyptian paintings and relief sculptures (see Chapters 2 and 3). In contrast to Egyptian style, however, the Minoan figures have natural curves, they turn more freely in space, and their movements are more dynamic. Works such as the

Toreador Fresco confirm that Minoan artists were influenced by Egypt, but that they also evolved their own distinctive style.

THE HAGIA TRIADA SARCOPHAGUS

The most elaborate image of a Minoan religious ceremony occurs on a sarcophagus found at the site of Hagia Triada (figure **4.6**). This is described here in some detail because it

4.6a Sarcophagus from Hagia Triada (front), *c.* 1400 B.C. Limestone with surface plastered and painted, 4 ft. 5 in. (1.35 m) wide. Herakleion Museum, Crete.

4.6b Back view of 4.6a.

Although the exact meaning of the imagery on the Hagia Triada sarcophagus cannot be identified, it clearly represents a sacrifical ritual. The scenes associate the double axe with killing the bull as well as with the presentation of offerings. They also point to the importance of music during funeral rites, which is confirmed by actual musical instruments found in Minoan burials.

MUSIC AND RITUAL

Surviving Minoan art indicates that ritual music in the Aegean —unlike that in Egypt—was the province of men. No written musical notes or texts of Aegean songs have survived, but several types of instruments have. Stringed instruments included the harp and the lyre, and the wind instruments were single- or double-reed pipes (**auloi**, in Greek); both types are depicted on the Hagia Triada sarcophagus. Horns were made from triton shells, and the sistrum (a type of rattle) was a popular percussion instrument. Singing was also an important part of Minoan religious ritual, which is illustrated in figure **4.8**.

Only the top half of this egg-shaped **rhyton** (drinking cup) is preserved. It is decorated with twenty-seven male figures. The leader wears a long tunic; workers carry farm implements; four are singing, as is indicated by the open mouths and depiction of the ribs, and one man shakes a sistrum. The scene is thought to represent a harvesting ritual, possibly related to gathering ripened olives, which were a staple of the Minoan (and later the Greek) economy.

4.7 John Younger, reconstruction of the Hagia Triada harp-player, as seen in figure 4.6a.

is a rare illustration in Minoan art showing figures enacting a ritual; it also reveals something about the kinds of musical instruments used by the Minoans.

The front left depicts a **libation** scene (in which a liquid is poured into a vessel). A woman in a fur skirt, possibly a priestess, pours liquid from one vessel into another (see figure 4.6a). The vessel stands on a platform flanked by vertical posts supporting double axes and birds. Behind the priestess, a second woman carries two jars suspended from a pole, and a man in a long yellow robe plays a type of harp (figure **4.7**). In the offering scene on the right, three men present models of calves and a boat to a figure (possibly the deceased) in front of what may be his tomb or a shrine.

On the other side of the sarcophagus (see figure 4.6b), a flute-player leads a procession of women. At the center, a bull is being sacrificed on a table, and its blood drips into a jar on the ground. Two small goats behind the table await their own sacrifice. To the right, a priestess places her hands over an altar, behind which is a post with double axes surmounted by a bird. At the far right, a second altar is built around an olive tree.

4.8 *Harvester Vase*, rhyton from Hagia Triada, 1650–1450 B.C. Steatite, 4¹/₂ in. (11.3 cm) diameter. Herakleion Museum, Crete.

THERA

On the volcanic island of Thera, north of Crete, archaeologists have discovered the ruins of a thriving civilization contemporary with the Minoans. During the heyday of Minoan power, Therans, like the inhabitants of Crete, had a high standard of living, with an economy based on agriculture and seafaring.

Although civilization on the island came to an end when the volcano erupted in the fifteenth century B.C., under the volcanic ash many elements of the culture were preserved—most notably, frescoes. These indicate a well-developed artistic

Defining Moment

The Eruption of Thera and Plato's Lost Atlantis

The ancient Aegean civilizations on Crete and Thera, which flourished from around 2000 B.C. to around 1200 B.C., were island cultures (map **4.1**). Sometime in the fifteenth century B.C., the area witnessed one of the most devastating volcanic eruptions ever known.

The Aegean island of Thera, now called Santorini, is located in the south of the Cyclades and is the surviving half of an active volcano. Thera's ancient culture was largely unknown until a Greek archaeologist, Spyridon Marinatos, began to excavate in the 1960s. Marinatos discovered building complexes, city streets, and walls up to 24 feet (8 m) high. Evidence was found of textile weaving and objects from many Mediterranean cultures, which indicate a well-established international trade on Thera. Pipes for transporting water, plumbing, and sewage systems attest to a good standard of living and are the earliest examples found so far anywhere in the world. Above all, archaeologists have unearthed a wealth of fresco paintings that reflect Theran life and ties to Minoan Crete. The frescoes illustrate a fleet, which was probably Minoan, dominating the Aegean Sea.

All of this, as well as parts of northern Crete, was destroyed when the volcano erupted. The inhabitants of Thera disappeared, and, as there is no trace of human remains on the island, it seems that they predicted the disaster and left in time. Ash and pumice from the explosion have been found as far away as modern Israel and Egypt, the Black Sea, and Turkey.

The enormity of the eruption on Thera has evoked comparisons with the eruption of Krakatoa, in Indonesia, in the nineteenth century. Most intriguing of all, Thera became associated with Plato's fourth-century-B.C. account of the Lost Atlantis. A mythic island in the Atlantic, Atlantis was said by Plato to have had its story related by Egyptian priests. It was reputed to have been powerful and to have sunk into the sea following a huge volcanic eruption. In reality, the devastation caused by the explosion on Thera completely wiped out Theran culture and contributed to the end of Minoan civilization, allowing the Mycenaeans to conquer Crete.

In 2004, an American researcher announced that he had found the Lost Atlantis off the coast of the island of Cyprus. He claimed that water sonars revealed man-made buildings on a hill sunk deep into the sea. But the main government archaeologist of Cyprus expressed doubts. Whatever the outcome, it is clear that the myth of the Lost Atlantis continues to intrigue researchers and will do so until the mystery has been solved.

READING SELECTION
Plato, *Critias*, the myth of Atlantis, PWC1-128-B

Critical Question Read Plato's account of the Lost Atlantis and decide if you think it is the same as Thera. What could have happened to the Therans when they escaped the eruption?

Map 4.1 The Aegean world, 2000–1200 B.C.

4.9 *Ship Fresco*, from Akroteri, Thera, *c.* 1650–1500 B.C., 15¾ in. (40 cm) high. National Archaeological Museum, Athens.

tradition; Theran artists were influenced by Minoan painting but developed their own, individual style.

The most important Theran fresco, called the *Ship Fresco* (figure **4.9**), dates to the second millennium B.C. There is disagreement among scholars over the exact meaning of this long painting, which extended across the upper part of three walls, but it has been a source of much information about Theran culture. It shows that ships were propelled by paddles and that dolphins swam in the Aegean. The ships, which are filled with warriors, are just setting out, most likely to engage in acts of piracy as well as to pursue peaceful trade. The *Ship Fresco* also contains examples of architecture and forest animals, such as deer, which provide clues to life on Thera.

Shortly after Thera's eruption, Greeks from the mainland invaded Crete. The invaders were the Mycenaeans, whose civilization lasted from around 1600 to 1150 B.C. It is not known for certain where the Mycenaeans came from, but they are thought to have been Indo-Europeans from the Caucasus who were great horsemen and who migrated to the east and west. From the beginning of the Mycenaean period, works of art and architecture on the mainland reflected Minoan influence.

MYCENAE AND THE HOMERIC HEROES

Mycenaean civilization takes its name from its main archaeological site at Mycenae in the northeast Peloponnese (southern Greece). But there were other important mainland sites, notably at Pylos, Tiryns, Corinth, and Athens. As in the Near East, Mycenaean cities were organized around fortified palaces often located on an elevated **citadel**. At Mycenae, the king and his consort were enthroned in a central room before a hearth where a sacred fire burned. Extending beyond the throne room were administrative offices and storage areas. Outside the palace, monumental city walls enclosed the main part of the citadel, which was inhabited by craftsmen. Beyond the citadel lay open land, which was farmed by peasants.

Above all, Mycenaean culture was a warrior culture. As such, it was celebrated in the two great epics attributed to the blind poet Homer, the *Iliad* and the *Odyssey*, which were not actually written down before the sixth century B.C. No one knows who Homer was, though he is believed to have lived in the eighth century B.C., when writing was revived at the end of the Dark Age. For centuries, professional poets had kept alive the Homeric epics by reciting them and singing them to the music of the harp. In contrast to the Egyptian ideal of eternity in the afterlife, the Homeric epics deal with mortal human heroes. The embodiment of the heroic ideal is Achilles, a warrior who chooses an early, heroic death over a long life.

The *Iliad* recounts the story of the Trojan War; the *Odyssey* tells of Odysseus's ten-year journey home after the war. The heroes of these epics are of two types. In the *Iliad*, Achilles is a great warrior, a kind of superhero, childish at times, unreasonably demanding, but also brave and skilled in fighting. Odysseus, the hero of the *Odyssey*, is crafty and intelligent. Like Achilles, he is a skilled warrior who fights alongside the Greek army at Troy. But when the war is over, Odysseus undertakes an epic quest and, like Gilgamesh (see Chapter 2), undergoes personal transformations as a result of his experiences. These include a series of memorable encounters with danger and temptation, and a visit to the Underworld. Whereas Achilles dies a heroic, youthful death, Odysseus returns home to his faithful wife, Penelope, in Ithaca, where he rules in peace and lives a long life. The *Iliad* and the *Odyssey* were studied in depth by the historical Greeks, and they continue to be an essential part of the Western educational curriculum today.

As with the Minoans, the Mycenaeans were known to the later Greeks, and indeed to the West, only in myth and legend. But in 1870 a successful German businessman, Heinrich Schliemann (1822–1890), set out to prove that the Trojan War actually happened. Inspired by reading Homer, Schliemann believed that there must have been some historical basis in the myths and legends surrounding the Trojan War. Having amassed a fortune, he was able to retire from business and pursue his goal. He first excavated at the site of Troy, a fortified city buried under the Greek and Roman town of Ilium on the northwest coast of Turkey.

HOMER'S *ILIAD*

Rage—Goddess, sing the rage of Peleus' son Achilles,
murderous, doomed, that cost the Achaeans [Greeks]
    countless losses,
hurling down to the House of Death so many sturdy souls,
great fighters' souls, but made their bodies carrion,
feasts for the dogs and birds,
and the will of Zeus was moving toward its end.
Begin, Muse, when the two first broke and clashed,
Agamemnon lord of men and brilliant Achilles.

(*Iliad*, lines 1–8)

The first eight lines of Homer's *Iliad* quoted here introduce the basic conflict of the epic. They take us into the middle of the action, rather than to the beginning of the story. The Greeks and their Minoan allies are waging war against the walled city of Troy. In the very first word—"rage"—Homer shows us the attitude of the youthful Achilles and his rash behavior, its consequences in causing the deaths of many warriors, and the violent, destructive character of war itself. Not only are brave soldiers killed, but their corpses are carrion, food for dogs and birds of prey.

Homer's reference to the "will of Zeus" reminds us of the Greek notion that, although humans have free will, their fate is controlled by the gods. This apparent paradox continues into later periods of Greek history and is a frequent theme in Greek literature and myth. It was an attempt to explain events and impulses that people could not control and to resolve inner, psychological conflicts that everyone experiences.

In the last two lines of the quotation, Homer asks his Muse, a goddess who inspires poetry, to begin the tale with the conflict between Achilles and Agamemnon, leader of the Greek army and king of Mycenae. Agamemnon had taken Achilles' war prize, a young Trojan woman, thus mirroring the legendary cause of the war itself. According to Greek legend, Agamemnon's brother, Menelaus, the king of Sparta, had married the beautiful Helen. When the Trojan prince, Paris, visited Menelaus, he was so struck by Helen's beauty that he abducted her and carried her off to Troy. Pledged to defend his brother's honor, Agamemnon led an army against the Trojans and ignited the war that lasted for ten years.

In the *Iliad*, Agamemnon and Achilles continue their feud. Achilles, the greatest of the Greek warriors, defies Agamemnon by refusing to fight and thus places the Greeks at a disadvantage. But when Hector, the bravest of the Trojan warriors, slays Achilles' best friend, Patroclus, Achilles returns to battle. Achilles had given his own armor to Patroclus, but Hector strips the armor and lays claim to Patroclus's naked body. Enraged by Hector's actions and devastated by the death of Patroclus, Achilles asks his mother, who is a goddess, to order him a new set of armor. She, in turn, asks Hephaestus, the blacksmith god, to forge weapons for her son. In a famous passage, Homer describes Achilles' new shield, which is decorated with images of city and country life, festivals and rituals, that mirror contemporary society.

Achilles now ceases to rage at Agamemnon, directing his anger instead at the Trojans. He slays dozens of enemy warriors, forcing them to take refuge inside the city. Finally, Achilles kills Hector in single combat. Achilles then strips Hector of his armor, and drags his nude body around the walls of Troy. Patroclus's spirit appears to Achilles and asks for proper burial rites.

In Greek religion, the soul of a dead person who was not properly buried was condemned to wander forever as a restless shade. Achilles thus arranges an elaborate burial for his friend. He then ransoms Hector's body to the Trojan king Priam. The *Iliad* ends with Hector's splendid funeral—the last line reads: "And so the Trojans buried Hector breaker of horses" (Bk. 24, last line).

HOMERIC LITERARY DEVICES

Homer's language is densely packed with action, which is intensified by colorful epithets (characterizing adjectives or short phrases), **similes** (comparisons using "like" or "as"), and metaphors (comparisons without "like" or "as"). We find, for example, epithets such as "well-greaved Greeks" (greaves being armor on the lower leg), "swift-footed Achilles," "crafty Odysseus," "wide-ruling Agamemnon," "god-like Priam," and "horse-breaking Hector." Achilles' spear is "far-shooting," the dawn is "rosy-fingered," and the sea is "wine-dark." Another device is repetition for the sake of emphasis.

In the following description of Priam's first sight of Achilles, note the use of repetition as well as of similes and metaphors. The Trojan king watches in fear as Achilles races toward the gates of Troy to fight his son, Hector:

And old King Priam was first to see him [Achilles] coming,
surging over the plain, blazing like the star
that rears at harvest, flaming up in its brilliance,—
far outshining the countless stars in the night sky,
that star they call Orion's Dog—brightest of all
but a fatal sign emblazoned on the heavens,
it brings such killing fever down on wretched men.
So the bronze flared on his chest as he raced—
and the old man moaned, flinging both hands high,
beating his head and groaning deep he called,
begging his dear son who stood before the gates,
unshakable, furious to fight Achilles to the death.

(Bk. 22, lines 31–41)

In vain, Priam pleads with Hector not to fight Achilles. Homer compares Hector to a coiled serpent waiting to strike its prey:

As a snake in the hills, guarding his hole, awaits a man—
bloated with poison, deadly hatred seething inside him,
glances flashing fire as he coils round his lair . . .
so Hector, nursing his quenchless fury, gave no ground,
leaning his burnished shield against a jutting wall.

(Bk. 22, lines 112–116)

And when Achilles pursues Hector, he is compared in another simile to a hound chasing a deer:

> And swift Achilles kept on coursing Hector, nonstop
> as a hound in the mountains starts a fawn from its lair,
> hunting him down the gorges, down the narrow glens
> and the fawn goes to ground, hiding deep in brush
> but the hound comes racing fast, nosing him out
> until he lands his kill. So Hector could never throw
> Achilles off his trail, the swift racer Achilles.
>
> (Bk. 22, lines 224–230)

MYCENAEAN ART AND ARCHITECTURE

Echoing the warrior character of the Homeric heroes is the massive, monumental architecture produced by the Mycenaeans. Unlike the Minoans, the Mycenaeans built defensive, fortified citadels as protection against invasion. The interior of the Mycenaean citadel contained a palace, royal tombs, and administrative centers. Most of the citizens were farmers, who lived on the slopes of the hill or in the valley below.

4.10 Lion Gate, Mycenae, Greece, 13th century B.C. Limestone, approx. 9 ft. 6 in. (2.9 m) high.
Note that the gate supports a triangular stone with a relief sculpture. This is composed of two lions guarding a Minoan column, which symbolizes the nature goddess worshipped on Crete, a motif that reflects contacts between the Minoan and Mycenaean cultures. At Mycenae, however, the faces of the lions were turned to the front, facing those who approach the entrance and denoting power.

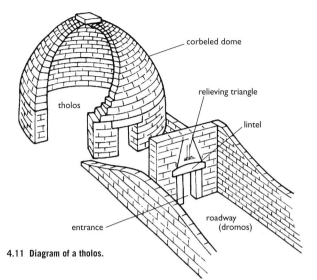

4.11 Diagram of a tholos.

Figure **4.10** illustrates the Lion Gate entrance to the walled Mycenaean citadel. It is a massive structure set between walls made of huge stone blocks. The large stone **courses** (layers of stone) of the wall increasingly project inward above the lintel to create a **corbel** arch.

A similar type of construction, known as a corbeled dome, was used for the monumental **tholos** tombs in which Mycenaean kings and queens were buried (figures **4.11** and **4.12**). The tholoi and earlier shaft graves at Mycenae contained gold

4.12 Entrance to the so-called Treasury of Atreus, Mycenae, Greece, 13th century B.C. Limestone.
Approached by a roadway, or **dromos**, the tholos was a round structure that tapered toward the top like a beehive. The door, which has not survived, was originally flanked by gypsum columns. Above the door, there is a triangular space, called a **relieving triangle** because it reduces the weight on the lintel; as with the Lion Gate, this space was originally filled in.

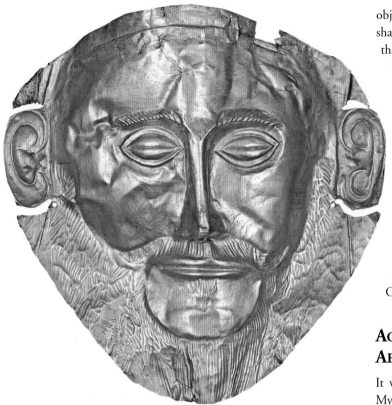

4.13 Mask of a ruler, erroneously called Agamemnon's mask by Schliemann, *c.* 1500 B.C. Gold, 12 in. (30.5 cm) high. National Archaeological Museum, Athens.

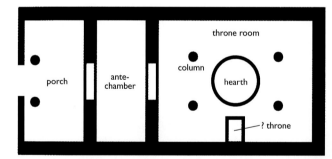

4.14 Plan of a Mycenaean megaron.

objects buried with the dead. Among these were works in the shape of bulls, indicating Minoan influence, and death masks that suggest a belief in the afterlife (figure **4.13**). Although little is known about Mycenaean religion, the Mycenaeans, like the Minoans, worshipped in palace shrines, rather than in separately built temples.

Inside the palace, the **megaron** was the main building within the Mycenaean citadel. The plan (figure **4.14**) shows the front porch with two columns, the **antechamber** (a room before, and leading into, another room), and the large throne room. Inside the throne room, the king sat facing the central hearth, which was surrounded by four columns. The reconstruction in figure **4.15** shows the elaborate painted decoration of the palace. The Minoan-style columns tapering toward the base are another indication of contact between Crete and mainland Greece.

AGAMEMNON AND THE *ORESTEIA* OF AESCHYLUS

It was from such a palace that Agamemnon and the other Mycenaean kings mentioned in the *Iliad* would have ruled. As the home of King Agamemnon, Mycenae was the most important Mycenaean city, which Schliemann excavated after Troy. Just as the story of the Trojan War had faded into myth and legend and was known only through the Homeric epics, so the story of Agamemnon and his family was known to the historical Greeks only through literature. The most complete surviving account of Agamemnon's return to Mycenae at the end of the war is a dramatic **trilogy** (set of three related plays), the *Oresteia*, by the fifth-century-B.C. playwright Aeschylus.

4.15 Reconstruction drawing of the Mycenaean megaron.

Although Aeschylus wrote many centuries after the events he described, his narrative is discussed here (fifth-century-B.C. Greek theater is explored further in Chapter 6). As with Homer, the power of Aeschylus's language, with its graphic imagery, emotional intensity, and taste for descriptions of violence, reflects the warrior culture of Mycenae.

The first play of the trilogy, *Agamemnon*, opens with a watchman guarding the palace of Mycenae and awaiting the signal that Agamemnon and his fleet are returning from Troy. When the signal finally comes, after ten years, the watchman's joy is muted by his knowledge of the famous curse on the House of Atreus: Atreus and Thyestes were brothers, but Thyestes seduced his brother's wife. Atreus took revenge by feeding Thyestes his own sons. Thyestes then cursed the descendants of Atreus, whose sons included Agamemnon and Menelaus.

Before setting sail for Troy, Agamemnon had insulted the moon goddess, Artemis, by killing one of her sacred stags. In revenge, Artemis calmed the winds to prevent the Greek ships from sailing. She demanded that Agamemnon atone for his insult by sacrificing his daughter, Iphigenia.

When Agamemnon returned to Mycenae at the end of the Trojan War, he found that his wife, Clytemnestra, had taken as a lover Thyestes' son, Aegisthus. Agamemnon himself had brought home as a war prize the Trojan princess Cassandra. She was cursed with the gift of prophecy but also with the fate that no one would ever believe her. Her warning that Clytemnestra would murder Agamemnon in his bath was thus ignored:

> Keep the bull from his mate! She hath caught him in the
> robe and gores him with the crafty device of her black horn!
> He falls in a vessel of water! It is doom wrought by guile
> in a murderous bath that I am telling thee.
>
> (Aeschylus, *Agamemnon*, lines 1125–1129)

Still angry at Agamemnon for having sacrificed their daughter, Clytemnestra fulfills Cassandra's prophecy. Her description of the murder is graphic indeed:

> Round him [Agamemnon], like as to catch a haul of fish, I
> cast a net impassable—a fatal wealth of robe—so that he
> should neither escape nor ward off doom. Twice I smote him,
> and with two groans his limbs relaxed. Once he had fallen, I
> dealt him yet a third stroke . . . Fallen thus, he gasped
> away his life, and as he breathed forth quick spurts of blood,
> he smote me with dark drops of ensanguined dew; while I
> rejoiced no less than the sown earth is gladdened in
> heaven's refreshing rain at the birthtime of the flower buds.
>
> (lines 1384–1392)

The play closes with Clytemnestra and Aegisthus ruling Mycenae—a reflection of the Mycenaean kingship system. Although kings ruled, they obtained legitimacy by marriage to a queen. On the death of Agamemnon, therefore, Aegisthus was free to marry Clytemnestra and become king of Mycenae.

The curse on the House of Atreus continues into the next generation and is the main theme of the second play of Aeschylus's trilogy, *The Libation Bearers*. Here the leading characters are Agamemnon's children, Electra and Orestes. Orestes has grown up away from the palace after his father's murder. Electra remains but is in perpetual mourning for her lost status as the king's daughter and for her father's death. Because she is female and fatherless, she cannot act. But the sun god, Apollo, orders Orestes to return to Mycenae and avenge Agamemnon's murder. Urged on by Electra as well as by Apollo, Orestes is in the difficult position of having to kill his own mother. Tortured by conflict but steady in his resolve, Orestes kills Clytemnestra and Aegisthus. The play ends with the Furies (goddesses who avenge crime) pursuing Orestes.

The last play of the trilogy, *The Eumenides* ("Kindly Ones"), deals with Orestes' quest for pardon. Pursued by the Furies to the city of Athens, Orestes goes on trial. Apollo himself presents the case to the jury. Reflecting the patriarchal bias of ancient Greece, the sun god argues that Clytemnestra is not really Orestes' blood relative because only a father can be a true parent. The mother, Apollo says, is merely the vessel and caretaker of the father's seed.

The jury fails to reach a verdict by reason of a tied vote. According to the rules of the Athenian court, a tie must be decided by Athena (goddess of war and wisdom), who casts her vote for acquittal. She then transforms the Furies into the Eumenides by promising them permanent sanctuary in Athens. Through the intervention of the gods, the curse on the House of Atreus is finally lifted, and Orestes becomes king of Mycenae.

HOMER'S *ODYSSEY*

Years after Agamemnon's return to Mycenae, the Greek hero Odysseus is still struggling to reach his family and his kingdom. His epic journey over land and sea and his descent into the Underworld are the subjects of Homer's *Odyssey*, which continues to inspire Western authors today. The very term "odyssey" has come to mean a spiritual, psychological, and physical journey that is heroic in character. As in the *Iliad*, Homer invokes the Muse in the opening lines, to sing not of Achilles' rage but of the crafty Odysseus, who wandered for years after the sack of Troy:

> Sing in me, Muse, and through me tell the story
> of that man skilled in all ways of contending,
> the wanderer, harried for years on end,
> after he plundered the stronghold
> on the proud height of Troy.
>
>   He saw the townlands
> and learned the minds of many distant men,
> and weathered many bitter nights and days
> in his deep heart at sea, while he fought only
> to save his life, to bring his shipmates home.
>
> (*Odyssey*, Bk. 1, lines 1–10)

Before departing for the Trojan War, Odysseus had ruled at Ithaca, an island in the Ionian Sea off the west coast of the Greek mainland. He bade farewell to his wife, Penelope, and son, Telemachus, and sailed for Troy.

At the beginning of the *Odyssey*, the war has been over for ten years. For seven of those years Odysseus and his men were imprisoned on an island by the goddess Calypso. In his absence, a number of suitors have tried to marry Penelope in order to rule Ithaca. Telemachus grows ever more afraid that he will lose his status as heir to the throne because, as at Mycenae, marriage to the queen would confer kingship on her new spouse and lower the rank of her children by Odysseus (see Box).

Eventually, Zeus orders Calypso to free Odysseus, who builds a raft and sets sail. But the raft is destroyed by Poseidon

(god of the sea), and Odysseus and his men are forced to land on another island. There he meets the king's daughter, Nausicaa, and is well entertained at the palace. A minstrel sings of heroes and gods, and of the wooden horse that made it possible for the Greeks to sack Troy. Unable to penetrate the city gates, the crafty Odysseus devised a plan: the Greeks built a huge wooden horse and offered it to the Trojans as a gift. But Greek soldiers hid inside and when the Trojans pulled it into the city, the Greeks brought:

> slaughter and death upon the men of Troy.
> He [the minstrel] sang, then, of the town sacked by Akhaians [Greeks]
> pouring down from the horse's hollow cave,
> this way and that way raping the steep city.
>
> (Bk. VIII, lines 551–554)

Odysseus describes the ordeals that he and his men have weathered since leaving Troy. A race of cannibal giants destroyed all but one of his twelve ships. The enchantress Circe transformed his men into swine. He journeyed through Hades, where he met the shades of deceased heroes who had fought at Troy. He successfully passed through the straits of Scylla (a monster who killed mariners) and Charybdis (a dangerous whirlpool). He resisted the irresistible Sirens' songs by filling his sailors' ears with wax and having himself tied to the mast of the ship. When he landed on the island of the Cyclopes (cannibal giants with a single eye), Odysseus and his men were captured and imprisoned in a cave. But Odysseus tricked the Cyclops Polyphemus into becoming drunk and then blinded him with a stake (see Box).

When Odysseus finally reaches Ithaca, Athena disguises him as a beggar. This allows him to discover what has been happening during his twenty-year absence. He meets his son Telemachus, reveals his identity, and together they plot to kill Penelope's suitors. In one of the most famous passages in the *Odyssey*, Odysseus is recognized by his old dog, Argos, who sees through his disguise:

> an old hound, lying near, pricked up his ears
> and lifted up his muzzle. This was Argos,
> trained as a puppy by Odysseus,
> but never taken on a hunt before
> his master sailed for Troy. The young men, afterward,
> hunted wild goats with him, and hare, and deer,
> but he had grown old in his master's absence.
> Treated as rubbish now, he lay at last
> upon a mass of dung before the gates—
> manure of mules and cows, piled there until
> fieldhands could spread it on the king's estate.
> Abandoned there, and half destroyed with flies,
> old Argos lay.
>
> But when he knew he heard
> Odysseus' voice nearby, he did his best
> to wag his tail.
>
> (Bk. XVII, lines 376–391)

Society and Culture

Women, Family, and the Rules of Marriage in the Homeric Age

Aristocratic nuclear families in the age of Homer consisted of the father, who was head of the household, his spouse, and their children. Adult sons, once married, lived at home with *their* wives and children. If a female slave had a son by a legitimate member of the family, that son had some rights, but fewer than the wife's sons. The son of a slave might inherit part of his father's property on his death, but generally property was divided among the wife's sons. If a father died before his son was grown, the son could lose his rights. This was the case with Orestes, providing him with a practical reason for killing Aegisthus and Clytemnestra. It was also a possibility that worried Telemachus.

Daughters were excluded from inheritance, and their fathers arranged their marriages, often for political or social reasons. The daughter had little say in the matter. The family of the bridegroom gave gifts to the bride's family, and the bride received a dowry from her family. Whereas the dowry was an investment in the future, the gifts were a sign of status. They were also a form of competition, in which several suitors might participate. Those who lost forfeited the gifts. Once married, the bride moved in with her husband's family.

In non-aristocratic families, money was the primary motive for marriage. A man might not marry until the age of thirty, but the average age of the bride was fifteen. Furthermore, in order to keep money in the family, marriages were arranged by a small group of close relatives.

According to the picture of Greek society painted by Homer, the Mycenaean period was one of relative social freedom for aristocratic women. Homer depicts wives as joining their husbands in conversation and participating with them in banquets. Women also ran the household economy and could go outdoors without a chaperone. These freedoms would be severely restricted after 800 B.C.

Society and Culture

The Cyclopes and Cyclopaean Masonry

The Cyclopes are the source of the term **cyclopaean masonry**, which denotes the huge stone blocks used in Mycenaean citadels. The later Greeks attributed the construction of such walls to giants, believing that no mere mortal was capable of lifting the stones. At Mycenae itself, cyclopaean masonry can be seen in the Lion Gate (see figure 4.10) and the walls of the dromos leading to the tholos tomb in figure 4.12. But in the corbeled enclosure at Tiryns (figure **4.16**), some 10 miles (16 km) from Mycenae, the monumental quality of these rougher stones is even more striking. Such enclosures, used to store weapons and for refuge in times of war, are the origin of the Homeric epithet for the city, "great-walled Tiryns."

4.16 Corbel vault, inside the citadel, Tiryns, Greece, *c.* 1300–1200 B.C.

The condition of the dog, weakened by neglect, is a metaphor for the state of Ithaca. Nevertheless, there is life in the old dog, as there is in the kingdom, and Odysseus quickly takes charge. Penelope, worn down by years of waiting and by the persistence of her suitors, has agreed to marry whoever can string Odysseus's bow and shoot an arrow through twelve axe heads. Still in disguise, Odysseus himself passes the test, kills the suitors and their mistresses, and convinces Penelope of his true identity. He then resumes control of Ithaca, preserves his son's heritage, and rules until his death.

READING SELECTION

Homer: *Iliad*, on the shield of Achilles, PWC1-205; *Odyssey*, in the Underworld, PWC1-211; *Odyssey*, on the Cyclops, PWC1-210; *Odyssey*, on the faithful dog, PWC1-215

Like all great works of literature, the *Iliad* and the *Odyssey* are timeless. Both portray aspects of their context, but also appeal to readers in different times and places. In the Homeric epics, as in Aeschylus's plays, we learn about Greek warrior culture and the structure of Greece's aristocratic and royal families, and we are told how gods and humans interact. But epics are also larger than life. They dramatize universal human themes and externalize internal human conflicts. Their characters are heroic, and their style is the result of poetic genius.

One lesson of the Minoan–Mycenaean civilizations is that myths and legends, like literature and the arts, are human products and therefore have meaning. It is important to take them seriously. Even though they may not be literally true in every respect, they contain grains of truth, as Evans and Schliemann demonstrated when they uncovered two "lost" civilizations and restored them to their place in history.

THE DARK AGE: *c.* 1150–900 B.C.

By around 1150 B.C., the Greek mainland had entered the period known as the Dark Age. This refers to an era of history about which there is very little information. As gaps in historical knowledge are filled in, however, so-called dark ages become less "dark." In the case of the Greek Dark Age, the Mycenaean palaces fell into disuse, widespread poverty resulted in a decline in technology and artistic patronage, and writing disappeared. Communities became mainly agricultural, and houses were flimsily constructed. Warfare was rampant, and it is probable that conflicts such as the Trojan War weakened the Mycenaean kingdoms. Despite the Dark Age, however, there is evidence of cultural continuity between Mycenaean civilization and historical Greece. In addition to the oral transmission of the epics, the Greek language persisted, and certain gods and pottery styles also survived.

At the close of the Mycenaean period, signs of cultural decline can be seen in the few surviving works of art. The *Warrior Vase* (figure **4.17**) found at Mycenae is flat and crude compared with the Minoan *Toreador Fresco*. Nevertheless, its imagery illustrates Mycenae's warrior culture.

The age of Homeric heroes disappeared with the Minoan–Mycenaean civilizations. Mycenaean citadels were destroyed

4.17
Warrior Vase,
c. 1200–1150 B.C.
Terra-cotta, 16 in.
(40.6 cm) high. National
Archaeological Museum,
Athens.
The repeated forms echo the relentless march of an army going to war. Accentuating the forward motion are the long, pointed noses and determined pace. The artist has carefully delineated the Greek armor, including elaborate helmets, shields and spears, and greaves. At the far left, a woman waves to the departing soldiers, reflecting another fact of warrior culture: that women, like Clytemnestra and Penelope, remain at home.

around 1200 B.C. by severe droughts resulting from changes in climate, by invaders whose identity is still debated, and possibly also by civil wars. Later legends describe invaders from the north called Dorians, who enslaved the native population. It was mainly in Athens that the cultural traditions of the Dark Age were retained and it is with Athens that we begin our exploration of historical Greece in the next chapter.

KEY TERMS

antechamber a room before, and leading into, another room.

ashlar rectangular blocks of stone.

aulos (plural **auloi**) a double-reed pipe.

capital the decorated top of a column.

chthonic relating to underground aspects of the earth.

citadel a fortified elevated area or city.

corbel brick or masonry courses arranged to form an arch or dome.

courses layers of stone.

cyclopaean masonry huge stone blocks used to construct walls, especially in the Mycenaean citadels.

dromos a roadway.

fresco a technique of applying water-based paint to a damp plaster surface, usually a wall or ceiling.

libation the pouring of a drink as an offering to a god.

Linear A undeciphered Minoan writing used for record-keeping and religious dedications.

Linear B readable Mycenaean script; an early form of Greek.

megaron the main building in the Mycenaean citadel.

pier a vertical support, usually rectangular.

relieving triangle in architecture, a space that reduces the weight on the lintel below it.

rhyton a drinking cup.

simile a comparison using "like" or "as."

symmetry a type of balance in which two sides of an object or picture are mirror images of each other.

thalassocracy rule through the control of the sea.

tholos (plural **tholoi**) a circular tomb of beehive shape.

trilogy a set of three related works of literature.

KEY QUESTIONS

1. How do scholars know that artistic works showing musical instruments are factual?
2. What three functions did Minoan palaces fulfill? Were Minoan palaces fortified? Why or why not, according to scholars?
3. How did the Mycenaean warrior culture view death?
4. What was the cause (according to the opening lines of Homer's *Iliad*) of the loss of countless Achaeans?
5. How does the *Iliad* begin? How does it end?
6. Watch the film *Troy* (2004) and read the relevant passages in Homer. Can you identify departures from the original text in the film?
7. Choose a passage from Homer with examples of metaphor, repetition, and epithets and discuss their usage.

SUGGESTED READING

Aeschylus. *Oresteia* (*Agamemnon*, *The Libation Bearers*, and *The Eumenides*), trans. H. Weir Smyth and H. Lloyd-Jones. Loeb Library Edition. Cambridge, MA: Harvard University Press, 1983.
  ▸ The trilogy of plays dealing with the House of Atreus.

Boardman, John. *Pre-Classical: From Crete to Archaic Greece*. Baltimore: Penguin, 1967.
  ▸ A standard work on style.

Homer. *Iliad*, trans. Robert Fagles. New York: Viking, 1991.
  ▸ The epic account of the Trojan War.

——. *Odyssey*, trans. Robert Fitzgerald. New York: Anchor Books, 1989.
  ▸ The epic journey of Odysseus at the end of the Trojan War.

Immerwahr, Sara A. *Aegean Painting in the Bronze Age*. University Park, PA: Pennsylvania State University Press, 1990.
  ▸ An illustrated study of Aegean frescoes.

Murray, Oswyn. *Early Greece*. Cambridge, MA: Harvard University Press, 1993.
  ▸ A study of the Mycenaean period.

Mylonas, George. *Mycenae and the Mycenaean Age*. Princeton, NJ: Princeton University Press, 1966.
  ▸ Mycenaean studies up to the 1960s by a Greek archaeologist.

Pedley, John Griffiths. *Greek Art and Archaeology*. New York: Harry N. Abrams, 1998.
  ▸ A general overview of ancient Greek art.

Pomeroy, Sarah B. *Goddesses, Whores, Wives, and Slaves: Women in Classical Antiquity*. New York: Schocken Books, 1995.
  ▸ An account of the roles and position of women in ancient Greece.

Renault, Mary. *The King Must Die*. New York: Random House, 1958/London: Arrow Books, 2004.
  ▸ A popular historical novel dealing with the myth of the Minotaur and the story of Theseus and the labyrinth.

——. *The Bull from the Sea*. New York: Longmans, 1962/London: Arrow Books, 2004.
  ▸ A historical novel based on the Minoan myth of Europa and the bull.

Woodford, Susan. *The Trojan War in Ancient Art*. Ithaca, NY: Cornell University Press, 1993.
  ▸ An illustrated discussion of the Trojan War as a subject of Greek art.

Younger, John G. *Music in the Aegean Bronze Age*. Philadelphia: Coronet Books Inc., 1998.
  ▸ A brief account of Aegean music, based mainly on the evidence of the Hagia Triada sarcophagus.

SUGGESTED FILMS

1927 *The Private Life of Helen of Troy*, dir. Alexander Korda
1956 *Helen of Troy*, dir. Robert Wise
1979 *Agamemnon*, dir. Peter Hall
2004 *Troy*, dir. Wolfgang Petersen

5 The Emergence of Historical Greece

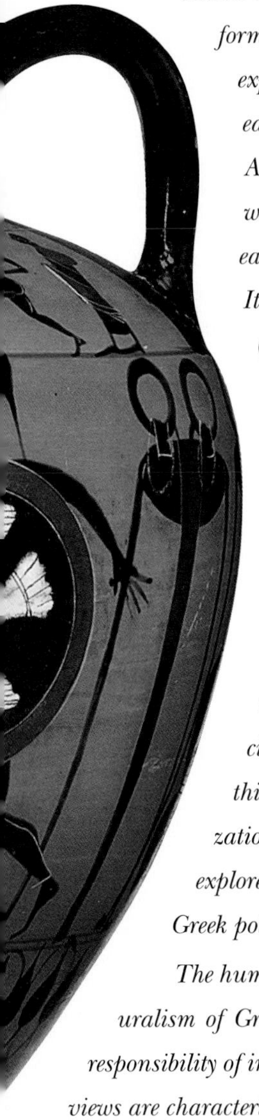

*I*n the eighth century B.C., Greece emerged from the Dark Age into its historical period. This transition coincided with a revival of writing and literacy, improved technology, and vigorous foreign trade, especially in metals. The use of Phoenician letters to stand for Greek sounds indicates contacts with the Near East.

The mainland Greeks called themselves Hellenes and their country Hellas. By the seventh century B.C., with a growing population and renewed agricultural prosperity, land became scarce. This led many Greeks to leave the mainland and form colonies in search of metals and commercial expansion (see map 5.1, p. 92). Colonies on the eastern Greek islands and on the west coast of Anatolia were known as Ionia. The Greeks also went southeast to Cyprus and Syria, and northeast to the Black Sea. Their colonies in southern Italy and Sicily were called Magna Graecia (meaning "Greater Greece"), but the people of Magna Graecia called the Hellenes Greeks, and Hellas, Greece.

In the early centuries of the historical period, Greeks created a new type of political organization, the **polis** (city-state). For the first time in the West, the notion of citizenship evolved, and male citizens were required to participate in their own governance. Many Greek city-states remained free of **tyrants** and kings. In this they differed from the other ancient civilizations considered so far. In what follows we will explore the major ideologies and events that affected Greek political thought.

The human focus of Greek religion and the evolving naturalism of Greek art mirrored the emphasis on the role and responsibility of individuals in guiding their own destiny. Similar views are characteristic of early Greek philosophy, which emphasizes the importance of empirical observation, reason, and intellect. These new cultural attitudes, along with a shared language, unified the mainland Greeks with their colonies and reinforced the ideal of the polis. As the city-state developed, Greece produced large-scale sculpture, painting, and stone architecture, reflecting a new and vital culture.

Key Topics

Evolving Ideas

Genealogy of the gods, views of the cosmos

Tyranny

Reason and observation

New types of warfare

Cultural Continuity

The *polis*

Oracles

Olympic Games

Cultural Unrest

Expansion through colonization

Economic disparities

Athens versus Sparta

TIMELINE	GEOMETRIC PERIOD *c. 1000–700*	ORIENTALIZING PERIOD *c. 700–600*	ARCHAIC PERIOD *c. 600–490*
HISTORY AND CULTURE	Greece emerges from Dark Age Revival of literacy Foreign trade, metals Increasing prosperity	Trade with the Near East Colonization begins Improved pottery techniques Influence of Near Eastern forms Warrior culture, hoplites	*Polis* develops Aristocratic warrior culture Idealization of male youth Solon and Lycurgus, lawgivers Athens and Sparta Beginning of philosophy and lyric poetry
RELIGION AND MYTH	Polytheism Anthropomorphic Olympians defeat Titans Afterlife in Hades Burial rites Myth of Pandora's Box Myth of Perseus and Medusa The Nine Muses		Modest grave markers
ART	Dipylon krater, *c.* 750 Geometric bronze horse, *c.* 750	*Chigi Vase*, *c.* 640 Olpe from Corinth, *c.* 600	*Sounion Kouros*, *c.* 580 Exekias, *Suicide of Ajax*, *c.* 540 *Anavysos Kouros*, *c.* 530 *Peplos Kore*, *c.* 530 Aristokles, *Stele of Aristion*, late 6th century Heracles vase, *c.* 520 Brygos painter, red-figure drinking cup, *c.* 500
ARCHITECTURE	Model of a shrine from Perachora, late 8th century		Temple of Aphaia, Aegina, *c.* 500 Doric and Ionic Orders
LITERATURE	Homeric epics (*Iliad* and *Odyssey*) written down Hesiod, *Theogony*, late 8th century		Lyric poets: Sappho (*c.* 640–580) Anacreon (*c.* 582–*c.* 485)
PHILOSOPHY			Pre-Socratics: Thales of Miletus (*c.* 625–*c.* 547) Pythagoras (*c.* 550–*c.* 500) Heraclitus (*c.* 540–*c.* 480)
MUSIC	No notation Part of rites Epics sung to music	Soldiers march to music	Lyric poetry sung to music

Several new styles of art evolved in the early historical period. In the Geometric period, lasting from around 1000 to 700 B.C., artists produced mainly small-scale sculptures and pottery decorated with geometric figures and designs. During the Orientalizing period (c. 700–600 B.C.) more fluid Eastern forms and subjects influenced painting and sculpture. And in the Archaic period (c. 600–490 B.C.) monumental stone architecture and lifesize sculpture appear.

During the Archaic period, the ideals of the Homeric warrior culture persisted, especially among aristocrats. Archaic artists expressed these ideals in a new type of image—the heroic male youth—which has survived mainly in sculpture. The quotation at the beginning of the chapter, for example, was inscribed on the statue of Kroisos, a young man "slain by Ares" (the war god) in the midst of battle. Just as Homer idealizes young men who choose heroic death over long life, so Archaic art memorializes the image and memory of youths who die bravely. This reflects one way in which the Greeks differed from the Egyptians, who believed in a material afterlife.

THE GREEK *POLIS*

By the end of the Greek Dark Age, disparate farming communities and villages began to gather around religious centers. These were led by rural priests and local landowners whose subsistence was based on agriculture and whose influence was limited by widespread poverty. The wealthiest among them functioned as judges in civil disputes, while criminal cases were decided by individual combat. Eventually, these rural communities evolved into the political center known as the *polis* (from which we get the English word "politics").

The *polis* (plural *poleis*) was composed of an urban area and its surrounding territory. The impetus for the formation of the *polis* came from people gathering together for mutual benefit rather than, as in the Minoan–Mycenaean era, Egypt, or the Middle East, from an imposed administration. As it developed, the central area of the *polis* became the **agora**, an open space for markets and public gatherings, which fostered a sense of social community and cultural identity. In the Geometric period, temples became standard structures in the *polis*, and although worship was held outdoors at sacred sites, mud brick shrines housed statues of the gods (figure **5.1**).

As the *polis* evolved, the rule of kings that had characterized the Minoan–Mycenaean era gave way to rule by heads of powerful families. This led to an **oligarchical** system (rule by a few), in which a class of aristocrats governed the city-state.

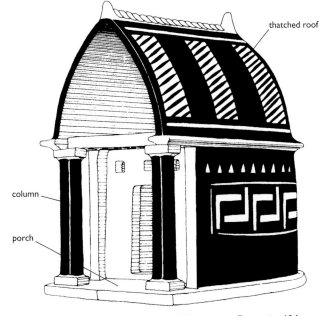

5.1 Model of a shrine from Perachora, late 8th century B.C. Terra-cotta, 13 in. (33 cm) high. National Museum, Athens.
Geometric period shrines consisted of a single room, a narrow front porch with two columns, and a thatched roof. The plan was rectangular on three sides with a curved wall at the back.

They governed through the institution of the assembly and an agreed structure of laws, or constitution. There was a wide variety of Greek *polis* types and forms of government, and many were already in existence by the Archaic period. The general principle of an independently governed city-state, each with its own economy and citizen army, was unique to Greek society.

ANCIENT GREEK RELIGION

Like the Egyptians and Mesopotamians, the Greeks believed in many gods and worshipped them in communal rituals. Rites included sacrifices, processions, music, and dance. Gods were everywhere in nature, and each *polis* had a patron god or goddess, who protected the city and demanded offerings in return. Athens, for example, had Athena as its patron goddess, whereas Olympia had Zeus, and Artemis was the patron goddess of the island of Aegina.

Nonetheless, in Greece there was more emphasis on the individual than in Egypt, where the pharaoh had absolute power and was regarded as a god on earth. Furthermore, the Egyptian gods were distanced from people in being shaped as animals, or as combinations of different species. The Greek gods were human in form (although they could change their shape) and had human personalities; they differed from humans mainly in being immortal.

The Greeks believed that when they died, their souls went to Hades, a dark Underworld populated by shades of the dead. There were no standard punishments for wrongdoing in

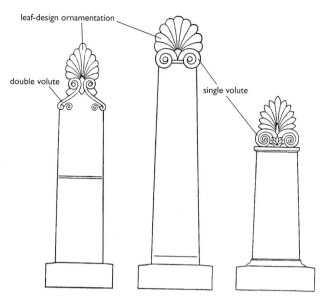

leaf-design ornamentation

double volute

single volute

5.2 *above* **Diagram of Attic grave stelae, 6th century B.C.**

5.3 Aristokles, *Stele of Aristion*, late 6th century B.C. Marble, 7 ft. 10 in. (2.4 m) high. National Museum, Athens.
The figure of Aristion is tightly enclosed in the rectangle of the stele and appears to be walking slowly. His head is slightly bowed, as if participating in his own funeral procession. The artist not only memorialized the warrior in this stele, he also preserved his own name, Aristokles, by inscribing it at the base. This reflects the growing sense of individual identity among artists in ancient Greece, and is consistent with the Greek notion of human centrality in the universe.

Hades unless one had offended the gods. In Egypt, on the other hand, Anubis (the jackal-headed god of embalmers) weighed the soul of the deceased to determine its worthiness (see Chapter 3).

As a result of different views of life and death, the burial monuments of Egypt and Greece also differed. Greek burial monuments were far more modest than the colossal Egyptian pyramids. Greeks marked their graves with a modest stele (vertical stone pillar) resting on a base (figure **5.2**).

The stele in figure **5.3** marked the grave of the warrior Aristion. Its style reflects the early Greek interest in showing that the figure, like the hero's memory, is alive. The folds of the clothing are flattened, but the more rounded arms and legs suggest the underlying anatomy. Traces of color indicate that the original was painted, which would have increased the figure's lifelike appearance.

HESIOD'S *THEOGONY*

During the late eighth century B.C., by which time Greek religion was well established, the poet Hesiod wrote the *Theogony*, an account of the genealogy of the gods. This work, like the Homeric epics, reflects the Greek focus on human individuality and shows the commitment of the Greek gods to human creativity. To assist Hesiod in composing his genealogy, the Muses give him a musical voice and a staff of laurel (the plant associated with fame and victory). They instruct him to begin with themselves,

> who gladden the great spirit of their father Zeus in Olympus with their songs, telling of things that are and that shall be and that were aforetime with consenting voice.

> (*Theogony*, lines 36–39)

First, according to Hesiod, the universe was Chaos (the Abyss), then came earth (Gaia), and then love (Eros). Gaia bore the heavens (Uranos), and together they bore six gigantic Titans. The Titans produced a third generation (including the Cyclopes; see Chapter 4). Chronos, a son of Uranos, castrated his father with his sickle, and from the blood emerged the three Furies (who pursued Orestes), a race of giants, and the wood nymphs (female nature deities). When Uranos's genitals were thrown into the sea, the goddess Aphrodite was born.

Chronos married his sister Rhea, who gave birth to five more children. But Chronos feared the prophecy that his offspring would one day destroy him, so he swallowed each infant as it was born. When Zeus was born, Rhea hid him in a cave on Crete and replaced him with a large, swaddled stone, which Chronos swallowed instead of the infant. When Zeus became an adult, he forced his father to cough up the other children and joined with his siblings to declare war on their divine ancestors. After ten years of cataclysmic battle, the younger generation of gods (Olympians) defeated their parents (Titans) and took control of the universe.

Hesiod's vivid description of the battle between the Olympians and the Titans is particularly rich in violent imagery. Note the use of repetition for emphasis in "to see with eyes" and "to hear with ears":

> The hot vapour lapped round the earthborn Titans: flame unspeakable rose to the bright upper air: the flashing glare of the thunder-stone and lightning blinded their [the Titans'] eyes for all that they were strong. Astounding heat seized Chaos: and to see with eyes and to hear the sound with ears it seemed even as if Earth and wide Heaven above came together.
>
> (lines 695–704)

The Olympian victory produced a new world order. No longer giants with cannibalistic tendencies, the gods were anthropomorphic (human in form), had human personalities and particular attributes, and socialized with humans (see Box).

Society and Culture

The Greek Gods and the Nine Muses

Zeus king of the gods (thunderbolt)

Hera goddess of marriage, wife and sister of Zeus (peacock)

Poseidon god of the sea (trident, a large three-pronged fork)

Hades god of the underworld (Cerberus, the triple-headed dog who guards Hades)

Demeter goddess of agriculture, sister of Zeus (grain)

Hestia virgin goddess of the hearth, sister of Zeus

Aphrodite goddess of love, beauty, and fertility

Eros god of love, son of Aphrodite (wings, bow and arrows)

Hephaestos blacksmith and crafts god, son of Hera

Athena virgin goddess of war, wisdom, and weaving, daughter of Zeus (armor, owl, gorgoneion)

Ares god of war (armor)

Apollo god of the sun, music, and prophecy (chariot of the sun, lyre)

Artemis virgin goddess of the moon (huntress, bow and arrow)

Hermes messenger (winged sandals, caduceus—a staff with entwined snakes that later became a symbol of medicine)

Dionysos god of wine and theater (grapes)

Hebe goddess of youth and cup-bearer to the gods

Attributes are shown in parentheses

The Nine Muses (daughters of Zeus)

Calliope epic poetry

Clio history

Erato erotic poetry

Euterpe music and lyric poetry

Melpomene tragedy

Polyhymnia sacred hymns

Terpsichore song and dance

Thalia comedy

Urania astronomy

Zeus frequently took mortal lovers (such as Europa in the Minoan origin myth; see Chapter 4), who gave birth to gods and demi-gods (half-gods).

GREEK GODDESSES AND GODS

Although there were six powerful Greek goddesses, all were subordinate to Zeus and reflected aspects of women as viewed by Greek men. Whereas the historical Greeks idealized men, they accorded women few rights and severely restricted their activities.

Athena, Artemis, and Hestia were virgin goddesses. Athena had the gender of a woman but a masculine character; Artemis preferred the company of women and could be deadly to men; Hestia tended the hearth. Aphrodite personified erotic love but without moral responsibility. Hera, the long-suffering and often vengeful wife of an unfaithful husband (Zeus), was a guardian of marriage. Hebe was essentially a servant.

The three major male gods—Zeus, Poseidon, and Hades—were brothers. Between them they divided up the universe: Zeus ruled the sky, Poseidon the sea, and Hades the Underworld. The war god, Ares, was handsome but not very intelligent. Apollo drove the sun across the sky in a horse-drawn chariot and was also a god of music. Dionysos was the god of wine and theater, and rites in his honor were typically orgiastic. Hephaestos, the lame crafts god, was married to Aphrodite, who was beautiful and unfaithful. She betrayed Hephaestos in a celebrated mythical romance with Ares.

PANDORA'S "BOX" AND HESIOD ON WOMEN

By modern standards, the Greeks were **misogynists** (people who dislike and distrust women). Hesiod, in particular, distrusted women and blamed them for causing men to work and suffer. He recounts the Greek myth of the first woman, Pandora, as the source of the world's evils. According to Hesiod, the Titan Prometheus stole fire from the gods and Zeus took revenge by creating Pandora, whose name literally means "all (*pan*) gifts (*dora*)." She disobeyed her creator by opening a jar, which allowed the evils of the world to escape. Hesiod calls her the source of the:

> deadly race and tribe of women who live amongst mortal men to their great trouble, no helpmeets in hateful poverty, but only in wealth. And as in thatched hives bees feed the drones whose nature is to do mischief—by day and throughout the day until the sun goes down the bees are busy and lay the white combs, while the drones stay at home in the covered skeps [farm baskets] and reap the toil of others into their own bellies—even so Zeus who thunders on high made women to be an evil to mortal men, with a nature to do evil.
>
> (*Theogony*, lines 591–600)

To the Greeks, Pandora was destined to disobey the gods but was also responsible for her actions. The fact that the gods created evil, placed it in the container, and tempted Pandora by telling her not to open it, was seen as a test. In failing the test, as the gods knew she would, Pandora came to represent the failings of all women.

THE ORACLE

An important feature of ancient Greek religion was the **oracle**, which refers both to the revelations of a god interpreted by a priest or priestess and to the place where the prophecy is spoken. Oracles were established throughout Greece and its colonies and, like the ideal of the *polis*, reinforced the sense of Greek cultural unity and continuity. The most famous oracle was located at the mainland site of Delphi.

After the Dark Age, the god Apollo was believed to preside over the Delphic oracle and answer questions through a priestess. She sat above a crevice in a rock and breathed gaseous fumes that rose from the opening. The fumes caused hallucinations and sent the priestess into a trance, which impressed visitors and created the illusion that she was divinely inspired. She answered questions in verse, which could be difficult to understand and thus seemed mysterious.

The Greeks called the Delphic oracle the *omphalos* (navel), meaning that it was the center of the world. It was located at Apollo's temple in the **precinct** (sacred area) overlooking a spectacular landscape (figure **5.4**). Foreigners as well as Greeks consulted the oracle on a wide variety of topics, including political decisions, the choice of a wife, future crops, and whether to make a career change or embark on a journey. Inscribed in a stone at the site was the famous phrase "know thyself," which advocated insight and self-knowledge. This saying is another instance of the Greek view that people, like Pandora, are responsible for their own lives even though fate is in the hands of the gods.

THE GEOMETRIC PERIOD: *c.* 1000–700 B.C.

POTTERY, PAINTING, AND SCULPTURE

The Geometric period is named for the geometric style of Greek pottery and sculpture that flourished between 1000 and 700 B.C. Beginning around 1000 B.C., toward the end of the Bronze Age, technological advances appear in Greek pottery, which resulted from an increase in prosperity and trade and an artistic revival. The potter's wheel improved, and pots were decorated with geometric designs. By the eighth century B.C., ceramic artists were painting human figures and narrative scenes on their wares (figure **5.5**).

5.4 Temple of Apollo at Delphi, 4th century B.C.

5.5 Krater from the Dipylon cemetery, *c.* 750 B.C. 4 ft. (1.23 m) high. National Museum, Athens.
This **krater** (a vessel for mixing wine and water) is decorated with a meander pattern just below the lid. The main scene is called a **prothesis** (lying-in-state of the dead) and is flanked by female mourners. The figures are flat, their torsos are triangular, and their legs and heads are in profile view. Below the prothesis a row of chariots seems to float in space. All four legs of each horse are visible, indicating that, as with Egyptian art, the artist represents the figure conceptually rather than naturalistically—that is, four legs are shown because we know that a horse has four legs and not because we would actually see them from this angle. The bodies of the charioteers are covered by shields.

The little horse in figure **5.6** is similar to those painted on the krater in its combination of animated stylization and hint of naturalistic form. The horse's head and torso are thin, cylindrical shapes, but the sturdy flanks convey a sense of organic structure. The shoulder merges smoothly into the broad, flattened neck, which continues into the lively curves at the top of the head. Note that the forelegs seem to face backward, which is not natural but which creates a pleasing symmetry with the back legs.

THE OLYMPIC GAMES

Founded toward the end of the Geometric period, the Olympic Games were first held in 776 B.C. in honor of Zeus at the god's precinct in Olympia, on the west coast of the Peloponnese (see map 5.1, p. 92). Greek-speaking men participated in the Games, and wars on Greek soil were halted so that athletes could travel safely to Olympia. Thus the Games provided the Greeks with another means of achieving a sense of cultural unity. The earliest games were devoted exclusively to the foot race. Later, longer races and other sports were added, including jumping, throwing the discus and javelin, wrestling, boxing, and foot races in armor (figure **5.7**).

The Olympic Games were held every four years; each four-year period was an Olympiad, which was the unit by which the Greeks counted time. In A.D. 394 the Christian Roman emperor Theodosius banned the Olympic Games on the grounds that they were pagan, and they were not reinstated until 1896.

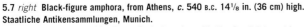

5.6 Geometric horse, *c.* 750 B.C. Bronze, 6¹⁵⁄₁₆ in. (17.6 cm) high. The Metropolitan Museum of Art, New York.

5.7 *right* Black-figure amphora, from Athens, *c.* 540 B.C. 14¹⁄₈ in. (36 cm) high. Staatliche Antikensammlungen, Munich.
Male athletes competed in the nude, in keeping with the Greek interest in the ideal male form. Winners were rewarded with honor, with laurel wreaths, and with statues intended to keep their memory alive. Women did not compete at Olympia.

THE ORIENTALIZING PERIOD: *c. 700–600* B.C.

The term "orientalizing" refers to a style of Greek art influenced by Eastern forms. Orientalizing style resulted from trade with the Near East and Egypt, which increased in the seventh century B.C. after three hundred years of relative isolation during the Dark Age. Greek colonization also encouraged cross-cultural exchange between Greece and the East. The port city of Corinth, north of Mycenae on the mainland, was particularly important in bringing Eastern influence to Greece.

POTTERY AND PAINTING

As in the Geometric period, the best surviving evidence of artistic, technological, and cultural developments in the Orientalizing period is pottery. Corinthian potters and painters absorbed Eastern forms and subjects (figure **5.8**). The animals parading on the beige background of this pitcher are no longer the flat, solid black figures of the Geometric style. The lively stylizations and their patterns are similar to those on the Achaemenid lions of ancient Persia (see Chapter 2).

The frontal eyes and upturned paws showing all five toes indicate that the conceptual imagery characteristic of Near

Eastern, Egyptian, and Greek Geometric style continued into the Orientalizing period. Similarly, fantastic animal combinations and elegant designs came from the East. Partly as a result of these Eastern forms, Greek paintings were animated and more freely drawn than in the Geometric period. Orientalizing vases thus reflect both the expansion of Greece through trade and the stylistic trend toward naturalism.

WAR, MUSIC, AND THE *CHIGI VASE*

During the latter part of the Orientalizing period, the Greek mode of warfare underwent important changes. Because there was continual conflict between the Greek city-states, fighting was a way of life. If we compare the image on the Mycenaean *Warrior Vase* (see thumbnail) with the detail of the *Chigi Vase* of the mid-seventh century B.C. (figure **5.9**), we can see that a new type of military formation has developed. The soldiers

Warrior Vase
see figure 4.17

5.8 *left* **Orientalizing olpe (pitcher), from Corinth, *c.* 600 B.C. Terracotta, 11½ in. (29.2 cm) high. British Museum, London.**

5.9 Detail of the *Chigi Vase*, a late proto-Corinthian oinochoe, *c.* 640 B.C. Vessel 10¼ in. (26 cm) high. Villa Giulia Museum, Rome.
As described in the Homeric epics, the soldiers carry shields and wear greaves (shin guards). The artist creates a sense of movement by repeating the advancing figures. At the same time, motion is arrested by the clashing groups. The figures on the left show the insides of the shields, which were carried on the left arm. The group to the right is distinguished by the shield designs. Prominent frontal eyes and opposing profiles emphasize the gaze of the warriors, which accentuates the intensity of conflict and also engages the gaze of the viewer.

Defining Moment

The Greek Phalanx

With the waning of the Dark Age in ancient Greece, a new type of warfare emerged based on the military formation known as the phalanx. Developed in the Spartan warrior culture, the phalanx was adopted by other city-states, including Athens, and was largely responsible for the Greek defeat of Persia in 479 B.C. (see p. 104).

In contrast to the relative disarray of previous formations, the phalanx was organized to protect the Greek fighters and inflict heavy casualties on the enemy. Phalanxes were made up of citizen-soldiers called hoplites after their large round shields. In addition to these shields, which extended from the shoulder to the knee, hoplites' armor consisted of a metal and leather breastplate, a helmet, and greaves. They were more heavily armed than the Homeric fighters: the two main offensive weapons were a long pike with an iron point at one end and a bronze point on the other, and a short sword with a double blade. The armor was heavy, weighing as much as 100 pounds (45.4 kg), so each soldier had to be in excellent physical condition. They waited until just before battle to put it on. At first, hoplites had to provide their own armor, but later in the fifth century B.C. it was supplied by the city-state. Participation in the hoplite ranks, therefore, required a specified economic status from its peasant soldiers. As foot-soldiers, the hoplites did not have as high a social standing as those who fought on horseback or in chariots.

In battle, the typical phalanx could be anywhere from eight to sixteen rows of hoplites arrayed over a quarter of a mile (400 m) across (figure **5.10**). They comprised a wall of armed men advancing at a brisk pace to the music of the double pipe or flute. They fought the enemy head on, fiercely, quickly, and efficiently. Most battles (although not necessarily wars) were short, allowing the hoplites to return to their civilian lives as soon as possible.

Throughout Greek history the power of the phalanx was legendary. Shields were used for protection, and also to carry the dead—hence the famous quotation from a Spartan mother to her hoplite son to return "with your shield or on it." Several centuries later, the Roman biographer Plutarch described the sight of a phalanx as "terrifying when they marched in step with the rhythm of the flute, without any gap in their line of battle, and with no confusion in their souls, but calmly and cheerfully moving with the strains of their hymn to their deadly fight" (*Lycurgus*, 22:2–3).

The hoplites were an integral part of the structure of the *polis* and they fought for the good of the *polis*, rather than for personal glory. According to some scholars, the unity of the phalanx, the sense of mutual cohesion and protection, as well as the effectiveness of the formation, influenced the idea that ordinary peasants, not just an aristocratic elite, could also work together in ruling the *polis*. The phalanx remained the military formation of choice until the rise of Rome and the development of the more flexible Roman legions.

Critical Question Is discipline (as used, for example, for troops) compatible with freedoms necessary for democracies?

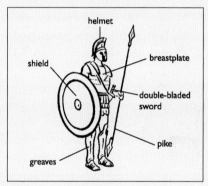

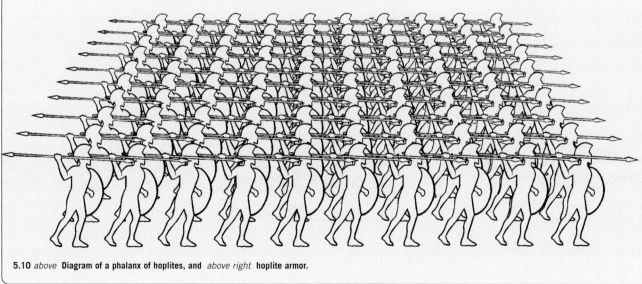

5.10 *above* **Diagram of a phalanx of hoplites, and** *above right* **hoplite armor.**

shown are **hoplites**, named for the *hoplon* (plural, *hopla*), a large wooden shield covered with a protective layer of bronze. Hoplites were foot-soldiers who fought next to each other and one behind the other, creating a **phalanx.** This was a formidable, densely packed military formation, with each soldier trained to step in and take the place of a fallen comrade. The image on the *Chigi Vase* is the earliest surviving representation of a hoplite phalanx, and it illustrates the way in which the *hoplon* shielded both its owner and the soldier next to him. The overlapping of the hoplites emphasizes the solidity of the phalanx and also reflects the painter's interest in the naturalism of three-dimensional space.

Notice that an unarmed boy between two phalanxes plays a double pipe (*aulos*) to signal the charge. This indicates that the hoplite army, like modern troops, marched in time. Music in ancient Greece was used not only in religious ritual and the recitation of epic poetry—it also inspired soldiers. Harmonious music was related to the harmony of the phalanx. In the *Theogony*, Hesiod says that Harmonia is the daughter of Aphrodite and Ares, thus embodying the ideal balance between love and war. She maintains the "harmony" of the phalanx, whereas her sisters, Panic and Fear, create disorder and disharmony, which lead to defeat.

THE ARCHAIC PERIOD: *c.* 600–490 B.C.

During the Archaic period, the Greeks continued a brisk trade with foreign cultures as well as expansion through colonization (map **5.1**). From early in the seventh century B.C., social unrest from a number of quarters began to disrupt the *polis*. Disputes over land, economic disparities, rural groups competing for power, and expanding trade were all factors. The unrest was often quelled by the emergence of a tyrant, a single ruler who seized power without the legal authority to do so. Some tyrants were relatively benevolent, but others were harsh and oppressive. By the end of the sixth century B.C., after a period of rule by tyrants, Athens abolished tyranny.

ATHENS AND SPARTA

Athens and Sparta were two city-states in ancient Greece that embodied extremes of the political spectrum during the Archaic period and would continue to do so. Their principal differences lay in the nature of their government structures and institutions as well as in their views of society and war. They also differed in their attitudes toward women.

ATHENIAN LAWGIVERS: DRACO AND SOLON   Athens's first lawgiver by tradition was Draco, who in the seventh century B.C. inscribed a set of laws in stone and made them available to the general population. Few of Draco's laws survive, but they are known for harsh penalties, such as death for trivial theft. Today we speak of a "Draconian" measure to convey unreasonable severity.

The next major lawgiver after Draco was Solon (*c.* 640–558 B.C.), an aristocrat who revised the constitution of the *polis* and laid the foundations of Athenian law for the remainder of its history. His laws were crucial to the Athenian concept of citizenship, and, in contrast to Draco, Solon has gone down in history as an exemplar of wisdom.

In order to avoid the social unrest that had led to tyranny in some *poleis*, Solon established a council of four hundred male citizens from a broad social spectrum and a court of appeals to ensure social justice for all citizens. He wanted to

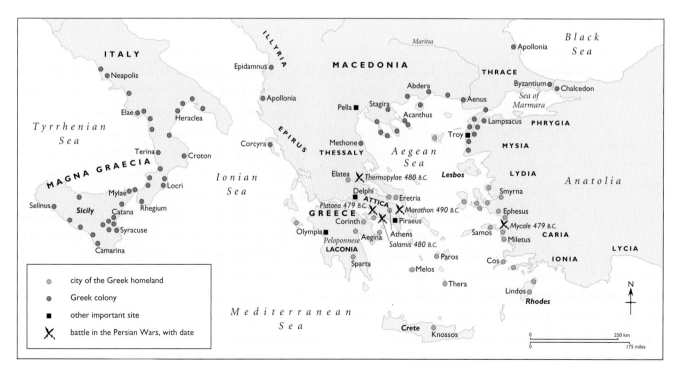

Map 5.1 Ancient Greece, *c.* **1000–490** B.C.

increase their participation in government, but had in mind only the citizens of Athens. Solon also effected the return of former citizens who had been sold into slavery to pay debts and he financed buying back their freedom.

To restart the economy, Solon abolished outstanding debts and revived industry and trade. He encouraged potters and other skilled workers to move to Athens, and he recommended exporting surplus goods, such as oil and wine, while retaining wheat to insure against famine. In addition, he altered the structure of social status in the *polis*, basing it on wealth rather than on inherited rank. So that his programs would continue beyond the present generation, Solon required fathers to educate their sons in a craft or trade. Once his reforms were in place, Solon retired from politics so that he would not be tempted to become a tyrant.

In the course of the next two centuries, coinage and currency reform calculated to favor Athenian trade and commerce were instituted. Laws against public displays of wealth (called sumptuary laws) were instituted. These were designed to reduce further the visibility and influence of the aristocracy.

WOMEN IN ATHENS Athenian men preferred that women be neither seen nor heard. The laws of Athens restricted women to the house, sharply limited their activity, and treated them intellectually and emotionally as children. The woman's primary function was to produce sons who would become Athenian citizens—hence the custom of a bride eating fruit with many seeds. If a family had no sons, the woman inherited the family property and became an attractive marriage prospect. Although all women entered into marriage with a dowry, which remained theirs for life, they were always under the control of a father, uncle, brother, or some other male family member.

The ideal marriage age for an Athenian female was considered to be fourteen, but for a man it was thirty. Both husbands and wives could sue for divorce, although the procedure was easier for the man: he had only to remove his wife from his household, whereas she needed a male relative to bring the issue to court.

SPARTA Sparta, like Athens, had an agrarian economy. But, unlike Athens, Sparta continued to rely exclusively on farming and its powerful hoplite army. It did not produce much literature or encourage the arts in the late Archaic period (although it had done so earlier). Sparta's laws are attributed to Lycurgus, who supposedly lived in the seventh century B.C. According to tradition, he advocated a strict oligarchy, in which a few citizens elected a council of five elders. These maintained tight control over the most intimate details of a person's life, including dress and grooming, diet, and decisions about marriage and childbirth. The term "spartan," referring to an austere way of life, comes from the social organization of Sparta in the late sixth century B.C.

The Spartan system was designed to provide the basics for its citizens, freeing them to concentrate on the welfare of the state. The socio-economic foundation that made this possible was the institution of the **helot**, a member of the native population enslaved by the Spartans. Helots worked the land and had no rights. Because they were engaged in a constant struggle for their freedom, their conquerors exercised rigid control over them. Helots were beaten every year as a sign of their subservience, and were forced to dress in animal skins to acknowledge their sub-human status.

From birth, Spartan boys trained to become warriors and remained such to the age of sixty. Boys left home at seven, and male infants considered unsuitable for war were left to die outside the city. Education was controlled by the state. The curriculum did not include reading, writing, or the arts (except for martial music), focusing instead almost entirely on physical survival skills. Those who failed to live up to the established standards of bravery were ridiculed, humiliated, and considered unmarriageable.

Spartan women also exercised regularly. They were not confined to household activities, as Athenian women were. The ideal marriage age for both men and women was considered to be eighteen, but up to the age of thirty, men lived in army quarters, visiting their wives secretly for purposes of procreation. Monogamy in Sparta was not as strictly enforced as in Athens, in part so that women could produce future Spartan citizens while their husbands were away at war.

ART AND ARCHITECTURE IN THE ARCHAIC PERIOD

While the Spartans were busy producing an ideal warrior state during the Archaic period, Athens and other cities created some of the most impressive works of art, poetry, and philosophy in Western history. The vigorous pottery industry in Corinth spread to Athens in this period. Corinth had invented the black-figure technique of vase decoration, in which artists painted black figures on a red clay background and incised details with a **burin** (a sharp instrument). Large-scale paintings most often depicted mythological and Homeric scenes, but none has survived.

VASE PAINTING One of the most impressive Athenian black-figure paintings shows the Homeric warrior Ajax preparing to commit suicide (figure **5.11**). The artist, Exekias, was the leading Athenian black-figure painter, known for insightful dramatic scenes conveying the psychology of his figures. In figure 5.11 Exekias depicts a well-known event from the end of the Trojan War. Ajax was a brave Greek chieftain who competed with Odysseus for the armor of the slain Achilles. Odysseus won the prize, and Ajax was driven temporarily mad by Athena, the Greek goddess of war, wisdom, and weaving. In his madness, he killed a herd of sheep and cattle, believing them to be men. When Ajax regained his sanity, he was ashamed before his family and friends and committed suicide.

5.11 Exekias, *Suicide of Ajax*, black-figure amphora, *c.* 540 B.C. Painted scene 9½ in. (24 cm) high. Musée des Beaux Arts, Boulogne, France.

Society and Culture

The Gorgon

In Greek myth, *the* Gorgon refers to Medusa, the only mortal of three monstrous Gorgon sisters, all with snakey hair, fangs, and bulging eyes. Medusa, who was originally beautiful, offended Athena, who made her ugly by turning her hair into snakes. The sight of Medusa was so terrifying that any man who looked at her turned to stone. Only by watching her indirectly in the reflection on his shield could the Greek hero Perseus overcome this obstacle and kill her. When he beheaded her, two sons were born from her blood—Chrysaor, the boy with the golden sword, and Pegasus, the winged horse.

The scene on the vase in figure **5.12** shows Perseus killing Medusa. She is in the bent-knee pose, which in Archaic art means that she is trying to run away. From the torso up Medusa is frontal, assertively displaying her monstrous attributes to the viewer. She wears a snakey tunic, snakes emanate from her head, and she glares fiercely at Perseus.

Perseus aims his sword directly at Medusa's neck but turns to avoid looking at her. After Medusa's death, Perseus gives her head, the **gorgoneion**, to Athena, who places it on her armor to terrify her enemies.

5.12 Amasis painter, *Perseus Decapitates Medusa*, black-figure olpe from Vulci. 10¼ in. (26 cm) high. British Museum, London.

Exekias's picture shows a solitary Ajax fixing his sword in the ground. Apart from the lone palm tree suggesting Athena's presence (in temples, her statues were erected near palm trees), Ajax is surrounded by empty space, which symbolizes his feeling of emotional emptiness and social isolation. Ironically, reinforcing our gaze as viewers are the frontal Gorgon head on the shield and the blank stare of the sightless helmet (see Box).

Some time around 530 B.C. the red-figure vase painting technique developed in Athens. This reversed the black-figure technique by outlining the figures, leaving them the red color of the vase, and painting the background black. Details were added in black with a brush, rather than being incised with a burin. As a result, red-figure artists painted more freely, and their paintings have greater depth than black-figure ones. Some vases, known as "bilingual," show a red-figure painting on one side and a black-figure painting on the other (figure **5.13**).

SCULPTURE Beginning in the late seventh century B.C., two main types of marble sculpture—the standing male youth (*kouros*) and the standing young female (*kore*)—were produced on mainland Greece and its eastern islands. At first, Greek artists traveled to Egypt to learn monumental stone carving, and their work shows Egyptian influence. But as with vase painting, Archaic sculpture soon developed in the direction of greater naturalism as a way of emphasizing lifelike qualities.

The Archaic *kouros* (Greek for "boy") represented an aristocratic youth of special achievement and was usually lifesize or larger and carved from a marble block. In the *Sounion Kouros* (figure **5.14**), the influence of Egyptian sculpture is evident in the tense, frontal pose and extended left leg (see thumbnail of the *Menkaure Triad*). Both statues retain the overall shape of the rectangular block of stone from which the artist carved the figures. But the *kouros* is nude and reveals more interest in anatomy. It is distinctively Greek, having scroll-shaped ears, bulging eyes, and hair

Triad of Menkaure
see figure 3.15

5.13 *above* **Two sides of a vase showing Heracles driving a bull,** *c.* **520** B.C. **21 in. (53 cm) high. Museum of Fine Arts, Boston.**
Heracles wears a lion skin—a symbol of strength. In Greek myth, Heracles was the son of Zeus and a hero of great intelligence. He was the only mortal admitted to Mount Olympus after his death.

5.14 *left* ***Sounion Kouros*, from the sanctuary of Poseidon, Sounion,** *c.* **580** B.C. **Marble, 9 ft. 10 in. (3 m) high. National Museum, Athens.**
This figure is named for its discovery in Poseidon's sanctuary at Sounion, a site near Athens.

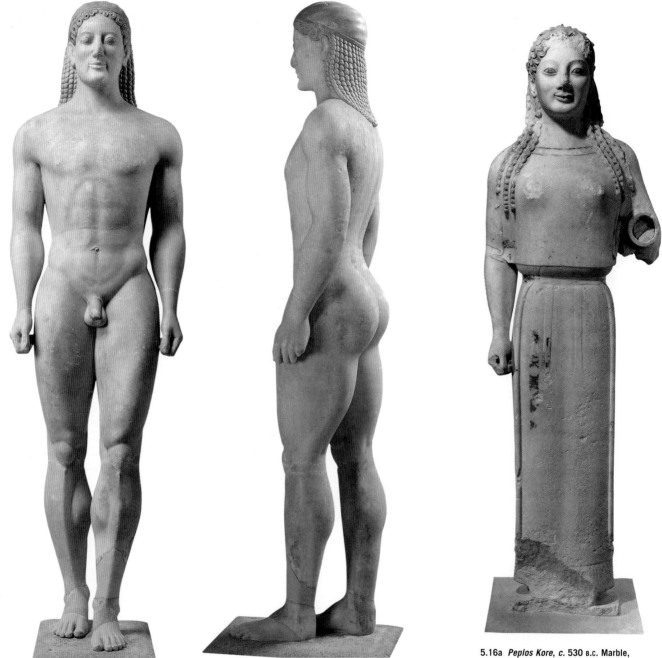

5.15 *Anavysos Kouros* (front and side), from Anavysos, Attica, *c.* 530 B.C. Marble, 6 ft. 4¹/₂ in. (1.94 m) high. National Museum, Athens.

This figure represents Kroisos, described in the inscription quoted at the beginning of the chapter. He embodies the ideal of the heroic, aristocratic youth who dies in battle. The artist urges viewers to pause and mourn the dead youth, whose image is preserved in marble.

5.16a *Peplos Kore, c.* 530 B.C. Marble, 4 ft. (1.21 m) high. Acropolis Museum, Athens.

composed of curls in the front and beads at the back. Horizontal lines define the rib cage as if it is on the surface of the torso, but the kneecaps and sternum emphasize the interior structure of the body. In contrast to the Egyptian figure of the pharaoh in the *Menkaure Triad*, the *Sounion Kouros* has open space between the arms and the body, and between the legs. This reduces the impression of immobility and eternity idealized in Egyptian royal sculpture.

The *Anavysos Kouros* (figure **5.15**) was carved about fifty years after the *Sounion Kouros* and shows the increase in naturalism over that time. It is more rounded than the *Sounion Kouros*, and the muscles and bone structure appear to be beneath the flesh rather than on its surface. The ears are no longer scroll-shaped, but resemble human ears. But both *kouroi* are tense and stand at attention. Both convey the impression of an inherent energy, as if they are ready to spring forth and take command of the three-dimensional space around them.

The *Anavysos Kouros* has a significant new feature that appears in Archaic sculpture—the Archaic smile (in the *Sounion Kouros*, the mouth is broken). As the lips curve

5.16b Painted reconstruction of a cast of the *Peplos Kore*. Museum of Classical Archaeology, Cambridge, U.K.

upward, the cheekbones push upward, indicating that Greek artists wanted their sculptures to represent living, breathing people. The smile also shows that naturalism was increasingly the standard guiding artists in their representation of the human figure.

Archaic sculptures of girls (*korai*, singular *kore*) were also depicted with a smile. But *korai* are not nude, and their poses are somewhat less assertive than those of *kouroi*. The *Peplos Kore* (figure **5.16a**), named after the smooth *peplos* (her outer garment; see Box), bends one arm in a gesture of offering. Traces of paint on the lips, eyes, and *peplos* are reminders that the ancient Greeks painted their statues to make them appear lifelike (figure **5.16b**).

Society and Culture

Archaic Greek Dress

The Doric *peplos* was a plain, sleeveless, rectangular wool garment (figure **5.17**). It was pinned at the shoulders and folded at the top. Another type of garment, the linen *chiton*, originated in Ionia and, paralleling the Ionic Order, was elegant and graceful. Like the *peplos*, the *chiton* was rectangular, but it did not fold over across the upper torso. At the shoulders, it was pinned or sewn, and buttoned at the top, leaving openings for the head and arms. Both the *chiton* and the *peplos* were belted when worn by adults, but not for small children.

The *peplos* could be worn over the *chiton*, as in the *Peplos Kore* (see figure 5.16a); it was open on the right side to free the right hand. Spartan women preferred the *peplos* because it was the more traditional, simpler garment, in line with the austerity of the culture. A *himaton* (mantle) was worn over the *chiton* and fell in an array of folds. Because the *chiton* was the least revealing Greek garment, it was generally worn in public.

Light skin was the ideal for Greek women (see the poem by Anacreon, pp. 102–103), because it showed that they were wealthy enough not to have to go outdoors. To enhance the lightness of their skin, many women used powder. Men wore shorter clothing than women, and prostitutes sported translucent materials. The most typical Greek shoe was the sandal, but Greeks who wanted to appear taller wore elevated shoes.

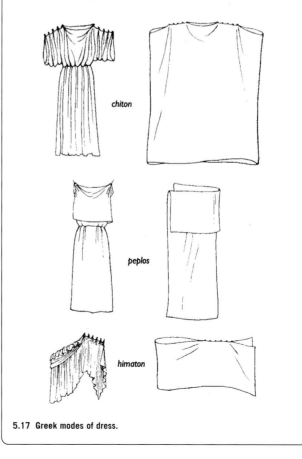

5.17 Greek modes of dress.

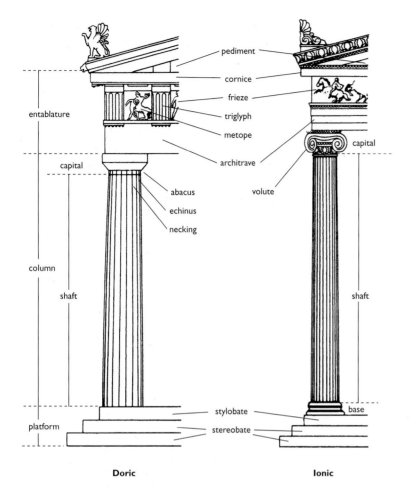

Doric   **Ionic**

5.18 The Doric and Ionic Orders.

ARCHITECTURE In the Archaic period, the Greeks built monumental stone architecture. To house statues of gods, they constructed temples which were of two main types, called Orders: the Doric Order originated on the mainland, and the Ionic Order originated in eastern Greece. The term "Order" refers to a system in which the parts of a structure are arranged in a particular sequence from the bottom to the top. These Greek Orders are diagrammed in figure **5.18**.

In the Doric Order, the columns rise directly from the top step (the **stylobate**), and their shafts bulge slightly (**entasis**) to give an impression of organic stretching. The Doric capital (consisting of the **necking**, the ovoid **echinus**, and the square **abacus**) was conceived of as the head (*caput* in Latin) of the column, and it provides a visual transition from the vertical shaft to the horizontal sections of the Order. The **entablature**, like the capital, is divided into three parts. A long horizontal **architrave** (meaning "high beam") supports the **frieze**, whose vertical **triglyphs** alternate with square **metopes**, which often contain relief sculptures. The thin **cornice** that completes the Order projects slightly to drain rainwater from the roof.

5.19 The basic elements of a Greek Doric temple façade.

Note that the Doric forms are heavier and plainer than their Ionic counterparts. Ionic columns are proportionally taller and slimmer; they have a round base and are decorated with elegant surface patterns.

In keeping with their focus on humanity, the Greeks conceived of the Orders in human terms. They associated the Doric Order with sturdy, masculine qualities, and the more graceful Ionic Order with feminine qualities. Unlike Egyptian columns, which were based on plant forms, the Greek Orders are geometric. Each part is designed to create a harmonious, unified relationship with every other part and to ensure smooth transitions between parts.

Greek temples, conceived on a more human scale than Egyptian ones, were rectangular in shape, with one or two interior rooms, a solid inner wall, and an outer wall of free-standing columns (the **peristyle**). They owed their gleaming white exteriors to the abundance of marble quarries in Greece and the precision of their carving to the well-trained artisans, sculptors, engineers, and architects who built them. Temples

were located in precincts sacred to a god, whose statue was placed in the main room (*naos*). Parts of the buildings were decorated with freestanding and relief sculptures, which were painted.

Figure **5.19** shows the basic elements of a Doric temple façade, which was designed to appear orderly, regular, and symmetrical. At the short sides of the Greek temple, a triangular **pediment** contained freestanding sculptures-in-the-round, which, like the metope reliefs, were usually painted. The imposing, sturdy appearance of the façade is characteristic of the Doric Order. Its columns have been compared to the military formation and orderly force of the hoplite phalanx.

THE TEMPLE OF APHAIA AT AEGINA The Doric temple on the island of Aegina in the Saronic Gulf (see map 5.1, p. 92) is a good example of late Archaic architecture (figure **5.20**). Figure **5.21** shows the plan of the temple, which has three steps supporting four outer walls of columns. There is a porch at either end and a long *naos*, the main room that housed the cult statue of Artemis, goddess of the moon.

5.20 The Temple of Aphaia, Aegina, *c.* 500 B.C. Marble.
The temple is dedicated to the mythic nymph Aphaia, who was loved by King Minos of Knossos. She eluded his advances by diving off a cliff into the sea. The moon goddess, Artemis, rescued Aphaia and brought her to Aegina. Artemis then became the island's patron goddess.

Few of the exterior sculptures have survived, but it appears that the pediment figures depicted a war scene, most likely from the Trojan War (figure **5.22**). As with all Greek pediments, the Aphaia artist had to accommodate the sloping sides of a triangular space. The central figure from the west pediment represents Athena in her aspect as the goddess of war. She is frontal, armed, and stands upright, filling the space under the top angle of the triangle (figure **5.23**). Her large size, frontality, and detached air convey her status; she is, literally, "above the fray" of battle.

5.23 *Athena*, from the Temple of Aphaia, Aegina, *c.* 500 B.C. Marble, 5 ft. 6 in. (1.68 m) high. Staatliche Antikensammlungen, Munich.

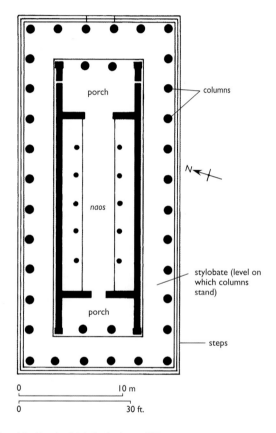

5.21 **Plan of the Temple of Aphaia, Aegina,** *c.* **500 B.C.**

5.22 *below* **Reconstruction diagram of the pediments from the Temple of Aphaia, Aegina.**

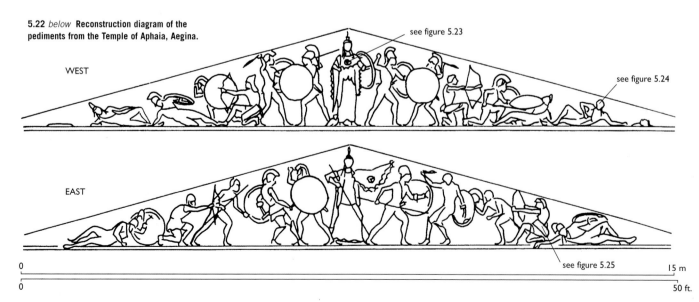

5.24 *above* **Dying Warrior**, from the west pediment of the Temple of Aphaia, Aegina, *c.* 500 B.C. Marble, 5 ft. 2¾ in. (1.59 m) long. Staatliche Antikensammlungen, Munich.

5.25 *Heracles*, from the east pediment of the Temple of Aphaia, Aegina, *c.* 490 B.C. Marble, 31 in. (79 cm) high. Staatliche Antikensammlungen, Munich.

The corners of the pediment are filled with dying warriors: The soldier in figure **5.24** is trying to extract an arrow from his chest. The sculptor has retained the Archaic smile to show that he is alive, rather than portraying him in pain. His stylized hair is also typical of late Archaic sculpture.

The kneeling figure of Heracles (figure **5.25**) from the east pediment would have fit into a space nearer the center than the *Dying Warrior*. Heracles is shown as an archer, tensely aiming his bow and arrow at an enemy. He wears short armor and a lion helmet, denoting his strength. As with the *Dying Warrior*, the *Heracles* has an Archaic smile, but here the muscles and the taut veins in his hands are visible beneath the flesh. Both sculptures thus reflect the transition from the rigid poses and surface patterns of the Archaic period toward naturalism.

PHILOSOPHY: PRE-SOCRATICS OF THE ARCHAIC PERIOD

In the sixth century B.C., different schools of Greek philosophy ("love of wisdom") began to emerge. Greek philosophy was the first in the Mediterranean world to diverge from religious thinking, seeking to explain the world empirically, that is, according to observation and reason, rather than according to a belief system, faith, or emotion. In so doing, Greek philosophers saw man as a rational being, capable of understanding himself in relation to the world. Greek philosophy thus shares with Greek art a kind of idealized naturalism.

The Archaic philosophers are known as pre-Socratic, because they pre-dated Socrates (469–399 B.C.), the great philosopher of fifth-century-B.C. Athens. Pre-Socratics are sometimes called Naturalist philosophers because they sought truth by observing nature, which was consistent with the sixth-century-B.C. artistic trend toward lifelike naturalism. Greek philosophers, like Greek artists, studied nature and tried to define it—the former in words and the latter in images.

Thales of Miletus (*c.* 625–*c.* 547 B.C.), who came from Anatolia, is considered to have been the first philosopher, although none of his writings survives. He founded the Ionian school of philosophy, which drew conclusions based on empirical observations. To this end, Thales studied astronomy and learned to predict eclipses of the sun and determine when the summer and winter solstices (the longest and shortest days of the year) would occur. He thus demonstrated that a rational logic is inherent in nature.

In his effort to reduce the origins of the universe to a single element, Thales concluded that all matter begins with water, which can be transformed into gas and ice. In other words, the three states of water—liquid, gas, and solid—encompass all the conditions of nature and therefore must comprise nature's basic unit of matter. Thales also believed that the earth was flat and that it floated on water.

Two other Naturalist philosophers at Miletus were Anaximander (610–*c.* 547 B.C.) and Anaximenes (active *c.* 545 B.C.), who both based their views of the cosmos on natural phenomena. Anaximander believed in the existence of a single intelligent force behind the universe and argued that the earth stands still because of its symmetrical location in the cosmos. Anaximenes reduced the cosmos to air in varying degrees of density. He used empirical experience to support his theories, whereas Anaximander preferred biological and legal models.

One of the most complex and obscure of the pre-Socratics was Heraclitus (*c.* 540–*c.* 480 B.C.), who lived in Ephesus, a Greek colony in western Anatolia. Because he believed that reality was in constant motion and that growth and unity are achieved from tension between opposites, Heraclitus is considered a Dualist. Some of his best known examples of dualism are: (1) seawater is both pure and polluted—it gives life to fish and is poisonous to humans, (2) a man cannot step in the same stream twice, and (3) the same road goes uphill and downhill.

PYTHAGORAS Pythagoras (*c.* 550–*c.* 500 B.C.), from the Ionian island of Samos, was the most influential pre-Socratic philosopher. His views impressed Plato, the great philosopher taught by Socrates (see Chapter 6), and infiltrated much of later Western philosophy. But Pythagoras is best known to students today as the author of the **Pythagorean theorem**: the square of the hypotenuse of a right-angled triangle equals the sum of the squares of the other two sides.

Pythagoras saw the universe in a more mystical way than the empiricists. He believed that people and animals are reborn after death and that their souls move into a new body where they have a new life (transmigration of souls). As a result he advocated vegetarianism to avoid eating a potential body that might otherwise be available to house a new soul. He established a communal school of philosophy in Crotona, in southern Italy. This and other philosophical, "Pythagorean" communities included women as well as men and were run by strict routines.

Pythagoras was a student of geometry and mathematics, who believed that numbers rather than elements defined the structure of the universe. He also thought that numbers formed the basis of musical harmony. From this he concluded that the earth was a sphere surrounded by stars and planets, which were attached to more distant spheres. The sphere containing the stars turned from east to west, whereas the sphere with the planets turned in the opposite direction. This movement of the spheres, in Pythagoras's view, created inaudible sounds, which formed a musical harmony in the universe.

LYRIC POETRY

Lyric poetry is named for the lyre, a stringed instrument resembling a small harp. One of the great achievements of ancient Greece, lyric poetry was an ancient poetic form originally sung to the music of the lyre (or the flute). But neither the texts nor the music were written down before the eighth century B.C. Lyric poems differ from the Homeric epics in being shorter and more intimate, and in dealing primarily with individual emotions. The modern term "lyrical" connotes the light, lilting pace of lyric poetry. The two most famous lyric poets of the Archaic period are Anacreon and Sappho.

ANACREON Anacreon (*c.* 582–*c.* 485 B.C.) was born in Ionia. His poems, which survive mainly in fragments, celebrate courtly subjects such as love, wine, and banqueting. But he could plumb the depths of emotion as well as be witty and to the point. On the inevitability of death, he writes:

> My temples are already gray and my head is white; graceful youth is no more with me, my teeth are old, and no long span of sweet life remains now. And so I often weep in fear of Tartarus [the Underworld]: for the recess of Hades is grim, and the road down to it is grievous; and it is certain that he who goes down does not come up again.

In another poem, Anacreon's speaker asks a painter to depict his absent mistress. He tells the artist to use **encaustic**, a type of paint in which beeswax is mixed with pigment. Its waxy texture and rich colors produce a lifelike effect, just as Archaic artists strove to make their sculptures seem alive. By the end of the poet's description, we should be able to visualize the image, and the painting ["the wax"] should be so true to life that it would talk:

> Come, best of painters! Paint, best of painters, master of the Rhodian art [painting]! Paint my absent girl according to my

instructions. First paint her soft black hair; and if the wax is able, make it smell of perfume. Paint her whole cheek and then her ivory brow beneath her dark hair. Do not part her eyebrows nor run them together, but let her keep, as in real life, the black rims of her eyes meeting imperceptibly. Now make her eyes as they are, from fire, both flashing like Athena's, and moist, like Cythere's [Aphrodite]. Paint her nose and her cheeks, mingling roses and cream. Paint her lips like Persuasion's, provoking kisses. Under her soft chin let all the Graces fly around her marble-white neck. Dress the rest of her in robes of light purple, but let her skin show through a little to prove the quality of her body. Enough—I can see her! Soon, wax, you will be talking too.

(Anacreonta 16)

And in a short, humorous poem, punctuated with sharp imagery, which matches the subject matter, Anacreon portrays an exchange between Eros and his mother Aphrodite:

Love [Eros] once failed to notice a bee that was sleeping among the roses, and he was wounded: he was struck in the finger, and he howled. He ran and flew to beautiful Cythere [Aphrodite] and said, "I have been killed, mother, killed. I am dying. I was struck by the small winged snake that farmers call 'the bee.'" She replied, "If the bee-sting is painful, what pain, Love, do you suppose all your victims suffer?"

(Anacreonta 35)

A lover of wine, song, and the Greek banquet known as the **symposium** (see Box), Anacreon wrote the following:

When Bacchus [the wine god Dionysos] comes, my worries go to sleep, and I imagine that I have the wealth of Croesus; I want to sing beautifully; I lie garlanded with ivy [an attribute of the wine god] and in my heart I disdain the world. Prepare the wine and let me drink it. Bring me a cup, boy, for it is far better that I should lie drunk than lie dead.

(Anacreonta 48)

Society and Culture

The Greek Symposium

In the Homeric age, Greek warriors feasted to songs and poems of battle. Under the influence of the Near East, these feasts became more elaborate and pleasure-oriented (as described by Anacreon). Libations and prayers were offered to the gods at the opening and closing of each gathering. In the Archaic period, the *symposion* (literally, a "drinking together" reserved for aristocratic men) preceded the feast. Figure **5.26** illustrates a wine cup of the type used at a symposium.

As in the image on the outside of the cup, Greeks drank (and dined) while reclining on a couch and leaning on the left elbow, a practice taken up later by the Romans (see Chapter 7). Women did not participate in the symposium, but female slaves, or *hetairai* (courtesans), might be hired to entertain. In the vase painting, we can see one woman offering a cup and two female musicians—one with a lyre and one with a double flute. The music accompanied lyric poetry.

The Greeks diluted their wine with water to achieve the alcohol content of today's beer, which meant they could drink for a long time. Because there was no plumbing, chamber pots were a standard feature of the symposium, and waste was thrown into the street.

5.26 Brygos painter, red-figure drinking cup, *c.* 500 B.C. 12½ in. (32 cm) diameter. British Museum, London.

SAPPHO   Sappho (*c.* 640–580 B.C.) is the only woman known to have achieved literary fame in the Archaic period. Unfortunately, only one of her poems has survived intact; the rest are fragmentary. Sappho was born on the island of Lesbos, from which comes the term "lesbian," after Sappho's reputed love for young girls. Whether or not this is accurate is much debated; she was probably married, and a few poems refer to her daughter Cleis: "I have a beautiful child who looks like golden flowers, my darling Cleis, for whom I would not (take) all Lydia or lovely . . . [missing text]" (Sappho 132).

Sappho's poems, like those of Anacreon, deal with subjective feelings, usually her own. In that way they are both personal and universal in their themes, the most consistent theme being love. Most of Sappho's poems were solos sung to the lyre, but some were written for female choral groups. Little is known of Sappho's life. She had a reputation for being quite ugly, which may have inspired her appreciation of beautiful girls. Her conviction that women should be educated suggests that she came from an aristocratic family and was herself well educated. In the following fragment, Sappho addresses a woman who lacked education:

> But when you die you will lie there, and afterwards there will never be any recollection of you or any longing for you since you have no share in the roses of Pieria [the nine Muses]; unseen in the House of Hades also, flown from our midst, you will go to and fro among the shadowy corpses.
>
> (Sappho 55)

In at least one fragment, the speaker declares her love for a boy: "Truly, sweet mother, I cannot weave my web, for I am overcome with desire for a boy because of slender Aphrodite" (Sappho 102).

In most of her poems, however, Sappho declares her erotic feelings for her female students. It is possible that they lived together only temporarily before marriage and that the homosexual aspects of this arrangement were conventional—as was the case generally with homosexual activity in ancient Greece (see Box). In the following relatively long fragment, Sappho's speaker compares her love for a young woman to Helen's passion for Paris:

> Some say a host of cavalry, others of infantry, and others of ships, is the most beautiful thing on the black earth, but I say it is whatsoever a person loves. It is perfectly easy to make this understood by everyone: for she who far surpassed mankind in beauty, Helen, left her most noble husband and went sailing off to Troy with no thought at all for her child or dear parents, but (love) led her astray . . . lightly . . . (and she?) has reminded me now of Anactoria who is not here; I would rather see her lovely walk and the bright sparkle of her face than the Lydians' chariots and armed infantry.
>
> (Sappho 16)

Society and Culture

Homosexuality in Ancient Greece

Homosexuality in ancient Greece was not thought of as a clear-cut category either socially or psychologically, as it is today. Indeed, the term itself did not exist. The Greeks followed certain conventions about who should be the active partner and who should be the passive partner in sexual relationships. Women, boys, slaves, and foreigners were supposed to be passive toward adult Greek men. The ideal homosexual relationship in Greece was between a man and an adolescent, both from good families, with no implication of financial gain or political favor. Such relationships existed simultaneously with heterosexual marriages, so that an older married man might become involved with a young man without incurring disapproval.

Less is known about female homosexuality in ancient Greece, although it is mentioned in the poems of Sappho and in fragments by other lyric poets of the Archaic period.

Sappho's emphasis on emotion, like Anacreon's attention to non-heroic experience, reflects the increasing focus of Greek culture on humanity. Similarly, the philosophical search for empirical evidence and the trend toward naturalism in painting and sculpture express the Greek interest in explaining the world scientifically and portraying natural form, especially that of idealized male youth. The small scale of Greek temples compared with those of Egypt mirrors the interest in human scale and proportion. In the development of the *polis*, Greeks emphasized individual rights and the role of citizens in self-governance. Even the Olympian gods are human in form and character.

At the end of the Archaic period, Greece was beset by invasions from Persia (modern Iran). The Greeks viewed the Persians as decadent foreigners ruled by tyrants, and Greece valiantly resisted being absorbed into the Persian Empire (see map 5.1, p. 92). In 499 B.C., with the support of Athens, eastern Ionian Greeks rebelled against Persian efforts to impose taxes on them.

Nine years later, the armies of the Persian king Darius I (ruled 522–486 B.C.) invaded the Greek mainland. But the Greek phalanxes used superior military strategy and defeated Darius in 490 B.C. at the Battle of Marathon. Led by the general Miltiades (c. 554–c. 489 B.C.), who joined the Ionian rebellion against Persia, 10,000 Athenians and 1000 allies defeated 25,000 Persians. Miltiades encouraged the Persians to attack the center of the Greek ranks and then ordered the Greek warriors to surround the Persians from either side and destroy them.

Ten years later, in 480 B.C., Darius's son Xerxes I (ruled 486–465 B.C.) mounted another attack on Greece. He overran Athens and defeated a small band of three hundred Spartans

Thematic Parallels

Sun Tzu and *The Art of War*

The art of war, as we have seen, was an important part of ancient Greek culture. In China, sometime around 500 B.C., the great general Sun Tzu wrote thirteen chapters, entitled *The Art of War*, which have been widely praised as a work of military genius and a guide to victory on the battlefield. The book has also been recommended as a roadmap to success in finance and in the art of love.

According to a second-century-B.C. Chinese chronicler, Sun Tzu demonstrated the effectiveness of his theories by training a group of ladies from the royal court of the King of Wu. At first, the ladies giggled instead of obeying orders, and Sun Tzu blamed himself for their inattention. But when they giggled a second time, he blamed the officers (the two leading ladies, who were the king's favorite concubines). Sun Tzu ordered the women to be executed. At this, the king protested, but Sun Tzu replied that a good general takes precedence over a king in military matters.

The two concubines were beheaded, and Sun Tzu appointed new leaders. The ladies stopped giggling and followed the commands of their officers. Sun Tzu then informed the King of Wu that his troops were properly trained and ready to be inspected. But the king declined to inspect the new battalion of well-trained ladies. When Sun Tzu accused him of being a man of words but not of action, the King of Wu recognized the general's genius and appointed him commander of his entire army.

Sun Tzu believed that the art of war is crucial to the safety of the state and that the real aim of war is peace. The calculations of the general, he said, determine the outcome of any conflict. Among Sun Tzu's strategic precepts, the following stand out: speed is essential, because weapons and morale grow dull with time; when an enemy is captured, he should be well treated; it is better to win without fighting and to seize the enemy's territory without destroying it; battles are won by avoiding mistakes and by creating tactical advantage.

In addition, there are only two kinds of attack in Sun Tzu's view: direct and indirect. Yet their combinations are infinite, and the element of surprise is important whatever the situation. Sun Tzu discussed the effect of terrain and weather on tactics, the crucial role of spies and intelligence, the use of fire, and the weak and strong characteristics of an army. Above all, he wrote, if you know your enemy and yourself, you need not fear a hundred battles.

China remained a warrior society for centuries after Sun Tzu wrote on the art of war. One of the most spectacular examples of this was discovered in 1974, when peasants in Xian, in Shaanxi Province, found fragments of a burial near an earth mound. When archaeologists excavated the site, they unearthed the burial of Emperor Qin ("Qin" being the source of the name "China"), who ruled from 221 to 210 B.C. The actual tomb chamber has still not been excavated because of fears that it may have been booby-trapped. But what has been unearthed has revealed an army of more than 7000 lifesize terra-cotta warriors dressed according to their rank, and horses (figure **5.27**). Among the warriors are infantrymen, archers, officers, and cavalrymen. At present, the site has been enclosed and turned into a vast museum open to visitors, who can observe the ongoing excavation and restoration of the figures. Qin's terracotta army was apparently not intended to be seen by the living; its function was to protect the emperor in the afterlife.

5.27 Emperor Qin's bodyguard, 221–210 B.C. Terra-cotta, lifesize. Emperor Qin's tomb, Lintong, Shaanxi Province, China.

and seven hundred allies who resisted at Thermopylae. The Persians then invaded and sacked Athens, but the citizens had already fled to the island of Salamis. Cornering the Persian ships between Athens and Salamis, the Athenians destroyed the invaders with their superior **triremes** *(warships with iron-covered prows). The final blow to the Persian invaders came in 479 B.C. at the Battle of Plataea, after which they retreated, and though they continued to threaten Greece, their strength was greatly reduced. This ended the Archaic chapter of Greek history.*

KEY TERMS

abacus   the square element of the Doric capital.

agora   an open public space in a city.

architrave   the lowest long horizontal part of the entablature, which rests directly on the capital of a column.

burin   a sharp instrument used for incising.

cornice   the topmost horizontal part of an entablature.

echinus (Greek, "hedgehog")   part of the Greek Orders above the abacus.

encaustic   a type of paint in which beeswax is mixed with pigment.

entablature   the portion above the capital on a column; it includes the architrave, the frieze, and the cornice.

entasis (Greek, "stretching")   the bulge in the shaft of a Greek column.

frieze   the central section of an entablature, often containing relief sculpture.

gorgoneion   the severed head of the Gorgon Medusa.

helot   a member of the native population enslaved by the Spartans.

hoplite   a heavily armed foot-soldier who fought in close formation (phalanx).

hoplon   a shield carried by a hoplite.

krater   a vessel in which wine and water are mixed.

metope   the square area between the triglyphs of a Doric frieze, often containing relief sculpture.

misogynist   someone who dislikes and distrusts women.

necking   the lowest of three elements comprising the capital of a Greek column.

oligarchy   a form of government by a few people.

oracle   the revelation of a god, the person who utters the revelation, or the place the revelation is spoken.

Order   one of the architectural systems—Doric, Ionic, Corinthian—used by the Greeks to build their temples.

pediment   the triangular section at the end of a gable-roof, often decorated with sculpture.

peristyle   the freestanding columns surrounding a building.

phalanx   a military formation in which heavily armed soldiers lined up close together in deep ranks, defended by a wall of shields.

polis (plural **poleis**)   a city-state in ancient Greece.

precinct   a sacred area.

prothesis   the lying-in-state of the dead.

Pythagorean theorem   a theory developed by Pythagoras: the square of the hypotenuse of a right-angled triangle equals the sum of the squares of the other two sides.

stylobate   the top step from which a Doric column rises.

symposium   a type of Greek banquet.

triglyphs   in a Doric frieze, the three verticals between the metopes.

trireme   an ancient Greek warship with an iron-covered prow.

tyranny   a form of rule in which power is concentrated in a single person.

tyrant   an illegitimate leader who exercises absolute power, often oppressively.

KEY QUESTIONS

1. The notion of citizenship evolved in the *polis*. Who were citizens and what was required of them?
2. How did the Olympic Games achieve a sense of cultural unity between warring *poleis*?
3. The *Theogony* reflects the Greeks' interest in _____.
4. The *Chigi Vase* is the earliest surviving representation of a hoplite phalanx. Describe the distinguishing features of a hoplite phalanx illustrated on this vase.
5. Compare the political organizations of Athens and Sparta.

SUGGESTED READING

Boardman, John. *Athenian Red Figure Vases. The Archaic Period.* London: Thames and Hudson, 1989.

——. *Athenian Black Figure Vases.* London: Thames and Hudson, 1974.

——. *Greek Sculpture. The Archaic Period.* London: Thames and Hudson, 1978.
  ▶ All of the above are standard surveys.

Brilliant, Richard. *Arts of the Ancient Greeks.* New York: McGraw-Hill, 1973.
  ▶ A survey of Greek art.

Carpenter, Rhys. *The Architects of the Parthenon.* Baltimore: Penguin, 1970.
  ▶ Architecture and aesthetics of the Parthenon.

Fullerton, Mark D. *Greek Art*. Cambridge, U.K.: Cambridge University Press, 2000.
▶ A general introduction to Greek art.

Murray, Oswyn. *Early Greece*. New York: Prometheus Books, 1979.
▶ Greece in the early stages of development.

Onians, John. *Classical Art and the Cultures of Greece and Rome*, New Haven, CT, and London: Yale University Press, 1999.
▶ An introduction to Greek and Roman art.

Pedley, John Griffiths. *Greek Art and Archaeology*. New York: Harry N. Abrams, 1997.
▶ A general introduction.

Pomeroy, Sarah, Stanley M. Burstein, Walter Donlan, and Jennifer Tolbert Roberts. *Ancient Greece: A Political, Social, and Cultural History*. New York and Oxford: Oxford University Press, 1999.
▶ Greek art in its social and political context.

Renault, Mary. *The Praise Singer*. New York: Pantheon Books, 1978.
▶ A popular historical novel about a sixth-century-B.C. singer in the age of the Archaic tyrants.

Scully, Vincent. *The Earth, the Temple, and the Gods: Greek Sacred Architecture*, rev. ed. New Haven, CT: Yale University Press, 1979.
▶ Greek architecture in the context of landscape.

Spivey, Nigel. *Greek Art*. London: Phaidon Press, 1997.
▶ A general survey.

Sun Tzu. *The Art of War*, trans. James Clavell. London: Hodder and Stoughton, 1981.
▶ A classic work on military strategy by a fifth-century-B.C. Chinese general.

SUGGESTED FILMS

1954   *Ulysses*, dir. Mario Camerini

1960   *The Giant of Marathon* (*La battaglia di Maratone*), dir. Jacques Tourneur

1963   *Jason and the Argonauts*, dir. Don Chaffey

1967   *Oedipus Rex* (*Edipo re*) (based on Sophocles), dir. Pier Paolo Pasolini

6 Ancient Greece: Classical to Hellenistic

" *What Herodotus the Halicarnassian has learnt by inquiry is here set forth: in order that so the memory of the past may not be blotted out from among men by time, and that great and marvellous deeds done by Greeks and foreigners and especially the reason why they warred against each other may not lack renown.*"

(HERODOTUS, BK. I, I)

With the defeat of the Persians in 479 B.C., Greece entered the Classical period. This was a time of great achievement in politics, philosophy, the visual arts, and theater, all of which have had a lasting impact on Western history. Poleis of different types had been established throughout mainland Greece and the Greek colonies, although, with a few exceptions, Greece maintained its agricultural base.

The Classical period is generally divided into Early Classical (c. 480–450 B.C.), High Classical (c. 450–400 B.C.), and Late Classical (c. 400–323 B.C.). Athens was the most important, and one of the most urbanized, of the fifth-century-B.C. poleis, and it was the focus of Greek cultural activity. After the Persian sack of Athens in 480 B.C., the city undertook building programs designed to revive confidence and project an image of cultural superiority. Athenian citizens enjoyed music, attended some of the most famous plays ever written, and participated in city-wide religious festivals. Poets thrived, and the philosophical interest in empirical observation that had begun in the Archaic period spread to medicine and science. For the first time in the West, historians such as Herodotus (c. 490–c. 425 B.C.), who is quoted at the opening of the chapter, began to record first-hand the events of their time and to explore their meaning.

The cultural expansion of Greece continued in the fourth century B.C. (the Late Classical period). In the latter decades of this century, Greece produced Alexander the Great of Macedon (356–323 B.C.), the greatest conqueror the world had ever known. His armies marched east to the Punjab, in modern Pakistan, where the influence of Classical style may be seen in Indian sculpture. Following Alexander's death in 323 B.C., his generals vied for power and broke up the unity of his empire. This ushered in the Hellenistic period, which lasted to the turn of the first century A.D., and the rise of the Roman Empire. During the Hellenistic period, new ethnic groups, especially from the east, infiltrated Greek territory. The scale of architecture increased, religious cults offered the possibility of a more appealing afterlife than Hades, and rule by kings replaced the polis.

Key Topics

High Points of Greek Civilization

The Parthenon

The age of Pericles

Socrates, Plato, and Aristotle

Theater

The Real and the Ideal

Philosophy in search of truth

Music and math

Science and medicine

Writing History

Herodotus

Thucydides

TIMELINE	EARLY CLASSICAL 480–450	HIGH CLASSICAL 450–400	LATE CLASSICAL 400–323	HELLENISTIC LATE 4TH TO 1ST CENTURY
HISTORY AND CULTURE	Persians defeated, 479 Delian League, 478 Hatred of tyranny Urbanization grows Beginning of cultural expansion	Age of Pericles History writing Athens the main *polis*; ruled by male citizens, 450–400 Peloponnesian War, 431–404	Philip II of Macedon Athens loses preeminent position Conquests of Alexander the Great Alexander the Great dies, 323	Rise of kings Main cities: Alexandria, Pergamon Libraries *Polis* declines, 1st century
RELIGION AND MYTH		Same as Archaic period (see Chapter 5)		Mystery cults expand Influence of eastern religions
ART	Kritios and Nesiotes, *Tyrannicides, c.* 477 Myron, *Discus Thrower, c.* 460 *Oedipus answering the riddle of the sphinx,* early 5th century	*Muse Playing a Kithara,* 445–430 Polykleitos, *Spearbearer, c.* 440	Praxiteles, *Aphrodite of Knidos, c.* 350 Caivano painter, *Birth of Helen, c.* 340	*Battle of Issos* (Roman copy of a Greek painting of *c.* 300) *Drunken Old Woman,* late 3rd century *Aphrodite of Melos, c.* 150 Agesander, Athenodorus, and Polydorus, *Laocoön Group,* early 1st century A.D. *Chiron Instructs Achilles,* 1st century A.D.
ARCHITECTURE	Temple building continues Theaters	Pericles' reconstruction of Acropolis, Athens: Phidias, Parthenon sculptures, *c.* 448–420 Temple of Athena Nike, *c.* 427–424 Erechtheum, *c.* 421–405	Large-scale architecture Temples	Pergamon Altar, *c.* 180–160 Olympeium, reconstructed 2nd century
LITERATURE, PHILOSOPHY, AND MEDICINE	Pindar (*c.* 518–after 446), *Odes* Parmenides (*c.* 515–after 450) Zeno (*c.* 490–after 445) Herodotus (*c.* 490–*c.* 425), "Father of History" Thucydides (*c.* 460/455–400)	Protagoras (*c.* 485–410): "Man is the measure of all things" Empedocles (*c.* 490–430) Herodotus, *History* Thucydides, *History of the Peloponnesian War* Hippocrates (*c.* 460–*c.* 377) (Hippocratic Oath) Democritus (*c.* 460–*c.* 370) Socrates (469–399)	Plato (*c.* 429–347), *The Republic; Dialogues; Apology* Aristotle (384–322), *Metaphysics; Ethics; Politics; The Poetics*	Epicurus (341–271) Diogenes (*c.* 404–325) Stoics Cynics Skeptics
THEATER	Great Dionysia, annual festival of Dionysos Development of tragedy Aeschylus (*c.* 525–456), *Oresteia* Beginning of comedy	Sophocles (*c.* 496–406), *Oedipus the King; Antigone* Euripides *(c.* 485–406), *Medea; The Bacchae* Old comedy: Aristophanes (*c.* 445–*c.* 388), *The Clouds; The Frogs; Lysistrata*	Old comedy continues	Decline of tragedy New comedy Poetry: Pastoral Lyrical
MUSIC	No notation Monophonic Greek modes: Dorian, Phrygian, Lydian, Mixolodian Accompanied theatrical performances			

HERODOTUS: THE "FATHER OF HISTORY"

In contrast to the mythic grandeur of the Homeric epics and the intimacy of the lyric poetry of the Archaic period, literature in Classical Greece is famous for laying the foundations of modern historical inquiry. (The Greek word *historiai* means "inquiries.") The seminal figure in this new approach to history was Herodotus. He was born in Halicarnassus, a Greek colony in Asia Minor, traveled widely, and lived for a time in Athens. Called the "Father of History," Herodotus recorded the Persian Wars and reported on his extensive journeys from western Asia through Egypt, Greece, and southern Italy. In addition to his own observations, he recorded hearsay and gossip, local legends, and traditions. Herodotus is remarkable for recognizing that writing history preserves the past and offers insights into human motivation. In particular, he wanted to understand why the Persians invaded Greece. His *History* concludes with the Battle of Plataea (479 B.C.) and the final Greek victory over Persia.

Herodotus's approach to history writing is marked by the effort to be objective. He sought to verify the truth of events and to record everything he heard. In so doing, Herodotus made another landmark contribution to the Greek exploration of the nature of humanity.

READING SELECTION

Herodotus, *History*, Sparta's last stand at the Battle of Thermopylae, PWC1-039

ATHENS FROM THE LATE ARCHAIC TO THE EARLY CLASSICAL PERIOD: *c.* 500–450 B.C.

Situated near the port of Piraeus, on the eastern coast of the Greek mainland, Athens was the most important city-state in the Classical period. Athenian sea power dominated the Aegean for most of the fifth century B.C. Athens had colonies throughout the entire region and the greatest fleet of all the Greek city-states. But the city itself was not large by modern standards. By 429 B.C., the population of Athens, which was about 7 square miles (18.1 sq km), numbered just over 100,000. The Athenian economy was based mainly on textiles, pottery, grapes, olives, wheat, and maritime trade. As the most democratic of the city-states, Athens was ruled by an assembly and a council of five hundred male citizens and ten generals. The laws traditionally attributed to Solon continued to prevail, and legal verdicts were decided by

a jury. Since jurors were paid, lower-income citizens could participate in the legal system without suffering financially.

The Athenians were proud of their democratic values. In the sixth century B.C., the general Peisistratus (*c.* 605–527 B.C.) had risen to prominence in Athens, seized power, and ruled as a tyrant. Beginning around 508 B.C., a new leader, the aristocratic Cleisthenes (*c.* 600–*c.* 570 B.C.), took up where Solon left off (see Chapter 5) and steered the Athenian laws further toward democracy. Cleisthenes feared that the *polis* risked domination by men of high social status backed by traditional tribal ties. To offset their power, Cleisthenes grouped male citizens according to where they lived (the **deme**), rather than according to their family of origin. He redefined the notion of kinship, challenging it as a justification for power. In a final effort to prevent tyranny, Cleisthenes is thought to have devised the system of ostracizing any man considered a danger to the state. This was carried out, beginning in 487 B.C., by asking citizens to write on a piece of pottery (an *ostrakon*) the names of men whom they believed to be inclined to usurp political power. When there was a clear choice, he was ostracized (exiled) for ten years.

THE EARLY CLASSICAL PERIOD: *c.* 480–450 B.C.

As internal Athenian politics progressed toward democracy, external politics continued to focus on the East. Despite having defeated the Persians, the Greeks still considered them a threat. In 478 B.C., therefore, the Greeks formed an alliance of city-states against Persia. This was called the Delian League, because the funds that supported it were kept on the island of Delos. Although all the *poleis* contributed to the league, Athens soon dominated it and eventually used the funds for its own benefit.

SCULPTURE

Early Classical sculpture continues the trend toward naturalism that we saw in the Archaic period (see Chapter 5). This is clear in the *Kritios Boy* (figure **6.1**). The Archaic smile has disappeared, making the youth seem more serious than, for example, the *Anavysos Kouros* (see thumbnail), and the *Kritios Boy*'s proportions and stance are more natural. Instead of standing stiffly to attention, the later figure is relaxed—he bends one knee and shifts slightly at the waist. This **contrapposto** pose shows that the Early Classical artist has rendered the natural movements of the body. In addition, the *Kritios Boy* is no longer frontal, for he turns his head slightly, and the surface stylizations of the *Anavysos Kouros* are replaced by a sense of organic structure.

In 477 B.C., in honor of two opponents of tyranny, Harmodius and Aristogeiton, Athens commissioned a pair of

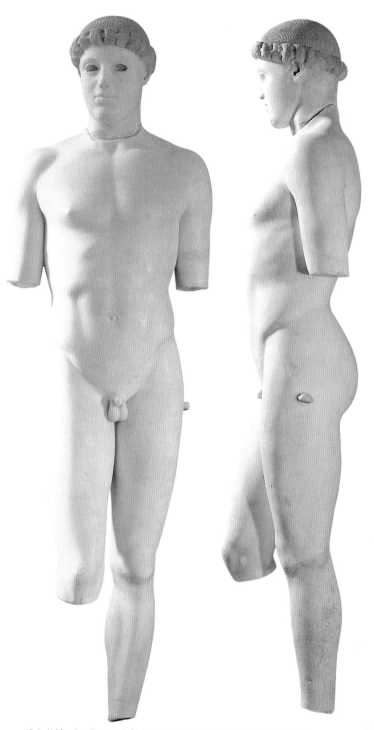

Anavysos Kouros see figure 5.15

agora, marking the political use of statuary to project a democratic image of the Athenian *polis*.

A slightly later Early Classical bronze (now known only from Roman marble copies) that illustrated the transition to naturalism is Myron's *Discus Thrower* (*Diskobolos*) (figure **6.3**). This sculpture probably honored a victorious athlete, but

6.1 *Kritios Boy* (front and side), *c*. 480 B.C. Marble, 33⁷/₈ in. (86 cm) high. Acropolis Museum, Athens.

6.2 *right and opposite (p. 113)* **Kritios and Nesiotes,** *Harmodius and Aristogeiton* **(the** *Tyrannicides***), partially restored copies of bronze originals that were erected in Athens in 477 B.C. Marble, 6 ft. 4³/₄ in. (1.95 m) high. National Archaeological Museum, Naples.**
Although the rule of Peisistratus was relatively benevolent and he instituted much-needed reforms, his son and successor, Hippias, was unpopular. Two Athenians, Harmodius and Aristogeiton, had assassinated Hippias's brother in 514 B.C. For this act against tyranny they were honored with statues in the *agora*. But in 480 B.C., just before their defeat, the Persians overran Athens and carried off the statues. The pair illustrated here are the new statues, recommissioned in the fifth century B.C.

bronze statues known as the *Tyrannicides* (tyrant-killers) (figure **6.2**) to replace an Archaic version that had been looted by the Persians. Note the change in the treatment of human form compared with the Archaic sculptures illustrated in the previous chapter. Although retaining some Archaic stylization, the *Tyrannicides* are structured organically and seem able to move freely in space. The statues were placed in the Athenian

his identity is not known. The work reflects both the political and cultural importance that the ancient Greeks attached to athletic competition and shows how the human body works. Myron has designed the sculpture so that it echoes the circular movement the athlete will make when throwing the discus.

The figure is caught as he turns, gathering momentum before spinning and launching the discus. What we are seeing, therefore, is not a static pose, but rather a captured movement. As in the *Tyrannicides*, there are traces of stylization in the *Discus Thrower*—the patterned ribcage and the smooth hair—but the body works as a logical unit. The absence of a facial expression and of any indication of strain or effort, however, reveals the Early Classical tendency to idealize figures. Myron's sculptures are not based on the features of an actual human model, but on an ideal appearance of the male nude.

6.3 *right* **Myron, *Discus Thrower* (*Diskobolos*), Roman copy of a Greek bronze, *c.* 460 B.C. Marble, 5 ft. 1 in. (1.55 m) high. Museo Nazionale delle Terme, Rome.**
The original statue, which was cast in bronze by Myron, has disappeared. This version is one of several later Roman copies in marble, which is given extra support by the tree trunk next to the leg.

PHILOSOPHERS ON THE REAL AND THE IDEAL: PARMENIDES AND ZENO

Early Classical philosophy echoes the combination of nature (the real) with idealization (the ideal) that we can see in the sculpture of the period. This is reflected, for example, in the views of Parmenides (*c.* 515–after 450 B.C.), even though they survive only in fragments. Born in Elea, a Greek colony in southern Italy, Parmenides was the leading Eleatic (from Elea) philosopher in the early fifth century B.C. The Eleatics rejected both the empirical evidence of the senses and mathematical abstraction. Parmenides studied biology and considered the nature of the real; he concluded that reality, like mathematics, was timeless and without motion. Parmenides believed that the idea of a thing was inseparable from its physical reality, a belief made material in such sculptures as the *Diskobolos*. As in Myron's sculpture, the real was seamlessly merged with the ideal.

Another Eleatic philosopher and an admirer of Parmenides, Zeno (*c.* 490–after 445 B.C.), was interested in progression and motion, which is also characteristic of the *Diskobolos*. Zeno used a series of **paradoxes** (statements that seem to contradict common sense) to support the views of Parmenides. Taking the example of a runner, Zeno observed that he has to run a half length before he can run a whole length, and a quarter length before a half length, and so on forever.

In a similar paradox, Zeno noted that a fast runner will never catch up with a slower runner who starts first; the fast runner will halve the distance between himself and the slow runner, and then halve what remains, and then halve it again, and so on forever, without ever catching the slow runner. In the case of Myron's athlete, the figure is represented in motion, but, because he is fixed in stone, he, like Zeno's runner, will never achieve his goal of throwing the discus.

POETRY: PINDAR ON ATHLETES

The best preserved **odes** (lyric poems) of Pindar (518–after 446 B.C.), the most important Early Classical poet, are dedicated to victorious athletes, reflecting the high esteem in which Greece held sports. These were not the popular team sports of today, but rather sports in which individual excellence was honored and memorialized in poetry as well as in sculpture.

Pindar traveled widely, attending the four great ancient Greek athletic festivals—the Olympian, Nemean, Pythian, and Isthmian Games. His early success as a poet won him commissions throughout Greece. In all, some forty-four of his odes survive. They were sung to music, either at the end of a competition or after a winner had returned home.

Pindar's *Olympian Ode II* celebrates Theron of Acragas, the victor in a chariot race held at the Olympic Games in 476 B.C. Because these games were sacred to Zeus, whose precinct and great temple were located at Olympia, Pindar opens his ode by praising the god:

> Ye hymns that rule the lyre! what god, what hero, aye, and what man shall we loudly praise? Verily Zeus is the lord of Pisa [a Greek city]; and Heracles established the Olympic festival from the spoils of war; while Theron must be proclaimed by reason of his victorious chariot with its four horses, Theron who is just in his regard for guests, and who is the bulwark of Acragas, the choicest flower of an auspicious line of sires . . . But, O thou son of Cronus and Rhea [Zeus], that rulest over thine abode on Olympus, and over the foremost of festivals, over the ford of the Alphaeus [a river]!
>
> (lines 1–30)

Note that Pindar's verse is packed with background information. He tells us that Zeus, the son of Rhea and Chronos, rules the Olympic Games, presides over Mount Olympos, and is the patron god of Olympia. Pindar reminds us of the tradition that

Heracles instituted the Olympic Games "from the spoils of war," alluding to the suspension of armed conflict so that Greek athletes could travel safely to the competition. Having paid homage to Zeus and Heracles, Pindar praises the family of Theron, a victor and an honor to his city.

THE HIGH CLASSICAL PERIOD: 450–400 B.C.

During the High Classical period, Athens was dominated by Pericles (*c.* 495–429 B.C.), a general and statesman who ruled the *polis* from 443 until his death (figure **6.4**). Under Pericles, the treasury of the Delian League was moved to Athens, and Pericles' political opponents accused him of diverting the funds to finance an Athenian building campaign. This aroused the anger of other city-states and eventually eroded Greek political unity.

6.4 Kresilas, *Pericles*, Roman copy of an original bronze of *c.* 429 B.C. Marble, 6 ft. (1.83 m) high. Vatican Museums, Rome.

6.5 The Acropolis, Athens, Greece.

Pericles presided over the rise of Athens to its central position in Greek art and politics. He used his power to finance works of architecture and sculpture designed to convey the importance of Athens. He decided to rebuild the Acropolis (literally the "upper city"), the elevated fortified rock that was the site of several temples and other important buildings (figures **6.5**, **6.6**, and **6.7**). But the Acropolis had lain in ruins since being sacked by the Persians. For Pericles, therefore, the reconstruction program celebrated the Athenian defeat of Persia and the cultural supremacy of Athens.

The reconstruction view in figure 6.6 conveys some idea of the original appearance of the Acropolis. Athenians proceeded to the Acropolis along the Sacred Way, which led to an impressive stairway. At the top of the stairs was the gateway called the Propylaia, which was begun in 437 B.C., with a Doric porch and an extension on either side. This structure marked a change from the previous function of the Acropolis—it had been a fortified citadel with a narrow entrance to deter invaders. But Pericles envisioned the area as a religious sanctuary. He wanted an imposing entrance, large enough to accommodate Athenians participating in religious processions and performing rituals dedicated to the gods.

6.6 Peter Connolly, reconstruction of the Acropolis, Athens, at the beginning of the 4th century B.C. Watercolor.

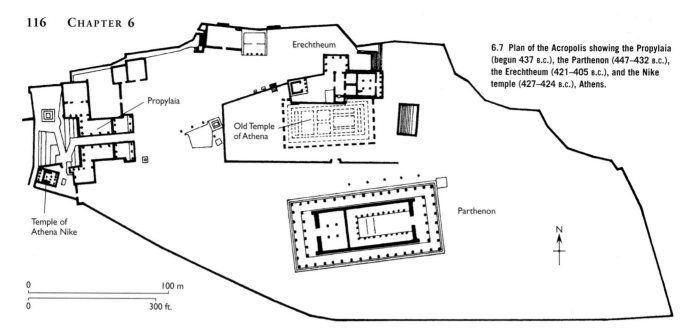

6.7 Plan of the Acropolis showing the Propylaia (begun 437 B.C.), the Parthenon (447–432 B.C.), the Erechtheum (421–405 B.C.), and the Nike temple (427–424 B.C.), Athens.

THE PARTHENON

To the east of the Propylaia on the Acropolis stands the Parthenon, a majestic temple dedicated to Athena (figure **6.8**). Figure **6.9** shows a cutaway reconstruction drawing.

The plan (figure **6.10**) shows the rectangular symmetry of the Parthenon, which has six columns on the front and back porches and a peristyle (a freestanding **colonnade**, or row of columns). Inside the peristyle is the *naos*, the main room containing the cult statue. To the west of the *naos*, a smaller room

with four interior Ionic columns housed the Athenian treasury. Since the Doric Order was a western, mainland Order and Ionic was eastern, the use of both in the Parthenon suggested the global reach of Athens under Pericles.

The Parthenon was designed with several architectural refinements to improve its appearance. The corner columns, for example, are closer together than the center columns, creating an impression of stability (as well as increasing the actual structural support) at the ends of each wall. The peristyle

6.8 Iktinos and Kallikrates, the Parthenon, Athens, 447–432 B.C. Marble, 111 × 237 ft. (33.8 × 72.2 m).
In Greek, *parthenos* means "virgin," which was an aspect of Athena, who was also the patron goddess of Athens. Today, the Parthenon is in ruins, although its restoration is an ongoing process. It was converted to a church by the Christians and to a mosque under Turkish domination in the sixteenth century. The Turks used the building to store gunpowder, which exploded in the seventeenth century and destroyed the interior.

6.9 *above* **Peter Connolly, cutaway reconstruction of the Parthenon, Athens. Drawing with watercolor.**

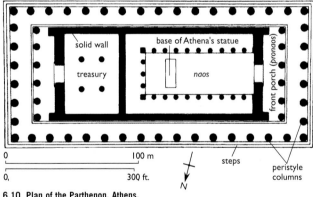

6.10 Plan of the Parthenon, Athens.

columns slant inward and the top step, the stylobate, is slightly convex. This corrects the natural tendency of the eye to perceive a long horizontal as concave.

THE SCULPTURAL PROGRAM OF THE PARTHENON   The Parthenon sculptures were designed by Phidias (*c.* 490–432 B.C.), who was a close friend of Pericles. The sculptural **program** (its design and meaning) of the temple was intended to reflect the political, religious, civic, and artistic superiority of the Athenian *polis*. Phidias decorated four main areas of the Parthenon with brightly painted sculpture: the *naos*, the outer Doric frieze, the inner Ionic frieze (around the *naos*), and the two pediments. The *naos* itself housed the colossal cult statue

of Athena; the flesh was made of ivory and the clothing and armor of gold (figure **6.11**).

The freestanding pediment sculptures illustrated two mythological events involving Athena. Her birth was shown on the east pediment, and her contest with Poseidon for the patronage of Athens was on the west pediment. The birth scene is diagrammed in figure **6.12**. Two of the most impressive figures from the east pediment are the reclining *Dionysos*, god of wine (figure **6.13**), and the *Horse of Selene* (figure **6.14**), a goddess of the moon.

The birth itself, which is now entirely missing, occupied the center of the pediment. According to Greek myth, Athena sprung full grown and armed for war from the head of Zeus—like an idea. On either side of Athena's birth, the gods await news of the event. The figure of Dionysos, who has not yet heard the news, faces the left corner of the pediment. He reclines in a relaxed manner, so that he fits naturally under the sloping frame of the pediment. His smooth, domed head, lack of facial expression, and youthful body are characteristic of the High Classical idealization of heroic male youth. The anatomical structure of the body is clearly visible, reflecting the Classical interest in human form.

At the left corner of the east pediment the horses of the sun god, Apollo, appear to be rising, an indication that Athena was born at dawn. At the far right corner, the *Horse of Selene* (a moon goddess) seems to descend, denoting the waning of the moon. This figure, like the *Dionysos*, creates a harmonious unity with its triangular space; note the curved triangle of the

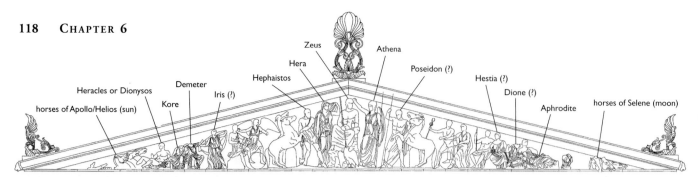

Heracles or Dionysos

horses of Apollo/Helios (sun)

Kore

Demeter

Iris (?)

Hephaistos

Hera

Zeus

Athena

Poseidon (?)

Hestia (?)

Dione (?)

Aphrodite

horses of Selene (moon)

6.12 *above* **Figures on the east pediment of the Parthenon, Athens.**
Most of the Parthenon sculptures are now in London. In the nineteenth century, when Greece was under Turkish domination, the British ambassador, Lord Elgin, was given permission to remove the works from the Acropolis and ship them to London. Today they are referred to as the Elgin Marbles. One shipment sank and the sculptures were lost; the remainder were sold to the British Museum and have been a subject of international controversy ever since. The Greeks are pressing for their return, but the British argue that no laws were broken by the removal of the works, that they are available for study and viewing, and that they are safer in London than in air-polluted Athens.

6.13 *right* **Phidias, *Dionysos*, from the east pediment of the Parthenon, Athens, *c.* 420 B.C. Pentelic marble, over lifesize. British Museum, London.**

6.11 Replica of Phidias's lost statue of Athena, from the *naos* of the Parthenon, Athens. Marble, 3 ft. 5¼ in. (1.05 m) high. Royal Ontario Museum.
It is most likely that the original statue was plundered for the value of its gold and ivory, but its appearance is known from descriptions and from ancient coins. Athena was shown armed for war, with a Gorgon head (the gorgoneion) on her breastplate. In her right hand she holds a Nike (goddess of victory), alluding to the Greek defeat of the Persians. Athena's imposing presence was a reminder of the invincible power of Athens protected by the goddess of war and wisdom. Athena was also a goddess of weaving, which was an artistic female pursuit in antiquity. She thus combined male and female qualities, as well as the ability to destroy (war), to create (the arts), and to administer justice (as in Aeschylus's *Libation Bearers*, in which she casts her vote for Orestes' acquittal).

cheek plate, and the triangular space of the mouth. As with the human figure, the horse has a convincing organic structure.

The metope sculptures are carved in relief. Although in ruins today, they depicted four mythological battles, each shown as a series of single combats and chosen to project the image of Greek cultural dominance. The battle between the Gods and the Giants illustrated the triumph of the Olympians over the more primitive, pre-Greek Titans; the battle between the Greeks and the Trojans, and between the Greeks and the Amazons (eastern warrior women), connoted victories of western civilization over the east; and the battle between the Lapiths (a Greek tribe) and the Centaurs (creatures that were half-man and half-horse) demonstrated the superiority of Greek reason over animal instinct (figure **6.15**).

The Ionic frieze continued around the solid side walls of the *naos* and treasury and over the front and back porches. In contrast to the triglyphs and metopes separating the Doric narrative into individual frames (see Chapter 5), the Ionic frieze is continuous. As such, it is well suited to the depiction of a procession, in this case the Great Panathenaic Procession

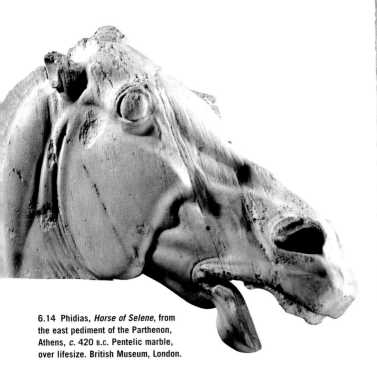

6.14 Phidias, *Horse of Selene*, from the east pediment of the Parthenon, Athens, *c.* 420 B.C. Pentelic marble, over lifesize. British Museum, London.

6.15 Phidias, *Lapith Battling a Centaur*, metope 30 from the Parthenon, Athens, *c.* 448–442 B.C. Pentelic marble, 4 ft. 4¾ in. (1.34 m) high. British Museum, London.
This illustrates the myth of the Lapiths and Centaurs. The Lapiths invited the Centaurs to a wedding, but the Centaurs became drunk and attempted to rape the Lapiths. The ensuing battle ended with the defeat of the Centaurs, indicating the victory of Greek civilization over the primitive, antisocial behavior of the Centaurs. In this metope, a Centaur temporarily has the upper hand. His horse part rears upward, and his entire body forms a series of energetic diagonals. Both figures show strain and tension, as they fight to the death.

in which all of Athens participated. The Panathenaia was held every four years in honor of Athena.

Figure **6.16** shows a detail of the horsemen on the Ionic frieze. They are carved in different poses to convey a sense of variety within a unified whole. At the left, rearing horses prepare to gallop forward. At the right, a dismounted youth turns to gaze at the group proceeding slowly behind him. The procession ends with the gods awaiting the presentation of a sacred *peplos* to Athena (figure **6.17**).

6.16 *below* Detail of the Great Panathenaic Procession, slabs 41 and 42, from the Parthenon frieze, Athens, *c.* 442–438 B.C. Marble, 3 ft. 5¾ in. (1.06 m) high. British Museum, London.
Phidias introduced two refinements in the Ionic frieze that enhance its harmonious appearance. He maintained a horizontal unity by placing all the heads at a relatively equal height (**isocephaly**), and he carved the lower section in deeper relief than the upper section. This improved visibility from below and created the impression of swift movement in the legs of the horses and youths. Over time, the Parthenon marbles have suffered considerable damage, but originally the sections were so precisely cut that the separations between them were not visible.

6.17 Phidias, *Hera and Zeus with Iris*, slab 5/28–30, from the Parthenon frieze, Athens, *c.* 442–438 B.C. Marble, 3 ft. 5¾ in. (1.06 m) high. British Museum, London. Notice that Phidias has maintained the isocephaly here by making the seated figures of Hera and Zeus as high as the standing figure of Iris. The large size of the king and queen of Mount Olympos reflects their importance compared with Iris, the rainbow-messenger goddess, as well as with the human figures and horses in figure 6.16. Hera turns toward the bearded Zeus, her veil an attribute of marriage. As with the horsemen, Hera and Zeus turn freely in space, as if engaged in casual conversation with each other.

THE TEMPLE OF ATHENA NIKE

The small Ionic temple dedicated to Athena Nike (Athena as a goddess of victory) was not begun until 427 B.C., two years after the death of Pericles (figure **6.18**). This elegant building overlooks the southern edge of the Acropolis, discreetly but decisively standing for Greek victory. Its nearly square *naos* originally housed small golden Nike statues. The front and back porches have four columns resting on three steps, and the continuous frieze, which survives only in fragments, represented gods and battle scenes. In its small scale, harmonious proportions, and symmetry, the Nike temple embodies the Classical architectural ideal.

THE ERECHTHEUM

Opposite the Parthenon to the north stands the complex Ionic Erechtheum (figure **6.19**). This temple is named after Erechtheus, a legendary king of Athens, but is dedicated to Athena Polias (Athena as goddess of the city). The Erechtheum is on uneven ground and thus has an irregular plan. Its most

6.18 Temple of Athena Nike. Acropolis, Athens, *c.* 427–424 B.C. Marble.

6.19 View of the Erechtheum, Athens, *c.* 421–405 B.C. Marble.

interesting feature is the south porch, with six **caryatids** (female figures that function as architectural supports), who wear the traditional *peplos* and support the entablature (figure **6.20**). Their human form is combined with architectural elements—for example, the folds of their garments resemble the flutes (grooves) of columns. Their crowns, like the capitals of columns, create a visual transition from vertical to horizontal and also perform a similar support function. In these figures, the Classical artists made explicit the association of the column with human form.

CLASSICAL PAINTING AND SCULPTURE UNRELATED TO THE ACROPOLIS

The architecture and sculpture of the Acropolis were not the only expressions of High Classical style in Greece. Concurrent with Pericles' building program, other artists worked on commissions unrelated to the Parthenon.

By the first half of the fifth century B.C., a new type of vase painting known as "white ground" had developed. White ground allowed artists even more freedom to paint lifelike figures than was possible with the red-figure technique. Artists working in white ground outlined figures in black, red, or brown and filled them in with green, blue, yellow, and purple

6.20 A caryatid (front and side), from the Erechtheum, Athens, 421–405 B.C. Marble, 8 ft. 7 in. (2.31 m) high. British Museum, London.

6.21 Achilles painter, *Muse Playing a Kithara on Mount Helikon*, *c.* 445–430 B.C. White ground lekythos, terra-cotta, 16 in. (40.7 cm) high. Staatliche Antikensammlungen, Munich. How far vase paintings such as this one reflect the lost monumental wall paintings of the period is not certain. However, a number of anecdotes about Greek painters indicate that illusionism was highly esteemed. One famous story describes a painting by Zeuxis of a boy carrying a bunch of grapes. The painted grapes were so convincing that real birds tried to eat them. What is clear is that this and similar anecdotes suggest that naturalism led to a taste for illusionistic tours-de-force by Greek painters.

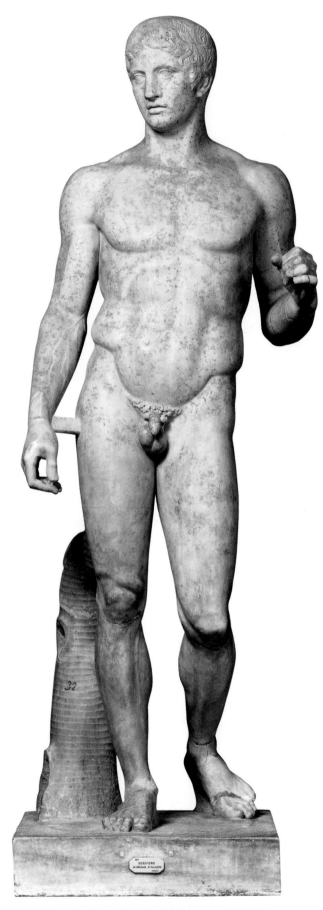

6.22 Polykleitos, *Spearbearer* (*Doryphoros*), Roman copy of a Greek bronze original, *c.* 440 B.C. Marble, 6 ft. 11½ in. (2.12 m) high. Archaeological Museum, Naples.

on a white background. White ground was most often used for *lekythoi*—tall, slim oil jars that were placed in graves. The scene in figure **6.21** shows a Muse sitting on a rock, playing a hand-held harp (*kithara*) and concentrating on the music; the little bird at her feet probably symbolizes the soul. The inscription *HELIKON* at the lower right refers to Mount Helikon, the mythological home of the nine Muses.

Perhaps the best-known High Classical work by an artist not involved in the Parthenon is the *Doryphoros* (*Spearbearer*) (figure **6.22**) by Polykleitos. He called his statue the *Canon*, indicating that it embodied his ideal of human **proportions**. In contrast to the stance of Archaic *kouroi*, the *Spearbearer* is relaxed, and he occupies a contrapposto pose, in which the waist twists slightly in response to the bent knee. Polykleitos believed that mathematical ratios determine order and harmony, and he represented this idea in the *Spearbearer*. The figure expresses the Classical ideal of youth and perfection of form and, at the same time, achieves a balanced harmony between motion and rest.

CLASSICAL PHILOSOPHY

Greek philosophy, which is first known from the Archaic period, continued to be an important part of Greek culture. During the fifth century B.C., a group of traveling philosophers hired to teach **rhetoric** (the art of eloquent argument), mathematics, and politics became popular. These were known as the Sophists—literally, "men of wisdom." They did not advocate any single philosophical point of view, but prided themselves on being able to argue any side of an issue. Eventually, however, the substance of their arguments gave way to artificial rhetoric, and they began to stress stylish form over content. The modern term "sophistry," referring to an argument that seems reasonable but is actually invalid, comes from the rhetorical style of the Greek Sophists.

PROTAGORAS Born in Thrace, in northern Greece, Protagoras (c. 485–410 B.C.) was the most famous Sophist. He was acquainted with Pericles and achieved fame in Athens, but was eventually exiled for questioning the existence of the gods. His main argument was that truth varies according to what each individual concludes from his own experience. This is a relativist view, which does not impose an objective set of rules defining the "real" and the "ideal," as had the Eleatic school. Protagoras thus exemplifies the Classical Athenian sense that men, not gods, are the standard by which everything is measured. He stated this notion explicitly in the famous saying attributed to him: "Man is the measure of all things."

EMPEDOCLES The philosopher Empedocles (c. 490–430 B.C.) of Sicily identified the four basic elements of matter as air, fire, water, and earth. He believed that the forces of love and strife caused evolution and that the most adaptive organisms would survive. In this view, he prefigured Darwin's theory of evolution (see Chapters 1 and 19). Empedocles' theory of four elements was applied by Greek physicians to the four humors (fluids) of the human body: blood, phlegm, yellow bile, and black bile.

DEMOCRITUS Democritus (c. 460–c. 370 B.C.), like Protagoras and in contrast to the Eleatics, was a relativist. Because he believed that atoms were the basic unit of matter, he is known as an Atomist (from the Greek word *atomos*, meaning "uncuttable"). Atoms, he thought, were unchanging, indivisible, and forever moving through space. They made up all physical matter, including the human body, but did not deteriorate with age. He also held that the soul was made of fire and was similar to the atom in that both animated the body, but also outlasted it.

The works of Democritus do not survive, but he is known to have described the physical universe and to have written about natural science, astronomy, mathematics, literature, and ethics. He believed that moderation (*metron*, or "measure") was the most ethical position and would lead to a happy life, hence the Greek maxim *metron ariston*—"measure is best." Later authors describe Democritus as the "laughing philosopher" because he laughed at the extremes of human frailty even as he recommended a life based on moderation.

6.23 Attributed to Lysippos, *Socrates*, Roman copy of a 4th-century-B.C. Greek original. Marble, 10 in. (27.5 cm) high. British Museum, London. Note that this Late Classical statue has a portrait-like quality absent in Early and High Classical style. Socrates is shown with his proverbial short stature, pug nose, fat torso, and beard, which fostered his reputation for ugliness.

SOCRATES AND PLATO Socrates (469–399 B.C.) and his student Plato (c. 429–347 B.C.) were the two leading Classical philosophers in Athens. Socrates was the son of a sculptor and a midwife; he was married to Xanthippe, whose nagging became legendary. (Today, therefore, a shrewish woman may be referred to as a "Xanthippe.") Unlike the Sophists, Socrates was not paid for his philosophy. He preferred to wander around Athens discussing philosophical issues with other citizens. Pretending to know nothing himself ("Socratic irony"), Socrates used a dialectic process of question and answer to elicit truth from his questioners. He was interested in inductive argumentation—that is, arriving at generalities from particular instances—which he used to lead his followers to conclusions he himself had already reached. This so-called "Socratic method" became a foundation of Western philosophy and the cornerstone of Plato's *Dialogues*.

Socrates did not write down his philosophy. His views are known mainly from what his most famous student, Plato, says he said. Plato presents Socrates as a man dedicated to pursuing the nature of the Good, the True, and the Beautiful, although Socrates, himself, was notoriously ugly (figure **6.23**). In this pursuit, Socrates discussed a wide variety of topics, ranging from the nature of love (*The Symposium*), rhetoric (*Phaedra* and *Giorgias*), metaphysics (*Parmenides*), death and the immortality of the soul (*Phaedo*), to the ideal state (*The Republic*, and later *The Laws*). In *Protagoras*, Socrates argues against the Sophists' view that there is no absolute truth and concludes that knowledge of the Good is the basis of virtue. And the deepest wisdom, according to Socrates, is insight into oneself. In his view, no one who knew right would act wrongly, making virtue synonymous with wisdom. To this end, he cites the wisdom of the inscription carved in stone at Delphi—"Know thyself"—which is also a cornerstone of Socratic philosophy.

Socrates' unconventional ideas led to his arrest in 399 B.C. for corrupting the youth of Athens and denying the existence of the gods. In his own defense, which is recorded in Plato's *Apology*, Socrates cross-examines his accusers. How, he asks, could he not believe in the gods, since it is well known that he believes in demi-gods, the illegitimate offspring of the gods? He points out, "You might as well affirm the existence of mules, and deny that of horses and asses" (*Apology*, 27).

The court found Socrates guilty and gave him a choice of exile from Athens or death by drinking the poison, hemlock. He chose death:

> . . . the difficulty, my friends, is not to avoid death, but to avoid unrighteousness; for that runs faster than death. I am old [he was seventy at the time] and move slowly, and the slower runner has overtaken me, and my accusers are keen and quick, and the faster runner, who is unrighteousness, has overtaken them.
>
> (*Apology*, 39)

Plato's *Crito* is set in the Athenian prison with the hour of Socrates' death approaching. His followers try to persuade him to escape and appeal to his obligations to his children. But Socrates replies that the issue is law and justice, not family. Having lived under Athenian law for seventy years, he refuses to escape on the grounds that he would be exchanging one evil for another—that is, escape and exile from Athens are as bad as death. He cannot break with the city-state that has nourished him his entire life and thus decides to obey the verdict of the court. Another reason for Socrates' decision to die was his refusal to do evil, even if others had been evil in their actions toward him.

THE REPUBLIC Plato's most famous dialogue, *The Republic*, outlines an ideal society based on justice and reason, but not on democracy. Plato's ideal state is authoritarian, and its rulers (guardians) require a lengthy period of education. He divides his state into three main classes: artisans (crafts workers) who labor and produce, soldiers who have physical power, and philosopher-kings who have wisdom. This social structure is a model of Plato's ideal individual—someone who is capable of productive work, who is morally and physically strong, and who is ruled by wisdom.

Plato's recommendations emphasize the importance of order and harmony in all areas of life. He bans from his Republic any person or activity that disrupts order or causes disharmony. For example, because music arouses the emotions, Plato outlaws all but martial music, which inspires soldiers in battle. He urges training the body as well as the mind, educating women along with men, and raising children in communal settings.

Plato believed in the existence of a realm of ideas, separate from the material world. This rather mystical notion of an ideal realm distinguished Plato's philosophy from both the empiricists and the relativism of the Sophists. The realm of ideas also had a bearing on Plato's view of visual artists. He believed that artists, unlike artisans, create illusions, which are a danger to the Republic because they are false.

The Platonic view—that the real world is merely a shadow of truth and that illusion is dangerous—has influenced thinkers and inspired metaphors throughout Western history. This notion is illustrated in the famous Allegory of the Cave (Book VII), in which Plato juxtaposes knowledge with illusion, comparing the former with light and the latter with darkness. Those who are chained inside the cave see only shadows, like screen puppets, but they believe the shadows to be real. When they leave the cave, they are dazzled by the brightness, but as their eyes grow accustomed to the light, they become capable of achieving true knowledge. Enlightenment, according to Plato, comes from intellectual rather than emotional knowledge. On occasion, he says, the enlightened must renounce intellectual pleasure and return to the cave, which they rule in order to improve the general condition of the state and not just that of the most educated citizens.

Plato taught in an olive grove near Athens, where he founded the Academy in 387 B.C. After his death in 347 B.C. his followers continued to teach there.

READING SELECTION

Plato: *Phaedo*, the body imprisons the soul, PWC1-145; *The Symposium*, on cosmic love, PWC1-158-C; *Apology*, "Know Thyself" and the Delphic Oracle, PWC1-141-A; *The Republic*, the Myth of Er, PWC1-127; *The Republic*, Allegory of the Cave, PWC1-122

MEDICINE

During the Classical period, Greek medicine, like Greek philosophy, marked a break from purely religious thinking, even though faith and prayer were still seen as aids to healing. Whereas pre-Greek medicine had used magic, ritual, and herbal potions to promote healing, the historical Greeks began to study empirical evidence based on clinical observation. From around 500 B.C., groups of doctors were practicing on the island of Cos and in Greek areas of western Anatolia.

HIPPOCRATES The best known Greek physician is Hippocrates (c. 460–c. 377 B.C.), who is called the "Father of Medicine." His name lives on in the Hippocratic Oath, which is taken by contemporary Western physicians before starting to practice medicine. They promise, among other things, to honor their teachers, to do no harm to their patients, and to respect confidentiality. A large body of Hippocratic texts, written by Hippocrates or based on his ideas, still survives. Their focus on observing and describing symptoms laid the foundation for later medical practice. The Hippocratic method of diagnosis reflects the Greek interest in the individual and in empirical inquiry.

In treating serious illness, Hippocrates recommends the following:

> examine the face of the patient, and see whether it is like the faces of healthy people, and especially whether it is like its usual self. Such likeness will be the best sign, and the greatest unlikeness will be the most dangerous sign.

In order to arrive at a diagnosis Hippocrates recommends questioning patients about their symptoms. He says that physicians should find out whether a patient has trouble sleeping or eating. They should also observe whether a patient's eyes are red, the complexion sunken, or the lips white. A bent nose, in the view of Hippocrates, indicates that death is near. When patients with fever grind their teeth and are delirious, according to Hippocrates, madness and death are imminent.

READING SELECTION
Hippocrates, *Hippocratic Writings*, the Oath, PWC1-529

Many Hippocratic texts deal with women and gynecology, but because women did not speak freely with male doctors, the information is less empirical and, therefore, less likely to be accurate than medical texts on other subjects. Greek women were not allowed to study medicine beyond the profession of midwife, but deliveries were performed more often by midwives, mothers, and grandmothers than by male doctors. The dangers of childbirth in historical Greece are clear from the high death rate of women aged sixteen to twenty-six, especially in Athens. Additionally, the social restrictions on Athenian women, who were confined to the house or accompanied by chaperones, were not conducive to healthy exercise.

Some of Hippocrates' views about female health stem from the inferior status of women and the idealization of young men. He asserts, for example, that pregnancy bestows a good complexion on the expectant mother if she is carrying a boy but a bad one if it is a girl. Male fetuses, he says, lean to the right of the uterus and females to the left; this reflects the age-old preference for right over left (consider, for example, the Latin word *sinister*, meaning "left").

Hippocrates differed from Mesopotamian and Egyptian physicians in taking a holistic approach to food. He believed that good health resulted from a proper balance of the four humors. He recommended that people suffering from wounds eat nothing and drink only water and vinegar. Plasters (salves) made from boiled beets, celery, and olive leaves could be applied to wounds, but fats, he said, should be avoided. Barley, millet, and flour are good for all diseases, he maintained, and lentils are indicated if a fever arises after taking a medication. Dry, strong meats help to restore a patient when a disease has subsided, and liquids should be added to the diet slowly.

In general, Hippocrates believed that healthy food and drink taken in small quantities best satisfied hunger and thirst. To build strength, he recommends eating dense flesh, such as pork and beef, because they thicken the blood. Fish, dog, fowl, and rabbit, on the other hand, were considered lighter meats. Best of all for humans, whether sick or healthy, in Hippocrates' view, are wine and honey, provided they are taken in moderation (see Box).

Society and Culture

A Greek Dinner Party: The Menu

The ancient Greeks took eating very seriously. Believing that body and mind are related, they felt that a good diet led to physical health. Phyllis Pray Bober, a modern scholar, has reconstructed a Greek symposium, complete with recipes and a menu based on the Greek ideal of a well-balanced diet.

Guests arrived wearing garlands and wreaths and washed their hands in bowls of scented water. They reclined on couches and were served and entertained (as in the Archaic period; see Chapter 5) by musicians and acrobats. The symposium began with a libation to the gods, but drinking during the main meal was generally restricted to honey water lightly flavored with vinegar; wine was saved for later. Appetizers included lamb meatballs, stuffed figs, toasted walnuts (the "acorns of Zeus") in a honey glaze, sausage, olives, and smoked eel and mackerel.

Lentil was a favorite type of soup (also recommended by Hippocrates). It was flavored with onion, parsnip, olive oil, thyme, and parsley and served with crusty bread. Sow's womb, stuffed with nuts, cracked wheat, calves' brains, onion, sausage, liver, and egg, was served with a balsamic vinaigrette containing olive oil and red wine. Additional meats included squid, whole pig, and hare with date sauces. Among the vegetables were stuffed fig leaves, turnips, cabbage, chard, leeks, artichokes, cucumber, zucchini, radishes, dandelion, nettles, and black-eyed beans.

For dessert, diners had flat cake poached in sweet wine, water, and honey. The top was embellished with fruit, and the cake was baked in the oven; once cooked, it was garnished with almonds. Honey and nut cake was made from almonds, hazelnuts, and walnuts mixed with honey. Generally, cheeses, fruits, and nuts were the dessert staples in ancient Greece.

MUSIC

Very little ancient music has been preserved, although it was an important part of everyday life. The Greeks believed that music had divine origins, and they associated the sun god Apollo with music. Music was thought capable of working miracles, of healing, of purifying, and of transporting listeners into states of ecstasy. Greeks performed religious rituals and recited poetry to music. In addition, music theory was an aspect of Greek philosophy and mathematics.

For the philosopher Pythagoras, music, like the cosmos, was organized according to a mathematical structure. He speaks of the musical **modes**, or scales, each consisting of an **octave** (the span between one note and the next of the same name). Octaves were divided into **tetrachords** of four notes each, with the notes separated by **intervals** (differences in pitch) of either whole or half steps. The feeling of the modes varied according to the order and sequence of its whole-step and half-step intervals. The native Greek Dorian mode, preferred by Plato because it inspired soldiers in battle, was strong and warlike. The more eastern Phrygian and Lydian modes came from Anatolia; the for-mer aroused the passions, and the latter was plaintive. The Mixolydian mode was elegiac.

Despite attempts to reconstruct ancient Greek music, nobody really knows how it sounded. It appears to have been monophonic—that is, consisting of a single line of melody. We do know, however, that music was an important part of Greek theater.

GREEK THEATER

Greek theater became a foundation of Western theater. Many Homeric myths and legends, such as the story of Agamemnon and the House of Atreus, were first dramatized in ancient Greece but later found their way into modern plays. Inspired by the rhythms of lyric poetry, Greek actors sang their lines, and music enriched the text. But much more is known about Greek theater than about the music that accompanied it.

In the Classical period, plays were performed throughout Greece, with the most important playwrights centered in Athens. Plays were performed at religious festivals, notably at the Great Dionysia, the festival of Dionysos (the wine god), which was held in Athens every year on March 10, and a prize was awarded for the best trilogy.

The Great Dionysia had evolved from outdoor cult performances in honor of the god. A chorus of singers and dancers performed in a horseshoe-shaped space (the *orchestra*, or

6.24 Peter Connolly, reconstruction of Dionysos Theater, on the south slope of the Acropolis, late 4th-century B.C. Watercolor.
Admission to a play in the fifth and fourth centuries B.C. cost two obols, which was about what a lower-class worker earned in a day. By the fourth century B.C., women as well as men attended the theater, and the audience ate and drank throughout the performance.

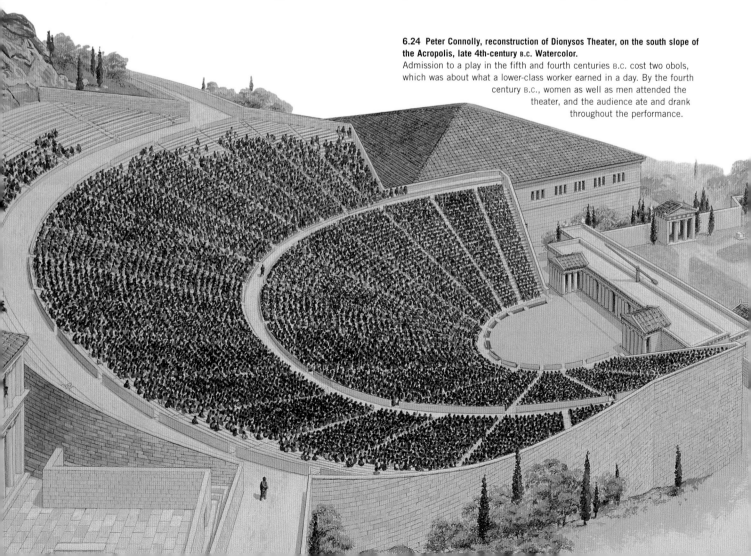

6.25 Plan of the theater at Epidauros, Greece, 4th century B.C.

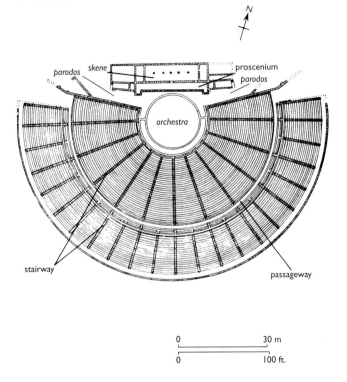

lifelike impression. They also disguised the fact that female as well as male roles were performed by men.

Figure **6.24** shows a reconstruction of a typical Greek theater. The large number of seats reflects the importance of the Great Dionysia. Superior acoustics made it possible to hear a pin drop on the stage from every seat. The area behind the orchestra was the *skene* (from which comes the word "scene"), a structure with three entrances, giving the actors access to the orchestra. The plan of the actual surviving theater at Epidauros, on the Greek mainland, is shown in figure **6.25**.

Some time in the early fifth century B.C., a crane-like device was created so that actors playing gods could be lowered onto the stage as if descending from the sky. Called by the Romans a *deus ex machina* ("god from a machine"), the term stuck and now means "out of the blue," referring to something that arrives at the last minute. Today we speak of a *deus ex machina* when a playwright (or film scriptwriter) resolves a plot complication by introducing some entirely unanticipated, and often jarring, element (character or event). In ancient Greek theater, the *deus ex machina* was always a god.

Another feature of Greek theater was the satyr play, from which we get the English word "satire." Satyr plays, which were performed for comic relief, made fun of the main tragedy and its heroic characters. The chorus was composed of satyrs— men with the ears and tail of a horse—who behaved in grotesque or obscene ways. Sometimes Silenus, the obese, drunken, orgiastic father of the satyrs, was also a character in the play. All three of the great Greek tragedians—Aeschylus, Sophocles, and Euripides—wrote satyr plays.

THE TRAGIC PLAYWRIGHTS

Playwrights in ancient Greece wrote tragedies and comedies. The term "tragedy" comes from *tragos*, meaning "one who wears a costume to perform in a ritual of Dionysos." Tragedies were usually written in verse form and dealt with serious, universal themes. The main character is generally a person of importance who falls by virtue of a character flaw. Fate, or destiny, is a crucial aspect of Greek tragedy. In refusing to accept fate, Greek tragic heroes often suffer from **hubris**, a word that denotes arrogant grandiosity.

AESCHYLUS The only surviving work by Aeschylus (c. 525– 456 B.C.) is the trilogy, *Oresteia* (see Chapter 4). Aeschylus won his first victory at the Great Dionysia in 468 B.C. and was the leading Greek playwright until his death at the dawn of the High Classical period. His themes emphasize human frailty and its consequences, but his plays generally end on an optimistic note. At the conclusion of the *Oresteia*, Orestes is absolved of his crime by an Athenian court and the favorable vote of Athena, the city's patron goddess. This outcome is a mirror of the moral evolution of the *polis* and is intended to show that Athens is ruled by divine as well as by human justice.

"dancing place"). At the center of the orchestra stood the god's altar. The theater itself (the *theatron*) was at first merely the slope of a hill and later stone seats were added. This arrangement grew into the modern theater-in-the-round, in which the audience sits around the stage in a semicircle rather than opposite the stage in rows.

The cult of Dionysos inspired the development of theater because, in addition to music, sacrifice, and ritual, it included mythological and heroic narratives. Dionysos was an orgiastic god, and the participants in his rites drank wine to increase their range of emotion and induce states of ecstasy. The rites themselves later became organized into theater and the participants in the rites became the actors.

The earliest festivals of Dionysos were accompanied by a **dithyramb** chorus (a group of actors who performed the dithyramb, a type of lyric poem sung and accompanied by flute music). In the sixth century B.C., according to tradition, the actor Thespis (from whose name derived the word "thespian," meaning "actor") began to converse with the chorus, thus introducing spoken dialogue and essentially inventing theater. Later, two actors and then three took on individual roles, and the chorus, usually representing a group of local townspeople, reacted to events as they unfolded.

Thespis is also credited with having introduced masks, for all Greek actors wore either a tragic or a comic mask, depending on their role. Masks consisted of linen strips glued together, slightly stiffened, and attached to the actor's face. As with Greek sculptures, the masks were painted to produce a

The organization of the *Oresteia* reflects certain Classical ideals and conventions. It avoids violence on the stage by the device of a messenger, who brings news of what has happened off-stage. Thus the audience, like the actors, is told of violent acts, but does not witness them. This allows the playgoers to visualize events for themselves and requires that the author use words to depict events. Aeschylus's success in creating such images comes from the power of his language and the simplicity of Greek tragic form. By restricting the number of actors on stage to two or three, Greek Classical theater intensified emotions in both the characters and the audience.

SOPHOCLES   The next great Athenian playwright of the fifth century was Sophocles (*c.* 496–406 B.C.). Only seven of his 123 plays survive, and all deal with heroes who struggle against themselves, against their fate, and against adversity. The story of Oedipus was well known to Greek audiences and is the subject of Sophocles' most famous play, *Oedipus the King*. It is the first of three in a trilogy dealing with the tragic fate of Oedipus. According to an oracle, Oedipus was destined to murder his father, King Laios of Thebes, and marry his mother, Queen Jocasta. To avoid this fate, Oedipus's parents take the infant to the mountains, drive a stake through his foot (Oedipus means "swollen foot"), and leave him to die. But he is discovered and reared by a shepherd and his wife. Later, when Oedipus learns of the oracle, he leaves home to avoid killing the shepherds, whom he believes to be his real parents.

Arriving at a crossroads, Oedipus argues with an older man over who will pass first, and he kills him. He journeys on and reaches the outskirts of Thebes, where a sphinx is terrorizing the countryside. According to Greek myth, the sphinx posed a riddle to all who passed its way: "What walks on four legs in the morning, two legs in the afternoon, and three legs in the evening?" Oedipus gives the correct answer—"Man"—which destroys the sphinx (figure **6.26**). When Oedipus reaches the court of Thebes, he receives the hand of the widowed queen, Jocasta, as a reward for solving the riddle of the sphinx, and becomes king. The play opens after Oedipus has fathered several children with Jocasta and a plague has fallen on the city of Thebes. A blind messenger, Teiresias, informs Oedipus that he has committed parricide and incest and that these crimes are the cause of the plague. At first appalled by the news, Oedipus finally realizes that the man he killed at the crossroads was his own father and that Jocasta is his mother. In a frenzy of guilt, spurred by the climactic discovery of his true identity, Oedipus blinds himself.

Sophocles' play exemplifies the vexing Greek notion that man has free will but is also ruled by fate. Dramatically, this sets up an ironic situation, because the audience understands the meaning of the oracle before the characters do. The **irony** of Oedipus's behavior is that he suffers the very fate he leaves home to avoid. In *Oedipus*, as in Greek tragedy generally, the

oracle represents the power of the unconscious mind, whereas free will is conscious choice. Because Oedipus does not understand the hidden meaning of the oracle—that is, because he lacks insight into his unconscious motivation—he is doomed to fulfill its prophecy. The blindness he inflicts on himself is retribution both for his refusal to see the truth and for his crimes. It is the result of his tragic insight (*anagnorisis*) and initiates the **falling action** of the play. At the end of the play, the **resolution** occurs when Oedipus goes into exile, which restores order to Thebes.

In *Antigone* (performed in 442 B.C.), Sophocles deals with the fate of Oedipus's daughter Antigone. After Oedipus goes into exile, his two sons, Eteocles and Polyneices, agree to take turns ruling Thebes, each for a year at a time. But Eteocles refuses to cede the throne to his brother when his year is up, leading Polyneices to form an alliance with an enemy of Thebes. He and Eteocles kill each other in the ensuing civil war. Their uncle Creon becomes king and orders proper funeral rites for Eteocles but not for Polyneices, whom he considers a traitor. Creon decrees that Polyneices' body be left unburied for animals to feed on, thus condemning his shade to wander forever.

Antigone defies her uncle Creon's order and secretly places earth over Polyneices. When Creon discovers that she

6.26 *Oedipus answering the riddle of the sphinx*, interior of a red-figure cup, from Vulci. Vatican Museums, Rome.
The sphinx is tensely perched on an Ionic column as a relaxed Oedipus ponders the riddle. He is shown wearing the hat and boots and carrying the stick of a traveler. The meaning of Oedipus's solution to the riddle is explained as a baby crawling on all fours, an upright adult on two legs, and an old person whose cane is the third leg.

has disobeyed him, he threatens her with death, even though she is engaged to marry his son, Haemon. But no amount of pleading sways Creon. He imprisons Antigone, who hangs herself. When Haemon also commits suicide, Creon repents of his decree and renounces the throne of Thebes.

In this story, Sophocles explores the conflict between Creon's blind tyranny and the rights of the individual, which was an important theme in the early days of the Greek *polis*, especially in Athens. Antigone is determined to obey the laws of the gods, which in her view take precedence over human law. She thus assumes the proportions of a tragic heroine. At the end of the play, Creon, like Oedipus, achieves self-knowledge, which evokes guilt and leads to atonement. He, too, therefore, fulfills the requirements of a tragic hero. Creon is, metaphorically, blinded by his own arrogance and places himself above divine law. He changes only when events force him to recognize his hubris, and insight overcomes his refusal to see.

EURIPIDES In contrast to Sophocles, Euripides (*c.* 485–406 B.C.) explores individual personal feelings. He is also known for his heroic female characters, in whom he juxtaposes extremes of human passion with the intimacy of softer emotions. The moods of his plays vary, often according to aspects of contemporary society he criticizes. In *Medea*, for example, which was produced in 431 B.C., the main character is a foreign enchantress who destroys her own family to rescue and follow the Greek hero Jason. Jason brings Medea to Corinth, where they have two sons. But when Jason decides to take a new wife, the daughter of the king, Medea is consumed with rage and insults the king, who banishes her from his land. Nor is she persuaded by Jason's argument that he loves her, but is marrying the princess only to improve the status and security of his existing family. Medea sends the princess a poisoned robe, which burns her flesh, and kills the king as he tries in vain to save his daughter. Finally, Medea takes revenge by murdering her two young sons to prevent the continuation of Jason's line.

A major theme of *Medea* is the tension between Greeks and foreigners. Medea embodies the Greek view of non-Greeks as irrational and driven by passion rather than by reason. She bemoans her fate as an outsider and a woman, with nowhere to go. As a woman, Medea is also a vehicle for Euripides to comment on Greek misogyny. His views angered a number of his contemporaries, and he later accepted voluntary exile from Athens.

Euripides' last play, *The Bacchae* (produced in 405 B.C.), deals with the power of emotion to engulf and destroy reason, possibly referring to ongoing wars on Greek soil. He increasingly believed that Athenians were unable to think for themselves.

In *The Bacchae*, the legendary Theban king Pentheus mocks Dionysos and his religious cult. The god takes revenge by

6.27 *Death of Pentheus*, House of the Vettii, Pompeii. Roman painting after a Greek prototype, mid-1st century A.D. 3 ft. 5½ in. (1.05 m) high.
This shows Pentheus kneeling before the frenzied Bacchae as they tear him limb from limb. His mother, at the right, ignores his pleas for mercy and tears out his shoulder.

tricking Pentheus into spying on his female followers (the Bacchae or Maenads), who are in a state of ecstatic frenzy. One of these is Pentheus's own mother, Agave. When she and the other women discover Pentheus, they are deluded into thinking that he is an animal and they tear him to pieces (figure **6.27**). Agave, like Oedipus, is ignorant of her victim's identity until it is too late.

Euripides' description of the frenzied murder is delivered by a messenger:

> the swiftness of their [the Bacchae's] feet
> Was as of doves in onward-straining race—
> His mother Agave and her sisters twain,
> And all the Bacchanals. Through torrent gorge,
> O'er boulders, leapt they, with the God's breath mad.
> . . . .
> Agave cried, "Ho, stand we round the trunk,
> Maenads, and grasp, that we may catch the beast
> Crouched there, that he may not proclaim abroad
> Our God's mysterious rites!" Their countless hands
> Set they unto the pine, tore from the soil:—
> And he, high-seated, crashed down from his height;
> And earthward fell with frenzy of shriek on shriek
> Pentheus, for now he knows his doom at hand.
>
> His mother first, priest-like, began the slaughter,
> And fell on him: . . .
> . . . with foaming lips and eyes that rolled
> Wildly, and reckless madness-clouded soul,
> Possessed of Bacchus . . .
> . . . his left arm she clutched in both her hands,

And set against the wretch's ribs her foot,
And tore his shoulder out—not by her strength,
But the God made it easy to her hands.

. . . .

In mangled shreds: with blood-bedabbled hands
Each to and fro was tossing Pentheus' flesh.
. . . His miserable head,
Which in her hands his mother chanced to seize.

(Bacchae, lines 1080–1140)

COMEDY

Comic theater originated in the Greek colonies of Sicily, where comic actors roamed the countryside, singing bawdy songs and participating in revels and processions in honor of Dionysos. Comedy (from *komos*, meaning "a light-hearted parade in honor of Dionysos") did not become part of the Great Dionysia until the 480s B.C., when five poets were permitted to compete. Greek comedy combined social, literary, and political satire and buffoonery with aspects of religious ritual.

ARISTOPHANES The most famous of the Greek comic playwrights is Aristophanes (c. 445–c. 388 B.C.), who makes fun of social and intellectual pretensions. *The Clouds*, produced in 423 B.C., satirizes Socrates and the false arguments of the Sophists. A potential student has the following exchange with his father about Socrates' theory of the gnat:

FATHER: . . . and what said your Master of the gnat?
STUDENT: . . . the entrail of the gnat
    Is small: and through this narrow pipe the wind
    Rushes with violence straight toward the tail;
    There, close against the pipe, the hollow rump
    Receives the wind, and whistles to the blast.
FATHER: So then the rump is trumpet to the gnats!
    O happy, happy in your entrail-learning!
    Full surely need he fear nor debts nor duns,
    Who knows about the entrails of the gnats.
STUDENT: And yet last night a mighty thought we lost
    Through a green lizard.
FATHER: Tell me, how was that?
STUDENT: Why, as Himself [Socrates], with eyes and mouth
      wide open,
    Mused on the moon, her paths and revolutions,
    A lizard from the roof squirted full on him.

(Clouds, lines 154–169)

In *The Frogs*, produced in 405 B.C., Aristophanes satirizes the Athenian tradition of dramatic competition. He places Aeschylus and Euripides in Hades, where they compete for the crown of tragedy. Each criticizes the other, but Aeschylus wins because his poetry is weightier—it literally weighs more—than that of Euripides. Aristophanes' chorus is composed of frogs, who sing in the Underworld. Their **onomatopoeic** refrain (in which words sound like the very thing to which they refer), "brekekekax, koax koax," replicates the natural sounds made by croaking frogs. It also reflects the musical basis of choral commentary and conveys some idea of the play's poetic rhythms.

THE PELOPONNESIAN WAR: 431–404 B.C.

Despite remarkable Athenian achievements during the High Classical period, conflicts with other Greek city-states, notably Sparta, arose in the second half of the fifth century B.C. One source of dissatisfaction stemmed from events following the Persian Wars, when Athens established the Delian League (477 B.C.). Sparta and other cities feared the power of the Athenian navy and the city's expansionist political ambitions; Corinth considered Athens a threat to its primacy in commerce and trade. In 431 B.C. the Peloponnesian War broke out between Athens and Sparta.

Pericles led Athens until his death only two years into the war. The best surviving primary source for the Peloponnesian War is the *History* written by the Athenian general Thucydides (460/455–400 B.C.). He fought in the war and contracted the plague, which had broken out in 430 B.C. Unlike Pericles, who died of the plague, Thucydides recovered. One of the most vivid passages in his account of the war is the description of the "plague of Athens." This epidemic entered the city in waves, coming first from Ethiopia, then from Egypt, and finally from the Persian Empire. In all, it killed 4400 hoplites, 300 cavalrymen, and an unknown number of the lower classes. By 427 B.C., one-third of the Athenian population had died and the city was seriously weakened.

Thucydides also recorded Pericles' stirring funeral oration praising Athenian soldiers killed in the fighting. From even the brief passage quoted here, it is clear that Pericles was a great orator and a charismatic leader. Rallying support for the war, Pericles extols the fallen fighters and the city of Athens for which they fought:

"We live under a form of government," he declares, "which does not emulate the institutions of our neighbors; . . . our government is called a democracy, because its administration is in the hands, not of the few, but of the many; yet while as regards the law all men are on an equality for the settlement of their private disputes."

(Thucydides, History, Bk. II. 36)

In addition to Athens being a democracy, in which all men were equal before the law, Pericles points out that the city is beautifully adorned. Games and sacrifices, he says, are provided for relaxation, Athenians are better trained for war than their enemies, and they honor the wisdom of their philosophers. Pericles implores the survivors to honor the dead and to celebrate the freedoms enjoyed in Athens. He argues that Athenians should not fear war, because they have the most to lose if they lose liberty.

Defining Moment

The Classical Ideal and Its Decline: The Peloponnesian War

In the history of Western civilization, one of the major defining periods was the brief moment in which Classical Athens rose to prominence. This period lasted about seventy-five years, from the Greek defeat of Persia in 479 B.C. to the devastation wrought by the Peloponnesian War, 431–404 B.C. The seeds of democracy, which had been sown by certain lawmakers and a general aversion to tyranny in the Archaic period (see Chapter 5), came to fruition in the fifth century B.C.

Athens specifically and the very notion of the *polis* differed from all previously known Mediterranean cultures. Greeks generally opposed kings and tyrants and evolved a political ideal requiring free male citizens to govern themselves. In Athens, this ideal in politics developed alongside vast building programs under the leadership of Pericles that were designed to embody the superiority of Athens. In addition to sculpture and painting, artists strove

6.28 *Warrior*, from Riace, Italy, 5th century B.C. Bronze with bone, glass paste, silver and copper inlaid, 6 ft. 6¾ in. (2 m) high. Museo Nazionale, Reggio Calabria, Italy.

for the ideal representation of the human figure, especially the male nude (figure **6.28**).

Eventually, however, other city-states began to resent Athenian power and its abuses of that power. *Poleis* allied themselves either with Sparta, which had a strong land army, or Athens, which had become a naval power. In 431 B.C. these alliances went to war, called "Peloponnesian" after the peninsula forming the southern part of Greece, which was united in a league headed by Sparta. The war strained the financial resources of Athens, which had been supplied by the Delian League. Pericles, in his famous funeral oration, had exhorted Athens to defend its democracy, though nobody could have predicted the length or eventual costs borne by either Athens or Sparta. Unfortunately, Pericles died of plague early in the war and it cannot be known how the outcome might have been different had he lived.

Critical Question What, if any, similarities can you describe between the political situation in fifth-century-B.C. Athens and the United States today?

READING SELECTION
Thucydides, *History of the Peloponnesian War*: Pericles' funeral oration and the plague, PWC1-066-B; Pericles' last speech, PWC1-067-A

One of the most entertaining antiwar works of literature dates to 411 B.C., twenty years into the Peloponnesian War. Written by Aristophanes, *Lysistrata* is about women who rebel against war by witholding sexual favors from their husbands. The main character, Lysistrata, instructs the women of Sparta and Athens to join in the following oath:

I will abstain from Love and Love's delights.
And take no pleasure though my lord invites.
And sleep a vestal [i.e., a virgin] all alone at nights.

. . . .

I will abjure the very name of Love.
So help me Zeus, and all the powers above.
If I do this, my cup be filled with wine.
But if I fail, a water draught be mine.

(*Lysistrata*, lines 213–228)

The women persist in their plan and eventually take over the Acropolis, effecting a humorous exchange of male and female roles. At the end of the play, once an agreement is in place, Athenians and Spartans dance to celebrate the peace.

In reality, however, Sparta defeated Athens in 404 B.C., and Athens lost its political and military power. However, this did not end Athenian supremacy in the arts, literature, and philosophy. After the war, new styles began to develop in the visual arts and fresh philosophical ideas emerged. The period following the Peloponnesian War, which occupied most of the fourth century B.C., is termed Late Classical.

THE LATE CLASSICAL PERIOD: c. 400–323 B.C.

Before the middle of the fourth century B.C., the powerful king of Macedon (north of Greece), Philip II (ruled 359–336 B.C.), rose to power. He quelled decades of political conflict, improved weaponry, disciplined the army, and instituted reforms that unified Macedon. By 338 B.C. Philip controlled most of Greece and had advanced to the Black Sea. In 337 B.C., he established the League of Corinth, an alliance designed to maintain Greek unity and prepare for an invasion of Persia. By this tactic, Philip projected his image as the legitimate ruler and defender of Greece.

Philip was assassinated in 336 B.C., at least in part because of an unpopular seventh marriage. He was succeeded by his son Alexander (356–323 B.C.), then nineteen years old (see Box). With a large army and new weapons, Alexander went on to conquer most of the known world, including Greece, Egypt, Mesopotamia, and the Persian Empire as far as the Punjab region of modern India. He had at his disposition 37,000 troops, 3000 royal guards, 1800 cavalry, a Greek army 9000 strong, and a fleet of nearly 200 ships (see Box).

Society and Culture

The Myth of Alexander's Birth

Alexander's mother, Olympias, was a foreigner, known in Greece for her violent and ambitious character. A worshipper in the cult of Dionysos, Olympias participated in the ecstatic frenzies of the Bacchantes. She kept pet snakes, which, as symbols of the earth, were used in the Dionysian nature cult. Olympias herself used the snakes in rites designed by women to frighten men.

When Philip II took a new wife, Alexander quarreled with him and left the court with his mother. When Philip's new wife gave birth to a son, Alexander's status as heir to the throne of Macedon was in jeopardy. Philip's assassination and the subsequent murder of his infant son were fortuitous for Olympias and Alexander, although their responsibility for these deeds has never been established.

In order to reaffirm her own relationship to Greece and Alexander's inheritance, Olympias traced her ancestors to Achilles and Helen of Troy. She wove mythical accounts of Alexander's birth, which were designed to legitimize his kingship and distance him from Philip. Olympias spread the rumor that when she became pregnant, her womb was sealed with a lion's mark, ensuring that Alexander would have the courage of a lion. She also claimed that she had been impregnated by Zeus's thunderbolt, which meant that Alexander was the son of the god rather than of Philip. This enabled Alexander, like many of the Homeric heroes, to boast a divine parentage.

Society and Culture

Warfare Technology and Science

The development of new weaponry and military engineering increased Philip of Macedon's power and that of his successors. Under Alexander, engineers devised mobile siege towers and long-distance catapults. Later engineers improved the accuracy of missiles by calculating the relationship of their weight to their range.

Hellenistic science was less innovative than its technology, but there were a few important scientists, notably Euclid (active c. 300 B.C.) and Archimedes (c. 287–212 B.C.). Euclid developed plane geometry in his *Elements*. He codified and systematized proofs and the form of reasoning in which a proof is logically deduced from a series of axioms. Archimedes wrote on the circle, the sphere, and the cylinder, and invented the compound pulley. The so-called Screw of Archimedes enabled water in irrigation canals to be raised for use on higher ground.

The Battle of Issos, in northern Syria, at which Alexander defeated the armies of the Persian king, Darius III, in 333 B.C., is memorialized in a Roman **mosaic** thought to be a copy of an original Greek painting of around 300 B.C. (figure **6.29**). The Greek conqueror is shown launching a frontal attack at the center of Darius's troops at the turning point of the battle. Darius wears a Persian helmet and towers over the fray as his charioteer attempts a retreat. Alexander, his breastplate decorated with a gorgoneion, charges in from the upper left on a powerful war horse. He raises his long Macedonian spear, which pierces a Persian soldier. This image of Alexander, as an energetic young man with flowing hair, became a model for portraits of rulers in Western art.

The Issos mosaic exemplifies the Greek interest in creating lifelike figures and natural, three-dimensional space. Shading and cast shadows reflect the fact that form in nature is made visible by shifts in light and dark. The rumps of the horses appear rounded as the lighter areas gradually shift to darker ones. Several figures, as well as horses, are **foreshortened** (shown in perspective)—that is, we see them as if they move spatially from front to back rather than from side to side. Note that the frame design is **illusionistic**—that is, it creates the illusion of three-dimensional geometric shapes, even though it is flat.

In addition to these formal techniques, the artist shows the psychological intensity of battle. In the foreground, a Persian watches himself die in the mirror reflection of his convex shield. The horses are visibly frightened and in disarray, and the anguished expressions of Darius and his men indicate their awareness of defeat. The artist thus evokes sympathy with the panic of the defeated Persians as well as admiration for the heroic Greek victory.

6.29 *The Battle of Issos*, from the House of the Faun, Pompeii, 1st century B.C. Mosaic, 8 ft. 10¾ in. × 16 ft. 9⅓ in. (2.71 × 5.12 m). Archaeological Museum, Naples.

A mosaic is an arrangement of small, colored stones or tiles called *tesserae*, which are embedded into a flat surface. In this example, the arrangement of the stones was termed "worm work" because they form curves similar to those made by crawling worms.

Alexander's vast empire (map **6.1**) reached to the western border of India. This laid the foundation for a period of Hellenization, a process by which Greek culture spread throughout the Mediterranean world and Greek became the dominant language.

At the same time, however, cross-cultural influences in politics, religion, and the arts led to new developments and widespread assimilation (see Box, p. 134). The death of Alexander in Babylon, in 323 B.C., marks the beginning of the Hellenistic period.

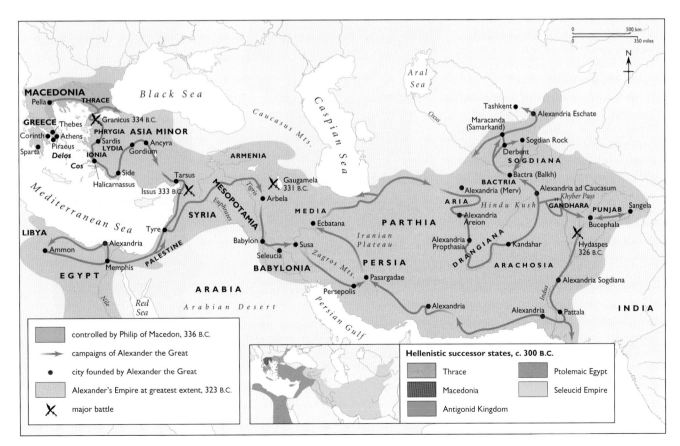

Map 6.1 Alexander's Empire, 323 B.C.

Cross-cultural Influences

Hellenism and the Far East

As Alexander the Great conquered the world, he spread Greek culture (Hellenism) to the Indian subcontinent (see map 6.1). Before turning back, Alexander founded the city of Karachi, now in Pakistan. Some of his soldiers remained in Bactria (parts of modern Afghanistan and Pakistan), located between the Hindu Kush and the Oxus River, which flows into the Aral Sea. Throughout the regions Alexander conquered, there is evidence of Greek art and architecture, but the clearest instance of Greek stylistic influence is found in the Buddhist art of Gandhara, across the Khyber Pass just north of the Indus River.

Siddhartha and the Origin of Buddhism

Buddhism, one of the world's great religions, arose in the region of modern Nepal. The sixth-century-B.C. prince Siddhartha Gautama (c. 563–483 B.C.), whose father was head of the Shakya clan, was raised in courtly luxury. But, at the age of twenty-nine, Siddhartha left the palace grounds and confronted the outside world. Appalled by human suffering, he embarked on a search for truth, first following an ascetic path and then deciding on a Middle Way.

Siddhartha was meditating under a pipal tree when the female demon Mara tried to seduce him. He resisted her temptations and became the Buddha. For the remainder of his life, the Buddha pursued a life of self-discipline, meditation, and quest for knowledge. He preached his first sermon in the Deer Park at Sarnath, which set in motion the Buddhist Wheel of the Law. The Buddha dedicated himself to the pursuit of spiritual truth and the alleviation of social ills. He advocated enlightenment as a means of providing release from reincarnation, making *nirvana* available to everyone. He founded monasteries and his missionary followers spread the new religion throughout the Far East.

Gandharan and Mathuran Sculpture

Figure **6.30** illustrates the impact of Hellenism on Far Eastern art. It shows a standing Buddha in a style prevalent in Gandhara

6.30 *Standing Buddha*, from the Bactro-Gandhara region, Pakistan, Kusana period, 1st century B.C.–1st century A.D. Schist, approx. 4 ft. 11 in. (1.5 m) high. Lahore Museum.

following Alexander's conquests. Influenced by the Classical style, the deeply carved folds define the left knee, and the head is depicted naturalistically. The garments and pose, however, are distinctly Buddhist—for example, the large round halo, the topknot (*ushnisha*), and the gesture of the right hand

(which is now missing). The Buddha's plain robe and lack of ornamentation signify his renunciation of the material world.

The Mathuran style, in contrast to the Gandharan, shows no evidence of Western Classical influence. Enormous figures of the Buddha from Mathura (between modern New Delhi and Agra, in India) convey a sense of monumental, otherworldly power (figure **6.31**). The imposing Mathuran Buddha has broad shoulders, little open space, and flat patterned drapery curves. Its rigid pose and aloof character are quite distinct from the more three-dimensional naturalism of Gandharan sculpture.

6.31 *Standing Buddha*, from Sarnath, c. A.D. 100. Red sandstone, 8 ft. 10¼ in. (2.70 m) high. Sarnath Museum.

READING SELECTION
Arrian, *Campaigns of Alexander*: cutting the Gordian Knot, PWC1-022; conquering an Indian army fighting with elephants, PWC1-023

After the Peloponnesian War and the conquests of Philip II and Alexander the Great, Athens was no longer the dominant military power in Greece. In philosophy and the arts, however, Athens retained its preeminent position. Styles of painting and sculpture became more illusionistic and emotional: the idealization of the young male hero began to wane as new, more specific types of representation evolved. The greatest fourth-century-B.C. philosopher was Aristotle, who wrote on a wide variety of topics, including the theater.

ARISTOTLE

Aristotle (384–322 B.C.) was born in Stagira, Macedonia, and moved to Athens to study with Plato. In 343 B.C. Aristotle left Athens for the Macedonian court of Philip II, where he became tutor to Alexander until Alexander came to power in 336 B.C. Aristotle then returned to Athens and founded the Lyceum, a school of philosophical studies based on his own, rather than on Plato's, ideas.

Unlike Plato, who believed in an immaterial realm of ideas, Aristotle was an empiricist. He believed that an idea and the thing to which the idea refers were one and the same. For Aristotle, nature and the physical world, including human experience, constituted reality. He discusses his quarrel with Plato's ideal realm primarily in the *Metaphysics*. In other works, Aristotle systematizes the study of nature by classifying and describing what can be observed. His writings include such topics as ethics, politics, rhetoric, logic, and science.

In the *Politics* and the *Ethics* (also called the *Nicomachean Ethics*), Aristotle sets out the ethical aspects of his political theory. In the *Ethics*, he argues that the aim of all conduct is the Good, which is a state of happiness, and that the greatest happiness lies in contemplating philosophical truth. He opens the *Ethics* as follows:

> Every art and every investigation, and likewise every practical pursuit or undertaking, seems to aim at some good: hence it has been well said that the Good is that at which all things aim.
>
> (*Ethics*, I, i)

The *Politics*, in which Aristotle famously calls man a "political animal," focuses on the city-state, its development, its citizens, and its constitution. For Aristotle the *polis* should be ruled not by the rich or the many, but by the good. He concludes that monarchy is the ideal political system, as long as the ruler is a good one. If there is no such ruler, Aristotle recommends government by an aristocracy of virtuous citizens.

However, given the reality of contemporary Greece and its aversion to tyranny, Aristotle admits that the political system closest to the Good is a relative democracy.

READING SELECTION
Aristotle: *Politics*, on the political animal, PWC1-505-B; *Poetics*, comparing the epic with tragedy, PWC1-014

Aristotle codifies the rules of tragedy in the *Poetics*, and he takes the example of Sophocles' *Oedipus* as a model. The basic elements of Greek tragedy, according to Aristotle, are unity of action, place, and time. This means that the action unfolds in a single location and that it is a continuous narrative within a short space of time. In addition, the personalities of the characters should be consistent with their behavior. Aristotle insists on the importance of language and plot: a plot should stand on its own as a powerful narrative, so that even without seeing the play readers would be affected by the story.

These requirements are met in the *Oedipus*. The action unfolds in Thebes within a brief period, and past events are reported by the characters. The messenger who informs Oedipus that he is the cause of the Theban plague is the seer Teiresias, whose physical blindness ironically highlights the psychological blindness of Oedipus and also foreshadows Oedipus's act of self-blinding. Oedipus is consistent in his willful refusal to see, whereas Teiresias, although blind, never fails to see clearly.

Aristotle states that tragic characters must be larger than life, just as the portrait-painter conveys a likeness:

> Since tragedy is a representation of men better than ourselves we must copy the good portrait-painters who, while rendering the distinctive form and making a likeness, yet paint people better than they are. It is the same with the poet. When representing people who are hot-tempered or lazy, or have other such traits of character, he should make them such, yet men of worth.
>
> (*Poetics*, xv, 15)

In other words, Greek tragic heroes are complex and neither perfectly virtuous nor entirely evil. They are generally the victim of a **tragic flaw**, which plunges them from a high station in life into misfortune. In *Oedipus*, the tragic flaw is the hero's *hubris* (grandiose pride), which convinces him of his ability to outwit fate. In attempting to avoid his fate rather than understand it, Oedipus inevitably brings it about. Once he comprehends what he has done, he undergoes a **catharsis** (literally an emotional "cleansing")—that is, he experiences fully his own responsibility for his actions and their consequences. He then works through his guilt and accepts the power of fate, which resolves the tragedy. The viewers of the play also experience a catharsis so that they, as well as the hero, gain insight into the human condition.

PAINTING AND SCULPTURE

In the fourth century B.C., the Greek interest in lifelike representation increased. Artists expanded the range of emotion, age, and character in their paintings and sculptures. With this expansion of types, the idealized male youth gave way to greater variety, and comic scenes appeared more frequently than before.

A Late Classical bell-krater of around 340 B.C. depicts the birth of Helen of Troy (figure **6.32**) in a humorous way. It shows a miniature nude Helen emerging like a movie starlet from a large egg as her mother and mortal father look on. She is no longer either a heroine of epic proportions or an ideal Classical figure.

If the Late Classical *Aphrodite of Knidos* (figure **6.33**) is compared with the *Spearbearer* (see figure 6.22), it is clear that the proportions have changed in the later work. Aphrodite is fleshier than Polykleitos's youth—her neck and waist are thicker—and her contrapposto (the shift at the waist) is slightly more pronounced. She stands by a *hydria* (water jar)

6.33 Praxiteles, *Aphrodite of Knidos*, c. 350 B.C. Marble, 6 ft. 8¾ in. (2.05 m) high. Vatican Museums, Rome.
According to the first-century A.D. Roman author Pliny the Elder, this statue was equally beautiful from all points of view and made Knidos famous. He relates the tale of a man who fell in love with the statue and embraced it. His act of passion was betrayed by a lustful stain left on the marble.

6.32 Caivano painter, *Birth of Helen*, red-figure bell-krater, from Campania, southern Italy, c. 340 B.C. National Museum, Naples.
According to Greek myth, Helen was the daughter of Zeus-disguised-as-a-swan and the mortal woman, Leda. The egg is thus the egg of a swan, hence its size. Leda's mortal husband was Tyndareus, whose stepdaughter was sought after by so many suitors that he feared the anger of those who would be rejected. Odysseus proposed that Tyndareus leave the decision to Helen, provided that all the suitors swore to avenge any affront to her chosen husband. They all agreed, and Helen picked Menelaus, the wealthy king of Sparta and Agamemnon's brother.

and grasps her garment, to cover her nudity as if suddenly aware that she is being observed.

Praxiteles was the first Greek artist who consistently portrayed the female nude. This particular example was rejected by the Greeks, who commissioned it, as being overly erotic and it was purchased instead by the Knidians, the inhabitants of the island of Knidos, in Ionia. They built a temple for the statue, which attracted many admirers. Some men were reported to have hidden in the precinct so that they could spend the night with the statue.

THE HELLENISTIC WORLD: 323 TO FIRST CENTURY B.C.

Alexander's untimely death at the age of about thirty-three left no obvious heir to rule his empire. At the beginning of the Hellenistic period, the empire was divided into three main areas by Alexander's generals: the Ptolemaic dynasty (which originated with Ptolemy I) ruled Egypt, the Seleucids (founded by Alexander's officer Seleucus I) ruled Persia, and Antigonus, called the One-Eyed, ruled Greece.

Throughout Greece, the *polis* gave way to kingship and small towns and cities became international urban centers. These benefited economically and were enriched culturally by thriving trade with the east, Africa, and Italy. Social divisions, ranging from royalty to an ever-increasing slave population, became more pronounced as the ideal of democracy faded. Women, on the other hand, especially in the upper classes, were accorded more social and economic freedom than they had enjoyed in Classical Athens.

In theater, tragedy ceased to be a popular form of entertainment. It was replaced by so-called New Comedy—usually light romances designed to distract audiences from the tensions of urban life.

Two main centers of Hellenistic culture were Alexandria, in Egypt, and Pergamon, on the west coast of modern Turkey. Alexandria was founded by Alexander the Great, after whom the city was named, and Pergamon adopted Classical styles and traditions. The latter city rose to power after its king, Attalos I (ruled 241–197 B.C.), vanquished the barbarian Gauls (in modern France and the Low Countries), who invaded in 238 B.C.

With an increase in literacy and developments in science, two huge libraries were established in Alexandria and Pergamon. The Pergamon library, rivaling that of Alexandria, housed some 200,000 texts written on calf-skin parchment ("pergamene paper"). In Alexandria, the Ptolemies encouraged scholars, scientists, physicians, and poets by building the Museum (Temple of the Muses), an institution dedicated to research. In conjunction with the Museum, Alexandria boasted the Great Library, which housed 700,000 papyrus manuscripts. The library's aim was to acquire every known Greek text.

MYSTERY CULTS

One source of Eastern influence in the Hellenistic world was the expansion of mystery cults. The Greeks had had mystery cults at Eleusis and Samothrace, as well as the cult of Dionysos, since the Bronze Age. In contrast to Olympian religion, however, these cults had a mystical flavor, practicing magic to protect against evil and performing secret rites. By the later fourth century B.C., aspects of Eastern religions began to infiltrate Greece.

Cults involving astrology came from Babylon, Zoroastrianism (see Chapter 2) came from Persia, and the pre-Greek belief in a Great Goddess began to be revived. The Egyptian mother-goddess, Isis, was worshipped first at Delos and later throughout the Mediterranean. Her role in the resurrection of Osiris (see Chapter 3) appealed to the new interest in life after death. The enormous attraction of immortality increased the power of such cults and later influenced the spread of early Christianity.

PHILOSOPHY IN THE HELLENISTIC PERIOD

Encouraged by wealthy and powerful rulers, Hellenistic philosophy flourished, although it has not exerted as strong an impact on Western thought as that of the Classical and Late Classical philosophers. Nevertheless, Hellenistic philosophers were influential later, especially during the Roman period. Terms used to describe Hellenistic schools of philosophy—Cynicism, Skepticism, Epicureanism, and Stoicism—live on in modern English nouns and adjectives. All denote ways of viewing human life.

The Cynics valued independence from desire and materialism, and they rejected religious and political institutions. In the view of the Cynics, traditional values of civilization were worthless. The most famous Cynic was Diogenes (*c.* 404–325 B.C.), who was known for public displays of vulgar behavior. He reportedly carried a lantern through the streets of Athens in search of an honest man. Today, we call someone a cynic if he or she tends to believe the worst about people, just as Diogenes thought he would never find the honest man.

The Skeptics questioned the basis for all conclusions, hence the English word "skeptical." They challenged the findings of science and prevailing philosophical ideas and argued that these disciplines could not furnish adequate explanations of reality. Because there is no certainty, according to the Skeptics, reality is relative and absolute judgments should be avoided.

In contrast to the Skeptics, the Stoics and the Epicureans did believe in certainty and were convinced of their respective approaches to life. Both were essentially materialists. The Stoics believed that universal reason, the *logos* (or "word" of God), determined the order of life. Thus, the ideal Stoic was disciplined and prepared to accept any fate. Epicureanism is named for Epicurus (341–271 B.C.), who advocated a calm mind, a healthy body, and a proper attitude toward the gods and death. Epicureans believed that sensory experience was superior to the intellect, that the gods were indifferent to humans, and that death was nothing more than a rearrangement of the body's atoms. As a result, since it is impossible to know the future, Epicureans devoted their lives to pleasure in the present.

HELLENISTIC POETRY

The main Hellenistic contributions to poetry were the **pastoral** (a poem dealing with the life and loves of shepherds) and the **idyll** (a short descriptive poem describing rural life). These poetic types were developed by Theocritus (*c.* 310–250 B.C.), a native of Syracuse, in Sicily, who wrote in hexameter verse (lines of six metrical feet). His pastorals describe the bucolic life and romances of rural dwellers, and his idylls create concise images of daily life and mythological tales. Theocritus's subject matter and poetic rhythms inspired the English Romantic poets in the eighteenth and nineteenth centuries (see Chapter 18).

In *Idyll* XI, entitled "The Cyclops," the one-eyed giant Polyphemus is a youth in love with the beautiful Galatea. Blinded by Odysseus (see Chapter 4), the Cyclops sits on a rock and finds consolation in music and song. Woefully aware of his ugly appearance, Polyphemus woos Galatea with his skill as a shepherd, feeding his sheep, making cheese, and producing the best milk in the land:

> O Galatea fair and white, white as curds in whey,
> Dapper as a lamb a-frisking, wanton as calf at play,
> And plump o' shape as ruddying grape, O why deny thy
>   lover?
>
> . . . .
>
> I've loved ye true; but Lord! to you my love as nothing is.
> O well I wot pretty maid, pretty maid, for why thou shun'st
>   me so,
> One long shag eyebrow ear to ear my forehead o'er doth go,
> And but one eye beneath doth lie, and the nose stands wide
>   on the lip;
> Yet be as I may, still this I say, I feed full a thousand sheep,
> And the milk to my hand's the best i' the land, and my
>   cheese 'tis plenty also;
> Come summer mild, come winter wild, my cheese-racks ever
>   o'erflow.
> And, for piping, none o' my kin hereby can pipe like my
>   piping,
> And of thee and me, dear sweet-apple, in one song oft I
>   sing,
> Often at dead of night.

(Theocritus, "The Cyclops")

In *Pastoral* I, the shepherd Thyrsis sings of Daphnis, another shepherd, who died of love. In the section cited here, Thyrsis complains that the wood nymphs ignored Daphnis:

> Country-song, sing country-song, *sweet Muses.*
> 'Tis Thyrsis sings, of Etna, and a rare sweet voice hath he.
> Where were ye, Nymphs, when Daphnis pined? ye Nymphs,
>   O where were ye?
>
> . . . .
>
> When Daphnis died the foxes wailed and the wolves they
>   wailed full sore,
> The lion from the greenwood wept when Daphnis was no
>   more.

(Theocritus, *Pastoral* I)

DEVELOPMENTS IN ARTISTIC STYLE

In the visual arts, the Hellenistic period brought about a further increase in the range of age, subject, and personality types. In Hellenistic sculpture and painting, figures move with increasing freedom as the space opens and expands. Hellenistic artists rejected Classical symmetry and created a greater variety of pose and gesture.

Compare, for example, the Hellenistic *Drunken Old Woman* (figure **6.34**) with the mid-second-century-B.C. *Aphrodite of Melos* (figure **6.35**). The former clutches a jug of wine and rolls her head backward in a stupor. Gone are all traces of Classical idealization, as wrinkles pattern the aged face. The figure evokes the belief in the Dionysian promise of immortality, which is indicated by the ivy (an attribute of the wine god) on the jug. The woman's drunken state

6.34 *above Drunken Old Woman*, late 3rd century B.C. Marble, 3 ft. (92 cm) high. Glyptothek, Munich.

6.35 *right Aphrodite of Melos*, *c.* 150 B.C. Marble, 6 ft. 8¼ in. (2.04 m) high. Louvre, Paris.

signifies the experience of ecstasy in the afterlife.

The *Aphrodite of Melos* retains idealized, although not Classical, form. Her youthful figure flows into an elegant S-shaped curve, and the smooth flesh merges gracefully into her garment. In contrast to the sense of weight conveyed by the old woman firmly planted on the ground, the Aphrodite swivels as if in continuous motion.

The Greek sculpture in which motion assumes its most powerful

emotional character is the Late Hellenistic *Laocoön Group* (figure **6.36**), which illustrates an event from the end of the Trojan War that is related in the *Odyssey*. Laocoön was a Trojan seer (prophet) who warned his fellow citizens not to admit the great wooden horse, which was filled with Greek soldiers, past the gates of Troy. When the gods sent huge serpents from the sea to devour Laocoön and his two sons, the Trojans concluded that Laocoön must be mistaken. They opened the gates to admit the horse, and the Greeks sacked Troy. In the statue, the curvilinear serpents weave among the human figures, strangling and biting them. In their struggle to escape, Laocoön and his sons echo the winding serpentine forms and grimace in pain.

In painting, as in sculpture, Hellenistic style increases formal movement as it turns away from Classical idealization. The wall painting depicting the centaur Chiron instructing Achilles on the lyre (figure **6.37**) shows the continuing taste for illusionism in the background architecture. Similarly, the use of shading, instead of line, to create form conveys the impression of the figures' three-dimensional volume. In the foreground, the rather uncomfortable-looking centaur tries to accommodate his horse part as he demonstrates on the strings of a lyre. Achilles does not conform to the proportional canon of Polykleitos, but his pose resembles that of the *Spearbearer* (see figure 6.22).

In accord with the large-scale political ambitions of rulers, Hellenistic architecture is generally monumental. One example of Hellenistic grandeur is the Great Altar at Pergamon, a section of which is illustrated in figure **6.38**. Constructed in the early second century B.C. under the ruler

6.36 *above* **Agesander, Athenodorus, and Polydorus of Rhodes,** *Laocoön Group*, **early 1st century** A.D. **Marble, 7 ft. 10½ in. (2.44 m) high. Vatican Museums, Rome.** Carved on the island of Rhodes, which was a major center of culture in the second century B.C., this sculpture disappeared in the fifth century A.D. and was rediscovered only in the sixteenth century. It was excavated in Rome and made a forceful impression on Michelangelo. The *Laocoön* influenced Western art and aesthetic theory for centuries to come.

6.37 *below* *Chiron Instructs Achilles in Playing the Lyre*, **from the Basilica, Herculaneum, 1st century** A.D. **Roman copy of a Hellenistic fresco. National Museum, Naples.**

6.38 North projection of the Pergamon Altar, *c.* 180/160 B.C. Marble, frieze 7 ft. 6½ in. (2.30 m) high. Pergamon Museum, Berlin.

6.39 Olympeium, Athens, reconstructed 2nd century B.C. Marble, 354 × 135 ft. (108 × 41.1 m); columns 55 ft. 5 in. (16.9 m) high.

Eumenes II (ruled 197–c. 160 B.C.), the altar celebrated the triumph of Greek civilization. Its vivid frieze, in which the Olympian gods battle the Titans, shares with the *Laocoön* a taste for violent struggle. The depiction of the battle was a metaphor for the recent defeat of the Gauls by the king of Pergamon, but it also alluded to the Greek victory over the Persians, which had remained in the cultural consciousness of Greece for centuries.

In temple architecture, too, scale increased and buildings became monumental. At the same time, the last of the three main Greek architectural Orders, the Corinthian, originally used only for interiors, now appeared on exterior columns. This more ornate Order had **foliate** (leaf-shaped) capitals, whose decorative qualities relieved the massive scale of Hellenistic temples.

In Athens, in the mid-second century B.C., the Seleucid ruler Antiochus IV (ruled 175–164 B.C.) commissioned the first use of the Corinthian Order in a large-scale building in the reconstruction of the Olympeium, a temple dedicated to Zeus. Originally a Doric temple built in the Archaic period (figure **6.39**), the surviving remains belong to a later reconstruction. The Olympeium today has only thirteen columns left, but even in its ruined state the monumentality of the temple is impressive.

Alexander's conquests bequeathed to the Hellenistic period a melting pot of cultural ideas and forms. Because of the new political climate in which kings held sway and democracies waned, the arts were used in the service of power. In 146 B.C., the Romans conquered Corinth and subordinated Greece to Roman rule. By 100 B.C., Greece was a province of Rome and in 86 B.C. the Romans sacked Athens. At the same time, however, Greek culture continued to exert an enormous influence on Rome and its vast empire, which are the subjects of the next chapter.

KEY TERMS

caryatid a supporting column carved to represent a woman; the male equivalent is an *atlantis* (plural *atlantes*).

catharsis "cleansing"; a term used by Aristotle to describe the emotional effect of a tragic drama on the audience.

colonnade a row of columns.

contrapposto a type of pose characterized by a twist at the waist.

deme a unit of local government.

dithyramb a type of lyric poem sung and accompanied by flute music.

falling action the means by which a complication in a literary work is unraveled and resolved.

foliate leaf-shaped.

foreshortened shown in perspective.

hubris arrogant grandiosity, often characterizing Greek tragic heroes.

idyll a short descriptive poem describing rural life.

illusionistic a type of representation in which objects appear real.

interval in music, a difference in pitch between two notes.

irony a literary device in which the implication of the words is the opposite of their literal meaning.

isocephaly the horizontal alignment of heads in a painting or sculpture.

mode in ancient music, an arrangement of notes forming a scale; Dorian mode: strong and military; Phrygian mode: passionate; Lydian mode: mournful; Mixolydian mode: elegiac.

monophonic consisting of a single line of music.

mosaic an image on a wall, ceiling, or floor created from small pieces of colored tile, glass, or stone.

octave in music, the interval between two notes of the same name, twelve semitones apart; in poetry, a stanza of eight lines.

ode a lyric poem.

onomatopoeic the use of words that sound like the objects to which they refer.

paradox a statement that seems to contradict common sense.

pastoral a poem dealing with the life and loves of shepherds.

program in art, a series of related images.

proportion the relation of one part to another and of parts to the whole in terms of scale.

resolution the outcome of a literary narrative.

rhetoric the art of eloquent argument.

tetrachord a series of four notes, with the first and last separated by the interval of a perfect fourth.

tragic flaw in theater, a characteristic of a hero that causes his or her downfall.

KEY QUESTIONS

1. Discuss the myths narrated in scenes on the Parthenon sculptures and their cultural meaning.
2. What theory of Empedocles prefigured Darwin's theory of evolution? What theory of Democritus prefigured atomic theory? Are these philosophers important because they are forerunners of modern thought or for other reasons?
3. What qualities did Plato wish to find in an ideal state (as outlined in his *Republic*)? Would his ideal state be a democracy?
4. What Classical ideals are seen in the *Oresteia*?
5. Compare two works of sculpture that show the differences between the Classical and Hellenistic ideals.

SUGGESTED READING

Bober, Phyllis Pray. *Art, Culture, and Cuisine. Ancient and Medieval Gastronomy*. Chicago and London: University of Chicago Press, 1999.
 ▶ A survey of feasts and menus from antiquity to the Middle Ages.

Carpenter, T. H. *Art and Myth in Ancient Greece*. London: Thames and Hudson, 1998.
 ▶ A general survey of Greek art and mythology.

Connolly, Peter, and Hazel Dodge. *The Ancient City*. Oxford and New York: Oxford University Press, 1998.
 ▶ Ancient architecture illustrated with clear, colorful reconstructions of ancient buildings in context.

Fox, Robin Lane. *Alexander the Great*. London: Allen Lane, 1973.
 ▶ A biography of Alexander the Great.

Hartnoll, Phyllis, *The Theater*. New York and London: Thames and Hudson, 1998.
 ▶ A brief history of the theater from Greek and Roman times to the present.

Kagan, Donald. *The Outbreak of the Peloponnesian War*. Ithaca, NY: Cornell University Press, 1994.
 ▶ A classic study of the causes of the Peloponnesian War.

——. *The Peloponnesian War*. New York: HarperCollins, 2003.
 ▶ A one-volume version of the author's standard four-volume study of the war.

Plato. *Apology*, in *Dialogues of Plato*, trans. B. Jowett. New York: Random House, 1932.
 ▶ Plato's account of Socrates' defense against the charge that he corrupted the youth of Athens.

Pomeroy, Sarah B. *Women in Hellenistic Egypt: From Alexander to Cleopatra*. New York: Schocken Books, 1988.
 ▶ An account of the role of women in the Hellenistic period.

Renault, Mary. *The Mask of Apollo*. New York: Longmans Green, 1966.
 ▶ A historical novel about an actor in the fourth century B.C.

——. *Fire from Heaven*. New York: Pantheon Books, 1969.
 ▶ A historical novel that brings to life Alexander the Great and his times.

Sophocles. *Oedipus the King*, trans. F. Storr. Loeb Library Edition. Cambridge, MA: Harvard University Press, 1981.
 ▶ Sophocles' play about the king of Thebes and his downfall, based on the myth that corresponds to Freud's account of the child's Oedipus Complex.

SUGGESTED FILMS

1939 *Trial and Death of Socrates* (in Italian), dir. Corrado d'Errico

1956 *Alexander the Great*, dir. Robert Rossen

1960 *Never on Sunday*, dir. Jules Dassin

1961 *Antigone*, dir. George Tzavellas

1962 *300 Spartans*, dir. Rudolpph Maté

1970 *Socrates*, dir. Roberto Rossellini

2004 *Alexander*, dir. Oliver Stone

7 Ancient Rome

"*Arms I sing and the man who first from the coasts of Troy, exiled by fate, came to Italy and Lavinian shores; much buffeted on sea and land by violence from above, through cruel Juno's unforgiving wrath, and much enduring in war also, till he should build a city and bring his gods to Latium; whence came the Latin race, the lords of Alba, and the walls of lofty Rome.*"

(VIRGIL, *Aeneid* BK. 1, LINES 1–7)

The early history of Rome is complex. Originally a village composed of huts by the River Tiber, Rome grew into a powerful city. Beginning in the Hellenistic period, Rome began its rise, and by the second century A.D. it had become a huge empire (see map 7.4, p. 163). The Roman Empire lasted for around five hundred years and stretched from Britain in the north to northern Africa and Egypt in the south, and from western Europe as far east as Mesopotamia, Assyria, and Armenia (in southern Russia). Because of its size and power, Rome was able to impose its language (Latin) on conquered territories—most of western Europe had no writing system until the Roman conquest in the first century A.D. At the same time, Rome was a vast melting pot; both the city and the empire absorbed influences from cultures throughout the Mediterranean region and beyond.

Several early kings of Rome—including the last three—were Etruscans, a people native to the Italian peninsula. They ruled from the ninth century B.C. until 509 B.C., a period corresponding to the evolution of Greece from the Dark Age through the Archaic era. In 509 B.C. Rome overthrew the last Etruscan king and became a republic, inspired in part by the democratic ideals of the Greek polis. The Roman Republic lasted until 27 B.C., when Octavian (63 B.C.–A.D. 14) came to power. Four years later, he changed his name to Augustus and became the first Roman emperor. The empire came to an end in A.D. 476, when barbarian tribes (Goths) from the north overran the city of Rome.

Key Topics

TIMELINE	ETRUSCAN CIVILIZATION 1000–509 B.C.	ROMAN REPUBLIC 509–27 B.C.	ROMAN EMPIRE 31 B.C.–A.D. 476
HISTORY AND CULTURE	Villanovan culture, 1000 B.C. Kings rule Etruria Powerful trading nation, 8th century B.C. Large naval fleet Advanced urban planning Irrigation Aristocratic, fashion-conscious, literate society Greek influence in art and architecture Improved status of women	Influence of Greek *polis* Latin language Ruled by senate and assembly of patricians Law of the Twelve Tables, *c.* 450 B.C. *Paterfamilias* and piety Punic Wars Caesar and the Gallic Wars, 58 B.C.: *Commentaries* Caesar crosses the Rubicon River, 49 B.C. Caesar killed, 44 B.C.	Octavian becomes Augustus, 27 B.C. *Pax Romana*: Rome "head of the world" (*caput mundi*) Latin language Rome falls to the Goths, A.D. 476
RELIGION AND MYTH	Greek gods given Etruscan names Belief in material afterlife Burials in the form of houses Borrowed Greek myths	Lares and Penates—household gods Roman names for Greek gods *Pontifex maximus* Ancestor worship	Founding myths: Aeneas, Romulus and Remus
ART	Bronze mirrors used by women *Achilles Ambushes Troilus, c.* 540 B.C. Cerveteri sarcophagus, *c.* 520 B.C. *Capitoline Wolf, c.* 500 B.C. Bronze hoplite, *c.* 450 B.C.	Sarcophagus of Lucius Cornelius Scipio Barbatus, *c.* 200 B.C. *Street Musicians* mosaic, *c.* 100 B.C. Wall-painting, Villa of the Mysteries, *c.* 60 B.C.	*Ara Pacis Augustae*, 13–9 B.C. Boscotrecase Villa wall-painting, *c.* 12 B.C. Patrician with two portrait heads, 1st century A.D. *Augustus of Prima Porta*, early 1st century A.D. *Gemma Augustea, c.* A.D. 10 Flavian woman as Venus, late 1st century A.D. Equestrian portrait of Marcus Aurelius, A.D. 164–166 Head of Constantine's colossal statue, A.D. 313
ARCHITECTURE	Temple of Apollo, Veii, *c.* 500 B.C. *Necropoleis* (cities of the dead)	Roman arches Appian Way, 312 B.C. Temple of Portunus, late 2nd century B.C. Pont du Gard, near Nîmes, late 1st century B.C. Roman forum Domestic buildings: villas and *insulae*	Colosseum, *c.* A.D. 72–80 Arch of Titus, *c.* A.D. 81 Trajan's Column, A.D. 113 Basilica Ulpia Pantheon, A.D. 125–128 Imperial forums
LITERATURE	Language not translated	Catullus (*c.* 84–*c.* 54 B.C.), poetry Virgil (70–19 B.C.), *Aeneid; Georgics; Eclogues* Horace (65–8 B.C.), lyric odes	Livy (59 B.C.–A.D. 17), *The History of Rome* Ovid (43 B.C.–A.D. 17), *Metamorphoses; Art of Love* Petronius (d. A.D. 65), *Satyricon* Tacitus (*c.* A.D. 56–120), *Annals; Histories* Juvenal (*c.* A.D. 55/60–after 127), *Satires* Suetonius (*c.* A.D. 69–after 122), *The Twelve Caesars*
THEATER		Comedy: actors masked Plautus (*c.* 250–184 B.C.), comedies Terence (*c.* 195–159 B.C.), comedies	
PHILOSOPHY, AND RHETORIC	Lost	Cicero (106–43 B.C.) Lucretius (98–*c.* 55 B.C.), *On the Nature of Things*	Marcus Aurelius (ruled A.D. 161–180), *Meditations* Seneca (*c.* 4 B.C.–A.D. 65), *Letters*, tragedies
MUSIC	No notation Music at dinner Music while cooking	Pipes (*auloi*), tambourines, cymbals	

MYTHS OF THE FOUNDING OF ROME

This chapter opens with the first seven lines of the *Aeneid*, an epic poem written by Virgil (70–19 B.C.). They allude to the two origin myths of Roman culture: Greek and native Italic. The Greek myth focuses on the tradition of Aeneas, the hero of the *Aeneid*, who linked Rome to the Homeric heroes and the gods. The Italic myth attributes the founding of Rome to Romulus and Remus and emphasizes the period of the republic.

VIRGIL'S *AENEID*

Virgil wrote the *Aeneid* to celebrate Rome's origins and to locate them within the Greek heroic tradition. Composed in hexameter verse (its lines have six metric feet) like Homer's *Iliad* and *Odyssey*, the *Aeneid* traces the long journey of the Trojan hero Aeneas, the "man" of whom Virgil sings. Virgil explains that he "sings arms and the man" to evoke the ancient oral traditions of the Homeric epics and link them with the founding of Rome.

The *Aeneid* begins with the end of the Trojan War and Aeneas's escape from the burning city of Troy after its sack by the Greeks. He carries his aged father, Anchises, and leads his young son, Ascanius, from the ravaged city (figure **7.1**). The fugitives carry away statues of the household gods, the **Lares and Penates**—spirits who protected Roman farms and homes. Romans worshipped these gods at certain times of year, at wedding festivals, and at meals. In Roman houses, statues of the Lares and Penates were placed over the hearth, where a fire burned steadily as a sign of family continuity from one generation to the next.

Like Odysseus, who also embarks on a journey after the Trojan War, Aeneas travels great distances and has many adventures before reaching his destination. Virgil relates that Aeneas arrives in Italy, where his descendants found Rome. His wife, Creusa, has died, but her shade (ghost) appears to Aeneas and informs him that a great destiny awaits him. The notion of divine destiny, like Rome's mythic descent from the gods, is a main theme of the *Aeneid*.

Aeneas was himself of divine origin: his mother was the goddess Venus. His father, the mortal Anchises, was a cousin of King Priam of Troy. The myth of Aeneas's parentage thus provided Rome with the desired link to the gods, and his heroic journey with a heritage of epic proportions.

Aeneas sets sail for Sicily, but a storm unleashed by the goddess Juno forces him off course to the northern coast of Africa (modern Libya). There, he and his men are welcomed by Dido, the Phoenician queen of the newly founded city of Carthage. Dido falls in love with Aeneas, who relates his adventures to her, just as Odysseus had described his adventures to the princess Nausicaa after being shipwrecked on her

7.1 Copy of a statue group of Aeneas, Ascanius, and Anchises.
The original group stood in the Roman forum of Augustus. Aeneas carries a small figure of Anchises, gazes back on his past as Troy burns, but strides forward toward his future destiny. Ascanius wears a cap from Phrygia, a civilization of ancient Anatolia; his elaborate costume, including the Phrygian cap, denotes the eastern locale of Troy.

father's island. Both Homer and Virgil use a similar literary device—that of making the hero rather than the author seem to be the narrator.

Like Nausicaa, Dido tries to keep the man she loves at her court with an offer of marriage. But Jupiter reminds Aeneas of his destiny and orders him to cut short his dalliance with Dido. Dido kills herself in despair as Aeneas sails from Carthage. In Book VI of the *Aeneid*, Aeneas returns to Italy—to Cumae, south of Rome. There he meets the Cumaean Sibyl, one of the female oracles who foretold the future in antiquity. She reveals Aeneas's destiny, which, like that of Gilgamesh (see Chapter 2), is to found a city. Then she escorts Aeneas to the Underworld, where he meets his father's shade. Anchises introduces his son to the future heroes of Roman history and describes Rome's destiny:

> Others, I doubt not, shall beat out the breathing bronze with softer lines; shall from marble draw forth the features of life; shall plead their causes better; with the rod shall trace the paths of heaven and tell the rising of the stars: remember thou, O Roman, to rule the nations with thy sway—these shall be thine arts—to crown Peace with Law, to spare the humbled, and to tame in war the proud!
>
> (*Aeneid*, Bk. VI, lines 847–853)

The "others" are Greeks. They are poets and philosophers, and their artists cast in bronze and carve in marble lifelike figures that seem to breathe. But the Romans will rule an empire, and their rule will be just, for they will "crown Peace with Law."

Not only is Rome descended from the gods and destined to command a mighty empire, therefore, but it will also gain legitimacy by imposing the rule of law.

In Book VII, Aeneas reaches Latium (where Latin was spoken), and marries Lavinia, the daughter of the king. A period of warfare follows (Books VIII–XI), until the gods preside over a truce between the Trojans and the Latins. In the final book (Book XII), Aeneas kills the local Latin king and founds the city of Lavinium (modern Pratica di Mare, on the west coast of Italy).

Ascanius assists his father in the struggle against the Latins. He is credited in Roman legend with being the founder and first king of Alba Longa, the city that preceded Rome—the "lords of Alba [Longa]" mentioned by Virgil were considered the descendants of Ascanius.

ROMULUS AND REMUS

The second, native Italic (non-Greek) myth deals directly with the founding of Rome, traditionally dated April 21, 753 B.C. The last king of Alba Longa had usurped power from the rightful king, Numitor, and sent Numitor's daughter, Rhea Silvia, to live with the Vestal Virgins, guardians of the hearth. In so doing, the king wanted to ensure that Numitor would have no descendants to reclaim Rome. Rhea Silvia would devote her life to keeping alive the fire in the temple of Vesta and preparing cakes for religious festivals. However, she is impregnated by Mars and gives birth to twin sons, Romulus and Remus. The role of the war god in creating the ancestry of Rome foreshadows the power of the Roman armies and the vast extent of their conquests. Numitor's usurper orders that the twins be killed, but, instead, the executioner abandons them on the banks of the Tiber. A she-wolf rescues Romulus and Remus, nursing them until, like the Greek king Oedipus, they are found and reared by a shepherd couple.

When Romulus and Remus grow up, they overthrow the usurper and restore Numitor to the throne. They decide to found a new city and mark out its boundaries on the Palatine (one of Rome's seven hills; see Box). They agree that one of them will rule the new city and that the choice will depend on an omen read from the flights of birds. But, in an act of arrogance, Remus shows contempt for his brother by jumping over the newly plowed foundations of the city walls. In revenge, Romulus kills Remus.

Society and Culture

The Seven Hills of Rome

Seven hills up to 150 feet (45 m) high stand near the River Tiber (map **7.1**). Rome's first settlement was on the Palatine, where Augustus, the first Roman emperor, built his house. Opposite the Palatine were the Quirinal and Viminal Hills. The remaining four are the Aventine, Capitoline, Caelian, and Esquiline.

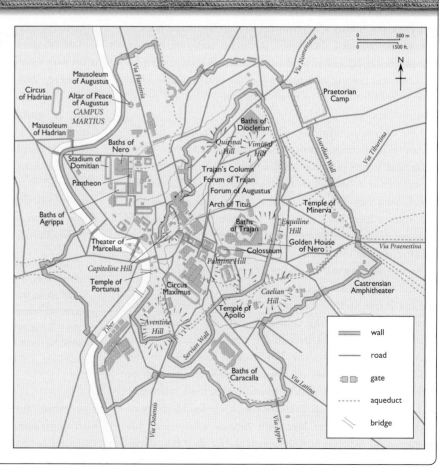

Map 7.1 Ancient Rome.

For Romans, the story of Romulus and Remus, like the epic account of Aeneas, reinforced a sense of destiny and divine lineage. Such founding myths would continue to define the self-image of Rome throughout its history. They connected Rome to the heroic Greek past and made its imperial expansion appear to have been decreed by the gods. As with Virgil's *Aeneid*, these ideas influenced the art, literature, and politics of both the republic and the empire.

The remainder of this chapter is divided into three historical periods: Etruscan civilization (ninth century to 509 B.C.), the Roman Republic (509–27 B.C.), and the Roman Empire (31 B.C.–A.D. 476).

THE ETRUSCANS: NINTH CENTURY TO 509 B.C.

The Etruscans inhabited most of the Italian peninsula between Florence and Rome (map **7.2**, p. 148). The region is known as Etruria, or Tuscany, after the Roman terms *Tusci* and *Etrusci*, designating the Etruscans. The ancestors of the Etruscans belonged to the Villanovan Iron Age culture, which flourished around 1000 B.C. Named after the town of Villanova, near Bologna, in northern Italy, this culture produced the earliest known evidence of Etruscan civilization. Archaeologists have discovered Villanovan burials of both men and women dating from as early as the ninth century B.C. These burials contained valuable personal possessions, including armor, elaborate jewelry, bronze mirrors, and everyday household objects. Such works reflect the high level of Etruscan craftsmanship and indicate a belief in a material afterlife.

From the eighth century B.C., Etruria became a powerful nation with a large naval fleet. Natural resources of iron ore, silver, and copper made Etruria an important center of trade in the Mediterranean. Abundant forests in the region provided wood for shipbuilding and houses, as well as for processing iron ore into metal. The Etruscans were pioneers in urban planning and skilled in augury (the ability to foretell the future from natural phenomena, such as the flights of birds, animals' entrails, and the weather).

Etruscan civilization was known in the Mediterranean world for its aristocratic taste. People enjoyed the cultural benefits of leisure time and were quite fashion-conscious. Little is known of Etruscan theater or music, but the Romans described their modes of entertainment. According to Roman accounts, the Etruscans were skilled dancers and cooked their meals to music. Etruscan wall-paintings show banquets with diners being entertained by dancers, musicians, and jugglers. They also depict sports and games.

GREECE AND THE ETRUSCANS

Etruscan civilization was influenced by Greek culture. The Etruscans adopted the names of the Greek gods and illustrated Greek myths. They borrowed elements of Greek architecture and sculpture, and imported thousands of Greek vases. The Etruscans also used the Greek alphabet, but their language was different from any other in their time or ours. They were literate, but their literature has not survived. As a result, much of what we know about the Etruscans comes from accounts by Greek and Roman writers.

The bronze statuette of a hoplite (figure **7.2**) shows the influence of Greek art and culture on the Etruscans as well as the evolution of an individual Etruscan style. Although the aristocratic hoplite originated in the Greek Archaic period, this figure wears tight-fitting Etruscan armor and a large helmet. It was made in around 450 B.C., which corresponds to the Greek Classical period. But the distinctively Etruscan character of the hoplite's slim proportions and flat surface patterns have more in common with Archaic than with Classical style. The lively, energetic stride that creates the impression of a warrior advancing into battle is typical of Etruscan sculpture. In addition, the delicate form reflects the skill of Etruscan artists in casting bronze.

7.2 **Statuette of a hoplite,** *c.* 450 B.C. Bronze. Archaeological Museum, Florence.

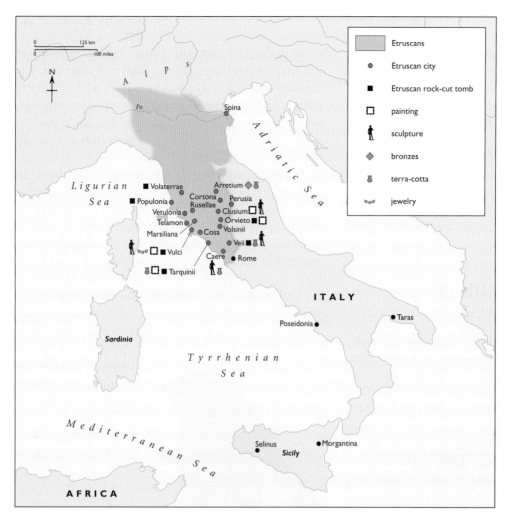

Map 7.2 Etruscan Italy, *c.* 500 B.C.

Legend:
- Etruscans
- ● Etruscan city
- ■ Etruscan rock-cut tomb
- □ painting
- sculpture
- ◆ bronzes
- terra-cotta
- jewelry

In temple architecture as in sculpture, the Etruscans developed their own forms but borrowed certain features from Greece. The favorite Etruscan building materials, in contrast to the Greek preference for marble, were wood, terra-cotta, and **tufa** (a soft, easily workable, volcanic rock that dries when exposed to the air). Figure **7.3** shows a reconstructed Etruscan temple dedicated to Apollo at Veii, northeast of Rome. The front porch (*pronaos*) has **Tuscan columns**, which are a form of Doric to which a round base has been added. The *pronaos* leads into the *cella* (the Roman equivalent of the Greek *naos*), which housed the cult statue. Unlike Greek temples, Etruscan ones are accessible only by a narrow flight of steps at the front.

The Veii temple stands on a raised platform (the **podium**), rather than at the top of steps

7.3 Reconstructed model of the temple of Apollo, Veii, Italy, *c.* 500 B.C.
The reconstruction is based on descriptions of Etruscan temples by the Roman architect Vitruvius (30 B.C.–A.D. 14). His treatise on architecture was written, like the *Aeneid*, in Augustan Rome.

that continue around the building and form a base, as in Greek temples. It has a broader, more gradually sloping roof than was found in Greece. Terra-cotta statues, some representing Greek gods in lively poses, were placed on the roof—a distinctive Etruscan practice not found in Greece.

ETRUSCAN WOMEN: THE ENVY OF ATHENIAN WOMEN

The aristocratic character of Etruscan society is related to the elevated position of women compared with Greece, especially Athens. In contrast to Athenian women, Etruscan women went out in public with their husbands and could attend theatrical performances, sporting events, and religious festivals. In art, scenes show women performing as athletes.

The attention to fashion among Etruscan women is indicated by the many bronze mirrors that have been excavated exclusively from female graves. Etruscan mirrors are typically decorated with mythological scenes, and the fact that they are inscribed with texts indicates that the women who used them could read (Figure **7.4**).

Because women went out in public, they wore mantles over their shirt-like *chitons*, as well as hats, boots, and elaborate jewelry. In the early periods of Etruscan history, women wore long braids tied with decorative clasps, often reaching to their feet. In the fifth century B.C., their shoes had gold laces and were elevated with wooden soles attached by hinges. To the dismay of Greek men, Etruscan footwear was particularly admired by Athenian women.

Literary accounts by Greek men confirm that they were offended by the fashionable dress and luxurious tastes of Etruscan women. For example, a fourth-century-B.C. Greek Sophist, Theopompus of Chios (active *c.* 380 B.C.), described Etruscan women as shamefully loose, lustful, given to appearing nude in public, and obsessed with opulence. The entire culture, he asserted, tolerated improper heterosexual and homosexual behavior. At the same time, however, Theopompus admitted that their attention to physical appearance made the Etruscans pleasing to look at, and he noted with amazement that Etruscans even frequented barber shops.

One distinctive way in which Etruscans improved their appearance was with the most advanced dental care of the time. From the seventh century B.C., Etruscans made dental bridges and dentures attached with gold wires to the jaw bone. (These are still studied by modern dentistry students.) False teeth were made of human teeth and, in at least one case, the tooth of an ox. These skills impressed the Romans, who themselves adopted dental care. In 450 B.C., Rome forbade burying the dead with gold in their teeth.

ETRUSCAN FUNERARY ART

Much of what is known about the Etruscans comes from their funerary art. They believed that demons escorted the dead to the Underworld and that the afterlife was a material one. In the Villanovan period, small funerary urns were designed to resemble houses. Later, much larger tombs were built in the form of houses and equipped with household furniture made of stone. Objects of everyday use, including mirrors and jewelry for women, armor for men, and toys for children, were buried with the deceased. Tombs were arranged in groups that resembled cities. These **necropoleis** ("cities of the dead")—at Cerveteri, Tarquinia, and elsewhere—resemble the large-scale Etruscan architecture that no longer exists.

7.4a Etruscan mirror with Bellerophon and the Chimera, 4th century B.C. Bronze, 9 in. (22.8 cm) high. The Metropolitan Museum of Art, New York.

7.4b Diagram of mirror.
The delicate engraving on this mirror shows the Greek hero Bellerophon riding the winged horse, Pegasus, and thrusting his spear into the upturned lion head of the monstrous chimera. The chimera's goat head has already been killed, but its snake part is unaware of the impending attack. The lion body is female, as indicated by the udders, which is an Etruscan element. Bellerophon's flowing hair, the lion's mane, the elaborate wings of Pegasus, and the sharp diagonals create the lively forms typical of Etruscan art. At the back, a single duck surrounded by foliage strolls by, reflecting the Etruscan interest in landscape.

7.5 *Achilles Ambushes Troilus*, **Tomb of the Bulls, Tarquinia, Italy,** *c.* **540** B.C. **Fresco.**
Troilus was a son of the Trojan king, Priam. In this scene, Troilus stops his horse at a date-palm tree. Achilles hides behind a large fountain, preparing to ambush and kill Troilus. Both Achilles and the horse are portrayed in a lively manner; the horse is enlarged, which compresses the figure of Troilus. This disregard for naturalistic proportions, together with the patterned fountain and stylized trees, is typical of Etruscan style in the sixth century B.C.

Tomb interiors were decorated with reliefs or paintings. Such images, especially in the sixth century B.C., typically illustrated aristocratic Etruscan banquets or Greek myths. The oldest excavated tomb site is at Tarquinia, northwest of Rome. There, in the Tomb of the Bulls, the rear interior wall is painted with a scene from the Trojan War (figure **7.5**). In Etruscan tomb paintings of banquets, diners recline on couches according to Greek custom. But unlike the Greeks, Etruscan husbands and wives dined together. This custom is reflected in the distinctive Etruscan ash-urns with sculptures of the deceased on the lid (figure **7.6**).

THE END OF ETRUSCAN RULE

Etruscan kings ruled Rome until 509 B.C., when Tarquin the Proud (Tarquinius Superbus) was expelled and a constitutional republic was established. Over the next two hundred years, Rome gradually assimilated elements of Etruscan culture, a process that was completed by the end of the first century B.C. Nevertheless, during the nearly five hundred years of republic and another five hundred years of empire, Etruscan ideas and art continued to influence Roman civilization. The Etruscans taught the Romans techniques of reading omens, engineering, and irrigation. They also provided a bridge between Roman and Greek culture by importing vases, borrowing architectural forms, and adopting the names of Greek gods and the Greek alphabet. In addition, according to literary sources, the Roman public theater traditions and gladiatorial combats were imported from Etruria.

7.6 Sarcophagus, from Cerveteri, *c.* **520** B.C. **Terra-cotta, 6 ft. 7 in. (2 m) long. Museo Nazionale di Villa Giulia, Rome.**
Etruscans cremated their dead and placed the ashes in urns of various sizes. Wealthier people commissioned the largest urns, most of which represented the deceased on the lid. As if to deny the fact of death, the Etruscans show the deceased couple very much alive. In this example, they share a blanket and recline on a dining couch. They seem engaged in lively conversation, an impression enhanced by the animated gestures, and stylized patterns in the hair and feet. Both husband and wife have Archaic smiles, which enliven the figures and reflect Greek influence.

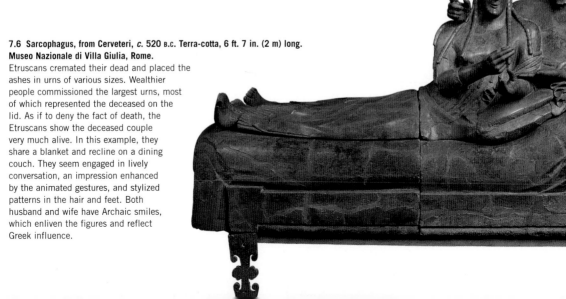

THE ROMAN REPUBLIC: 509–27 B.C.

The geographical position of Rome (map **7.3**)—at a crossroads of trade between the Mediterranean, the Greek settlements in Sicily (Magna Graecia), and the Etruscans—proved commercially and politically advantageous in the coming centuries. What began as a small village on the banks of the Tiber grew into the capital of a vast empire (figure **7.7**). By the late republic, the population of Rome had grown to around one million, international trade was thriving, and a large number of people had grown wealthy through trade and commerce. Grains were imported from Africa, and oil from Spain. Generally these were shipped in large Greek amphorae, reflecting Rome's commercial ties with Greece and other Mediterranean regions. Wine came from Campania, a fertile area in the south of the Italian peninsula, where many prosperous Romans had country houses.

7.7 *Capitoline Wolf*, *c.* 500 B.C. Bronze, 33½ in. (85.1 cm) high. Capitoline Museum, Rome.
The Italic legend of Rome's founding inspired the image of the she-wolf nursing Romulus and Remus. This became the symbol of Rome and it remains so today. During the republic and the empire, other versions of the subject were exhibited on the Capitoline Hill, which also housed a live wolf. In this particular statue, the wolf is an original Etruscan bronze guardian figure, but the twins were added during the Renaissance. Nevertheless, the twins were also added in antiquity, as is evident from Roman coins.

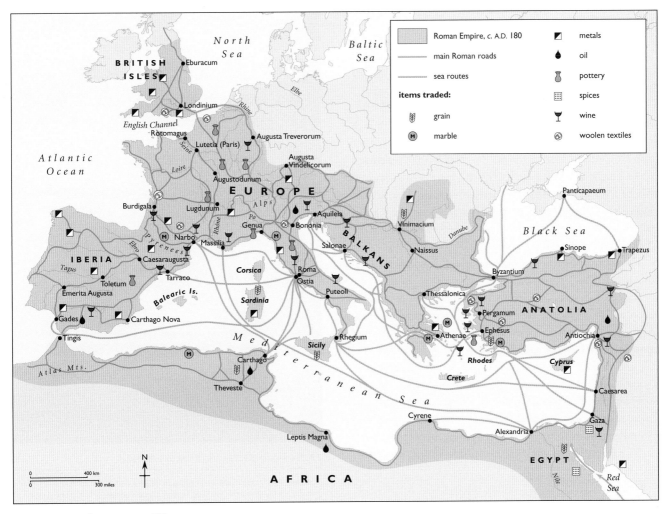

Map 7.3 Roman trade routes, *c.* A.D. **200.**

CHRONOLOGY AND HISTORY

The traditional date of Rome's founding is 753 B.C., but it remained a small village until the late sixth century B.C., when Etruscan rule transformed it into a great city. After the ousting of the last Etruscan king in 509 B.C., Rome established a republic comparable to the oligarchies in some of the Greek city-states.

The political divisions of the Roman Republic were based largely on the class structure of Roman society. The two main governing bodies were the aristocratic, patrician senate (*senatus*) and the plebeians, who made up the popular assembly of citizens (*comitia centuriata*). Two patrician magistrates (later called consuls) were elected each year (up to around 300 B.C.) by male citizens. Most of the power, however, lay with the senate, which had grown to three hundred members by the third century B.C. A senator indicated his rank by wearing a white toga (an Etruscan style) with a purple band.

The senate was located in the **forum**, originally an open market area and public meeting-place derived from the Greek *agora* (see Chapter 5). Under the Etruscans, the forum contained the king's palace and the temple of the Vestal Virgins. During the republic, however, the forum expanded. It became a political center, where citizens gathered to hear announcements from the senate. They worshiped in shrines and temples located in the forum and did their marketing in the shops. During the empire, the number of forums increased as each emperor built a new one in his own name to glorify himself and the power of Rome.

Around 450 B.C. Rome issued the Law of the Twelve Tables, which granted all citizens equal rights before the law, although it prohibited marriage between patricians and plebeians. Now known only from later fragments, the Twelve Tables included certain democratic features of Greek law, but the language and style of legal thought were distinctively Roman. The Roman emphasis on the rule of law and its imposition on Roman society—and later on all parts of its empire—were part of the sense of destiny described by Virgil.

The governing patricians were conceived of as fathers of the Roman "family." Patricians were expected to oversee the welfare of the state, in return for which they would be accorded due respect by the plebeians. This paternalistic view of politics mirrored the view of the family. In the Roman family, the father—the *paterfamilias*—ruled and protected his wife and children, and they, like the plebeians, owed him their loyalty. The Romans termed this devotion *pietas* (roughly meaning "piety" or "a sense of duty"), which was considered an essential virtue and a central theme of Roman life. *Pietas* is a main theme of the *Aeneid*, for Aeneas must follow his destiny out of respect for the gods and his father—hence his epithet, *pius Aeneas*.

A third social class arose during the republic. It was made up of families of *equites* (knights, or horsemen), who were wealthy enough to own horses. As part of the Roman cavalry, the *equites* were important to the army, and, as their power increased, they demanded more rights. From the early second century B.C., the *equites* were a class with a high economic and political status, second only to the senatorial class. However, their military function was phased out in favor of more expert horsemen. Despite the social stratification, in 90 and 88 B.C. the senate enacted legislation granting equal rights and citizenship to every free man in Italy.

The history of Rome's rise from a small settlement to a world power is one of continual warfare and conquest. In 390 B.C., Rome was attacked by Gauls, a northern tribe that eventually settled in the area that became modern France. In response, Rome built tufa walls around the city to improve its defense. Figure **7.8** shows a wall constructed during the republic of ashlar tufa blocks, each about 18 inches (45 cm) high. Cut into the wall is a round arch (figure **7.9**), a structural system first devised in ancient Babylon (see Chapter 2), used in the Hellenistic period, and developed by the Romans for many types of architectural construction. In this case, the arch

7.8 Santa Maria di Falleri gate, Rome, 241–200 B.C.
The little head above the keystone may be that of Janus, the Roman god of gateways. His double face (one in the front and one in the back of his head) permitted him to watch travelers as they came and went. It is from Janus that we call the first month of the year "January," when we look forward to the New Year and back over the past year.

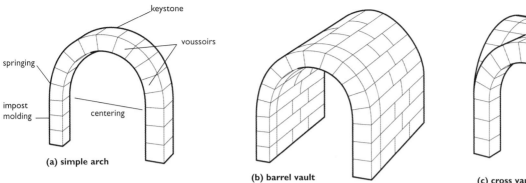

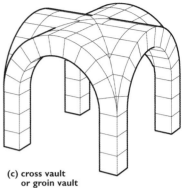

(a) simple arch

(b) barrel vault

(c) cross vault or groin vault

7.9 Roman arch construction.

The simple arch (a) is composed of wedge-shaped stones (**voussoirs**), which seem to spring upward from the **impost** molding to form the curve of the arch. They are held in place at the center by the **keystone**. The extension of the simple arch through space creates the **barrel vault** (b), and two intersecting barrel vaults create a **cross-vault** (also called a **groin vault**) (c). When a simple arch is rotated, the result is a **dome**, which in Rome rested on a round supporting structure called a **drum** (d). In the round arch, the weight is transferred from the keystone outward and downward to the **springing** points, which push outward on the piers. The **centering** holds each stone in place while the arch is being completed and makes it possible to cap large interiors with domes. Such techniques reflect the Roman interest in the utilitarian use of space in contrast to the Greek emphasis on the exterior appearance of its architecture.

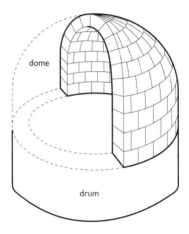

(d) dome on a drum

spans a road, one of many built by the Romans—hence the popular expression, "All roads lead to Rome."

Roads were one of the most important features of ancient Rome. They linked different parts of the empire, making trade and travel relatively easy and encouraging cultural unity. The most famous of the roads leading to Rome is the Appian Way (figure **7.10**), which was constructed in 312 B.C.

7.10 The Appian Way, constructed 312 B.C.

7.11 Pont du Gard, over the Gardon River, near Nîmes, France, late 1st century B.C. Stone, 162 ft. (49.38 m) high, 883 ft. (269 m) long.
Aqueducts served the combined purpose of transporting water over long distances and providing a bridge for travel. The Pont du Gard, made of large stones assembled without mortar, was designed to carry water through a pipe, or channel, at the top. Located 13 miles (21 km) from Nîmes, in the south of France, the Pont du Gard is one of many surviving aqueducts built outside Rome.

By the end of the fourth century B.C., Rome had developed sophisticated engineering techniques that made possible not only an elaborate system of roads, but also impressive **aqueducts** (figure **7.11**) that brought water to homes and public baths. The earliest aqueduct, which carried water to Rome from a spring over 7 miles (11.3 km) away, the Aqua Appia, was built on the Appian Way. Eleven aqueducts were built between 312 B.C. and A.D. 226, the longest being 59 miles (95 km) long. The Segovia aqueduct in Spain, still functioning today, is built of around 20,400 stone blocks.

In the course of the fourth century B.C., Rome took control of the Latin League, a group of settlements allied against the Greeks and the Etruscans. Rome later conquered the Greek area of southern Italy (called Magna Graecia) and, by 275 B.C., controlled all of Italy south of the Po valley.

THE PUNIC WARS

During the second and third centuries B.C., Rome fought three wars against Carthage, which was a major naval power and controlled trade throughout the western Mediterranean. These were called the Punic Wars, after *Poeni*, meaning "Phoenicians,"

people from the Arabian peninsula who had settled in parts of northwest Africa. The first war (264–241 B.C.) was a struggle for control of Sicily, which Rome feared it would lose to the Carthaginian Empire. In the second war (219–202 B.C.), Rome aimed to prevent Carthage from dominating Spain. The Carthaginian general Hannibal (247–183 B.C.) invaded the Italian peninsula from Spain and reportedly led a herd of elephants over the Alps. But Rome defeated Hannibal and took control of parts of Spain.

Rome's leading orator (public speaker), Marcus Porcius Cato, known as Cato the Censor (234–149 B.C.), fought in the second Punic War. He was elected censor in 184 B.C.; as censor he devoted himself to a program of moral reform among the aristocracy and advocated conservative values. Cato's writings, some of which survive, as well as his public speeches, urged Rome to return to a simpler, agricultural way of life. Cato visited Carthage after the war and was impressed by its prosperity. He believed that the city still posed a serious threat to Rome's independence.

Cato's declaration *Carthago delenda est* ("Carthage must be destroyed") was fulfilled when Rome defeated and sacked Carthage at the end of the third Punic War (149–146 B.C.). With the threat of Carthage removed, Rome stepped into the power vacuum left by the death of Alexander the Great in 323 B.C., and by 129 B.C., it controlled provinces in the eastern Mediterranean, Macedonia, and parts of western Asia. Internal power struggles and civil wars had marked much of the first century B.C. For the next hundred years, Rome permitted temporary dictatorships as a means of dealing with political crises. One of the final contenders was the Roman patrician general Gaius Julius Caesar (100–44 B.C.).

JULIUS CAESAR

In 58 B.C., Julius Caesar launched a series of conquests in western Europe against the Gauls and Goths that took Roman culture and the Latin language as far north as Britain. He memorialized his military campaigns in his *Commentaries on the Gallic War*, which describe life in the Roman army in a matter-of-fact style and offer detailed, sometimes entertaining, accounts of the peoples he conquered.

Caesar writes in the third person, creating an impression of objectivity. For example, after a difficult, stormy crossing of the English Channel, he describes how the Britons fought with chariots:

> First of all they drive in all directions and hurl missiles, and so by the mere terror that the teams inspire and by the noise of the wheels they generally throw ranks into confusion. When they have worked their way in between the troops of cavalry, they leap down from the chariots and fight on foot . . . Thus they show in action the mobility of cavalry and the stability of infantry.
>
> *(Gallic War, Bk. 4.33)*

Caesar describes the inhabitants of Kent, in southeastern England, as "by far the most civilized." Clearly impressed by their customs, he writes:

> Of the inlanders most do not sow corn, but live on milk and flesh and clothe themselves in skins. All the Britons, indeed, dye themselves with woad, which produces a blue color, and makes their appearance in battle more terrible. They wear long hair, and shave every part of the body save the head and the upper lip. Groups of ten or twelve men have wives together in common, and particularly brothers along with brothers, and fathers with sons; but the children born of the unions are reckoned to belong to the particular house to which the maiden was first conducted.
>
> *(Gallic War, Bk. 5.33)*

In 49 B.C. Caesar crossed the River Rubicon in northern Italy, which was then the boundary of the corporate Roman state, and declared war on the senate. He defeated his rival, the general Pompey (106–48 B.C.), and took control of Rome. Caesar pursued Pompey to Egypt, where he met Queen Cleopatra (see Box). Their celebrated affair produced a son, Caesarion, who was later murdered by Octavian.

As ruler of Rome, Caesar instituted a number of civic improvements. Streets were cleaned, heavy daytime traffic was

Cleopatra, Queen of Egypt

Cleopatra (c. 68–30 B.C.), the Egyptian queen celebrated in plays, operas, songs, and films throughout Western history, was, like Helen of Troy, renowned for her beauty. But she was also a shrewd politician. She became queen in 51 B.C. and co-regent with her younger brother, Ptolemy XII. Although engaged to marry her brother, Cleopatra fell in love with Julius Caesar. She contrived to meet him in a scene famous in cinema history by arranging to be carried into his presence rolled up in a carpet. Their son, Caesarion, was named after his Roman father. Cleopatra left Egypt and went to Rome to live with Caesar, but after Caesar's murder in 44 B.C., she returned to Egypt and resumed her role as queen.

In 41 B.C., Cleopatra met the Roman leader Mark Antony, who had married the sister of Octavian (later Augustus). Mark Antony, a rival of Augustus, deserted his wife and went to live with Cleopatra in Egypt; they had three sons. When Rome declared war on Cleopatra and defeated her forces in 31 B.C. at the Battle of Actium (on the west coast of the Greek mainland), Cleopatra managed to escape with sixty Egyptian boats, and Mark Antony again followed her to Egypt. The Romans attacked Alexandria in 30 B.C., and, seeing no hope of winning, Antony and Cleopatra committed suicide.

According to tradition, Cleopatra died by placing a poisonous asp on her breast, but there is no evidence that this was in fact her method of suicide. In Egypt she was remembered as a great queen and associated with Isis as a goddess who gave birth to kings.

banned, and traders were forbidden to display their wares in public. Caesar reformed the Roman calendar, introducing the 365-day year we use today and adding an additional day every four years. One of his greatest achievements was unifying the civil law code, called the *Ius Civile*. The laws of the Twelve Tables had become complex and disordered, and Caesar enlisted legal experts to unify and simplify them. On the military front, he extended Roman conquests to parts of Asia Minor, and in 47 B.C. he uttered the famous words: *Veni, Vidi, Vici* ("I came, I saw, I conquered").

Caesar's power in Rome increased to the point where the senate suspected that he planned to become king. In 44 B.C., on the Ides of March (the 15th of the month), a group of senators gathered to assassinate him. When he recognized his friend Marcus Junius Brutus (c. 78–42 B.C.), who was a committed republican, Caesar uttered the well-known phrase *Et tu Brute!* ("You, too, Brutus!"). It was this event that gave rise to the expression "Beware the Ides of March" (from Shakespeare's *Julius Caesar*; see Chapter 15).

RELIGION AND ART

Roman ceremonies and festivals were important from earliest times. Presiding over the rituals was the *pontifex maximus*. This official title translates literally as "the greatest bridge-builder," but its original meaning is not known. In the early period, when Rome was ruled by kings, the *pontifex maximus* was the highest priest. He assisted the king in matters relating to the state cult, advised on religious rituals, established certain important dates, and supervised the Vestal Virgins. At first the *pontifex* was a patrician, but the position was later open to plebeians as well. The title was conferred on every emperor, and in the late fifth century A.D. on the Christian pope. The solemn nature of Roman religion meant that vows made to the gods were taken very seriously. Obligations to the divinities were mirrored by the sense of *pietas* toward the state and the *paterfamilias*.

Roman religion was **syncretistic**—that is, it assimilated features of other belief systems. Like the Etruscans, the Romans adopted the Greek pantheon, but they gave the gods Roman names and a Roman character (see Box). As Rome overran more and more territory, it absorbed customs from different cultures and borrowed from local religious cults, such as the Egyptian cult of Isis and the Phrygian cult of the Mother Goddess. This openness to assimilation both appealed to the conquered people and infused Roman religion with new ideas.

Romans cremated their dead and placed them in ash-urns or buried them in stone sarcophagi. Unlike the Etruscans, however, Romans rarely included effigies on the lid (figure **7.12**). In this example, the influence of Greek motifs is readily

Society and Culture

The Roman Gods

Roman God	Greek Equivalent
Jupiter	Zeus
Hera	Juno
Neptune	Poseidon
Pluto	Hades
Ceres	Demeter
Vesta	Hestia
Venus	Aphrodite
Cupid	Eros
Vulcan	Hephaestos
Minerva	Athena
Mars	Ares
Phoebus	Apollo
Diana	Artemis
Hermes	Mercury
Bacchus	Dionysos

apparent. The ends of the flat lid curve into Ionic volute shapes, and the side is decorated with a Doric frieze. Triglyphs alternate with rosette designs in the metopes, below which an inscription proclaims the virtuous life of the deceased.

Ancestor worship was an important part of Roman religion. For centuries, the inhabitants of Italy had made death masks of their ancestors and displayed them during funerals. Under

volute

cornice

Doric frieze

rosette

metope

triglyph

7.12 Sarcophagus of Lucius Cornelius Scipio Barbatus, from the graves of the Scipios, Via Appia, near Rome, *c.* **200** B.C. **Tufa, 4 ft. 7 in. (1.4 m) × 9 ft. 1 in. (2.77 m). Vatican Museums, Rome.**

7.13 Patrician with two portrait heads, copy of a republican statue, 1st century A.D.; the patrician head is a later addition. Marble, 5 ft. 5 in. (1.65 m) high. Palazzo dei Conservatori, Rome.
Republican portraits were typically individual marble busts (showing the figure from the head to the shoulders). But this is a more complex example, illustrating a patrician wearing a toga and carrying two ancestor busts to show the importance of his family. They are carved to reveal their actual features and somber expressions. The pose of the patrician suggests that he is walking slowly, as if in a funeral procession, but the one bent leg combined with the straight, support leg is reminiscent of the Greek *Spearbearer* (see figure 6.22).

7.14 Temple of Portunus, Rome, late 2nd century B.C. Stone.

rectangular and accessible only by steps at the front. Surrounding the solid walls of the single *cella* are **engaged columns** (columns attached to a wall); the only freestanding columns, which are Ionic, are located on the *pronaos*. In contrast to Greek temples, which were designed in relation to the surrounding landscape, the Roman temple, like the Etruscan, stands on a podium and dominates an urban space.

ART AND ARCHITECTURE OF EVERYDAY LIFE

The Romans devoted a great deal of time, energy, money, and engineering to domestic architecture. Inside the city, most people lived in apartment blocks, called *insulae* ("islands"; see Box, p. 158, and figure 7.15). The poorer classes occupied low-lying *suburbia*, literally the area "below the city" (compare the word "suburbs"). Those who could afford it built second homes (**villas**) in the countryside.

Much of our knowledge of Roman domestic architecture and everyday life (see Box, p. 158, and figure 7.16) comes from the ruins of Pompeii and Herculaneum. These two towns south of Rome were completely buried in volcanic ash in A.D. 79, when Mount Vesuvius suddenly erupted. People were literally stopped "in their tracks" as the lava flowed over them. They remained buried until the eighteenth century, when an Italian farmer accidentally discovered traces of the cities on his land.

Augustus, Virgil wrote the *Aeneid* to demonstrate the divine ancestry of Roman culture. And Roman portraits, influenced by Hellenistic realism, express a desire to keep alive the memory of the deceased through a lifelike image (figure **7.13**).

Roman temples, such as the late second-century-B.C. Temple of Portunus (the god of harbors), combine elements of Greek and Etruscan architecture (figure **7.14**). The temple is

Rome Builds in Concrete

As the hub of a vast and long-lasting empire built on conquest and assimilation, Rome and its territory needed large-scale buildings to accommodate crowds of people. Huge audiences filled the Colosseum, aqueducts carried water over long distances, public baths provided recreation and relaxation spaces, and domestic architecture (both urban and in the country) came into its own. The Greeks had built mainly in marble, the Egyptians in limestone, sandstone, and granite, and the Mesopotamians had imported much of their stone. When the Romans developed the inexpensive and easily acquired material of concrete, they made possible new types of building on a scale that corresponded to their imperial ambitions.

Roman concrete was a mixture of rubble and gravel combined with mortar made from *pozzolana* (volcanic ash) and water. It could be shaped around a wooden frame and reinforced with stones and bricks. Large spaces could thus be enclosed, as is evident in buildings such as the Pantheon, basilicas, country villas, and apartment blocks (figure **7.15**). Limestone was generally used for solid foundations, and tufa was available when a soft material was required.

The use of concrete expanded in the early years of the Roman Empire under Augustus, Vespasian, and Hadrian. Architects constructed arches, vaults, and domes in concrete and reinforced them with brick facing. As concrete is not an attractive material, the Romans faced the exteriors of these structures with tile and **travertine** (a type of limestone that turns yellow as it ages). Later, colored marble, from the Aegean and North Africa, was used to decorate private houses and some public buildings. White marble was a Greek-inspired fashion. It was quarried at Carrara, in Italy, from around 50 B.C. and became the favorite facing material of the empire. Hence the assertion that Augustus found Rome a city of brick and left it a city of marble.

Critical Question Do all innovations in technology and science improve cultural development? Is there a necessary link between developing technological innovations and using these innovations?

7.15 Reconstruction of an *insula* (apartment block), Ostia, near Rome, 2nd century A.D. Brick and concrete.

A Roman Bakery

Except for the occasional banquet, dining in ancient Rome was a simple affair. The average Roman ate a breakfast of bread and cheese, had a quick lunch at a food-stand, and for dinner had a two-course meal. Meat, fish, fruit, and cakes were standard fare. The main drink was wine diluted with water, which could be sweetened with honey. Romans did not drink tea, coffee, or hard liquor.

Bread was one of the most popular foods, originally baked at home and, from the second century B.C., in bakeries. It could then be delivered to a house or purchased directly from the shop. Figure **7.16** shows a reconstructed bakery at Pompeii. At the right, the hour-glass-shaped mill made of volcanic stone stands on a round base. Grain was poured into the top, ground into flour by turning the upper section against the lower section, and made into dough.

Brick ovens had a space for storing fuel and a chimney. For good luck, Romans often placed a relief or a painting of an erect phallus on the wall by their ovens.

7.16 Peter Connolly, detail of reconstructed baker's shop, Pompeii. Watercolor.

7.17a
Peter Connolly,
reconstruction of an upper-
class Roman house based on
examples from Pompeii. Watercolor.

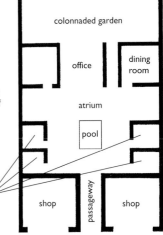

7.17b *right* **Plan of
an upper-class Roman house.**
This reconstruction shows an upper-
class house built on one floor. It was fronted
by shops (*tabernae*, compare "taverns") that open
onto the street. One entered the interior of the house through
a passageway between the shops, coming first to the central atrium. At
the center of the atrium, a pool collected rain water from an opening in the roof
(the *compluvium*) and drained it into a cistern under the floor (the *impluvium*).
On either side of the atrium were bedrooms. The dining room (*triclinium*) and
office (*tablinum*) were behind the atrium, with a colonnaded garden at the back.

WALL-PAINTINGS Upper-class houses in Pompeii were decorated with wall-paintings and mosaics. Surviving Roman wall-paintings are divided by scholars into four Pompeian styles based on their chronology. The first two styles belong to the republic and the last two to the empire. The earliest style is the First, or Masonry, Style, which can be seen in figure **7.17**. It consists of imitation marble, which enlivened the walls with rectangles of color.

Second Style paintings were three-dimensional and often created architectural illusions (figure **7.18**). Here, the artist makes the wall appear to extend into a deep space defined by a receding row of columns, which cast shadows. To the left, a striking mask reflects the Roman fascination with theater and suggests that the scene represents a stage set. The peacock enhances the illusion of depth, as its tail seems to fall out of the picture into the real space of the viewer.

At the Villa of the Mysteries, on the outskirts of Pompeii, there is a group of paintings illustrating a mysterious initiation ritual. Lifesize figures are shown against a background of Pompeian red (figure **7.19**). They turn freely on an illusionistic ledge that seems to occupy a real space between the actual wall and the painted wall. Painted architectural divisions, such as the **pilasters** (square columns) and the geometric horizontal frieze above them, are characteristic of the Second Style.

Third Style painting (see figure 7.27) tends to depict either tiny scenes surrounded by broad monochrome spaces framed with thin, decorative architectural motifs or large-scale villas and landscapes. In the Fourth Style, artists used features of all three previous styles.

7.18 *right* **Second Style Roman painting, from the villa at Oplontis, Italy,
1st century B.C.** Fresco.

7.19 Fresco, Villa of the Mysteries, south wall, outside Pompeii, *c.* 60 B.C., 5 ft. 3 in. (1.62 m) high.

A MUSICAL MOSAIC The mosaic in figure **7.20** decorated a villa in Pompeii. It shows street musicians from a Roman comedy and is thought to illustrate a scene in a play. It also depicts some of the musical instruments popular in Rome. Roman actors, like their Greek counterparts, wore masks, and Roman musicians played Greek instruments. Here, the woman wears a white mask and plays a double flute (the *aulos*, which the Romans called a *tibia*). The men wear darker masks and dance to the music of a large tambourine and small cymbals. As in Greek theater, Roman performances included music, but in the absence of musical notations, it is not known how Roman music sounded.

7.20 *Street Musicians*, from the Villa of Cicero, Pompeii, *c.* 100 B.C. Mosaic, 16⅞ × 16⅛ in. (42.5 × 41 cm). National Museum, Naples.

PHILOSOPHY: LUCRETIUS

Romans were more legally than philosophically inclined. They were interested in civic and military duty rather than abstract philosophical thought. Nevertheless, they adapted from Greece the Stoic and Epicurean philosophies—although the latter had few followers. Stoicism, which was the prevailing philosophy during the empire, is discussed later in this chapter.

The only significant Roman follower of Epicurus during the republic was the poet Lucretius (98–c. 55 B.C.). His long work, *On the Nature of Things* (*De rerum natura*), combines verse with philosophy. He concludes from the atomism of Democritus (see Chapter 6) that it is best to follow the live-and-let-live attitude of Epicurus. For example, Lucretius argues that human autonomy makes happiness possible, that religion is superstition, and that the gods—should they exist—do not affect the course of human life.

His disregard of the gods notwithstanding, Lucretius opens his poem with a passionate appeal to the goddess Venus to inspire the work. It is a hymn to the beauty of nature and to the creative powers of the goddess. Like Virgil, Lucretius links Venus to the founding of Rome:

> Mother of Aeneas and his race, darling of men and gods,
> nurturing Venus, who beneath the smooth-moving heavenly
> signs fill with yourself the sea full-laden with ships, the earth
> that bears the crops, since through you every kind of living
> thing is conceived and rising up looks on the light of the
> sun: from you, O goddess, from you the winds flee away, the
> clouds of heaven from you and your coming; for you the
> wonder-working earth puts forth sweet flowers, for you the
> wide stretches of oceans laugh, and heaven grown peaceful
> glows with outpoured light.
>
> (*On the Nature of Things*, Bk. I.1–10)

Lucretius's purpose is extensive. He describes the behavior of atoms (the basic unit of nature) and conceives of the universe as composed of matter and void:

> For since the first-beginnings of things wander through the
> void, they must all be carried on either by their own weight
> or by a chance blow from another atom. For when in quick
> motion they have often met and collided, it follows that they
> leap apart suddenly in different directions; and no wonder,
> since they are perfectly hard in their solid weight and
> nothing obstructs them from behind.
>
> (Bk. II.80–88)

According to Lucretius, atoms alone comprise the mind and the spirit and themselves have no feeling. There is, therefore, no need to fear death. "The sum of things," he writes,

> is ever being renewed, and mortal creatures live dependent
> one upon another. Some species increase, others diminish,
> and in a short space the generations of living creatures are
> changed and, like runners, pass on the torch of life.
>
> (Bk. II.76–80)

THEATER: ROMAN COMEDY

As the Roman Republic declined, literature flourished. New genres developed, in part as a result of Greek influence. One example of this is the popularity of Hellenistic New Comedy (see Chapter 6), which influenced the early Roman comedies of Plautus (c. 250–184 B.C.) and Terence (c. 195–159 B.C.). Terence was the more elegant of the two; Plautus was known for his bawdy, slapstick humor, verbal punning, stock characters, and lively plots. The lyrics of both Plautus and Terence were set to music.

The first lines of *The Braggart Soldier* (*Miles Gloriosus*), convey a sense of Plautus's literary style. The scene opens in front of two houses on a street in the Greek colony of Ephesus, in modern Turkey. A pompous Pyrgopolynices is proud of his huge shield and claims to be a brave soldier. He enters with Artotrogus, who portrays the popular stock character of a flatterer.

> PYRGOPOLYNICES: Look lively—shine a shimmer on that shield of
> mine
> Surpassing sunbeams—when there are no clouds, of
> course.
> Thus, when it's needed, with the battle joined, its gleam
> Shall strike opposing eyeballs in the bloodshed—bloodshot!
> Ah me, I must give comfort to this blade of mine
> Lest he lament and yield himself to dark despair.
> Too long ere now has he been sick of his vacation.
> Poor lad! He's dying to make mincemeat of the foe.
> . . . Say, where the devil is Artotrogus?
> ARTOTROGUS: He's here—
> By Destiny's dashing, dauntless, debonair darling.
> A man so warlike, Mars himself would hardly dare
> To claim his powers were the equal of your own.
> PYRGOPOLYNICES [preening]: Tell me—who was that chap I saved
> at Field-of-Roaches?
> Where the supreme commander was Crash-Bang-Razzle-
> Dazzle
> Son of Mighty-Mercenary-Messup, you know, Neptune's
> nephew?
> ARTOTROGUS: Ah yes, the man with the golden armour, I recall.
> You puffed away his legions with a single breath
> Like wind blows autumn leaves, or straw from thatch-
> roofed huts.
> PYRGOPOLYNICES: A snap—a nothing, really.
>
> (*The Braggart Soldier*, lines 1–17)

READING SELECTION

Plautus, *The Pot of Gold*, on why it is best to marry a poor wife, PWC1-220

RHETORIC: CICERO

The art of rhetoric (logical argument) was an important part of Roman education. The greatest and most influential Roman orator of the first century B.C. was the upper-class citizen Marcus Tullius Cicero (106–43 B.C.). He began his career as a lawyer, and his courtroom arguments, especially those defending accused murderers, made his reputation as a master of rhetoric. He published his legal speeches as well as works on religion, and moral and political philosophy.

In 63 B.C. Cicero was elected consul, and he became famous for his political speeches. After his death, some nine hundred of his letters, which reveal an intimate picture of his personality, were also published. Cicero had studied Greek, but his culture was thoroughly Roman. A strong supporter of the republic and its laws, Cicero hated tyranny and had the following to say after the assassination of Julius Caesar:

> We recently discovered, if it was not known before, that no amount of power can withstand the hatred of the many. The death of this tyrant [Caesar], whose yoke the state endured under the constraint of armed force and whom it still obeys more humbly than ever, though he is dead, illustrates the deadly effects of popular hatred; and the same lesson is taught by the similar fate of all other despots, of whom practically no one has ever escaped such a death. For fear is but a poor safeguard of lasting power; while affection, on the other hand, may be trusted to keep it safe forever.
>
> (Cicero, *On Duties*, Bk. II.23:7)

READING SELECTION

Cicero, *Select Political Speeches*, the value of literature, PWC1-040

THE POETS

One of Rome's major poets, Gaius Valerius Catullus (c. 84–c. 54 B.C.) was born in Verona, in northern Italy. He moved to Rome around 62 B.C. and frequented an upper-class, somewhat degenerate social set. He fell in love with Clodia, the sister of one of Cicero's enemies and the wife of a consul. Their romance, as reflected in Catullus's brief poems, was fraught with heights of passion, bouts of distrust, and despair caused by Clodia's infidelities. He addresses her in the poems as Lesbia. Here Catullus is at his most ardent:

> We should live, my Lesbia, and love
> And value all the talk of stricter
> Old men at a single penny.
> Suns can set and rise again;
> For us, once our brief light has set,
> There's one unending night for sleeping.
> Give me a thousand kisses, then a hundred,

> Then another thousand, then a second hundred,
> Then still another thousand, then a hundred;
> Then, when we've made many thousands,
> We'll muddle them so as not to know
> Or lest some villain overlook us
> Knowing the total of our kisses.
>
> (Catullus, No. 5)

In this famous poem, Catullus is tormented by ambivalence:

> I hate and love. Perhaps you're asking why I do that?
> I don't know, but I feel it happening and am racked.
>
> (No. 85)

The other major Roman poet of the period was Virgil (see p. 145), whose bucolic *Eclogues* were influenced by the idylls of Theocritus, and whose *Georgics* praise country life. The following passage from the *Georgics* describes the orderly lifestyle of bees:

> They alone have children in common, hold the dwellings of their city jointly, and pass their life under the majesty of law. They alone know a fatherland and fixed home, and in summer, mindful of the winter to come, spend toilsome days and garner their gains into a common store. For some watch over the gathering of food, and under fixed covenant labour in the fields; some, within the confines of their homes, lay down the narcissus' tears and gluey gum from tree-bark as the first foundation of the comb, then hang aloft clinging wax; others lead out the full-grown young, the nation's hope; others pack purest honey, and seal the cells with liquid nectar. To some it has fallen by lot to be sentries at the gates, and in turn they watch the rains and clouds of heaven . . . All aglow is the work, and the fragrant honey is sweet with thyme . . . The aged have charge of the towns, the building of the hives, the fashioning of the cunningly wrought houses . . . All have one season to rest from labour, one season to toil.
>
> (Virgil, *Georgics*, 4:152–184)

Virgil's friend and fellow poet Quintus Horatius Flaccus (65–8 B.C.), known as Horace, wrote odes inspired by Greek lyrics. He found a wealthy backer, Maecenas, to whom he dedicated his first ode. He compares different paths to fame and glory, beginning with Olympic athletes and Roman politicians, and concluding with lyric poets:

> Maecenas, sprung from an ancient line of kings,
> my stronghold, my pride, and my delight,
> some like to collect Olympic dust
> on their chariots, and if their scorching wheels
> graze the turning-post and they win the palm of glory
> they become lords of the earth and rise to the gods;
> one man is pleased if the fickle mob of Roman citizens
> competes to lift him up to triple honors;
>
> . . . .
>
> As for me, it is ivy, the reward of learned brows,
> that puts me among the gods above. As for me,
> the cold grove and the light-footed choruses of Nymphs
> and Satyrs set me apart from the people

if Euterpe lets me play her pipes, and Polyhymnia*
does not withhold the lyre of Lesbos.
But if you enrol me among the lyric bards
My soaring head will touch the stars.

*Euterpe and Polyhymnia are two of the nine Muses

(Horace, Ode I)

READING SELECTION
Horace, *The Art of Poetry*, on how to write poetry, PWC1-235

THE END OF THE REPUBLIC

Several factors led to Rome's evolution from a republic to an empire. One was an increase in economic and social conflicts between the patricians who were in control of the senate; another was the rise of the *equites*, who were opposed to the senators; and a third problem arose as small farmers were forced by wealthy landowners to sell their farms. When the small farmers then migrated from the country to the city, they lost their livelihoods and created a new, impoverished class. Civil war, following Caesar's assassination in 44 B.C., added to the unrest until Octavian defeated his rival Mark Antony and

took control of Rome. Octavian claimed to be in favor of the republic and promised to restore order, but in fact he became the first of a long line of emperors. Some emperors were good rulers, a few were dissolute or insane, or both; others were merely incompetent. All had absolute power.

Octavian was Caesar's grandnephew and had been adopted as his son so that he could inherit Caesar's fortune and power. In 27 B.C. Octavian took the title *Augustus*, which combines connotations of dignity, reverence, divinity, and prosperity. He maneuvered to have Caesar deified (declared a god), making himself *divi filius* ("son of the god"). The republic drew to a close when Augustus assumed the power of veto over all laws passed by the senate. In 12 B.C., Augustus was declared *pontifex maximus*.

THE ROMAN EMPIRE: 27 B.C.–A.D. 476

Augustus succeeded in restoring peace. Known as the *Pax Romana* ("Roman Peace"), this lasted for two hundred years, during which time Rome became *caput mundi* ("head of the world") (map **7.4**) and survived the worst of its emperors. Peace freed the Romans from having to finance wars, permitting them to undertake cultural programs—in the arts, architecture, and literature—of

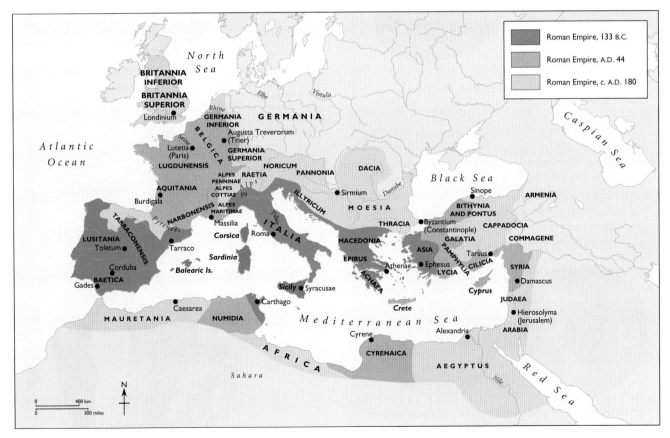

Map 7.4 The expansion of the Roman Empire, 133 B.C.–*c.* A.D. 180.

monumental dimensions. Even the distant provinces of the empire recognized the benefits of Roman rule, which included economic prosperity and the increasing ease of attaining Roman citizenship.

Society and Culture

Greek and Roman Coinage

Coins are more than units of monetary exchange. They are also a relatively inexpensive means of circulating images to an entire population. Ancient Greeks and Romans understood this, as we do today (see the symbols on the U.S. quarter, for example). Among the Greek coins were the Owls of Athena, showing the profile head of the goddess of wisdom on the **obverse** (the front), and an owl, an attribute of Athena, on the **reverse** (the back) (figure **7.21**). Then, as now, the owl was a symbol of wisdom—hence the term "wise old owl." Next to the owl is an olive branch, Athena's gift to Athens, whose economy depended on the olive tree. The *A TH E* alludes to both the goddess and her city.

7.21 Athenian tetradrachm, *c.* 530–490 B.C. Silver, 1 in. (2.4 cm) diameter. Museum of Fine Arts, Boston.

Figure **7.22** shows a Roman coin minted by Augustus. Following the Greek model, the Augustan coin depicts the emperor's profile on the obverse and an emblematic image on the reverse. The emblem consists of an elephant on a triple arch surmounting an aqueduct. Both structures refer to the architectural achievements of Rome and its vast empire. Elephants, which were imported from Nubia and India, symbolized strength and long life. In Rome they were the exclusive property of the emperor.

7.22 Roman coin with the head of Augustus, and Augustus and an elephant on an arch resting on an aqueduct, 17 B.C. British Library, London.

IMPERIAL AUGUSTAN IMAGERY

Augustus was a genius in the use of imagery for political propaganda. One particularly successful technique was aligning himself in the public mind with his adoptive father, Julius Caesar. To this end, Augustus completed the building projects begun by Caesar and added new ones of his own. He built theaters, aqueducts, roads, race tracks, temples, and other public buildings throughout Roman territory. He also built the forum of Augustus in Rome and minted coins showing himself as a just and benevolent ruler (see Box).

A major example of Augustan iconography is the *Augustus of Prima Porta* (figure **7.23**). This large-scale portrait idealizes the new emperor. He appears handsome and youthful in a pose reminiscent of Polykleitos's *Spearbearer* (see figure 6.22). The meaning of this statue is intentionally political, for it depicts Augustus in the role of a victorious general, an *imperator*—the title Julius Caesar had earned with his military victories. Unlike Caesar, Augustus was not a great general, but he

7.23 *Augustus of Prima Porta,* after a bronze of *c.* 20 B.C., early 1st century A.D. Marble, 6 ft. 8 in. (2.03 m) high. Vatican Museums, Rome.

7.24 *Ara Pacis Augustae*, Rome, 13–9 B.C. Marble, outer wall approx. 34 ft. 5 in. × 38 ft. × 23 ft. (10.5 × 11.6 × 7 m).

nonetheless adopted the title for himself. From that time on, only the emperor was allowed to celebrate military triumph as commander-in-chief.

The breastplate of the statue is decorated with reliefs referring to Augustus's defeat of the Parthians (a Near Eastern culture inhabiting Bactria, in modern Afghanistan) in 20 B.C. Augustus raises his right arm as he addresses the troops. The little Cupid by his right leg alludes to the *Aeneid* and the legend that Rome was founded by the son of Venus (who was also Cupid's mother). Both Augustus and Cupid are thus shown as having a divine genealogy—Cupid by virtue of Greek and Roman myth, and Augustus through Rome's descent from Aeneas.

Augustus created his most outstanding example of political imagery, the *Ara Pacis Augustae* (Altar of Peace of Augustus), between 13 and 9 B.C. (figure **7.24**). The *Ara Pacis* was constructed on the Campus Martius (Field of Mars) in Rome. It conveyed the impression of Augustus as the man who brought peace through military triumph. The altar itself is enclosed in a rectangular wall decorated with a frieze glorifying Augustus and his reign.

The detail of the frieze in figure **7.25** illustrates a procession of the imperial family and court. This evokes the characteristic Roman link between rulers and the *paterfamilias* and reflects Augustus's campaign to restore family values to the city. Children are shown together with adults, including senators

7.25 Detail of the procession from the *Ara Pacis*, Rome, 13–9 B.C. Marble, 5 ft. 3 in. (1.6 m) high. Rome.

7.26 *Gemma Augustea*, c. A.D. 10. Onyx cameo, 7½ in. × 9 in. (19 × 23 cm). Museum of Art History, Vienna. The iconography of this cameo reflects Augustus's desire to ensure the succession of his stepson Tiberius. The surface of the "gem" is divided into two registers. At the top, Augustus is enthroned in the center beside the helmeted personification of Rome. Rome gazes at Augustus, who looks toward Tiberius as he leaves his chariot at the far left. The armed figure beside Rome is the young Germanicus, Tiberius's adopted son and a renowned warrior ready to fight for the empire. At the right, Augustus is crowned with the symbol of the city of Rome, and a personification of Italy sits on the ground with images of plenty. In the lower register, Roman soldiers defeat a group of foreigners and take them prisoner.

wearing togas—a reminder that Augustus encouraged large families because Rome's elite population had been decimated by civil war. At the left of the procession, an elderly Augustus, his head covered, wears the priestly costume of *pontifex maximus*. This alludes to his piety, which provides yet another link between the emperor and Aeneas.

Augustan imagery not only harks back to his divine descent, it also looks forward to his future successor. When Augustus died in A.D. 14, his wife, Livia (58 B.C.–A.D. 29), received the title *Julia Augusta*, designating her power and influence. Her administrative skill and commitment to civic virtue endeared her to the Romans. Although she had no children by Augustus, she did have two sons, Tiberius and Drusus (who died in 9 B.C. after falling from a horse), by her previous marriage. For political stability as well as dynastic continuity, both Livia and Augustus wanted to ensure that Tiberius would be the next emperor.

Announcing the end of Augustus's reign and the beginning of the next is the imagery on the so-called *Gemma Augustea* (Gem of Augustus) (figure **7.26**). A summation of Augustan propaganda, this large cameo shows Augustus ruling over a loyal, victorious army and a prosperous land. His reputation for maintaining civic order extends to the order of imperial succession, which is blessed by the gods. Augustus himself is compared to the supreme god, Jupiter, in whose guise he is shown. Note the eagle, Jupiter's emblem, beneath Augustus's

throne. This foreshadows his own posthumous deification, and that of all subsequent emperors.

AUGUSTUS AS A PATRON OF LITERATURE As with visual imagery, Augustus patronized literature in the service of politics. He welcomed Virgil's *Aeneid* and became a friend and patron of the historian Titus Livius, known as Livy (59 B.C.–A.D. 17). Born in Padua, in northern Italy, Livy wrote a history of Rome in 142 books, which describes the mythic founding of the city, its kings, the early republic, and the beginning of the empire up to 9 B.C.

Livy idealized Roman tradition and wanted to record the events that had led to the rise of the greatest city in the world. At the same time, he criticized the social unrest of his own time, which he attributed to moral decline.

READING SELECTION
Livy, *The History of Rome from Its Foundation*, Romulus and Remus and the wolf, PWC1-042

Augustus also befriended Horace and Maecenas and on several occasions asked Horace to write for him. The poet obliged with a *Secular Hymn* and a new collection of odes. Both praise Rome and refer to its divine origin. In the third stanza of the *Secular Hymn*, Horace addresses the Sun:

Life-giving Sun, who with your gleaming chariot
display and then conceal the day, born for ever new
and for ever the same, nothing can you see greater
    than the city of Rome.

(Horace, *Secular Hymn*, lines 9–12)

And later in the same poem:

O you gods, since Rome is your work, since through you
Trojan troops once reached the Etruscan shore, that small
    band
Commanded to change its city and household gods
    and find safety in flight
when the chaste Aeneas, who outlived his fatherland,
and carved a free path for his people,
unscathed through the burning city [Troy] to give them
    more than they had lost—
O you gods, grant good character to our young,
and peace and quiet to the old, and to the race of Romulus
prosperity, posterity,
    and every glory,
and whatever the noble blood of Anchises and Venus
prays for with offerings of white oxen,
let Rome receive, first in war, but merciful
    to a fallen enemy.

(lines 37–52)

The third major poet of the Augustan period was Publius Ovidius Naso (43 B.C.–A.D. 17), known as Ovid. He studied rhetoric—his father wanted him to be a lawyer—but decided to write poetry instead. Ovid's *Metamorphoses* has become a standard source for Greek and Roman mythology and has inspired later poets and artists. The *Metamorphoses* deals with the transformations of the gods, including the disguises assumed by Zeus in his pursuit of mortal women. For example, Ovid gives his own account of Zeus's abduction of Europa, which had previously been described by Hesiod (see Chapter 4):

Majesty and love do not go well together, nor tarry long in
the same dwelling place. And so the father and ruler of the
gods, who wields in his right hand the three-forked lightning,
whose nod shakes the world, laid aside his royal majesty
along with his sceptre, and took upon him the form of a bull
. . . His color was white as the untrodden snow, which has
not yet been melted by the rainy south-wind. The muscles
stood rounded upon his neck, a long dewlap hung down in
front; his horns were twisted, but perfect in shape as if
carved by an artist's hand . . . Agenor's daughter [Europa]
looked at him in wondering admiration, because he was so
beautiful and friendly . . . The disguised lover rejoiced and,
as a foretaste of future joy, kissed her hands . . . And now
he jumps sportively about on the grass, now lays his snowy
body down on the yellow sands . . . The princess even dares
to sit upon his back, little knowing upon whom she rests.
The god little by little edges away from the dry land, and
sets his borrowed hoofs in the shallow water; then he goes
further out and soon is in full flight with his prize on the
open ocean. She trembles with fear and looks back at the
receding shore, holding fast a horn with one hand and

resting the other on the creature's back. And her fluttering garments stream behind her in the wind.

(Ovid, *Metamorphoses*, 2.845–875)

Ovid's knowledge of the arts of seduction, among other things, inspired his *Art of Love* (*Ars Amatoria*), which opens as follows:

If anyone among this people knows not the art of loving, let
him read my poem, and having read be skilled in love. By
skill swift ships are sailed and rowed, by skill nimble
chariots are driven: by skill must Love be guided.

(Ovid, *The Art of Love*, I.1–4)

For this poem, or for other reasons Ovid never acknowledged, he was banished by Augustus to Tomi (modern Constanza), a town on the west coast of the Black Sea. He died there after ten unpleasant years of exile, during which he continued to write poetry.

READING SELECTION
Ovid: *The Art of Love*, on where to find women, PWC1-250; *Metamorphoses*, Caesar becomes a god, PWC1-260

PAINTING IN THE AGE OF AUGUSTUS Under Augustus, painters developed the Third Pompeian Style of wall painting. Like the First and Second Styles, the Third survives on walls of villas that belonged to wealthy Romans. The best early Third Style paintings are from a dismantled villa at Boscotrecase (figure **7.27**). They consist mainly of delicate landscapes framed by thin painted architectural dividers and flat rectangles of solid red or black.

ART AND ARCHITECTURE AFTER AUGUSTUS

The use of art and literature for political purposes continued throughout the Roman Empire. After the death of Augustus, with the succession of Tiberius, the Julio-Claudian dynasty (named for Julius Caesar and the later emperor, Claudius) was in place (see Box, p. 169).

THE JULIO-CLAUDIANS Late in the Julio-Claudian dynasty, around A.D. 60, the Fourth Style of wall-painting appeared and continued for several generations. It combines elements of the Second and Third Styles, and shows the influence of Hellenistic art in the lifelike figures and three-dimensional space. Fourth Style subject matter was often taken from Greek myths or Homeric epics, which reinforced perceptions of Rome's heroic ancestry (figure **7.28**).

Nero (ruled A.D. 54–68) was the last emperor of the Julio-Claudian dynasty. He is famous for both his artistic interests and his delusions of grandeur. The allegation that Nero "fiddled while Rome burned" alludes to a fire that swept the city in

7.27 Red room, north wall, from Boscotrecase Villa, near Pompeii, *c.* 12 B.C. Fresco, 10 ft. 10¼ in. (3.31 m) high. Archaeological Museum, Naples. Note the fine detail in the framing and in the foliage above the scene. Perspective lines at the top contribute to the three-dimensional illusion of the wall, and enhance the impression that the viewer is looking through the wall at figures in a distant countryside.

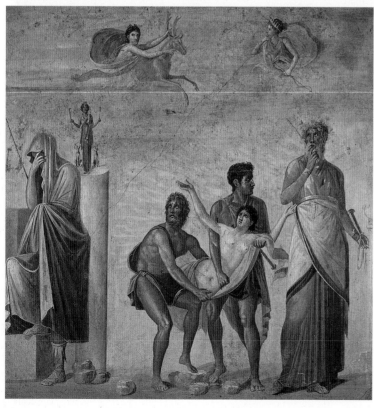

A.D. 64. Instead of rebuilding the destroyed houses of the general population, Nero constructed for himself a huge country villa. It was known as the Golden House, because of its beauty and lavish gold decoration. The original design consisted of an octagonal core, from which radiated numerous rooms embellished with gems and mother-of-pearl. The entrance portico was a mile (1.6 km) long, the pool was set in a space as wide as a pasture, and baths were equipped with saltwater from the ocean and sulphur water from natural springs. In the dining room, a golden dome revolved above

7.28 *Iphigenia Carried to her Sacrifice*, fresco after a 4th-century-B.C. Greek painting, from A.D. 63. National Museum, Naples.
This shows Agamemnon's daughter Iphigenia being carried to her sacrifice (see Chapter 4). Her frantic gestures are characteristic of Hellenistic style. An old priest stands at the right looking skyward at Artemis riding a stag, a reminder that the goddess demanded Iphigenia's death as recompense for Agamemnon's having killed her sacred stag. A statue of Artemis, flanked by a pair of animals, stands on a column. At the left, Agamemnon covers his head and turns from the sight of Iphigenia's forthcoming death.

an ivory ceiling. At the emperor's command, perfume and flowers floated down from the ceiling onto the guests.

Nero also commissioned a colossal, 120-foot (36-m)-high statue of himself, which was known as the Colossus. But his self-aggrandizing character so offended the Romans that he was forced to commit suicide. A period of civil disruption followed, during which three generals became emperor in the space of a year.

In A.D. 69, Vespasian assumed power and tried to correct the abuses of Nero's reign. The senate officially damned Nero's memory and dismantled both his Golden House and the colossal statue. Vespasian decapitated the Colossus and replaced Nero's head with that of the sun god. He also turned Nero's vast private gardens into a public park. For these and similar actions, Vespasian was said to have given Rome back to the Romans.

THE FLAVIANS Vespasian (ruled A.D. 69–79) was a member of the plebeian Flavian dynasty, who wanted to be thought of as a man of the people. The crowning architectural achievement of his reign was the enormous Colosseum (figures **7.29** and **7.30**), which was designed for violent public entertainments. As an affront to the memory of Nero, the Colosseum stood on the site of his pond and was named after his colossal statue.

On the exterior (see figure 7.29) the first three stories are composed of rows of round arches separated by decorative, engaged columns belonging to three different Orders. Each set of columns appears to support an entablature, but in fact both

7.29 *below* **Colosseum, Rome, *c.* A.D. 72–80. Stone and concrete, originally faced with travertine and tufa, 159 ft. (48.5 m) high.**
This huge oval amphitheater has a concrete core that was originally faced with tufa and travertine. The bloodthirsty tastes of Roman spectators were satisfied by combat between gladiators or between gladiators and lions and other wild animals kept in cages below the central floor. The Colosseum could also be flooded for mock naval battles, and a sophisticated drainage system allowed for the removal of water and blood after the spectacles. In case of inclement weather, awnings were stretched across the top of the amphitheater.

7.30 Interior of the Colosseum, Rome.

columns and entablature are part of a decorative façade and are attached to the underlying arch and pier. At ground level the Order is Tuscan Doric, which conveys an impression of sturdy support. The lighter, more elegant Ionic and Corinthian Orders are on the second and third tiers, respectively. The top level is a solid wall pierced by small square windows.

Romans entered the Colosseum through one of seventy-six ground-level arches into barrel-vaulted (see figure 7.9) corridors, which permitted an easy flow of human traffic. Spectators, fashionably dressed women and men (see Box), ascended a stairway to their seats, of which there were some 50,000. At the end of a gladiatorial contest, one of the twelve Vestal Virgins seated near the imperial box would signal whether the loser should be spared or killed by the gesture of a thumbs up or a thumbs down.

Vespasian's successor, Titus (ruled A.D. 79–81), is known for his victory over the Jews and his destruction of Solomon's Temple (previously rebuilt by King Herod) in Jerusalem (see Chapter 2). After his death and deification, Titus was honored by his brother Domitian (ruled A.D. 81–96), the last of the Flavian emperors, with an imposing triumphal arch (figure 7.32). This typically Roman structure marked a place of passage through which a triumphant emperor entered the Roman forum. The Arch of Titus celebrated his sack of Jerusalem, and it is decorated with reliefs depicting his army carrying off the spoils of war. Such triumphal arches with single openings were constructed throughout the Roman Empire, and among their later descendants are the Triumphal Arch in Paris, the Washington Square Arch in New York City, and Marble Arch in London.

Society and Culture

The Flavian Coiffure

Under the Flavian emperors (ruled A.D. 69–96), elegant hairstyles became popular. Figure 7.31 shows a Flavian woman as Venus. Her hair is piled on top of her head in a mass of neatly arranged curls. Her perfectly coiffed portrait head is juxtaposed with a semi-nude torso, reminiscent of Greek sculpture—a merging of Greek and Roman traditions typical of the Roman Empire. Note also that wide hips, a departure from the proportions of the Classical ideal, are accentuated by the sharp contrapposto. The stance and gesture convey self-confidence and assertiveness, which were characteristic qualities of Roman matrons. And such elaborate attention to the hairstyle reflects the more public lifestyle of Roman women compared to their Greek counterparts. Upper-class Roman wives owned more slaves than Athenian women, which freed them to shop, attend performances, accompany their husbands on social occasions, and even pursue intellectual achievement and the arts.

7.31 Portrait of a Flavian woman as Venus, late 1st century A.D. Marble, over lifesize. Capitoline Museum, Rome.

7.32 Arch of Titus, Rome, *c.* A.D. 81. Marble, 50 ft. (15 m) high.

7.33 *below* Trajan's Column, Rome, A.D. 113. Marble, 125 ft. (38 m) high.

TRAJAN: *OPTIMUS PRINCEPS* The emperor Trajan (ruled A.D. 98–117) rose in the ranks of the army and became a Roman consul. Because of his reputation as a good emperor, he was known as *optimus princeps* ("best leader"). He was celebrated for his victory over the Dacians, a tribe that inhabited the region of modern Romania along the Danube River and was known for its goldwork. With the proceeds of his booty, Trajan built a huge retirement colony for his soldiers in North Africa and his forum in Rome.

Dominating Trajan's forum is a monumental freestanding column (figure **7.33**) symbolizing Trajan's defeat of the Dacians. It rests on a podium and is decorated with an innovative spiral frieze of historical reliefs (figure **7.34**). Figure **7.35** shows the section of Trajan's forum containing the Basilica Ulpia, named for Trajan's family. The basilica, a characteristic Roman structure, was a large rectangle with a wide central aisle (the **nave**) separated from the side aisles by rows of columns, with an **apse** (the curved section) at each end. Basilicas were used for social gatherings, business transactions, administration, and law courts (figure **7.36**), and took their name and design from Hellenistic royal audience halls.

In the next chapter, we shall see that the Roman basilica became the basis for the architectural design of early Christian churches.

7.34 *above* **Detail of the frieze, Trajan's Column, Rome.**
This segment of Trajan's Column illustrates a Roman military tactic called the *testudo*, or "turtle." As the soldiers besiege a Dacian fort, they raise their shields to create a protective shell against enemy weapons. Peering over the walls at the onslaught are small Dacian soldiers whose oval shields seem flimsy compared with those of the powerful Roman formation. Dead soldiers lie on the ground below.

7.35 *right* **Plan of the Basilica Ulpia and other parts of Trajan's forum.**
One of the apses contained law courts and a statue of the emperor. This
was a way of linking the emperor with the senate and the rule of law in
the public mind.

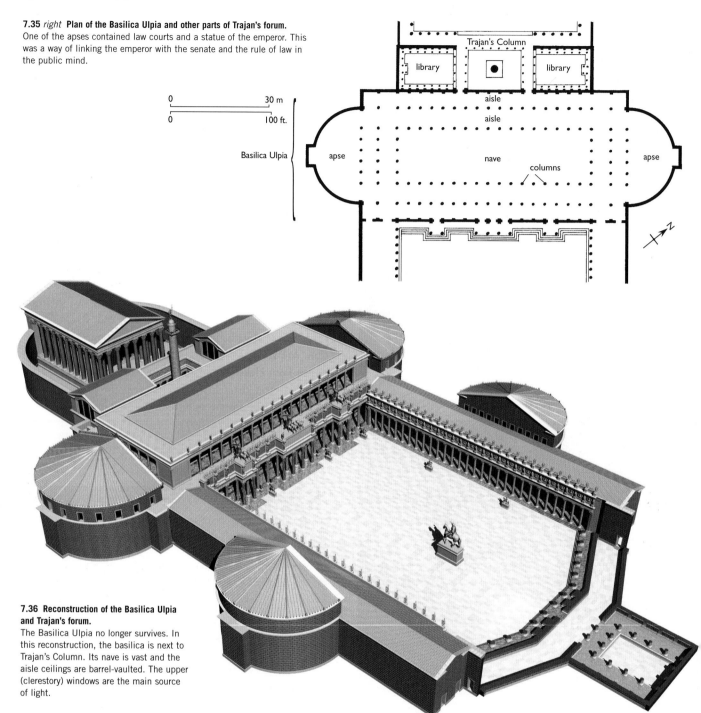

Basilica Ulpia

0 ____ 30 m
0 ____ 100 ft.

**7.36 Reconstruction of the Basilica Ulpia
and Trajan's forum.**
The Basilica Ulpia no longer survives. In
this reconstruction, the basilica is next to
Trajan's Column. Its nave is vast and the
aisle ceilings are barrel-vaulted. The upper
(clerestory) windows are the main source
of light.

HADRIAN: THE PANTHEON   Trajan was succeeded by the
emperor Hadrian (ruled A.D. 117–138), whose admiration for
the Greeks influenced art styles during his reign. He built an
enormous villa at Tivoli, outside Rome, and decorated it with
copies of Greek statues and floor mosaics.

In Rome, Hadrian commissioned the Pantheon (meaning
"all the gods"), a large, round temple dedicated to the five
known planetary gods plus the sun and the moon and a
remarkable feat of engineering. In the exterior view (figure
7.37), the large round **drum** (the central space), the **dome** at
the top, and the Greek temple front are visible (figure **7.38**).

The interior (figure **7.39**) is a huge circular space. The
curved walls are decorated with Corinthian columns and pilasters, niches containing statues of the gods, and different
colored stone—tufa, travertine, brick, and pumice. The Pantheon's unique feature is the huge dome, whose square **coffers**
(the recessions in the ceiling) decrease its weight. At the center
is the round **oculus**, 27 feet (8.23 m) in diameter, designed
to allow outdoor light into the interior. The light circles the
interior as the earth rotates around the sun, evoking the sun's
journey across the sky.

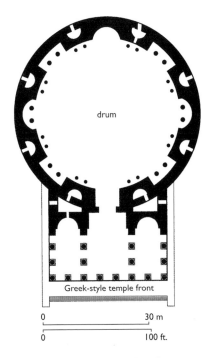

7.37 *left* Exterior of the Pantheon, Rome, A.D. 125–128. Marble, brick, and concrete.

drum

Greek-style temple front

0   30 m
0   100 ft.

7.38 *above* Plan of the Pantheon, Rome

MARCUS AURELIUS: EMPEROR AND STOIC PHILOSOPHER

Marcus Aurelius (ruled A.D. 161–180) was the second member of the Antonine dynasty. He is the subject of the major surviving **equestrian monument** (figure on horseback) of ancient Rome (figure **7.40**), which portrays him as a victorious fighter crushing his enemies. Originally, a small figure of a defeated enemy cowered beneath the raised foreleg of the horse. The emperor was, in fact, continually fighting Germanic, barbarian invaders. Like Hadrian, Marcus Aurelius admired the Greeks, which is reflected in his Greek-style beard. At the same time, however, as with the *Augustus of Prima Porta* (see figure 7.23), Marcus Aurelius wears a Roman military mantle and gestures as if speaking to his troops.

Marcus Aurelius wrote a collection of thoughts that reflect Roman Stoicism. Known as the *Meditations* and written in Greek, these are short instructions to himself. They recommend that he accept his fate with the dignity expected of a loyal Roman:

> Begin each day by telling yourself: Today I shall be meeting with interference, ingratitude, insolence,

7.39 *right* G. P. Pannini, *Interior of the Pantheon, c.* 1734. Oil on canvas, 4 ft. 2 in. × 3 ft. 3 in. (1.28 m × 0.99 m). National Gallery of Art, Washington, D.C.

disloyalty, ill-will, and selfishness—all of them due to the offenders' ignorance of what is good or evil. But for my part I have long perceived the nature of good and its nobility, the nature of evil and its meanness . . . therefore none of those things can injure me, for nobody can implicate me in what is degrading.

(Marcus Aurelius, *Meditations*, 2.1)

Hour by hour resolve firmly, like a Roman and a man, to do what comes to hand with correct and natural dignity, and with humanity, independence, and justice. Allow your mind freedom from all other considerations. This you can do, if you will approach each action as though it were your last.

(*Meditations*, 2.5)

Marcus Aurelius's dissolute and depraved son, Commodus, did not live up to his father's ideals. He was murdered in A.D. 192, and a new dynasty, the Severans, came to power.

7.40 Equestrian portrait of Marcus Aurelius, Rome, A.D. 164–166. Gilded bronze, 11 ft. 6 in. (3.5 m) high.

ROMAN AUTHORS AFTER AUGUSTUS

During the reign of the Julio-Claudian dynasty (A.D. 14–68), Rome entered its Golden Age of literature. But praise of Augustus gave way to a somewhat anti-imperial tone, because many authors were aristocrats who resented imperial rule. They believed that the emperors had usurped the power wielded during the republic by the patrician senate.

HISTORY: TACITUS The greatest historian after Livy was Publius Cornelius Tacitus (*c.* A.D. 56–120), who was born two years after Nero became emperor. Tacitus was a member of the provincial aristocracy of the region that now includes southern France and northwest Italy. He became a Roman orator and a provincial governor in Anatolia. Like Livy, Tacitus was devoted to Rome but favored the republic over the empire. Tacitus's *Annals* trace Roman history from the reign of Tiberius to Nero's death in A.D. 68. His *Histories* begin with the death of Nero and end with the assassination of Domitian in A.D. 96. Book I of the *Annals* criticizes Roman history writing as biased, first by fear of an emperor's power and then by hatred of his deeds:

while the glories and disasters of the old Roman commonwealth have been chronicled by famous pens, and intellects of distinction were not lacking to tell the tale of the Augustan Age, until the rising tide of sycophancy deterred them, the histories of Tiberius and Caligula, of Claudius and Nero, were falsified through cowardice while they flourished, and composed, when they fell, under the influence of still rankling hatreds. Hence my design, to treat a small part (the concluding one) of Augustus' reign, then the principate of Tiberius, and without partiality, from the motives of which I stand sufficiently removed.

(*Annals*, I.1)

READING SELECTION

Tacitus, *Annals*, Nero and the burning of Rome, PWC1-010

BIOGRAPHY: SUETONIUS Another type of literature that became prominent in imperial Rome was biography. Gaius Suetonius Tranquillus, known as Suetonius (*c.* A.D. 69–after 122), was secretary to Hadrian and thus had access to state archives. He wrote a series of highly entertaining biographies, *The Twelve Caesars*, which are filled with historical and personal anecdotes. Suetonius depicts the ambivalent character of the Roman emperors, who could be fair and generous, but even the best of them could at any moment switch into the hubristic grandiosity that comes with absolute power.

Suetonius had the greatest admiration for Augustus, describing him as a talented youth fully deserving of Julius Caesar's confidence. According to Suetonius, Augustus had simple tastes, even as emperor, living in a plainly furnished household, sleeping on an ordinary bed, and wearing home-made clothes. He also wore the white toga with a purple stripe of the republican senate and, reflecting a touch of vanity, kept a pair of thick-soled shoes to make him appear taller than he was. Physically, according to Suetonius, Augustus was:

> remarkably handsome and of very graceful gait even as an old man; but negligent of his personal appearance. He cared so little about his hair that, to save time, he would have two or three barbers working hurriedly on it together, and meanwhile read or write something, whether they were giving him a haircut or a shave.
>
> (*The Twelve Caesars*, "Augustus," 79)

READING SELECTION
Suetonius, *The Twelve Caesars*, "Augustus," PWC1-050-B

Suetonius begins the life of Nero by listing his accomplishments. He then proceeds to his follies and vices, including the ridiculous musical ambitions that gave rise to his reputation for fiddling while Rome burned. Suetonius says that Nero tried to develop his singing voice:

> He would lie on his back with a slab of lead on his chest, use enemas and emetics to keep down his weight, and refrain from eating apples and every other food considered deleterious to the vocal chords. Ultimately, though his voice was still feeble and husky, he was pleased enough with his progress to nurse theatrical ambitions.

When singing in Naples, then a Greek city, Nero became so

> captivated by the rhythmic applause of some Alexandrian sailors from a fleet which had just put in, that he sent to Egypt for more. He also chose a few young knights, and more than 5000 ordinary youths, whom he divided into claques to learn the Alexandrian method of applause—they were known, respectively, as "Bees," "Roof-tiles," and "Brick-bats"—and provide it liberally whenever he sang.
>
> (*The Twelve Caesars*, "Nero," 20)

On the subject of Nero's insane vices, Suetonius is eloquent:

> Not satisfied with seducing free-born boys and married women, Nero raped the Vestal Virgin Rubria . . . Having tried to turn the boy Sporus into a girl by castration, he went through a wedding ceremony with him—dowry, bridal veil, and all—which the whole court attended; then brought him home, and treated him as a wife . . .
>
> The passion he felt for his mother, Agrippina, was notorious; but her enemies would not let him consummate it, fearing that, if he did, she would become even more powerful and ruthless than hitherto. So he found a new mistress who was said to be her spit and image; some say that he did, in fact, commit incest with Agrippina every time they rode in the same litter—the state of his clothes when he emerged proved it.

> Nero practiced every kind of obscenity, and at last invented a novel game: he was released from a den dressed in the skins of wild animals, and attacked the private parts of men and women who stood bound to stakes . . . According to my [Suetonius's] informants he was convinced that nobody could remain sexually chaste, but that most people concealed their secret vices; hence, if anyone confessed to obscene practices, Nero forgave him all his other crimes.
>
> ("Nero," 28–29)

Nero was alleged to have murdered his adoptive father (the emperor Claudius), his mother, an aunt, at least one wife, and several other family members. Shortly before his own death at the age of thirty-two, Nero had changed the name of the month of April to Neroneus after himself and was about to change the name of Rome to Neropolis. When he finally killed himself, the senate rejoiced.

STOIC PHILOSOPHY: SENECA Stoic philosophy was introduced to Rome in the late republic by Greek philosophers, but it took on a new cast during the empire. The major Roman Stoic author was Lucius Annaeus Seneca (*c.* 4 B.C.–A.D. 65), who was born in Spain to a wealthy Roman family. He was educated in Rome, where he learned philosophy and rhetoric, and for a time he was a senator. Seneca wrote tragedies inspired by Greek plays, moral essays in the form of letters, and Stoic treatises on nature.

Seneca had the misfortune of being hired as Nero's tutor, and there is some controversy over the degree to which he compromised his moral principles in order to survive. For example, in his letter *On Anger*, Seneca advises his nephew Novatus on how to allay anger, "the most hideous and frenzied of all the emotions." Throughout, Seneca subtly warns of the political dangers in expressing anger against imperial abuse.

Nonetheless, Seneca tried to improve Nero's character by comparing the ruler to a physician and to a ship's captain. He observes that a wise man is "kindly and just toward errors," and a "reformer of sinners," just as a physician tries to heal the sick. Similarly, according to Seneca, when a "skipper finds that his ship has sprung her seams," he does not become angry at the ship or the crew but, rather, rushes to the rescue.

Seneca cites the example of another insane emperor, Caligula, who murdered the son of a Roman soldier because he disliked his appearance. When the soldier, Pastor, pleaded for his son's life, Caligula sentenced him to death as well. Then, in order not to appear completely callous, Caligula invited Pastor to dinner on the very day of his son's burial. Pastor accepted the invitation, because, writes Seneca, he had another son. Pastor was thus an ideal Stoic, capable of restraining his anger in order to save the life of his second son.

Seneca's tragedies reflected his philosophy and influenced Classical theater in fourteenth-century Italy (see Chapter 13), later inspiring Shakespeare as well (see Chapter 15). In A.D. 65,

Seneca was accused of conspiring against Nero and was forced to commit suicide.

READING SELECTION

Seneca, *Moral Epistles*, on whether philosophers should withdraw from the world, PWC1-525-C

SATIRE: JUVENAL AND PETRONIUS The leading Roman author of satirical poems, Decimus Junius Juvenalis, better known as Juvenal (*c.* A.D. 55/60–after 127), wrote sixteen lengthy satires during the reigns of Trajan and Hadrian. His attacks on life in Rome are strongly ironic and pessimistic. Juvenal insulted and reviled the rich, women, homosexuals, foreigners, and inferior literature. At the same time, he idealized the republic. In the third satire, Juvenal attacks the Greeks for being foreigners:

> And while we're discussing Greeks, let us consider
> not the gymnasium crowd, but some bigwig philosophers,
> like that elderly Stoic informer who destroyed his friend and
>   pupil:
> *he* was brought up in Tarsus, by the banks of the river
> where Bellerophon fell to earth from the Gorgon's flying nag
>   [Pegasus].
> No room for honest Romans when Rome's ruled by a junta
> of Greek-born secret agents, men who—like all their race—
> never share friends or patrons, but keep them to themselves.

(Juvenal, Satire 3.114–121)

On the infidelity of women, Juvenal writes:

> The bed that contains a wife is always hot with quarrels
> and mutual bickering: sleep's the last thing you get there.
> In bed she attacks her husband, worse than a tigress
> robbed of its young, and to stifle her own bad conscience
> bitches about his boy-friends, or weeps over some fictitious
> mistress. She always keeps a big reservoir of tears
> at the ready, and waiting for her to command in which
> manner they need to flow: so you, poor worm, are in heaven,
> thinking this means she loves you, and kiss her tears away—
> but if you raided her desk-drawers, the letters, the
>   assignations
> you'd find that your green-eyed adulteress has amassed!

(Satire 6.268–278)

READING SELECTION

Juvenal, *Satires*, on sex-crazed women, PWC1-242

The other leading satirist, Petronius Arbiter (died A.D. 65), was a member of Nero's inner circle and the emperor's authority on taste. He was falsely accused of disloyalty and exiled to Cumae, where he killed himself. His colorful and obscene

Satyricon contains descriptions of life under Nero and reflects his talent for capturing local speech patterns and conveying humorous images of Roman society. In the "Eumolpus" (part of the *Satyricon*), one of Petronius's characters recites a short verse on hair as a metaphor for growing old:

> Poor boy,
> One moment your hair
> Was shining gold
> And you were more beautiful
> Than Phoebus or his sister [Diana].
> Now you are shinier
> Than a bronze
> Or the round cap
> Of a mushroom after rain.
> You run nervously
> From the laughter of ladies.
> Death's sooner than you think,
> You must believe—
> See now, Death has begun at the top.

(Petronius, *The Satyricon*, "Eumolpus")

In another section of the *Satyricon*, "Dinner with Trimalchio," Petronius satirizes the host's vulgar display of wealth. Trimalchio epitomizes the newly rich social climber:

> The orchestra played, the tables were cleared, and then three white pigs were brought into the dining-room, all decked out in muzzles and bells. The first, the master of ceremonies announced, was two years old, the second three, and the third six. I was under the impression that some acrobats were on their way in and the pigs were going to do some tricks, the way they do in street shows. But Trimalchio dispelled this impression by asking:
>   "Which of these would you like for the next course? Any clodhopper can do you a barnyard cock or a stew and trifles like that, but my cooks are used to boiling whole calves."

("Dinner with Trimalchio")

READING SELECTION

Petronius, *Satyricon*, an extravagant banquet, PWC1-237

THE DECLINE AND FALL OF THE ROMAN EMPIRE

For generations, historians have argued about the reasons for the decline of the Roman Empire. If Roman literature is any indication, it would appear that moral corruption and depraved rulers had a hand in the fate of Rome. But other factors also contributed, including the barbarians beyond the boundaries of the empire and the internal anarchy that erupted when the last Severan emperor died in A.D. 235. In an effort to quell civil unrest and restore imperial control, the emperor

Diocletian established a **tetrarchy** of four co-rulers. But the turmoil persisted, and several emperors were assassinated by the army, which was itself in disarray. At the same time, the rise of Christianity (see Chapter 8) provided an alternative to paganism and posed a challenge to the empire.

The late empire begins with the rule of Constantine I (ruled A.D. 306–337). He legalized Christianity and in A.D. 330 established a new capital in Byzantium (Istanbul, in modern Turkey). Under Constantine, who tried to assimilate the popular appeal of Christianity, Christian churches began to be constructed in Rome. We can see how different Constantine's political image was from that of Augustus by comparing the head and hand of his colossal marble statue (figure **7.41**) with the more human scale of the *Augustus of Prima Porta* (see figure 7.23).

Not even Constantine, however could maintain the Roman Empire as it had been since 27 B.C. In A.D. 410, a German tribe, the Visigoths, took advantage of the weakened empire and sacked Rome. This was followed by a period of invasion throughout Europe and a second sack of Rome in A.D. 455. Rome's final demise came in A.D. 476, when the city fell to barbarian Goths. In the next chapter we turn to the development of Christianity and its roots in Judaism, against the background of pagan cults prevalent in the Mediterranean world.

7.41 Elbow, head, knee, and hand of Constantine's colossal statue, Palazzo dei Conservatori, Rome, A.D. 313. Marble, head 8 ft. 6 in. (2.6 m) high.
This statue once stood in the apse of Constantine's Basilica. At over 30 ft. (9 m) high, with stylized hair patterns, an abstracted gaze, and an upwardly pointing finger, the statue was an image of awe-inspiring, divine power.

Thematic Parallels

Deadly Games: Gladiators and Mesoamerican Ball-players

There is little question that the gladiatorial games held at the Roman Colosseum and attended by thousands were often deadly. To the degree that they pleased the crowds, these events may be considered to have been popular entertainment. But the games had originated as religious rituals, perhaps as substitutes for human sacrifices offered to the gods.

Another deadly contest, which remained explicitly religious, took place in some early Mesoamerican cultures (map **7.5**), especially during the Classic and early post-Classic periods (600–1200). This was the ritual ball game, the meaning of which is debated by scholars. Both the Roman and the Mesoamerican contests had elements of theater, spectatorship, and ritual violence. But the ball courts do not appear to have had seats; spectators would have had to watch from the walls surrounding the court (figure **7.42**).

The nature of the sites also differed. The Roman Colosseum was built over Nero's pond largely for political reasons; the ball courts were oriented according to the symbolic meaning of a local landscape.

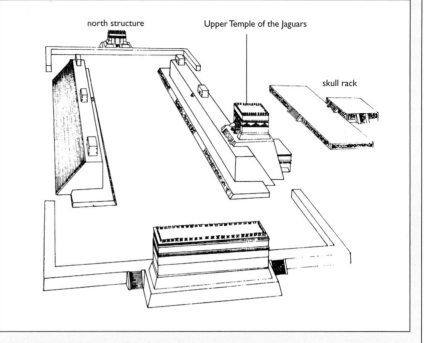

7.42 Diagram of the ball court at Chichén Itzá, Mexico.

Often they continued a natural line of sight from a nearby mountain.

According to descriptions of the Meso-american ball game by Spanish conquerors, players wore heavy padding and used only their hips and arms (not their hands or feet). The object was to knock a heavy rubber ball through elevated narrow hoops attached to the inner walls of the court. The ball game appears to have combined athletic skill with

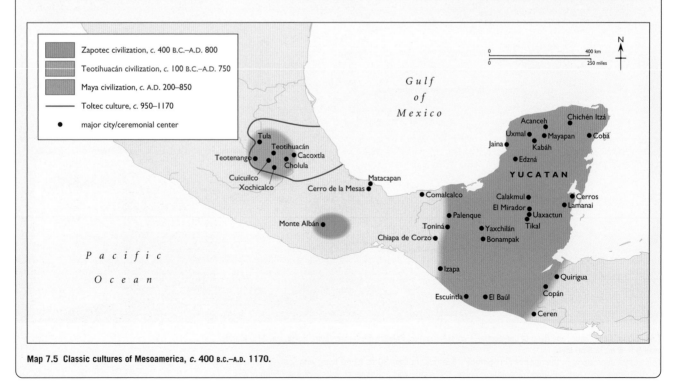

Map 7.5 Classic cultures of Mesoamerica, c. 400 B.C.–A.D. 1170.

ritual. Sacrifices involved offering human blood to the gods, and allusions to war suggest that captives might have been players. In some cases people gambled on the outcome of a game. The Mesoamerican ball game was also played by the Native American Hohokam culture of Arizona, suggesting cultural interchange between the two regions.

The game itself is described in the pre-Columbian Mayan creation epic, the *Popol Vuh*, which, like *The Epic of Gilgamesh* and the Homeric tales, was transmitted orally for centuries and written down only much later (in the seventeenth century). According to the *Popol Vuh*, the ball game, played by two sets of Hero Twins against the lords of Xibalba (the Underworld), is a metaphor for life and death. A first set of twins, One-Hunahpu and Seven-Hunahpu, had angered the lords of Xibalba (One Death and Seven Death) because their game made too much noise. One and Seven Death complain:

What's happening on the face of the earth? They're just stomping and shouting. They should be summoned to come play ball here. We'll defeat them, since we simply get no deference from them. They show no respect, nor do they have any shame. They're really determined to run right over us!

(*Popol Vuh*)

The twins were invited to play against the gods and were killed. The head of One-Hunahpu was hung from a calabash tree and caused it to bear fruit. Blood Gatherer, the daughter of an Underworld god, passed by, and the head impregnated her with its spit. The head then addressed Blood Gatherer as follows:

It's just a sign I have given you, my saliva, my spittle. This, my head, has nothing on it—just bone, nothing of meat. It's just the same with the head of a great lord: it's just the flesh that makes his face look good. And when he dies, people get frightened by his bones. After that, his son is like his saliva, his spittle, in his being, whether it be the son of a lord or the son of a craftsman, an orator. The father does not disappear, but goes on being fulfilled. Neither dimmed nor destroyed is the face of a lord, a warrior, craftsman, orator. Rather he will leave his daughters and

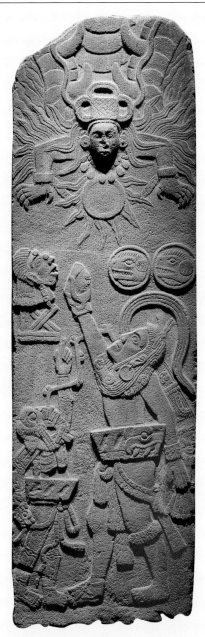

7.43 *above* **Bilbao Monument 3, from Guatemala, c. A.D. 600. Stone, 9 ft. 6 in. (2.9 m) high. Ethnographic Museum, Berlin.**

sons. So it is that I have done likewise through you.

(*Popol Vuh*)

(Note the image of spittle as an impregnating force; hence the modern term to be "the spitting image" of a parent.)

Blood Gatherer was exiled from the Underworld and gave birth to a new set of Hero Twins (Hunahpu and Xbalanque), who are doubles of the first twins and the heroes of the Maya creation myth. These new twins have magic powers. When they reach adulthood, they become famed ball-players and call for a rematch against the Underworld gods. This time, the Hero Twins win by trickery and skill. Eventually they are transformed into heavenly bodies.

In the actual ball games of Mesoamerica, losers appear to have been sacrificed, whereas in Roman gladiator contests life or death could depend on the "thumbs up or thumbs down" of a Vestal Virgin or the will of an emperor. The player in figure **7.43** wears a yoke around his waist and offers a human heart to a god. Echoing his gesture is the small skeleton beside him. A large figure with flames and rays resembling the sun hovers over the scene.

Decorating the walls of the ball courts were complex, flat reliefs illustrating various stages of the games and their aftermath (figure **7.44**). This drawing of a scene depicted on a ball court shows a figure at the left holding the severed head of another. At the right, the decapitated body kneels with serpents, symbolizing blood, and a large flower extending upward from his neck. This imagery reflects the Mesoamerican notion that life and death are intermingled rather than being two completely different states.

7.44 Drawing of a relief illustrating the ball game in the Great Ball Court of Chichen Itzá, Mexico.

KEY TERMS

apse the curved section at the end of a nave.

aqueduct a structure designed to transport water.

barrel vault a vault made by extending a round arch through space.

centering a means of holding stones in place during the construction of an arch.

coffer a recessed geometric panel in a ceiling.

cross-vault (or **groin vault**) a vault made by the intersection of two barrel vaults.

dome a hemispherical roof or ceiling; made by rotating a round arch.

drum the circular support of a dome.

engaged column a column that is attached to a wall.

equestrian monument a portrait of a ruler on horseback.

forum the public center of an ancient Roman city.

impost the support of an arch attached to a wall.

keystone in a round arch, the top center stone holding the voussoirs in place.

Lares and Penates Roman household gods.

nave in basilicas, a wide central aisle separated from the side aisles by rows of columns.

necropolis (plural **necropoleis**) a city of the dead.

obverse the front of a coin.

oculus a round opening in a wall or ceiling.

pilaster a square column.

podium (plural **podia**) the masonry forming the base (usually rectangular) of a temple, arch, or other building.

reverse the back of a coin.

springing the upward thrust of an arch.

syncretism a process through which differing belief systems are assimilated.

tetrarchy a form of government by four co-rulers.

travertine a type of pale limestone, used in Roman building, that turns yellow as it ages.

tufa soft, easily workable, volcanic rock, used in Etruscan building.

Tuscan column a form of Doric style, used by the Etruscans.

villa a country estate.

voussoir a wedge-shaped stone used in round arches.

KEY QUESTIONS

1. Judging from the funerary art, what view of the afterlife was held by Etruscans?
2. What aspects of Roman life and Roman art reinforce the concept of *paterfamilias*?
3. What military action did Cato and Caesar consider essential for Rome's rise to power?
4. How were Roman buildings constructed to accommodate large crowds, and how were they used?
5. When Aeneas meets his father in the Underworld, what does Anchises predict for Rome's future? Is his prediction correct? How does Virgil's characterization of Rome differ from his characterization of Greece?
6. Why is Aeneas called *pius Aeneas* by Virgil?
7. How does Caesar describe the Britons?

SUGGESTED READING

Balsdon, J. P. V. D. *Life and Leisure in Ancient Rome.* London: Weidenfeld and Nicolson, 2002.
▶ A study of everyday life in Rome.

Bonfante, Larissa (ed.). *Etruscan Life and Afterlife.* Oxford: Aris and Phillips, 1986.
▶ Everyday life and religion in ancient Etruria.

——. *Etruscan Dress*, 2nd ed. Baltimore: Johns Hopkins University Press, 2003.
▶ A study of form and meaning in Etruscan dress.

Brendel, Otto. *Etruscan Art.* Harmondsworth, UK: Penguin, 1978.
▶ A classic work on Etruscan art.

Brilliant, Richard. *Roman Art from the Republic to Constantine.* London: Phaidon, 1974.
▶ An account of Roman art in context.

——. *Pompeii A.D. 79.* New York: Outlet, 1979.
▶ An account of Pompeii and the eruption of Mount Vesuvius.

Brown, Frank E. *Roman Architecture.* New York: George Braziller, 2000.
▶ A brief interpretive study of Roman architecture.

Chauveau, Michel. *Cleopatra: Beyond the Myth*, trans. David Lorton. Ithaca and London: Cornell University Press, 2002.
▶ A brief biography of the Egyptian queen.

Friedel, David, Linda Schele, and Joy Parker. *Maya Cosmos*. New York: William Morrow, 1993.
  ▸ On the religion of the ancient Maya.

Harris, Robert. *Pompeii*. London: Hutchinson, 2003.
  ▸ A historical novel about an aqueduct engineer sent to investigate suspicious water activity just before the eruption of Mount Vesuvius.

Johnston, D. *Roman Law in Context*. Cambridge, UK: Cambridge University Press, 1999.
  ▸ A study of ancient Roman law in its social, political, and economic context.

Lyttleton, Margaret, and Werner Forman. *The Romans: Their Gods and Their Beliefs*. New York: Orbis Publications, 1984.
  ▸ An introduction to ancient Roman religion.

Miller, Mary Ellen. *The Art of Mesoamerica*. London, 1996.
  ▸ A survey of Mesoamerican art.

Noble, David Grant. *Ancient Ruins of the Southwest*. Flagstaff, AZ: Noble Northland Publishing, 2000.
  ▸ A survey of the surviving ruins of the Native American Southwest.

Pasztory, Esther. *Pre-Columbian Art*. London: Weidenfeld and Nicolson, 1998.
  ▸ A general introduction to pre-Columbian art.

Popol Vuh, trans. Dennis Tedlock. New York: Simon and Schuster, 1996.
  ▸ A translation of the major Mayan epic.

Ramage, Nancy H., and Andrew Ramage. *Roman Art*. London: Laurence King Publishing, 1996.
  ▸ A general introduction to Roman art in context.

Shelton, Jo-Ann. *As the Romans Did*. New York: Oxford University Press, 1988.
  ▸ A study of Roman life and culture.

Zanker, Paul. *The Power of Images in the Age of Augustus*. Ann Arbor, MI: University of Michigan Press, 1990.
  ▸ A study of the political role of imagery under Augustus.

SUGGESTED FILMS

1917   *Cleopatra*, dir. J. Gordon Edwards

1934   *Cleopatra*, dir. Cecil B. de Mille

1946   *Caesar and Cleopatra*, dir. Gabriel Pascal

1951   *Quo Vadis?*, dir. Mervyn Leroy

1953   *Julius Caesar* (based on Shakespeare), dir. Joseph Mankiewicz

1959   *Ben Hur*, dir. William Wyler

1959   *Spartacus*, dir. Stanley Kubrick

1963   *Cleopatra*, dir. Joseph Mankiewicz

1964   *The Fall of the Roman Empire*, dir. Anthony Mann

1973   *Antony and Cleopatra*, dir. Charlton Heston

1976   *I Claudius* ("Masterpiece Theater" television series)

1979   *Caligula*, dir. Tinto Brass, Giancarlo Lui, and Bob Guccione; screenplay by Gore Vidal

1999   *Titus* (based on Shakespeare), dir. Julie Taymor

2000   *Gladiator*, dir. Ridley Scott

8 Pagan Cults, Judaism, and the Rise of Christianity

> " *For unto us a child is born, unto us a son is given: and the government shall be upon his shoulder: and his name shall be called Wonderful, Counsellor, The mighty God, The everlasting Father, The Prince of Peace.*"
>
> (ISAIAH 9:6)

As the Roman Empire was beginning its rise to power, a new religion, Christianity, was taking root in the Mediterranean region. The pivotal figure of the new faith was Jesus, who died around A.D. 33. According to the Christian religion, Jesus was crucified outside Jerusalem, which was then part of the Roman Empire. At first, the followers of Jesus seemed to be members of one of the many cults flourishing throughout the Near East in the Hellenistic period. But, like the Roman Empire, Christianity grew into a powerful force. Eventually it spread to Rome itself, outlasting the empire and becoming central to Western civilization.

Christianity stems in large part from Judaism, especially the Hebrew Scriptures (written texts). The opening quotation of this chapter is from Isaiah, a prophetic book in the Hebrew Bible (called the Old Testament by Christians). Writing in the eighth century B.C., the prophet Isaiah declared that the birth of a child would usher in a new era and an age of peace. This child would be the Jewish Messiah. The word Messiah, meaning "anointed" in Hebrew and translated as Christos in Greek, at first meant someone who had been given special powers by God. It later came to mean "savior" or "deliverer."

Isaiah's imagery associates the notion of a child's birth with the beginning of a new age. This idea was basic to both Judaism and Christianity, and it echoes the theme of rebirth after death found in the Egyptian myth of Osiris (see Chapter 3). The thematic similarities between these religions are another example of cross-cultural influences in the Mediterranean region, but before we discuss these world religions, we will consider a few of the pagan cults popular during the period of the Roman Empire.

183

TIMELINE	PAGAN CULTS	JUDAISM	EARLY CHRISTIAN PERIOD A.D. 33–600
HISTORY AND CULTURE	Cults throughout the Mediterranean Syncretism Astrology Osiris and Isis Cybele and Attis Greek mysteries: Eleusinian, Orphism Mithraism (Persia) Animal sacrifice	4000 years old Abraham, Moses Ten Commandments Prophets, Twelve Tribes Rule of kings: Saul, David, Solomon, Herod the Great Assyrian conquest, 722 B.C. Babylonian Captivity, 586 B.C. Jews return to Jerusalem, 538 B.C. Theocracy Diaspora	Life of Jesus (d. A.D. 33) Titus razes Temple of Solomon, A.D. 70 Zealots at Masada Teachings of Jesus Mission of Paul, Acts of Apostles Roman persecutions of Christians Constantine's new eastern capital at Byzantium, A.D. 330 Edict of Milan, A.D. 313 Christianity established as official religion of Rome under Theodosius
RELIGION	Mysticism Neoplatonism 	Covenant, Ark of the Covenant Exodus One God, Yahweh (Jehovah)	Death and Resurrection of Christ Christ as Messiah Typology Creeds established Missionaries and monasteries Heresies: Aryan, Manichean Gnosticism Transubstantiation Trinity Baptism
ART	*Mithras Slaying the Sacred Bull*, c. A.D. 200 	Wall-painting of a menorah, 3rd century A.D. *Moses and the Crossing of the Red Sea*, c. A.D. 250	Relief from the Arch of Titus, A.D. 81 *Token of St. Agnes*, 4th century A.D. *Good Shepherd*, c. A.D. 300 *The Sacrifice of Isaac*, c. A.D. 320 Sarcophagus of Junius Bassus, c. A.D. 359
ARCHITECTURE		First Temple of Solomon, Jerusalem, 10th century B.C. Second Temple of Solomon, Jerusalem, 516 B.C.	Old St. Peter's, Rome, c. A.D. 330 Santa Costanza, outside Rome, c. A.D. 350 Santa Maria Maggiore, Rome, A.D. 432–440
LITERATURE	Plotinus (c. A.D. 205–269/270), *Enneads* 	Hebrew Bible: 39 books, including Genesis, Exodus, Psalms, Song of Solomon, Isaiah, Ezekiel Dead Sea Scrolls	New Testament: 27 books–4 gospels, Acts, 21 epistles, Revelation Gnostic Gospels St. Augustine, *Confessions*, c. A.D. 397; *The City of God*, A.D. 413–426 St. Ambrose (A.D. 339–397), *De officiis ministrorum* St. Jerome (c. A.D. 347–c. 420), Vulgate St. Gregory (c. A.D. 540–604), *Book of Pastoral Rules*
MUSIC	Used in rituals	Used in liturgy (religious services) Lyre, harp with Psalms of David Responsorial singing	Used in Mass and other church services Ambrose founds Latin hymnody Gregorian chant: monophonic plainsong for liturgy

PAGAN CULTS

Rome assimilated many different cultures under the mantle of its huge empire. It also tolerated various religious cults, as long as they did not interfere with the authority of the emperor.

From ancient Babylon came an interest in astrology, which was also popular in Rome. From Egypt came the cult of Isis, who had restored her brother-spouse, Osiris, to life after his murder and dismemberment by Set (see Chapter 3). Images of Isis nursing the infant Horus made her a popular maternal figure, and the Romans dedicated a temple to her as early as the second century B.C. From Phrygia, in modern Turkey, came the cult of Cybele, the Great Mother Goddess, who was believed to have power over life and death. Her cult, which centered around the myth of Attis, was present in Rome by the late third century B.C. Cybele fell in love with Attis, a handsome mortal youth. When he died, she restored him to life, just as Isis had restored Osiris. But Attis betrayed the goddess, and she had him castrated.

MYSTERIES

From Greece came secret religions, called **mysteries**, or mystery cults. Unlike other cults that welcomed any believer, the mysteries were accessible only to the initiated. The Eleusinian Mysteries, for example, were celebrated in honor of the agricultural goddess, Demeter, and her daughter, Persephone. Orphism was based on the myth of Orpheus, a legendary musician torn to pieces by Maenads (frenzied female followers of Dionysos; see Chapter 6) when he tried to interfere with their cult. Adherents of Orphism believed in reincarnation and in retribution in Hades for those who had led immoral lives.

In general, the mystery cults used agricultural cycles and seasonal rebirth as metaphors of everlasting life. They promised immortality for all people, not only for the deified emperor, and they satisfied the natural wish to see justice done—which could not always be fulfilled in one's lifetime—by promising reward or punishment after death. Rituals performed in the mystery religions included communal meals, in which the body of a god was symbolically eaten; animal sacrifice; initiation and purification ceremonies; and entering into ecstatic, visionary states.

MITHRAISM

The most prevalent religion in Persia (modern Iran) was Mithraism, whose hero, Mithras, was born on December 25. Mithras killed a sacred bull (figure **8.1**) and fertilized the earth with its blood. Followers of Mithras were thus baptized in the blood of a bull. Mithraism's emphasis on masculinity and its exclusion of women appealed to the ideals of Roman soldiers. By the third century A.D., the cult had spread to North Africa and to Europe, as far north as Britain. Under the emperor Commodus (ruled A.D. 180–192), Mithraism became an imperial cult, but by the fourth century A.D. it began to die out.

8.1 *Mithras Slaying the Sacred Bull*, from the mithraeum at Marino, south of Rome, *c.* A.D. 200. Fresco.

One of many images of Mithras slaying the sacred bull, this shows the hero wearing a Phrygian cap, ankle-length, baggy trousers, a short tunic, and a flowing cape decorated with a star-studded night sky. He kneels on the bull, pulls back its head, and plunges a knife into its neck, while a dog and a snake eagerly lick the blood dripping from the wound. To the left and right of a cave entrance are torchbearers; one torch points upward and the other downward. (On Roman sarcophagi, the upright torch symbolized eternal life and the downward one death.) Faces of the sun and moon are visible above vertical rows of Mithraic scenes. Mithras exchanges a glance with the sun, reflecting the association of light with the forces of good in Mithraism. The migration of this motif to the art of the Roman Empire reflects the widespread influence of Mithraic religion.

NEOPLATONISM

Another source of religious thought was Neoplatonism, which was based mainly on the writings (*Enneads*) of the Egyptian philosopher Plotinus (c. A.D. 205–269/270), who settled in Rome. His views were mystical both in his sense of the divine and in his Platonic notion of a higher Good, which he called the One. For both Plato and Plotinus, the material world was a mere reflection of the Good and the One, or God. Through meditation, Plotinus believed, it was possible to unite with God. But he also considered God to be beyond the reach of human language and indefinable, except by what he is not.

READING SELECTION
Plotinus, *Enneads*, treatise on beauty, PWC1-072

THE ISRAELITES AND JUDAISM

Judaism has been in existence for around 4000 years. The Hebrew Bible (see Box) begins with the beginning: "In the beginning God created the heaven and the earth," making creation the result of God's Word: "And God said, Let there be light: and there was light." "And God said, Let the waters under the heaven be gathered together unto one place, and let the dry land appear: and it was so" (Genesis 1:1, 3, 9).

The word "Judaism" refers to the belief system of the Hebrews; the word "Israelites" refers to the inhabitants of ancient Israel, who shared certain beliefs with other Mediterranean peoples but differed from them in important ways. At first, the Israelites believed in more than one god, but later, from around the eighth to seventh century B.C., they were monotheistic. Their one god was Yahweh (Jehovah), the one and only God. The name *Yahweh* was so revered that it could not be spoken, nor could images of him be created, which inhibited the development of Jewish pictorial art. Other Mediterranean religions at the time had no such prohibitions.

Prophecy was part of Israelite practice, especially from the eighth to the fifth century B.C., which is reflected in the writings of Isaiah and others. Some warned that the end of time was near and that there would be a final day of judgment. The prophets were united by a shared hope for a better future at the coming of a Messiah and by a belief in living an ethical life. These general principles evolved over a long period, during which history, tradition, faith, fact, and fiction converged.

HISTORY, CHRONOLOGY, AND TRADITION

Much of early Jewish history is unknown. The first biblical figure who can, to some degree, be located in a historical context is Abraham. According to tradition, around 2000 B.C.

Society and Culture

The Hebrew Bible and the Dead Sea Scrolls

There are three main parts to the Hebrew Bible: the Torah, the Prophets, and the Writings. The first five books—Genesis, Exodus, Leviticus, Numbers, and Deuteronomy—make up the Torah, which is also called the Law or the Pentateuch. The Pentateuch, accepted as divinely inspired from the fifth century B.C., begins with the Creation and the Fall of Man, and concludes with the early history of the Jewish people.

The books of the Prophets, accepted in the first century B.C., elaborate on Jewish history and develop religious ideas. The early Prophets are Joshua, Judges, 1 and 2 Samuel, and 1 and 2 Kings. The later Prophets are Isaiah, Jeremiah, Exekiel, Hosea, Joel, Amos, Obadiah, Jonah, Micah, Nahum, Habakkuk, Zephaniah, Haggai, Zechariah, and Malachi.

The Writings consist of wisdom and visionary texts, poetry, stories, and histories. These are Psalms, Proverbs, Job, Song of Songs, Ruth, Lamentations, Ecclesiastes, Esther, Daniel, Ezra, Nehemiah, and 1 and 2 Chronicles. Most of the Writings were accepted in A.D. 90, but the Psalms were not considered divinely inspired until ten years later.

The books of the Apocrypha were written between 200 B.C. and A.D. 100. These are wisdom texts, stories, and histories that are not accepted as sacred. Later, however, the Catholic Church included them in the Greek version of the Hebrew Bible, known as the Septuagint. Literally the "Seventy," the Septuagint was, according to tradition, commissioned by Ptolemy II of Egypt (ruled 285–246 B.C.). He reportedly asked seventy-two Hebrew elders to translate the Bible into Greek in seventy-two days.

In 1947, a startling new discovery revealed a group of writings hidden in eleven caves near the Dead Sea, in modern Jordan (see map 8.1, p. 189). Written in Hebrew, Aramaic, and Greek on papyrus scrolls, these works have been dated by carbon-14 to between 250 B.C. and A.D. 70. They contain sections of the Hebrew Bible, two versions of Isaiah, and apocryphal and non-sacred writings. The authors of the texts belonged to the militant monastic Qumran community, which lived apart from the Jewish community in Jerusalem. This group is identified with the Essene sect, to which Jesus is thought by some to have belonged.

Abraham was a Hebrew who led his people from their home, believed by some to have been the Sumerian city of Ur (see Chapter 2). Tradition also has Abraham settling in Canaan, an area later called Palestine (see map 8.1, p. 189). Abraham's grandson, Jacob, changed his name to Israel; his twelve sons produced descendants who became the Twelve Tribes of Israel, and the Hebrews became the Israelites.

According to the biblical book of Genesis, Jacob's son Joseph was sold by his brothers into slavery in Egypt, where he became renowned as the pharaoh's dream interpreter. Joseph interpreted two of the pharaoh's dreams as omens of widespread famine and instructed him to store food for the future. When Joseph's prediction came to pass, the pharaoh invited his family to Egypt, where they prospered and multiplied. But a new pharaoh came to power and enslaved the Israelites. Eventually, around 1250 B.C., Moses, who had grown up at the pharaoh's court, led the Israelites on a forty-year journey—the **Exodus**—out of Egypt, to freedom. According to the Bible, they traveled through the Sinai Desert to the Promised Land of Canaan.

MOSES Moses is associated with one of the most important tenets of Judaism, namely the **covenant**, a solemn pact between God and the Jews. The covenant established an exclusive relationship, in which God chose the Jews to be his people (hence the expression "Chosen People") and the Jews promised fidelity to God. They agreed that Yahweh would be their one and only God and that they would worship only him. This notion is reflected in the first of the Ten Commandments, a set of religious and ethical rules that God is believed by Jews and Christians to have given to Moses (see Box). Like Hammurabi, who received the laws of Babylon from the sun god Shamash (see Chapter 2), Moses went up a mountain (Mount Sinai) to receive the **Tablets** (also called the **Tables**) **of the Law**.

8.2 *Wall-painting in a Jewish catacomb*, Villa Torlonia, Rome, 3rd century A.D. 3 ft. 11 in. × 5 ft. 9 in. (1.19 × 1.8 m).
A menorah, with illuminated candles, stands on either side of the Ark of the Covenant, which is below a painted curtain. This corresponds to God's instructions in Exodus (26:1), where he calls for "ten curtains of fine twined linen, and blue, and purple, and scarlet." Note that the Ark resembles a miniature temple with a crowning pediment, indicating the influence of Greek and Roman architecture on this artist's conception of the Ark.

Society and Culture

The Ten Commandments

The Ten Commandments embody the ethical and religious rules of Judaism. The first four describe the relationship between God and the Israelites:

1. *Thou shalt have no other gods before me.*
2. *Thou shalt not make unto thee any graven image, or any likeness of any thing that is in heaven above, or that is in the earth beneath, or that is in the water under the earth.*
3. *Thou shalt not take the name of the Lord thy God in vain.*
4. *Remember the Sabbath day, to keep it holy.*

(Exodus 20:3–8)

The last six commandments establish social order:

5. *Honor thy father and thy mother.*
6. *Thou shalt not kill.*
7. *Thou shalt not commit adultery.*
8. *Thou shalt not steal.*
9. *Thou shalt not bear false witness against thy neighbor.*
10. *Thou shalt not covet thy neighbor's wife . . . nor any thing that is thy neighbor's.*

(20:12–17)

To house the Tablets of the Law, Moses and his followers built a sacred container, the **Ark of the Covenant**, and carried it with them to the Promised Land. The Ark also housed a **menorah** (a candelabrum with seven candlesticks, three on each side and one in the center) and other holy objects (figure **8.2**). In the book of Exodus, God tells Moses how to design the menorah:

And thou shalt make a candlestick of pure gold: of beaten work shall the candlestick be made . . . And six branches shall come out of the sides of it . . . Three bowls made like unto almonds [almond blossoms], with a knop [calyx] and a flower [petal] in one branch; and three bowls made like almonds in the other branch, with a knop and a flower; so in the six branches that come out of the candlestick.

(Exodus 25:31–33)

One of the most dramatic events in Exodus is the parting of the Red Sea, a miracle that allowed the Israelites to escape their Egyptian pursuers:

And Moses stretched out his hand over the sea; and the Lord caused the sea to go back by a strong east wind all that night, and made the sea dry land, and the waters were divided.

And the children of Israel went into the midst of the sea upon the dry ground and the waters were a wall unto them on their right hand, and on their left.

And the Egyptians pursued, and went in after them to the midst of the sea, even all Pharaoh's horses, his chariots, and his horsemen . . .

And the Lord said unto Moses, Stretch out thine hand over the sea, that the waters may come again upon the Egyptians, upon their chariots, and upon their horsemen . . .

And the waters returned, and covered the chariots, and the horsemen, and all the host of Pharaoh . . .

But the children of Israel walked upon dry land in the midst of the sea; and the waters were a wall unto them on their right hand, and on their left.

(Exodus 14:21–29)

Although figurative imagery was prohibited, the parting of the Red Sea was nonetheless illustrated in a monumental wall-painting of around A.D. 250 in Dura Europos, a town in modern Syria where Roman soldiers were garrisoned. The work is a major example of the presence of a Jewish pictorial tradition under Roman rule. Several Mithraic and Roman shrines, in addition to Christian and Jewish places of worship, were discovered at Dura Europos, indicating a mix of different religions.

The *Crossing of the Red Sea* (figure **8.3**) illustrates the biblical text. Moses and his brother Aaron stand firmly on dry land, their togas reflecting Roman influence. Above, the hand of God descends from heaven to divide the water. At the right, the pursuing army, stripped of its arms, begins to drown. Leaping fish add an element of lively visual description.

MONARCHY AND CONFLICT Over the next two centuries, the Twelve Tribes established a monarchy with Saul as its first king. His armies defeated the Philistines, thought to have been a Sea People who settled in the Near East around 1100 B.C. Under David (ruled *c.* 1000–960 B.C.) and his son, Solomon (ruled *c.* 960–933 B.C.), the Israelites prospered. Solomon built the Temple, which is described in detail in the Bible. Located on the site of the Temple Mount in modern Jerusalem, it was rectangular and constructed of cedar wood from Lebanon. A front porch led to a holy inner sanctuary that contained the Ark of the Covenant. Two bronze columns flanked the entrance, and the entire surface of the Temple was covered with gold.

Solomon instituted certain repressive financial policies that led to class conflict and caused Israel to split into two kingdoms. After his death, ten of the tribes formed the kingdom of Israel in the north, while the remaining two tribes retained the kingdom of Judah in the south, with Jerusalem as its capital (map **8.1**). This division weakened the power of Israel.

In 722 B.C. the kingdom of Israel was conquered and its people were dispersed by the Assyrians (see Chapter 2). In 586 B.C., Nebuchadnezzar II of Babylon attacked Jerusalem and razed the Temple. He exiled the citizens of Judah to Babylon, hence the term for this period—the Babylonian Captivity (also known as the Babylonian Exile). In 538 B.C., the Persians conquered Babylon and permitted the Israelites (now called Jews) to return to Jerusalem. Those who chose to return rebuilt the Temple in 516 B.C., were ruled by a theocracy (government by priests), and accepted the visionary and prophetic texts written before the period of exile as the word of God. Those who did not return from exile are known as the Jews of the Diaspora (the Dispersion). They remained in Babylon and eventually spread to different regions of the ancient world.

Between the fourth and first centuries B.C., Judah was conquered first by Alexander the Great, who Hellenized the region, and later by the Romans. Rome placed Judah under the rule of local kings. Among these was Herod the Great (ruled 37–4 B.C.). He expanded the second Temple of Solomon, a reconstruction of which is shown in figure **8.4**.

8.3 *Moses and the Crossing of the Red Sea*, detail, from Dura Europos, Syria, *c.* A.D. 250. Fresco. National Archaeological Museum, Damascus.

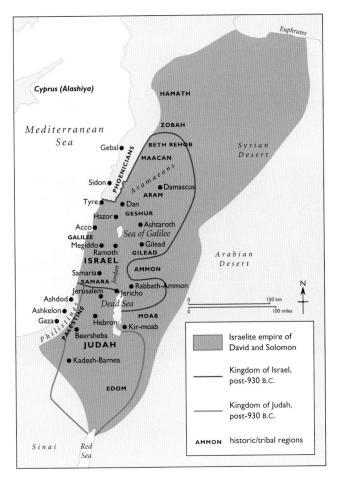

Map 8.1 Ancient Israel.

citizens, weak and unarmed, butchered wherever they were caught. Round the Altar the heap of corpses grew higher and higher, while down the Sanctuary steps poured a river of blood and the bodies of those killed at the top slithered to the bottom. The soldiers were like men possessed and there was no holding them, nor was there any arguing with the fire.

(Josephus, *The Jewish War*)

READING SELECTION
Josephus, *The Jewish War*, on religion in Roman Judea, PWC1-011

8.4 Reconstruction model of the second Temple, Jerusalem.
Note the engaged Corinthian columns and pilasters, reflecting Hellenistic elegance. Decorating the upper section of the building is a continuous gilded frieze, with finials crowning the projecting cornice.

THE SECOND TEMPLE DESTROYED The Jews rebelled against Roman domination in A.D. 66 and fought until A.D. 70, when the Roman emperor Titus (see Chapter 7) defeated them and destroyed the second Temple. Only one group of so-called Zealots continued to resist. They held out at Masada, a mountain fortress near the Dead Sea. Rather than submit to Roman rule, the Zealots committed suicide.

Like all victors in the ancient world, Titus looted the city, an action memorialized in a relief from the interior of his triumphal arch in Rome (figure **8.5**). The destruction of the Temple was recorded by Flavius Josephus (*c.* A.D. 37–100), a Jewish soldier and statesman who wrote in Greek. He had impressed the emperors Vespasian and Titus and was granted Roman citizenship. According to Josephus, the Temple was destroyed against the wishes of Titus:

As the legions charged in, neither persuasion nor threat could check their impetuosity: passion alone was in command. Crowded together round the entrances many were trampled by their friends, many fell among the still hot and smoking ruins of the colonnades and died as miserably as the defeated. As they neared the Sanctuary they pretended not even to hear Caesar's commands and urged the men in front to throw in more firebrands . . . everywhere was slaughter and flight. Most of the victims were peaceful

8.5 Relief from the Arch of Titus, Rome, A.D. 81. Marble, 6 ft. 7 in. (2 m) high.
This shows Titus's soldiers carrying off the spoils of war as they head for the triumphal arch at the far right.
Prominently depicted is the large menorah, whose capture symbolizes the triumph of Rome over the Jews.

One wall of the Temple escaped destruction; in modern Jerusalem it is called the Wailing Wall, because it remains a place of mourning. Following the Temple's destruction, the surviving Jews were again dispersed, this time by the Romans, who wanted to avoid future rebellion. Nevertheless, the Jews maintained their cultural unity and, in the absence of a great temple, began to worship in synagogues, led by rabbis (teachers).

With the institution of the synagogue came new religious views and practices. Forms of worship changed from sacrifice to prayer and religious study. Previously, presiding over worship had been restricted to a small number of priests, but it now became a possibility for more people. In contrast to ancient Egypt, where worshippers were relegated to a court-yard, and Greece, where worship was held outside the temple, Jewish ceremonies took place inside the synagogue, and rituals were enacted in the presence of the congregation. The syna-gogue remains the typical Jewish place of worship today.

THE HEBREW BIBLE AS LITERATURE

The Bible, like the *Iliad* and the *Odyssey*, has had an enormous influence on Western literature. Parts of the Hebrew Bible were first written down in around the tenth century B.C., having been transmitted orally prior to that date. The Bible includes a number of different genres and literary devices. In Exodus, for example, the device of repetition enhances the poetic quality of the story of the crossing of the Red Sea,

suggesting the rushing waters and relentless advance of the Egyptian army. Repetition also creates the impression of a divinely inspired **litany** (a form of prayer in which a leader and a congregation speak alternately during a service).

Poetry is the genre of the Psalms of David and the Song of Solomon. Perhaps the best known psalm is the twenty-third:

The Lord is my Shepherd; I shall not want.
  He maketh me to lie down in green pastures: he leadeth me beside the still waters.
  He restoreth my soul: he leadeth me in the paths of righteousness for his name's sake.
  Yea, though I walk through the valley of the shadow of death, I will fear no evil: for thou art with me; thy rod and thy staff they comfort me.
  Thou preparest a table before me in the presence of mine enemies: thou anointest my head with oil; my cup runneth over.
  Surely goodness and mercy shall follow me all the days of my life: and I will dwell in the house of the Lord forever.

The Song of Solomon (also called the Song of Songs) is essentially a collection of love poems. They are lyrical in style, obscure in meaning, and rich in pastoral metaphor:

I am the rose of Sharon, and the lily of the valleys.
  As the lily among thorns, so is my love among the daughters.
  As the apple tree among the trees of the wood, so is my beloved among the sons. I sat down under his shadow with great delight and his fruit was sweet to my taste.

(2:1–3)

And the beginning of Chapter 4:

> Behold, thou art fair, my love; behold thou art fair; thou hast doves' eyes within thy locks: thy hair is as a flock of goats, that appear from mount Gilead.
>
> Thy teeth are like a flock of sheep that are even shorn, which came up from the washing; whereof every one bear twins, and none is barren among them.
>
> Thy lips are like a thread of scarlet, and thy speech is comely; thy temples are like a piece of a pomegranate within thy locks . . .
>
> Come with me from Lebanon, my spouse, with me from Lebanon; look from the top of Amana, from the top of Shenir and Hermon, from the lions' dens, from the mountains of the leopards.
>
> (4:1–3, 8)

There is a great deal of mythic grandeur in the Hebrew Bible, as there is in epic poetry. One cultural purpose of myths is to explain what otherwise seems inexplicable. For example, in Genesis, the story of the Tower of Babel—a Mesopotamian ziggurat (see Chapter 2)—explains why people around the world speak different languages. This was not, however, always the case:

> And the whole earth was of one language, and of one speech.
>
> And it came to pass, as they journeyed from the east, that they found a plain in the land of Shinar; and they dwelt there.
>
> And they said to one another, Go to, let us make brick, and burn them thoroughly. And they had brick for stone and slime had they for mortar.
>
> And they said, Go to, let us build us a city and a tower, whose top may reach unto heaven; and let us make us a name, lest we be scattered abroad upon the face of the whole earth.
>
> And the Lord came down to see the city and the tower, which the children of men builded.
>
> And the Lord said, Behold, the people is one, and they have all one language; and this they begin to do: and now nothing will be restrained from them, which they have imagined to do.
>
> Go to, let us go down, and there confound their language, that they may not understand one another's speech.
>
> So the Lord scattered them abroad from thence upon the face of all the earth: and they left off to build the city.
>
> Therefore is the name of it called Babel; because the Lord did there confound the language of all the earth: and from thence did the Lord scatter them abroad upon the face of all the earth.
>
> (Genesis 11:1–9)

To punish the human race for its hubris in daring to invade the sky, God made its speech garbled so people could no longer communicate with each other. As a result, cooperation came to an end, work stopped, and the tower was never completed. The builders scattered over the earth and formed different language groups. The story of the Tower of Babel demonstrates

God's power to destroy as well as to create. In order to reaffirm his supremacy in a universe created by his Word, he reduced the power of human speech by breaking up its unity.

The writings of the prophet Ezekiel are visionary in nature and are said by the Bible to have been directly inspired by God's own Word:

> The word of the Lord came expressly unto Ezekiel the priest, the son of Buzi, in the land of the Chaldeans by the river Chebar; and the hand of the Lord was there upon him.
>
> And I looked, and, behold, a whirlwind came out of the north, a great cloud, and a fire infolding itself, and a brightness was about it, and out of the midst thereof as the color of amber, out of the midst of the fire.
>
> Also out of the midst thereof came the likeness of four living creatures. And this was their appearance; they had the likeness of a man.
>
> And every one had four faces, and every one had four wings.
>
> And their feet were straight feet; and the sole of their feet was like the sole of a calf's foot: and they sparkled like the color of burnished brass.
>
> And they had the hands of a man under their wings on their four sides; and they four had their faces and their wings.
>
> Their wings were joined one to another; they turned not when they went; they went every one straight forward.
>
> As for the likeness of their faces, they four had the face of a man, and the face of a lion, on the right side: and they four had the face of an ox on the left side; they four also had the face of an eagle.
>
> (Ezekiel 1:3–10)

Ezekiel's poetic vision of four divine creatures, part human and part animal, would inspire later Christian imagery.

CHRISTIANITY: THE BIRTH OF JESUS THROUGH THE FOURTH CENTURY

The period of Rome's decline roughly corresponds to the rise and spread of Christianity. It is a religion grounded in Judaism and, like Judaism, has a strong ethical message and is based on Scripture. The Christian texts reflect a belief in the power of God's Word and its sacred character. As with Judaism, the power and promise of faith is a central feature of Christianity. But in contrast to the Jews, who are still awaiting the Messiah, Christians believe that the Messiah is Jesus, a Jew born between 6 and 4 B.C., who died at the age of thirty-three.

The life and teachings of Jesus were not recorded until between A.D. 70 and 100. There is thus no first-hand account of him. His life marks the major division of the traditional Western calendar into B.C. (Before Christ) and A.D. (*anno domini*, Latin for "in the year of our Lord," denoting the time after the birth of Jesus). The main Christian text is the New Testament, which takes Jesus to be the Messiah prophesied by Isaiah and builds on the foundation of the Hebrew Bible (see Box).

Although Jesus did not leave any writings, his message and life are recorded in the four Gospels of the New Testament—Matthew, Mark, Luke, and John. Jesus preached the Jewish belief in a single God who created the human race, but he went beyond contemporary Jewish thinking by placing greater emphasis on faith and forgiveness, on the promise of eternal life, and on God's compassion. Christians are thus expected to perform works of charity in the community. Jesus gathered around him his twelve devoted apostles, performed miracles, and claimed to be the Messiah prophesied by Isaiah.

In the Sermon on the Mount, recorded in the Gospel of Matthew, Jesus sets forth his ethical principles. He promises the poor and unfortunate a blessed future in heaven, he revises Old Testament law, and he advances the notion that one can sin in thought as well as in deed. He also announces that he has come to fulfill the prophecy of a Messiah (see Box):

Society and Culture

The New Testament

The New Testament was written in Greek and accepted as **canonical** by the middle of the second century A.D. It is organized into the Gospels, the Acts, the Epistles, and the Apocalypse (or Revelation).

The four Gospels were written by the Evangelists (literally "bearers of good news"), Matthew, Mark, Luke, and John. The first three are biographies of Jesus. They are called **synoptic** ("seen together") because they are similar enough to be placed side-by-side and viewed together at a glance. Matthew opens with the genealogy (the "begats") of Jesus to demonstrate his descent from the House of David. Mark focuses on the miracles of Jesus. Luke describes Jesus' childhood in the most detail and includes the miraculous birth of John the Baptist.

John's is the most philosophical gospel. It opens with: "In the beginning was the Word, and the Word was with God, and the Word was God." Jesus is thus the *Logos*, the Word of God made flesh (human) by the power of God's speech. John conveys the originality of Jesus' message and the ways in which it departs from traditional thinking. He uses the metaphor of light to express the intellectual newness of Jesus' teachings: "That was the true Light, which lighteth every man that cometh into the world" (1:9). John the Baptist, by contrast, was not *the* light, but rather, "He was . . . sent to bear witness of that Light" (1:7). And whereas Moses had introduced the law, Jesus brought grace and truth: "For the law was given by Moses, but grace and truth came by Jesus Christ" (1:17).

The Acts of the Apostles, written by Luke toward the end of the first century A.D., span a period of some thirty years. They chronicle the apostles' mission to spread Christianity to the world beyond Jerusalem. They include miracles performed by the apostles and end with Paul under house arrest in Rome.

The Epistles are in the form of letters, the first fourteen of which are attributed to Paul. They are Romans, 1 and 2 Corinthians, Galatians, Ephesians, Philippians, Colossians, 1 and 2 Thessalonians, 1 and 2 Timothy, Titus, Philemon, Hebrews, James, 1 and 2 Peter, 1, 2 and 3 John, and Jude.

The Apocalypse, from the Greek word for "revealing," or Revelation, is a visionary book and the last of the New Testament. It was written between A.D. 75 and 90 by John the Divine on the Greek island of Patmos. The Apocalypse is a vision of the end of the world and the Second Coming of Christ. John describes seeing the enthroned Christ surrounded by fire and light, twenty-four elders clothed in white and wearing gold crowns, and four beasts that echo those envisioned by Ezekiel (see p. 191):

And before the throne there was a sea of glass like unto crystal: and in the midst of the throne, and round about the throne, were four beasts full of eyes before and behind.

And the first beast was like a lion, and the second beast like a calf, and the third beast had a face as a man, and the fourth beast was like a flying eagle.

And the four beasts had each of them six wings about him; and they were full of eyes within.

(Revelation 4:6–8)

The enthroned Christ in the form of a Lamb holds a book with seven seals. When they are opened, the cataclysm at the end of time is revealed. The first four unleash the Four Horsemen: Conquest, War, Famine, and Death.

And I saw . . . a white horse: and he that sat on him had a bow; and a crown was given unto him: and he went forth conquering, and to conquer . . .

And there went out another horse that was red: and power was given to him that sat thereon to take peace from the earth, and that they should kill one another: and there was given unto him a great sword.

And when he had opened the third seal . . . I beheld . . . a black horse; and he that sat on him had a pair of balances in his hand.

And I heard a voice . . . say, A measure of wheat for a penny, and three measures of barley for a penny; and see thou hurt not the oil and the wine . . .

And I looked, and behold a pale horse: and his name that sat on him was Death, and Hell followed with him. And power was given unto them over the fourth part of the earth, to kill with sword, and with hunger, and with death, and with the beasts of the earth.

(6:2–8)

Finally John envisions the New Jerusalem, illuminated by God's light and "prepared as a bride adorned for her husband" (21:2).

And seeing the multitudes, he went up into a mountain: and when he was set, his disciples came unto him:

And he opened his mouth, and taught them, saying:

Blessed are the poor in spirit: for theirs is the kingdom of heaven . . .

Blessed are the meek; for they shall inherit the earth.

Blessed are the peacemakers; for they shall be called the children of God . . .

Think not that I am come to destroy the law, or the prophets; I am not come to destroy, but to fulfil.

(Matthew 5:1–9, 17)

And referring to the Old Law, he says:

Ye have heard that it hath been said, An eye for an eye, and a tooth for a tooth:

But I say unto you, That ye resist not evil: but whosoever shall smite thee on thy right cheek, turn to him the other also . . .

Be ye therefore perfect, even as your Father which is in heaven is perfect.

(5:38–39, 48)

Jesus also teaches his followers how to pray and recites what is known as the Lord's Prayer:

Our Father which art in heaven, Hallowed be thy name.

Thy kingdom come. Thy will be done in earth, as it is in heaven.

Give us this day our daily bread.

And forgive us our debts, as we forgive our debtors.

And lead us not into temptation, but deliver us from evil: For thine is the kingdom, and the power, and glory, for ever. Amen.

(6:9–13)

In the last verses of the Sermon, Jesus offers some of his most famous lessons for right conduct, some direct and others as allegories (stories told in symbolic form):

Judge not, that ye be not judged . . .

And why beholdest thou the mote that is in thy brother's eye, but considerest not the beam that is in thine own eye? . . .

Give not that which is holy unto the dogs, neither cast ye your pearls before swine, lest they trample them under their feet . . .

Ask, and it shall be given you; seek, and ye shall find; knock, and it shall be opened unto you:

. . . whatsoever ye would that men should do to you, do ye even so to them: for this is the law and the prophets.

Enter ye in at the strait gate: for wide is the gate, and broad is the way that leadeth to destruction . . .

Beware of false prophets, which come to you in sheep's clothing, but inwardly they are ravening wolves.

Ye shall know them by their fruits . . .

A good tree cannot bring forth evil fruit, neither can a corrupt tree bring forth good fruit.

(7:1–18)

Society and Culture

The Typological Reading of History

In the Christian typological view of history, events and personages of the Old Testament are interpreted as prefigurations, or types (from the Greek *tupoi*, meaning "examples"), of corresponding events and personages of the New Testament. Jesus, for example, calls himself the New Solomon in the Gospel of Matthew. Jesus is also called the New Adam and was, according to tradition, crucified on the site of Adam's burial. Both Solomon and Adam, therefore, are types for Christ.

Mary is the New Eve and redeemed Eve's sin as Jesus redeemed Adam's. Moses receiving the Tablets of the Law on Mount Sinai is compared with Jesus delivering the Sermon on the Mount. The parting of the Red Sea is paired with the rite of baptism, because both are miracles involving water. And the story of Jonah's three days in the whale and release is paired with the resurrection of Jesus after three days in the tomb.

Typology became so widespread that ever-increasing numbers of events and personages from the Old Testament were paired with those in the New Testament. The underlying purpose of the typological system was to demonstrate God's divine plan encompassing all of time. According to this plan, Jesus fulfills the prophecy of a Messiah.

DEATH AND RESURRECTION

One of the basic original tenets of Christianity was the sacrificial death and resurrection of Jesus. Through his sacrifice, he was believed to have redeemed humanity from Original Sin, which had caused the Fall of Man. The Fall, according to the Bible, alienated people from God, from their original state of grace, and from the paradise that Adam and Eve enjoyed in the Garden of Eden. God sent his "only begotten son," Jesus, conceived through the Incarnation and born to the Virgin Mary, to assume the fate of humanity. As a man, Jesus was destined to suffer and die on the Cross (see Box, p. 194). Christians believe that, in so doing, he took on the sins of Adam and Eve and the guilt of the human race and reconciled the faithful to God. This reconciliation included the promise of an afterlife.

BAPTISM AND THE EUCHARIST

As Christianity evolved, a number of rites became basic to Christian worship. Two of the most important, though neither was entirely new, were baptism and the Eucharist. Baptism had been practiced in Mithraism; but in Christianity, water rather than blood was used. Jesus himself was baptized in the River Jordan by John the Baptist. For Christians, the rite of baptism came to symbolize rebirth into the faith.

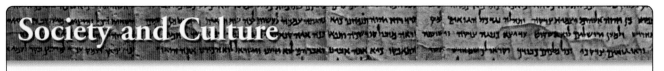

Society and Culture

Principal Events in the Life of Jesus

Childhood

Annunciation: The angel Gabriel announces Jesus' birth to the Virgin Mary and tells her that Jesus' father is God (celebrated on March 25). Joseph is Jesus' earthly father; Mary, Joseph, and Jesus constitute the Holy Family.

Visitation: Mary is three months pregnant when she visits her cousin Elizabeth, who is six months pregnant with John the Baptist.

Nativity: Jesus is born in Bethlehem (celebrated on December 25).

Adoration of the Magi: Three wise men, often described as kings, are led to Bethlehem by a star. They bring gifts of gold, frankincense, and myrrh (celebrated on January 6).

Presentation in the Temple: Jesus is presented to Simeon, the old priest at the Temple in Jerusalem. God has promised Simeon that he will see the Savior before he dies.

Massacre of the Innocents: King Herod decrees the murder of all boys under the age of two in Bethlehem and its vicinity because of a prophecy that one will destroy his kingdom.

Flight into Egypt: Warned by an angel of Herod's plans to massacre the infants, the Holy Family escapes to Egypt.

Jesus among the Doctors: At twelve, Jesus astounds the Temple priests with his wisdom.

Adult Life

Baptism: Jesus is baptized by John the Baptist in the River Jordan.

Temptation of Jesus: Jesus rejects the Devil's offer of wealth and earthly power.

The Calling of the Apostles: Jesus calls the twelve apostles (his followers) to his service. He calls Matthew the tax collector and the brothers Peter and Andrew, who are fishermen. Jesus promises to make them "fishers of men."

Miracles: In the Marriage at Cana, Jesus turns water into wine. In the Transfiguration, Jesus appears in glory in a blaze of light on Mount Tabor, in Galilee, and God announces that Jesus is his son. In the Resurrection of Lazarus, Jesus restores the brother of Mary and Martha to life.

The Passion

The events leading to, and including, the death of Jesus are:

Entry into Jerusalem: Jesus enters Jerusalem on a donkey. This begins his approach to death and is celebrated on Palm Sunday, a week before the Resurrection.

Last Supper: Jesus' last meal with his apostles. He tells them to remember him by eating bread (his body) and drinking wine (his blood), which institutes the ritual of the Mass (the Eucharist).

Betrayal of Judas: The apostle Judas Iscariot accepts thirty pieces of silver in exchange for identifying Jesus to the Romans.

Kiss of Judas: Judas identifies Jesus with a kiss in the Garden of Gethsemane.

Jesus Before Pilate: The Roman governor of Jerusalem, Pontius Pilate, condemns Jesus to death.

Flagellation: Jesus is whipped by Roman soldiers.

Mocking: Jesus is taunted for his claim to be King of the Jews. He is made to wear a crown of thorns and a scarlet robe.

Way to Calvary: Jesus is made to carry his own cross to Calvary (Golgotha, the Hill of the Skulls outside Jerusalem), where he will be crucified.

Crucifixion: Jesus is executed on the Cross between two thieves.

Lamentation: Mourning over Jesus' body. In art, this usually includes Mary his mother, Mary Magdalene, and the youngest apostle, John.

Entombment: Jesus is placed in the tomb, later called the Holy Sepulcher.

Resurrection: Jesus rises from the tomb, which is guarded by Roman soldiers.

Three Marys at the Tomb: The three Marys discover that the tomb is empty.

Noli me tangere: Mary Magdalene sees the risen Jesus and reaches out to touch him. He commands her not to touch him. (Noli me tangere is Latin for "do not touch me.")

Ascension: Jesus ascends to heaven.

Pentecost: The apostles are given the gift of tongues so that they can travel the world spreading Jesus' message to communities speaking different languages.

Christianity eliminated the orgies and animal sacrifices of paganism and established rituals that were more symbolic. From early worship in private houses, the table became the altar, and Jesus' Last Supper was reenacted in the central rite of the Mass, or Communion—that is, the Eucharist, which means "thanksgiving" in Greek. During Mass, the bread (or a wafer) is transformed into Jesus' body, and red wine becomes his blood. This miracle later came to be known as transubstantiation.

THE MISSION OF ST. PAUL

St. Paul (died *c.* A.D. 67) was a crucial figure in the spread of Christianity. Originally named Saul, he was born in Tarsus, in Cilicia (now in Turkey). He was a Jew and a Roman citizen who persecuted Christians, but he became a Christian after hearing the voice of Jesus asking why he was persecuting him. Saul was on the way to Damascus, in Syria, and in some accounts he saw a bright light and fell from his horse. On conversion, Saul changed his name to Paul. He believed in the Incarnation (that Jesus was born as a human being), the Trinity (three equal parts of the godhead—Father, Son, Holy Ghost), and redemption (that Jesus saved humanity by assuming

Original Sin). For Paul, therefore, Jesus was both human and divine and equal to God.

In his devotion to Jesus, Paul undertook to spread the Christian message to Jews and gentiles (non-Jews) throughout the Mediterranean world (map **8.2**). Beginning around A.D. 40, Paul traveled to Syria, Cyprus, Asia Minor, Greece, and Rome, where, emphasizing the importance of faith and the love of God, he converted many gentiles. In addition to preaching, Paul wrote the Epistles, which are letters to groups of believers and Christian leaders to reinforce previous teaching and overcome immorality. The Epistles are now part of the New Testament and a foundation of Christian religion. When Paul arrived in Rome, according to tradition, he was imprisoned and beheaded in the persecution of Christians ordered by the emperor Nero.

EARLY CHRISTIANITY IN ROME

Like Judaism, Christianity was considered a threat to the power and authority of Rome. Adherents of both faiths were persecuted for refusing to worship pagan gods and for denying the divinity of the emperor. The times of greatest persecution of Christians in the first century A.D. were under Nero in 64 and Domitian in 93. Later, in 111, Trajan declared Christians traitors to the Roman Empire; in 250 Decius (ruled 249–251) ordered Christians to be executed for refusing to sacrifice to the emperor; and in 257 Valerian (ruled 253–260) launched a full-scale persecution, burning and beheading thousands of Christians.

In 284, Diocletian (ruled 284–305) tried to stabilize the empire by instituting a **tetrarchy**. This form of governance established four equal rulers at the far ends of the empire. The tetrarchy lasted for ten years but failed to re-establish Rome's former power. At first, Diocletian tolerated Christianity, but when Christians refused to join the Roman army, he turned against them. In 303, Diocletian ordered the destruction of all Christian places of worship and Christian texts, and in 304, he demanded the death or imprisonment of anyone known to be a Christian. This created a large number of **martyrs** (people who die for their beliefs). Eventually, the Church conferred sainthood on most martyrs as well as on other Christians considered to have led holy lives.

In its early stages, Christianity appealed to the lower classes of Roman society, including slaves. But from the second century, the middle class, intellectuals, and aristocrats—more women than men—were drawn to the new religion. The broad appeal of Christianity came in large part from its advocacy of universal equality before God. The promise of salvation was not restricted by gender or class; Jesus himself had had prominent female followers. In addition, women were integrated with men during services, and some assumed leadership roles in the new cult. In Paul's Epistle to the Romans (16:1–15), he mentions a number of female as well as male followers of Christ who help him spread the gospel (see Box, p. 196).

Although under continual threat of persecution, Christians could safely worship in the **catacombs**, underground burial places that the Romans held sacred. Built by law outside the city walls, the catacombs consisted of complex passageways and up to four stories of small chambers. Bodies were placed in niches in the walls and sealed in with tiles or blocks of stone.

Because of the restrictions placed on Christians, their art developed only minimally before the fourth century. In fact, it

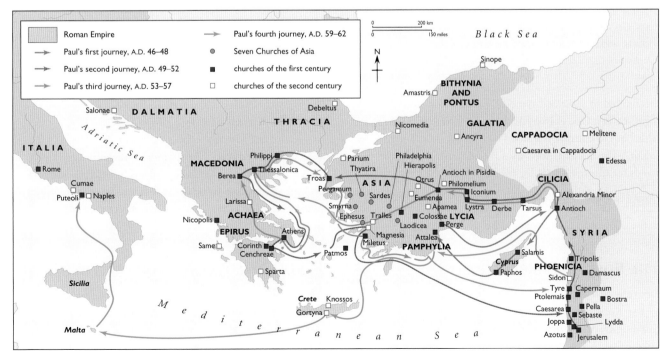

Map 8.2 Paul's missionary journeys, A.D. 46–62.

Society and Culture

Women in the Bible

The role of women in the Bible is complex and varied and has been reinterpreted many times. In addition, the biblical narrative is interwoven with cultural and political histories that influence views of women in different times and places. Nevertheless, there are some important general observations to be made. Women in the Bible have many symbolic meanings and can personify wisdom, compassion, and even nations.

Typically of lower status than men, a number of women—for example Delilah, in the story of Samson and Delilah—control men through the power of seductiveness. In the Hebrew Bible, foreign women are seen as especially dangerous in this respect unless, like Ruth, they accept the covenant with Yahweh. Ruth was a Moabite who not only assumed her husband's culture and religion but also followed her mother-in-law, Naomi, after her husband's death: (". . . Whither thou goest, I will go . . . thy people shall be my people, and thy God my God"; Ruth 1:16). In contrast, when Israelite women marry foreign men and adopt different religions, they are compared to treacherous nations. Women are thus described as devious as well as faithful.

Royal women, priestesses, widows, and temple prostitutes sometimes escape the traditional status imposed by their gender. Queen Esther, for example, personifies the wise, devoted, and courageous spouse who saves her people. The same may be said of the apocryphal heroine Judith, who rescued the Hebrews from the Assyrian army, although she did so by deception and seduction.

The four Gospels of the New Testament, in which women are the first witnesses to the Resurrection, accord women a new status. Jesus accepts women equally with men. In the Acts and Epistles, women are mentioned as missionaries, apostles, prophets, and church leaders who perform services.

---

was limited to signs and symbols, partly as a means of avoiding discovery. One example is the word *ICHTHUS*, Greek for "fish," but to Christians it stood for "Jesus Christ, Son of God, Savior." The I stands for "Jesus," or *Iesus* in Greek; the CH stands for *Christos*; the U for *Uios*, or "Son"; the TH for *theou*, or "of God"; and the S for *Soter*, or "Savior." Eventually, the fish came to symbolize the Eucharist, and the symbol appears in the catacombs with images of bread and wine.

THE ROLE OF CONSTANTINE

From the first to the third century, the number of Christians in the Roman Empire grew from a small segment of the community to a tenth of the population—approximately 5 million. Christians formed larger groups in the cities, especially Rome, and smaller ones along the borders of the empire.

In 313, Constantine (ruled 306–337) issued the Edict of Milan, which granted tolerance to all religions, especially Christianity. The edict essentially ended persecutions and paved the way for Christianity to become the official religion of Rome. According to Constantine's biographer, the Palestinian theologian Eusebius (*c.* 260–*c.* 339), who was the bishop of Caesarea (in modern Israel), the emperor was himself converted and baptized. The event believed to have inspired Constantine's conversion is part of a complex Christian narrative known as the Legend of the True Cross.

According to the legend, in 312, when Constantine was preparing for battle, he had a vision (or a dream, depending on the text). He saw an angel carrying a small cross with the words *in hoc signo vincis* ("In this sign, you conquer"). True to the vision, Constantine carried a small cross before him into battle and routed the enemy without effort.

Although the only source for Constantine's conversion is the account of Bishop Eusebius, which could be considered biased, it is clear that Constantine made it possible for Christianity to expand and develop throughout and beyond the Roman Empire. Constantine also took as his emblem the *Chi-Rho*, "Chr" in Greek and the first two letters of Jesus' Greek name, Christos. It is written as a superimposed *X* (*Ch* in Greek) and *P* (*R* in Greek). The emblem adorned Constantine's shield and became a motif in Christian art. In addition, Constantine encouraged the construction of many churches, freeing Christians to worship openly, seek converts, publish texts, and create large-scale works of art.

In the year 330, Constantine established a new capital at the port city of Byzantium to take advantage of its potential as a center of commerce. Changing the name of the city to Constantinople, he made it his eastern capital, while Rome remained the western capital of the empire. The two centers gave rise to differences in doctrine as well as to divergent artistic styles. The western style, discussed below, is generally referred to as Early Christian; the eastern style, known as Byzantine, is explored in the next chapter. Today, the head of the Western Church is the pope in Rome, and the Eastern (or Orthodox) Church is led by a patriarch.

Toward the end of the fourth century, Theodosius I (ruled 379–395) proclaimed Christianity as the official religion of Rome. The emperor persecuted pagans, ordered their works of art and architecture to be destroyed, and banned sacrifices to pagan gods. The ascendancy of Christianity over paganism was now complete.

EARLY CHRISTIAN ART AND ARCHITECTURE

After the Edict of Milan and Constantine's conversion, art and architecture began to reflect Christian ideas. Content shifted from mythological and imperial subjects to Christian ones. And whereas Roman art had continued the naturalism of Hellenistic Greece, Early Christian art became progressively two-dimensional. Striving to express a spiritual rather than a material realm, Christian artists moved away from naturalism by flattening space and increasing the stylization of their figures. The transition was gradual but steady, and many Early Christian images have traces of Roman features.

PAINTING AND SCULPTURE Because Christian art is highly symbolic, any discussion of it must include the iconographic aspect of its imagery as well as its style. The word **iconography** means how the subject matter is "written." It relates not only to the apparent meaning of an image, but also to its themes and underlying symbolism.

A good example of a Christian image with both a surface meaning and a symbolic meaning is the little disk called the *Token of St. Agnes* (figure **8.6**). Originally from the inside of a cup or bowl, this was found in the catacombs. It shows a frontal figure of St. Agnes, a popular martyr in Rome, with outstretched arms. She is flanked by two columns, each surmounted by a dove.

The symbolic meaning of the image on the disk is more complex than what we see at first glance. The saint's pose is one of prayer, a type known as an *orans* (a praying figure). But in a Christian context, this pose alludes to the Crucifixion, because Agnes's outstretched arms visually echo Christ's arms on the Cross. In Christian art, the dove stands for the Holy Ghost,

8.6 *below Token of St. Agnes*, Catacomb of San Pamfilo, Rome, 4th century A.D. Gold-glass.

Polykleitos, *Spearbearer* see figure 6.22

8.7 *Good Shepherd, c.* A.D. 300. Marble, 39 in. (99 cm) high. Vatican Museums, Rome.

and the architectural columns can refer to the church building. The symbolic meaning of the image is thus that St. Agnes is a mirror of Christ in having died for her faith and that faith, like a column, is supportive. In this context, faith supports the Christian Church and is reinforced by the Holy Ghost.

Another image that alludes to Christ is the Good Shepherd, whose flock symbolizes the Christian congregation (figure **8.7**). This was derived in part from the pastoral traditions of Greece and Rome and from the Archaic Greek type of a youth carrying a sheep on his shoulders. Classical influence can be seen in the contrapposto stance, which is reminiscent of the *Spearbearer* (see thumbnail). The shepherd is beardless, which is a Roman rather than Greek fashion, and he wears a Roman

8.8 *The Sacrifice of Isaac*, Via Latina Catacomb, Cubiculum C, Rome, *c.* A.D. 320. Fresco.
The sacrificial meaning of this event is accentuated by the central position of the altar and wood-burning fire. Themes of obedience and the sacrifice of a son by a father recur in the New Testament story of Jesus. His death, like Isaac's, is presented as the will of God; and both are saved by God, though in different ways. Isaac became a type for Jesus, and his potential sacrifice was seen as a prefiguration of Jesus' actual sacrifice on the Cross. The man and the donkey may simply be a scene of everyday life, or they may refer to Jesus' entry into Jerusalem.

depth: by turning the ram so that it is seen from the rear, the artist compresses its form and makes it appear to occupy three-dimensional space. The cast shadows add to the impression of a natural, horizontal surface. At the same time, however, the altar tilts unnaturally upward, which flattens the space. This shift in perspective reveals the tension between naturalism and the Early Christian preference for the flat space of a spiritual world.

Another expression of the transition between Roman and Early Christian style can be seen in the fourth-century sarcophagus of the Roman consul Junius Bassus (figure **8.9**). The style is primarily Roman, but the iconography is Christian. Like the Romans, the early Christians did not include an image of the deceased on the lids of their sarcophagi. Instead, they carved narrative scenes on the sides. The figures resemble Roman sculpture, and the head types are reminiscent of Roman portrait busts. In some cases, however, such as the Adam and Eve in the lower tier (second from the left), the proportions are not Classical. The architectural divisions consist of different Orders of Greek columns, but the twisted columns allude to Solomon's Temple.

ARCHITECTURE There are two main types of Early Christian church plan: the longitudinal basilica and the centrally planned building. Although there are no surviving fourth-century basilican churches, there are drawings that show the typical plan (figure **8.10**) that evolved from the Roman basilica (see Chapter 7). Figure **8.11** is a diagram of the interior and elevation of Old St. Peter's, which remained the most important Christian church in the West until the sixteenth century.

The plan was in the form of a Latin cross, with an atrium at the entrance, as in Roman domestic architecture (see figure 7.17). The large central nave, side aisles, and **clerestory** (upper story) windows of the Roman basilica were retained. A new feature, the **transept** (the cross-section corresponding to the arms of the cross), separated the nave from the curved apse. In contrast to pagan temples, the interior of the church building,

tunic. The artist has emphasized the intimate relationship between the shepherd and his sheep (and implicitly between Jesus and his followers), which endows the original Greek subject with a Christian meaning. In John 10:11 Jesus says, "I am the good shepherd."

After the Edict of Milan, the number and scale of Christian paintings increased. The *Sacrifice of Isaac* (figure **8.8**) from the catacombs illustrates a well-known event from the Old Testament book of Genesis. It shows Abraham preparing to sacrifice his son Isaac as a sign of obedience to God. In the biblical text, Isaac is saved when an angel intervenes. Although the figure of the angel in the painting has faded, Abraham can be seen gazing toward either the angel or the hand of God staying Isaac's death. Isaac kneels at the right, and the ram, which will be sacrificed in his stead, is at the left.

Note the transitional nature of this painting, which is partly Roman in style and partly Early Christian. Abraham wears Roman costume and is shown in a contrapposto stance. Foreshortening (rendering in perspective) creates the illusion of

Sacrifice of Isaac   Arrest of Peter   Jesus between Peter and Paul   Jesus before Pilate   Latin inscription

Job on the dunghill   Temptation of Adam and Eve   Jesus' entry into Jerusalem   Daniel in the lion's den   Paul led to his martyrdom

8.9 Sarcophagus of Junius Bassus, *c.* A.D. **359. Marble, 3 ft. 10½ in. (1.18 m) high. Lateran Museum, Rome.**

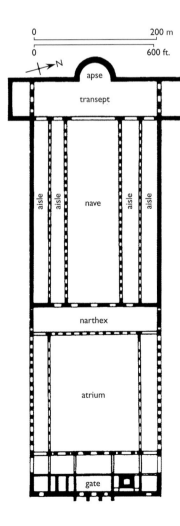

0 — 200 m
0 — 600 ft.

N

apse

transept

aisle | aisle | nave | aisle | aisle

narthex

atrium

gate

8.10 *Plan of Old St. Peter's*, Rome, *c.* A.D. 330.

In Matthew 16:18–19, Jesus tells Peter: "Thou art Peter, and upon this rock I will build my church; and the gates of hell shall not prevail against it. And I will give unto thee the keys of the kingdom of heaven." Because the Greek word for "rock" is "petros," Jesus' declaration is grammatically ambiguous. Tradition has maintained that Jesus gave Peter the keys to heaven and the mission to found the Church. As a result, Peter is considered to have been the first Roman pope and Old St. Peter's stood on the traditional burial site of St. Peter.

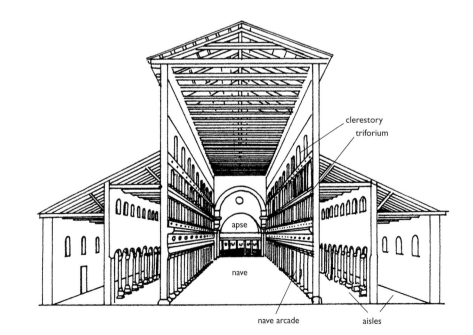

clerestory
triforium

apse

nave

nave arcade   aisles

8.11 Section showing the interior and elevation of Old St. Peter's, Rome, *c.* A.D. **330.**

8.12 Interior of Santa Maria Maggiore, Rome, A.D. 432–440.

like the Roman basilica, was designed to accommodate large crowds.

Old St. Peter's was destroyed in the sixteenth century to make way for the present church, New St. Peter's. But the appearance of an early Christian basilican church can be gained from the interior view of Santa Maria Maggiore in Rome (figure **8.12**). It combines Early Christian elements with those derived from the Roman basilica. As in Old St. Peter's, Santa Maria Maggiore has a large central nave, side aisles, a transept, and an apse. But the coffered ceiling, similar to that in the dome of the Pantheon (see figure 7.39), differs from the wooden roof of Old St. Peter's.

At the far end of the nave, leading to the apse, is a round arch derived from the Roman triumphal arch. But instead of signifying the triumph of a pagan emperor, it now alludes to the triumph of Jesus. The apse, which in the Roman basilica had housed the law courts and the emperor's colossal statue, has become a sacred space for the Christian altar. The long horizontal of Santa Maria Maggiore's nave draws the gaze of the worshipper toward

8.13 Exterior of Santa Costanza, outside Rome, c. A.D. 350.

8.14 Interior of Santa Costanza, outside Rome, c. A.D. 350.
The two visible sections showing the ceiling mosaics reflect the Christian assimilation of pagan iconography. Cupids, birds, and animals are juxtaposed with a scene of grape-harvesting. The grapes refer both to the wine of the Eucharist and to the orgiastic cults of Dionysos. This use of the grapes as an allusion to two religious rites is a good example of iconographic syncretism.

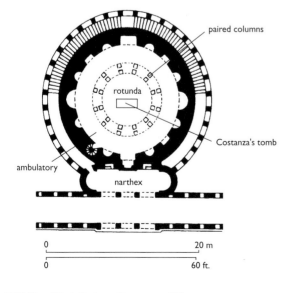

8.15 Plan of Santa Costanza, Rome, c. A.D. 350.

the apse, and the gold mosaics on the walls reflect light, denoting the presence of the divine.

The second type of church design is based on the Greek cross, which has four arms of equal length. Such centrally planned buildings had traditionally been used as **baptisteries** (where baptisms are performed), **martyria** (built over tombs of martyrs), and **mausolea** (large round tombs). Thus the fourth-century church of Santa Costanza was originally built by Constantine to mark his daughter's tomb but was later converted to a church. Its monumental, imposing exterior (figure **8.13**) contrasts with the lighter, more decorative interior (figure **8.14**). The vaulting is brick, and twelve pairs of smooth-shafted columns ring the domed core (figure **8.15**). Colored granite columns support miniature entablatures; their ornate marble capitals combine Ionic volutes with Corinthian foliage. The interior is designed so that worshippers enter first into a darkened space. They are then drawn toward the center, where light from the clerestory windows dramatically illuminates Costanza's tomb.

THE SPREAD OF CHRISTIANITY

As Christianity expanded, the Church established **creeds**, or doctrines, and disseminated them throughout the Mediterranean world. Christianity was less tolerant of other religions than paganism was. Since Christians were convinced of the truth of their beliefs and the reality of their experience of God, they sent missionaries to share their message and convert people to their faith. In the second century, missionaries traveled as far east as India, and by the fifth century, according to tradition, St. Patrick had converted Ireland, and St. Columba, Scotland. Beginning in the fourth century, the Church convened numerous councils to plan ways of combating **heresy** (belief or practice that is contrary to established Church teaching).

THE ARIAN HERESY

One of the most vexing problems of early Christianity concerned the nature of Jesus. According to the Libyan priest Arius (c. 250–c. 336), who preached and wrote songs, Jesus was less divine than God and his nature was different. Arius argued that Jesus was God's instrument and was created by God, which meant he was not eternal. In effect, Arius was challenging the Trinity by denying Jesus' equality with God. To resolve this controversy, in 325, Constantine convened the Council of Nicaea, in Bithynia (in modern Turkey) and exiled the Arian leaders. But Arianism remained popular, prompting further councils—in 343, 351, 353, 355, 357, 359, and 362. Finally, in 381, the emperor Theodosius convened the Council of Constantinople, and the Trinity was proclaimed doctrine. Nevertheless, the Arian heresy persisted for nearly a hundred years more.

MANICHEES, BOGOMILS, CATHARS, AND ALBIGENSIANS

Heresies have continued to challenge Church doctrine throughout its history. Manichaeism, founded by Mani in the third century (see Chapter 2), argued that conflict between good and evil was derived from the light and dark forces of Zoroastrianism. Mani taught that Satan had stolen light particles from the world and imprisoned the human mind. The aim of religious practice was to release these particles of light. In order to bring this about, according to the Manichees, the Hebrew prophets, the Buddha, and Mani himself, as well as Jesus, had been sent by God.

The Bogomil heresy developed in the eighth century in the Balkans, in eastern Europe. Originally a Manichee sect, the Bogomils believed that the world and its inhabitants had been created by Satan and that only the soul was God's creation. The Bogomils were declared heretics in the tenth century but were not completely eradicated until the fifteenth.

In the twelfth century, the Cathars, in the south of France, Germany, and northern Italy, took up Mani's notion of the duality of good and evil. They taught that material things, including the established Christian rites, were evil. Cathars living around Albi were called Albigensians; they believed that Jesus was an angel and thus neither God nor human. They denied the doctrine of the Resurrection and Jesus' assumption of human sin. Such heresies, like Arianism, were enormously popular. They were eradicated only after numerous Church councils and, eventually, the massacre of their followers.

GNOSTICISM

At first, Gnosticism was considered a heresy by the Church, but by the second century, it had become a separate Christian sect. It was an extremely complex version of Christianity, and its origins and beliefs are still being studied. The name comes from the Greek word *gnosis*, meaning "knowledge." Gnosticism developed over a long period and was influenced by both Judaism and the New Testament. It, in turn, influenced Zoroastrianism, Manichaeism, and the early heresies.

Gnosticism, like the mystery religions, held that secret wisdom possessed by ascetics could lead to salvation. The source of knowledge, however, was not a pagan god or a state of ecstasy, but the wisdom of the apostles transmitted by teachers from one generation to the next. Gnosticism distinguished between a Demiurge (creator god) and a Supreme Divinity (Divine Being). Jesus was seen as the messenger of *gnosis*, or divine knowledge. He was not believed to have been "God made Man" but, rather, a phantom who assumed a human shape or a being who entered the body of a human. Gnosticism attempted to solve contradictions between good and evil. According to the Gnostics, evil did not come from the Supreme Divinity or from Original Sin, but from the Demiurge, who trapped humanity in ignorance. Their goal was thus to seek the knowledge that would bring them to a state of pure spirituality.

The Gnostics wrote gospels that differ from those in the Bible and the Apocrypha. In the Gnostic Gospel of Thomas there are secret sayings attributed to Jesus, which are metaphorical, and often enigmatic. One of the main themes is enlightenment.

Gnosticism differed from orthodox Christianity in according equality to women. For although we have seen that during the second century in Rome, the Christian message included equality between men and women (see p. 196), this later changed. One of the main forces in this change was the misogyny of St. Paul and other early Christian authors who postdate the Bible.

THE BEGINNINGS OF MONASTICISM

An important development in the early Church was the growth of monasticism, beginning around 300. The monastic movement originated with the conviction that to achieve salvation one must withdraw from the corrupt world. Although he did not establish a formal monastery, St. Anthony of Egypt

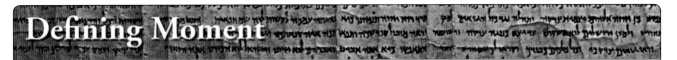

Defining Moment

St. Anthony and the Beginnings of Monasticism in the West

The idea of monasticism apparently originated in India and infiltrated the West through monks traveling along trade routes. The origins of Christian monasticism are attributed to St. Anthony, whose life is known mainly from a biography by the Greek author St. Athanasius.

Anthony was born in Koma, in Egypt. His parents died when he was around twenty years old. About six months later, he entered a church and heard a reading from the Gospel of Matthew: "If thou wilt be perfect, go and sell all thou hast" (19:21). Anthony was struck by the words and renounced his worldly possessions.

Anthony withdrew from the world around 270 and went to live an isolated existence in a tomb near Koma. Visited by visions of demons, he suffered extreme moral conflict for some fifteen years (figure **8.16**). Around the age of thirty-five, he left the tomb and retired across the River Nile to the mountain of Pispir (modern Der-el-Memum), living in an ancient fortress. He remained there for twenty years, resisting all human contact. But his holiness and learning attracted ascetics who looked to him for spiritual leadership, and finally he emerged.

Anthony then spent time organizing groups of monks, and these would later develop into great monastic communities during the Middle Ages. He also fought heresy—especially the Arian heresy—and the Roman persecution of Christians. According to Athanasius, Anthony preached lengthy sermons on the ascetic life and on his own battle with demons. He died at the age of 105, having spent his last forty-five years in relative isolation.

Critical Question Is the task of the journey or is the reward of finding the right goal more important? Would it matter if one were never to reach a desired goal? Would the journey still have meaning?

8.16 Paul Cézanne, *Temptation of St. Anthony*, 1874–1877. Oil on canvas, 18½ × 22 in. (47 × 56 cm). Musée d'Orsay, Paris.
Cézanne produced several pictures on the theme of St. Anthony's temptation. This one is the third in his series and shows the saint at the left cowering beneath an overpowering horned red devil. The real source of the temptation, however, is the large Venus-like woman surrounded by small boys, who exposes herself to Anthony.

(c. 251–355) is generally considered the founder of monasticism in the Roman Church (see Box). He renounced his possessions in his early twenties and for the next thirty-five years lived as a hermit. His resolve in resisting attacks from demons has been the subject of many later creative works, notably, paintings by the nineteenth-century French artist Paul Cézanne (see figure 8.16) and Gustave Flaubert's novel *The Temptation of St. Anthony*. Anthony's piety attracted scores of disciples eager to learn from him, and so, in 305, he reluctantly returned to the world.

During the next several hundred years, as Christians followed Anthony's example, monasticism grew. Separate religious communities were established, where monks lived, worked, and prayed according to a particular **rule** (a systematic regimen).

Anthony's counterpart in the Eastern Church was Pachomius of Egypt (c. 290–346). Born a pagan, Pachomius converted to Christianity and founded a monastery near the River Nile, at Tabennisi. A few decades later, Basil the Great, bishop of Caesarea (c. 330–379), and his friend Gregory of Nazianus (c. 329–c. 389) preached against Arianism and urged Christians to take up the monastic life. They built hospitals, churches, and living quarters for the poor. The rule of Basil became the basis of monasticism in the Eastern Church. Community life was rigorous and founded on obedience, daily routines of prayer and worship, manual work, poverty, chastity, and charity.

CHRISTIAN AUTHORS: THE FOUR DOCTORS OF THE CHURCH

Because Christianity is based on Scripture, early Christian writers were enormously important in establishing Church doctrine. Four of these writers are known as the Four Doctors of the Church, because they laid down the most fundamental precepts of Christianity. They are Ambrose, Jerome, Pope Gregory I, and Augustine, all of whom were classically educated. They warned against heresy and paganism, and wrote extensively.

Ambrose (339–397), born in Trier, in modern Germany, was the son of a Roman administrator in Gaul. He became a lawyer and practiced Roman law before converting to Christianity. In 374, when he was thirty-four, he became bishop of Milan, in northern Italy, a post he held until his death. Ambrose had a strong social conscience, caring for the poor and preaching against injustice. He particularly objected to the abuses of the Roman emperors. Of his many writings, the most significant is *De officiis ministrorum*, which is influenced by the rhetorical style of Cicero and emphasizes the importance of leading an ethical Christian life.

Jerome (*c.* 347–*c.* 420) was born in Italy, south of Rome. He is considered the most distinguished scholar of the early Church. He wrote treatises attacking heretics and pagans and commentaries on the Bible. He also translated the Bible from Hebrew and Greek into Latin. At the time, Latin was the *volgare*, or common, everyday speech—Jerome's translation is thus called the "Vulgate" and is still the standard Bible of the Roman Catholic Church. Jerome traveled widely, and founded a monastery in Bethlehem. He led the life of a hermit, practicing asceticism and self-denial.

Gregory the Great (*c.* 540–604) was the son of a Roman senator, but he renounced his wealth and gave his belongings to the poor. He was committed to monasticism, founding six monasteries in Sicily and one, St. Andrew's, in Rome, which he joined at the age of thirty-four. Gregory believed that bishops were shepherds of souls, and he described the life they should lead in *Liber regulae pastoralis* (*Book of Pastoral Rules*). His belief in the notion of Purgatory—a place where souls can be purged of sin in preparation for entry into heaven—became part of Church doctrine. Gregory's social, political, and economic skills, combined with his piety, led to his being elected pope as Gregory I in 590.

READING SELECTION
Gregory the Great, *Dialogues*, St. Benedict, the father of western monasticism, struggles against sin, PWC2-101-B

The most influential of the Four Doctors was Augustine (354–430). Born in Tageste, in modern Algeria, to a Christian mother and a pagan father, Augustine studied Plato and Plotinus in Carthage. He led a dissolute life, and was fascinated by magic and astrology. At first an adherent of Manichaeism, Augustine went to Rome and met Ambrose, who inspired him to become a Christian. He was baptized in 387. Augustine then returned to North Africa to preach, entered the administration of the Church, and became bishop of Hippo in 396.

Around 397, Augustine wrote the *Confessions*, an autobiography of his spiritual journey from paganism to Christianity. He was eloquent and charismatic, and believed that God's grace, more than good works, determined salvation. For Augustine, evil was created by the human race, not by God. No doubt drawing on his own experience as a sinner, Augustine argues the power of Original Sin and insists that faith is the best weapon against evil. In describing his boyhood, he enumerates his sins and his curiosity, implores God, and shrewdly observes the hypocrisy of parents:

> And yet I sinned, O Lord my God, creator and arbiter of all natural things, but arbiter only, not creator, of sin. I sinned, O Lord, by disobeying my parents and the masters of whom I have spoken . . . I was disobedient, not because I chose something better than they proposed to me, but simply from the love of games. For I liked to score a fine win at sport or to have my ears tickled by the make-believe of the stage, which only made them itch the more. As time went on my eyes shone more and more with the same eager curiosity, because I wanted to see the shows and sports which grown-ups enjoyed. The patrons who pay for the production of these shows are held in esteem such as most parents would wish for their children. Yet the same parents willingly allow their children to be flogged if they are distracted by these displays from the studies which are supposed to fit them to grow rich and give the same sort of shows themselves. Look on these things with pity, O Lord, and free us who now call upon you from such delusions.
>
> (Augustine, *Confessions*, 1.10)

READING SELECTION
Augustine, *Confessions*, on his conversion, PWC2-009-C

Augustine's other great work is *The City of God*, written in twenty-two books, after the Visigoths sacked Rome in 410. He wrote partly in response to pagans, who blamed the destruction of Rome on the Christian God. Augustine argued that Rome's destruction was simply another event on the way to the Second Coming of Christ. *The City of God* is based on the architectural metaphor of dividing the universe into two cities. The City of God is inhabited by those destined for eternal life in heaven; the City of Man is inhabited by those destined for hell. Throughout, Augustine alludes to Classical works such as the *Aeneid*, to Roman history, to the Bible, and to contemporary Christian authors. Book One opens with God's divine plan:

Most glorious is and will be the City of God, both in this fleeting age of ours, wherein she lives by faith, a stranger among infidels, and in the days when she shall be established in her eternal home.

(*The City of God*, Preface)

The City of Man, on the other hand, is the source of the pagan enemy:

For it is from this earthly city that the enemies spring against whom the City of God must be defended.

(*The City of God*, 1.1)

The City of God concludes with Augustine's lengthy discourse on the end of time. He does not claim to know exactly how things will be, but he is certain that the virtuous will see God in the heavenly city:

Therefore it is possible, and very probable, that we shall see the corporeal bodies of the new heaven and the new earth in such as way that, wherever we turn our eyes, we shall, through our bodies that we shall be wearing and plainly seeing, enjoy with perfect clarity of vision the sight of God everywhere present and ruling all things, even material things.

(*The City of God*, 22.29)

READING SELECTION

Augustine, *The City of God*, on the two cities, PWC2-001

MUSIC IN THE EARLY CHURCH

Music had been an important part of Jewish services in the Temple of Solomon and continued to be so in the synagogues. A **cantor** chanted Bible readings, and psalms were sung **responsorially**—a soloist alternated with congregational responses. This involved the congregation in the service, creating an atmosphere for worship and reinforcing a sense of religious community. As described in the Psalms of David, the lyre and harp sometimes accompanied singing. The early Church discontinued this use of instruments in worship, on the grounds that they were pagan and could incite passion; the Church Fathers were particularly opposed to anything associated with luxury. However, the chanted style of singing was to develop into the most important form of early Christian music, namely, **plainsong** (or **plainchant**).

Two forms of service developed in the early Church. The first was a reenactment of Jesus' Last Supper, and gradually a standard text narrating the Eucharist or Mass was established. Much of this was chanted to music. Some sections—known as the "Ordinary"—always used the same words, but other parts —known as the "Proper"—changed according to the Church year and its feasts. The second type of service was a meeting devoted to singing psalms, reading the Bible, and prayer.

At first, the language of worship was Aramaic, but as the apostles and missionaries of the Church began to spread the gospel, Greek, the international language of the time, was adopted. It was not until the fourth century that Latin came to be used in the Western Church, a usage that persisted in Roman Catholicism until the 1960s. Thus the texts of the main body of Western religious music are in Latin.

Little remains of early church music, partly because notation did not come into use anywhere until at least the seventh century—songs and chants were transmitted orally from generation to generation. However, it is known that Ambrose wrote Latin hymns, and several have survived. He is considered the founder of Latin hymnody. There is also a body of plainsong called Ambrosian chant, which he may have developed.

It is Pope Gregory I whose name has gone down in history for his contribution to the Church's **liturgy** (form of worship). During his reign, the chants used in the Western Church were collected and standardized for use in the Mass and throughout the Church year, for celebrations such as Easter and saints' days. Now known as "Gregorian chant," this body of some 3000 melodies is a highly significant part of church music.

Plainsong, as the term suggests, is a plain line of music, sung unaccompanied. Like earlier forms of chant, it is monophonic (it has a single strand of melody). Its range of **pitch** (height or depth of notes) is small, and it has no **meter** (regular divisions into set numbers of rhythmic beats). Gregorian chant has an austere, timeless quality, with phrases rising and falling gently in patterns somewhat like speech. In some chants there is one note per text syllable ("syllabic chant") and in others the syllable is held for several notes ("**melismatic** chant"). This distinction between syllabic and melismatic music would later become a major issue in church music, as the authorities sought to cut down on musical diversions so as to assert the primacy of the religious text.

In the next chapter we follow the development of the Christian Church, which eventually split into Eastern and Western factions, each with its own version of doctrine and liturgy. During the seventh century, under the influence of Muhammad in Saudi Arabia, a new world religion—Islam—would arise. This, in turn, would lead to new forms of art and architecture.

KEY TERMS

Ark of the Covenant the original container for the Tablets containing the Ten Commandments.

baptistery a building in which baptisms are performed.

canonical authorized; used with reference to a collection of writings or works applying to a particular religion or author.

cantor in Jewish worship, the singer who chants Bible readings, prayers, or parts of the liturgy.

catacomb an underground burial place or cemetery, held sacred by the Romans.

clerestory in a church or temple, an upper story of the nave, above the aisle, that is pierced with windows to admit light.

covenant a formal agreement; the conditional promises made between God and his people in the Bible.

creed a formal statement of the beliefs of a particular religion or philosophy.

Exodus the forty-year journey made by the Israelites, led by Moses, out of Egypt to freedom; also, the second book of the Hebrew Bible.

heresy a belief or practice that is contrary to established Church teaching.

iconography the apparent meaning of an image and its underlying symbolism.

litany a type of prayer in which a leader and a congregation speak alternately.

liturgy rites of worship.

martyr a person who dies for his or her beliefs (the meaning of the Greek word is "witness").

martyrium (plural **martyria**) a structure built over the tomb of a martyr.

mausoleum (plural **mausolea**) a large, elaborate round tomb.

melismatic music in which several notes are sung to one syllable.

menorah a candelabrum with seven candlesticks, three on each side and one in the center.

meter in music, regular division into set numbers of rhythmic beats.

mystery (or **mystery cult**) cultish religion, based on ancient myths, of a type that was common in Greece and throughout the Roman Empire.

pitch in music, height or depth of a tone.

plainsong (sometimes called **plainchant** or **Gregorian chant**) unaccompanied monophonic music sung to Latin texts as part of a church service.

responsorial a style of music in which a soloist alternates with congregational or choral responses.

rule in monasteries, a systematic regimen.

synoptic referring to three books of the New Testament, the Gospels of Matthew, Mark, and Luke, which are considered to form a group.

Tablets (Tables) of the Law the stones on which were inscribed the laws given to Moses on Mount Sinai.

transept in a church, the cross-section corresponding to the arms of the Cross.

KEY QUESTIONS

1. What rituals did Christianity borrow from mystery cults and Judaism? What term is used to describe these borrowings?
2. Why did Rome consider both Judaism and Christianity as threats?
3. What sources do scholars use for the life of Jesus? When were these sources written?
4. What is a good example of a Christian image with both a surface meaning and symbolic meaning?
5. What changes in art occurred when its content shifted from mythological and imperial subjects to Christian subjects?
6. How would you distinguish between a valid original source, tradition, legend, myth, and literature?

SUGGESTED READING

Augustine, St. *The City of God*, ed. D. Knowles. New York: Penguin Books, 1972.
  ▶ The classic work by the Bishop of Hippo on his vision of salvation.

——.*Confessions*, trans. R. S. Pine-Coffin. New York: Dorset Press, 1986.
  ▶ An autobiography of the saint from his early childhood through his conversion to Christianity.

Brown, P. *Power and Persuasion in Late Antiquity: Towards a Christian Empire.* Madison, WI: University of Wisconsin Press, 1992.

▸ The relationship of early Christianity to imperial Rome.

———. *The Rise of Western Christendom.* New York: Blackwell, 1996.

▸ On the transition from pagan Rome to the rise of the Western Church.

Elsner, Jas. *Imperial Rome and Christian Triumph.* New York: Oxford University Press, 1998.

▸ On the transition from the Roman Empire to early Christianity in art and culture.

Fox, Robin Lane. *Pagans and Christians.* Harmondsworth, U.K.: Penguin Books, 1986.

▸ On paganism in the ancient world and the rise of Christianity.

Frend, W. H. C, *The Rise of Christianity.* Philadelphia: Augsburg Fortress, 1983.

▸ A history of early Christianity.

Geist, Sidney. *Interpreting Cézanne.* Cambridge, MA: Harvard University Press, 1988.

▸ An original, biographical approach to Cézanne's imagery that includes the *Temptation of St. Anthony* pictures.

Grabar, André. *The Beginnings of Christian Art, 200–395,* trans. Stuart Gilbert and James Emmons. London: Thames and Hudson, 1967.

▸ A standard work on early Christian art.

Pagels, Elaine. *The Gnostic Gospels.* New York: Vintage Books, 1989.

▸ A study of the Gnostic Gospels.

Pritchard, J. B. *Ancient Near Eastern Texts Relating to the Old Testament.* Princeton, NJ: Princeton University Press, 1969.

▸ A compilation and discussion of ancient Near Eastern texts relating to the Hebrew Bible.

Smart, Ninian (ed.). *Atlas of the World's Religions.* Oxford and New York: Oxford University Press, 1999.

▸ A survey of the major world religions showing their geographical spread and development.

SUGGESTED FILMS

1932   *The Sign of the Cross,* dir. Cecil B. de Mille

1953   *The Robe,* dir. Henry Kosta

1956   *The Ten Commandments,* dir. Cecil B. de Mille

1959   *Solomon and Sheba,* dir. King Vidor

1966   *The Bible,* dir. John Huston

1972   *Augustine of Hippo (Agostino di Ippo),* dir. Roberto Rossellini

1981   *Raiders of the Lost Ark,* dir. Steven Spielberg

1988   *The Last Temptation of Christ,* dir. Martin Scorsese

2000   *Joseph—King of Dreams,* dir. Robert C. Ramirez and Rob La Duca

9 The Byzantine Empire and the Development of Islam

> " *The entire ceiling is overlaid with pure gold . . . Who can recount the beauty of the columns and the stones with which the church is decorated: One might imagine that he had come upon a meadow with its flowers in full bloom. For he would surely marvel at the purple of some, the green tints of others, and at those from which the white flashes, and again, at those which Nature, like some painter, varies with contrasting colors.*"
>
> (PROCOPIUS OF CAESAREA, *The Buildings*, I.1)

The end of the Pax Romana in A.D. 193 was followed by decades of civil war until Diocletian became emperor in 284. Among the formidable challenges he faced in stabilizing the Roman Empire were the Germanic tribes to the north (see Chapter 10). By 300, the Huns, Vandals, and Goths had reached the boundaries of the empire along the Danube and Rhine rivers. The Goths then separated into Visigoths in the west and Ostrogoths in the east.

In 330, in another attempt to stabilize the declining Roman Empire and protect its wealthier eastern regions, Constantine established a new imperial capital in Byzantium, which he renamed Constantinople. But in 410 the Visigoth king Alaric attacked and plundered Rome. The sixth-century Byzantine historian Procopius of Caesarea (c. 500–565) described the brutality of the Visigoths, who slaughtered men, women, and children, and burned and looted the city. What is now known as the Byzantine Empire is the Eastern Roman Empire that persisted after the fall of Rome itself in 476. People in the Eastern Empire considered themselves Romans and their culture as a continuation of that of Rome.

In 451–452, Attila, king of the Huns (ruled 434–453), invaded Germany, Gaul, and northern Italy, but he did not advance on Rome. Three years later the city was invaded by the Vandal leader Gaiseric (ruled 428–477), who further impoverished Rome by blocking a grain shipment from North Africa. In 476, the official date of the fall of Rome, the German Goth Odoacer (ruled 476–493) dealt the city a devastating blow and took control of the entire Italian peninsula. He ruled from the strategically important Italian port city of Ravenna, on the Adriatic coast. In 493, the king of the Ostrogoths, Theodoric (ruled 493–526), killed Odoacer and seized power in Ravenna. Under Theodoric, Ravenna began its political, religious, and artistic rise to prominence.

In the quotation that opens this chapter, Procopius is describing the interior of the church of Hagia Sophia in Constantinople. The splendor of this huge Byzantine church, with its gold mosaics, reflective light, and expansive space, was meant to project the piety, wealth, and power of the ruler. A similar taste for elaborate surface decoration characterized Islamic design, despite profound differences between the Christian and Muslim religions, their cultures, and their approaches to imagery.

Key Topics

The Byzantine Empire

After the fall of Rome

The founding of
  Constantinople

Justinian and Theodora

Nika Riots

Law Code of Justinian

Art as power

Church music

The Development of Islam

Muhammad's vision

A succession of caliphs

Schisms in the Islamic world

Islamic philosophy and
  science

Islamic poetry and art

The Five Pillars and *jihad*

Controversies

The Consolation of Philosophy

Popes and patriarchs

Iconoclasm

*The Incoherence of the
  Incoherence*

The Guide for the Perplexed

TIMELINE	END OF THE WESTERN ROMAN EMPIRE AND OSTROGOTHIC RULE 193–526	BYZANTINE EMPIRE 476–1453	ISLAM c. 600–c. 1700
HISTORY AND CULTURE	Diocletian becomes emperor, 284 Constantine's eastern capital renamed Constantinople, 330 Alaric sacks Rome, 410 Attila the Hun invades, 451–452 Odoacer causes the fall of Rome, 476 Theodoric comes to power, 493 Ravenna rises to prominence	Capital Constantinople Justinian comes to power, 527 (rules with Theodora) Arab and Bulgarian encroachments, 7th–8th century Golden Age begins under Basil I (ruled 867–886) Army in power: Comnenus (ruled 1081–1118) Michael Palaeologus (ruled 1259–1282) Ottoman Turks begin to erode Byzantine power, c. 1302 Turks sack Constantinople, 1453; rename it Istanbul	Muhammad (c. 570– 632) Muhammad leaves Mecca: *Hijra*, 622 Succession of caliphs, from 632 Umayyad dynasty founded, 661 Abbasid dynasty in power, 750–1258 Islam spreads, 8th century Muslims ousted from Spain, 1492
RELIGION	Arianism under Theodoric Boethius (c. 480–524) on theology	Eastern Orthodox Christianity Patriarch as head of Church Iconoclastic Controversy, 726–843	Allah, the one true God of Islam Qur'an (Koran) (114 *suras*) Hadith Five Pillars of Islam *Ka'bah*, Mecca Sunnis and Shi'ites Mystical devotional movement: Sufism
ART	Mosaics in Sant' Apollinare Nuovo, Ravenna, early 6th century	Mosaics in San Vitale, Ravenna, 6th century Icon showing Christ blessing, 6th century *Barberini Ivory*, late 6th century	Calligraphy from the Qur'an, 11th or 12th century Glass bottle, mid-14th century Kashani, Ardabil carpet, 16th century
ARCHITECTURE	Mausoleum of Theodoric, Ravenna, early 6th century Sant' Apollinare Nuovo, Ravenna, early 6th century	San Vitale, Ravenna, 6th century Monastery of St. Catherine, Mt. Sinai, 530 Hagia Sophia, Constantinople, 537 Mt. Athos monastery, 963 St. Mark's, Venice, begun 1063	Dome of the Rock, Jerusalem, completed 691 Córdoba Mosque, 786–987 Alhambra, Granada, 1343–1391 Tomb of Timur Leng, Samarkand, c. 1403 Taj Mahal, Agra, 1630s
LITERATURE		Procopius (c. 500–565), *History of the Wars of Justinian; Secret History* Justinian Law Code, 534 Icasia (poet) (born c. 810) Michael Psellus (1018–1078) Anna Comnena, *Alexiad*, c. 1148	*The Thousand and One Nights*, recorded by late 8th century Omar Khayyam (c. 1048–c. 1131), *Rubáiyát* Sufi poets: Jalal al-Din Rumi (c. 1207–1273) Hafiz (1326–1390)
PHILOSOPHY	Boethius, *The Consolation of Philosophy*, c. 523		al-Kindi (c. 800–c. 870) al-Farabi (c. 870–c. 950), *The Ideas of the Inhabitants of the Virtuous City* al-Ghazali (1058/9–1111), *Deliverance from Error* Averroës (1126–1198), *The Incoherence of the Incoherence* Maimonides (1135–1204), *The Guide for the Perplexed*
MATHEMATICS AND MEDICINE	Boethius on mathematics and music		Mathematics: al-Khwarizimi (c. 780–c. 850) Medicine: al-Razi (c. 865–932) Avicenna (980–1037), *Canon of Medicine* al-Hazen (d. 1038)
MUSIC	Boethius on mathematics and music	Eastern (Orthodox) liturgy (hymns and psalms) Western (Roman) liturgy (the Mass and Divine Office) Plainchant Responsorial and antiphonal performance	Chanting of Qur'an, call to prayer Sufism: whirling dervishes, *qawwâli* Court music: *maqams, taqsims*

RAVENNA UNDER THEODORIC

Since A.D. 404, Ravenna had been an alternative capital to Rome on the Italian peninsula. In addition to its strategic location on the coast, Ravenna was smaller than Rome and was not the center of the empire. As a result, barbarian tribes were less likely to attack Ravenna than Rome. Under Theodoric, Ravenna was a thriving center of culture and an Ostrogoth capital until 526. In 510, Theodoric appointed the statesman and philspher Anicius Manlius Torquatus Severinus Boethius (*c.* 480–524) to a consulship. Boethius wrote the last great theological treatise in the tradition of imperial Roman literature.

BOETHIUS ON THEOLOGY

Boethius became Theodoric's adviser. But when he defended a former consul charged with treason, Theodoric arrested him and condemned him to death. While he was in prison Boethius wrote *The Consolation of Philosophy*, which became enormously popular in the West. Boethius argued that through philosophy one could arrive at a vision of God. In this view, he was influenced by Plato, Aristotle, Cicero, and Augustine. Boethius attempted to resolve the long-standing conflict between the notion of free will and an omnipotent divinity by distinguishing between human time and divine time. God, according to Boethius, sees all of time simultaneously, whereas people experience time sequentially—as past, present, or future. The fact that God has foreknowledge does not, therefore, eliminate human choice. The *Consolation* is written in the form of a dialogue between the author and the fictional speaker, Lady Philosophy. This literary device allowed Boethius to address various sides of philosophical issues and also to feel less isolated by conversing with an imaginary companion.

READING SELECTION
Boethius, *The Consolation of Philosophy*, on the wheel of Fortune, PWC2-012

BOETHIUS ON MUSIC

In addition to philosophy, Boethius wrote on physics, astronomy, and music. His treatise on music, *De institutione musica*, was influenced by Plato's theories, especially the notion that music and mathematics are related. He organized music according to a three-tiered hierarchy. At the top was the "unhearable" music of the planetary spheres described by Greek philosophers (see Chapter 5). Then came human music based on Platonic "harmonia" and finally, of lesser value in Boethius's view, instrumental music and popular songs. His treatise on music, like the *Consolation*, was extremely influential during the Middle Ages, providing something of a synthesis and a transition between Classical and Christian ideas.

THEODORIC AND THE VISUAL ARTS

Theodoric's reign was, on the whole, prosperous, and relatively tolerant of religious minorities. He instituted social reforms and patronized the arts. Two of his major artistic commissions in Ravenna were his own tomb (figure **9.1**) and the Palace Church of Sant' Apollinare Nuovo (figure **9.2a**). The church walls are decorated with mosaics designed to express the piety of Theodoric. The detail of the nave wall shown here depicts a long row of male saints wearing Roman togas. They are proceeding toward an enthroned Christ flanked by angels. Figure **9.2b** shows the palace of Theodoric, its frontal white columns echoing the saints' togas. This visual correspondence between the saints and the architecture reflects the combined secular and religious significance of the palace. Above the triple-arched entrance, alluding to Roman triumphal arches, is the inscription *PALATIUM* (meaning "palace"). Behind the palace the rooftops of Ravenna can be seen.

9.1 Mausoleum of Theodoric, Ravenna, early 6th century.
Theodoric's mausoleum is the typically round funerary structure of antiquity. Its massive dome measures 36 by 10 feet (11 × 3 m) and rests on a circular drum. Note the round exterior arches resting on narrow projecting ledges in the manner of Roman arches cut into city walls (see figure 7.8). The tomb itself, which was destroyed in the Middle Ages, was made of porphyry, a stone traditionally reserved for emperors.

9.2a *above* **Mosaics on the south wall of the nave, Sant' Apollinare Nuovo, Ravenna, early 6th century.**
St. Apollinaris was the first bishop of Ravenna. He was martyred and venerated in the nearby port city of Classe.

9.2b **Theodoric's palace, detail of the mosaics on the south wall of the nave, Sant' Apollinare Nuovo, Ravenna, early 6th century.**

THE BYZANTINE EMPIRE: AN OVERVIEW—FOURTH TO THIRTEENTH CENTURY

Constantine planned to take advantage of the strategic position of his new capital, Constantinople. Byzantium was located on the Bosphorus, between the Black Sea and the Aegean Sea (see map 9.1), which flows into the Mediterranean. Constantine believed that from Byzantium he would benefit from readily accessible trade routes and be better able to defend the declining Roman Empire. In fact, however, his move laid the foundation for the rise of the Byzantine Empire. It also reinforced the division between the Eastern and Western Churches, which led to the final schism in 1054.

In 527, a powerful new emperor came to power in Constantinople. Justinian I (ruled 527–565) succeeded his uncle, Justin I (ruled 518–527), who had come from a peasant family in Macedonia. But Justinian was well-educated and had worked in the imperial administration. He ruled together with his empress, Theodora, and greatly expanded the empire. In 562, he conquered Italy, and eventually he controlled the Near East, North Africa, Egypt, Asia Minor to the west coast of the Black Sea, and Greece to the Danube River (map **9.1**). The Byzantine Empire flourished, and Justinian presided over a vast artistic program, which included church building, mosaic decoration, and other works.

During the seventh and eighth centuries, Arabs and Bulgarians conquered parts of the Byzantine Empire. This led to a repressive social and economic system, with private armies in control of most of the land. In the ninth century, however, a period known as the Golden Age of the empire began when Basil I (ruled 867–886) established the Macedonian dynasty. He improved the economy, encouraged the development of an intellectual community, and sent missionaries to eastern Europe. By the tenth century, Russia had adopted Christianity.

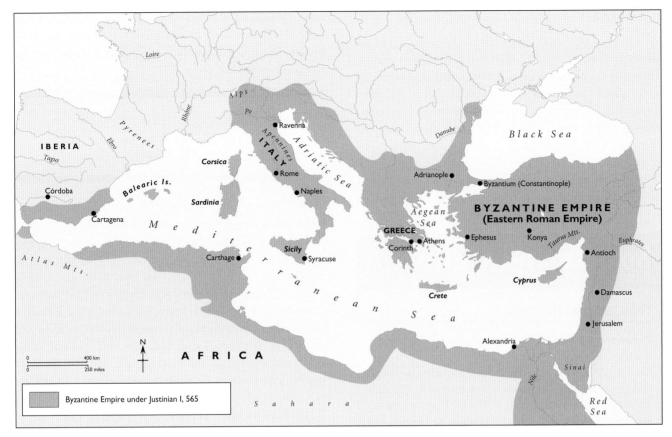

Map 9.1 The Byzantine Empire, 565.

At the end of the eleventh century, the army took over the administration of the empire. Its economy was primarily agrarian, with **serfs** (peasant workers) living on the land and turning over a portion of their income to the landowners. In 1081, another new dynasty of rulers, the Comneni, led by General Alexius I Comnenus (ruled 1081–1118), gained power. His daughter, Anna Comnena (1083–c. 1153), wrote the *Alexiad*, which is a biased account of his reign (see Box).

READING SELECTION

Anna Comnena, *Alexiad*, Byzantium meets the crusaders, PWC2-200-A

In 1261, after nearly a century of unrest, a new dynasty was founded by the aristocratic Michael VIII Palaeologus (ruled 1259–1282). A ruler in Nicaea, he blinded the legitimate emperor and seized control of Constantinople. His successors maintained power for two hundred years. But beginning around 1302, the Ottoman Turks (named for their leader, Osman) gradually eroded Byzantine power and encroached on its territory. This culminated in the sack of Constantinople in 1453 and the establishment of the Ottoman Empire. The Ottomans renamed the city Istanbul.

Society and Culture

Byzantine Scholarship, Ninth to Eleventh Century

Byzantine scholars, among them the clergy and educated aristocrats, kept alive the Classical Greek texts. Michael Psellus (1018–1078), a statesman who wrote on science, mathematics, history, law, and rhetoric, was particularly devoted to the works of Plato and Aristotle. In general, Byzantine scholarship was not innovative. Its main contribution was in preserving, editing, and commenting on Classical literature. During the eighth century, the principal innovations in philosophy and science came from the Arab world.

A few women, despite severe social and legal restrictions on their freedom, also participated in Byzantine intellectual life. One was the poet Icasia (born c. 810), who was celebrated at court but eventually retired to a convent. Anna Comnena studied Classical literature, and her history of her father's reign is evidence of a high level of literacy and strong, independent opinions. According to the *Alexiad*, Comnenus shared power with his mother; he made the military decisions and she administered the civil service and ran the finances of the empire. Anna Comnena's secret efforts to eliminate her brother, John II Comnenus, so that she herself could rule, failed. He became co-emperor with his father in 1092, and she entered a convent.

JUSTINIAN I

In 527, with Justinian I's rise to power, the boundaries of the Byzantine Empire expanded. Justinian wanted to be seen as Constantine's successor and to restore Constantinople to its former glory. He therefore ruled from Constantinople, which he considered his personal city, although he launched enormous artistic programs throughout the empire, including Ravenna. With Theodora (see Box), Justinian ruled in the autocratic style typical of Byzantine emperors.

Byzantine rulers considered themselves God's emissaries on earth, and their power was absolute. This form of government,

called **autocracy** (rule by an individual), was believed to have been divinely ordained. To reinforce the notion of the ruler's divinity, Byzantine emperors wore purple and gold as the Roman emperors had done.

READING SELECTION
Procopius, *The Secret History*, on the scandalous past of Theodora, PWC1-006

In 532, a rebellion against Justinian's autocratic policies broke out during a horserace in Constantinople. The Nika Riots, so-called after the shouts of *nika, nika*, meaning "victory," were suppressed by the emperor's faithful general Belisarius (c. 505–565). Three years later, Belisarius captured North Africa for Justinian, and between 535 and 561 he recovered Italy from the Goths. Procopius accompanied Belisarius on his military campaigns and recorded them in his *History of the Wars of Justinian*. But despite Justinian's imperial gains, which included taking control of the silk market in the West (see Box), he overspent his resources and weakened the empire.

THE BARBERINI IVORY: AN IMAGE OF IMPERIAL TRIUMPH

A good example of Justinian's political iconography can be seen in the *Barberini Ivory* (figure **9.3**). This carving shows

Society and Culture

Theodora and the Court

Theodora (c. 500–548) is sometimes identified as the daughter of a stable owner, sometimes of an animal trainer in the circus. She herself had been a dancer, actress, and courtesan before becoming the emperor's concubine; two years later they were married and she became empress. A woman of high intelligence and driving ambition, she was a close adviser to Justinian and urged him to exert his power. During the Nika riots, Theodora reportedly said to Justinian, "there is the sea, and there are the ships," should he wish to escape the mob. She herself, ever vain, would stay, because "purple makes a superb shroud."

Like Justinian, Theodora opposed paganism and approved the shutting down of Plato's Academy and Aristotle's Lyceum in Athens. Her early life notwithstanding, as empress she was engaged in moral reform, and she founded a home for rehabilitated prostitutes. Theodora also influenced certain laws in the Justinian Code that benefited women. At the time, marriage between people of different social classes was illegal—which made it impossible for Justinian to marry Theodora. That law had been eased before the new laws were issued, but with the Code, any woman who renounced the theater could marry a high-ranking man. The Code also ended all proscriptions on marriages between the upper and lower classes.

The lavish life at Justinian's court contrasted markedly with the style of Theodora's humble beginnings. Some 4000 servants attended the imperial couple, and access to them was guarded by eunuchs and slaves. A huge civil service, composed of well-educated men, administered the empire. Justinian's otherwise faithful historian Procopius (c. 500–565) chronicled the rampant abuses at court in a *Secret History*, which was not intended for publication. Procopius objected to a woman of low-class origin ascending the throne and believed Theodora had bewitched Justinian. As an actress, she was naturally viewed at the time as a prostitute. She was well known for her striptease and her talents as a comic mime and contortionist. Procopius, who was not only elitist but also a misogynist, thoroughly disapproved of Theodora and was extremely hostile to her.

9.3 *Barberini Ivory*, late 6th century. 3³⁄₈ × 10⁹⁄₁₆ in. (34.2 × 26.8 cm). Louvre, Paris.

Society and Culture

Justinian and the Silk Routes

The Silk Routes (map **9.2**) had long been traveled by merchants and caravans bringing silks, ceramics, lacquer ware, and furs from Asia to Rome. They also took Western gold, ivory, glass, and wool to the East. The particularly profitable silk trade was controlled by a Persian monopoly. With a view to improving his own economy, Justinian persuaded Indian Buddhist monks to teach him the secret of making silk. He hired the monks to transport mulberry trees and worms' eggs to Constantinople. By learning how to feed the silkworms on mulberry leaves, he broke the Persian monopoly on silk in the West.

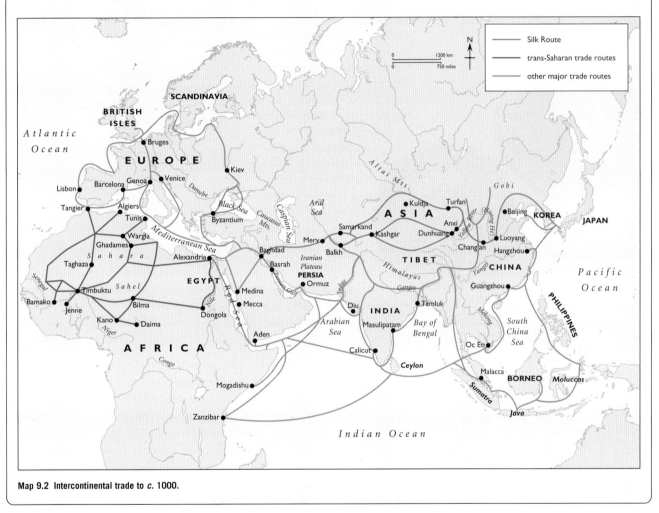

Map 9.2 Intercontinental trade to *c.* **1000.**

the emperor as an equestrian in the tradition of Roman emperors such as Marcus Aurelius (see figure 7.40). Justinian wears a jeweled crown and controls a vigorous horse rearing over a female figure. She personifies fertility and prosperity, which are indicated by her pendulous breasts and the fruit in her lap. To the left, a Roman soldier carries a small figure of Nike offering a laurel wreath to the emperor, and an Asiatic prisoner follows behind the horse. Above Justinian, a young Christ in beardless Roman tradition is flanked by angels.

The lower tier of the ivory is filled with defeated enemies. Among these are Asians wearing Phrygian caps and leggings and an African carrying a large tusk. The Asians are accompanied by a lion and the African by an elephant; both are bearing tribute. Another Nike dominates the center, alluding to Justinian's military and imperial triumphs.

JUSTINIAN'S LAW CODE

One of Justinian's most lasting accomplishments was commissioning a revision of the Roman law code, which had grown exceedingly complex since the republic and needed reorganizing. The revision consisted of four parts: the *Codex* reviewed all imperial decrees from Hadrian to Justinian; the *Digest* summarized past legal opinions and arguments; the *Institutes* were laws that dealt with people, things, actions, and crimes against

Defining Moment

The Code of Justinian

The legal code that was to become the foundation of law in most western European countries during the twelfth to eighteenth centuries was initiated by the Emperor Justinian (figure **9.4**). In February 528, Justinian appointed a commission of ten headed by the pagan legal scholar Trebonianus (d. 545) to devise new imperial constitutions. His aim, as asserted in the preface of the Code, was that:

Imperial majesty should not only be adorned with military might but also graced by laws, so that in times of peace and war alike the state may be governed aright and so that the Emperor of Rome may not only shine forth victorious on the battlefield, but may also by every legal means cast out the wickedness of the perverters of justice, and thus at one and the same time prove as assiduous in upholding the law as he is triumphant over his vanquished foes.

(Justinian, *The Digest of Roman Law: Theft, Rapine, Damage, and Insult*)

The result of some ten years of labor was to gather together Roman law into one body, known as the Justinian Code or the *Corpus Iuris Civilis* (*Body of Civil Law*). Justinian's code was a compilation of early Roman laws and legal principles, illustrated by individual cases, and combined with new laws. Significant as the Code was in its own time, it achieved even greater significance thereafter. In the late eleventh century, the discovery of two manuscripts of the complete text of Justinian's Code revolutionized the study of law in western Europe. Comprehensive and systematic Roman civil law became a model for western Europeans struggling to create their own legal systems. The view that law should be based on a philosophical system comes directly from Justinian's Code. This was the most widely used law until the emperor Napoleon commissioned the Napoleonic Code in 1804.

Critical Question How can a society devise fair civil laws? Is it just to base laws on traditional beliefs and the customs of those already in power?

9.4 Solidus with a portrait of Justinian on the front and a representation of Victory on the reverse, 527–565. Gold, ⅛ oz. (4.27 g). Preussischer Kulturbesitz, Münzkabinett, State Museums, Berlin.

people; and the *Novels* listed all laws enacted after the Code was instituted.

Under the revised code, promulgated in 534, disputes were settled by the courts, and new individual rights placed a few limits on the ruler's absolute power. It further distinguished between two theoretically independent jurisdictions, granting the emperor (*imperium*) authority in secular matters and the clergy (*sacerdotum*) authority in matters pertaining to the Church. Justinian, however, remained the head of both Church and state.

READING SELECTION
Justinian, *Digest of Roman Law*, on sexual harassment in ancient Rome, PWC1-045

THE ARTS IN RAVENNA

Although Justinian never visited Ravenna, his artistic program was designed to make his presence and his image known in that part of the Byzantine Empire. Two of Justinian's major achievements were mosaics at Sant' Apollinare Nuovo (figure **9.5**) and the church of San Vitale.

San Vitale has a centralized Greek cross plan (figures **9.6** and **9.7**). In the apse Justinian commissioned a pair of mosaics honoring himself and Theodora. In figure **9.8** Justinian is shown dressed in the royal purple of Roman emperors. He is flanked by clergymen, including Archbishop Maximian holding a jeweled cross. All wear Roman togas. To the left, Justinian's soldiers carry a shield with the *CHI-RHO* monogram, reflecting Justinian's role as Constantine's legitimate successor and showing that his power is sustained by the army as well as by the Church. His central position and direct frontal gaze convey his power, just as the halo denotes his divine status.

The figures in Theodora's mosaic (figure **9.9**) are set slightly back in space, which makes her appear less imposing than the emperor. She, too, wears purple and has a halo. At her left is a group of richly clothed and elaborately jeweled ladies-in-waiting, and at her right are clergymen. One of them pushes aside a curtain to reveal a baptismal fountain. Theodora herself offers a gold chalice, a gesture echoed by the three Magi embroidered at the bottom of her robe. Her mosaic, like Justinian's, projects an image of wealth, power, and piety—all of which served the political purpose of empire.

9.5 North wall of Sant' Apollinare Nuovo, Ravenna, early 6th century.

A long procession of virgin saints and martyrs approaches the enthroned Virgin Mary. She wears a toga and holds Jesus on her lap. In this iconography, Mary is the Queen of Heaven and Christ its King. His small size and adult appearance embody the notion of the miraculous baby-king, which is a fundamental aspect of Christian imagery. Leading the procession are the three Magi. Their names,

like those of the virgins, are inscribed above each one: Balthasar, Melchior, and Caspar. Note their Asiatic costume—red Phrygian caps, flowing capes, and patterned leggings—denoting the luxury of the East. Their bowed poses indicate that they are paying homage to Christ. Palm trees identify the locale as the Near East.

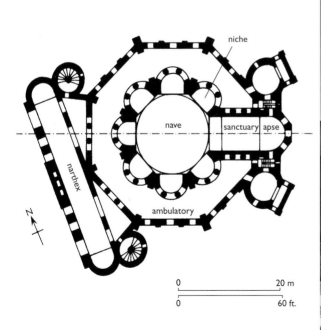

9.6 Plan of San Vitale, Ravenna, 6th century.

9.7 Exterior of San Vitale, Ravenna, 6th century.

San Vitale is a small, complex, octagonal church, with a brick exterior. It has a circular nave surrounded by seven niches, which are fronted by arches and surrounded by an ambulatory. Opposite the **narthex** on the west side is the apse at the east end.

9.8 *above* Mosaic of Justinian, apse of San Vitale, Ravenna, 6th century.

9.9 Mosaic of Theodora, apse of San Vitale, Ravenna, 6th century.

MUSIC IN THE WESTERN AND EASTERN CHURCHES

There are no surviving musical notations from sixth-century Ravenna. Nevertheless, as the liturgy in the Western Church differed from that in the Eastern Church, and as manuscripts do survive from later periods, one can assume that their music was also different. Both Western and Eastern church buildings had been constructed in Ravenna—Theodoric's basilican, Latin cross plan in Sant' Apollinare Nuovo and Justinian's centralized Greek cross plan in San Vitale—reflecting the city's status as a meeting point of the cultures of West and East.

Since the fourth century, when Christianity had been legalized and encouraged under Constantine, increasingly large gatherings had been assembling for services. Gradually the great urban centers—especially Rome, Byzantium, Antioch, and Alexandria—began to develop their own forms of worship. Liturgical texts were written down, standardized, and circulated. The Western Church, led from Rome, focused primarily on the Mass. In the sixth century the essential structure of the Roman liturgy was established, specifying, for example, set forms for the prayers of the officiating priest in the Mass, and the texts of Bible readings for different times of the year. The second important liturgical and musical element in the Western Church was the Divine Office—meaning other regular church services, both monastic and non-monastic. The most significant, musically speaking, were Matins, Lauds, and Vespers.

The Mass was still heavily based on plainchant, enhanced by **antiphonal** singing (alternation of two groups of singers) as the choir processed in at the start of the service and again for the offertory and communion within the Mass. After the Bible readings, solo chants were sung with simple congregational or choral responses. Psalms continued to form a regular part of services; they were performed either responsorially (a soloist alternated with the congregation or choir) or antiphonally. The latter style led to the development of a new genre, the **antiphon**—a separate chant with a Latin text and a simple melody to be sung with the psalm.

Antiphonal psalm singing was also characteristic of the Eastern Church as its liturgies developed in Byzantium, Antioch, and Alexandria. But, unlike the Western Church, the Eastern Church assigned a prominent and permanent place to the hymn. Early hymn tunes probably had semipopular origins, deriving from secular songs or folk music. Thus their melodies were simpler and their style more rhythmic than other church music. Hymn texts were written in short stanzas, so within a hymn each verse had the same number of lines, the same pattern of stresses, and sometimes the same rhyming scheme. One hymn tune could be used for all the texts with a matching poetic structure, an interchangeability that still applies to the hymnals of the twenty-first century.

HAGIA SOPHIA

Justinian's personal church and the main church of Constantinople was Hagia Sophia ("Holy Wisdom") (figure **9.10**). It was designed by two Greek mathematicians—Anthemius of Tralles and Isidorus of Miletus. Their interest in circular form is apparent in the medley of domes, curved arches, and **lunettes** (half-moon shaped wall sections), which give the building a

9.10 Anthemius of Tralles and Isidorus of Miletus, exterior of Hagia Sophia, Constantinople (Istanbul), Turkey, finished 537. 184 ft. (55.2 m) high.
Note the four minarets, which were added after Constantinople fell to the Ottoman Turks in 1453. The church was then converted to a mosque.

9.11 Anthemius of Tralles and Isidorus of Miletus, interior of Hagia Sophia, Constantinople.

dynamic, organic character. The plan in figure **9.12** gives some idea of its size and complexity. At 184 feet (55.2 m), it is taller than the Roman Pantheon (see figure 7.37), and, like large basilican churches, it has an arcade on either side of the nave.

The dazzling splendor of the interior (figure **9.11**) is achieved with gold mosaics and reflected light. Procopius described the huge dome as a suspended gold sphere. In contrast to the Roman Pantheon, the huge dome of Hagia Sophia towers over a cubed space. To make a graceful transition from the round dome to the square cube, Byzantine architects devised a feature called the **pendentive**. This is a curved triangle between the lunettes and the dome, which leads from the outline of the dome to the solid cubed base. Since the two

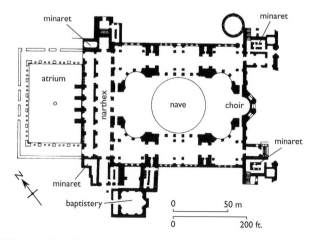

9.12 Plan of Hagia Sophia, Constantinople.

lower stories belong to the cube, the lunettes, which have one horizontal and one curved border, are shared by the rectangular wall and the dome.

ICONS AND THE MONASTERY OF ST. CATHERINE

Justinian built many churches throughout his empire. On Mount Sinai, in the Sinai Desert where Moses is believed to have received the Ten Commandments, Justinian commissioned a monastic church dedicated to St. Catherine (figure **9.13**). The church, the *Katholikon*, visible behind the fortified wall, was built in 530 for hermits who had been living on the mountain. Members of the monastery, located in the valley below the fortress, not only worked and prayed, but also painted **icons**. The Byzantine icon was typically a painting that represented Christ, an individual saint, or a religious event. Icons were usually on wood panel and shown against a rich, gold background.

9.14 Icon showing Christ blessing, monastery of St. Catherine, Mount Sinai, 6th century. Encaustic on board, 33 × 18 in. (84 × 45.5 cm).
This type of Christ—the *Pantokrator*, Greek for "Ruler of All"—emphasizes Christ's universal power. From the ninth century, bust-length figures of the *Pantokrator* appear on interiors of domes, where they tower over the space below just as Christ dominates the universe.

9.13 Fortress enclosing the monastery of St. Catherine, Sinai Desert, Egypt, 6th century.

During church services, icons were a means of reinforcing the worshipper's identification with holy figures. These are usually frontal, gazing directly at the viewer. In figure **9.14** a Greek-style, bearded Christ looks at us as if through a window. His large scale and gesture of blessing convey his power as well as his compassion. The jeweled book with a cross embedded in the cover reminds the viewer of Christianity's basis in Scripture and of Jesus' teachings. Traces of shading on Christ's face reflect the continuing impact of Roman and Hellenistic traditions of naturalism.

THE EASTERN ORTHODOX CHURCH

Christianity had been practiced as early as the second century in Byzantium, and with Constantine's move there in 330 the city became predominantly Christian. In 451, the bishop of Constantinople assumed the office of patriarch, and the patriarch of Constantinople would vie with the Roman pope for power for centuries to come. Although Latin was the official language of the whole Western Church, the Eastern (also called Orthodox) Church used different languages in different areas. In Constantinople, Greek was the official Church language; Syriac was used in regions influenced by Syria, and Egyptians used Coptic; Armenians and Georgians similarly worshipped in their own local languages; and in the Caucasus, there was an Albanian liturgy. These variations in the use of language influenced the evolution of different forms of worship. Nevertheless, the Greek rite of Constantinople remained the major Eastern liturgy.

One example of a difference between Roman and Eastern liturgy can be seen in events celebrated to commemorate Christ's birth. Christ's Nativity, celebrated on December 25, is the more important event in the Roman Church calendar, whereas in the Eastern Church it is the Epiphany, celebrated on January 6. This date was in some cases associated with Christ's baptism, and in others with the journey of the Magi. As a result, in Byzantine church decorations, scenes of the Magi bearing gifts for Christ are more often represented than the Nativity.

Orthodox priests, unlike those of the Western Church, were allowed to marry. But as in the Roman Church, some chose to set themselves apart for divine service. Some Eastern Orthodox monastics adhered to the ascetic ideal of isolation, whereas others formed communities of monks. The Eastern Church's monasteries, which consisted of independent self-governing units, grew wealthy and powerful in the course of its history. The most famous Greek Orthodox monastery was founded in 963 and is located on Mount Athos (known as Holy Mountain) in northeastern Greece. By the thirteenth century, the monastery could accommodate up to 8000 monks, who lived, worked, prayed, and painted holy images inside its walls. Today it consists of some twenty individual monasteries. Women were, and still are, excluded from the peninsula on which Mount Athos is located, a regulation that extends even to female animals.

THE ICONOCLASTIC CONTROVERSY

One of the most heated debates between the Eastern and Western Churches, the Iconoclastic controversy, raged for over a century, from 726 to 843. In 726, as the new religion of Islam threatened Christianity, the Byzantine emperor Leo III (ruled 717–741) decreed the destruction of all icons and other images of holy figures. Evoking the authority of the second commandment against graven images, Leo hoped that **iconoclasm** (literally "breaking of images") would attract converts from among the Jews and the Muslims (followers of Islam), both of whom discouraged figurative art. One argument against representational art, especially sculptures of human figures, was that people would worship images of saints rather than the saints themselves. As a rule, iconoclasm was supported by the emperors, the bishops, the army, and members of the civil service. Monks and the Roman Church, on the other hand, were in favor of images.

Leo III's son, Constantine V (ruled 741–775), continued his father's policies and persecuted **iconophiles** (those who supported religious imagery). Between 775 and 780, the Empress Irene, who was regent for Constantine VI until he was old enough to assume the throne, reversed the iconoclastic policy. In 787, the Council of Nicaea decreed that icons could be displayed in private houses and churches. But when Constantine VI (ruled 780–797) assumed power in 790, he placed his mother under house arrest. In 797, Irene took back the throne, had her son blinded and killed, and ruled until she was herself deposed and exiled in 802.

Despite the efforts of Irene and the Council of Nicaea, a second wave of iconoclasm swept the Eastern Church when the Armenian general Leo V (ruled 813–820) was elected emperor by the army. Leo removed icons from all public buildings, including churches, and persecuted iconophiles. After Leo's assassination in 820, his successor, Michael II (ruled 820–829), relaxed the persecutions. But they were again revived by his son Theophilus. With the death of Theophilus in 842, his mother, acting as regent, influenced the election of an iconophile monk, Methodius, as patriarch in 843. He held a celebration of icons on the first Sunday of Lent in the year of his election, thereby ending the Iconoclastic controversy. The intense debate over this issue, however, reinforced the split between the Eastern and Western Churches.

THE PERSISTENCE OF BYZANTINE STYLE

With the resolution of the Iconoclastic controversy, there was a revival of image-making in the Byzantine Empire. Byzantine style continued to influence church architecture in northeastern Italy and central and eastern Europe. One of the most impressive cities to have been influenced by Byzantium is Venice, on the northeast coast of Italy. Its Cathedral of St. Mark, begun in 1063, dominates the main square, the Piazza San Marco (figure **9.15**). Based on a centralized Greek cross plan, Saint Mark's has five gilded domes. The spectacular interior of the main dome is decorated with creation scenes from Genesis (figure **9.16**).

9.15 *above* Exterior of St. Mark's, Venice, begun 1063.

9.16 Creation Dome of St. Mark's, Venice.

The Byzantine Empire had various periods of growth and decline, but its culture persisted until 1453—well into the Renaissance period (see Chapter 13). With the fall of Constantinople, Greek scholars emigrated to Italy and other areas of western Europe. Their departure contributed to a revival of interest in Greek Classical texts, which had an enormous influence, first in Italy and eventually throughout the Western world. In Russia, the Byzantine style lasted well into the sixteenth century.

THE RISE AND EXPANSION OF ISLAM: SEVENTH TO SEVENTEENTH CENTURY

One of the major challenges to the Byzantine Empire had been the rise to power of the new religion of Islam in the seventh century. It originated on the Arabian peninsula, an impoverished area surrounded by several large empires. In the fifth and sixth centuries, Arabia had been primarily a desert, nomadic culture, although some regions were ruled by kings.

Islam is the most recent of the world's major religions. It began with the prophet Muhammad (*c.* 570–632) and expanded rapidly. By 750 Islam dominated the area from the Indus River, Central Asia, and the borders of China to North Africa, Spain, and Portugal (map **9.3**). In 725, Muslim armies reached Tours, in central France, but were repelled by Frankish forces. Islamic rulers controlled most of Spain, however, until the fall of Granada in 1492. Some of the greatest examples of Western Islamic art and architecture can be found there today.

THE LIFE OF MUHAMMAD

Since Islam begins with Muhammad, we begin with his life. He was born a member of the Quraysh tribe in Mecca, the most prosperous Arabian city. His father died before his birth, and his mother died when he was still a child. He was raised by a grandfather and an uncle among Bedouin nomads but later returned to Mecca. Muhammad worked for several years as a merchant and at the age of twenty-five married his wealthy, forty-year-old employer, Khadijah, with whom he had six children. Their daughter Fatima later married a religious leader and was venerated by Muslims. After Khadijah's death in 619, Muhammad married Ayisha, who was to play an active role in early Islam. In 632, Muhammad died in her house, which later became a major Islamic shrine.

In the late sixth century, hundreds of pagan gods, the god of the Hebrews and the Christians, the Zoroastrian Ahura Mazda, and the Arabian Allah were worshipped in the Near East. It was in this context that Muhammad, then around the age of forty, began praying in isolation and had a dream vision in which the voice of the archangel Gabriel called on him to "recite." Muhammad asked what he should recite, and Gabriel instructed him to recite in the name of the Lord Allah, who created the human race from clots of blood.

Gabriel also told Muhammad to repeat that Allah (which means "the one God") was the most bountiful, and by the pen taught people what they did not know. According to the traditional account of this event, Muhammad awoke convinced that Gabriel's words had been inscribed on his heart. The emphasis on the pen in Muhammad's vision is of interest in the light of the tradition that he himself could not read or write. He, as well as the religion he founded, attributed enormous importance to the power and beauty of the written word.

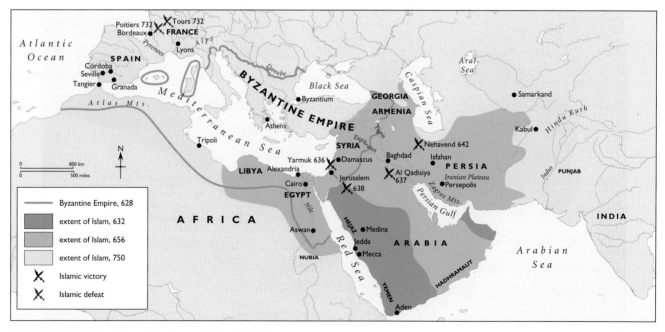

Map 9.3 The Byzantine Empire and the expansion of Islam, 622–750.

Muhammad's vision was followed by twenty years of revelations from Allah, which Muhammad memorized and scribes recorded. In 610, Muhammad declared Islam the last and final of God's three revelations of truth, the first being Judaism and the second Christianity. He taught that the Jews had corrupted the Scriptures, that the Christian belief that Jesus was the son of God was blasphemous, and that the Trinity was a false concept. Islam honors Abraham, Moses, and Jesus as prophets, but considers Allah the one true God. Islam's unquestioning submission to Allah is consistent with Judaism's story of Abraham's strict obedience to God's will, even to the point of being ready to sacrifice his son Isaac. The term *Islam*, in fact, means "submission." Muslims trace the genealogy of Islam, through Muhammad, to Abraham's other son, Ishmael.

Muhammad preached his message and was gradually accepted in Mecca as Allah's prophet. But his stance against idolatry and his growing influence alarmed the ruling classes. In 622, in the face of overt hostility, Muhammad left Mecca and went to Yathrib, later called Medina. His departure is known as the *Hijra* ("Great Emigration") and marks the opening date of the Islamic calendar—the Muslim year 1 corresponds to the Western year 622.

Eight years later, in 630, Muhammad returned to Mecca with an army, fought three successive battles, and converted most of the population to Islam. He transformed the pagan *Ka'bah* ("Cube") into the central and most holy site of the new religion. The *Ka'bah* itself is a sacred black stone believed to have been first erected by Adam. Abraham and Ishmael, according to Islam, then fulfilled God's order to construct a sanctuary around it.

In 632, Muhammad died without an heir. A succession of **caliphs** (Muslim rulers, or delegates of Allah) then led the Islamic world.

SUNNIS AND SHI'ITES

Soon after Muhammad's death, Islam split into two main factions—the Sunni and the Shi'ites—which led to a struggle for power. The Sunnis, who were in the majority, venerated the first three caliphs: Abu Bakr, who died in 634; Umar, the ally of Abu Bakr (ruled 634–644); and Uthman (ruled 644–656). Sunnis believed that religious guidance came from the Qur'an (Koran), the sacred text of Islam. They also believed that leaders should be chosen on the basis of piety and competence but not necessarily because of blood ties to the prophet.

Within the Sunni faction, a mystical, devotional movement arose called Sufism. Its followers were named for the rough woolen cloth worn to denote their ascetic lifestyle. The Sufi believed in emotional union with God, which was achieved through meditation and prayer, but this was considered by orthodox Muslims to border on blasphemy. Sufism has been a force in the arts, especially poetry and music.

The Shi'ites (from the term "Shi'a" of Ali, or faction of Ali) rejected the authority of the three caliphs and followed Muhammad's first cousin Ali (c. 600–661). He had married Muhammad's daughter Fatima and became caliph in 656 after Uthman was assassinated. The Shi'ites believed that religious guidance must come from a leader who, like Ali, had blood ties with Muhammad and thus shared in his religious charisma.

Ali and Fatima are considered by Shi'ites to embody the Islamic ideals of wisdom, humility, spirituality, and willingness to wage war to gain converts. But Ali's legitimacy as caliph was challenged by Mu'awiya, who was related to Uthman. A military leader in Syria and a member of the wealthy Umayyad clan from Mecca, Mu'awiya asserted his own legitimacy on the grounds of family prominence and military and leadership credentials.

Mu'awiya succeeded in undermining Ali's authority and in 661 Ali was assassinated by an angry follower. One of Ali's sons, al-Hasan, ruled for six months but resigned in the face of Mu'awiya's superior strength. With Mu'awiya's assumption of the caliphate—he ruled from 661 to 680—the Umayyad dynasty was founded. In 680, Mu'awiya was attacked by Ali's other son, al-Hasayn, who was killed by Umayyad forces at Karbala. He became the first martyr commemorated by the Shi'ites.

Both the Shi'ites and Sunnis believed in conquest to put other nations under Islamic rule, but they did not generally conquer to make converts. From 661 to 750, the Umayyad dynasty ruled from Syria and spread Islam through military conquest to Pakistan in the east and Spain in the west. The Umayyads encouraged scholarship, founded schools and libraries, and commissioned translations of Greek texts—especially Aristotle—into Arabic. In 750, the Umayyads were overthrown by the Sunni Abbasid dynasty, which moved the capital of Islam to Baghdad, in modern Iraq, and retained power until it was conquered by the Mongols in 1258. The Abbasid period, lasting from 750 to 1258, is sometimes called the Classical period of Islam.

THE FIVE PILLARS OF ISLAM

Muhammad is considered the "Seal of the Prophets"—that is, he is the final prophet of Allah and his law. Muslims believe that Muhammad transmitted Allah's code of ethics and the basic tenets of Islam. These include the conviction that the world is Allah's creation and a reflection of his presence. People are made in Allah's image, and their immortal souls are received into heaven if they have followed Islamic law. This law is stated in the Five Pillars of Islam; note the architectural metaphor used to describe the base on which the religion rests:

1. Repeat the creed (*shahada*) daily: there is no God but Allah and Muhammad is his prophet.
2. Pray to Allah five times a day in the direction of Mecca (the *salat*)—at daybreak, noon, mid-afternoon, sundown, and nightfall.

3. Give to charity (*zakat*); Muslims are required to donate a percentage of their income to the poor.

4. During the holy month of Ramadan (the ninth of the lunar year), refrain from food and drink, medicine, tobacco, and sex during daylight hours (*sawm*).

5. Make at least one pilgrimage to Mecca (*hajj*) in a lifetime and pray at the *Ka'bah*.

Early in the history of Islam, men were required to join the *jihad*, or holy war, against "infidels" (non-Muslims). For some Muslims, *jihad* is an additional "pillar," of which there are two types. The Greater Jihad is the individual's personal struggle to achieve a state of piety; the Lesser Jihad is Holy War. It obliges Muslims to combat pagans, Jews, and Christians and force them to accept an Islamic state. This belief and subsequent armed warfare in Allah's name has proven extremely effective. Aside from Spain and Portugal, the areas of the world conquered by Lesser Jihad in the seventh and eighth centuries are still largely Muslim today.

THE QUR'AN (KORAN) AND THE HADITH

The Qur'an, or Koran, is the most sacred Islamic Scripture. Literally "the Recital," the Qur'an was completed after Muhammad's death under Umar, the second caliph. By around 650 it was declared official by the third caliph, Uthman. The Qur'an is composed of 114 *suras* (chapters), each opening with the *basmala*: "In the name of Allah, the Compassionate, the Merciful." The *suras* are written in verse (*aya*) form, and become shorter as the text proceeds. The longest sura has 286 *ayas*, and the last has three. The Qur'an was originally written in Kufic script, which has only a few vowels and does not differentiate between certain consonants. This has given rise to various interpretations (figure **9.17**).

Whatever the interpretation of particular passages in the Qur'an, however, the text is considered the concrete revelation of Allah's eternal Word in Arabic. Ideally it should not be translated or read in any other language. Verse 43:1 of the Qur'an, for example, reads as follows:

> In the Name of Allah, the Compassionate, the Merciful
> *Ha mim.* By the Glorious Book!
> We have revealed the Koran in the Arabic tongue that you may grasp its meaning. It is a transcript of Our eternal book, sublime, and full of wisdom.
>
> (Qur'an, 43:1)

The Hadith, which are later than the Qur'an, are a collection of Muhammad's sayings and include accounts of his life. They are meant to instruct the faithful in how to live an ethical life according to the precepts of Islam.

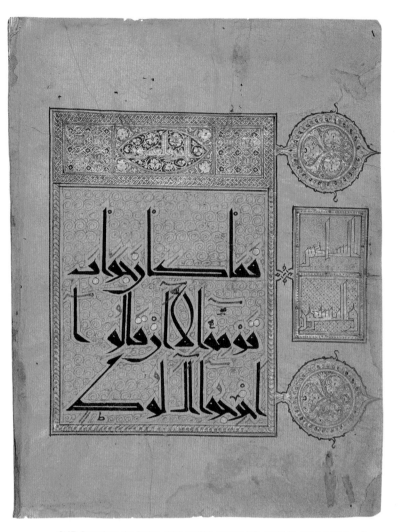

9.17 Page from the Qur'an, 11th or 12th century. 9³⁄₄ × 7³⁄₈ in. (24.7 × 18.7 cm). Bayerische Staatsbibliothek, Munich.
To express the truth of the Qur'an Muslims have evolved a high level of calligraphy (literally, "beautiful writing"), through which Allah's Word is conveyed. The striking black, angular Kufic script is particularly elegant. Framing the page is a pattern of spirals; rich gold designs are found in the top panel and in the shapes to the right.

The Qur'an, like the second commandment of the Hebrew Bible, forbids figurative imagery because it is seen as a route to idolatry. Although Muslim rulers have often been patrons of figurative painting, especially for courtly audiences, Islamic devotional art completely avoids the figure. Islamic styles are characterized by elaborate designs and countless varieties of pattern. The abstract quality of the written word and of calligraphy shown in figure 9.17 recurs in most Islamic works, including monumental architecture, crafts, and the decorative arts.

READING SELECTION
The Qur'an: the believer's duties, PWC2-212; on women, PWC2-213; on Jews and Christians, PWC2-214

ISLAMIC ART AND ARCHITECTURE

The most important type of Islamic architecture is the mosque. But Muslims have also built shrines, monumental tombs, and elaborate palaces. These, like Islamic pictorial images, are typically decorated with complex surface patterns and rich color.

THE DOME OF THE ROCK

The late-seventh-century Dome of the Rock on Temple Mount in east Jerusalem is the earliest surviving Islamic shrine and the second most important Islamic site after Mecca (figure **9.18**). Its plan, like that of San Vitale in Ravenna, is octagonal (figure **9.19**) with four entrances, and a tall, gilded dome towers over the sacred rock inside (figure **9.20**). Elaborate arches resting on multicolored columns surround the rock. The walls are covered with inscriptions from the Qur'an. The patterns, typical of Islamic decoration, consist mainly of floral forms and the merging of repetition and variety reflects the Islamic concept of the infinite and the oneness of the universe.

A shrine rather than primarily a place of community worship, the Dome of the Rock has no large space for prayer.

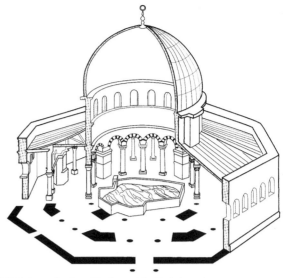

9.19 Cutaway drawing of the Dome of the Rock, Jerusalem.

It was built by Abd al-Malik (ruled 685–705), a caliph of the Umayyad dynasty, and designed to serve a political as well as a religious function. It was meant to proclaim that just as Muhammad, the true prophet of Allah, had superseded Abraham, Moses, and Jesus, so Islam had superseded Judaism and Christianity as the definitive world religion.

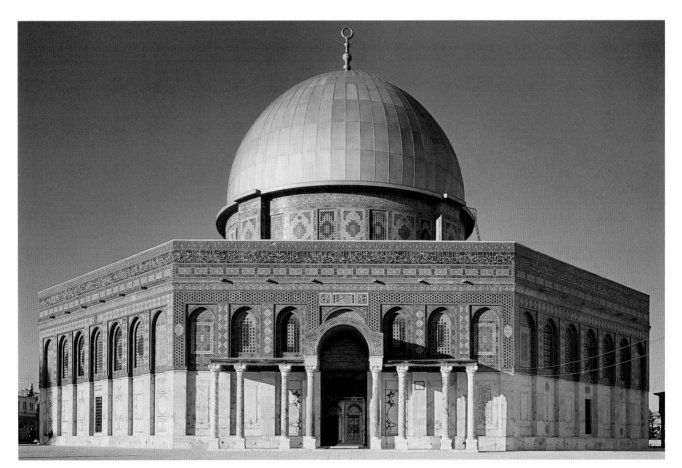

9.18 Exterior of the Dome of the Rock, Jerusalem, completed 691.
For Muslims this is the site from which Muhammad rose to the Seventh Heaven, passing on his way his predecessor prophets Abraham, Moses, and Jesus. Later commentators claimed that Muhammad ascended to heaven on the winged horse Buraq. For Jews, Temple Mount is the site of the Sacrifice of Isaac and the first Temple of Solomon.

MOSQUES

Like the early Christians, Muslims first worshipped in private surroundings, notably the court of Muhammad's house in Mecca. Later the mosque became the main Islamic structure of Islam. Mosques, of which there are two main types, are oriented so that worshippers pray facing the direction of Mecca. Masjid mosques are for daily prayer, and Jami, or Friday mosques, are used on the Muslim holy day, which is Friday. The latter contain a *minbar* (pulpit), from which the *imam* (spiritual leader) preaches. The *minbar* is the only piece of furniture inside the mosque. Fountains are used for ritual purification and prayer rugs are placed on the floor—people have to remove their shoes before entering. The exteriors of most mosques have tall, thin towers (**minarets**), from which a **muezzin** (crier) calls the faithful to prayer five times a day.

A good example of a mosque in the West can be seen in the Great Mosque at Córdoba, in Spain (figure **9.21**). The plan shows the large open space of the *sahn* (courtyard), which had been a feature of Muhammad's own house. At the far end, a *mihrab* (niche) is set into the *qibla* (prayer wall) facing Mecca.

Although converted to a church after the Christian reconquest of Spain, the Córdoba Mosque retains its original two-tiered, horseshoe-shaped arches on the interior. They were designed for increased height and enhanced illumination (figure **9.22**). The alternating red and white voussoirs of the arches create a lively formal pattern typical of Islamic taste. Further elegant ornamentation can be seen in the *mihrab* (figure **9.23**), which was added in the tenth century.

9.21 Plan of the Córdoba Mosque, Spain, built in three stages; originally 786–787, with additions in 832–848 and 961–987.

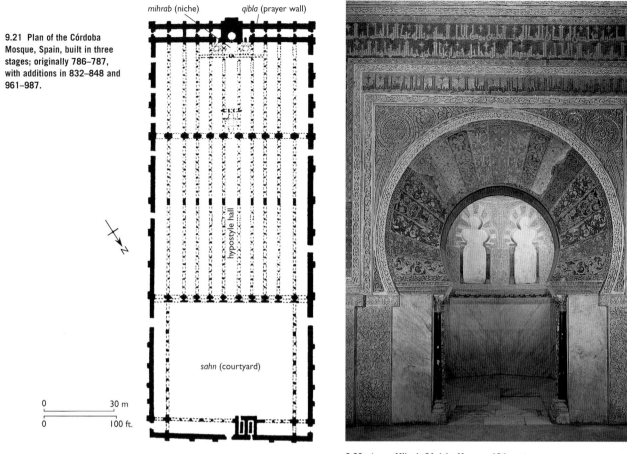

mihrab (niche)   qibla (prayer wall)

hypostyle hall

sahn (courtyard)

0 ——— 30 m

0 ——— 100 ft.

9.23 *above* **Mihrab**, Córdoba Mosque, 10th century.

9.22 Arches of the Córdoba Mosque, 8th century. Columns 9 ft. 9 in. (2.97 m) high.

TOMBS

The melon- or slightly more elongated onion-shaped domes of mosques are a distinctive feature of Islamic architecture also used in tombs. The fifteenth-century mausoleum of Timur Leng, or Tamerlane (*c.* 1336–1405), in Samarkand, Uzbekistan, supports a dome over 30 feet (9.1 m) high (figure **9.24**). The rich colors of the dome and exterior walls were created using the vivid glazed tiles that are typical of much Islamic architecture. Kufic script on the dome proclaims that Allah alone is eternal.

Perhaps the most famous of all Islamic mausoleums is the seventeenth-century Taj Mahal (figure **9.25**). It was built by the Mughal ruler Shah Jahan in honor of his wife Mumtaz (the "chosen one of the palace"), who died in childbirth. The Taj Mahal sits like a jewel on the banks of the River Jumna, near

9.24 *right* **Mausoleum of Timur Leng (Tamerlane), Samarkand, Uzbekistan, *c.* 1403.**
Timur Leng was a much-feared Mongol conqueror who defeated the Mongol empire originally established by Jenghis (Genghis) Khan (*c.* 1162–1227). In 1398, Timur's armies invaded the Punjab and overran the Muslim areas of north India. He also conquered Persia, Armenia and Georgia in southern Russia, Syria, and parts of Asia Minor. From 1369 until his death in 1405 he ruled at Samarkand, in Uzbekistan.

9.25 Taj Mahal, Agra, India, 1630s.

Agra, in India. It is a graceful, octagonal structure, with four minarets and four pavilions, surrounded by gardens. The white marble facing, accented with color and patterns carved and inlaid into the surface, exemplifies the rich artistic culture that flourished in India under the Mughal dynasty.

SECULAR ART

Islamic palace architecture is highly complex and lavishly decorated. At the Alhambra in Granada, in southern Spain, the fourteenth-century Court of the Lions is particularly elaborate (figure **9.26**). As at the Córdoba Mosque, the arches rest on short columns, but here some are paired for extra support. The plaster and wood carvings around the arches and on the walls and ceilings are more complex than at Córdoba. They are enhanced by shimmering, outdoor light. The Alhambra is actually two palaces, the Palace of the Myrtles, which was used for public receptions, and the private Palace of the Lions. Throughout the complex, fountains serve the practical purpose of cooling the air and the aesthetic purpose of reflecting light and creating the murmur of rushing water.

Islamic attention to minute, decorative detail lends itself to certain types of crafts, notably glasswork and carpets. The carpet in figure **9.27** shows the taste for intricate design patterns and rich color. This is one of

9.26 *above* **Court of the Lions, Granada, Spain, 1343–1391.**
The architecture of the Alhambra and its surrounding stark landscape and hardy peasants inspired the nineteenth-century American author Washington Irving (1783–1859). He memorialized the Alhambra in his engaging classic work of fantasy, *Tales of the Alhambra.*

9.27 **Masaud Kashani, Ardabil carpet, from northwest Iran, 16th century. Silk and wool, 30 ft. 5¾ in. × 17 ft. 6¼ in. (10.51 × 5.34 m). Victoria and Albert Museum, London.**

9.28 Bottle, from Syria, mid-14th century. Glass with enamel and gilt, 19½ in. (49.7 cm) high, 9¾ in. (24.8 cm) diameter. Freer Gallery of Art, Smithsonian Institution, Washington, D.C.

the earliest surviving knotted carpets of Middle Eastern origin. Its layout is related to book design, having a central medallion in a field of nearly symmetrical patterns.

Glasswork is an ancient technology some 4000 years old; it reached a high degree of development in Syria under the Roman Empire. Made by heating and fusing sand and silicates and adding magnesium for transparency, glass was cooled slowly in an oven. It was shaped by blowing through a long tube, and threads of color could be added (figure **9.28**). In this example, areas of design are set off from the elegant enamel used to decorate the surface. A rich blue forms the background for calligraphic inscriptions, and the red rosettes in white circles are the emblem of the Syrian ruler who commissioned the work.

which originated in Sufi tradition and is regularly performed at Muslim shrines, stage concerts, and other events. Further, many kinds of sung poetry in the Muslim world (including those used in *qawwâli*) can be interpreted—often depending on performance context—as expressing either worldly, romantic love, or else mystical love for God. In that sense, the range of Muslim devotional music, everywhere from Morocco to Bangladesh, is in fact vast.

Muslim rulers have been patrons of secular music, which is an important artistic medium of the courts. Inspired by Greek musical texts, Muslim scholars wrote treatises on music theory, which became a branch of Islamic science and philosophy. Regional music, both Classical and folk, also flourished throughout the Muslim world.

By the twelfth century, according to treatises, Arabic music was based on a system of melodic modes, later called **maqam** (a specific scale having certain phrases and patterns). Popular instruments at the time included the stringed *'ud*, from which the later Western lute was derived, and the *nay* (a cane flute), still in use today.

Improvised preludes often preceded fixed compositions and evolved into **taqsim** (an improvised elaboration of *maqams* in a free-rhythmic style). It is possible that modern *taqsims*, even those played on a recently invented instrument like the steel-stringed *bouzouq*, might sound like older Arabic music. This is not certain, however, because there are no surviving notations of ancient Arabic music.

ISLAMIC MUSIC

Orthodox Islam frowns on music as a distraction from piety. As an institutionalized religion, therefore, Islam has not encouraged music, apart from its use in chanting the Qur'an or the call to prayer, both of which have a musical quality and are suited to the patterns of Arabic melody. Music and dance are not permitted in mosques.

MUSIC LISTENING SELECTION
Islamic call to prayer (*Adhan*). CD track 2

However, music is widely used in devotional contexts throughout much of the Islamic world. Music has been cultivated with particular enthusiasm by members of Sufi sects, who regard song as a means of intensifying devotional fervor and, ideally, attaining a state of mystical union with God. The **whirling dervishes** associated with the Mevlevi Sufis of Turkey represent one example of such practices. In India and Pakistan, many Muslims are also fond of **qawwâli** (devotional song),

ISLAMIC LITERATURE

The collection of prose stories from the Arabic world perhaps best known to Westerners is *The Thousand and One Nights* (*The Arabian Nights*). The tales were originally transmitted orally and probably derived from Indian and Persian traditions. The basic core of some eleven stories was written down by the late eighth century, with elements of folktales and legends added over time. The earliest surviving complete manuscript is from fourteenth-century Syria, but tenth-century Arab historians refer to collections of a thousand stories, which no longer exist. Some of the most popular tales, such as "Aladdin and the Magic Lamp," were not known until the eighteenth century. In any case, what is now called the *Arabian Nights* developed from a long tradition of lively and imaginative narrative that interwove fantasy with details of everyday life.

The story of the *Arabian Nights* is, itself, about story-telling. Its narrator is Shahrazad, wife of the Persian king Shahrayar. The king had killed all of his previous wives on their wedding night because he believed that all women were unfaithful. Shahrazad stays alive by entertaining the king with a story each night until he finally learns to trust her.

The pace of the narrative is regularly varied with verse, and throughout there is a whimsical sense of enchantment. Each tale opens with a statement designed to engage the king, who is called "O happy King"—for example, the One Hundred and Sixty-First Night: "I heard, O happy King, that the tailor told the king of China that the barber told the guests that he had said to the caliph . . ." The Forty-Sixth Night begins:

> "I heard, O happy King, that the second dervish said to the girl:
>
> "When I took the sword and went up to her, she winked at me, meaning, 'Bravo! This is how you repay me!' I understood her look and pledged with my eyes, 'I will give my life for you.' Then we stood for a while, exchanging looks, as if to say:
>
> > Many a lover his beloved tells
> > With his eyes' language what is in his heart.
> > 'I know what has befallen,' seems to say,
> > And with a glance he does his thoughts impart.
> > How lovely are the glances of the eyes,
> > How graceful are the eyes with passion fraught.
> > One with his looks a lover's message writes,
> > Another with his eyes reads what his lover wrote.

> *(The Arabian Nights)*

Islam has an extensive poetic tradition. One of the best known Persian poets in the West is Omar Khayyam (*c.* 1048–*c.* 1131). He was also an astronomer, as much of his imagery shows. His *Rubáiyát*, here freely translated by Edward Fitz-Gerald, consists of individual quatrains, rich in metaphor; the work later influenced English poetry. Note that the first, second, and fourth lines rhyme:

> Awake! for Morning in the Bowl of Night
> Has flung the Stone that puts the Stars to Flight:
> And Lo! the Hunter of the East has caught
> The Sultan's Turret in a Noose of Light.

Many verses recommend enjoying the fleeting pleasures of life:

> Dreaming when Dawn's Left Hand was in the Sky,
> I heard a Voice within the Tavern cry,
> "Awake, my Little ones, and fill the Cup
> Before Life's Liquor in its Cup be dry."
>
> Ah, my Beloved, fill the cup that clears
> Today of past Regrets and future Fears—
> *Tomorrow?*—Why, To-morrow I may be
> Myself with Yesterday's Sev'n Thousand Years.

On philosophers and philosophy:

> Oh, come with old Khayyam, and leave the Wise
> To talk; one thing is certain, that Life flies;

> One thing is certain, and the Rest is Lies;
> The Flower that once has blown forever dies.
>
> Myself when young did eagerly frequent
> Doctor and Saint, and heard great Argument
> About it and about: but evermore
> Came out by the same Door as in I went.
>
> With them the Seed of Wisdom did I sow,
> And with my own hand labour'd it to grow:
> And this was all the Harvest that I reap'd—
> 'I came like Water, and like Wind I go.'

And on the inevitable march of time:

> The Moving Finger writes; and, having writ,
> Moves on: nor all thy Piety nor Wit
> Shall lure it back to cancel half a Line,
> Nor all thy Tears wash out a Word of it.

Sufi poetry, which is less familiar to Westerners than the *Arabian Nights* and the *Rubáiyát*, emphasizes mystical union with God. This union is sometimes achieved through ecstasy and intoxication from wine and love. Both are generally seen as metaphors for the intense love of God. Wine-drinking is also celebrated as a way of flouting the strict rules of orthodox Islam, which prohibits all alcohol. The Sufi combination of secular and religious images of love is reminiscent of the Song of Songs in the Hebrew Bible (see Chapter 8).

The Sufi poet Jalal al-Din Rumi (*c.* 1207–1273) was born in Balkh, in modern Afghanistan, and moved to Konya, in what is now Turkey. He wrote around 30,000 verses and performed ecstatic dances while reciting poetry, and it was his followers who set up the Sufi sect of whirling dervishes that still exists today. In the poem "Only Breath," Rumi describes a universal state of being:

> Not Christian or Jew or Muslim, not Hindu, Buddhist, sufi, or zen. Not any religion
> or cultural system. I am not from the East or the West, not out of the ocean or up
> from the ground, not natural or ethereal, not composed of elements at all. I do not exist,
> am not an entity in this world or the next, did not descend from Adam or Eve or any
> origin story. My place is placeless, a trace of the traceless. Neither body or soul.
> I belong to the beloved, have seen the two worlds as one and that one call to and know,
> first, last, outer, inner, only that breath breathing human being.
> There is a way between voice and presence where information flows.
> In disciplined silence it opens.
> With wandering talk it closes.

> *(Rumi, "Only Breath")*

The Persian Sufi poet Hafiz (1326–90) wrote **ghazals**, which had been popular at Middle Eastern courts before Islam.

They are written in concise lyrical couplets with strict meter and a double rhyme scheme. *Ghazals* are typically about love, which is interpreted either as divine or romantic love. In "The only dervish in the world who can't dance," Hafiz bewails his distance from the "Beloved," which in this translation means "God." Note that each couplet has a separate theme:

> I am perhaps the only dervish in the world who can't dance,
> Because my heart is like a frightened deer.
>
> In Winehouse Street I walk around weeping, with hanging head,
> Ashamed of how little I've accomplished and how little I have done.
>
> The Golden Age of Egypt didn't last forever and neither did Alexander's reign.
> O dervish, don't add your troubles to an already troubled world.
>
> Friend, face it, you're a slave, so don't go complaining about
> The lack of love in your life: move on!
>
> Hafiz, it's not every beggar who has touched the hem of the Beloved's shirt:
> All the gold in the Sultan's bank wouldn't fit into His hand.

(Hafiz, "The only dervish in the world who can't dance")

ISLAMIC SCIENCE, MEDICINE, AND PHILOSOPHY

From their beginnings, Islamic philosophy and science were linked as a single discipline. They flourished in the Golden Age that lasted from around the ninth to the end of the twelfth century under the Abbasids. Academic centers in Seville and Córdoba (Spain), Cairo (Egypt), Baghdad (Iraq), and Damascus (Syria) revived Greek texts of Aristotle, Plato, and the Neoplatonists through Arabic translations. Islamic scholars also studied Indian and Chinese texts, and Christian theology was another important source of influence. Like their Western contemporaries, Islamic philosophers sought to reconcile reason and revelation. However, they did not make logic an end or a discipline in its own right, as Western philosophers later began to do.

SCIENTISTS AND PHYSICIANS

The Islamic view of God as an architect and mathematician inspired an interest in mathematics and astronomy. Geographers and astrologers studied the earth and the movements of the planets and stars. A leading Islamic mathematician, al-Khwarizimi (*c.* 780–*c.* 850), made several important contributions that are still in use today. He introduced the concept of algorithms and helped bring the Indian development of the concept of zero and Arabic numerals to the West. Al-Khwarizimi also invented algebra.

During the period of intellectual expansion from the ninth through the twelfth century, Islamic medicine and medical schools were among the most progressive in the world. Islamic physicians studied infectious diseases, particularly of the eye, and learned to perform cataract surgery. In the eleventh century, the Egyptian al-Hazen (d. 1038) improved the practice of optics and devised new ways to grind lenses. He also measured the density of the earth's atmosphere and investigated how it affected astronomy.

Physicians studied drugs and their properties and encouraged clinical observation. Al-Razi (Rhazes) (*c.* 865–932), a physician who ran the hospital in Baghdad, wrote the first known clinical account of the difference between measles and smallpox. Like the Greek philosopher Socrates, whom he greatly admired, al-Razi believed in the importance of detailed study and precise description. His major work was a medical encyclopedia, which he filled with his own clinical observations and conclusions as well as with comparative medical views of physicians in Iran, Syria, India, and Greece.

The Persian physician Avicenna, or Ibn Sina (980–1037), was also a philosopher who studied Aristotle and Plato as well as the Qur'an. His approach to philosophy and religion was from a scientific point of view. For example, Avicenna defined prophecy as a form of knowledge through which one could describe visionary experience. In medicine, Avicenna discovered a relation between pulse beats and diagnosis. He believed that in medicine, as in philosophy, reality is observable. He constructed a hierarchical system to demonstrate that reality could be ranked according to ontology: that is, each entity is responsible for the existence of the entity below it. Because this is observable, he argued, there can be no infinity and no vacuum. And he concluded that existence is, itself, the equivalent of proof. Avicenna founded the medical curriculum that prevailed in the West until the nineteenth century. His *Canon medicinae* (*Canon of Medicine*) became a standard medical text (figure **9.29**).

Moses ben Maimon, known as Maimonides (1135–1204), was a Jewish physician, philosopher, and jurist trained in Islamic medicine. Originally from Córdoba, he was forced from Spain by persecutions of the Jews and went to Egypt as personal physician to the vizier (Muslim state minister) of the sultan (Muslim ruler) Saladin. An authority on Jewish Law, Maimonides understood the then unknown importance of hygiene in warding off disease. Influenced by the philosophy of Aristotle, Maimonides wrote *The Guide for the Perplexed* around 1204. This was an attempt to resolve the apparent conflict between theism and paganism, which he considered primitive. Revelation requires that through the quest for human perfection we approach God's likeness, he argued. For Maimonides, it is God who demands continual moral and intellectual improvement in people, which can be obtained by seeking God through nature and the laws of mathematics.

9.29 Page from Avicenna, *Canon medicinae*, with text and anatomical drawings, fourteenth-century copy in Al Quanum manuscript. National Museum, Damascus, Syria.

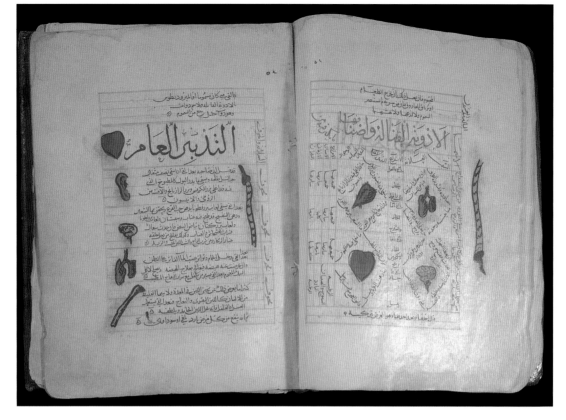

PHILOSOPHERS

From the late eighth to the middle of the ninth century, Islamic philosophy was centered in Baghdad's House of Wisdom, a hub of scholarship under the patronage of the caliphs. The House of Wisdom welcomed thinkers from around the Islamic world and encouraged them to find ways to increase the power of the Islamic Empire. A leading philosopher of this period, al-Kindi (*c.* 800–*c.* 870), argued that although the concept of scriptural revelation was valid, it needed to be demonstrated. In this he was influenced by Neoplatonism and Plotinus's notion of the One (see Chapter 8), which stated that original creation emanated from nothing (*ex nihilo*). Al-Kindi also studied Greek musical theory and wrote on the ways in which people could be affected by music. He recorded properties of medicines and perfumes and conducted experiments in physics, optics, and pharmacology.

The philosopher al-Farabi (*c.* 870–*c.* 950) commented on Aristotle and wrote on linguistics. He also produced the first work discussing Islamic political theory in relation to Islamic religion. In *The Ideas of the Inhabitants of the Virtuous City*, which was influenced by St. Augustine's *City of God*, al-Farabi attempted to reconcile secular law with divine law.

Two major Islamic thinkers of the twelfth and thirteenth centuries with opposing views were the Persian theologian al-Ghazali (1058/9–1111) and the Arabic philosopher Averroës (1126–1198). Al-Ghazali's autobiographical *Deliverance from Error* has similarities with the *Confessions* of Augustine. Both authors repented their earlier views and dedicated their lives to the study of God and visionary revelation. Al-Ghazali says that his teaching had been motivated by ambition rather than by the wish to serve God. Following a mental breakdown, al-Ghazali resigned as a college professor in Baghdad and became a Sufi. He argued in favor of the Sunni against the Shi'ites and believed that although philosophy could assist math and logic, it could not lead to a knowledge of God. His *Incoherence of the Philosophers* recommended that theologians use logic to rebut heresy, thus placing philosophy in the service of theology. Reason and philosophical logic, in al-Ghazali's view, should be subordinated to revelation, because God can only be known by emotional and spiritual experience. His theological position, published in *Revival of the Religious Sciences*, earned him the reputation of having revived the power of Islam.

Averroës was born in Córdoba and became a judge in Seville, in southern Spain. He took issue with al-Ghazali's views and argued in *The Incoherence of the Incoherence* that theology can neither lead to empirical knowledge nor correctly interpret divine law. Accused of heresy, Averroës was banished in 1195. The last of the great medieval Islamic philosophers, Averroës wanted to draw a clear distinction between theology and philosophy. He recommended a return to Aristotelianism and the elimination of Neoplatonic mysticism from Islamic philosophy. His work had a more profound impact on later Christian thinkers than on Islamic theologians, and his commentaries on Aristotle and Plato's *Republic* became well known in the West.

For several centuries after the fall of Rome, when western Europe was beset by turmoil from barbarian invasions and urban culture was in decline, Islamic philosophy and science were highly developed. For a time, Classical thought was kept alive through Arabic translations of ancient Greek texts. Later, during the Middle Ages, Aristotle's logic and Plotinus's mysticism began to appeal to Christian thinkers. With the dawn of the Italian Renaissance beginning in the fourteenth century (see Chapter 12), however, there would be a widespread revival of interest in the philosophy of Plato and in Classical culture.

KEY TERMS

antiphon in music, a liturgical chant with a Latin text sung with a psalm.

antiphonal in music, a style of composition using two or more groups of performers to create effects of echo or contrast.

autocracy absolute rule by one person.

caliph a Muslim ruler or leader.

ghazal a Middle Eastern poem in couplets having strict meter and a double rhyme scheme.

icon a sacred image.

iconoclasm the destruction of religious images.

iconophile someone who supports religious imagery.

lunette a half-moon shaped wall section.

maqam in Arabic music, a specific scale having certain phrases and patterns.

minaret a thin tower on the exterior of a mosque.

muezzin in Islam, a crier who calls the faithful to prayer from a minaret.

narthex a vestibule or porch across the west end of a church.

pendentive an architectural feature resembling a curved triangle between the lunettes of a dome.

qawwâli a genre of Muslim devotional song, generally with lyrics in Urdu, popular in north India and Pakistan, typically sung by two to four vocalists, with hand-clapping, harmonium, and barrel-drum accompaniment.

serf a peasant worker unable to leave the land.

taqsim in Arabic music, an improvised elaboration of *maqams* in a free-rhythmic style.

whirling dervish a Sufi ascetic who seeks divine ecstasy through whirling to music.

KEY QUESTIONS

1. Byzantine rulers considered themselves God's emissaries. Their power was absolute. This form of government is called _____ and literally means _____.
2. How might a ruler enforce such a concept through art and architecture?
3. What were the arguments that led to the Iconoclastic controversy? What was its resolution?
4. What schisms developed in the Islamic world after the death of Muhammad?
5. What is the most important type of Islamic architecture? Why?
6. What interests developed in the academic centers of the Islamic world from around the ninth to the end of the twelfth century under the Abbasids? Why is this age considered a Golden Age?

SUGGESTED READING

Boethius. *The Consolation of Philosophy*, trans. V. E. Watts. New York: Penguin Books, 1969.
  ▸ An account of Boethius's philosophy.

Comnena, Anna. *The Alexiad of Anna Comnena*, trans. E. R. A. Sewter. London: Penguin Books, 1969.
  ▸ A translation of Comnena's biased view of Byzantine history.

Demus, Otto. *Byzantine Art and the West*. New York: New York University Press, 1970.
  ▸ A study of Byzantine style in art.

Elias, Jamal J. *Islam*. London: Routledge, 1999.
  ▸ A general overview of Islam.

Evans, James Allan. *The Empress Theodora: Partner of Justinian*. Austin, TX: University of Texas Press, 2002.
  ▸ A brief, up-to-date study of Theodora and her time.

Graves, Robert. *Belisarius*. London: Penguin Books, 1975.
▸ An interpretive account of the life of Belisarius.

Hourani, A. *A History of the Arab Peoples*. London: Faber and Faber, 1991.
▸ The beginnings of Islam and its early development.

Irwin, Robert. *Islamic Art in Context*. New York: Harry N. Abrams, 1997.
▸ A study of Islamic art in its cultural context.

Khayyam, Omar. *Rubáiyát of Omar Khayyam*, trans. Edward FitzGerald. Edinburgh: Riverside Press, n.d., and New York: Thomas Y. Crowell, 1859.
▸ The loosely translated poems of Omar Khayyam.

Kitzinger, Ernst. *Byzantine Art in the Making: Main Lines of Stylistic Development in Mediterranean Art, 3rd–7th Century*. Cambridge, MA: Harvard University Press, 1978.
▸ A survey of the development of Byzantine art.

The Koran, trans. and ed. N. J. Dawood. London: Penguin Books, 1956.
▸ A standard translation.

Lowden, John. *Early Christian and Byzantine Art*. London: Phaidon, 1997.
▸ A well-illustrated account of early Christian and Byzantine art.

Mainstone, Rowland J. *Hagia Sophia: Architecture, Structure and Liturgy of Justinian's Great Church*. London: Thames and Hudson, 1988.
▸ A thorough discussion of Hagia Sophia's architecture and its relationship to liturgy under Justinian.

Manuel, Peter. *Popular Musics of the Non-Western World*. New York and Oxford: Oxford University Press, 1988.
▸ A general introductory survey.

Mathews, Thomas. *Byzantium*. New York: Harry N. Abrams, 1998.
▸ Places the art of Byzantium in its cultural context.

Nett, Bruno, Charles Capwell, Philip V. Bohlman, Isabel K. F. Wong, and Thomas Turino. *Excursions in World Music*. Englewood Cliffs, NJ: Prentice Hall, 1992.
▸ A survey of Western and non-Western music.

Rumi. *The Essential Rumi*, trans. Coleman Barks and John Moyne. New York: HarperCollins, 1995.
▸ Rumi's poems in English translation.

Von Simpson, Otto G. *Sacred Fortress: Byzantine Art and Statecraft in Ravenna*. Princeton, NJ: Princeton University Press, 1987.
▸ On politics and art in Ravenna during the Byzantine period.

Walther, W. *Women in Islam*. Princeton, NJ: Markus Wiener Publishers, 1995.
▸ The effect of Islam on women.

Weitzmann, Kurt, et al. *The Icon*. New York: Marboro Books, 1982.
▸ A study of the style and meaning of Byzantine icons.

SUGGESTED FILMS

1910 *Justinian and Theodora*, dir. Otis Turner

1924 *The Thief of Bagdad*, dir. Raoul Walsh

1940 *The Thief of Baghdad*, dir. Michael Powell, Ludwig Berger, and Tim Whelan

1958 *The Seventh Voyage of Sinbad*, dir. Nathan Juran

1973 *The Golden Voyage of Sinbad*, dir. Gordon Hessler

10 The Early Middle Ages and the Development of Romanesque:

565–1150

> " The Emperor Charles [Charlemagne], who left us in command
> Of twenty thousand he chose to guard the pass,
> Made very sure no coward's in their ranks.
> In his lord's service a man must suffer pain,
> Bitterest cold and burning heat endure;
> He must be willing to lose his flesh and blood.
> Strike with your lance, and I'll wield Durandel [Roland's sword]—
> The king himself presented it to me—
> And if I die, whoever takes my sword
> Can say its master has nobly served his lord."
>
> (Song of Roland, VERSE 88)

I n western European history the term "Early Middle Ages" refers to the period from the end of Justinian's reign (565) to around 1000, when the Romanesque style of architecture began to emerge. From the sixth through the ninth centuries, Europe's economy declined. This was largely a result of weakened, decentralized government within the lands of the Roman Empire, and of invasions of that empire by Germanic tribes and Vikings from the north. Poverty and disease were widespread. Monumental architecture and other costly pursuits declined along with the general economy. Literacy also declined and the largest segment of society consisted of farmers, landowners, and local warlords.

Early medieval society was dominated by the Church, with its increasing power and expanding network of monasteries. From the ninth century, two complex but loosely organized social systems, **manorialism** and **feudalism**, also became important. The Church was the primary spiritual force and to some degree it influenced politics. Manorialism guaranteed the basic needs of everyday life, while feudalism protected people from external dangers. These systems continued in some form to the end of the thirteenth century.

The quotation that opens this chapter is from the French epic poem the Song of Roland, which was inspired by wars fought by Christian soldiers. A work of literature rather than of history, the poem exemplifies the medieval code of **chivalry**, in which men promised service and loyalty to a lord in return for protection. Such men evolved into a warrior class and followed certain rules of behavior. **Vassals** had land in return for duties involving allegiance to their lords and **knights** performed military service for the right to own land. The loyalty of knights to their lords provided armies that defended a lord's power and territory. In the episode cited above, the French knight Roland has pledged his allegiance to the emperor Charlemagne. Roland thinks of dying with honor as he prepares to fight Muslim forces amassing on the border between France and Spain.

Key Topics

Religion

Monasticism

Missionaries

Pilgrimage

Crusades

Structuring Society

Feudalism

Manorialism

The code of chivalry

The palace school

Structuring Power

Charlemagne's Classical
  revival

Ottonian rulers

Northern Europe: Vikings and
  Goths

The Arts

Literature: sagas and epics

Music: antiphonal singing

Mystery, miracle, and morality
  plays

Secular theater: Hroswitha of
  Gandersheim

Visual arts: manuscripts,
  metalwork, churches,
  monasteries

TIMELINE	EARLY MIDDLE AGES 565 TO c. 1000	ROMANESQUE PERIOD c. 1000–1150
HISTORY AND CULTURE	Economic and cultural decline No central government Agrarian economy Feudalism and manorialism Growth of monasteries Merovingian and Carolingian dynasties Charles Martel stops Muslim invasion of France, 734 Charlemagne (768–814) Carolingian Renaissance Viking, Magyar, and Muslim invasions Ottonian rule, from 936	Revival of monumental architecture Improved technology and commerce Urbanization Capetian dynasty founded in France, 987 Pilgrimage roads Crusades
RELIGION AND MYTH	Norse myth Christianity Bede, *Ecclesiastical History of the English People*, 731 Monastic schooling: Alcuin of York adopts *trivium* and *quadrivium*, late 8th century Alcuin reforms monasteries, late 8th century	Norse myth Christianity
ART	Sutton Hoo purse cover, 7th century Book of Kells, late 8th century Cross of Muriedach, early 10th century	Rune stones, *c.* 1000 Picture stones, *c.* 1000 Gospel Book of Otto III, *c.* 1000 Bayeux Tapestry, *c.* 1070–1080 Chessmen, 12th century Reliquary of Thomas à Becket, *c.* 1190 Hildegard of Bingen illumination, *c.* 1200
ARCHITECTURE	Charlemagne's Palace Chapel, Aachen, 792–805 Benedictine monasteries	Sainte Marie Madeleine, Vézelay, *c.* 1089–1206 Cluny monastery reconstruction, *c.* 1157
LITERATURE	Legend of King Arthur Oldest-known English poem: "Caedmon's Hymn," 7th century Einhard (*c.* 770–840), *Life of Charlemagne* *Beowulf*, 7th–10th century *Song of Roland*, late 8th century, first recorded 11th or 12th century Icelandic sagas: *Njal's Saga*, 10th century	*Mabinogion*, recorded by 1100 Romances Herrad, *The Garden of Delights*, 12th century Hildegard of Bingen (1098–1179), *Scivias; Book of Divine Works* Geoffrey of Monmouth, *History of the Kings of England* (1135–1139) Snorri Sturluson (1179–1241), *Edda*
THEATER	Traditions of Roman comedy, pagan festivals, and Christian liturgy German *scop* (5th–7th century) Feast of Fools Boy Bishop ritual Theatrical elements in the Mass Mystery, miracle, and morality plays Secular theater: Hroswitha (*c.* 935–*c.* 1002)	*Play of Adam*, 12th century *Everyman*, recorded 15th century
MUSIC	Charlemagne adopts Gregorian chant, 8th century Parallel organum develops, 9th century Antiphonal singing Tropes added to existing chants, by 925 Notation using neumes	Gregorian chant Melismatic organum develops, 11th century Guido of Arezzo (*c.* 991–1050) invents four-line staff for notation

THE EARLY MIDDLE AGES

MONASTERIES

The Christian monastic movement, which had begun in the third century with St. Anthony (see Chapter 8), underwent a period of expansion during the Early Middle Ages. Monasteries became cultural centers, encouraging the arts and the study and preservation of religious texts. Their ordered way of life consisted of communal worship, prayer, and contemplation, which provided a spiritual model for society at large.

Monasteries were self-supporting communities of monks and nuns, supervised by abbots and abbesses, respectively. In addition, some members of the monastic community worked as clerks, secretaries, accountants, and lawyers, running day-to-day operations. The administrative skill of the monastic workers and their ability to use successful farming practices to good effect made many monasteries wealthy. Their increasing wealth enabled them to provide social services, such as caring for the poor and the sick. These good works, in turn, led more people to enter monasteries, inspired more converts to Christianity, and increased the importance of the Church in medieval society.

EARLY MEDIEVAL SOCIAL STRUCTURE

The social structures that developed in the Early Middle Ages were a response to the problems of decentralized government. They represented an effort to create stability and order after the fall of Rome.

FEUDALISM Feudalism evolved from the sixth and seventh centuries when **freemen**, who lacked social or political ties, sought protection from more powerful people. The word "feudalism" refers to a fluid political, military, and social organization based on mutual obligations between warlords, or princes, and vassals, who swore allegiance (**fealty**) to them. The vassals could be summoned at any time to fight for the lord, and they eventually developed into a knightly warrior class that followed a code of chivalry. Groups of vassals thus amounted to standing armies, maintaining horses, arms, and armor in case of war. Both the lord and the vassal were bound to each other through honor and loyalty. By the ninth century even clerics, including abbots and bishops, swore allegiance to local lords. This led to new sources of conflict, because the Church, although pleased to receive the protection that feudalism provided, objected to its clergy becoming vassals to a secular authority.

MANORIALISM The manorial system of the Early Middle Ages was organized around the **manor**. This was a group of farms and villages, including grazing land for animals and forests for hunting. A landowner (the lord) allowed peasants to live and work on the land, and to collect wood for their fires, in exchange for a percentage of their produce and other obligations. By the ninth century, peasants had split into two main classes: the freeman and the serf. The freeman owned property, but turned it over to the lord in return for protection and certain economic and legal rights. The serf, who was tied to the land, could own animals but not the land he cultivated.

Peasants made up nearly 90 percent of the medieval population. They typically lived at or below subsistence level in small one-room houses. Women and girls did most of the weaving and spinning to produce textiles. They also helped to farm the land, baked bread, salted meat in order to preserve it, and brewed ale. Peasant families were the most susceptible to famine and disease. Their poor living conditions led some peasants to enter monasteries, while others took up a wandering life of begging or searched for more generous lords.

Later in the Middle Ages, the manor coalesced into a one-family property. As the working population grew and the lord's territory diminished in size, peasants worked more for themselves and less for the lord. This resulted in individual families owning more property, which they could pass on to their descendants.

GERMANIC TRIBES

In addition to the uncertain lives of medieval peasants, the nomadic lifestyle of Germanic tribes contributed to the weakened social and political structure in the Early Middle Ages, as it had previously contributed to the fall of Rome. Although the skilled, non-urban, Germanic fighters were sometimes tolerated and occasionally used by Rome to fend off other attackers, they were generally considered to be barbarians. Forced westward by the warlike Huns of what is now Mongolia, these tribes moved rapidly through Europe. The Goths were divided into Visigoths (west Goths) who went to Spain and France, and Ostrogoths (east Goths), who moved into the Balkans and thence to Rome. Franks went south and west into what is now France; Burgundians and Alemanni moved into Burgundy and part of modern Germany; Angles, Saxons, and Jutes migrated from what are now Denmark and the Netherlands to England; and Vandals moved west across the Rhine, through Spain, across North Africa and Sicily, and up through Italy (map **10.1**, p. 242). The Huns reached as far as northern France by around 450.

The Goths and Vandals became Christian, but because they were Arians (see Chapter 8), they came into conflict with the Roman Church. The Franks were to have the most significant impact on Western history, for they gave rise to the Merovingian and Carolingian dynasties.

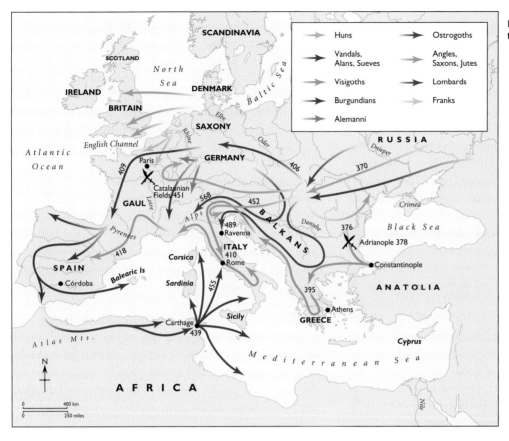

Map 10.1 Movements of Germanic tribes, 370–568.

THE MEROVINGIAN AND CAROLINGIAN DYNASTIES

The Franks, a Germanic people from what is now Belgium and from the lower Rhine, occupied Gaul (modern France, Belgium, the Netherlands, part of Germany, and north Italy). Four Frankish rulers were particularly influential for the development of Western culture: Clovis, Charles Martel, Pepin the Short, and Carolus Magnus, who became known as Charlemagne. Clovis was a warlord who belonged to the Merovingian dynasty; the other three were in the Carolingian line.

Clovis (ruled 481–511) was the first Frankish king and founder of the Merovingian dynasty, which was named after his ancestor Merovich. According to Church tradition, Clovis was a pagan when he ascended the throne, but he called on Christ to aid him in battle and his victory inspired him to become a Christian. His Christian wife, Clotilde, encouraged him to convert to Christianity by inviting the bishop of Reims (in northern France) to teach Clovis the gospel. His conversion is described in the *History of the Franks* by the bishop of Tours, Gregory (*c.* 538/539–593), although some historians consider Gregory's account biased.

READING SELECTION

Gregory, *History of the Franks*, the conversion of Clovis, PWC2-056-C

In 732, Charles Martel (Charles the Hammer) (*c.* 688–741), who was **mayor of the palace** of Austrasia (the eastern part of the Frankish kingdom), raised an army and took Neustria and Burgundy from the Church. This action angered the Church, but in fact it gave Charles the means to defend the Church from attacks by the Lombards, another Germanic tribe, who came from the Danube region and ruled in northeast Italy. Charles Martel's most significant military triumph was the defeat of Muslim armies moving northward in their campaign of conquest, having conquered most of North Africa and Spain. In 734, he stopped their advance at Tours, near Poitiers, in central France. With this victory, Charles Martel enabled most of Europe to remain Christian.

The Carolingian rulers developed an administrative system designed to restore centralized power to their domain and at the same time maintain the feudal system of allegiances. They also standardized the obligations of counts and dukes in exchange for a **benefice** (originally land granted for services, but later extended to ecclesiastical offices as well). However, the real administrative officers were household ministers known as *missi domini*.

Map 10.2 Europe on the death of Charlemagne, 814.

The ruler gave land to the counts and dukes and in return expected loyalty. In fact, however, the counts and dukes were themselves ambitious and amassed their own followers, often having different aims than the ruler. Further weakening the ruler was the system of succession: instead of transferring power and territory to his eldest son, the ruler divided his land among all his legitimate sons.

By the eighth century, the holder of the office of mayor of the palace wielded more power than the counts. In 751, one of Charles Martel's sons, Pepin the Short (c. 714–768), used that office to overthrow the last Merovingian king, Childeric III (ruled c. 743–751). Pepin established the Carolingian dynasty, which was named for his father. He seized parts of Italy (later called the Papal States) from the Germans and the Lombards and returned them to the pope. In recognition of Pepin's service to the Church, the pope proclaimed him the first legitimate Carolingian king.

The Carolingian ruler who had the greatest impact on medieval culture was Pepin's son Charlemagne (768–814). He expanded the borders of the Frankish lands and forced his conquered enemies to become Christian. When he died, his empire included most of continental western Europe (map **10.2**).

CHARLEMAGNE AND THE CAROLINGIAN RENAISSANCE

Charlemagne was inspired by the achievements of Rome, notably in law, politics, literature, and the visual arts. He saw himself as a ruler in the imperial Roman tradition (figure **10.1**) and accordingly launched a Classical revival, now known as the Carolingian Renaissance (rebirth). Although he himself could not write, Charlemagne promoted literacy and encouraged the accurate use of Latin in official documents. He also improved the economy and standardized coinage and church music.

Charlemagne's life and achievements are recorded in the *Vita Caroli* (*Life of Charlemagne*), a biography by the Frankish scholar Einhard (c. 770–840). Modeled on Suetonius's *Lives of the Caesars* (see Chapter 7), Einhard's account includes personal observations and historical facts. He writes as follows of the impressive appearance of Charlemagne, who stood over 6 feet 3 inches (1.9 m) tall:

> He used to wear the national, that is to say, the Frank, dress—next his skin a linen shirt and linen breeches, and above these a tunic fringed with silk; while hose fastened by

10.1 Equestrian statuette of Charlemagne, from Metz (the capital of Austrasia), 9th century. Bronze with traces of gilt, 9½ in. (24.1 cm) high. Louvre, Paris.

bands covered his lower limbs, and shoes his feet, and he protected his shoulders and chest in winter by a close-fitting coat of otter or marten skins. Over all he flung a blue cloak, and he always had a sword girt about him, usually one with a gold or silver hilt and belt; he sometimes carried a jeweled sword, but only on great feast days or at the reception of ambassadors from foreign nations.

(Einhard, *Life of Charlemagne*, 23)

Charlemagne fought the Lombards in northern Italy, the Saxons in Germany, and the Muslims who were expanding into southern Gaul. He instituted a program aimed at converting as many people as possible to Christianity and sought to protect Christian shrines, such as the Holy Sepulcher (Christ's tomb), that were located in Muslim-ruled Palestine. At the same time, however, he maintained diplomatic ties with the court of Harun-al-Rashid, the Abbasid caliph of Baghdad (the caliph of the *Arabian Nights*; see Chapter 9). Within his own borders, Charlemagne encouraged the presence of Jews, who, he believed, would promote commerce. In recognition of Charlemagne's efforts on behalf of Christianity, Pope Leo III (papacy 795–816) crowned him Holy Roman Emperor on Christmas Day in the year 800 (see Box).

Defining Moment

The Coronation of Charlemagne

The only time that a pope has ever bowed to an "earthly king" was at the coronation of Charlemagne on Christmas Day in 800 (figure **10.2**). The coronation of Charlemagne is significant because it marked the arrival of a new inheritor of the Roman legacy and a competitor of the Byzantine Empire. The event also marked the union of the Roman and the German, of the Mediterranean and the northern civilizations—the beginning of a concept of nations unified by a common culture. The Holy Roman emperors strengthened the power of the popes to enthrone, and at times to dethrone, emperors.

After inheriting the kingdom of the Franks, Charlemagne worked toward bringing order to what is now called Europe. In Charlemagne's realm, the Franks had been regressing toward barbarianism and neglecting education. In 771, the northern half of Europe was still pagan and lawless under the Saxons and the Norse tribes; meanwhile,

10.2 *The Coronation of Charlemagne as Holy Roman Emperor by Pope Leo III in Rome (25 December 800),* from the *Grandes Chroniques de France, 1375–1379.* Illumination, Bibliothèque Nationale, Paris.

in the south, the Roman Church strove to assert its power against the Lombard kingdom on the Italian peninsula.

In 772, Charlemagne launched a thirty-year campaign, during which he conquered and Christianized the powerful Saxons in

the north. He subdued the Avars, a Tatar tribe on the Danube, and compelled the rebellious Bavarian dukes to submit to him. When possible, however, he preferred to settle matters peacefully. For example, Charlemagne offered to pay the Lombard king, Desiderius, for return of lands to the pope. But Desiderius refused, and Charlemagne seized his kingdom in 773–774.

By the year 800, Charlemagne was the undisputed ruler of western Europe. His vast realm covered what are now France, Switzerland, Belgium, the Netherlands, half of present-day Italy, Germany, part of Austria, and the Spanish March ("border"), which reached to the Ebro River. By establishing a central government in western Europe, Charlemagne restored much of the unity of the old Roman Empire and sowed the seeds of modern Europe.

Critical Question Why is a county, district, or municipality officer who inquires into deaths called a coroner? How does "coroner" relate to "coronation"?

READING SELECTION
Einhard, *Life of Charlemagne*, the coronation of
Charlemagne, PWC2-032

LITERARY EPIC: *SONG OF ROLAND*

Despite Charlemagne's ultimate victory over the Muslims, his forces were defeated in 778 by the Basques at the Battle of Roncesvalles in northern Spain. This episode is included in the epic *Chanson de Roland* (*Song of Roland*), an anonymous poem of 4000 ten-syllable lines. It glorifies the loyalty and bravery of Charlemagne's commanders as well as Charlemagne's determination to rout the Muslims and preserve Christianity.

The *Song of Roland* is the most famous example of the *chanson de geste* (literally a "song of deeds"), and the name suggests that the deeds in question are heroic and therefore worthy of being told and retold. In keeping with medieval ideals, the heroes of these *chansons* fight in service to a lord and are devout Christians. Although not written down until the eleventh century, the *Song of Roland* had been recited orally at early medieval courts ever since the time of Charlemagne. Wandering performers, among them **minstrels** who sang secular songs, kept alive the heroic deeds of Charlemagne's French knight, Roland, who warned his lord of the Muslim threat.

As with many epics, the *Song of Roland* is a mixture of tradition and legend. Its heroes perform larger-than-life deeds, their faith is unwavering, and their loyalty to Charlemagne is unquestioning. The epic is composed from the point of view of the French, and it exalts Christianity while depicting the Muslims as evildoers. It also extols the virtue of chivalry, the code of behavior that required knights to fight and die for their lord and have faith in God. In the eyes of the poet, Roland exemplified the chivalric code.

In one of the most dramatic episodes in the poem, Charlemagne has crossed the Pyrenees from Spain back into France. Arrayed along the border are troops chosen by Charlemagne as a rearguard. His trusted count, Oliver, overlooks Spain from a hilltop and sees that the Saracens (Muslims) have assembled a great force:

> Their helmets gleam with gold and precious stones.
> Their shields are shining, their hauberks [chain mail coats]
>   burnished gold,
> Their long sharp spears with battle flags unfurled.
>
> (verse 81)

Defending his king and Christendom, Roland attacks. But he loses his warhorse, Veillantif, and is forced to proceed on foot. When he sees the corpses of his friends strewn over the battlefield, Roland recognizes the imminence of his own death. As he dies, his last thoughts are of honor, penance, and faith in God:

> His ears give way, he feels his brains gush out.
> He prays that God will summon all his peers;
> Then, for himself, he prays to Gabriel.
> Taking the horn, to keep it from all shame,
> With Durandel clasped in his other hand,
> He goes on, farther than a good cross-bow shot,
> West into Spain, crossing a fallow field.
>
> (verse 168)

> In the green grass he lies down on his face,
> Placing beneath him the sword and Oliphant [an elephant-
>   tusk horn];
> He turns his head to look toward pagan Spain.
> He does these things in order to be sure
> King Charles [Charlemagne] will say, and with him all
>   the Franks,
> The noble count conquered until he died.
> He makes confession, for all his sins laments.
> Offers his glove to God in penitence.
>
> (verse 174)

READING SELECTION
Song of Roland, the death of Roland, PWC2-163-B

CHARLEMAGNE'S PALACE

Charlemagne's palace was located at Aachen, near the border between modern France and Germany. It was designed by his chief architect, Odo of Metz. In contrast to the Merovingian kings, Charlemagne wanted one palace identified as the cultural center of his kingdom. This, he believed, would be an advantage in maintaining political stability—and, indeed, the Palace (or Palatine) chapel would remain the site of German coronations until the sixteenth century.

Although the fortress-like palace was destroyed, it is thought to have had a huge royal hall, some 140 by 60 feet (42.7 × 18.3 m), lavishly decorated on the interior. A long gallery connected the hall to the royal chapel. All that remains of the original royal complex is the chapel (figures **10.3** and **10.4**). Its centralized, octagonal plan and interior design were inspired by the Church of San Vitale in Ravenna (see Chapter 9). Charlemagne had visited Ravenna, and he instructed Odo to take mosaics from San Vitale and use them at Aachen.

THE PALACE SCHOOL

In order to revive learning and literacy, Charlemagne established a palace school and staffed it with outstanding scholars from different parts of Europe. The most important of these scholars was Alcuin of York (c. 732–804), an Anglo-Saxon from Northumbria, in England. Alcuin had been educated at

10.3 Odo of Metz, interior of Charlemagne's Palace Chapel, Aachen, 792–805.
This section of the octagonal interior of Charlemagne's Palace Chapel shows the massive squared piers on the ground floor supporting round arches inspired by Roman architecture, with voussoirs of alternating color. Behind the arches is the ambulatory, which supports the second-story gallery, from where Charlemagne could view Mass being celebrated. Outdoor light enters the chapel from the upper clerestory windows.

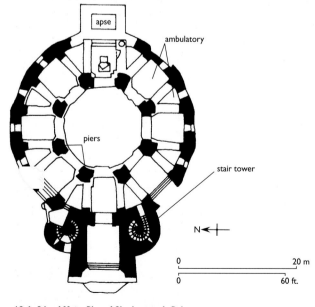

10.4 Odo of Metz, Plan of Charlemagne's Palace Chapel, Aachen (Aix-la-Chapelle), Germany, 792–805.
Note that the chapel's exterior wall is composed of sixteen segments.

the cathedral school in York and was appointed its master in 766. In 782 Alcuin moved to Aachen, where he established the curriculum at the palace school and promoted similar curricula throughout Charlemagne's empire.

At York, Alcuin had been influenced by the writings of the Venerable Bede (*c.* 673–735), a biblical scholar, known as the "Father of English History." Bede had written on language and science, lives of saints, and monastic histories. He completed his *Historia Ecclesiastica Gentis Anglorum* (*Ecclesiastical History of the English People*) in 731.

Alcuin was also influenced by Classical texts. He studied the Latin grammar of the Roman scholar Aelius Donatus and adopted his curriculum: the *trivium*, which consisted of grammar, rhetoric, and dialectic (logical argument) and the *quadrivium*, which consisted of arithmetic, geometry, music, and astronomy. This became the standard medieval course of study in schools until the Renaissance, some four hundred years later. Alcuin himself read Greek authors on philosophy, rhetoric, history, mathematics, and Greek musical theory.

CAROLINGIAN MANUSCRIPTS

Medieval manuscripts, often containing religious texts, were books written by hand. They played a key role in Charlemagne's cultural revival and helped to keep literacy alive throughout the Middle Ages. Biblical and other sacred texts were frequently **illuminated** (decorated with painted images). The most valuable manuscripts had pages of purple **parchment** (the treated and dyed skin of a sheep or calf), on which texts were copied in letters of gold and silver. Manuscript illumination was not only a significant art form in its own right, but was considered a way of enhancing and honoring God's Word.

Under Alcuin, penmanship was simplified and made more readable than the unpunctuated Roman **cursive** script used in the Merovingian era. The new Carolingian **minuscule** resembled modern-day lowercase writing. As a result, it was possible for Charlemagne to improve communication throughout his empire and make administration more efficient. In addition, more people, especially the clergy, learned to read and write.

Figure **10.5** shows a page from a manuscript produced at Charlemagne's palace school. St. Mark is seated at his desk before a parted curtain. He is in the process of writing his Gospel, which lies open on the desk. At the same time, he turns to receive the first words of the text from a lion (Mark's iconographic symbol), depicted as if dictating the already-written text from heaven. The two realms, heaven and earth, are separated by the rod holding a curtain, which opens to reveal the evangelist as the lion reveals the Word of God. At the corners above the arch (the **spandrels**), the artist has illustrated an angel at the left and John the Baptist at the right. The figure of St. John probably alludes to the description of Christ's Baptism in the Gospel of Mark.

The style of the illumination reflects the influence of various cultures. Patterning and stylization combine elements from Byzantium and Ireland (see below), but suggestions of organic form and perspective indicate some knowledge of Greco-Roman naturalism. Such cross-cultural infusions, especially when applied to different disciplines, tend to encourage periods of high cultural achievement. This was true of Charlemagne's reign, and it would occur again on an even grander scale during the Renaissance in Italy (see Chapters 13 and 14).

MUSIC IN THE CAROLINGIAN PERIOD

Charlemagne's approach to music, especially church music, was another expression of his interest in assembling the best minds from different regions of Europe. He brought Roman monks to Aachen to revise the liturgy and develop musical accompaniment. He believed that music as well as literacy would inspire the faithful.

10.5 *St. Mark*, from the Gospel Book of St. Médard of Soissons, France, early 9th century. Gold ink on vellum, 14³/₈ × 10¹/₄ in. (36.5 × 26 cm). Bibliothèque Nationale, Paris.

St. Benedict and the Benedictine Rule

Benedict was born in Nursia, in southern Italy, and studied in Rome. Around 500, he retired from the world to live as a hermit in a cave, but his piety attracted a group of followers. In 525, Benedict went to Monte Cassino, near Rome, and founded the Benedictine Order, to which he imparted a set of rules for monastic living. He required that members of his Order take vows of poverty and chastity, agree to live communally in one place, and obey the abbot. The daily schedule in a monastery was governed by routines to be followed at designated times during the day. These included a series of daily prayers, scriptural readings, celebration of Mass, and manual labor. Monks would rise at two in the morning and retire around five or six in the evening.

Benedict's sister, St. Scholastica (c. 480–543), also chose a religious life. She founded a convent of Benedictine nuns near her brother's monastery and met with him on a yearly basis to discuss issues relating to the rule.

Charlemagne adopted plainsong, sung without instrumental accompaniment, as his official church music (see Chapter 8). Singing in church was reserved for men, and the emperor himself participated. There are no surviving examples of musical notation from Charlemagne's court, but one can imagine how the haunting rise and fall of Gregorian chant filled the chapel.

During the ninth century, a new musical style known as **organum** developed. Whereas plainsong was monophonic ("single-sounded"), consisting of a single melodic line sung by one or more persons, organum was **polyphonic** ("many-sounded"), with two or more melodic lines performed at once. The result, documented in *Musica enchiriadis*, a musical handbook of around 900, was a fuller texture. In the earliest form

of organum, two voices moved in parallel, simultaneously singing the same piece of plainsong and using the same rhythms, but with one voice four or five notes lower than the other. Later, a third or fourth vocal line was added at the octave. These particular intervals between the lines of music—fourths, fifths, and octaves—sound bare and melancholy to modern ears.

In the eleventh and twelfth centuries, the style evolved. A lower voice sang the plainsong melody in long notes; this was named the **tenor**, from the Latin *tenere*, "to hold." Above it, a higher voice sang shorter notes in melismatic style—that is, with several notes sung to a single syllable (see Chapter 11).

MONASTICISM UNDER CHARLEMAGNE

By Charlemagne's era, monastic communities had been established throughout Europe. The monks, and to some degree the nuns, who lived in monasteries and convents, composed sacred music. Through copyists and illuminators in the monastic **scriptoria** (rooms for writing), Classical and Christian texts remained in circulation. Charlemagne encouraged the expansion of monastery and church schools with their own libraries throughout the empire. Further, since the standard of monastic life had declined by the beginning of his reign, Charlemagne decided to institute reform. In particular, he wished to implement the early-fifth-century rule of St. Benedict (c. 480–547; see Box). The task fell to Alcuin of York, who was a member of the Benedictine Order.

The earliest surviving Benedictine monastery plan is preserved at St. Gall, in Switzerland (figure **10.6**). No known monastery actually adheres to this plan; it may be that of an ideal monastery. This complex design shows all the buildings necessary for the community of monks, including a church, cloister, school, living quarters, stables, land for the monks to work, an infirmary, and a cemetery. The typical monastery was thus a self-sufficient community. Its economy was based on agriculture, though the monks often made craft items and wine, which could be sold outside the monastery.

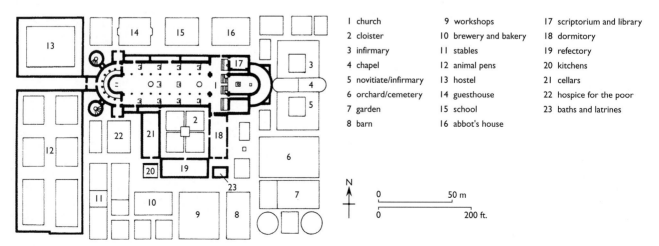

1 church	9 workshops	17 scriptorium and library
2 cloister	10 brewery and bakery	18 dormitory
3 infirmary	11 stables	19 refectory
4 chapel	12 animal pens	20 kitchens
5 novitiate/infirmary	13 hostel	21 cellars
6 orchard/cemetery	14 guesthouse	22 hospice for the poor
7 garden	15 school	23 baths and latrines
8 barn	16 abbot's house	

10.6 Plan of the Benedictine monastery of St. Gall, Switzerland, *c.* 820, drawn from five pieces of parchment.

Cross-cultural Influences

Monasticism

Monasticism began in the Far East before taking hold in the West. It was practiced in India in the first millennium B.C. and was espoused by the Buddha in the sixth century B.C. as a way of achieving spiritual enlightenment. From the third century B.C., there were Buddhist missionaries in the Near East and Greece, where they influenced the development of Christian monasticism.

In India, monks and nuns inhabited living spaces (*viharas*) cut into caves. These were located outside the main cities, but close to small villages and trading routes.

Because monks did not own land or personal possessions, many begged for support and food.

The thirty Buddhist *viharas* at Ajanta, northeast of Bombay, are the best-known monastic quarters in India. Inside the *viharas*, Buddhists built *chaitya* halls with columns and a curved apse (figure **10.7**). The apse contained a statue of the Buddha and a **stupa**, a round structure that evolved from the Buddha's burial mound. Relief sculptures decorating the capitals of the columns and the walls illustrate important Buddhist events.

As Buddhism spread throughout the Far

East, the number of monasteries increased. In Japan, for example, the best-known Buddhist monastery complex is Horyu-ji in Nara (figure **10.8**). This view shows the elaborate architectural design of the monastery, which includes temples, *kondos* (halls), **pagodas** (tiered towers that contained relics), cloisters, and living spaces.

Like Christian monastics, Buddhist monks at first espoused poverty and isolation from society, but as the movement grew, they formed self-sufficient communities owning land and the buildings on it. Buddhist monks also spent time in prayer, study, and work.

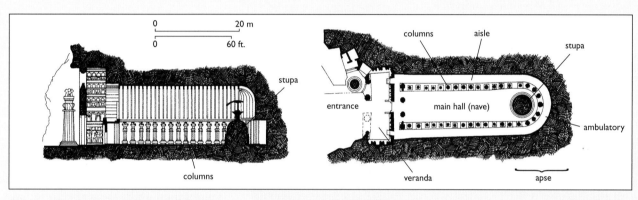

10.7 *above* **Generic plan and section of a *chaitya* hall.**

10.8 Horyu-ji monastery complex, Nara, Japan, 7th century.

FROM THE CAROLINGIAN TO THE OTTONIAN PERIOD

When Charlemagne died in 814, his only surviving son, Louis I, the Pious (ruled 814–840), came to power. Louis did not want to weaken the empire by dividing it equally among his three sons by his first wife. Instead, he appointed the eldest, Lothair (d. 855), as his imperial successor and gave parts of France and Germany to his other two sons. But Louis remarried and, in 823, had a fourth son, Charles the Bald, who was also entitled to a share of the kingdom. This further division of the imperial realm diminished the power of the empire and left it open to waves of invasion from Vikings, Magyars (modern Hungarians), and Muslims. A dark age followed, which was a period of illiteracy and widespread poverty, and it saw a decline in monumental architecture. Charlemagne's achievements receded into legend, and his reign reemerged in works of literature, such as the *Song of Roland*, as a time of mythic grandeur.

In the tenth century, a more stable government took hold in Germany under a series of rulers, three of whom were named Otto, giving rise to the term Ottonian Empire. Otto I, the Great (ruled 936–973), expanded his power base by defending the pope and being proclaimed emperor in return. Like Charlemagne, Otto encouraged a revival of ancient Roman culture, including the arts and literature. A page from the *Gospel Book of Otto III* gives some idea of the artistic revival in the Ottonian period (figure **10.9**).

Despite the relative political stability and cultural achievements promoted by the Ottonian rulers, rivalry between Rome and the Eastern (Byzantine) Empire continued. As a result, the Ottonian Empire never truly evolved into an independent political state. The conflict was only partly resolved in 1122 by the Concordat of Worms, which ended the Investiture controversy. Thereafter, the pope had the authority to invest clergy with control of spiritual matters, while the emperor could bestow secular authority and land.

THEATER IN THE EARLY MIDDLE AGES

Like literacy, theater declined after the fall of Rome. Invasions and political instability had made organized theater difficult to maintain. Nevertheless, the traditions of Roman comedy, pagan festivals, and Christian liturgy all provided sources from which theater began to revive. In addition, there were traveling entertainers, such as minstrels, jugglers, acrobats, and animal-trainers, who performed in public squares and at the courts. The most popular performing animals were bears and apes.

From the fifth to the seventh centuries, a type of German performer called a **scop** sang tales of Germanic heroes. The *scop* tradition died out in the eighth century, when the

10.9 *Jesus Washing the Feet of Peter*, from the *Gospel Book of Otto III*, *c.* 1000. Tempera on vellum, image 8⅜ × 6 in. (21.3 × 15.2 cm). Bayerische Staatsbibliothek, Munich.
In this scene, St. Peter protests the humility of Jesus, who washes the feet of his followers. Jesus reprimands the apostle and glares sternly at him. Their gestures and glances animate their exchange and energize the narrative. At the left, eight apostles await their turn, while, at the right, one apostle laces his sandal as another arrives with a fresh basin of water. Jesus is a commanding presence, centered between two colorful green columns and towering over the apostles. Byzantine influence can be seen in the re-use of Greco-Roman art, which the Ottonian illuminator has flattened and thus made less three-dimensional.

Church declared it a threat to the Christian faith. Pagan seasonal rites, on the other hand, were absorbed into the liturgical calendar. Thus the spring maypole festival coincided with the Resurrection of Jesus, and the date of the Nativity, December 25, was associated with pagan rites of winter. Comedy and revelry were also incorporated into the Church from popular rites, including the burlesque Feast of Fools celebrated by minor clerics. On Holy Innocents' Day (December 28 in the liturgical calendar), equality was celebrated in the Boy Bishop ritual, when choirboys impersonated members of the clergy.

LITURGY AND DRAMA

Certain aspects of Church liturgy lend themselves to the establishment of a dramatic tradition. The prime example is that liturgy marks religious events cyclically—that is, according to days of the calendar—rather than according to historical chronology. Thus the Nativity is celebrated *every* December 25 without fail, year after year. Congregations would build up the expectation of revisiting each such story annually. In addition, priests began to introduce visual elements into the liturgy— symbolic gestures, such as making the sign of the Cross— which could easily be recognized by a congregation unable to read. In the performance of Mass itself, the priest created an atmosphere of dramatic expectation, engaging the congregation in the narration of the events of Jesus' Last Supper, acted out with bread and wine. Enhancing the drama were antiphonal songs, sung either by two alternating groups of singers or by a group of singers and an individual.

Antiphonal singing eventually led to inserting, first, music and, later, music with words into the text of a service. These insertions, called **tropes**, consisted of newly composed verses with melodies, and they were added between sections of existing chant. An Easter trope from around 925 is the earliest to have survived. This exchange between angels and the Three Marys who discover the empty tomb of Jesus is both dramatic and direct:

> ANGELS: Whom seek ye in the tomb, O Christians?
> THE THREE MARYS: Jesus of Nazareth, the crucified,
>   O Heavenly Beings.
> ANGELS: He is not here, he is risen as he foretold.
>   Go and announce that he is risen from the tomb.
>
> (Easter trope)

By the late tenth century, liturgical theater had become widespread in Europe. Over the next two hundred years, plays would be performed, first inside the church and then, from the twelfth century, outside in the square in front of the church. Attributes such as the keys of St. Peter, wings of angels, and the devil's horns, tail, and pitchfork allowed viewers to identify stock characters. There were three main types of religious plays performed in the Middle Ages. **Mystery plays** dramatized biblical events, **miracle plays** focused on miraculous events, and

in **morality plays** the human struggle between good and evil was given dramatic form.

The twelfth-century *Play of Adam*, a mystery play, presents the Creation and Fall of Man. In "Creation," God makes the earth and animals but wants a creature to worship him and keep his world in order:

> To keep this world, both more and less,
> A skillful beast then will I make
> After my shape and my likeness,
> The which shall worship me to take.
>
> (*Play of Adam*, lines 21–24)

In the "Fall of Man," responsibility for sin falls squarely on Eve, through the guile of Satan. She tells Adam that they will be as great as God if they eat the apple:

> We shall be as gods, thou and I,
> If that we eat
> Here of this tree. Adam, forthy [therefore]
> Let not that worship for to get,
> For we shall be as wise
> As God that is so great,
> And as mickle [worthy] of price;
> Forthy eat of this meat [i.e. the apple].
>
> (lines 92–99)

The most widely known medieval morality play is *Everyman*. This was not written down until the fifteenth century, but had already been performed for centuries. It is composed in rhyming couplets, combining allegorical characters and personifications with moral lessons. The plot is simple: the life of Everyman is a pilgrimage from the earthly world to death and salvation. As with Greek tragedy (see Chapter 6), a prologue introduces the main theme. Here, the words of the Prologue are spoken by a messenger:

> I pray you all give your audience,
> And hear this matter with reverence,
> By figure [in form] a moral play:
> The *Summoning of Everyman* called it is,
> That of our lives and ending shows
> How transitory we be all day [always].
>
> (*Everyman*, lines 1–6)

At the outset of the play, God is displeased with the behavior of mankind. He summons Death to instruct Everyman in the pilgrimage he must make. Death is only too willing to oblige:

> Lord, I will in the world go run overall [everywhere],
> And cruelly outsearch both great and small;
> Every man will I beset that liveth beastly
> Out of God's laws, and dreadeth not folly.
> He that loveth riches I will strike with my dart,
> His sight to blind, and from heaven to depart [separate]—
> Except that alms be his good friend—
> In hell for to dwell, world without end.
> Lo, yonder I see Everyman walking.

Full little he thinketh on my coming;
His mind is on fleshly lusts and his treasure,
And great pain it shall cause him to endure
Before the Lord, Heaven King.

(lines 72–84)

Everyman gradually comes to realize that friends, relatives, and worldly possessions will not bring salvation. Rather, the only way to satisfy God at the reckoning of the Last Judgment is with Confession, Good Deeds, and Christian Knowledge, all of which are personified in the play. Having learned his moral lesson, Everyman is received into heaven:

ANGEL: . . . Hereabove thou shalt go
        Because of thy singular virtue.
        Now the soul is taken the body fro [from],
        Thy reckoning is crystal-clear.
        Now shalt thou into the heavenly sphere,
        Unto the which all ye shall come
        That liveth well before the day of doom.

(lines 895–901)

NON-LITURGICAL DRAMA: HROSWITHA OF GANDERSHEIM

Only one group of non-liturgical plays has survived from the tenth century. These are of interest partly because they were written by the first female playwright on record, and partly because they are the earliest known examples of non-liturgical drama. The author is Hroswitha (c. 935–c. 1002), a canoness at Gandersheim Abbey in northern Germany. She came from an aristocratic family and, as her plays indicate, had received a Classical education.

Hroswitha was a prolific author, but her works were not published until the sixteenth century. She wrote two historical epics praising Otto I and Otto II, eight legends in verse, and six morality plays in rhymed prose. Inspired by the Roman comedies of Terence (see Chapter 7), Hroswitha intended to use the appeal of sophisticated, worldly dialogue to convey the moral lessons of the Bible and Christianity.

In *Dulcitius*, for example, Hroswitha engages the reader in the ecstasy of martyrdom with humor bordering on slapstick. The setting is the palace of Diocletian during the fourth-century Christian persecutions. Governor Dulcitius, having heard that Christians indulge in exotic orgies, attempts to seduce three recently converted Christian virgins: Agape, Chione, and Irena. But when he approaches them, he becomes delusional and kisses pots and pans instead of the girls. When he comes to himself and sees that the pots have blackened his face, he sends the young women to their death.

Hroswitha was the first author in the West to use the Faust legend, in which a man sells his soul to the devil for earthly wealth and power. This, as we shall see, became a popular theme in Western literature.

NORTHERN EUROPE: BRITAIN, IRELAND, SCANDINAVIA, AND ICELAND

Christianity arrived in northern Europe somewhat later than in central and southern Europe. Roman missionaries had brought the faith to Britain in the second or third century A.D. However, in the fifth century, the pagan Germanic Angles, Saxons, and Jutes invaded England and wiped out most of the Christians. Then, in 596, Pope Gregory I, who was devoted to the spread of monasticism, dispatched Augustine (d. *c.* 604), the prior of St. Andrew's monastery in Rome. Augustine, later known as Augustine of Canterbury, went with forty missionaries to reestablish Christianity in England.

Augustine arrived in Kent, in the southeast, the following year. He converted the king of Kent, Ethelbert (d. 616), whose Frankish wife Bertha was herself a Christian. Ethelbert was thus England's earliest Christian king. Augustine founded an abbey at Canterbury and became its first archbishop. By the seventh century, monasticism was well established in England.

The *History* of the Venerable Bede describes these events, including the story told in the oldest-known English poem, "Caedmon's Hymn." According to Caedmon (650?–680?), an illiterate cowherd and lay brother (an unordained member of a monastery) at Whitby, a voice instructed him to sing of the Creation. Whitby, a dual monastery housing both men and women, was founded and ruled by the abbess St. Hilda (614–668).

READING SELECTION
Bede, *Ecclesiastical History of the English People*, Augustine's conversion of King Ethelbert, PWC2-051-C

IRELAND AND THE BOOK OF KELLS

Because of its isolation and distance from the main centers of European power, Ireland remained Christian even when England was dominated by the pagan Anglo-Saxons. According to Irish tradition, St. Patrick (c. 390–c. 461) Christianized the country in the early fifth century. Monasticism took hold in the sixth century and became a strong force. Two saints were particularly important in the monastic movement of Ireland and Scotland. St. Brigid, the abbess of Kildare (d. *c.* 525), was believed to have performed many miracles during her lifetime and is credited with expanding monasticism in Ireland. St. Columba (543–615), whose rule was extremely strict, left Ireland around 563 to convert the pagan Picts of Scotland. He founded a monastery on the island of Iona.

10.10 *Canon Table*, Book of Kells, late 8th century. Illumination on vellum, 13 × 9½ in. (33 × 24 cm). Trinity College, Dublin.

Note the appearance of the four Evangelists in symbolic form. The upper corners are formed by the stylized wings of the angel of Matthew and the eagle of John. The lion of Mark and the bull of Luke are shown in the space between the two small arches.

Irish monasteries maintained a high level of learning. They kept alive the Latin language by reading and copying Classical as well as Christian texts. As the number of monasteries expanded, they became repositories of texts and housed some of the greatest examples of manuscript illumination. Those that have survived managed to escape the Viking raids.

The best-known Irish manuscript is the Book of Kells, generally dated to the late eighth century. It contains the four Gospels, whose text pages, designed to enhance the Word of God, are richly decorated. But there are also pages that completely or primarily consist of images. It is likely that the Book of Kells and other important manuscripts were placed on altars for special occasions.

The page illustrated in figure **10.10** depicts a Canon Table, a type of image created by Eusebius, the fourth-century bishop of Caesarea (see Chapter 8), to demonstrate parallels between the Gospels. The texts are arranged in four vertical rows separated by columns filled with colorful, intertwined designs. Intricate patterns above the columns include fanciful, interlacing animal, human, and abstract forms. Some are pagan and some are Christian.

A characteristic example of Irish art that predates Christianity is the simple, upright stone marker, generally placed in a graveyard or near a monastery. After the conversion of the Irish, these markers were made in the form of the Cross and decorated with Christian scenes, for instructive purposes

10.11 Cross of Muriedach, Monasterboice, County Louth, Ireland, early 10th century. Stone.
This view shows the Crucifixion, framed by a circle symbolizing the universal Church at the crossing point.

(figure **10.11**). Here, as in the Book of Kells, the surfaces are filled with interlace ornament.

ANGLO-SAXON METALWORK AND LITERATURE

The Anglo-Saxon invaders of England brought with them great skill in metalworking and a particular style of animal art. Examples of both can be seen in the Sutton Hoo purse cover, which was discovered in East Anglia (figure **10.12**). The purse was filled with gold coins and was one of several objects found in a pagan ship burial. Such elaborate burials were reserved for Anglo-Saxon kings and the nobility. A similar rite, in which the deceased is placed in a ship and sent out to sea, is described in the oldest surviving Anglo-Saxon epic poem, *Beowulf.*

BEOWULF

The epic of *Beowulf* is a heroic narrative of some 3000 lines. It was composed between the seventh and tenth centuries in Anglo-Saxon (Old English). Although the setting is the warrior culture of medieval Scandinavia, strains of Christian morality permeate the text. *Beowulf* is the story of a Geat (Swedish) prince who travels to Denmark, where most of the action takes place. His mission is to destroy Grendel, the monster ravishing the land, devouring its inhabitants, and attacking the royal hall of Denmark:

> So times were pleasant for the people there
> until finally one, a fiend out of hell,
> began to work his evil in the world.
> Grendel was the name of this grim demon
> haunting the marches, marauding round the heath
> and the desolate fens.

(lines 99–104)

10.12 Purse cover, from Sutton Hoo, East Anglia, 7th century. Gold, garnets, and enamel, 8 in. (20.3 cm) long. British Museum, London.
The intricate interlace and animal designs are made of sections of gold and garnets held in place by gold strips. The individual sections are known as *cloisons*, meaning "compartments."

Grendel is descended from Cain, the first man to commit murder in the Bible, which links him to a genealogy of evil:

> he had dwelt for a time
> in misery among the banished monsters,
> Cain's clan, whom the Creator had outlawed
> and condemned as outcasts.
>
> (lines 104–107)

> So, after nightfall, Grendel set out
> for the lofty house, to see how the Ring-Danes
> were settling into it after their drink,
> and there he came upon them, a company of the best
> asleep from their feasting . . . Suddenly then
> the God-cursed brute was creating havoc:
> greedy and grim, he grabbed thirty men
> from their resting places and rushed to his lair,
> flushed up and inflamed from the raid,
> blundering back with the butchered corpses.
>
> (lines 115–125)

Beowulf is committed to defending his men, reflecting the bond between the Germanic chieftain and his band of warriors. Like Roland, Beowulf is motivated by bravery and honor. When Beowulf kills Grendel, the monster's mother takes revenge by killing several of Beowulf's men. Beowulf then pursues Grendel's mother to a swamp, destroys her, and returns home to rule for fifty years. When a dragon preys on his subjects, Beowulf is driven to fight by pride, a fatal flaw like the hubris of the Greek tragic heroes that results in his death.

The poetic power of *Beowulf* comes from its skillful use of language. The narrative is enriched by the use of concrete, compound words called **kennings**—the "Spear-Danes," the "Ring-Danes," the "shadow-stalker" (Grendel), the "poison-breather" (Grendel's mother), the "Weather-Geats" (Swedes), and the "tail-turners" (cowards who run from battle), to cite but a few. Subhuman monsters inhabiting murky swamps, a sense of impending doom, the strident clash of battle, larger-than-life heroism, and majestic royal feasts create an atmosphere of poetic mystery.

The epic concludes with Beowulf's warrior funeral and the recognition that with the death of their lord his people face an uncertain, dreary future:

> The Geat people built a pyre for Beowulf,
> stacked and decked it until it stood four-square,
> hung with helmets, heavy war-shields
> and shining armour, just as he had ordered.
> Then his warriors laid him in the middle of it,
> mourning a lord far-famed and beloved.
> On a height they kindled the hugest of all
> funeral fires; fumes of woodsmoke
> billowed darkly up, the blaze roared
> and drowned out their weeping, wind died down
> and flames wrought havoc in the hot bone-house,
> burning it to the core. They were disconsolate
> and wailed aloud for their lord's decease.
>
> (lines 3137–3149)

THE LEGEND OF KING ARTHUR

One of the most popular stories of the Early Middle Ages is the legend of King Arthur and his knights of the Round Table. The literary origins of the Arthur legend are found in pre-Christian Britain, but aside from brief references in several sources to a brave warrior called Arthur, the earliest written account in which he is a king presiding over a group of loyal followers is the Welsh *Mabinogion*. This collection of tales, written down by 1100, is filled with mystery, magic, folklore, and echoes of Irish and Welsh myth. Arthur appears in five of the stories; his queen is Guinevere (Gwenhwyvar in Welsh). He rules over the most virtuous and splendid court in an uncertain setting, somewhere in Britain (see Box).

The following passage from "The Dream of Rhonabwy" gives some idea of the imaginative atmosphere pervading these tales. A rider from an opposing army approaches Arthur and

---

Society and Culture

The Legend of King Arthur through Time

Arthur's first recorded appearance as a king occurs in the Welsh *Mabinogion*, but Arthurian themes later appeared in France and Germany, where they were interwoven with local legends. The French author Chrétien de Troyes wrote four poems about Arthur in the second half of the twelfth century. He added the story of the knight Percival and the search for the Holy Grail—the cup used by Christ at the Last Supper. Geoffrey of Monmouth's *History of the Kings of England* (1135–1139) presents an extensive account of King Arthur as a heroic warrior who brought peace and prosperity to Britain. He also describes Arthur's murder by his evil nephew Mordred.

In the thirteenth century, the *Prose Lancelot* became popular. Lancelot, Arthur's French knight, was associated with the Holy Grail through his pure son, Sir Galahad. (Lancelot had fallen from grace because of his adulterous affair with Arthur's queen, Guinevere.) In the fifteenth century, there was a resurgence of interest in the legend in Britain with Thomas Malory's *Le morte d'Arthur* (*The Death of Arthur*) (1469–1470), and in Victorian England in the late nineteenth century, it was revived again with Alfred, Lord Tennyson's long poem *The Idylls of the King* (1885).

In the twentieth century, the American poet Edwin Arlington Robinson wrote an Arthurian trilogy. The English author T. H. White retold the legend in *The Once and Future King* (1939–1958), which would form the basis for Alan J. Lerner and Frederick Loewe's musical, *Camelot* (1960), named for the legendary seat of Arthur's court. To the present day, King Arthur and his court are associated with the political ideals of even-handed justice and peace maintained by a force of knightly, chivalrous warriors. And Camelot has become a generic term for a Golden Age in which government is fair and just.

asks him to call off the flock of ravens that are killing his troops and devouring his dead knights. Note the use of vivid, fanciful color—especially gold and black—to convey the mystery of the setting:

> After that came a rider on a handsome black high-headed horse: from the top of its left leg it was pure red, and from the top of its right leg down to the hoof pure white, and both horse and rider were clothed in spotted yellow armour speckled with Spanish linen; his cloak and that of the horse were in halves, white and pure black with purple-gold fringes. He carried a gleaming gold-hilted three-grooved sword, with a belt of yellow gold-cloth and a clasp from the eyelid of a pure black whale with a tongue of yellow gold; on his head he wore a helmet of yellow linen with gleaming crystals, and on the crest the image of a griffin with a powerful stone in its head, while in his hand he carried a ridge-shafted ash spear coloured with blue lime, the blade covered with fresh blood and riveted with pure silver.

(*The Mabinogion*, "The Dream of Rhonabwy")

Society and Culture

Chivalry and Medieval Paradigms of Women

According to the chivalric code depicted in romances, the knight was not only brave and loyal to his lord and faithful to God, but he was devoted to a particular woman—his lady. The woman in question was most likely of noble or royal status. "Romantic" knights performed feats of valor to impress their ladies and defend their lords.

The chivalric code was related to the Christian cult of the Virgin Mary that developed around 1050. As the mother of Jesus, the Virgin became a maternal ideal—nourishing, compassionate, willing to intercede with God on behalf of humanity, and free of sin. Eve had disobeyed God and eaten the forbidden fruit, thus causing the Fall of Man and becoming the paradigm (model) of the sinful woman. The Virgin had obeyed God and was thus seen as sinless—a "new Eve."

The third female paradigm was Mary Magdalene, a composite of several women in the Bible and medieval glosses. She, like the Virgin, was the object of a growing cult, in her case because she exemplified the average woman. Mary Magdalene was given special status as the first person to see Christ after his Resurrection. She thus combined Eve's sinfulness with redemption, offering a model for human imperfection and the possibility of human salvation.

In romance literature, as in the medieval code of chivalry, women tended to be seen in terms of religious, secular, or legal paradigms. The religious models were Eve, the Virgin Mary, and Mary Magdalene; the secular models were the queen, the lady, and the commoner; and the legal models depended on the social status of maiden, wife and mother, and widow.

From the sixth or seventh century, the Arthurian legend was elaborated, Christianized, and romanticized on the European continent, first in France and then in Germany. From around 1150, the legend appealed to the growing taste for the literary form known as the **romance**, which was distinct from the *chanson de geste*. The romance, so-called because it was thought (incorrectly) to have originated in Roman tradition, was a long tale, in which a knight performed heroic feats to impress his lady. Ideally, in terms of setting up emotional tension, the knight's lady was married to someone else and thus unattainable (see Box).

READING SELECTION

Geoffrey of Monmouth, *History of the Kings of Britain*, King Arthur, PWC2-063-C; Malory, *Death of Arthur*, Arthur becomes king, PWC2-316-B

THE VIKINGS: NINTH TO TWELFTH CENTURY

The Vikings, who repeatedly invaded Europe during the Early Middle Ages, belonged to the heroic cultures described in *Beowulf*. They came from Norway, Sweden, and Denmark. With longboats propelled by oars and equipped with square sails, the Vikings could navigate rough waters fairly easily. In the ninth century, they overran northern Britain and France, parts of Spain, and central and eastern Europe. On the north coasts of Europe they established trading centers, but they were also pirates, raiding, looting, and kidnapping (map **10.3**). Like the Anglo-Saxons, the Vikings were literate. They used the runic alphabet, which consisted of sixteen letters, to inscribe records, memorials, and poetry on large upright **runestones** (figure **10.13**).

When Christian missionaries arrived in the Viking lands, they brought the scripts used for manuscripts, and the unconnected runic letters gradually fell into disuse. Before 965, when Harald Bluetooth of Denmark converted to Christianity, the Vikings were pagans. Their mythology mirrored both their Nordic climate and their warrior culture.

NORSE MYTHOLOGY   Like other pagan cultures, the pre-Christian Norse were polytheists. As we saw in Chapter 1, the Norse creation myth begins when frost from the north and fire from the south meet and produce Ymir, the ice giant, and a cow. The cow licks off Ymir's ice, and his children are born.

The Norse universe was divided into three tiers, with spaces between them. Asgard, at the top, was the home of the Aesir, the warrior gods, who inhabited the halls of Valhalla (figure **10.14**). There, deceased warriors feasted and fought while awaiting Ragnarök, the great battle at the end of time. The ruler of Valhalla was Odin, god of wisdom and poetry; his

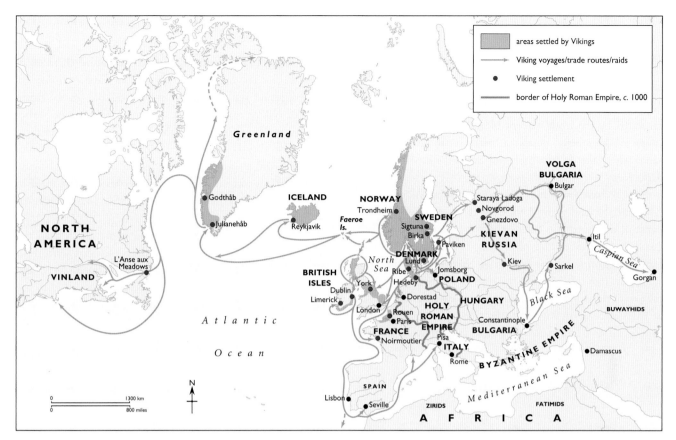

Map 10.3 The Viking world, *c.* 1000.

10.13 Rune-stone, Karlevi, Öland, Sweden, *c.* 1000.
This rune-stone was raised in memory of a Viking chieftain and contains a runic text in verse.

10.14 *right* Memorial picture stone, from Lillbjärs, Sweden. Paint on stone (the paint is modern), 33³⁄₄ in. (86 cm) high. National Antiquities Museum, Stockholm. Like rune-stones, many picture stones were memorials. This one illustrates the deceased in the guise of a mounted warrior being welcomed to Valhalla. At the right, a woman offers him a drinking horn. Below, two men ride in a Viking ship—possibly a reference to a ship burial. Both scenes are framed with an interlace pattern.

wife, Frigg, was a goddess of fertility. Vanaheim, home of the Vanir (fertility gods), and Alfheim, where the light elves lived, were also in Asgard.

The second level, connected to Asgard by a rainbow called the flaming bridge, was Midgard (Middle Earth). This was the home of the human race. Encircling Midgard was a vast ocean inhabited by the world serpent biting its own tail. This tier contained Jotunheim, inhabited by the Jotun (giants); Nidavellir, where the dwarfs lived; and Svartalfheim, land of the dark elves.

The bottom level, nine days down from Midgard, was Niflheim, the land of the dead. Cold and dark, it was the residence of the monstrous female Hel, the half-white, half-black guardian of the citadel of death. The dragon Nidhogg feasted on corpses at the bottom of Niflheim. He also consumed the roots of Yggdrasil, the great and timeless ash tree at the axis of the world, whose roots encompassed the three levels of the universe. At Ragnarök, the tree would hide a single couple, Lif and Lifthrasir. From these sole survivors (as with the biblical story of Noah and the flood), the human race would regenerate.

DRESS AND CHESS   Despite the fiercely masculine character of their warrior culture, the Vikings were not averse to displays of wealth and status reflected in clothing and jewels (figure **10.15**). Viking women wore long, pleated dresses, either short-sleeved or sleeveless, that were lined for warmth. Over the dresses, they wore shawls and woolen tunics clasped with a brooch on the chest or shoulder (figure **10.16**). Beads suspended from the brooches could be made of colored glass, silver, or semi-precious stones. Married women wore head-scarves.

The fashions of Viking men were more lavish than the women's. Furs and heavy cloaks, which provided warmth in winter, were worn over gathered trousers, linen shirts, and belted tunics. A purse or a knife was usually attached to the belt. Men as well as women wore gold and silver rings, but men also wore neck rings. Both men and women wore leather shoes and boots with decorative trimmings.

In their leisure time, the Vikings enjoyed the game of chess, which was invented in sixth-century India and brought to Europe along the Silk Routes (see Box, p. 215). The largest surviving set of medieval European chessmen dates to the twelfth century and comes from the Outer Hebrides, islands off Scotland but then part of Norway (figure **10.17**).

10.15 Viking dress.

10.16 Trefoil brooch, from Oslo, Norway. Bronze, gold, and silver, 20½ in. (8.1 cm) high. National Antiquities Museum, Stockholm.
This elaborate silver and bronze brooch, decorated with interlaced patterns, is in the shape of a box. The cross at the center indicates that it was made for, or by, a Christian.

10.17 Chessmen, from the island of Lewis, Outer Hebrides, Scotland. 12th century. Walrus ivory, tallest figure 26 in. (10.2 cm) high. British Museum, London.
The design of the pieces, particularly the foliate interlace on the pawn, reflects the cross-cultural influences that resulted from continual invasions, colonization, and trade. Norway itself was a center of trade in walrus ivory, of which the chessmen are made.

ICELAND AND THE SAGAS: NINTH TO TWELFTH CENTURY

Around 870, not wishing to live under King Harald Fairhair of Norway or pay the taxes he levied on them, many Vikings departed in search of new land. They settled in Iceland, northwest of Britain, where they established a society of landowning farmers, including people from Ireland, northern Britain, and the Hebrides Islands. Much of the work was done by slaves, who had been captured from different parts of Europe in Viking raids. Many of the women had been kidnapped from Scotland and Ireland.

The Icelandic settlers pushed westward. In the tenth century, Erik the Red founded a colony on Greenland, and his son, Leif Erikson (called Leif the Lucky), sailed to the east coast of Newfoundland, where Norse settlements have been discovered. Icelanders also went to North America (now New England), as is recorded in the *Vinland Sagas*. Named "Vinland," or "Wineland," after the abundance of grapes, New England impressed the Icelanders with its fields of grass and wheat, rivers rich in fish, and climate warmer than their own.

READING SELECTION

Vinland Sagas, the Norse discovery of America, PWC2-108-B

Iceland was first ruled by an oligarchy of clans (family groups), headed by a chieftain. Around 930, they established a parliamentary government and instituted the **Althing**. This

was a general assembly governed according to a law code prepared by an expert on Norwegian law. The Althing convened every year on the plain of Thingvellir, about 30 miles (48 km) east of Reykjavik, to resolve disputes and decide judicial and constitutional issues. Thirty-nine chiefs held power, which could be inherited, bought, or even borrowed. At the time Icelandic religion was pagan, but by 1000 Christianity had been officially adopted.

As in Scandinavia, Christian missionaries to Iceland brought a new script that made it easier to write down traditional stories previously transmitted orally. As a result, the rich Norse poetic tradition was committed to parchment and preserved. The two main types of verse are **scaldic** and **eddaic**. Scaldic recounts tales of kings and heroes, and eddaic relates myths and legends.

Snorri Sturluson (1179–1241), a politician, historian, and poet, is best known for the *Poetic Edda*, a group of poems setting forth the Norse creation myths. At the beginning of the "Prophecy of the Seeress," for example, the narrator announces that she will set forth the fate of the world:

Hear me, all ye hallowed beings,
both high and low of Heimdall's children:
thou wilt, Valfather, that I well set forth
the fates of the world which as I first recall.

(*Poetic Edda*, verse I)

The children of Heimdall comprised members of three social classes: nobility, freemen, and slaves. Valfather is Odin, the "father" of the deceased in Valhalla. The poet thus calls on all of society to hear the will of Odin. As in *Beowulf*, the use of kennings—such as "Valfather," a combination of father and Valhalla—enriches the language.

Kennings are also a feature of the Icelandic **sagas**. The sagas are a mix of history, legend, myth, and folk tradition written down after Iceland converted to Christianity. Like the *Song of Roland*, they purport to record heroic events of the past—in this case, the settlement of Iceland in the ninth century. The most famous of the sagas, *Njal's Saga*, is a good example of the genre. Direct and straightforward, it reflects the rugged, warrior-based, agricultural lifestyle of the Icelanders. After being introduced, characters may be either dropped or carried through the tale, but their inner motivations are never identified. What motivates them is implied through descriptive detail, such as a raised or lowered eyelid, an action, or a brief comment. The sagas reflect the harsh landscape, blood-feuds, fears of eerie pagan spirits, and sense of fate that characterized the heroic period of Iceland.

The basic plot of *Njal's Saga* is simple. It recounts the events leading to Njal Thorgeirsson's death, when enemies trap him and his family and burn them alive in their home. The opening of Chapter 25 shows how characters are introduced by their genealogy, a reflection of the family-based organization of Icelandic society. Note, too, the use of kennings in the names:

> A man called Valgard the Grey lived at Hof, beside Rang River. Valgard the Grey was the son of Jorund the Priest, the son of Hrafn the Fool, the son of Valgard, the son of Ævar, the son of Venumd the Word-Master, the son of Thorolf Creek-Nose, the son of Thrand the Old, the son of Harald War-Tooth, the son of Hraerek the Ring-Scatterer and of Aud, the daughter of Ivar-of-the-Long-Reach, the son of Halfdan the Brave.
>
> He had a brother called Ulf Aur-Priest. Ulf Aur-Priest was the ancestor of the Oddi family. He was the father of Svart, the father of Lodmund, the father of Sigfus, the father of Saemund the Learned. One of Valgard the Grey's descendants was Kolbeing the Young.
>
> (*Njal's Saga*)

Descriptions of battle are brutal and matter-of-fact:

> Kol lunged at him with a spear. Kolskegg had just killed someone, and had no time to raise his shield; the spear struck the outside of his thigh and went right through it. Kolskegg whirled round and leapt at him, swung at his thigh with the short-sword, and cut off Kol's leg.
>
> "Did that one land or not?" asked Kolskegg.
>
> "That's my reward for not having my shield," said Kol. He stood for a moment on one leg, looking down at the stump.
>
> "You don't need to look," said Kolskegg. "It's just as you think—the leg is off."
>
> Then Kol fell dead to the ground.

And a few lines later:

> Gunnar . . . hurled himself at the Easterner; with one sweep he sliced him in two at the waist. Next he threw the halberd at Bork, sending it right through him and pinning him to the ground. Kolskegg cut off Hauk Egilsson's head, and Gunnar sliced off Ottar Egilsson's forearm.

ROMANESQUE ON THE EUROPEAN CONTINENT: ELEVENTH AND TWELFTH CENTURY

The term Romanesque, or "Roman-like," refers to the period of architectural revival that began before the new millennium, in the tenth century. Invasions had died down somewhat, and new social and political structures evolved from feudalism. The Church was to remain the most stabilizing force in western Europe for several more centuries.

Society and Culture

Farming—New Technology and Inventions

A major technological development that benefited the medieval peasant was the moldboard plow. This type of plow was drawn by oxen or horses and could penetrate the soil more deeply than the older scratch plow. The moldboard plow turned over the soil, forming ridges and impressions in which seeds could be more deeply planted. The newer plow was particularly effective in northern Europe, where rain made the soil heavier and more compacted than in the south. Another advantage of the moldboard was its impact on crop rotation. Previously, peasants rotated crops by leaving one out of every two fields fallow each year. The new system used three fields, only one of which was left fallow. This meant that more land could be cultivated.

The waterwheel had been invented in China and carried west by Muslim traders, but was not commonly used in Europe before the eighth century. Then it was employed to power mills, and eventually it would also facilitate brewing, fulling cloth, and making paper.

Europeans in the Early Middle Ages also discovered how to make their horses work more efficiently. From the horseriders of the Asian Steppe Westerners learned to harness their horses with stiff, padded collars, which enabled the horses to draw heavy weights without choking. As in Asia, horses in Europe began to be shod with iron nailed to their hoofs, protecting their feet and lengthening the time they could work. Stirrups, also known in China from the fourth century, began to be used in Europe during the Middle Ages.

Centers of commerce, banking and manufacturing enterprises, and organizations (**guilds**) of workers in particular crafts arose. Guilds were established as a means of ensuring that workers were well trained and that their families were protected if a worker died. These organizations would grow and become a central aspect of the medieval economy. During the Gothic period, when cities competed to build great cathedrals (see Chapter 11), the guilds took on an even more important role.

Trade also expanded during the early medieval period. Cloth was imported from the north, silks from China, and spices from the Middle East. As the economy improved, populations increased. Towns began to emerge, gradually leading to the growth of cities. Meanwhile, new plowing and farming techniques improved the life of the peasants (see Box).

ROMANESQUE ART AND ARCHITECTURE

Romanesque architecture first developed in France, where Hugh Capet (ruled 987–996) founded the Capetian dynasty, which lasted over three hundred years. From around 1000,

10.18 Reconstruction of the third Abbey Church at Cluny, France, *c.* 1157 (original monastery founded 910).

the main Capetian power base was Paris, which became a political and cultural hub of Europe. In France, as under Charlemagne, the monastery was an important and influential institution.

THE MONASTERY AT CLUNY The largest monastery, and a force in maintaining the power of the Church, was the French Benedictine monastery founded at Cluny, in Burgundy (figure **10.18**). The monastery was rebuilt twice after being destroyed by fire and invasion. This third version, destroyed in 1798 after the French Revolution (1789), has been reconstructed to show its elaborate twelfth-century complex. Members of the Order worshipped in the large church, which was considered an expression of Heavenly Jerusalem on earth. They held meetings in the chapter house where the archives were kept, ate in the refectory, and sang in the choir of the church. Scribes and illuminators worked in the scriptorium. Other buildings included the pantry, a warming room (calefactory), a hospital, and an inn for visitors. Like St. Gall, Cluniac monasteries were self-sufficient communities run by an abbot.

Beginning around 900, the Cluniacs set out to standardize monastic practices. They insisted on strict ethics, devotion to spiritual rather than worldly pursuits, and a celibate clergy. They were also against the selling of spiritual **benefices** (a practice known as **simony**).

Some of the popes elected in the eleventh century supported the reforms advocated at Cluny. One of the major papal decisions, made in 1059, was to form the College of Cardinals, which ensured that popes would be elected by members of the Church acting independently of national politics. And from 1073, when Gregory VII (papacy 1073–1085) was elected, the Cluniac reforms were instituted in Rome and officially adopted by the Church.

The Cluniac Order, which broke away from the Benedictine Order, spread throughout Europe as its reforms gathered support. Many of its churches and abbeys became

stopping places along the pilgrimage routes that were traveled by thousands of penitents in search of salvation (see Box, p. 262). Monasteries were also havens for people hiding from political enemies. And children from large aristocratic families were often urged into the religious life, so they would renounce their claim to a share of the family's inheritance.

Early Benedictines emphasized the importance of manual labor, but the Cluniacs were more interested in learning, art, and music. In the tenth century, Odo of Cluny (abbot 927–942) encouraged his monks in choral singing, himself composing hymns and antiphons. At that date plainsong was notated using **neumes** (diagonal marks placed over the word to be sung, each indicating a note or group of notes). As pitch and intervals were not specified in this system, training took years and monks had to memorize long passages—the notation was just a memory aid. Later, in the early eleventh century, another Benedictine monk and musician, Guido of Arezzo (*c.* 991–1050), immeasurably improved notation by inventing a four-line staff on which to place the notes, so it was clear when the melody went up or down (figure **10.19**).

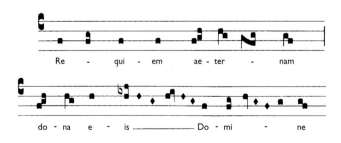

10.19 Guido of Arezzo's musical staff.

Society and Culture

The Pilgrimage Roads

In the course of the Middle Ages, large numbers of Christians made pilgrimages to holy sites. The most important of these sites was the Holy Sepulcher in Jerusalem. But Jerusalem was a long and arduous journey from western Europe, and many pilgrims traveled instead to nearer sites. In Europe, the two main destinations were Rome and Santiago de Compostela, in northwest Spain. Rome was the Christian capital of western Europe, and the church in Santiago was dedicated to St. James, the first of Christ's apostles to be martyred. Beheaded in A.D. 42 by King Herod Agrippa I (ruled A.D. 41–44), James's body was said to have been miraculously moved (**translated**) to Santiago de Compostela.

Many other churches throughout Europe contained sacred **relics**, which are either the physical remains of saints or martyrs, or items associated with them. These objects were enshrined in **reliquaries** (sacred containers) and venerated by the faithful. Relics were believed capable of bringing about miracles, but one had to see or touch the actual object.

The cathedral of Canterbury, in the English county of Kent, became a major pilgrimage site after its archbishop, Thomas à Becket, was assassinated there on December 29, 1170. Becket had been appointed chancellor to King Henry II (ruled 1154–1190) in 1155 and archbishop in 1162. Once the closest of companions, the two men fell out over matters of taxation and judicial authority. Henry, who had overhauled the entire legal and administrative systems of his kingdom, wanted power over the Church courts, an ambition that was vigorously opposed by Becket and the Church. Four of Henry's knights killed the archbishop as he worshipped at the altar of Canterbury Cathedral. After negotiating with the Church, Henry performed a penance that would absolve him of Becket's death. Becket's remains were removed to the Trinity Chapel in Canterbury Cathedral and venerated by thousands of people. The Church canonized Becket in 1173 (figure **10.20**).

10.20 Reliquary of Thomas à Becket, *c.* 1190. Limoges *champlevé* enamel, 11¼ × 15½ × 4⅝ in. (28 × 38.5 × 11.5 cm). Private collection.

Limoges, in France, was famous for its enamel workmanship. *Champlevé* is a technique in which shallow indentations are made in a metal surface, filled in with ceramic, and fired in a kiln. In use since Roman antiquity, the process was typically reserved for reliquaries and other liturgical objects during the Middle Ages. The scenes on this reliquary are divided into two horizontal narratives. Below, Becket is attacked by three knights as he prays at the altar; at the far right two clergymen raise their hands in horror. Above, Becket is lowered into his tomb, and to the right he ascends to heaven accompanied by angels.

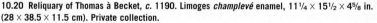

Guido's staff made it possible for the singers to sight-read the notes of music they had never previously heard.

The integration of sculpture with architecture and piety at Cluny is reflected in the decoration of its Abbey Church. By adorning architectural surfaces with sculpture, as well as by encouraging music and illuminating manuscripts, the members of the Cluniac Order expressed their belief that the arts should engage worshippers and strengthen their faith. One example can be seen in the capitals that depict musical tones (figure **10.21**). Music, a subject of philosophical and mathematical enquiry for Plato and the Neoplatonists, here becomes an expression of God's presence on earth.

Not all clerics approved of the time, money, and work that the Cluniac Order put into the arts. The influential abbot Bernard of Clairvaux (1090–1153) took an opposing view. He established a monastery at Clairvaux in France that demanded a rigorous lifestyle of prayer and self-denial. Bernard held that mystical experience and the power of grace and free will in

10.21 *right* **Third Musical Tone, capital from the Abbey Church, Cluny, 1088–1095. Farinier Museum of the Abbey, Cluny.**
The third tone is personified as a musician playing a hand-held harp, or lyre. As in illuminated manuscripts, text and image here reinforce each other. The inscription identifies the third tone with Christ's Resurrection. The harp itself had been the instrument of David, who was seen as a typological precursor of Christ. Harps were also Christian symbols of the Cross.

attaining salvation were of paramount importance. His treatise on monastic decadence, claiming that the arts distracted from piety, was specifically directed against Cluny.

READING SELECTION

Bernard of Clairvaux, *An Apologia for Abbot William*, monastic decadence, PWC2-155-B

MONASTICISM AND WOMEN IN THE ARTS A significant result of monasticism in the twelfth century was the increasing literacy of certain women. Some women, especially aristocrats, became patrons of the arts and there are records of women, such as Ingeborg of Denmark (wife of Philip II Augustus, king of France) and Melisende (queen of the crusader state of Jerusalem), who commissioned **psalters** (psalm books). Matilda of Canossa, who ruled the Italian regions of Emilia and Tuscany, commissioned an illustrated book of Gospels.

But it was in the convents that women, freed from the constraints of marriage and the dangers of childbirth, had the greatest contact with learning and the arts. Christina of Markyate (d. *c.* 1155) was prioress of a convent near London and a visionary. The St. Albans Psalter is thought to have been a gift to her from the abbot of St. Albans. As such, it would indicate her refined taste in works of art. Herrad, the twelfth-century abbess of Hohenberg, in Alsace, wrote an encyclopedia of world history entitled *The Garden of Delights* for her nuns to read.

Perhaps the best-known religious woman of the twelfth century was the noble German mystic Hildegard of Bingen (1098–1179). Instructed by a vision to found a community of nuns in the Rhineland, she composed music to accompany hymns and wrote Latin poetry and treatises on herbs and medicine. Her morality play, *Ordo virtutum*, also in

Latin, deals, like *Everyman*, with the conflict between good and evil. Her two visionary books are *Scivias* (a composite of two Latin words "you know" and "the way," meaning "the ways of God") and *Liber divinorum operum* (*Book of Divine Works*).

Hildegard is also credited with supervising the illustration of her books and, although the originals have been lost, later copies exist (figure **10.22**). The visionary character of the image is clear, as a red-skinned woman in a long red robe with

10.22 Hildegard of Bingen, illustration from a 13th-century copy of "The Vision of Divine Love, who holds the Lamb of God, and Tramples upon Discord and the Devil," from the *Book of Divine Works*, c. 1200. Illumination on parchment, 13³⁄₄ × 6¹⁄₂ in. (34.5 × 16 cm). Biblioteca Statale, Lucca, Italy.
In the small rectangle below the main image, Hildegard's vision descends in the form of red flames through an opening in the frame. Seated between her confessor and a nun wearing black, Hildegard writes her vision on a tablet.

gilded folds stands on a serpent (Satan) and a monster (Discord). She carries the Lamb of God and a scroll of prophecy. Emerging from the top of her head is the head of an older, protective male figure. At the sides are elaborate wings, in which appear the head of an eagle (left) and a woman's red face (right). The flattened gold space thrusts the figures forward and accentuates the otherworldly character of the scene.

MUSIC LISTENING SELECTION
Hildegard of Bingen, "O viridissima Virga." Oxford Camerata, conductor Jeremy Summerly, CD track 4

SAINTE MARIE MADELEINE AT VÉZELAY The Romanesque church at Vézelay, in Burgundy, France, is known for its sculptural decoration and elaborate vaulted ceiling. It was designed by an architect who trained at Cluny and is dedicated to Mary Magdalene, whose relics were housed there. (Vézelay is one of two French churches claiming to have Mary Magdalene's entire, intact body.) An important church on the pilgrimage routes, it had to accommodate the large crowds traveling to venerate her relics. Figure **10.23** shows a generic Romanesque church plan derived from the Roman basilica (see Chapter 7).

10.24 Church of Sainte Marie Madeleine. Vézelay, France, *c.* 1089–1206.

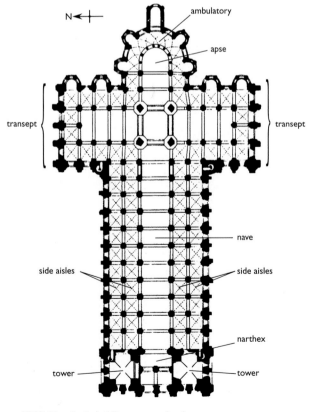

10.23 Plan of a typical Romanesque church.

The addition of an **ambulatory** (the curved passageway that surrounds the apse) allowed pilgrims to proceed from the side aisles of the apse, leaving the clergy to worship undisturbed at the high altar.

Vézelay, like most Christian churches, is oriented with its apse to the east and the main entrance to the west. This expresses the idea that the church building is a metaphor of the Christian world, with the Holy Land in the east and Europe to the west. The main altar, with a crucifix placed on or above it, was located in the apse, corresponding to Jerusalem as the site of Christ's Crucifixion.

The façade at Vézelay retains the Roman round arch and the massive walls and small windows that are found in contemporary castles and palaces (figure **10.24**). The interior view of the nave (figure **10.25**) shows the groin-vaulted ceiling—again, a style developed by the Romans. The alternating brown and white voussoirs of the **transverse arches** create an impression of lightness, despite the massive Romanesque walls. Each arch, which rests on a pier support consisting of **column clusters**, frames a **bay** (the repeated section of the wall). Second-story clerestory windows are the main source of natural light.

In addition to being an important pilgrimage site, Vézelay was a crusade church. It encouraged the first two of the eight crusades undertaken by the Western Church between 1095 and 1291 against the Muslims (see Box). Pope Urban II planned to preach the First Crusade at Vézelay in

10.25 Nave looking east, Church of Sainte Marie Madeleine, Vézelay, 1135–1140.

Society and Culture

The Crusades

The crusades originated as armed pilgrimages to rescue lands from various non-Christian cultural groups, and crusaders believed they would receive pardons and improve their chances of salvation. In eastern Europe, crusaders campaigned against the Slavs, in Livonia against the Bulgars, and, to a lesser degree, they campaigned against the Jews throughout Europe. Associated with notions of chivalry, the crusades were related to stories of the Holy Grail (the cup that Christ used at the Last Supper) and its quest. But the major crusades were launched to rescue the Holy Land from the Muslims.

In 638 the Muslims had conquered Jerusalem, where they built several mosques. In 1091, the Byzantine emperor asked Pope Urban II (papacy 1088–1099) for help in recapturing Jerusalem. Four years later, Urban II proclaimed the First Crusade in a rousing anti-Muslim sermon. Thousands of soldiers from France, Italy, and Germany answered his call and traveled to Constantinople to join forces with Orthodox Christians. Every Muslim living in Jerusalem was killed, and the Dome of the Rock (see Chapter 8) was converted to a church. Many crusaders remained in the Holy Land, building castles and becoming wealthy through international commerce.

By the middle of the twelfth century, Muslims had begun to retake the Holy Land. This led to the Second Crusade (1147–1149), preached by Bernard of Clairvaux. Led by King Louis VII of France (ruled 1137–1180) and the Holy Roman Emperor, this crusade ended in failure. Nearly forty years later, in 1187, Jerusalem was reconquered by the Muslims. The Third Crusade (1189–1192) also failed, mainly because of political rivalry between the European rulers leading it.

The Fourth Crusade (1202–1204) was launched against Egypt, but Venice wanted to protect its profitable Egyptian trade and thwarted the crusaders. Instead of attacking Egypt, they sacked Constantinople, even though it was a Christian city. This led to a fifty-year period during which the West controlled Byzantium.

The strange Children's Crusade (1212) was undertaken by thousands of children between the ages of ten and fourteen. They set out for Palestine, but most died or were captured and sold into slavery.

In the Fifth Crusade (1218–1221), Egypt was captured, but only temporarily. The Holy Roman Emperor Frederick II (ruled 1212–1250) captured Jerusalem in the Sixth Crusade (1228–1229), but lost it again in 1244. The Seventh (1249–1254) and Eighth (1270–1272) Crusades were led by Louis IX of France (ruled 1226–1270), later St. Louis. Both failed, and by 1300 interest in the crusades had subsided.

Although at first fought in the name of religion, the crusades were motivated partly by political and economic considerations. One factor was colonialism, similar to the Germanic impulse to dominate the Slavs, the English to control the Irish, and, in 1492, the reconquest of Muslim Spain by Christians. Despite overt animosity, however, the crusades were a source of cultural contact between Islam and the West. Muslim science, math, philosophy, and elements of Muslim architecture began to infiltrate and influence west Europeans in those fields. Economically the crusades were sometimes enormously rewarding, for successful crusaders returned home with huge amounts of booty, including fruits, spices, and other luxurious materials from the East. Crusades, like pilgrimages, could also be an excuse for travel at a time when many Europeans wished to see more of the world.

archivolts   tympanum   lintel

trumeau   door jamb

10.26 Central entrance, Church of Sainte Marie Madeleine, Vézelay, 1130s.

10.27 *The Mystical Mill*, capital from the Church of Sainte Marie Madeleine, Vézelay, 1104–1120.
An Old Testament prophet pours grain into a wheel-powered mill and St. Paul receives the flour. The meaning of this image is typological: Old Law becomes New Law through the teachings of Christ, just as the rough grain is transformed into refined flour.

1095 (he actually preached it elsewhere). Then, in 1146, Bernard of Clairvaux preached the Second Crusade at Vézelay; and forty-four years later the English king, Richard the Lion Heart, and the French king, Philip II Augustus, departed for the Third Crusade from the church.

Vézelay's role as a crusade church is reflected in the iconography of its sculptural decoration. The façade sculpture is concentrated around the central entrance (figure **10.26**). The **tympanum** merges two scenes—Christ's Ascension (when he rises to heaven) and Pentecost (when the Holy Spirit descends on the apostles to empower them for their mission to spread the gospel, as told in Acts, Chapter 2). The flame-like designs represent the tongues of fire that came down from heaven and gave the apostles the miraculous ability to speak in different tongues, and they allude to the fiery character of the Holy Spirit's inspiration. Each apostle holds a book, indicating that the Christian message is based on Scripture.

Christ dominates the scene. Framed by a **mandorla** (an oval of light around the entire body), he is the central figure and by far the largest. His frontality and extended arms, from which rays of light emanate, indicate that he is welcoming the faithful to his mission and to the church. The flat, stylized, rhythmic curves of Christ's draperies are typical of Romanesque sculpture.

Illustrated in the **archivolts** (the attached arches around the tympanum) are signs of the zodiac and the labors of the months (depicted either as seasonal workers or as their tools). The horizontal **lintel** shows people from around the world awaiting conversion. At the far right, for example, members of an imaginary Indian race have large ears, signifying that though they can hear sound, they are deaf to moral truth. To their left, a Pygmy tries to mount a horse with the help of a ladder. The figures at the left include a group with bows and arrows—weaponry no longer in general use in Europe. Next to them a bull is being led to a pagan sacrifice.

Below the lintel, on the **trumeau** (the vertical stone between the doors), John the Baptist stands with the Lamb of God. He refers to the rite of baptism as the sign of accepting the Christian faith. Positioned at the church entrance, the sculpture conveys the message that salvation is to be found within.

The decoration of capitals with narrative reliefs was a Romanesque development (figure **10.27**). Such scenes functioned as sermons in stone for the illiterate population. In the course of the Middle Ages, as we shall see in the next chapter, these visual sermons became more numerous and more elaborate.

THE BAYEUX TAPESTRY: ROMANESQUE NARRATIVE

One of the most significant historical events of the Romanesque period was the Norman conquest of England in 1066. William the Conqueror, ruler of Normandy in France, was descended from Viking invaders, and when he defeated the Anglo-Saxons at the Battle of Hastings, he established the rule of Norman kings in Britain. This event is recorded in the remarkable work of embroidery known as the Bayeux Tapestry (figures **10.28** and **10.29**).

It is not known who designed or executed the tapestry, but it may have been commissioned by William's half-brother, Bishop Odo of Bayeux, for the cathedral. The narrative, which reads from left to right, occupies the central field, with a Latin text explaining what is happening. Above and below the main narrative are fallen warriors and fanciful animals like those seen in manuscripts such as the Book of Kells (see figure 10.10).

Like the *Song of Roland*, the Bayeux Tapestry is an epic, but it is a visual rather than a literary epic. Both works are lengthy, secular narratives. The Tapestry is some 230 feet (70 m) long, its heroic characters change the course of history, it combines fact with fiction, and it presents the French view of events. Both works are also expressions of the impulse to make artistic records of significant historical and religious experiences, which is particularly characteristic of the Romanesque period.

10.28 Bayeux Tapestry, detail showing William of Normandy giving the order to build a fleet, *c.* 1070–1080. Wool stitching on linen, 20 in. (50.8 cm) high. Musée de l'Evêché, Bayeux, France.

The inscription reads: "King William ordered ships to be built." William can be seen enthroned inside his castle with Bishop Odo. A courtier at the left gestures in response, and a man with a carpentry tool receives the order and turns to go. He points toward the figure outside the castle, who is chopping down a tree.

10.29 Bayeux Tapestry, detail showing the longboats landing on the south coast of England, *c.* 1070–1080. Wool stitching on linen, 20 in. (50.8 cm) high. Musée de l'Evêché. Bayeux.

This scene shows William's arrival in England. The inscription says that the soldiers and horses are disembarking. The longboats used by William to cross the rough waters of the English Channel were similar to those used by the Vikings. Men lower the sails as the horses are led from the boats. At the right, a series of empty boats indicates that they arrived earlier and their passengers are now on dry land. At the left, a boat is just arriving as its prow and lead warrior come into view. By this technique of showing different stages of arrival, the artist creates a sense of narrative time.

In the next chapter, we survey the Gothic period that evolved from Romanesque. New architectural developments led to taller, wider cathedrals decorated with huge, elaborate stained glass windows. In sculpture, a new naturalism prefigured the Renaissance. In English politics, the king's absolute power was limited officially so that he had some responsibility to certain of his subjects. And as churches and cathedrals took over education, there was a gradual rise in literacy and the beginnings of a professional class.

Thematic Parallels

Pilgrimage

We have seen that the notion of pilgrimage, whether conceived of as a literal or a spiritual journey, occurs across cultural boundaries. Christian pilgrimages inspired the construction of numerous churches to accommodate the large crowds traveling through Romanesque Europe. In addition to churches, inns and hostels were required, which led to thriving economic activity along the pilgrimage roads.

We have also seen the importance of pilgrimage in Islam, where the *hajj* is one of the Five Pillars (see Chapter 9). Figure **10.30** shows a view of the *Ka'bah* at the Great Mosque of Mecca, illuminated at night. Muslims perform the *tawaf*, a ritual in which they circumambulate (proceed around) the *Ka'bah* seven times. (Circumambulation is also a feature of Buddhism, whose adherents circumambulate the stupa, and some Christians circumambulate while praying or meditating.)

Another pilgrimage that draws millions of people is the Indian *Kumbh Mela* (figure **10.31**). This ancient festival is mainly a Hindu event, but it is open to all faiths. Its dates vary with astrological signs and the summer and winter solstices. The main site of the *Kumbh Mela* is at the meeting-point of the Yamuna and Ganges rivers at Allahabad in Uttar Pradesh. But it is also celebrated on the Ganges at Hardwar, at Ujjain on the banks of the Shipra, and at Nasik on the River Godavari. The pilgrims bathe in the river's holy water, which washes away sin and leads to salvation. As such, the *Kumbh Mela* can be compared with the Christian rite of baptism, originally performed by John the Baptist in the River Jordan. In both faiths, the symbolic notion of spiritual cleansing is expressed by literal cleansing—whether by bodily immersion in a holy river or by sprinkling holy water on a person's head.

10.31 *Kumbh Mela* celebrations, Hardwar, India.

10.30 The Ka'bah, Great Mosque of Mecca, Saudi Arabia.

KEY TERMS

Althing in medieval Iceland, a general assembly governed according to a law code.

ambulatory in a church, the curved passageway that surrounds an apse.

archivolts the attached arches around the tympanum.

bay a space in a building defined by piers.

benefice originally land granted for services, the word later included ecclesiastical offices.

chivalry a code of values in which knights promised service and loyalty to a lord in return for protection.

column cluster a group of attached columns.

cursive handwriting in flowing strokes with the letters joined together.

edda a type of Icelandic poetry that recounts myths and legends.

fealty an oath of allegiance sworn by a vassal to a lord.

feudalism in medieval Europe, a fluid political, military, and social organization based on mutual obligations between lords and their vassals, who swore allegiance to them.

freeman a property-owning peasant, who turned the property over to a lord in return for protection and certain economic and legal rights.

guild an organization of workers within a particular craft.

illumination the decoration of biblical and other sacred manuscript texts with painted images.

kennings concrete, compound words used to enrich a narrative.

knight in the Middle Ages, a man who carried out military service in return for the right to hold land.

lintel a horizontal cross-beam.

mandorla an oval of light around the entire body.

manor in the Middle Ages, a group of farms and villages.

manorialism in medieval Europe, a social system organized around a manor in which a landlord allowed peasants to live and work on the land in exchange for a percentage of their produce and other obligations.

mayor of the palace in Merovingian France, the king's major-domo (prime minister) and often the real ruler.

minstrel a wandering performer who sang secular songs in medieval courts.

minuscule a small cursive script.

miracle play a medieval religious play dramatizing miracles.

morality play a medieval religious play that gives dramatic form to the human struggle between good and evil.

mystery play a medieval religious play based on a Bible story.

neume in plainsong, a diagonal mark indicating a note or group of notes over the word to be sung.

organum a form of plainsong in which two or more melodic lines are sung at once; a type of polyphony.

pagoda in Buddhist architecture, a multi-tiered tower that contains relics.

parchment the treated and dyed skin of a sheep or calf used for manuscripts.

polyphony a form of music in which two or more melodic lines are sung at once.

psalter a psalm book.

relics the physical remains of saints and martyrs or objects associated with them.

reliquary a container housing a sacred relic.

romance a medieval tale in a Romance language depicting heroic deeds.

rune-stone a large, upright memorial stone engraved with runic text.

saga an Icelandic story that mixes history, legend, myth, and folk tradition.

scaldic a type of Norse poetry that recounts tales of kings and heroes.

scop a type of German performer who sang tales of Germanic heroes in the fifth to seventh centuries.

scriptorium (plural **scriptoria**) a room for writing, usually in a monastery.

simony the selling of spiritual benefices.

spandrel in architecture, the triangular area between (1) two adjacent arches or (2) the side of an arch and the right angle that encloses it.

stupa in Buddhist architecture, a round structure derived from the Buddha's burial mound.

tenor in medieval music, the low voice singing long held notes of plainchant in polyphonic pieces.

translate in religion, to transfer or remove to another place.

transverse arch in a church or cathedral, an arch that spans the nave.

trope a passage, with or without words, inserted in Gregorian chant.

trumeau the central vertical support of a lintel or tympanum above a wide doorway.

tympanum in Christian architecture, the curved triangular area between an arch and the lintel below it.

vassal in the Middle Ages, a man who held land in return for duties of allegiance to a lord.

KEY QUESTIONS

1. How and why was the feudal system of allegiances maintained in the Middle Ages?
2. What actions of Charlemagne influenced learning in medieval culture?
3. How does the fact that the *Song of Roland* was written from the French point of view affect the portrayal of the Muslims?
4. How do plainsong and organum differ?
5. How did Irish monasteries help keep Classical learning alive during the Middle Ages? What other functions did monasteries perform?
6. Summarize the heroic qualities of *Beowulf.*

SUGGESTED READING

Alexander, Jonathan J. G. *Medieval Illuminators and their Methods of Work.* New Haven, CT, and London: Yale University Press, 1993.
▸ A well-illustrated study of manuscript illumination.

Beowulf: A New Verse Translation, trans. Seamus Heaney. New York: Farrar, Straus and Giroux, 2000.
▸ A modern translation of *Beowulf* by a Nobel prize-winning poet.

Bragg, Melvyn. *Credo.* London: Hodder and Stoughton, 1996.
▸ A fictional account of the Early Middle Ages and Romanesque period.

Braunfels, Wolfgang. *Monasteries of Western Europe.* London: Thames and Hudson, 1972.
▸ A basic study of monasticism and its art.

Cahn, Walter. *Romanesque Bible Illumination.* Ithaca, NY: Cornell University Press, 1983.
▸ A scholarly study of manuscript painting.

Cawley, A. C. (ed.). *Everyman and Medieval Miracle Plays.* London: Orion, Phoenix Editions, 1993.
▸ A study of *Everyman* and medieval theater.

Diebold, William. *Word and Image.* Boulder, CO: Westview Press, 2000.
▸ A brief, original approach to early medieval art.

Einhard. *The Life of Charlemagne,* with a Foreword by Sidney Painter. Ann Arbor, MI: University of Michigan Press, 2001.
▸ A brief, early medieval biography of Charlemagne.

The Mabinogion, trans. Jeffrey Gautz. London: Penguin Books, 1976.
▸ A translation of the Celtic tales.

Mâle, Emile. *Religious Art in France, the Twelfth Century: A Study of the Origins of Medieval Iconography.* Princeton, NJ: Princeton University Press, 1978.
▸ A classic study of medieval art and iconography.

McKitterick, R. (ed.). *Carolingian Culture: Emulation and Innovation.* London: Cambridge University Press, 1993.
▸ On the origins and rise of Carolingian art and culture.

Njal's Saga, trans. Magnus Magnusson and Hermann Pálsson. London: Penguin Books, 1960.
▸ The most popular of the Norse sagas.

Petzold, Andreas. *Romanesque Art.* New York: Pearson, 1995.
▸ A general introduction to Romanesque art and its context.

The Plays of Hroswitha of Gandersheim, trans. Larissa Bonfante with the collaboration of Alexandra Bonfante-Warren. Wauconda, IL: Bolchazy-Carducci Publishers, 1986.
▸ An annotated edition of the plays of Hroswitha.

The Poetic Edda, trans. Lee M. Hollander. Austin, TX: University of Texas Press, 1986.
▸ A translation of the Norse poem.

Sawyer, P. *The Oxford Illustrated History of the Vikings,* Oxford: Oxford University Press, 1997.
▸ A well-illustrated survey of Viking history, culture, and art.

Schapiro, Meyer. *Romanesque Art: Selected Papers.* New York: George Braziller, 1976.
▸ A classic work of medieval scholarship.

Stokstad, Marilyn. *Medieval Art.* Denver, CO: Westview Press, 2004.
▸ A standard survey of medieval art.

SUGGESTED FILMS

1931 *A Connecticut Yankee in King Arthur's Court* (based on Twain), dir. David Butler
1933 *Charlemagne,* dir. Pierre Colombier
1942 *Arabian Nights,* dir. John Rawlins
1949 *A Connecticut Yankee in King Arthur's Court* (based on Twain), dir. Tony Garnett
1951 *Murder in the Cathedral,* dir. George Hoellering
1953 *Knights of the Round Table,* dir. Richard Thorpe
1964 *Becket,* dir. Peter Glenville
1968 *The Lion in Winter,* dir. Anthony Harvey
1978 *La Chanson de Roland (The Song of Roland),* dir. Frank Cassenti
1987 *Juniper Tree* (old Icelandic tale), dir. Nietzcha Keene
1998 *Canterbury Tales,* dir. Jonathan Myerson

11 The Development and Expansion of Gothic: 1150–1300

" *We will not sell, refuse, or delay right or justice to anyone . . .*
We will appoint only such justices, constables, sheriffs, or bailiffs
as know the law of the realm and intend to obey it."

(*Magna Carta*, 1215)

The term Gothic refers to a style of art and architecture and to the period of their development in western Europe, which lasted from the middle of the twelfth century into the fourteenth century in Italy and later in other European countries. Today, the term is purely descriptive, but when it was first coined, in early-sixteenth-century Italy, the word Gothic had negative connotations associated with the Germanic Goths, who had sacked Rome. To the Italians, Gothic style seemed "barbaric" but, in fact, Gothic style is one of the most remarkable Western achievements. The term is now associated with the towering cathedrals that first appeared in France in the mid-twelfth century and rapidly spread throughout Europe.

The Gothic period is also significant for developments in economics, religion, philosophy, and literature, as well as in society and politics. One example of a small but important step forced on the English king in the early thirteenth century can be seen in the above quotation. The Magna Carta (Great Charter) marks the first time that a king's power was officially limited so that he was no longer above the law. The two clauses of the Magna Carta cited above are a small part of a much larger document, but they clearly reflect the demand to be ruled by law rather than by royal whim.

Key Topics

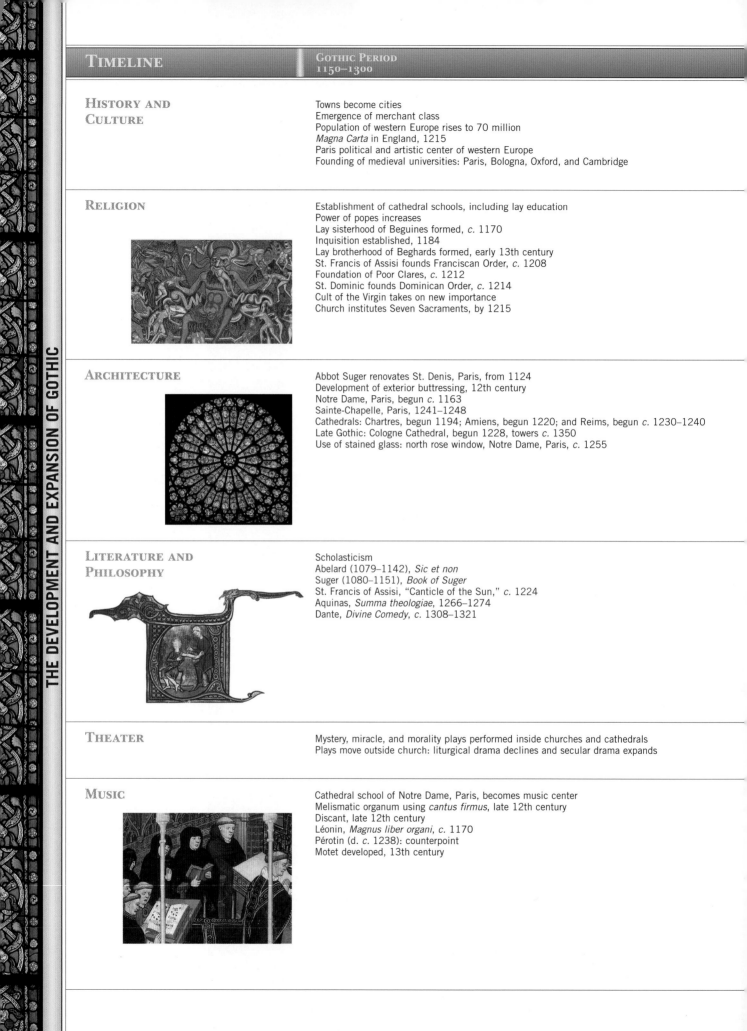

TIMELINE	GOTHIC PERIOD 1150–1300

HISTORY AND CULTURE

Towns become cities
Emergence of merchant class
Population of western Europe rises to 70 million
Magna Carta in England, 1215
Paris political and artistic center of western Europe
Founding of medieval universities: Paris, Bologna, Oxford, and Cambridge

RELIGION

Establishment of cathedral schools, including lay education
Power of popes increases
Lay sisterhood of Beguines formed, *c.* 1170
Inquisition established, 1184
Lay brotherhood of Beghards formed, early 13th century
St. Francis of Assisi founds Franciscan Order, *c.* 1208
Foundation of Poor Clares, *c.* 1212
St. Dominic founds Dominican Order, *c.* 1214
Cult of the Virgin takes on new importance
Church institutes Seven Sacraments, by 1215

ARCHITECTURE

Abbot Suger renovates St. Denis, Paris, from 1124
Development of exterior buttressing, 12th century
Notre Dame, Paris, begun *c.* 1163
Sainte-Chapelle, Paris, 1241–1248
Cathedrals: Chartres, begun 1194; Amiens, begun 1220; and Reims, begun *c.* 1230–1240
Late Gothic: Cologne Cathedral, begun 1228, towers *c.* 1350
Use of stained glass: north rose window, Notre Dame, Paris, *c.* 1255

LITERATURE AND PHILOSOPHY

Scholasticism
Abelard (1079–1142), *Sic et non*
Suger (1080–1151), *Book of Suger*
St. Francis of Assisi, "Canticle of the Sun," *c.* 1224
Aquinas, *Summa theologiae*, 1266–1274
Dante, *Divine Comedy*, *c.* 1308–1321

THEATER

Mystery, miracle, and morality plays performed inside churches and cathedrals
Plays move outside church: liturgical drama declines and secular drama expands

MUSIC

Cathedral school of Notre Dame, Paris, becomes music center
Melismatic organum using *cantus firmus*, late 12th century
Discant, late 12th century
Léonin, *Magnus liber organi*, *c.* 1170
Pérotin (d. *c.* 1238): counterpoint
Motet developed, 13th century

THE ECONOMY, POLITICS, AND RELIGION

The Gothic period saw an increasing trend toward the urbanization that had begun in the Romanesque era. As trade and commerce expanded, towns began to grow into cities. Old Roman cities, in decline since the fall of the empire, became revitalized. Early medieval manors attracted fairs and markets, which encouraged commerce, improved the economy, increased the population, and spurred the development of yet more towns. From 1000 to 1300, the population of western Europe doubled, rising to about 70 million. By 1300, western Europe had become a network of small cities. The biggest, with populations of 100,000 or more, were in Italy—especially Milan, Venice, Genoa, Naples, and Florence. In France, Paris had a population of 80,000 in 1300. In the Netherlands (Holland and Belgium), too, cities soon became thriving centers of commerce and trade.

In this new economic atmosphere, people became more entrepreneurial. A rural society based on networks of loyalty and allegiance to a lord was replaced by towns, by workers demanding better working conditions, and by individual ambition. A new merchant class evolved, with bankers, moneylenders, and other wealthy businessmen enjoying lives of luxury. But conflicts also arose—between the landowners and the city dwellers, between the rich and the poor, and between different groups within the clergy.

The role of the monastery as a center of learning was taken over by cathedral schools, especially in France. These schools had been established to teach the liberal arts to members of the clergy, but in the late twelfth century the pope required that lay people (those not ordained) be admitted to the schools free of charge. This improved literacy among the population, which helped promote a higher level of professional life. In addition, the cathedral schools were centers of intellectual debate. Scholars argued about the validity of faith versus reason, about whether literature should be written in Latin or the vernacular (everyday language), and about the nature and value of Arabic contributions to learning. Eventually, universities would replace cathedral schools as the main centers of learning in Europe.

In England, in 1215, after King John (ruled 1199–1216) had lost English territories in France, dissatisfied barons wanted to retain their power. They forced the king to sign the *Magna Carta*, the first document to recognize that kings as well as their subjects (in this case the nobility) had moral and social responsibilities and were subject to certain laws. Taxes, according to the *Magna Carta*, could be levied only by general consent, and freemen could no longer be arrested, imprisoned, or exiled without due legal process.

The Church consolidated its power through the papacy, sometimes antagonizing rulers by encroaching onto the secular arena. Innocent III (papacy 1198–1216) wielded significant political influence, especially in England, France, and the territories around Rome. He supported crusades to the Holy Land and Egypt (see Chapter 10) and fought heresy in Europe. In an effort to combat the Albigensian heresy (see Chapter 8), Innocent sent preachers to persuade the Albigensians to accept the doctrines of the Roman Church. In 1208, when this failed, he launched a crusade against them.

In 1215, Innocent convoked the Fourth Lateran Council, the largest in the Middle Ages. It was attended by over 1200 bishops and abbots, two Eastern patriarchs, and many representatives of secular rulers. The Council passed seventy decrees and condemned two sects for heresy—Cathars and Waldensians. The latter originated in France and followed the Bible but opposed the Church hierarchy. Among the doctrinal issues covered, the Council decreed that all adult Christians should attend Mass and confession at least once a year.

By 1215, the Church had instituted the Seven Sacraments: Baptism (by which one enters the faith), Confirmation (by which one is confirmed in the faith), the Eucharist (the Mass, in which bread and wine are transformed into Christ's body and blood, a process known as **transubstantiation**), Penance (confession and atonement), Marriage, Last Rites, and Ordination (for the priesthood). These Sacraments were conceived of as points of progression in the Christian faith.

At the close of the thirteenth century, Boniface VIII (papacy 1294–1303) was elected to the papacy. He believed in the absolute power of the Church and demanded authority over secular rulers. His views angered the French king, Philip IV, the Fair (ruled 1285–1314), also called Philip the Handsome—in French, Philippe le Bel—who ordered his arrest. Boniface barely escaped, but he was captured in 1302 by Philip's army and severely beaten before being allowed to return to Rome. He died the following year, and the power of the papacy began to decline.

MONASTIC DEVELOPMENTS IN THE THIRTEENTH CENTURY

One result of urbanization was the development of the **mendicant** (literally "begging") Orders, which consisted of **friars** (brothers) who wandered from town to town. In contrast to monks, who isolated themselves in self-sufficient monastic communities, the friars worked in the outside world. They did not own possessions, and relied on townspeople for their subsistence. The two main figures in this new movement were Dominic Guzmán (*c.* 1170–1221) of Old Castile, in Spain, and Francis (*c.* 1182–1226) of Assisi, in Italy.

ST. DOMINIC

Dominic was a nobleman who espoused poverty and founded the Dominican Order, also called the Black Friars because of their black robes. He traveled through Italy, Spain, France, and Hungary, establishing friaries. The Dominican Order was devoted to intellectual work, especially preaching and studying religious texts. The Order was forbidden to have possessions—except its churches and residences—and thus had to beg. Dominican friars followed a strict rule requiring a Spartan, regulated regimen of prayer, worship, abstinence, and self-denial. Since they espoused a strictly orthodox view of Christianity, the Dominicans became zealous **Inquisitors** (officials appointed to combat heresy) (see Box). In their zeal, the

Dominicans established an institute designed to save women from the dangers of Albigensian ideas.

ST. FRANCIS OF ASSISI

St. Francis espoused a different approach to Christianity from that of St. Dominic. According to traditional accounts of the life of St. Francis, he defied his wealthy father by publicly renouncing his possessions and removing his clothes in the market square of Assisi. He thus rejected both his father and

Defining Moment

The Inquisition

The Inquisition was an official body established in 1184 under Pope Lucius III by the papal bull *Ad abolendum* to combat heresies that had been plaguing the Church since the fourth century. This was a defining moment in Western history, for the Inquisition would become a source of fear and terror in the countries where it thrived. For the arts and sciences, the Inquisition represented a regressive, conservative force that discouraged innovation, empiricism, and intellectual inquiry. Judicially, the Inquisition embodied everything that goes against the grain of modern democracy.

In 1232, under Frederick II, Holy Roman Emperor and king of Sicily, the Inquisition was empowered to pursue, arrest, and bring to trial heretics throughout Frederick's empire. But the extent of its zeal alarmed Gregory IX (papacy 1227–1241), who insisted that campaigns against heresy were the province of the Church. He therefore appointed the mendicant Orders, especially the Dominicans, to comb Church territory and warn heretics to repent.

Heretics were tried before a jury of clerics and laymen based on the evidence of two witnesses. The accused had no right to counsel, and sentences could not be appealed. At first the identity of the accusers was kept secret, but under Boniface VIII (papacy 1294–1303) this was changed.

Beginning in 1252, under Innocent IV (papacy 1243–1254), torture was permitted as a means of forcing the accused to confess. Penalties ranged from making pilgrimages or wearing the cross of infamy to

the loss of all possessions or life imprisonment. And when the inquisitors handed heretics over to the civil authorities, it was tantamount to a demand that the accused be put to death.

In 1484, Innocent VIII, in his bull *Summis desiderantes* of December 5, describes the motives for establishing the Inquisition:

Desiring with supreme ardor, as pastoral solicitude requires, that the Catholic faith in our days everywhere grow and flourish as much as possible, and that all heretical depravity be put far from the territories of the faithful, we freely declare and anew decree this by which our pious desire may be fulfilled, and, all errors being rooted out by our toil as with the hoe of a wise laborer, zeal and devotion to this faith may take deeper hold on the hearts of the faithful themselves.

It has recently come to our ears, not without great pain to us, that in some parts of upper Germany, as well as in the provinces, cities, territories, regions, and dioceses of Mainz, Köln, Trier, Salzburg, and Bremen, many persons of both sexes, heedless of their own salvation and forsaking the Catholic faith, give themselves over to devils male and female, and by their incantations, charms, and conjurings, and by other abominable superstitions and sortileges, offences, crimes, and misdeeds, ruin and cause to perish the offspring of women, the foal of animals, the products of the earth, the grapes of vines, and the fruits of trees, as well as men and women, cattle and flocks and herds and animals of every kind,

vineyards also and orchards, meadows, pastures, harvests, grains and other fruits of the earth; that they afflict and torture with dire pains and anguish, both internal and external, these men, women, cattle, flocks, herds, and animals, and hinder men from begetting and women from conceiving, and prevent all consummation of marriage; that, moreover, they deny with sacrilegious lips the faith they received in holy baptism; and that, at the instigation of the enemy of mankind, they do not fear to commit and perpetrate many other abominable offences and crimes, at the risk of their own souls, to the insult of the divine majesty and to the pernicious example and scandal of multitudes.

The notorious Spanish Inquisition was not instituted until the late fifteenth century under Ferdinand V and Isabella (the rulers who financed the voyage of Columbus to the New World). Initially, Jews were the target, then the Moors who had been forcibly converted, and finally Protestants (from the sixteenth century). The Spanish Inquisition, which was independent of Rome, was a tightly run, highly efficient organization under the leadership of an Inquisitor General. In Spain, the Inquisition instituted *autos-da-fé* (burnings of heretics), but in northern Europe and England the Inquisition had little influence. When the French overran Spain in the early nineteenth century, the Inquisition was finally suppressed.

Critical Question What is "due process"? Why would "due process" be incompatible with the practices of the Inquisition?

his father's profession—that of a textile merchant. Instead, Francis identified with Jesus, and sought a new father in God. He founded the Franciscan Order and established a convent in Portiuncula, near Assisi. He traveled through the towns of Italy, preaching poverty and asserting God's presence in nature. In 1224, while praying on Mount La Verna, Francis saw a vision of the crucified Christ in the form of a seraph (a type of angel). Marks resembling Christ's Crucifixion wounds—called the **stigmata**—miraculously appeared on Francis's hands, feet, and side.

After receiving the stigmata, Francis wrote the "Canticle of the Sun," praising God in nature as a metaphor of the human family:

> Praised be You, my Lord, with all your creatures, especially
>   Sir Brother Sun, . . .
> Praised be You, my Lord, through Sister Moon and the
>   stars, . . .
> Praised be You, my Lord, through Brother Wind, . . .
> Praised be You, my Lord, through Sister Water, . . .
> Praised be You, my Lord, through Brother Fire, . . .
> Praised be You, my Lord, through our Sister Mother Earth, . . .
> Praised be You, my Lord, through our Sister Bodily Death.

("Canticle of the Sun")

READING SELECTION
St. Francis of Assisi, "Canticle of the Sun," In Praise of God's Creation, PWC2-148

From the thirteenth century, St. Francis became a popular subject of painting. His love of nature and his genius as a communicator extended to birds and other animals, and this aspect of his character is reflected in the iconography of many Franciscan works of art (figure **11.1**).

Despite Francis's insistence on poverty, the Franciscan Order became wealthy. It then split into two groups: Conventualists and Observants. The Conventual Franciscans accepted their wealth and managed their money well. But the Observant Franciscans followed the original rule and refused to have possessions or own land. The pope sided with the Conventualists, largely because the papacy itself and the Church in Rome were enormously wealthy and wanted their wealth to grow.

WOMEN MONASTICS IN THE THIRTEENTH CENTURY

Inspired by the message of St. Francis, the noblewoman Clare (1194–1253) followed his teachings and attracted a group of her own followers, known as the **Poor Clares**. In 1215, Francis established her as the abbess of a convent, also at Portiuncula. Like the Franciscans, the Clares followed a strict rule and expanded in the fourteenth century. In contrast to the Franciscans, however, the Poor Clares were confined to convents and did not wander from town to town as the Franciscans did.

In late-twelfth-century Belgium, a group of lay women, the **Beguines**, formed a sisterhood, which quickly spread to France, Germany, and the Netherlands. Although not nuns,

11.1 Master of the Bardi Saint Francis Dossal, *Saint Francis Preaching to the Birds***, Bardi Chapel of Saint Francis, Church of Santa Croce, Florence,** *c.* **1250. Tempera on panel.**
In the company of two other friars, Francis preaches to a group of alert birds standing up and taking notice of the saint's words. Today, visitors to Assisi are invariably struck by the thousands of birds flying around the city.

they established Christian centers devoted to prayer, education, social work, and helping the poor and the dying. In addition, the Beguines worked as weavers, fullers (workers who increased the weight of cloth by shrinking and pulling it), and dyers of cloth. Unlike the Poor Clares and other monastic communities, the Beguines had no abbess and they worked in the outside world. They could also own property and were allowed to marry as long as they lived outside the beguinage. A male counterpart of the Beguines, the **Beghards**, was also dedicated to doing good work for the community and to leading a spiritual life. The establishment of such lay groups reflected an expansion of religious life among the laity in northern Europe during the later Middle Ages.

THE CENTRAL ROLE OF PARIS

In the Gothic period, the city of Paris was the political and artistic center of western Europe. It was the residence of the king, a commercial hub, and the site of an important university as well as a cathedral and its school. Nearby, at St. Denis, was a royal Benedictine monastery, the burial place of French kings and associated in the popular imagination with Charlemagne. The monastery's abbey church was dedicated to the fifth-century martyr St. Denis, traditionally identified as the first bishop of Paris, and contained his relics. St. Denis was, therefore, a major pilgrimage site. In addition, a large trade fair of considerable commercial importance was held in the area every year. For all these reasons, crowds of visitors flocked to the church of St. Denis, which soon needed more space to accommodate them.

ABBOT SUGER AND ST. DENIS

The abbot of St. Denis in the early twelfth century was Suger (1080–1151). He came from a poor family that pledged him to the Church when he was ten. Suger attended school with the future king, Louis VI (ruled 1108–1137), and became his friend and adviser, remaining as adviser to Louis VII (ruled 1137–1180). He was named abbot of St. Denis in 1122. Influenced by Bernard of Clairvaux's call for monastic reform (see Chapter 10), Suger tightened discipline at the abbey and insisted on following a strict version of the Benedictine rule.

A man of small stature but great intelligence, political skill, and vanity, Suger decided in 1124 to rebuild the abbey church of St. Denis. This proved to be a momentous decision that changed the course of intellectual and artistic history in the West. Unlike Bernard, who opposed the display of art in churches, Suger believed that the more lavish the art, the more inspiring it was to the faithful. His views were reinforced by reading Neoplatonic texts, which extolled light as an expression of the divine. (At the time these writings were mistakenly believed to be by St. Denis himself.) Suger also, of course,

realized that his building program would increase the power and popularity of his king.

Suger documented the renovation in his *Book of Suger, Abbot of Saint Denis*. He added two towers at the entrance and a triple portal (figure **11.2**), and extended the length of the nave. The enlarged choir was surrounded with a double ambulatory to permit an easy flow of pilgrims (figure **11.3**). The outer ambulatory had seven **radiating chapels**, which allowed Masses to be celebrated and relics to be displayed without interfering with the services that were taking place at the high altar. Each chapel had two tall, pointed windows, called **lancets**, so that outdoor light could stream into the interior (figure **11.4**).

Suger's alterations included two of the most important structural developments of Gothic style. The first was the design of the vaults of the ambulatory, which, in contrast to the heavy vaulting systems of the Romanesque period, were **rib vaults**, made by the intersection of pointed arches (figure **11.5**). The pointed arch permitted greater height and a sense of greater delicacy than the Romanesque round arch. The second development was an increase in the size of windows

11.2 Façade of St. Denis, Paris, mid-12th century.

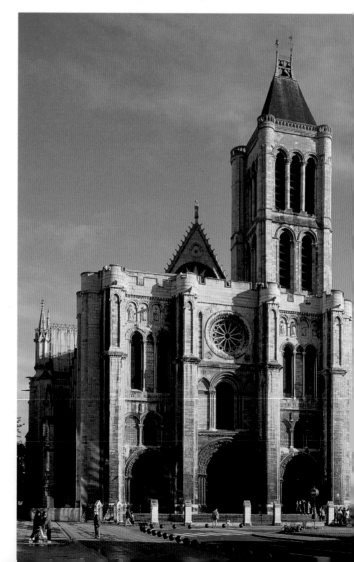

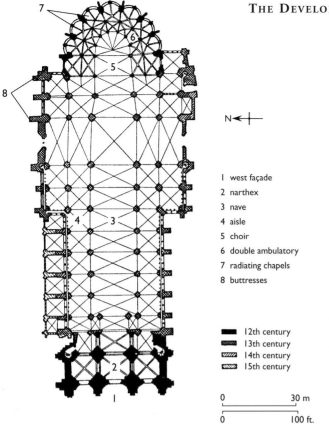

N ← +

1 west façade
2 narthex
3 nave
4 aisle
5 choir
6 double ambulatory
7 radiating chapels
8 buttresses

▬ 12th century
▨ 13th century
▧ 14th century
▩ 15th century

0   30 m
0   100 ft.

11.3 Plan of St. Denis, Paris.

11.4 Interior of the ambulatory, St. Denis, Paris.

made possible by the ribbed vault construction. Coupled with greater use of **stained** (colored) **glass**, it flooded the interior with light and color.

For Suger, the dazzling play of light and color indicated God's presence at St. Denis. To this, he added his own taste for precious gems and gold decoration. And, indeed, he did transform St. Denis into a vision that elevated the soul to new heights of mystical experience. Suger defended the expense of his project as a necessary aid to salvation.

The door to the church was a metaphor for the entrance to heaven. Accordingly, Suger decorated the central portals on the west façade with gilded bronze reliefs. These he described in the following verse:

> Whoever thou art, if thou seekest to extol the glory of
>   these doors,
> Marvel not at the gold and the expense but at the
>   craftsmanship of the work.
> Bright is the noble work; but, being nobly bright, the work
> Should brighten the minds so that they may travel,
>   through the true lights,
> To the True Light where Christ is the true door.
> In what manner it be inherent in this world the golden
>   door defines:
> The dull mind rises to truth through that which is material
> And, in seeing this light, is resurrected from its former
>   submersion.

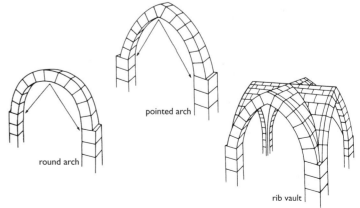

pointed arch

round arch

rib vault

11.5 Diagrams of arches and the rib vault.

THE CATHEDRAL OF NOTRE DAME IN PARIS

Suger's ideas about light, color, and space launched the Gothic style. In addition to expanding the window area and using pointed arches (rather than the round Romanesque arch), Gothic builders after Suger developed flying buttresses. These are visible in the side view of the cathedral of Notre Dame, Paris (figure **11.6**). They were added around 1200, when the thrust (the downward and outward force) of the interior arches began to make the walls buckle.

Notre Dame is located, as was the king's palace, on the Ile de la Cité, a small island in the River Seine, which divides Paris into its Left and Right Banks. Notre Dame was begun around 1163 and consecrated in 1177. Its towers were added from 1220 to 1225, but the building was not completed until the second half of the thirteenth century. Note the curve of the apse at the eastern (back) end to the right, the elaborate transept wall, and the towers at the western entrance

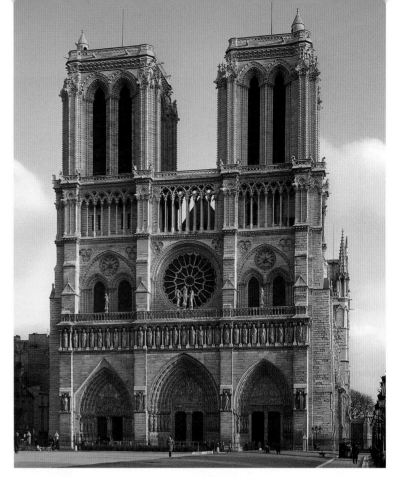

11.7 *above* **West façade of Notre Dame, Paris, 1220–1250.**

11.6 **Notre Dame, Paris, 12th century.**

11.8 Nave of Notre Dame, Paris, 1180–1250.
The nave wall is three stories high. The lower story (the nave arcade) consists of heavy piers supporting pointed arches. The second story, called the triforium, is a series of shorter pointed arches, and the third story, called the clerestory, is the main source of light. The clerestory windows are larger than their Romanesque predecessors, and the proportions are taller and thinner (see thumbnail). In this view we are looking east, toward the curved apse illuminated by three stories of windows, reflecting Suger's philosophy that light and color glorify the interior of the church building.

(to the left). The slim projections at the top of the buttresses are called flyers, because they resemble wings.

The façade of the cathedral (figure **11.7**) is symmetrical, with tall towers and pointed arches that carry our gaze heavenward. Compared with St. Denis, the wall surface decoration is more animated, and it is also divided into geometric sections. Triple portals are surmounted by a **gallery** (row of figures) of Old Testament kings, including Christ's typological precursors David and Solomon. Above these, the **rose window** (a large, round window in Gothic cathedrals) is flanked by double lancets framed by a larger single arch.

In the interior (figure **11.8**) soaring vaults are locked in place by circular keystones. Note that the wall of the nave is

Romanesque nave of Sainte Marie Madeleine, Vézelay
see figure 10.25

divided into repeated sections, called bays. Each bay is separated from its neighbor by a pier and slim columns rising from the capital of the pier and continuing into the ribs of the vaults. The reconstruction in figure **11.9** shows how the buttressing system is designed to counter the thrust of the ceiling vaults. The bay is shown in relation to the aisle and the entire exterior buttress in the sectional drawing in figure **11.10**.

flying buttress   clerestory window   cross-rib   transverse arch

11.9 Reconstruction showing the Gothic system of buttresses and flying buttresses.
At each point of contact at the inside wall, the thrust is carried on the exterior by the buttress.

By the time the north rose window (figure **11.11**) was in place, Gothic builders had developed the **rayonnant** (radiant) style, in which shapes of glass seem to radiate from the small circle at the center. The area occupied by supporting architectural elements has been reduced and the glass windows now take up more space. The geometric regularity of the design creates the impression of an ordered universe. By filtering outdoor light through colored glass, Gothic cathedrals suggested the transforming power of faith.

Gothic cathedrals were thought of as mirrors of the Christian universe. As such, they devoted space to the grotesque, the deformed, and the monstrous aspects of nature and human fantasy. Such images appear on capitals and under the feet of holy personages. But they are most consistently represented as **gargoyles** (figure **11.12**).

BUILDING THE CATHEDRAL

Building a Gothic cathedral was a major architectural, economic, and social undertaking. Reflecting the hierarchical structure of the Church, a cathedral is the seat of a bishop and has authority over a larger territory than a parish

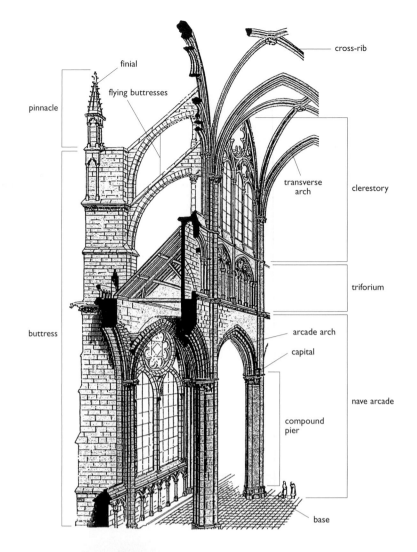

11.10 *above* **Sectional diagram of Notre Dame, Paris.**

11.11 *left* **North rose window, Notre Dame, Paris,** *c.* 1255. 43 ft. (13.1 m) diameter.

11.12 *above* **Gargoyle on the balustrade of the Grande Galerie, Notre Dame, Paris, 19th-century replica of a 12th-century original. Stone.**
Gargoyles originally served as water spouts of the cathedral's drainage system, keeping water from eroding the walls—water is expelled through their mouths. The term itself is related to "gargle," which comes from the French word *gorge*, meaning "throat." Their exclusion from the sacred space of the interior, like their monstrous forms, reflects their association with evil.

11.13 *above* **Table of guilds, from Orvieto, Italy, 14th century. Museo dell'Opera del Duomo, Orvieto.**
The table shows various trade guilds, including tailors, barbers, bread-makers, vintners, and eyeglass makers, whose workers and their families benefited from the building of a cathedral.

church or an abbey church. The greater size of the cathedral thus indicates its greater importance in the Church hierarchy. Generally, the site chosen for a cathedral in the Middle Ages was the high point of a town, so that the building would be visible from a distance. In addition, the bells, located in the towers, could be heard for miles around, announcing the hours of worship.

Constructing a cathedral usually brought prosperity to a medieval town. The work created jobs for a large number of workers and a stream of income for their families. Patronage of the cathedral was also a community affair. Some of the financing came from the royal family, some was provided by contributions from the clergy, and some came from local people wishing to atone for their sins or hoping for a miracle. Contributions from the associations of craftsmen who worked on the project provided another source of money. These associations were the guilds (see Chapter 10), which oversaw the training, maintenance, and population of specific trades and industries (figure **11.13**). Guilds also provided care and education for the families of workers if a worker died. Each guild had a patron saint, and each worker learned his trade by a system of apprenticeship.

Figure **11.14** shows builders at work. Stonemasons on top of the wall lay and level the bricks; at the left, a man operates a pulley lifting mortar to the masons. In the center, a carver completes a capital, and at the right, a woodcutter removes the bark of a log on a sawhorse.

11.14 Matthew Paris,
Building a Cathedral, **from the**
Life of Saint Alban and Saint
Amphibalus*, c.* **1250. Trinity**
College, Dublin.

11.15 Thomas de Cormont, interior of Sainte-Chapelle, Paris, 1241–1248. 32 ft. × 99 ft. 6 in. (9.75 × 30.3 m).

Supervising the enormous numbers of workers was the master mason—the **master-builder**. Since building a cathedral could take several generations, the master-builder worked from **templates**—diagrams of architectural sections, which could be passed on to a successor. Thus if one master-builder died or retired, a new one was able to continue building according to the original design.

SAINTE-CHAPELLE: THE KING'S CHAPEL

One of the greatest Gothic expressions of mystical atmosphere created through light and color is the French royal chapel, Sainte-Chapelle, in Paris (figure **11.15**). It was commissioned by Louis IX (later St. Louis, ruled 1226–1270) and was adjacent to the king's palace on the Ile de la Cité. The chapel was divided into a lower section, dedicated to the Virgin Mary and used by members of Louis's household, and an upper section for the royal family. The upper section is composed of tall, thin, gilded columns extending to the blue, star-studded, vaulted ceiling. Visible on the lower piers are statues of the twelve apostles. At the far end is the gilded reliquary tabernacle for which Sainte-Chapelle was built. It contains relics of the Crucifixion—the Crown of Thorns, the sponge (Jesus was given a sponge filled with vinegar to drink while he was on the Cross), and fragments of the lance that pierced his side and the True Cross.

With its nearly transparent wall of red and blue glass and its tall, slim, gilded columns, Sainte-Chapelle embodies Suger's conception of a church interior. Indeed, in this chapel, which is clearly fit for a king, the mystical treatment of light espoused by Suger and by the Neoplatonists he read marks a high point of Gothic style.

MUSIC AT THE CATHEDRAL SCHOOL OF NOTRE DAME

The cathedral school in Paris followed the curriculum that Alcuin of York had developed for Charlemagne (see Chapter 10), which included the study of Aristotle and the Church Fathers. It was also an important center of music in the twelfth and thirteenth centuries. Traditional church music had been the plainchant sung responsively by a chorus (the choir) and an individual or by two choirs. In the early tenth century, the trope had been inserted into the liturgy.

Composers at Notre Dame brought earlier organum techniques (the earliest form of polyphony) to fruition in the late twelfth century. In the organal or melismatic style, a chant melody (the *cantus firmus*) was sung by the tenor voice, with each note held for several seconds, like a drone. Above the chant, another voice sang an elaborate faster moving line, with several notes to each syllable of text.

A second style was known as **discant** (from the Latin for "singing apart"). In this, the tenor voice sang shorter notes, while one or more higher voices sang only slightly more rapid notes above it. These parts, rather than rising and falling at the same time (as in earlier parallel organum), often moved in different directions, and functioned as simultaneous melodies. The technique came to be called *punctus contra punctum*, literally "point against point," or counterpoint.

The most important new musical form developed in the thirteenth century was the **motet**. Just as extra words had earlier been added to plainchant to create tropes, now new text was added to the upper voice (or voices) of organum to create the motet. (The term derives from the French *mot*, meaning

11.16 Miniature from a Book of Hours, showing a church service with singing, from Paris, 15th century. Illuminated manuscript, decorated area 6½ in. (16.7 cm) high. British Library, London.
The integration of music in church services is shown here as a priest prays before the altar surrounded by a choir of singing monks. At the left, a group reads from an open book, the notes clearly visible on the page. The exuberance of the music is shown not only by the singers around the altar, but also by the seated figure in the initial D and the monks in the border area. The border is filled with floral and foliate designs, indicating that music both fills space and flows through it.

"word.") Both sacred and secular motets were composed, and the religious and profane could be combined within one work—so, for example, the tenor might perform the notes and Latin text of a chant while a higher voice sang the words of a French poem. By the fifteenth century the motet would evolve into a polyphonic setting of a Latin religious text, normally in three parts.

The increasing complexity of church music in this period can be compared with the new, more complex architecture of cathedral interiors. Both the music and the architecture were designed to express the soaring quality of faith and the expansiveness of God's presence in the universe (figure **11.16**).

The two main figures associated with church music in the late twelfth and early thirteenth centuries are Léonin (*c.* 1163–1190) and Pérotin (d. *c.* 1238). They and their contemporaries at the Notre Dame School standardized the use of six regular rhythmic patterns, which replaced the free-flowing earlier chant styles. Units of three formed the basis of all the patterns—like the triple architectural sections of Gothic cathedrals, anything structured in threes was considered sublime because it mirrored the Trinity.

Léonin compiled the *Magnus liber organi (The Great Book of Organum)* (*c.* 1170), the most important collection of Gothic liturgical music. It contained over a hundred pieces of organum interleaved with plainsong, arranged, for maximum convenience, in the order of the Church year. Pérotin, who became head of the music school at Notre Dame Cathedral toward the end of the twelfth century, is believed to have revised and re-notated the *Magnus liber*. While Léonin's organum was florid and generally for two voices (tenor and *duplum*, or "second"), Pérotin often used three or four voices, with shorter melismas. As all the singers were men, the vocal parts lie at roughly the same pitch and weave in and out, sometimes imitating each other's melodies. One consequence of having four simultaneous lines of music within a narrow range

is that the interest begins to switch from the horizontal strands of music to the vertical—to the way the notes coincide as chords. Regular, persistent rhythms give the music a hypnotic quality that is enhanced by the scale of the later pieces; some last for twenty minutes and in their grandeur match the magnificence of the architectural setting in which they were sung.

THE UNIVERSITY OF PARIS

Our modern universities originated in the Middle Ages and were products of urbanization. With the rise of cities, administrative workers who could read and write were needed. These, along with a new interest in legal studies, science, and mathematics, contributed to the growth of an educated class.

The medieval university was more organized than the informal schools of Aristotle, Plato, and other ancient philosophers. At first, students and teachers came together as a group, like masters and apprentices in an academic guild. But soon universities were granted charters and became official institutions that could borrow and invest money. Students who had a reading knowledge of Latin entered university as early adolescents. They usually spent four years there. When students finished a course of study they were awarded certificates and

Society and Culture

Medicine in the Middle Ages

As in ancient Greece and Rome, the practice of medicine in the Middle Ages was a mix of tradition, superstition, folklore, astrology, and ignorance of human anatomy. Medical ingredients consisted mainly of herbs and ointments sold in apothecary shops (pharmacies). Textbooks were in Latin, which most people could not read, and only a few doctors who treated the wealthy had university training in Hippocratic medicine. Some, especially surgery students, were apprenticed to a practicing doctor. Barber-surgeons, who treated more people, formed a guild-based profession.

The majority of the population was treated by herbalists, midwives, and healers, who had no university training. Through the fourteenth century, only midwives dealt with women in childbirth, but with the invention of forceps men began delivering babies. Although monks cultivated herbs for medicinal purposes, the Church barred the clergy from medical studies. It also discouraged empirical investigations of the human body.

Most doctors diagnosed illness by examining a patient's urine. Because the body was believed to be composed of four humors (fluids)—blood, phlegm, yellow bile, and black bile—it was assumed that an imbalance of the humors would show itself in the

urine. Doctors also examined blood to see how it flowed and clotted. As a result, it was generally believed that blood-letting could bring the humors into the correct balance (figure **11.17**). In fact, however, blood-letting often resulted in death from loss of blood.

11.17 Aldobrandino of Siena, blood-letting scene, from *Li livres dou santé* (*The Books of Health*), France, 13th century. Manuscript illumination, initial box 2 1/8 in. (5.5 cm) wide. British Library, London.
This illustration from an Italian health manual was published in thirteenth-century France. It shows a doctor, wearing a professional cap and long gown, cutting a patient just above the elbow. The patient looks away, apparently to avoid the sight of blood, which flows into a bowl on the floor. Medieval manuals on surgery and the treatment of broken and dislocated bones also survive.

could go on to complete the level of Master. Thereafter they could pursue a doctorate (the ancestor of the PhD degree) in law, theology, or medicine (see Box, p. 286). The requirements were rigorous and a degree in theology could take over twenty years of study.

By the end of the twelfth century, the University of Paris was an intellectual center, and it is still, as the Sorbonne, the major university in France. Other important medieval universities that are well known today include Bologna (in northern Italy), and Oxford and Cambridge (in England). Students at these medieval universities were exclusively men. Although they enrolled for the benefits of having a degree, they criticized the poor living conditions and the lack of money for books, food, and lodging. They had no heat or hot water, and only candlelight to read by.

As with the cathedral schools, the curriculum in medieval universities was based on the one devised by Alcuin of York for the palace school of Charlemagne (see Chapter 10). In the Gothic period, Alcuin's focus on rhetoric and dialectic became the basis of a system of thought called **scholasticism**.

SCHOLASTICISM: PETER ABELARD AND THOMAS AQUINAS

Scholasticism tried to impose a sense of order on the world and to deal with the apparent contradiction of faith and reason. This was a form of logic inspired by the writings of Aristotle and Augustine. Aristotle's works had been preserved in Arabic commentaries and in translations made from Greek into Arabic by Arabic scholars. Eventually these texts were translated into Latin and could be read by Western scholars.

The scholastic method began with a question and sought the answer by demonstrating a series of incorrect or contradictory responses. Its approach to questioning an idea consisted of three steps: (1) posing a question, (2) discussing different aspects of the question based on Classical and Christian authors and biblical texts, and (3) achieving a resolution. Scholasticism was thus a closed system, designed to uphold Church doctrine rather than to explore new ideas.

Within scholasticism, there were two main points of view: the **realist** and the **nominalist**. Realists based their arguments on Plato's notion that universal ideas exist separately from the physical world and the mind. The nominalists disagreed with Plato and argued that only some things are real. An accomplished lecturer at the Paris Cathedral School, William of Champeaux (c. 1070–1121), espoused realism. His brilliant student Peter Abelard (1079–1142) claimed that universal ideas did exist but could be understood only by being expressed in language. He exposed contradictions in Church doctrine and in the scriptures by using the scholastic method of logic. He argued, for example, that three and one could never be the same. By this reasoning, Abelard concluded that the concept of the Trinity as three persons in one was not logical (see Box).

Society and Culture

Abelard and Héloïse

Peter Abelard was the major figure in the growth of the University of Paris. He began teaching at the cathedral school in 1113, lecturing on logic and theology. He challenged the Church in *Sic et non* (*Yes and No*), in which he brilliantly demonstrated contradictions in the Bible and in the writings of Christian authors and brought to light the differences between faith and reason. But instead of trying to reconcile the contradictions, he allowed them to remain as open questions.

Abelard's challenge to the Church was not only intellectual, it was also personal. While he was teaching in Paris he met and fell in love with Héloïse (c. 1098–1164), an accomplished theologian. She was a brilliant and beautiful young woman, who was living with her uncle, Fulbert, a canon (church official) of Notre Dame Cathedral, and was being tutored by university scholars. Abelard rented a room from Fulbert and began an affair with Héloïse. Their son, Astralabe, was born around 1118 after Héloïse went to live with Abelard's family. At first, Héloïse refused Abelard's offer of marriage on the grounds that a scholarly life was preferable to a domestic one. Eventually, however, they did marry, so enraging Canon Fulbert that Abelard sent Héloïse to the safety of a convent. Soon thereafter Fulbert's men attacked and castrated Abelard.

Abelard entered the monastery of St. Denis in Paris, but he was expelled by Suger when he challenged the monks on a matter of historical accuracy. He continued to teach, but was accused of heresy by both Bernard of Clairvaux and Pope Innocent II. The abbot of Cluny, Venerable Peter, defended Abelard, who then joined the abbey. When Abelard died, Peter sent his body to Héloïse for burial. Héloïse, meanwhile, had become abbess of her convent. Astralabe was raised by Abelard's sister, who lived in Brittany, and he became a canon at the cathedral of Nantes. Abelard recorded his affair with Héloïse in his *Historia calamitatum* (*Story of My Misfortunes*).

READING SELECTION

Héloïse, *The Letters of Abelard and Héloïse*, on the hypocrisy of religion and discrimination against women, PWC2-021; Abelard, *Story of My Misfortunes*, on his love affair with Héloïse, PWC2-018

Abelard's views were taken up by the leading proponent of scholasticism of the thirteenth century, Thomas Aquinas (c. 1225–1274). Born in Italy to a noble family, he became a Dominican friar, wrote extensively, and is widely considered the greatest of the medieval philosophers. His most influential work is the *Summa theologiae*. Aquinas sought to resolve the conflicts between faith and reason, and reason and revelation. He argued that because some aspects of Christian doctrine—such as the immortality of the soul, the existence of God, the Trinity, and the notion of Christ as God who became human—are not empirically (through the five senses) or logically provable, we must go beyond reason and embrace faith. In other words, the knowledge we acquire from our senses leads us to intuit the existence of God and the immortal soul.

Aquinas was the first thinker to propose a systematic reconciliation of Christianity with the philosophy of Aristotle. His aim was not only to resolve the dualisms inherent in the Church—faith, reason, revelation—but also to synthesize the ideas in the Bible and in the writings of Christians, Muslims, and Aristotle. He argued for faith as an absolute and for accepting God's revealed truth. His well-known statement, quoted from Tertullian, *Credo quia absurdum est* ("I believe because it is absurd"), sums up his conviction that reason alone is not sufficient to account for the mysteries of the universe.

READING SELECTION
Aquinas, *Summa theologiae*, on natural law, PWC2-007-C

Thomas Aquinas and the scholastic system of thought were in conflict not only with Abelard but also with Duns Scotus (*c.* 1265–1308). An Oxford-educated Franciscan friar, Duns Scotus challenged Aquinas's synthesis of faith and reason. According to Duns Scotus, Christian mysteries, such as the existence of God and the Holy Ghost, are not provable. Rather, faith was the only route to understanding such mysteries.

Duns Scotus proposed the preeminence of free will and the notion that human behavior is determined by a sense of justice, which is a matter of secular reason rather than faith. He argued that people act out of a motivation combining what is good for the individual with the common good.

In these various approaches to understanding the nature of the world, medieval thinkers were attempting to reconcile what they could observe and prove with what seemed inexplicable. They wanted to explicate Church doctrine to the point where there was no further room for questioning. Like the Gothic cathedral, followers of scholasticism combined hierarchy, structural logic, and mysticism with reason. On the other hand, some scholars, such as Peter Abelard and Duns Scotus, resisted the closed scholastic system and sought new ways of thinking about the world. As we will see in the next chapter, these thinkers were laying the foundation for the deeper questioning stance that would lead to the development of the Renaissance.

THE DEVELOPMENT OF GOTHIC STYLE OUTSIDE PARIS

The Gothic style in architecture quickly spread beyond Paris. If we compare the façades of three French cathedrals—at Chartres (begun 1194), at Amiens (begun 1220), and at Reims (façade begun *c.* 1230–1240)—we can see that they share basic structural elements (figures **11.18**, **11.19**, **11.20**). All have triple portal entrances and are divided horizontally and vertically into three sections; two soaring towers flank the center, which contains a rose window.

11.18 Façade of Chartres Cathedral, France, begun 1194.

11.19 Façade of Amiens Cathedral, France, begun 1220.

11.20 Façade of Reims Cathedral, France, begun *c.* 1230–1240.

11.21 Central portal of Chartres Cathedral, France, *c.* 1194.

As the style progresses, the pointed arches become increasingly vertical, the amount of glass increases as the amount of solid wall decreases, and spaces become deeper. There is also much more surface decoration.

In every case, the portals are surrounded by sculptures designed to create a transition from the material world outside to the sacred space inside. Conceived of as the Heavenly Jerusalem on earth, the Gothic cathedral was a vision of eternity in stone and glass. The portal sculptures, for example, were designed to inspire worshippers to deepen their faith. A case in point is the central portal on the entrance façade of Chartres Cathedral (figure **11.21**).

THE CENTRAL PORTAL OF CHARTRES: A VISION OF THE END OF TIME

The sculptures that embellish the center door of Chartres's west façade are divided into two main groups. The vertical figures at the door jambs represent Old Testament kings and queens. The relief sculptures above the door come from St. John the Divine's apocalyptic vision described in Revelation, the last book of the Bible. Christ appears on the tympanum in a mandorla of light, surrounded by the four symbols of the Evangelists—Matthew the angel, Luke the bull, Mark the lion, and John the eagle. Below, on the lintel, are the twelve apostles. Carved on the three archivolts are one set of twelve angels and the twenty-four Elders of the Apocalypse. This is John's vision of the Second Coming of Christ, who returns to earth to judge humanity for all time. He holds a book in his left hand, alluding to the textual basis of his teaching, and blesses with his right.

The typological iconography is based on the notion of prophecy and prefiguration on the one hand and fulfillment on the other (see Chapter 8). Old Testament royalty prefigures Christ the new king and, by extension, Mary the new queen, to whom the cathedral is dedicated. The door jambs and their statues comprise a literal and symbolic foundation on which the New Testament rests. In this case, the end of the world and of time reminds viewers of their own mortality and cautions them to follow the teachings of the Church.

THE CULT OF THE VIRGIN

Although the cult of the Virgin developed in the Romanesque period, it took on new importance in the Gothic period. Chartres had been a pilgrimage site since the ninth century when King Charles II, the Bald, donated a relic of the tunic worn by the Virgin at the Nativity. In the stained glass window known as the *Belle Verrière*—literally, "beautiful stained glass window" (figure **11.22**)—Mary is shown as the Queen of Heaven. She is enthroned and crowned, with the Holy Ghost (the white dove) suspending a halo behind her head. She is the largest and most important figure, befitting her lofty position in the hierarchical structure of the Church. Three angels kneel on either side of her, four swinging censers (incense containers) and two holding large candlesticks. The architectural detail above the Holy Ghost identifies Mary as a symbol of the church building itself.

In this complex iconography, Mary is not only the Queen of Heaven and the church building, she is also the throne of Christ. He, in turn, is suspended between her knees, defying gravity and occupying a flattened, non-material space. His depiction as a miniature man exemplifies the Christian notion of Christ as a miraculous baby-king.

11.22 *Notre Dame de la Belle Verrière*, Chartres Cathedral, *c.* 1220.
Stained glass windows were made by fitting together pieces of colored glass and fusing them with lead strips. A few details, such as facial features, were painted in, and the glass sections were set in frames and held in place by vertical and horizontal rods. The rich blues and reds are characteristic of the windows at Chartres.

11.23 *Vierge dorée (The Gilded Virgin)*, south portal, Amiens Cathedral, France, *c.* 1250. Stone, over lifesize.

Another image of the Virgin and Christ, created some thirty years after the *Belle Verrière*, shows an increasing concept of Mary's humanity in her relationship to her son (figure **11.23**). She is still a queen; three angels in a cruciform arrangement support her halo, and an architectural detail appears over her head. Although the symbolism here is similar to that of the *Belle Verrière*, Mary now holds a more baby-like Christ and turns to face him. She responds to him as an infant rather than as a king. There is even the suggestion of a turn at her waist, indicating a human body beneath the clothing. Compared with the regal, hierarchical figures of the *Belle Verrière*, these are more human and interact as would a normal mother and child.

11.24 Cologne Cathedral, Germany, begun 1228, towers planned *c.* 1300 and built *c.* 1350.

LATE GOTHIC: COLOGNE CATHEDRAL

Although Gothic style began in France, it soon spread throughout western Europe, especially to England, Germany, the Netherlands, Italy, and the non-Muslim parts of Spain. The basic French style was retained, but certain national characteristics were added. In some countries, the style lasted for several centuries. In Cologne in Germany, for example, a cathedral was begun in 1228, but its towers were not constructed until around 1350 (figure **11.24**). (The entire cathedral was in fact completed only in the nineteenth century.) The towers demonstrate the Late Gothic taste for tall, thin spires and animated surfaces.

Gothic style became international in scope and expanded beyond Church patronage to regional courts. The courtly Gothic style, called International Gothic, continued in parts of northern Europe well into the fifteenth century.

THEATER AND LITERATURE IN THE GOTHIC PERIOD

From the middle of the eleventh century to around 1300, liturgical drama continued to develop. Mystery, miracle, and morality (*Everyman*) plays were performed inside churches and cathedrals throughout Europe, although in Muslim Spain such drama was forbidden.

According to surviving manuals, plays were acted by males only—either choirboys or members of the clergy. Lines were chanted rather than spoken, generally in Latin. Because the cathedral was considered a microcosm of the universe, it was easily transformed into a vast theatrical environment. The choir loft became the setting for heaven and the underground crypt for hell. Staging used mechanical apparatuses to move the star leading the three kings to Bethlehem, to lower a dove or the angel Gabriel when re-enacting the Annunciation, or to create tongues of flame for Pentecost.

As dramatic productions moved outside the church, liturgical plays began to decline and secular drama expanded. Comedy, as we saw in Chapter 10, grew out of liturgical events such as the Feast of Fools. But the full expansion of comedy would not come until the late Middle Ages, when theater had become more detached from both the liturgy and the church interior.

In literature as in theater, Romanesque themes and genres continued to flourish in the Gothic era, even as new ones developed. In the eleventh century, troubadours recited poetry and wandering minstrels sang *canzoni* (love poems) in Provençal, the language of the south of France. *Canzoni* were popular at the courts, as was the **lay** (*lai*, in French), a short poem sung to the accompaniment of the harp. The earliest surviving lays are by Marie de France (active *c.* 1170), a poet born in Brittany who lived mainly in England. She wrote twelve lays in Old French rhyming couplets. They were inspired by the legends of Lancelot and King Arthur, and their themes were love, infidelity, and moral conflict.

Marie de France also composed *Ysopet*, seventy-five tales based on the ancient Greek fables of Aesop. According to the Greek historian Herodotus (see Chapter 6), Aesop was a slave in sixth-century-B.C. Egypt. His fables, in which the characters are animals rather than people, contain moral messages. Marie de France's *Ysopet* thus reflects her acquaintance with Classical authors.

READING SELECTION
Marie de France, "Lanval" and "Les Deus Amanz" ("The Two Lovers"), PWC2-169

DANTE AND THE *DIVINE COMEDY*

In Italy, Dante Alighieri (1265–1321) wrote the great medieval poem, which he titled *Commedia*, now known as the *Divine Comedy*. It is an epic vision of a journey in three parts through hell (*Inferno*), purgatory (*Purgatorio*), and heaven (*Paradiso*). Each of these three parts of the Christian universe is divided into nine regions. Dante calls his traveler the Pilgrim, although it is clear that the Pilgrim represents the author.

The poem is composed of one hundred *cantos*, thirty-three in each section and a prologue. Dante wrote the *Divine Comedy* in the vernacular (called *volgare* in Italian)—that is, in Italian, not Latin. He used a verse form known in Italian as *terza rima*, in which each stanza has three lines (*terzine*, or tercets) with a rhyme scheme of ABA, BCB, CDC. The line that does not rhyme in one stanza thus recurs and *does* rhyme in the next stanza. For example, the non-rhyming B of ABA rhymes in BCB; then the C, which does not rhyme in BCB, becomes the rhymed line in CDC. This strictly controlled poetic structure reflects the influence of Thomas Aquinas and the hierarchy of scholasticism. The repeated groupings of three also echo the Trinity and the three-part organization of Gothic cathedrals.

Dante was born in Florence, and he was devoted to the city. His family saw to it that he was well educated. He studied rhetoric at the University of Bologna, read Classical and Christian texts, knew the leading intellectuals of his time, and was deeply involved in politics. His marriage to Gemma Donati was arranged by the couple's parents when he was eleven years old and she was around ten. They had three children. In 1302, Dante was exiled from Florence for political reasons.

DANTE AND BEATRICE Dante was nearly ten years old when he first saw Beatrice Portinari, who was about a year younger than he. For the rest of his life he was infatuated with her, and she inspired much of his poetry. Aside from a few passing remarks, Dante and Beatrice were involved only in the poet's imagination, where he raised Beatrice to a level of divine perfection that exists only in myth and art.

In 1287, when she was twenty-one, Beatrice married a member of the wealthy Bardi family and went to live in the countryside. Dante then addressed a number of poems to her, but he was rebuffed and decided to devote himself solely to writing about her. In 1290, when she was twenty-four, Beatrice died and thereafter, for Dante, resided in heaven. In the *Divine Comedy*, it is Beatrice who guides the Pilgrim through paradise and sends Virgil to guide him through hell and purgatory.

THE POEM The *Divine Comedy* was written between about 1308 and 1321, during Dante's exile from Florence. It is, first and foremost, a pilgrimage of the poet's soul. Dante the author writes about Dante the pilgrim, fusing present and future time just as the cathedral expressed both earthly and spiritual time.

The poem is also a rich tapestry of medieval politics, for along the way Dante mentions events in Florentine history and describes encounters with famous political and religious figures, meting out the punishments or rewards he thinks they deserve.

The *Divine Comedy* opens on Good Friday in the year 1300. The events are condensed into a single liturgical week, beginning on the day of the Crucifixion. On Easter Sunday morning, Dante emerges from hell (as Christ rose from the dead) into purgatory. Three days later, on the Wednesday after Easter, Dante enters paradise, and he concludes his journey on Thursday. Throughout, the poet uses the metaphor of light and dark to symbolize good and evil, salvation and damnation, enlightenment and sin, the divine and the primitive, respectively. At the outset of the first *canto*, which opens like a dream, Dante writes:

> Midway along the journey of our life
>   I woke to find myself in a dark wood,
>   for I had wandered off from the straight path.
>
> How hard it is to tell what it was like,
>   this wood of wilderness, savage and stubborn
>   (the thought of it brings back all my old fears),
>
> a bitter place! Death could scarce be bitterer.
>   But if I would show the good that came of it
>   I must talk about things other than the good.
>
> (*Inferno*, Canto I, lines 1–9)

Dante sees a figure approaching and asks if he is a shade (ghost) or a living man:

> "No longer living man, though once I was,"
>   he said, "and my parents were from Lombardy [in
>   northern Italy]
>   both of them were Mantuans by birth.
>
> I was born, though somewhat late, *sub Julio* [late in the reign
>   of Julius Caesar]
>   and lived in Rome when good Augustus reigned,
>   when still the false and lying [pagan] gods were worshipped.
>
> I was a poet and sang of that just man [Aeneas],
>   son of Anchises, who sailed off from Troy
>   after the burning of proud Ilium [another name for Troy]."
>
> (Canto I, lines 67–75)

The former man is Virgil, the Roman poet from Mantua and author of the *Aeneid* (see Chapter 7), who will be Dante's guide. Dante thus suggests that his journey through hell is inspired by the journeys of Aeneas and Odysseus, making himself an epic hero traveling through a Christian universe.

THE CIRCLES OF HELL Dante's hell is a hierarchy arranged in descending circles of sin and ascending degrees of punishment. The first circle is Limbo, which is inhabited by the unbaptized, including the great figures of pagan antiquity. In the second circle, Dante sees carnal sinners whirling in eddies of uncontrollable winds. Among them are the famed adulterous lovers Paolo and Francesca, whose romance was inspired by the Arthurian story of Lancelot and Guinevere. The third circle contains gluttons, who are condemned to roll in mud; in the fourth circle are the avaricious (money-hungry), and in the fifth are the wrathful. In the sixth circle, heretics are burned alive. The seventh circle contains people who have committed suicide and those who have sinned against their neighbors and against God, art, and nature.

In the eighth circle, containing the fraudulent, Dante notices dark compartments in which different tortures are carried out. Seducers are whipped by demons, and those who bought their clerical offices are held upside down and the soles of their feet are burned. People guilty of giving evil counsel are engulfed in flames; among them is Odysseus, the wily strategist of the Homeric epics. He is punished in Dante's Christian hell for deceiving the Trojans with the wooden horse (see Chapter 4).

Nearing the lowest depths of hell in the ninth circle, Dante encounters the Lake of the Treacherous. Their sins range from betrayal of family, nations, and guests to treason against lords and benefactors. Among the treacherous, Dante sees one of the most despicable and dramatic figures in Western literature—Count Ugolino of Pisa—who is embedded in ice. Ugolino had been a traitor during his lifetime, and in hell he eats the brain of his partner in treachery, the archbishop Ruggieri. Ugolino had been imprisoned along with his sons, who had died of starvation. In hell, too, Ugolino sees his sons die, and then returns to his own gruesome meal. Dante gives him the words: "hunger proved more powerful than grief" (Canto XXXIII, line 75).

> He spoke these words; then, glaring down in rage,
>   attacked again the wretched skull with his teeth
>   sharp as a dog's, and as fit for grinding bones.
>
> (Canto XXXIII, lines 76–78)

Dante and Virgil finally reach Satan's realm in Canto XXXIV, the conclusion of the *Inferno*. This is the center of the earth, the location of the worst betrayers, including Brutus and Cassius, who betrayed Julius Caesar, and Judas, who betrayed Christ. Satan himself has three heads and is half wedged in ice. Here is Dante's lurid description:

> If once he was as fair as now he's foul
>   and dared to raise his brows against his Maker,
>   it is fitting that all grief should spring from him.
>
> Oh how amazed I was when I looked up
>   and saw a head—one head wearing three faces!
>   One was in front (and that was a bright red),
>
> the other two attached themselves to this one
>   just above the middle of each shoulder,
>   and at the crown all three were joined in one:
>
> The right face was a blend of white and yellow,
>   the left the color of those people's skin
>   who live along the river Nile's descent.

11.25 Detail of Hell, from a mosaic in the vault of the Baptistery. Florence, Italy, 13th century.

In this image, located in the Baptistery of Dante's native Florence, Satan is surrounded by flames and has features similar to the Satan of the *Inferno*. He has a distorted human face with large horns, and two serpents emerge from his ears and thighs. Souls are being chewed, swallowed, and expelled only to suffer the same fate over and over. Some are tortured by dozens of little devils, lizards, and toads, while others are engulfed in flames. At the left, appearing particularly downcast, are a few souls who have just begun to confront their unfortunate future.

> Beneath each face two mighty wings stretched out,
>   the size you might expect of his huge bird
>   (I never saw a ship with larger sails):
>
> Not feathered wings but rather like the ones
>   a bat would have. He flapped them constantly . . .
>
> In each of his three mouths he crunched a sinner,
>   with teeth like those that rake the hemp and flax,
>   keeping three sinners constantly in pain.
>
> (Canto XXXIV, lines 34–57)

Satan's hideous appearance is the opposite of his former beauty. Whereas he had been Lucifer (God's bearer of light) in heaven, he is now immersed in the darkness of hell. His former beauty has become monstrous, and his angel wings have turned into bat wings. His triple head is an intentional reversal of the Holy Trinity. Satan is thus an eternal, cannibalistic torturer who has sunk to the depths of evil. Such imagery abounded in the Middle Ages, both as a warning to would-be sinners and as a means of rich literary and artistic expression (figure **11.25**).

Having confronted the full force of Satan's hideous nature, Dante is told by Virgil that they must depart. For the first time, at the end of the *Inferno*, the travelers rise rather than descend. They climb through a hole and welcome the sight of the night sky. Each of the three main sections of the *Divine Comedy* ends with the image of a star, denoting a hopeful outcome.

PURGATORY Dante's purgatory is reserved for souls on their way to heaven. They have died in a state of grace but need time, often hundreds of years, to atone for their sins. Purgatory is a mountain island arranged, like hell, in levels, but it begins with the gravest sins at the bottom—pride is the first sin and lust is the last. Now Dante and Virgil are on the ascent. At the summit of purgatory, Virgil can go no further, for it marks the limit of human wisdom and he is among the unbaptized. From here on Dante is in paradise, the site of divine revelation, wisdom, faith, and purity of soul.

Just before the summit of purgatory, Dante is terrified by a wall of flame. Virgil reassures him that the wall is all that separates him from Beatrice and that beyond the wall lies the last stairway to the top of purgatory. Dante and Virgil fall asleep (note that at the opening of the *Inferno*, Dante awoke from sleep) and awaken to ascend the summit.

The conclusion of the *Purgatorio* takes place on the mountaintop and lasts for six *cantos*. Here Dante sees a figure associated with Countess Matilda of Canossa, who had ruled parts of Italy from around 1065 to 1115 and was a patron of the arts (see Chapter 10). She enchants Dante with her singing.

As Matilda fades, a vision of St. John the Divine from the book of Revelation comes into view. The twenty-four Elders parade before him, followed by Ezekiel's vision of the four creatures with six wings (see Chapter 8). Two additional groups, one, dancing personifications of the theological virtues—faith, hope, and charity—and the other of the cardinal virtues—prudence, temperance, justice, and fortitude—surround a chariot. Dante sees that Beatrice rides in the chariot, and he hears angels singing verses from the *Aeneid*. Virgil, denied the vision of paradise for having lived in a pagan era, is forced to depart.

PARADISE Beatrice, who resides in the ninth heaven, takes over from Virgil and guides the poet through paradise, which is based on the seven planets described in medieval astronomy.

These are the Sun and Moon, Mercury, Venus, Mars, Jupiter, and Saturn. Beyond the planets are the fixed stars and, further still, the Empyrean Heavens. This final segment of the *Divine Comedy* opens, like the *Iliad* and the *Odyssey*, with an invocation of the gods and Muses:

> O good Apollo, for this last task, I pray
>   you make me such a vessel of your powers
>   as you deem worthy to be crowned with bay . . .
>
> O power divine, but lend to my high strain
>   so much as will make clear even the shadow
>   of that High Kingdom stamped upon my brain,
>
> and you shall see me come to your dear grove
>   to crown myself with those green leaves [the poet's laurel]
>   and my high theme shall make me worthy of.

> *(Paradiso*, Canto I, lines 13–27)

Now Dante is in the realm of visionary light and weightlessness. He no longer climbs against the force of gravity, but ascends the planets from the moon to Saturn, and finally to the ninth sphere—the Empyrean Heavens. He does this without physical effort or travel time, listening along the way to the Platonic music of the spheres (see Chapter 6). Throughout the *Paradiso*, Dante is struck by the power of God's divine light that pervades the heavens. As in hell and purgatory, Dante meets historical personages; but now they are immaterial spirits. Among these are the Roman emperor Constantine, the Byzantine emperor Justinian, the Dominican Thomas Aquinas, and St. Benedict, whose monastic rule spread throughout Europe. Higher spheres are inhabited by the apostles, Christ, the Virgin Mary, and the hierarchy of angels.

At the summit of paradise, Dante again receives a new guide, St. Bernard of Clairvaux. Bernard shows the poet his last vision of Beatrice, who resumes her place at God's eternal fountain. Bernard had been a most devoted follower of the Virgin, and the fact that he is Dante's guide demonstrates the power of Mary's cult in the Middle Ages. Dante has Bernard name the Virgin

> The Queen of Heaven, for whom in whole devotion
>   I burn with love, will grant us every grace
>   because I am Bernard, her faithful one.

> *(Canto XXXI, lines 101–103)*

Thematic Parallels

Views of Paradise

Most religions have a view of life after death. But the image of that life, whether based on reward and punishment as in Christianity, or a more neutral view, varies. Paradise is generally the destination of those who are rewarded for a lifetime of faith and good works. But this too differs according to a particular religion and, to some extent, according to the culture in which that religion arose. For example, in Greek mythology there is no paradise or immortality for ordinary mortals. These are the province of the gods and the Muses, with the exception of Heracles, who was admitted to Mount Olympos. Indeed, one of the reasons Christianity appealed to the pagan Mediterranean world was its promise of paradise for the faithful.

In Norse myth, paradise is Valhalla—the destination of brave warriors who await Ragnarök, the battle at the end of time. This image is consistent with Viking warrior society.

In Hinduism, first practiced in India, there is no paradise in the Western sense. Instead there is nirvana (a state of perfect bliss). Most Hindus believe in reincarnation, which is a cycle of rebirth depending on one's behavior in a previous life. Related to the strict caste system of India, reincarnation accounts for one's birth into a particular level of society—Brahmins, the spiritual and social elite, are at the top. Each class is seen as merely one step in the long cycle of reincarnation, which ends with release from the cycle. When Hindus attain nirvana, their souls become one with the cosmos, and they are freed from the material constraints of the world. Outside the caste system are the Untouchables, or "outcastes."

When Buddhism originated in India in the sixth century B.C., the notion of nirvana was adopted. Later, however, around the fifth century A.D., a number of sects arose that sought to avoid the repeated cycles of rebirth and to simplify the route to nirvana. These sects promised an afterlife in a splendid paradise, which could be attained directly through faith rather than having to endure several lifetimes of reincarnation.

Muslims, like Christians, believe that the end of the world will come and that there will be a final judgment according to the way one has lived life. The Qur'an describes the last day as filled with noise and disruption. Those who have led a good life will be rewarded with an afterlife of pleasure, whereas those whose lives are found wanting will be committed to a dark abyss (or hell). In contrast to Christianity, however, Muslim souls are not eternally damned. They spend time in hell according to the amount and nature of their sins but can eventually enter heaven. Only heretics burn forever in hell. According to the Qur'an, paradise is a lush garden, flowing with rivers and filled with fruit, flowers, and beautiful virgins. A more mystical view interprets heaven as closeness to God and a state of eternal spiritual well-being. The Islamic paradise is not necessarily high up in the heavens, but can be interpreted as being on a transformed earth.

READING SELECTION

The Qur'an, on infidels burning in hell and dark-eyed virgins attending the faithful in heaven, PWC2-220

Bernard asks the Virgin to intercede on behalf of Dante so that he might see God. The vision of God swells Dante's soul, but he cannot describe it, for human words are dark compared to God's light. He concludes the *Paradiso* with the following verse:

> Here my powers rest from their high fantasy,
>   but already I could feel my being turned—
>   instinct and intellect balanced equally
>
> as in a wheel whose motion nothing jars—
>   by the Love that moves the Sun and the other stars.

(Canto XXXIII, lines 142–146)

Dante is considered the most important figure in Italian literature, and his influence on later Western authors has been enormous. The *Divine Comedy* is the poetic equivalent of the *Summa* of Thomas Aquinas. But Dante's creation is imaginative —a personal, historical, and artistic vision—whereas Aquinas's *Summa* is a compendium of his philosophical and theological thought. Dante's poetry, like the Gothic cathedral, gives concrete expression to the universe of the Christian spirit. It also embodies Suger's notion that the arts, the experience of the senses, and human creativity are ways of understanding the divine. Dante's poetry is as rich in metaphor and allusion as Suger's church was in gold, gemstones, stained glass, and light.

READING SELECTION

Dante, *Divine Comedy*, Vol. 1, *Inferno*: Canto I, Dante begins his journey through hell and meets Virgil, PWC2-022-B; Canto III, the gates of hell, PWC2-023-B; Canto V, Paolo and Francesca, PWC2-024

In Italy, Dante and the Divine Comedy *can be seen as occupying a pivotal place in the gradual transition from the Middle Ages to the early Renaissance period. On the one hand, he writes in the hierarchical tradition of the medieval scholastics and on the other he conveys a sharp sense of personality and history. In addition, by choosing Virgil as the guide on his epic journey, he heralds the fourteenth-century revival of Classical texts that would propel Italy and, later, parts of northern Europe into a new era.*

KEY TERMS

Beghards in medieval northern Europe, a group of lay men dedicated to leading a spiritual life and working for the community.

Beguines in medieval northern Europe, a group of lay women who established spiritual centers.

discant in medieval music, a style in which the lower, tenor voice sings in a steady rhythm, while one or more higher voices sing slightly faster melodies above.

friar a member of a mendicant ("begging") Order.

gallery a row of figures.

Inquisitors officials appointed by the Roman Church to combat heresy.

lancet a tall, narrow arched window.

lay a short poem, sung to the accompaniment of a harp.

master-builder one who supervises the building of a cathedral.

mendicant a member of a religious order who wandered from town to town begging.

motet a polyphonic choral work, generally written in Latin for church performance; some early motets were secular and multilingual.

nominalism in philosophy, the belief that universals (general ideas, abstract concepts) are nothing more than names; the opposite of realism.

Poor Clares nuns who belong to the Order of Abbess Clare.

radiating chapels chapels placed around an ambulatory.

rayonnant a style in Gothic rose windows in which shapes of glass radiate from the small circle at the center.

realism in philosophy, the belief that universals (general ideas, abstract concepts) have an objective existence; the opposite of nominalism.

rib vault a vault made by the intersection of pointed arches.

rose window a large, round window in Gothic Cathedrals.

scholasticism a system of thought developed in the Gothic period that addressed the apparent contradiction of faith and reason.

stained glass pieces of colored glass held in place in windows by strips of lead.

stigmata marks resembling Christ's wounds on the Cross.

template a diagram of an architectural section used by master-builders.

transubstantiation in the Mass, a process in which bread and wine are believed to be transformed literally into Christ's body and blood.

KEY QUESTIONS

1. What document was the first to recognize that kings as well as their subjects had moral and social responsibilities and were subject to certain laws?
2. Explain the relationship between the crusades, the concept of heresy, and the Inquisition.
3. Whose ideas about light and color launched the Gothic style? What were these ideas, and how does the

construction of the Gothic cathedral illustrate them?
4. Summarize the controversy between the realists and the nominalists.
5. Who was the first thinker to propose a systematic reconciliation of Christianity with the philosophy of Aristotle? Summarize what the statement *Credo quia absurdum est* means and how it relates to this reconciliation.

SUGGESTED READING

Baldwin, J. W. *The Scholastic Culture of the Middle Ages: 1000–1300.* New York: Houghton Mifflin, 1971.
  ▸ A discussion of medieval scholasticism.

Branner, Robert. *Chartres Cathedral,* New York: Norton, 1969.
  ▸ A classic study of the cathedral: style and iconography.

Burge, James. *Héloïse and Abelard: A New Biography.* San Francisco: HarperSanFrancisco, 2004.
  ▸ An account of the famous medieval romance.

Camille, Michael. *Gothic Art: Glorious Visions.* New York: Harry N. Abrams, 1996.
  ▸ A survey of Gothic art in Europe.

Clanchy, M. T. *Abelard: A Medieval Life,* Oxford: Blackwell Publishers, 1997.
  ▸ A biography of Abelard.

Dante. *The Inferno of Dante,* trans. Robert Pinsky. New York: Farrar, Straus and Giroux, 1996.
  ▸ A modern verse translation juxtaposed with the original.

Follet, Ken. *Pillars of the Earth.* London: Pan Books, 1990.
  ▸ A historical novel about the lives and families of cathedral builders, by an author of popular thrillers.

Gilson, Etienne. *Héloïse and Abelard.* Ann Arbor, MI: University of Michigan Press, 1960.
  ▸ A discussion of the story of Héloïse and Abelard in its social context.

Herlihy, D. *Medieval Households.* Cambridge, MA: Harvard University Press, 1985.
  ▸ Everyday life in the Middle Ages.

Hollister, C. Warren. *Medieval Europe.* New York: McGraw-Hill, 1997.
  ▸ A general survey of the period.

The Lais of Marie de France, trans. R. Hanning and J. Ferrante. Durham: Labyrinth Press, 1982.
  ▸ A modern translation in free verse of the *lais* of Marie de France.

Mâle, Emile. *Religious Art in France: the 13th Century—A Study of Medieval Iconography and its Sources.* Princeton, NJ: Princeton University Press, 1984.
  ▸ A classic study of Gothic iconography.

Panofsky, Erwin. *Gothic Architecture and Scholasticism.* New York: Meridian Books/London: Thames and Hudson, 1957.
  ▸ On the relationship between Gothic architecture and scholastic thought.

———. *Abbot Suger on the Abbey Church of St. Denis and its Art Treasures,* Princeton, NJ: Princeton University Press, 1979.
  ▸ An account of Suger's innovations and the origin of Gothic style.

Shahar, S. *The Fourth Estate: A History of Women in the Middle Ages.* London: Methuen, 1983.
  ▸ On the roles and lifestyles of medieval women.

Stock, B. *The Implications of Literacy.* London: Methuen, 1983.
  ▸ The effect of literacy on the Middle Ages.

Voelkle, William. *The Stavelot Triptych: Mosan Art and the Legend of the True Cross.* New York: The Pierpont Morgan Library, 1980.
  ▸ A monograph on one of the central reliquaries of medieval art.

Von Simpson, Otto. *The Gothic Cathedral: Origins of Gothic Architecture and the Medieval Concept of Order.* Princeton, NJ: Princeton University Press, 1988.
  ▸ A study of the sources of Gothic style in the context of medieval thought.

SUGGESTED FILMS

1938 *Alexander Nevsky,* dir. Sergei Eisenstein
1950 *The Black Rose,* dir. Henry Hathaway
1950 *Francis, God's Jester (The Flowers of St. Francis),* dir. Roberto Rossellini
1961 *Francis of Assisi,* dir. Michael Curtiz
1971 *Blanche,* dir. Walerian Borowczyk

1972 *Brother Sun, Sister Moon,* dir. Franco Zeffirelli
1986 *The Name of the Rose,* dir. Jean-Jacques Arnaud
1993 *Anchoress,* dir. Chris Newby
1993 *Francesco,* dir. Liliana Cavani
1993 *The Hour of the Pig,* dir. Leslie Megahey

12 The Transition from Gothic to Early Renaissance: 1300–1450

66 *The impulse to make the climb . . . took hold of me while I was reading Livy's History of Rome . . . and I happened upon the place where Philip of Macedon . . . climbed Mount Haemus in Thessaly . . . I could see the clouds under our feet, and the tales I had read of Athos and Olympus seemed less incredible as I myself was witnessing the very same things from a less famous mountain."*

(PETRARCH,
Familiares, BK. 4.1)

The fourteenth century was a period of sharp contrast and transition in art, literature, and music, as well as in society. In art, the Gothic style expanded in some regions and declined in others. Authors increasingly depicted everyday life, and composers wrote more secular music than before. Cities continued to grow, guilds became more powerful, and a significant merchant class developed. At the same time, however, Europe struggled with a series of catastrophes. War and famine ravaged the countryside, peasant rebellions eroded the feudal and manorial systems, banks failed, and plagues wiped out a large percentage of the population.

New challenges to the authority of the Church arose not only from theologians and scholars but also from ambitious kings. As political power became more centralized under aggressive rulers, a sense of national identity emerged. This was reinforced by the increasing use of the vernacular in literature and theater.

On the Italian peninsula, which was culturally and geographically identified with Rome, a new interest in the Classical tradition appeared in the late thirteenth century, and in the following two centuries it became the basis of a complex intellectual and artistic trend called **humanism**. With the Classical revival, Italy led Europe into the Renaissance.

The quotation that opens this chapter embodies the transition from the Middle Ages to the early Renaissance in Italy. It comes from the Italian author Francesco Petrarca (Petrarch, in English; 1304–1374). On reading Livy's History of Rome (see Chapter 7), Petrarch felt impelled to climb Mount Ventoux, in the south of France. There, exhilarated by the vista below, Petrarch recalls the past. In a single moment, the view from the French mountain reminds him of three mountains famous in antiquity: Mount Haemus (scaled by Philip of Macedon, the father of Alexander the Great), Mount Athos (the site of a Byzantine monastery), and Mount Olympos (the home of the Greek gods). Petrarch's rapturous response to nature and antiquity exemplifies the ideals of the humanist movement and heralds Renaissance culture.

TIMELINE	LATE MIDDLE AGES 1300–1450	EARLY RENAISSANCE IN ITALY 1300–1450
HISTORY AND CULTURE	Rise in urban populations Guilds become more powerful Increase in international trade Bubonic plague devastates Europe, 1348 Political power more centralized under kings Peasant revolts in France, 1356, and England, 1381 Ciompi rebellion in Italy, 1378 Hundred Years War (1337–1453) between England and France	Emergence of humanism Interest in original Latin and Greek texts Revival of Classical tradition New educational curriculum developed Italy divided into regions with courts, monarchies, and republics
RELIGION	Challenges to the Church from secular rulers, especially in France Challenges from within: William of Ockham (c. 1285–c. 1349) and Wycliffe (c. 1330–1384) Great Schism divides Church, 1378–1417 Publication of the first English-language Bible, 1388	Scholasticism persists The effects of the plague
ART	Pisano, *Adoration of the Magi*, c. 1260 Cimabue, *Enthroned Madonna and Child*, c. 1285 Traini, *Triumph of Death*, 1330s Limbourg brothers, *Très riches heures du duc de Berry*, c. 1415	Giotto, *Enthroned Madonna*, c. 1310; Arena Chapel frescoes, c. 1305–1310 Duccio, *Maestà*, 1308–1311 Lorenzetti, Palazzo Publico frescoes, 1338–1339 Andrea da Firenze, *Triumph of St. Thomas Aquinas*, c. 1365
ARCHITECTURE	Palazzo Publico, Siena, completed 1309 House of Jacques Coeur, Bourges, 1443–1451	
LITERATURE AND PHILOSOPHY	Chaucer, *Canterbury Tales*, c. 1386 Christine de Pisan, *Book of the City of Ladies*, 1405	Petrarch, *Africa*, 1343 Boccacio, *Decameron*, 1349–1351
THEATER	Folk comedy introduced into liturgical drama Wakefield Master, *The Second Shepherds' Play*, early 15th century Plays begin to be set in the present Theater becomes more independent of the Church	Mussato, *Ecerinis,* 1314
MUSIC	Development of *ars nova*, 14th century Music becomes increasingly secular Machaut (c. 1300–1377), *Mass of Notre Dame*, secular songs	Landini (c. 1325–1397), secular love-songs

THE LATE MIDDLE AGES

The late Middle Ages witnessed an increase in international trade that promoted the economies of medieval cities. At the same time, many peasants renounced farming, preferring to work for hard currency rather than in exchange for low-level subsistence. Some, recognizing that new opportunities were opening up in towns, set out to learn a trade. Larger numbers of skilled laborers increased the economic power of the guilds, which also benefited as their members demanded a role in the political life of the city.

A merchant class developed as enterprising individuals took advantage of the opportunities in trade and commerce. To facilitate the new merchant economy and to regulate the workday, clocks, which were invented in the thirteenth century, were installed in the major cities. No longer were church bells the primary markers of time.

Along with a rise in urban populations, the growth of monumental church architecture, which had begun in the Romanesque period, continued. In addition, secular building increasingly included hospitals, orphanages, and public bath houses (which required bringing in water supplies). Guildhalls and town halls also sprang up. After 1300, secular universities supplanted cathedral schools as the primary centers of higher learning, and they attracted more students to the cities. Bridges and paved roads made travel and trade easier.

But urbanization brought its own problems. Fires destroyed houses made of wood, crime was on the rise, and disease became more prevalent, especially in crowded areas. In Venice, the first public houses of prostitution opened in 1360.

Causing further disruption in the late Middle Ages, workers began staging social protests. Many demanded better pay and more political rights. In 1356, for example, French peasants revolted against excessive taxation levied on them by wealthy landowners. In Italy, the Ciompi rebellion of 1378 was the most important of several workers' revolts. Wool-workers in Florence, the Ciompi—like their counterparts in Germany and France—wanted membership in the guilds and access to guild privileges. The Ciompi were successful, and three new guilds were established for wool-workers, making them eligible for political office and improving their social status (see Box). Three years after the Ciompi rebellion, peasants in England rose up against laws that kept them bound to landowners. Indirectly, their anger was fueled by a religion that preached submission and poverty while ambitious popes sought worldly power and enriched the Church.

Society and Culture

The Wool Industry in Florence

In the fourteenth century, the most sophisticated textile production was located in Florence, in Tuscany. High-quality English wool and dyes were imported and used in the manufacture of cloth. Workers washed the wool in the Arno, the river that runs through Florence, and sent the clean wool to the countryside for carding, combing, and spinning. Carding and combing cleaned the fibers and removed knots from the threads to prepare them for spinning. The spun wool was then returned to weavers in the city. Wool was dyed in separate workshops, fulled in nearby mills, and then packaged for export.

In the thirteenth century, the spinning wheel, which had previously been used in the East, was brought to Europe. In figure **12.1**, the spindle is hand-held instead of being attached to a wheel. The woman at the lower right combs the wool, the central figure holds two cards (flat boards with sharp projections), and the third works a hand spindle. At the top, a fourth woman weaves on a loom. Patterns on the wall and floor allude to those created by cloth-makers, particularly the weavers.

12.1 *Carding, spinning, and weaving*, from Boccaccio, *Le Livre des cleres et nobles femmes*, early 15th century. Manuscript illustration, 2⅝ in. (6.6 cm) wide. British Library, London.

THE HUNDRED YEARS WAR

The late Middle Ages unfolded against the backdrop of a long and devastating war between England and France. Called the Hundred Years War, it was actually fought from 1337 to 1453. At dispute were the succession to the French throne and the control of territory and industry in northern Europe.

In 1328, the French king Charles IV died leaving no heir to the throne. The English king, Edward III (ruled 1327–1377), then fifteen years old, was the grandson of Philip IV, the Fair, of France. On the grounds of his heritage, at a time when the immediate French successors had died out, Edward claimed the French throne. But the French nobility and Church instead appointed Philip VI, a member of the Valois dynasty (to which Philip IV had belonged). Philip VI ruled from 1328 to 1350, and the Valois remained on the French throne for nearly three hundred years.

Joan of Arc

Although Joan of Arc, Jeanne d'Arc in French (1412–1431), lived in the fifteenth century, she is essentially a figure of the late Middle Ages. She was born to a peasant family in the French village of Domrémy during the Hundred Years War. As an illiterate girl of twelve, she heard voices from God instructing her to remain a virgin and rescue France from the English. This meant defending Charles VII's claim to the French throne. When she was seventeen, Joan persuaded a neighboring lord to present her to the king. At first, the king doubted that her voices were really sent by God, but his cause seemed doomed, so he was willing to try anything and agreed to equip her with armor and weapons. She rode into battle with the French troops at Orléans, giving them a new sense of national pride and inspiring them to victory. In Reims, she personally crowned Charles king.

Joan's subsequent battles were less successful, and in 1430 she was captured by the Burgundians (English allies from Burgundy, in central France), sold to the English, and handed over to the Inquisition in Rouen, in northern France. Charles did nothing to help her. The transcript of her trial has survived, showing that she was questioned about her voices, accused of heresy, witchcraft, idolatry, and transvestitism, and tortured. Condemned as a heretic, she was burned at the stake in the public square of Rouen.

Very much too late—in 1456—King Charles reviewed Joan's trial and declared her innocent. In 1920, Pope Benedict XV made Joan a saint. The appeal of her story has inspired many literary works, including Christine de Pisan's hymn (1429), George Bernard Shaw's play *Saint Joan* (1923), and several twentieth-century films.

England and France also vied for control of Flanders (modern Belgium, Holland, and part of northern France) and its profitable wool industry. Battles ravaged the countryside and mercenary soldiers looted villages. Peasants who survived the war often lost their homes and animals. Adding to the number of deaths among both the combatants and the civilians was the use of gunpowder. It had been known in China as early as the third century B.C., was perfected in the Far East by A.D. 1000, and by 1313 traders had imported large amounts of it to Europe.

As the Hundred Years War continued into the early decades of the fifteenth century, it looked as if France had lost. But unexpected help arrived in 1429 when a young peasant, Joan of Arc, rallied the dispirited French troops and defeated the English at the Battle of Orléans, a city south of Paris (see Box). The English were forced to renounce most of their claim to French land, which made France more secure. In the end, France and England consolidated their national boundaries as growing nationalist sentiments on both sides reinforced their long-standing animosity, and both countries established strong, centralized monarchies.

CONFLICT IN THE CHURCH

Challenges to the Church were another source of unrest in the late Middle Ages. In the fourteenth century, these challenges were both political and philosophical. Secular rulers, particularly the French king, objected to the political claims of the pope. In addition, two English philosophers, William of Ockham and John Wycliffe, took issue with prevailing Church thought.

THE GREAT SCHISM Boniface VIII was elected pope in 1294. Six years later, in 1300, he proclaimed a Jubilee Year (Holy Year). Thousands of pilgrims, drawn by the promise of pardon for their sins, flocked to Rome, where the spectacle of large crowds created the impression that the city, the papacy, and Boniface himself were comfortably in power. But Boniface's political ambitions threatened Philip IV, the Fair, of France, who ordered the pope's death (see Chapter 11). Philip then saw to it that Boniface's successor was a Frenchman, Clement V (papacy 1305–1314). In 1309, Clement moved the papal court from Rome to Avignon, a city in the south of modern France, which at the time belonged to the Angevin king of Naples. With the papacy now in Avignon, it was strongly influenced by France.

The popes remained at Avignon for nearly seventy years (from 1309 to 1377), a period that came to be known as the Church's "Babylonian Captivity"—a reference to the Babylonian exile of the Israelites (see Chapter 8). Finally, in 1377, the Avignon pope Gregory XI (papacy 1370–1378) returned to Rome. When Gregory died, the College of Cardinals elected an Italian pope, Urban VI (papacy 1378–1389).

Soon after his election, Urban tried to curtail the power of the cardinals (Church officials appointed by the pope). In return, the cardinals—who were mainly Frenchmen—claimed that Roman mobs had forced them to elect Urban because he was Italian. The cardinals then elected a new pope, Clement VI (papacy 1378–1397), who was French. Now there were two popes, one claiming authority from Avignon and the other from Rome, causing the division in the Church known as the Great Schism.

The popes struggled for control for the next thirty-five years, until the Avignon pope John XXIII convened the Council of Constance (1414–1418) in Switzerland at the instigation of Sigismund, who had become Holy Roman Emperor in 1411. Determined to reform the Church, combat heresy, and end the Great Schism, the council elected Martin V (papacy 1417–1431) and returned the papal court to Rome. The Avignon popes, called **antipopes**, were never legitimized in the eyes of the Roman Church, and the papacy in Rome continued to abuse its office by seeking wealth and secular power.

PHILOSOPHICAL CHALLENGES TO THE CHURCH As the Church faced external political threats, tensions increased from within. The English philosopher William of Ockham (c. 1285–c. 1349) was, like Duns Scotus (see Chapter 11), an Oxford-educated Franciscan friar, who took issue with Thomas Aquinas. Ockham denied the existence of universals except as they are constructed by the human mind. He also disagreed that a divine spark could ignite faith and an understanding of God. Nor did he accept the relationship between faith and reason that Aquinas proposed. Rather, he thought that these were completely separate.

In Ockham's view, facts could be determined only from empirical observation and should not be taken on pure faith. This idea was, of course, an attack on the unquestioned authority of the Church. At the University of Paris, Ockham openly challenged the scholastic realists. He considered their ideas needlessly complex, especially the **syllogistic** system of Aquinas, in which a formal argument is analyzed according to a major and minor premise and a conclusion that follows logically from them. He argued the merits of shaving down every issue to its simplest form, a concept known as **Ockham's razor**. Ockham's emphasis on experience was, in part, inspired by the ideas of St. Francis, and he was excommunicated for advocating the Franciscan rule of poverty at a time when the Church sought more and more wealth and power.

Another influential fourteenth-century Englishman was John Wycliffe (c. 1330–1384), who taught at Oxford University. Objecting to the rampant corruption of the Church and rejecting scholasticism, he preferred the simplicity of the Bible's message over the dialectic of theologians. Furthermore, he questioned the infallibility of the pope and denied the doctrine of transubstantiation (the belief that the wafer and wine are transformed into Christ's body and blood during Mass). The Eucharist, he argued, should be understood symbolically and spiritually, and he dismissed the Church's literal view as pure superstition.

Wycliffe was condemned, but not otherwise punished, by the Church because he was protected by the duke of Lancaster, John of Gaunt. Later he was accused of having incited the English Peasants' Revolt of 1381 and was forced to retire from teaching. Nonetheless, he continued preaching until the end of his life. When Gaunt died, Wycliffe was posthumously convicted of heresy, and his corpse was exhumed and burned. One result of Wycliffe's influence and his appeal to the common people was the publication of the first English-language Bible.

THE BLACK DEATH

By 1346, Europe had received news of a virulent plague raging in the Far East and spreading through the Middle East. The following year, ships from the East brought rats carrying infected fleas to Sicily. From there, the plague spread through mainland ports of Italy to overcrowded cities. A panicked population fled to the countryside, carrying the infection with them. The so-called Black Death would ravage Europe for the next several years (see map 12.1, p. 305).

Even before the arrival of the Black Death, parts of Europe from Spain to Scandinavia were suffering severe food shortages. A number of harvests had failed, and bad weather with little sunshine (needed for evaporation) limited salt production. Without salt, meat could not be preserved. At the worst, famine led to a few documented instances of cannibalism. Several important Italian banks failed, which caused severe economic problems. Meanwhile, the plague tore across Europe, and by the time it subsided a huge percentage of the population of Europe had died (see Box, p. 304).

Reactions to the plague vacillated between a *carpe diem* (seize the day and enjoy life) attitude and a fervent belief that penance and atonement were the only routes to salvation. In the absence of medical knowledge, the plague was attributed to astrological occurrences, polluted water, an angry God, heretics, Arabs and other foreigners, and people with deformities or leprosy. In Germany, Jews were blamed for the epidemic and thousands were massacred (figure **12.2**).

One result of the Black Death was a new interest in medicine. Another was increased religious fervor and a preoccupation with death. At the height of the plague, a belief that the dead danced on their graves to entice the living intensified. This is reflected in the popular image of the *danse macabre*, or Dance of Death, which was a feature of many fourteenth-century theatrical productions.

12.2 The burning of lepers as mass poisoners on behalf of the Jews, from *Chroniques de France ou de St. Denis*, late 14th century. Manuscript illumination, 7 in (17.8 cm) wide. British Library, London.
Even before the Black Death, Jews were accused of using lepers to poison wells owned by Christians (leprosy cannot in fact be transmitted via water). In this illustration from a French manuscript, lepers are burned at the stake as punishment for allegedly spreading the plague.

Defining Moment

Plague Devastates Europe

Plague is a great equalizer, killing rich and poor alike. Some scholars argue that the plague of 1348 altered the economic and social structures of Europe and led to the rise of cities, capitalism, and belief in individual freedom. Others argue that the arts witnessed a conservative backlash in Italy, from which art styles did not recover until around 1400. Some who survived the plague began to question traditional beliefs, and a new skeptical attitude toward the Church emerged. Some adopted a philosophy of enjoying life while there was still time. And others became fearful and more devout.

The Black Death, according to some accounts, arose in Asia by around 1346 and was brought to Europe from the Genoese trading station of Kaffa in the Crimea (on the coast of the Black Sea). Another account suggests that the Mongols were besieging Kaffa when disease broke out among their forces and compelled them to abandon the

siege. This account further says that the Mongol commander catapulted some of the plague victims into the town. As soon as the Mongols had departed, merchants who left Kaffa for Constantinople carried the plague with them. It then spread from Constantinople along the trade routes to Italy. Another version of the origins of the Black Death attributes it to an outbreak of the plague in China. In October 1347, several Italian merchant ships returned from the Black Sea, one of the key trade links to China. When the ships docked in Sicily, many of those on board were already dying.

Plague mainly affected rodents, but fleas also transmitted the disease to people, who, once infected, rapidly communicated it to others. Symptoms included high fever, vomiting, hemorrhaging, and a painful swelling (or bubo, hence the term "bubonic plague") of glands and lymph nodes. Bleeding under the skin produced spots that were red at first and then turned black (hence the name

"Black Death"). Contemporary chroniclers observed different symptoms but did not know that they were part of the same disease. A pneumonic form spread into the lungs and caused vomiting of blood. Another form, called septicemia, was caused by bacilli entering the bloodstream. A rash appeared within hours, and death occurred in a day, even before the swellings appeared. Boccaccio, in the Introduction to the *Decameron*, wrote of the devastation caused by the plague in Florence, and of the speed with which it took people to their death:

What more remains to be said, except that the cruelty of heaven (and possibly, in some measure, also that of man) was so immense and so devastating that between March and July of the year in question, what with the fury of the pestilence and the fact that so many of the sick were inadequately cared for or abandoned in their hour of need because the healthy were too terrified to approach

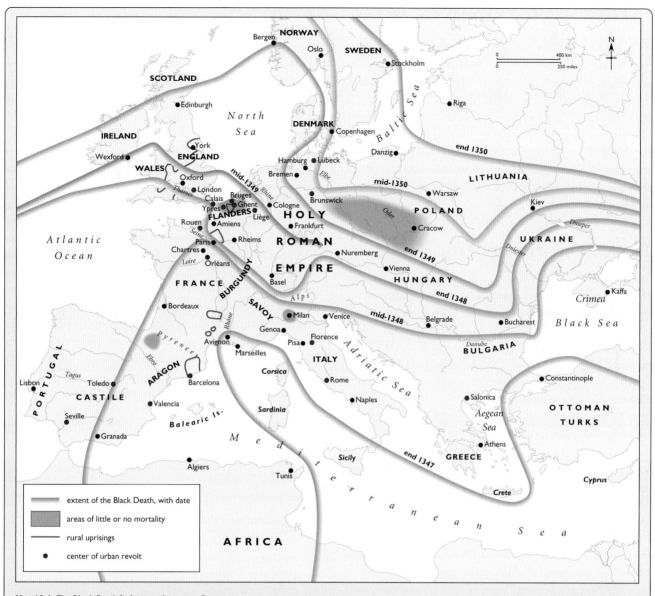

Map 12.1 The Black Death in fourteenth-century Europe.

them, it is reliably thought that over a hundred thousand human lives were extinguished within the walls of the city of Florence? Yet before this lethal catastrophe fell upon the city, it is doubtful whether anyone would have guessed it contained so many inhabitants.

Ah, how great a number of splendid palaces, fine houses, and noble dwellings, once filled with retainers, with lords and with ladies, were bereft of all who had lived there, down to the tiniest child! How numerous were the famous families, the vast estates, the notable fortunes, that were seen to be left without a rightful successor! How many gallant gentlemen, fair ladies, and sprightly youths, who would have been judged hale and hearty by

Galen, Hippocrates, and Aesculapius (to say nothing of others), having breakfasted in the morning with their kinfolk, acquaintances, and friends, supped that same evening with their ancestors in the next world!

(Boccaccio, *Decameron*, Introduction)

In the winter of 1348, the disease seemed to disappear, but only because fleas were dormant. The following spring, the plague attacked again, killing new victims. After five years 25 million people were dead—one-third of Europe's population in the fourteenth century (map **12.1**).

The death of such a large proportion of the population tore apart the existing economic and social structures. A shortage of

peasants and laborers caused wages to rise as peasants and serfs gained greater bargaining power. For the first time in history, wealthy landlords were at the mercy of those who survived and were healthy enough to work their land. Without the many architects, masons, and artisans who had been killed by the plague, cathedrals and castles remained unfinished for decades. Governments lacked officials, since priests and scholars were in short supply, ancient manuscripts were put to one side, and documents began to be written in the vernacular.

Critical Question What is cognitive dissonance? Does it take an extreme event to cause cognitive dissonance or does it often happen when ideas conflict?

LATE GOTHIC TRENDS IN ART

In art, as in society, the late Middle Ages was a period of contrasts. Gothic style in architecture continued to develop, especially in the north. In painting, several trends overlapped, reflecting the social disparity between courts and commoners. Some scholars have noted that the emerging naturalism evident, for example, in the *Vierge dorée* at Amiens (see figure 11.23), declined and did not revive for several generations. Subject matter as well as style after the Black Death conveyed both a fear of damnation and a delight in worldly luxury.

THE ICONOGRAPHY OF DEATH

Beginning around 1300, decades before the plague, a growing preoccupation with death overtook western Europe. In the Italian town of Pisa, for example, in the Camposanto, the cemetery beside the cathedral, Francesco Traini (*c.* 1321–1363) painted a huge fresco, nearly 20 by 50 feet (6.1 × 15.2 m), entitled the *Triumph of Death*. The detail in figure **12.3** shows a group of crippled figures gesturing anxiously, apparently pleading with Death for deliverance.

In the fourteenth century, a type of burial monument called a **transi tomb** developed. The lid of the transi tomb showed the deceased in a state of physical decay. The term comes from the Latin preposition *trans*, meaning "through," suggesting both "crossing over" in the sense of "dying" and the transitory nature of life on earth. Transi tombs were thus a type of *memento mori* (reminder of death).

A related image representing decay appears in the statue of *Frau Welt* (*Mrs. World*) of around 1300, in Germany (figure **12.4**). The iconography of the statue gave concrete form to fire-and-brimstone sermons warning that unrepentant souls would suffer the fires of hell, and all flesh would become food for worms. Inspired by an ancient belief that snakes are born from the human spinal cord after death, many German tombs depicted the deceased crawling with snakes and toads.

Frau Welt differs from images on transi tombs in being beautiful from the front while depicting decay and being covered with snakes and toads at the back. In this case, the traditional association of these creatures with death and the devil is also applied to the image of the deceptive woman embodied by the Greek myth of Pandora and the biblical Eve. *Frau Welt* thus exemplifies medieval misogyny. She represents both the physical corruption of human flesh and the moral corruption associated with women.

The medieval legend of the Three Quick and the Three Dead gave rise to a standard iconographic image in the fourteenth century (figure **12.5**). According to the legend, three living figures encounter three dead figures. The first dead man says that in life he was rich and handsome; the second that death is a great equalizer and God's mirror, in which the living can see their future; and the third, like the medieval *Everyman* play (see Chapter 10), urges penance and good works. Often the dead carry inscriptions warning the living: "I was once as you are, and you will be as I am now."

The manuscript illustrated here contains a poetic version of the standard text:

Vous serez commes nous sommes
d'avance mirez-vous en nous
puissance, honneur, richesse ne sont rien
à l'heure de la mort
il n'y a que les bonnes oeuvres qui comptent.

A loose translation reads:

You will be as we are
consider us mirrors of your future.
Power, honor, and wealth are as nothing
at the hour of death;
only good works count.

12.3 Francesco Traini, *Triumph of Death*, detail showing cripples and an inscription, Camposanto, Pisa, Italy, 1330s. Fresco, entire painting approx. 20 × 50 ft. (6.1 × 15.2 m).

12.4 *right and far right*
Frau Welt **(side and back),
Worms Cathedral, Germany,
c. 1300.**

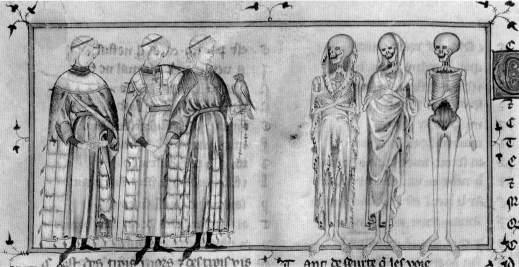

12.5 *The Three Quick and
the Three Dead*, **from the
Psalter of Maria of Brabant,
c. 1300. Bibliothèque
Nationale, Paris.**
Three living figures
confront three grinning
skeletons, two in rags and
one a mere "bag of
bones." Note that the feet
overlap the lower frame,
which is characteristic of
flattened medieval style.
But there is also some
shading in the draperies
and the skulls, reflecting
an emerging interest
in naturalism.

THE ICONOGRAPHY OF WEALTH

Among the royal courts, the late Gothic style of painting evolved into the International Gothic style, which appealed to courtly tastes and continued into the fifteenth century. Although the subject matter of International Gothic painting was often Christian, it reflected the opulence of the European courts. One of the most luxurious regional courts where International Gothic flourished was that of Jean, duc de Berry, brother of the French king, Charles V (ruled 1364–1380). Jean levied outrageously high taxes on his subjects to finance his passion

for collecting works of art, jewels, and other objects of value. His most famous commission is the Book of Hours (an illustrated prayer book) known as the *Très riches heures du duc de Berry* (*The Very Rich Hours of the Duke of Berry*). It was richly illuminated in the International Gothic style by the Limbourg brothers (active 1400–1415).

Figure **12.6** is typical of International Gothic style north of Italy. It shows the rich detail of Jean's castle, the surrounding landscape, and contains his royal emblems. The wealth reflected in the illuminations stood in stark contrast to the everyday existence of the average person. Courts, especially north of the Alps, were centers of artistic and musical patronage, but they also indulged a last gasp of medieval excess, including extravagant dress and cuisine (see Box, p. 310), in the lifestyle of the very wealthy.

To a great degree, the courts set an example of taste that was emulated by the wealthiest commoners (see Box). With the rise of international trade in the late Gothic period, some merchants amassed large fortunes as a result of their skill in business. By the fifteenth century, one such merchant in France, Jacques Coeur (*c.* 1395–1456), lived in truly luxurious surroundings (figure **12.7**).

From Bourges, an important city in the cloth trade, Jacques Coeur ran a successful international enterprise between the Middle East and western Europe. He oversaw some three hundred agents, who managed his warehouses, messengers, and a carrier pigeon service. He also owned a fleet of boats for trading and shipping in the Mediterranean. Coeur was a skilled financier, who loaned money to King Charles VII of France (ruled 1422–1461) when the Hundred Years War with England depleted the treasury. In this capacity, Coeur frequented the French court and his house reflects his taste for late Gothic International style luxury.

12.6 Limbourg brothers, *The Temptation of Christ*, from *Très riches heures du duc de Berry, c.* 1415. **Illumination on vellum, 6¾ × 4½ in. (17 × 11.4 cm). Musée Condé, Chantilly, France.**
Christ stands on a tall rock, alluding to the future Church as the "Rock of Ages." He confronts a black, winged Satan and rejects the offer of worldly wealth. The elaborate castle with its turrets, delicate crenellations (the notches along the top of the wall), and moat, belonged to the duc de Berry. The swans gliding along the stream are one of Jean's royal emblems, and, at the lower right, a lion seems to have treed a creature that is part bear and part ape. The bear was also a Berry emblem.

12.7 House of Jacques Coeur, Bourges, France, 1443–1451.

Jacques Coeur's house in Bourges, in northeastern France, is a good example of late Gothic-style domestic architecture. The entrance wall is decorated with elaborate windows and turrets. Two simulated balconies show servants depicted in relief gazing at the street below. Delicate stone tracery designs are carved on the archivolts of the double entrance, the narrower one for pedestrians and the wider one for horses. The entrance leads to a courtyard, around which were arranged the living spaces and Coeur's private chapel. Reinforcing his identification with royalty, Coeur commissioned an equestrian portrait of himself on an interior portal. He thus projected the image of his house as both his home and his castle. In 1450, after being accused of poisoning the king's mistress, however, Coeur was banished from the country.

Society and Culture

Daily Life in the House of a Prosperous Merchant

In the Middle Ages, housing was relatively rudimentary. There was little heat, windows were openings in the wall, and entire families slept together. But at the end of the thirteenth century, as wealthy merchants came in contact with the courts and began to want more creature comforts and privacy for themselves, domestic interiors improved. More bedrooms were constructed for the family as well as for the servants, fireplaces improved heating, doors were sturdier, and windows were covered with oil cloth or shutters. Instead of remaining plain stone or wood, interior walls were plastered or paneled and some were hung with tapestries, which added insulation and improved

the decor. In the absence of plumbing, people washed in portable basins, and each morning chamber pots were emptied from a window.

Merchants and their wives were generally literate, which was useful for accounting and record-keeping. Children were educated at home for a few years and then sent to school. The literate populace began buying and reading books, the favorites being romances and the chivalric tales of Roland, Arthur, and the Holy Grail. Lives of the saints, prayer books, health manuals, and cookbooks were also popular.

If the owner of the house was a merchant or craftsman, a shop and an office usually occupied the ground floor. Households were led by the husband, who was expected to

work hard to support his family. The housewife had to clean the bedchamber and make sure her husband had clean linen and clean feet. She kept the fire going without letting smoke build up in the house, cared for the children and servants, stocked what was needed to run the house, did the spinning and weaving, and entertained guests. Families who could afford it had their infants fed by wet nurses.

Husbands were permitted to beat their wives for disobedience but did not have the right to kill them. However, women could face death for infanticide or witchcraft. In addition, sumptuary laws (which determined appropriate dress) were applied more strictly to women than to men. Dressing lavishly or above one's social position was unacceptable.

Society and Culture

A Late Gothic Feast

The discussion and sample meals are based on Phyllis Pray Bober's *Art, Culture, and Cuisine*.

As the period of opulence in Gothic courts waned, rulers indulged in unrestrained displays of wealth, including lavish banquets and rich cuisine. Exotic spices, herbs, and other delicacies imported from the East were popular. Surviving cookbooks and health manuals based on ancient Greek medicine reflect increasing culinary sophistication, especially among the upper classes.

Forks were not in general circulation in the late Middle Ages, but the use of spoons replaced drinking soup directly from the bowl. Male diners no longer sliced their own meat from a communal roast; instead, carving was the function of a separate carver. Vegetables and fruit were considered good for the health. The best wines were said to come from Greece and Cyprus, and in addition to wine, the French drank cider. The English preferred mead (an alcoholic honey drink), ale, and beer. Children also drank alcohol.

A late Gothic English court banquet might look as follows: the table is set with a different tablecloth for each course. Large napkins, spoons, and knives are laid at every place. A basin of scented water is provided for washing one's hands. Married couples share a wine goblet; each spouse drinks from one side only. The same goes for soups and stews, which means that spouses have to be seated next to each other. If children are present, they are dressed up to serve, and they sound a trumpet to announce the arrival of each new dish.

Royal banquets could have from three to five main courses. In England, such feasts usually began with a roast (beef or lamb), boiled for a short time and then cooked on a spit. The meat was served with a sauce made of currants, hazelnuts, cloves, ginger, mace, cinnamon, peppercorns, salt, breadcrumbs, red wine, and vinegar. Next, to balance the heated roast, came minced and strained chicken, colored with saffron (an expensive condiment derived from the crocus), and served cold with a mixture of fruit, nuts, and cinnamon.

A capon served with a sauce made of herbs, goose fat, liver, onion, and sugar might follow, and it could be accompanied by a peas pudding pie, wholemeal breads, fritters, wines from Bordeaux, and a gingerbread house or castle, made in the manner of a Middle Eastern honey cake.

Other popular roasted dishes were salmon and venison. Salmon was served with the medieval version of potato chips (*cryspes*), which were made of flour, egg whites, and yeast deep-fried in fat. Other accompaniments were salad (with oil and vinegar, salt, onion, garlic, shallots, fennel, and herbs), almond custard, pears in syrup, dried fruits, and quail pie. Venison roasts were served with currant jelly and red wine vinegar sauce.

A particularly impressive course was the cockentrice, the front half of a capon attached to the rear of a piglet and served as if it were a single species. Figure **12.8** illustrates the custom of "endoring" meats and fowl—that is, reconstituting them with their skin and feathers after they have been cooked. The feet and beaks were usually gilded. Such dishes were designed to arouse the admiration of the diners as well as to whet their appetites.

Banquets usually concluded with hot or cold spiced wine, named Hippocras, after the Greek physician Hippocrates (see Chapter 6), who believed that certain foods were necessary to balance the body's humors.

Of course, a Gothic feast was less pleasurable to a creature on the menu. Here is the "Minstrel's Song of the Swan," an example of medieval irony illustrating the point of view of the cooked bird:

Once I was white as snow
by far the fairest high and low
Now I'm darker than a crow.

REFRAIN: Alas, alack, I am black,
to repeat burned to a crisp.

Once I swam upon a lake
all my beauty wide awake
I was a pretty swan.

On the water I should lie
bare below the airy sky
Not spiced with peppercorn.

How the searing fire burns
as the spit turns and turns
So to table I must go.

Laid out on a silver platter
I liked flying high much better
than the teeth of hungry eaters.

12.8 *Presenting the Peacock*, detail of miniature in the *Histoire du Grand Alexandre* (*The Romance of Alexander the Great*), late 14th century. Illumination on parchment. Musée du Petit Palais, Paris.

THEATER IN THE FOURTEENTH CENTURY

Liturgical drama continued to be performed in the fourteenth century, but the weakened position of the Church caused by the Schism, as well as by the political and philosophical challenges to its power, led to some major new developments. Most importantly, folk comedy was introduced and mixed with the more pious message of a play. This can be seen in the best-known mystery play of the period, *The Second Shepherds' Play*, which is attributed to the Wakefield Master and was performed in England in the early 1400s. The play is divided into two parts. In the first, a scoundrel steals a sheep. When the shepherds discover a sheep in the thief's house, his wife claims it is her own infant. The shepherds bring gifts to the child, but soon realize that it is actually their stolen sheep. They retaliate by swaddling the thief in a blanket and hurling him back and forth between them. In the second part of the play, an angel appears to the shepherds and announces the birth of Christ.

The slapstick humor in the first part of the play engages the audience; the second part leaves the audience with the uplifting message that Christ is born. The two parts of the play are linked by the simple motifs of sheep and shepherds, both of which can allude to Christ. Christ is at once a sacrificial lamb and the shepherd of a flock, giving the play a symbolic typological character. The opening farce prefigures the more serious second part, thereby combining popular drama with liturgical drama.

Comic scenes were also incorporated into Passion plays. In addition, choral segments called *laude* ("praises") were integrated into the narrative. Thus, even the tragic events leading to Christ's death might now include music and humor.

A second development in late medieval theater was setting plays in the present. This technique encouraged viewers to identify with the time and place of the story. In *The Second Shepherds' Play*, for example, shepherds and sheep were familiar parts of village life, and most people had, at some time, come across a scoundrel or a thief.

In a third development, the idea that a play could be an entertainment independent of the Church gained acceptance. Even in miracle plays celebrating the Feast of Corpus Christi ("body of Christ," held in honor of the Eucharist) there was more community participation than before. For example, processions of guild members carried the Host (the wafer representing the body of Christ) through the city. In addition, as lay people became involved in theater, secular drama began to evolve.

With the increase in the use of the vernacular, Latin declined as the primary language of theater, including liturgical drama. This shift to everyday speech led to a greater use of spoken dialogue (Latin had been chanted). Laymen who did not speak Latin could now participate in liturgical as well as secular plays. Also, by virtue of the vernacular, national differences began to infiltrate theater, and individual plays started to reflect the culture of the language in which they were written.

Among the few surviving records of how plays were performed in the medieval period is a director's scroll listing actors' cues and stage directions from a play in fourteenth-century Germany. Elaborate portable staging devices were moved from town to town, assembled in the public square, and dismantled at the end of the performance. Scenery was designed in individual units to accompany specific scenes and could be reused from one play to another.

MUSIC

Music continued to play a prominent role in Christian liturgy, but, as in theater, the most important late medieval innovations lay in secularization. In England, for example, a secular song that dates to around 1250, "Sumer is icumen in" ("Summer is a-coming in"), has survived:

> Sumer is icumen in,
> Lhude sing cucu,
> Groweth sed and bloweth med,
> And springth the wde nu.
> Sing cucu.

This brief text is significant because its subject is nature rather than liturgy. Also, it was written in English instead of Latin and is the earliest known polyphonic song for six voices. The words are sung in a **round**, a form in which each voice enters in turn with the same music after the previous one has sung several measures.

ARS NOVA

Ars nova, literally "new art," is the term used to describe the new, more secular musical style of fourteenth-century music. The term comes from a treatise of the same name, written around 1322 by the French composer, poet, and theorist Philippe de Vitry (1291–1361). One innovation described both in *Ars nova* and in another treatise of around 1330, *Ars novae musicae (The Art of New Music)*, is dividing a beat into two, rather than three. This new rhythmic structure was a departure from the triple division preferred by the Church. De Vitry also codified recent developments in notation.

The leading composer of *ars nova* was Guillaume de Machaut (c. 1300–1377), who was an ordained priest, a politician, and a poet as well as a musician. He traveled widely in France and Bohemia, working for the Church and noble patrons, including King John of Bohemia and Jean, duc de Berry. Eventually Machaut became canon of Reims Cathedral in northern France.

Machaut's music reflects the prevailing contemporary taste for secular compositions and the new interest in nature. In addition to traditional motets and early medieval lays, Machaut composed romantic ballads for three voices and wrote rounds, love songs, and drinking songs, which were enormously popular with courtly audiences.

Machaut's compositions illustrate an important feature of *ars nova*—namely, the attempt to create a formal structure. In place of the loose, open-ended, meandering chants or repetitive melodies of earlier styles, *ars nova* composers wrote fixed song-like pieces. One technique for achieving a more unified composition was the use of repeated rhythmic patterns, or **isorhythms**. Machaut's *Messe de Notre Dame* (*Mass of Our Lady*) shows careful attention to formal unity. It was written for the Ordinary of the Mass (the part of the Mass that is unchanging; see Box). It is polyphonic, written for four voices, and thematically cohesive. In general, Machaut's polyphony, with its greater use of thirds, has a soft, warm sound, which is more pleasing to the modern ear than the earlier, austere organum styles.

Society and Culture

The Ordinary of the Mass

The Ordinary of the Mass consists of the following sections:

1. Kyrie eleison, which translates as "Lord have mercy on us. Christ have mercy on us."
2. Gloria, which is a hymn praising God and Christ.
3. Credo, which means "I believe"; the words of the creed, or belief statement of the Church, follow.
4. Sanctus and Benedictus, which are based on praise in Isaiah 6:3 and Psalm 118:26, respectively.
5. Agnus Dei, meaning "Lamb of God," which is sung at the opening of communion.

Musical instruments used in the fourteenth century included strings, percussion, and wind, as shown in figure 12.9. The two women at the top play a lute (on the right) and a viol (on the left). The lower figures, from left to right, play bagpipes, drums, and trumpets. In the center, flanked by a tambourine-player on the left and a clapper-player on the right, is the personification of Music herself. She plays a hand-held organ and, like King Solomon, sits on a lion throne. Above the figure of Music, in a round frame, is Solomon's father, King David, who plays a psaltery (a type of harp). By placing David in a separate frame, the artist removes him in time and space from the contemporary figures on the page. David also serves as a reminder of the tradition that he introduced music into Jewish religious services.

LITERATURE IN ENGLAND AND FRANCE

As with music, fourteenth-century literature in England and France became increasingly secular. The greatest author in England, Geoffrey Chaucer, depicted characters drawn from everyday life. And in France, the Italian-born Christine de Pisan wrote seriously about women in a way that reflected the Classical tradition and has been seen as a forerunner of feminism.

12.9 *Music and Her Attendants*, from Boethius, *De arithmetica*, 14th century. Manuscript illumination. Biblioteca Nazionale, Naples.

GEOFFREY CHAUCER

Geoffrey Chaucer (c. 1342–1400) grew up in London, where his father, John Chaucer, was a vintner who bought wine for King Edward III (ruled 1327–1377). Through his connections, John arranged for his son to become a page at court. In 1359, Geoffrey fought with Edward's troops against the French and was captured and ransomed (with the king's help) the following year. He married, had a family, and traveled around Europe in the king's service.

Chaucer read widely in the Classics and was familiar with recent Italian authors, including Dante. A prolific writer, he began his classic work, *The Canterbury Tales*, around 1386 when he moved to Kent (the county in which Canterbury is located) to serve in parliament. He was the first commoner to be buried in London's Westminster Abbey.

Chaucer sets *The Canterbury Tales* in 1386 and uses the context of a pilgrimage to examine life in medieval England. Each character represents a particular social class or profession and as such is a window into society. The work begins in the spring and the opening lines, like "Sumer is icumen in" and Petrarch's account of climbing Mount Ventoux, exemplify the emerging interest in nature:

> When in April the sweet showers fall
> And pierce the drought of March to the root, and all
> The veins are bathed in liquor of such power
> As brings about the engendering of the flower . . .
>
> (Prologue, lines 1–4)

Chaucer is about to embark on a pilgrimage when a group of twenty-nine "sundry folk" arrives at the Tabard Inn where he is staying in Southwark, by the River Thames. Their destination is Canterbury and the relics of Thomas à Becket (see Chapter 10). Each pilgrim recounts a tale that reveals the character and status of the teller. Thus "The Knight's Tale" is a chivalric romance, the Pardoner (a cleric who pardons people's sins for money) tells an exemplary story, and the Parson sermonizes. The Miller (one who grinds grain into flour) and the Reeve (an officer on a medieval English manor) are exuberantly bawdy. The Prioress is inspired by legends of the saints, and the Wife of Bath (a Roman town in England) exposes social hypocrisy.

These people are not, however, entirely stock characters. They have well-rounded personalities with good and bad qualities. Chaucer makes this clear as he introduces each one in the Prologue. He also takes the opportunity to criticize hypocrisy and corruption in the Church. The Nun Prioress, for example, appears dainty, pious, and well-mannered, but under her habit she wears a necklace and a gold brooch inscribed with the words *Amor vincit omnia* ("Love conquers all"). The Monk adorns his robe with fur and a gold clasp and eats and drinks to excess:

> I saw his sleeves were garnished at the hand
> With fine grey fur, the finest in the land,
> And on his hood, to fasten it at his chin
> He had a wrought-gold cunningly fashioned pin;
> Into a lover's knot it seemed to pass.
> His head was bald and shone like looking-glass;
> So did his face, as if it had been greased.
> He was a fat and personable priest.
>
> (Prologue, lines 193–200)

The Friar is charming but corrupt, a tippler and a womanizer who prefers the material benefits of wealth to the spiritual rewards of caring for the sick and the poor:

> He knew the taverns well in every town
> And every innkeeper and barmaid too
> Better than lepers, beggars and that crew,
> For in so eminent a man as he
> It was not fitting with the dignity
> Of his position, dealing with a scum
> Of wretched lepers; nothing good can come
> Of commerce with such slum-and-gutter dwellers,
> But only with the rich and victual-sellers.
>
> (Prologue, lines 240–248)

Chaucer uses humor and a vivid sense of irony to expose human foibles. A good example is the Wife of Bath. She has made three pilgrimages to Jerusalem, but has been widowed five times because of her habit of marrying old men for their money. Chaucer describes her unappealing appearance and her seductive ways: "Her hose were of the finest scarlet red." She had "gap-teeth," "large hips," and a red face, "And knew the remedies for love's mischances,/An art in which she knew the oldest dances . . ." (Prologue, lines 475–476).

In the end, Chaucer completed only twenty-three tales. All are rooted in medieval society and set in the religious context of a pilgrimage, but they are down-to-earth rather than romantic or chivalric. Chaucer's women are not idealized, his men are not heroic, and his nuns and priests are corrupt. He wrote in the vernacular, in a local London dialect (now called Middle English) from which modern English evolved. The following, which can be compared with the first quotation in this section, are the first four lines of the Prologue in the original:

> Whan that Aprille with his shoures sote
> The droghte of Marche hath perced to the rote,
> And bathed every veyne in swich licour,
> Of which vertu engendred is the flour . . .
>
> (Prologue, lines 1–4)

READING SELECTION

Chaucer, *The Canterbury Tales*, Prologue, PWC2-324-B

12.10 *Christine de Pisan presenting
her poems to Queen Isabel,
c. 1410–1415. Manuscript
illumination, 7 in. (17.7 cm) wide.
British Library, London.*
The setting is an intimate interior
inhabited by women. Christine
kneels before Isabel and presents
her with a large book of poems,
implying that both are literate. The
room is filled with rich, royal details.
Patterns of gold fleurs-de-lis
(emblems of French royalty) are
embroidered in the blue wall
hanging, the women wear the latest
fashion, and the ceiling is gilded.
On the back wall, an open window
shows the type of small panes of
glass used in the Middle Ages. One
dog sleeps at the foot of the bed
and another sits by Isabel. The
elaborate, delicate detail of this
manuscript reflects the wealth and
luxury of International Gothic style
that also characterized the
illuminations of the Limbourg
brothers (see figure 12.6).

CHRISTINE DE PISAN

Christine de Pisan (1364–*c.* 1430) was a scholar and poet who was born in Venice. When her father was appointed astrologer and physician to Charles V of France (ruled 1364–1380), she accompanied him to the court. There she learned to write and to read Latin. She married a court notary when she was fifteen, and, when he died, she wrote to support their three children. She published a world history of women from antiquity to the fourteenth century (1404), a defense of women against misogyny, and a poem about Joan of Arc. Between 1399 and 1415 she wrote fifteen books, including a history of Charles VII and a treatise on weaponry. Among her best-known works is the *Cité des dames* (*Book of the City of Ladies*) (1405), a history of powerful and virtuous women (figure **12.10**).

Christine de Pisan was very much a figure of the late Middle Ages. To a degree, she accepted the traditional role of the woman, instructing women how to advise their husbands in business and how to be loving enough to keep them at home. She recommended that wives focus on the household, treat their husbands well, and avoid wasting money. At the same time, however, she herself was quite independent, well educated, and aware of the benefits of literacy. Without them, she could not have supported her family by writing. Furthermore, she cited as models examples of educated women and powerful goddesses of antiquity. In so doing, she exhibited intellectual affinities with the new humanist developments that emerged in Italy at the turn of the fourteenth century.

READING SELECTION
Christine de Pisan, *Book of the City of Ladies*, refuting ideas of ancient authors alleging the inferiority of women, PWC2-190

HUMANISM IN ITALY

Humanism was an intellectual and cultural movement that began in Italy in the late thirteenth century, and was manifested in an interest, first, in original Latin and, later, in Greek texts. In Padua, in northeastern Italy, a group of lawyers started to examine Roman law. They read Cicero, the great Roman orator, and studied his summation courtroom speeches. Around the same time, also in Padua, the plays of the Roman Stoic philosopher Seneca were revived. The fascination with antiquity grew and spread, so that by the early fourteenth century a few intellectuals were beginning to build libraries of Classical texts. The texts they sought were not the Arabic translations and commentaries that had been carried to Europe in the Middle Ages. Rather, the humanists set out to rediscover Greek and Roman authors in their original form. In addition to searching for the great Classics in law and literature, humanists collected works of philosophy, history, biography, and autobiography.

Reading the Classical texts in the original languages was an aspect of the new interest in chronological, rather than liturgical, time and in understanding human motivation. Humanity and its place in nature became the focus of inquiry, as it had been in ancient Greece. Intellectuals turned from Aristotle to Plato and revitalized the intellectual spirit by opening up the fixed dialectic of scholasticism. The rediscovery of Plato's dialogues, with Socrates as the spokesman, sparked an interest in the human mind. Stepping back from the medieval emphasis on faith, humanists (who were usually devout Christians) sought knowledge through experience. Eventually, this new view of humanity led to a spirit of exploration in science, medicine, mathematics, philosophy, and geography.

The Byzantine and Gothic styles were rejected sooner in Italy than in the rest of western Europe. Humanist artists began to study Roman architecture and sculpture and revived the Classical approach to human form. By the beginning of the fifteenth century, wealthy collectors were sending agents to Greece to buy original Greek sculpture and Classical Greek manuscripts.

Despite the focus on antiquity, however, aspects of Byzantine and Gothic style continued to appeal to those of conservative taste. The Dominicans, for example, preferred more decorative artists who emphasized mysticism and, following St. Dominic, the authority of the Church hierarchy. The Franciscan Order, in contrast, tended to favor monumental artists who were interested in humanity and the natural world. This was consistent with the teachings of St. Francis and his devotion to nature.

In education, a new curriculum developed as humanism evolved. Classical as well as Christian texts supplemented Alcuin's more limited early medieval *trivium* and *quadrivium* (see Chapter 10). The idea that women should be educated and literate gained credence from the early fourteenth century, and in the most enlightened humanist schools of the fifteenth century, girls were educated along with boys (see Chapter 13).

Politically, fourteenth-century Italy was not the unified nation it is today (see map **12.2**). Some regions were governed by princely and ducal courts, others were monarchies, and a few were republican communes with guild members participating in self-rule. The last of these, modeled on the Roman Republic, was the system of choice for the humanists. Among the main centers of humanism were Padua (the site of a distinguished university founded in 1222), Florence (whose *studium*—university—had a chair of Greek studies by 1390), and Naples and Rome (where ancient ruins were most in evidence). Siena was also an important artistic and theological

Map 12.2 Fourteenth-century Italy.

center in the fourteenth century. But as a city dedicated to the cult of the Virgin, Siena adhered more closely to Byzantine style in the visual arts.

LITERATURE AND MUSIC

As the humanist revival developed in Padua, dramatists began writing plays inspired by Roman theater. In 1314, for example, the author Albertino Mussato (1261–1329) produced *Ecerinis*, a tragedy in the style of Seneca (see Chapter 7). The subject, however, was not Roman; it was the story of a tyrant, Ezzelino da Romano, who had ruled Padua. Mussato, inspired by the humanist preference for republicanism, used the play to warn against the dangers of tyranny. Later, in imitation of an ancient Roman ceremony, Mussato was crowned poet laureate of Padua.

In music, the late medieval trend toward secularization continued. The leading Italian musician of the fourteenth century was Francesco Landini (*c.* 1325–1397). Although he was blind, he excelled as a poet, composer, and performer on the lute, organ, and flute. Most of Landini's compositions were *ballate*—that is, secular love-songs in two or three parts, which could be rendered vocally or instrumentally. They are distinguished for their suave-sounding harmonies, which anticipate the chord-based, "common-practice" tonal system of later periods.

PETRARCH AND BOCCACCIO Dante, as we have seen, was a man of the Middle Ages. He created an *Inferno* that mirrored the scholastic hierarchy and the soul's journey from sin to salvation. At the same time, Dante chose as his guide the Roman poet Virgil; both convey a sharp sense of history and politics as they travel through the circles of hell. Dante is thus a pivotal figure, at once immersed in medieval culture and an admirer of his pagan predecessor who was denied salvation by the Church.

The first thoroughly humanist literary giant was Petrarch (1304–1374). He was born in the central Italian town of Arezzo but lived primarily in Avignon, in the south of France. Although he studied law, he settled on a career as a writer and amassed a large private library of Classical manuscripts. He was a prolific writer, whose works include poetry, prose, songs, and letters to dead authors such as Seneca, Cicero, Virgil, and Homer. Although he himself never learned Greek, he recommended that others do so. In 1341, he was crowned poet laureate in Rome.

As Dante had his Beatrice, so Petrarch had his Laura. This was his pseudonym for a married woman with whom he fell in love at a glance. They never met, and Laura died of the plague in 1348. She was the object of most of Petrarch's love poetry, mainly sonnets. Each Petrarchan sonnet is composed of fourteen lines, beginning with an eight-line octave followed by a six-line sestet. The octave poses a question and describes a situation, or expresses a set of feelings, and the sestet offers a comment or conclusion. The main themes are female perfection and the tortures of love.

In the following sonnet, Petrarch questions his intensely conflicted reaction to love and its power over him. For Petrarch, love is a series of apparent contradictions (**oxymorons**)—a living death, a sweet torment—and he the lover is adrift at sea, buffeted by the wind, wise and foolish, hot and cold:

> If it's not love, then what is it I feel:
> but if it's love, by God, what is this thing?
> If good, why then the bitter mortal sting?
> If bad, then why is every torment sweet?
>
> If I burn willingly, why weep and grieve?
> And if against my will, what good lamenting?
> O living death, O pleasurable harm,
> how can you rule me if I not consent?
>
> > [end of octave]
>
> And if I do consent, it's wrong to grieve.
> Caught in contrasting winds in a frail boat
> on the high seas I am without a helm,
>
> so light of wisdom, so laden of error,
> that I myself do not know what I want,
> and shiver in midsummer, burn in winter.
>
> > [end of sestet]
>
> (Petrarch, "If it's not love, then what is it I feel?")

Compared with Dante's mystical account of Beatrice in paradise, Petrarch's sonnet describes love on a more human level. He is unsure, ambivalent, and confused, echoing the psychological exploration of love that characterizes his poetry.

Petrarch's humanism is also evident in his passionate response to nature. The quotation that opens this chapter is taken from an allegorical letter that he wrote in 1336, describing his ascent of Mount Ventoux after reading Livy. Petrarch's account of breathing the pure air, surveying the vast expanse of landscape, and watching the clouds below him inspired wealthy Italians to build country villas giving onto distant scenic views.

In 1343 Petrarch completed a draft of his epic poem *Africa*. Inspired by Homer and Virgil, *Africa*, like the *Iliad*, the *Odyssey*, and the *Aeneid*, opens with an invocation of the Muse. Petrarch asks for inspiration in telling the story of a great cultural hero.

> Muse, you will tell me of the man renowned
> for his great deeds, redoubtable in war,
> on whom first noble Africa, subdued
> by Roman arms, bestowed a lasting name.
>
> (Petrarch, *Africa*, lines 1–4)

The hero of the epic is Scipio Africanus the Elder, who defeated Hannibal in the Second Punic War between Rome and Carthage (see Chapter 7). Of two possible heroes, Julius Caesar and Scipio, Petrarch chose the more republican-minded Scipio over the more tyrannical Caesar. Petrarch's Scipio combines the characteristics of a Christian saint and a triumphant Roman general.

Petrarch drew on Livy for historical background and on Virgil for epic style, thus departing from literary practice for medieval romances, *chansons de geste*, and chivalric legends.

Stylistically, *Africa* exhibits the humanist interest in models and ideas drawn from Classical antiquity. It is filled with allusions to Roman myth and history, and it is also meant to demonstrate the virtues of the Roman Republic.

Reading Livy inspired Petrarch to write *De viribus illustribus* (*On Famous Men*), which heralded another feature of Renaissance humanism—namely, the interest in fame. In the Middle Ages, immortality was conceived of mainly in spiritual terms, but humanists strove for worldly fame and the promise that their achievements would live on in the cultural memory. Petrarch describes his own moral struggle between earthly ambition and spirituality in his autobiographical *Letters of Old Age*.

READING SELECTION
Petrarch, *Canzoniere*, lyric poetry, PWC3-073-C

Petrarch's younger contemporary and friend Giovanni Boccaccio (1313–1375) shared his humanist philosophy and credited Petrarch with having restored ancient Rome to its rightful place in the heritage of Italy. He also took Petrarch's advice and learned Greek. Boccaccio was the illegitimate son of a Florentine banker employed by the prominent Bardi bank and an unknown mother. His father later married a distant relative of Dante's Beatrice Portinari.

When Boccaccio was thirteen, his father was transferred to the Naples branch of the bank. At the time, Naples was one of the preeminent intellectual centers of Europe; an interest in classicism had emerged some years previously at the court of Holy Roman Emperor Frederick II (ruled 1212–1250). In the early fourteenth century, the king of Naples was Robert the Wise (ruled 1309–1343), a serious patron of the arts. Boccaccio worked alongside his father at the bank in Naples where,

though he disliked the job, he met people from all walks of life. Later he drew on them to create the characters in his stories.

Boccaccio's most famous work is the *Decameron*, written in the vernacular and set at the time of the Black Death. Ten (whence the title *Deca*, meaning "ten") young people depart for the countryside to escape the plague. They pass the time telling stories that include vivid, satirical descriptions of contemporary society and the Church. In particular, the stories condemn the Inquisition and discrimination against women. For Boccaccio, nature meant human nature as well as landscape, and his tales thus reflect various psychological reactions to the Black Death.

READING SELECTION
Boccaccio, *Decameron*: Day 1, Story 6, criticizing the Inquisition in Rome, PWC3-103; Day 3, Story 1, on the custom of placing young women in convents against their will, PWC3-104

THE VISUAL ARTS

The visual arts, like literature, were invigorated by humanism. For example, the sculpture of Nicola Pisano (*c.* 1220/1225–*c.* 1284) demonstrates the developing taste for naturalism (figure **12.11**), although Gothic elements persist. Pisano's name indicates that he spent most of his career in Pisa, but he was originally from the south of Italy, where he came into contact with Classical taste at the court of Naples. In painting, the shift away from medieval style is illustrated by a comparison of two altarpieces depicting the Virgin and Christ—one by Cimabue and the other by Giotto.

12.11 Nicola Pisano, *Adoration of the Magi*, baptistery pulpit, Pisa, *c.* 1260. Marble, approx. 34 in. (86.4 cm) high.
Pisano retains Gothic patterning in the beards, the horses' manes, and the angel's wings, but the draperies now define the organic structures of the body. Mary, who resembles a Roman matron more than a medieval Queen of Heaven, occupies a believable three-dimensional space. Christ is himself a believable infant, with his pudgy proportions and eagerness to receive the king's gift. He sits firmly on his mother's lap as she rests her hand protectively on his shoulder. Evidence of medieval style can still be seen in the unnatural scale of the horses compared with the human figures and in the angular drapery folds.

PAINTING: CIMABUE AND GIOTTO The last great Byzantine painter in Italy was Cenni di Pepi, known as Cimabue (*c.* 1240–*c.* 1302). His monumental *Enthroned Madonna and Child* of around 1285 was commissioned for the high altar of the church of Santa Trinità in Florence (figure **12.12**). Its large size and imposing grandeur convey the power of Byzantine imagery. The Virgin and Christ are seated on a jeweled throne held aloft by eight angels in a flattened gold space. Below the throne, four Hebrew figures—Abraham, David, Jeremiah, and Isaiah—are shown with scrolls signifying prophecy. The message here, as on the central west portal of Chartres Cathedral (see figure 11.21), is that the new era ushered in with the birth of Christ rests on the foundation of the Old Testament. Christ and *his* message are thus seen typologically as the fulfillment of prophecy.

The predominance of gold, not only in the background and on the throne, but also in the drapery folds, is characteristic of Byzantine style. In addition, the proportions of Christ are more adult than baby like. He thus retains the medieval character of a miraculous infant, small in size but endowed with adult form and intelligence.

Cimabue, and his place in the history of Italian art, inspired the following lines in the eleventh *canto* of Dante's *Purgatorio*:

> O empty glory of human powers! How short the time
> its green endures at its peak, if it be not
> overtaken by the crude ages! Cimabue thought to hold
> the field in painting, and now Giotto has the cry,
> so that the fame of the former is obscured.

(Dante, *Purgatorio*, Canto XI, lines 91–95)

In this passage, Dante laments the fact that earthly fame is short-lived. He notes that Cimabue's reputation as the greatest living painter in Italy was soon overshadowed by that of his successor, Giotto di Bondone (*c.* 1266–1337). A comparison of Giotto's *Enthroned Madonna* of around 1310 with Cimabue's makes clear why Dante thinks Giotto is the greater artist (figure **12.13**). Similar though these altarpieces are in serving a devotional purpose, a careful viewing of Giotto's reveals several innovations that struck his contemporaries—and future art historians—as revolutionary.

Giotto has retained the gold background characteristic of Byzantine altarpieces, and the throne, with its pointed arches and tracery, is Gothic in style. However, in comparison with Cimabue's work, Giotto represents space in a more three-dimensional way, and the throne does not appear to move upward. Giotto's Christ is more naturally baby-like than Cimabue's. He sits solidly on his mother's lap, and she holds him rather than presenting him to the viewer, as Cimabue's Virgin does. Giotto's Christ is nevertheless a miraculous baby, wise beyond his years, for he carries a scroll and blesses the faithful. But his proportions are more naturalistic, and rolls of baby fat are visible around his neck and wrists.

12.12 Cimabue, *Enthroned Madonna and Child*, *c.* 1285. Tempera on panel, 12 ft. 7 in. × 7 ft. 4 in. (3.84 × 2.24 m). Galleria degli Uffizi, Florence.
The favorite medium for altarpieces was tempera on wood panel. Tempera paint is a mixture of pigments with water thickened with egg yolk. The technique was painstaking, requiring months of preparation. First the wood (usually poplar) had to be cut, reinforced with glue, sized to prevent warping, and sanded. The artist then drew in, and inked, the outlines of the image. Gold leaf was applied to background areas, halos, and other decorative details, and then polished. When the picture had been completely painted, it was left to dry. Once dry, the surface was varnished.

The Virgin, as in Nicola Pisano's relief (see figure 12.11), is a solid, matronly figure. Her drapery is heavy, and it defines her form by a new technique of shading called "chiaroscuro" (literally "light-dark"). Chiaroscuro makes form visible, as it is in nature, by gradations in light and dark rather than through outlining (there are no outlines in nature), as in Byzantine style. Looking closely at the folds of Mary's white robe, one can see that they curve as if she is shifting her torso to one side, which suggests the contrapposto pose of antiquity (see Chapter 5). Like the more natural depiction of light and dark, the weightier figures reflect the force of gravity. The depiction of three-dimensional space and the use of contrapposto indicate a revival of Classical naturalism. Giotto thus pierced the picture plane, which had been two-dimensional for nearly the first thousand years of Christian style. He conceived of a painting not as a flat devotional space, but as a stage on which human characters perform and human as well as divine events unfold.

PETRARCH AND BOCCACCIO ON GIOTTO In his last will and testament, Petrarch proudly bequeathed a painting of the Virgin and Christ by Giotto to his patron, Francesco da Carrara. Petrarch wrote that although the ignorant (unenlightened) may not understand its beauty, "masters of the art will marvel at it." In other words, Petrarch applies a light–dark metaphor to intelligence and ignorance while also alluding to Giotto's use of chiaroscuro.

Boccaccio echoes these sentiments in the sixth story of the *Decameron*. Citing the Western theme of the ugly genius (such as Socrates), he writes: "Nature has frequently planted astonishing genius in men of monstrously ugly appearance." Giotto, who was known for his ugliness, was, according to Boccaccio,

> a man of such outstanding genius that there was nothing in the whole of creation that he could not depict with his stylus, pen, or brush . . . Hence, by virtue of the fact that he brought back to light an art which had been buried for centuries beneath the blunders of those who, in their paintings, aimed to bring visual delight to the ignorant rather than intellectual satisfaction to the wise, his work may justly be regarded as a shining monument to the glory of Florence.
>
> (Boccaccio, *Decameron*, 6.5)

GIOTTO'S NARRATIVE PAINTING Giotto's most famous and best-preserved fresco cycle is located on the walls of the Arena Chapel in Padua. It testifies to his reputation for returning naturalism to painting. The chapel was commissioned by Enrico Scrovegni, the richest man in Padua, whose father Dante had confined to hell for the sin of usury. Enrico financed the chapel as a means of atonement and to ensure his own entry into heaven.

12.13 Giotto di Bondone, *Enthroned Madonna (Ognissanti Madonna)*, *c.* 1310. Tempera on panel, 10 ft. 8 in. × 6 ft. 8¼ in. (3.25 × 2.03 m). Galleria degli Uffizi, Florence.
Giotto was a Florentine, although his reputation as the greatest living artist took him to many Italian cities. He was also a skilled businessman, earning money on the side from real estate. The father of some six children, Giotto was one of the first Christian artists to portray children as they look and behave in the real world.

Figure **12.14** shows the chancel arch and part of the side walls as seen on entering the chapel. The barrel-vaulted ceiling is painted to resemble a star-studded blue sky. On the side walls, the top row of narrative scenes portrays the lives of Mary and her parents (Anna and Joachim), and the life of Christ is depicted in the second and third rows. The scenes on the chancel arch are like the prologue of a play: they announce the beginning of the narrative and foreshadow future events.

Above the opening of the arch, God is shown summoning the host of heaven, including Gabriel, and setting in motion the story of Christ. On either side of the arch opening is the *Annunciation*, split into two panels, with Gabriel at the left and Mary at the right. Below the *Annunciation*, at the right, is the *Visitation* (when Mary, who is three months pregnant, visits her cousin Elizabeth, who is six months pregnant); and the *Betrayal of Judas* is at the left. The former scenes foreshadow the

12.14 Giotto, Arena Chapel, looking toward the chancel arch, Padua, Italy, c. 1305–1310. Frescoes.

births of Christ and John the Baptist and the latter shows Judas receiving a bag of silver to betray Christ. The remainder of the narrative unfolds horizontally on the side walls in chronological sequence.

12.15 Giotto, *Last Judgment*, Arena Chapel, Padua, *c.* 1305–1310. Fresco.
To the left of the Cross below Christ, the penitent figure of Enrico Scrovegni presents a model of the chapel to three holy figures. Including the patron in a work he financed would become standard practice in Renaissance art. Notice as evidence of Giotto's wit that a little soul is trying to hide behind the Cross and sneak from hell over to the side of the saved. Evidence of Giotto's taste for illusionism appears in the painted white cloak of the monk assisting Scrovegni. It seems to overlap the doorway arch as if actually falling out of the fresco into the space of the viewer.

12.16 Giotto, *St. Francis rejecting his father's wealth*, Bardi Chapel, Church of Santa Croce, Florence, *c.* 1318. Fresco.
The preferred technique for painting walls in the Renaissance was fresco, in which waterpaint is applied to damp lime plaster. It is a durable technique requiring speed and skill. Because plaster dries within twenty-four hours, the artist has to prepare only that part of the wall to be covered in one day. A layer of lime and sand is applied, a coat of plaster is added, and then the surface is painted. As the plaster dries, the paint is absorbed and bonds with the wall.

Turning to leave the chapel, viewers confront the huge *Last Judgment* on the entrance wall (figure **12.15**). This is Giotto's vision of the end of time, which corresponds to the conclusion of the viewer's visit to the chapel. Its structure follows the conventional arrangement of the Last Judgment in Western art. Christ occupies a central position in heaven, surrounded on either side by apostles and angels. In the lower section to the right of Christ (our left), the saved climb from their tombs and ascend to heaven in an orderly manner. On the lower right (Christ's left), a fiery hell awaits the damned who tumble downward in disorder. A monstrous Satan simultaneously swallows and expels several souls, while devils torture others. A number of figures are shown hanging, a form of death that depends on gravity and thus emphasizes that hell is down.

Giotto's genius for conveying human drama can be seen in his later fresco cycle illustrating the life of St. Francis of Assisi (figure **12.16**). Located in Florence, in a chapel commissioned by the Bardi banking family, it reflects the irony of wealthy citizens who idealize the vows of poverty taken by the saint. In this scene, Francis rejects his father's wealth. He has removed his clothes and is wrapped in a bishop's cloak, signifying his transition from the everyday world to the Church. His father's rage is shown by his jaw jutting forward in fury, and his separation from Francis by an empty space. Giotto thus juxtaposes

the solid form of the building with the literal and figurative void between father and son.

Here, as in the Arena Chapel frescoes, Giotto places his figures in a solid, three-dimensional setting. In contrast to Early Christian and medieval figures, these turn freely in space and interact with each other rather than facing the viewer directly. They participate, like actors on a stage, in a dramatic narrative, combining Christian subject matter with natural human emotion.

PAINTING IN SIENA Florence's rival city was Siena, which considered itself the city of the Virgin. It was ruled by a Council of Nine, the *Nove*, who represented the city's wealthy merchants. Like Florence, Siena supported the arts for both religious and political purposes. The cathedral was the main source of religious patronage, and the town hall—the Palazzo Pubblico—of political patronage.

The leading painter in Siena was Duccio di Buoninsegna (*c.* 1260–*c.* 1319). He was commissioned in 1308 to produce a large altarpiece, the *Maestà* ("majesty"), for the cathedral. Rather than standing with its back to a chapel wall like the enthroned madonnas of Cimabue and Giotto, the *Maestà* was placed under the dome and was visible from all sides. The back was decorated with scenes of Christ's Passion and the front with the enthroned Virgin, saints, and angels (figure **12.17**).

12.17 *above* **Duccio,** *Maestà*, **1308–1311. Tempera and gold leaf on panel, 7 × 13 ft. (2.13 × 3.96 m). Museo dell'Opera del Duomo, Siena.**
Note the predominance of gold, the rich color, and the elaborate detail of the throne. Although Duccio has eliminated the gold drapery folds used by Cimabue and there is some evidence of chiaroscuro, the flavor of the image is Byzantine. Related to the powerful cult of the Virgin, the work was intended to evoke a devotional response and to emphasize the compassion of the Virgin rather than to create a dramatic narrative.

Mary is shown as a queen surrounded by a heavenly court, the sides of her throne expanding outward as if to embrace the faithful. In the inscription on the base of the throne, Duccio asks her to bring peace to Siena and long life to himself as recompense for his altarpiece.

Siena's town hall (figure **12.18**), completed in the first decade of the fourteenth century, is an imposing structure with Gothic arches, a tower, and fortress-like crenellations. For the interior of the Palazzo Pubblico the Council of Nine commissioned frescoes that were politically motivated and designed to suggest that their rule was fair. The humanist commitment to just government can be seen, for example, in the frescoes by Ambrogio Lorenzetti (*c.* 1290–1348), who died during the Black Death. In *The Effects of Good Government in the City* (figure **12.19**), the bustling merchant town of Siena can be seen

12.18 **Palazzo Pubblico, Siena, completed 1309.**

12.19 Ambrogio Lorenzetti, *The Effects of Good Government in the City*, Palazzo Pubblico, Siena, 1338–1339. Fresco, total length approx. 23 ft. (7 m).

in full swing. Under good government, according to Ambrogio, there is peace and prosperity. Traders offer their wares for sale, students attend school, shops are open for business, musicians and dancers perform in the street, and builders are hard at work on the roof tops. To show the effects of bad government,

Ambrogio painted the allegory in figure **12.20**, which personifies Tyranny and its evil companions. By juxtaposing two types of government, Ambrogio exemplifies humanist political philosophy and projects the image of Siena as a well-ruled commune under the Council of Nine.

12.20 Ambrogio Lorenzetti, *Allegory of Bad Government*, Palazzo Pubblico, Siena, 1338–1339. Fresco.
Tyranny is the large central figure with fangs and a horned black hood. Surrounding his head are the vices of Avarice, Pride, and Vainglory. Seated on his right (reading from the viewer's left) are Cruelty, with an infant killed by a snake; Treason, holding a creature that is part-lamb, part-scorpion; and Fraud, with cloven feet. On Tyranny's left, an agitated, wolf-headed centaur represents Frenzy, Discord saws herself in half, and War is armed for battle. The figure in white is labeled Justice; she has been tied up and her scales broken.

DOMINICAN ICONOGRAPHY AND SCHOLASTIC RESISTANCE TO HUMANISM

After the Black Death, there was no fourteenth-century artist who rivaled the innovations of Giotto, Duccio, or Ambrogio Lorenzetti. At the same time, scholasticism persisted amid the widespread anxiety and preoccupation with death that followed the plague. The scholastic concern for salvation is portrayed in a set of huge frescoes by Andrea da Firenze (Andrea di Bonaiuti; *c.* 1337–1377). They are located in the Spanish Chapel, a Dominican chapter house in the Florentine church of Santa Maria Novella.

Andrea's *Triumph of St. Thomas Aquinas* of around 1365 is organized hierarchically and has none of Giotto's dramatic narrative, Duccio's compassion, or Ambrogio's humanist politics (figure **12.21**). Below an angel-filled sky sits St. Thomas Aquinas in direct confrontation with the viewer. He presides over the scene, flanked on his left by Old Testament figures and by New Testament figures on his right. Below, a long arcaded bench decorated with delicate tracery and pinnacles is occupied by personifications of the Virtues, the Liberal Arts, and the Sciences. In these three tiers—the heavens, St. Thomas, and the earthly world—Andrea has produced the pictorial equivalent of an orderly scholastic dialectic. His image conveys the power of the Church as the route to salvation.

It would take Italy a few more generations to recover fully from the devastating effects of the Black Death, which had added to the problems already besetting Europe. With recovery would come a cultural, intellectual, and artistic expansion that began at the turn of the fifteenth century. Throughout Europe, despite lingering Gothic influence, the Renaissance style would broaden the innovations introduced by the early humanists.

12.21 Andrea da Firenze, *Triumph of St. Thomas Aquinas*, Spanish Chapel, Santa Maria Novella, Florence, *c.* 1365. Fresco, approx. 38 ft. (11.58 m) wide.

KEY TERMS

antipope the name given to a rival pope, often resident in Avignon, but not legitimized by the Roman Church.

humanism an intellectual and artistic trend, beginning in the late thirteenth century and based on a renewed interest in the Classical tradition.

isorhythm in fourteenth-century music, the use of a repeated rhythmic scheme, usually applied to a plainsong melody.

Ockham's razor the principle of reducing—shaving—an assumption to its simplest form.

oxymoron a figure of speech using an apparent contradiction.

round a musical form in which each voice enters in turn with the same music after the previous one has sung several measures.

syllogism a logical system of deductive reasoning, in which a conclusion follows from a major and a minor premise.

transi tomb a tomb with an effigy of the deceased in a state of decay.

KEY QUESTIONS

1. What does the term "Great Schism" mean? Summarize the main problems present in this schism.
2. How did the Black Death affect the visual art and literature of this period?
3. What qualities make *ars nova* a new, more secular musical style?
4. How does Chaucer satirize society through his characters?
5. How did humanism affect the visual arts and literature of this period?

SUGGESTED READING

Allmand, C. *The Hundred Years War: England and France at War, c. 1300–1450*. Cambridge, U.K.: Cambridge University Press, 1988.
  ▸ A survey of the origins and effects of the war.

Barolsky, Paul. *Giotto's Father and the Family of Vasari's Lives*. University Park, PA: Pennsylvania State University Press, 1992.
  ▸ A brief interpretive view of Giotto's relationship to his father and its implications for his art.

Baxandall, Michael. *Giotto and the Orators*. Oxford: Oxford University Press, 1971.
  ▸ A study of Giotto and literature relating to him.

Bober, Phyllis Pray. *Art, Culture, and Cuisine*. Chicago and London: University of Chicago Press, 1999.
  ▸ Feasts and menus from the fourteenth century.

Boccaccio, *The Decameron*, trans. G. H. McWilliam. London: Penguin Books, 1972.
  ▸ Ten tales set at the time of the Black Death.

Burckhardt, Jacob C. *The Civilization of the Renaissance in Italy*, trans. S. G. C. Middlemore, 3rd rev. ed. London: Phaidon, 1950.
  ▸ A classic study of the Italian Renaissance

Chaucer, Geoffrey. *The Canterbury Tales*, trans. Nevill Coghill. London: Penguin Classics, 1977.
  ▸ A long poem in which pilgrims pass the time by recounting the stories of their lives. A window on medieval society.

Christine de Pisan. *The Book of the City of Ladies*, trans. Earl Jeffrey Richards. New York: Persea Books, 1982.
  ▸ A book by a medieval woman on the position of women during the Middle Ages.

Cohen, Kathleen. *Metamorphosis of a Death Symbol*. Berkeley and Los Angeles: University of California Press, 1973.
  ▸ A study of medieval transi tombs, their iconography, and meaning.

Cole, Bruce. *Giotto and Florentine Painting, 1280–1375*. New York: Harper and Row, 1975.
  ▸ A brief study of Giotto and his impact on Florentine painting.

Gordon, Mary. *Joan of Arc*. New York: Viking Press, 2000.
  ▸ A brief biography of St. Joan by a well-known author.

Meiss, Millard. *Painting in Florence and Siena after the Black Death*. Princeton, NJ: Princeton University Press, 1951.
  ▸ A classic account of the character of the Black Death and its effects on art and society.

——. *French Painting in the Time of Jean de Berry: The Late Fourteenth Century and the Patronage of the Duke*. London: Thames and Hudson, 1975.
  ▸ A study of International Gothic painting in France.

Schneider, Laurie (ed.). *Giotto in Perspective*. Englewood Cliffs, NJ: Prentice Hall, 1974.
  ▸ A critical history of the artist, from the fourteenth to the twentieth century.

Tierney, B. *The Crisis of Church and State 1050–1300.* Englewood Cliffs, NJ: Prentice Hall, 1964.
  ▸ Annotated original documents of the period.

Tuchman, Barbara. *A Distant Mirror.* New York: Alfred A. Knopf, 1978.
  ▸ An account of the Middle Ages.

White, John. *The Birth and Rebirth of Pictorial Space*, 2nd ed. Boston: Faber and Faber, 1967.
  ▸ On the development of linear perspective.

Ziegler, Philip. *The Black Death.* London: Penguin Books, 1991.
  ▸ A recent account of the Black Death.

SUGGESTED FILMS

1922 *Robin Hood*, dir. Allan Dwan

1928 *The Passion of Joan of Arc (La Passion de Jeanne d'Arc)*, dir. Carl Theodor Dreyer

1938 *The Adventures of Robin Hood*, dir. Michael Curtiz and William Keighley

1948 *Joan of Arc*, dir. Victor Fleming

1952 *Ivanhoe*, dir. Richard Thorpe

1957 *Saint Joan*, dir. Otto Preminger

1962 *Procès de Jeanne d'Arc (The Trial of Joan of Arc)*, dir. Robert Bresson

1991 *Robin Hood*, dir. John Irvin

1991 *Robin Hood: Prince of Thieves*, dir. Kevin Reynolds

1999 *The Messenger: The Story of Joan of Arc*, dir. Luc Besson

13 The Early Renaissance in Italy and Northern Europe

66 How great and wonderful is the dignity of the human body . . . how lofty and sublime the human soul, and . . . how great and illustrious is the excellence of man himself made up of these two parts. "

(GIANNOZZO MANETTI, *On the Dignity of Man*)

The word Renaissance (meaning "rebirth") refers to the revival of interest in, and admiration for, Greek and Roman antiquity. This began in the late thirteenth century in Italy and appeared somewhat later in northern Europe, contributing to the waning of the Middle Ages. History evolves slowly, however, and the medieval worldview persisted throughout Europe even after the beginnings of Renaissance thought.

It took several generations for Europe to recover from the Black Death of 1348, from bank failures, and from the other economic problems of the fourteenth century. But by the turn of the quattrocento (1400s), a new era was emerging. Economic recovery, resulting from increasing trade between Italy and the north of Europe (see map 13.1) and a rise in banking, improved living conditions for all social classes. Prosperity, in turn, led to an expansion of artistic patronage, which was no longer restricted to the Church and the courts, as it had been during the Middle Ages. New patrons appeared, especially among wealthy merchants, guilds, and individual families, who were ambitious for power and prestige. These new sources of secular patronage reflected new ideas about the role of the individual in society and in the cosmos.

The city of Florence, in Tuscany, was the center of the humanist movement in the early decades of the fifteenth century. Humanist chancellors who ran the city favored a form of government that was based on the republic of ancient Rome and fifth-century-B.C. Athenian democracy. Eventually, however, Florence became an oligarchy, ruled by a few families, notably the Medici, who dominated the political, financial, intellectual, and artistic life of Florence for most of the century. Having amassed a vast fortune through banking and moneylending, the Medici spent huge sums on art and architecture, helping to establish Florence as the cultural center of Italy. They also supported humanist poets, musicians, and philosophers.

Outside Florence, too, humanist Italian courts patronized artists, architects, and writers, as well as scientists and philosophers. Like the Medici, these rulers, who included the popes, used the arts to express their wealth, power, and intellectual ambition.

Although humanism emerged first in Italy with the revival of Classical antiquity, it soon spread to parts of northern Europe, especially Germany and the

TIMELINE	ITALY 1400–1500	NORTHERN EUROPE 1400–1500
HISTORY AND CULTURE	Economic recovery Mercantile economies City-states and courts Florence key cultural center Turks take Constantinople, 1453 Trade and exploration Production of books; increase in literacy Spread of humanism Patronage by Church, wealthy individuals, and guilds Medici family: rulers and patrons	Economic recovery Mercantile economies Countries ruled by monarchs Bruges leading commercial city Trade and exploration Gutenberg perfects printing press, 1440s Expansion of humanism Patronage by Church, wealthy individuals, and guilds
RELIGION	Dominican backlash against humanism: Antoninus (1389–1459) and Savonarola (1452–1498) Humanist popes	
ART	Brunelleschi/Ghiberti, *Sacrifice of Isaac* reliefs, 1401–1402 Donatello, *John the Evangelist*, c. 1409–1411; *David*, 1420–1440 Masaccio, *Trinity*, 1425–1428; *Virgin and Child*, 1426; *Tribute Money*, 1420s Fra Angelico, *Mocking of Christ with the Virgin and St. Dominic*, 1438–1445 Uccello, *Battle of San Romano*, 1440s Rossellino, tomb of Leonardo Bruni, begun 1444 Gozzoli, *Procession of the Magi*, 1459 Piero della Francesca, *Battista Sforza* and *Federico da Montefeltro*, c. 1472 Botticelli, *Birth of Venus*, c. 1480 Verrocchio, *Colleoni*, c. 1481–1496 Leonardo, *Last Supper*, c. 1495–1498	van Eyck, Ghent altarpiece, 1432; *Man in a Red Turban*, c. 1433; *Arnolfini Portrait*, 1434 Petrus Christus, *St. Eloy in His Studio*, 1449 Fouquet, *Portrait of Charles VII*, after 1451 Schongauer, *Elephant*, c. 1485
ARCHITECTURE	Brunelleschi, dome of Florence Cathedral, begun 1420 Rossellino, plan of Pienza, 1460s Mantegna, Camera Picta, Mantua, 1474 Giuliano da Sangallo, Santa Maria delle Carceri, Prato, 1485–1490	
LITERATURE	Bruni, *Panegyric of the City of Florence*, 1401; *History of the Florentine People*, 1415 Manetti (1396–1459), *On the Dignity of Man* Ficino (1433–1499), commentaries on Plato and translations of Plotinus Alberti, *On Painting*, c. 1435; *Book of the Family*, 1436; *On Architecture*, 1452 Pico della Mirandola, *Oration on the Dignity of Man*, 1486	Gutenberg Bible, 1450s William Caxton (c. 1422–1491), illustrated books
THEATER	Merging of Classical subject matter and form Laschi, *Achilles*, 1390	Increased use of farce and comedy *Pierre Pathelin*, c. 1470 Morality plays increasingly portray human nature
MUSIC	Humanist tastes encourage listener response Move from sacred to secular Lorenzo de' Medici founds music school Isaac spends ten years in Florence under Lorenzo's patronage, from 1485 *Intermedio* and *frottola*	Main center of music patronage: court of Philip the Good (1396–1467) in Burgundy Secular song: *chansons* Dunstable (c. 1390–1453), motets, secular songs Dufay (c. 1400–1474), development of "cyclic Mass," motets, chansons Josquin Desprez, *Ave Maria . . . virgo serena*, c. 1485 Four-voice texture becomes the norm

Netherlands. Nevertheless, the visual arts of the north retained a more Gothic flavor than in Italy. In music, on the other hand, the north was more innovative than the south, as patronage became increasingly secular and composers developed new styles.

As the quotation by the humanist philosopher Giannozzo Manetti at the opening of this chapter suggests, the essence of humanism is its interest in man. Whereas medieval thinkers made a sharp distinction between the body and the soul, fifteenth-century humanists conceived of man as a totality—which includes the physical appearance, the mind, and the soul. Manetti argued that because man was made in God's image, he must also be endowed, like God, with a creative mind and a "sublime soul." This Renaissance view of humanity was consistent with the revival of Classical culture.

THE EXPANSION OF HUMANISM

The development of humanism (see Box, p. 333) coincided with advances in technology, new approaches to the arts and sciences, a greater awareness of the world through geographic exploration, and an expansion of international trade (map **13.1**).

ADVANCES IN TECHNOLOGY

In 1425, in the German city of Mainz, Johannes Gutenberg (*c.* 1398–1468) perfected movable type, and by the 1450s, he had printed the entire Bible on a printing press. The technology of printing enabled ideas to circulate at a faster rate than previously, which had enormous cultural ramifications. Books, which had hitherto been painstakingly copied by hand, could now be replicated and printed in large quantities. The increase in the number and availability of books was accompanied by a gradual rise in literacy as the reading public grew (see Box, p. 332).

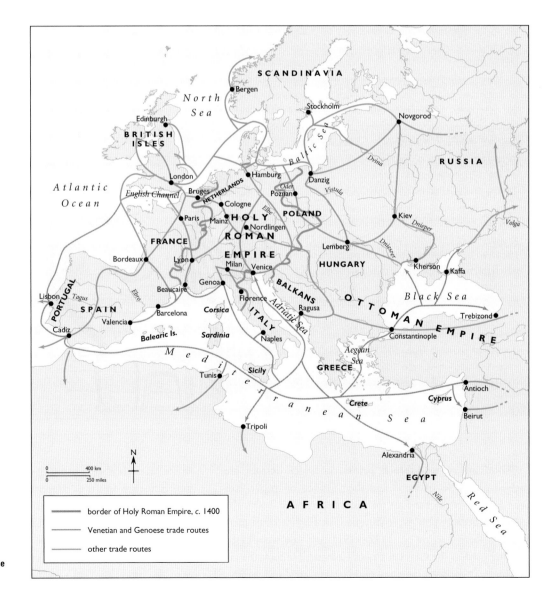

Map 13.1 European trade in the fifteenth century.

Defining Moment

The Printing Press

In the early fifteenth century, commercial centers of business, royal courts, and banks needed scribes to record transactions. Scribes, however, were expensive and few were available. The improvement of the printing press in mid-fifteenth-century Europe solved this problem and brought about one of the most radical changes in Western intellectual and commercial history. The printing revolution made reading a part of everyday life and changed the face of education, law, and politics. It popularized the discoveries of the New World and contributed to the reproduction of more accurate charts and maps, which, in turn, facilitated further discovery. Printing also led to the standardization of languages by selecting and repeating particular usages and spellings.

Many existing technologies were linked to foster the printing press: the punch of the goldsmith, the manufacture of paper (parchment was not porous enough to take the ink), wine and linen press construction, metallurgy, ink and oil production. It was in the Rhine Valley in Germany in the 1440s that Johannes Gutenberg began using the printing press in conjunction with a series of blocks, each bearing a single letter on its face. The press employed by Gutenberg was a hand press, in which ink was rolled over the raised surfaces of hand-set letters fitted into a wooden frame, which was then pressed against a sheet of paper (figure **13.1**). Gutenberg's innovative system allowed the mass reproduction of movable type. The letter blocks were arranged in a type tray, which was then used to print a page of text. If one letter was damaged, it could be replaced. When the printing of the copies of a page was finished, the type could be reused for the next page or, indeed, the next book.

At first, typefaces imitated hand lettering. However, as humanists rediscovered works from Classical antiquity, they popularized new typefaces modeled after the curved, more readable letters of the Romans.

Before the invention of the printing press, books had been copied mainly in monasteries, where monks wrote them out. Books were scarce, because it could take a year to copy a Bible by hand. With the Gutenberg press plus two or three people who could read and a few operatives to work the machinery, it was possible to create several hundred copies of the Bible—or any other long text—in a year. Each sheet of paper still had to be fed into the press individually, which limited reproduction speed, and the type had to be set manually for each page, which placed a restriction on the number of different pages that could be created in a day.

Printing technology spread rapidly, and by 1480 more than 110 towns, mainly in Italy and Germany, had established presses. The printing press helped to spread intellectual ideas across Europe. Because many craftsmen had died of the plague, the European economy needed "how to" books, and the printing press made pos-sible the transmission of accurate technical information. At the same time as the concept of authorship emerged, writers could be sure of reaching readers, who would then hold them responsible for information. Printing also made possible new forms of cross-cultural exchange independent of travel and generally contributed to greater knowledge among the populations of Europe.

Critical Question　If a new technology becomes popular, do old technologies simply fade away or do they find new relevance? (For example, before the advent of writing and books, people had to memorize poetry if it was to pass to the next generation. Now that we have computers, are books becoming obsolete?)

13.1 Artist's impression of Johannes Gutenberg, based on the carvings on his tomb, showing him reading proofs while his assistant works the printing press. Woodcut.

Woodcuts or woodblock prints, in which images are incised on blocks of wood and then printed on paper, had been known in the Far East for centuries. Around 1400, the technique became popular in Europe. The English cloth merchant William Caxton (c. 1422–1491) first saw woodblock printing used in the German city of Cologne. He took the art to Bruges, in modern Belgium, and later returned to London, where he established a printing concern in Westminster. Caxton's influence on the development of printing was enormous; and his woodcut illustrations of texts such as Chaucer's *Canterbury Tales* (see Chapter 12) are still popular today.

At first, religious texts were the most commonly printed books, but in time popular secular works and Classical texts were also produced. In 1429, for example, twelve hitherto lost

The Humanist Movement

The origins of the intellectual movement known as humanism are found in the late thirteenth century, when a group of attorneys in the northern Italian city of Padua became interested in Roman law, especially the works of Cicero. Dramatists revived the Roman plays of Seneca, and a new interest in ancient texts, stored but neglected in monasteries, emerged. Philologists (those who study language) began to analyze texts as a means of interpreting ancient thought. This thirst for the original writing of Greek and Roman authors led some to collect and translate texts and eventually to amass large libraries of Classical manuscripts.

For the humanists, man and his place in the world were a focus of attention and inquiry, just as they had been for the ancients. The authors Petrarch and Boccaccio were the leading figures in fourteenth-century humanism. They extolled the benefits of studying Latin and Greek, and their own writings reflect the influence of Classical thought. In addition, they admired new developments in the arts, especially the painting of Giotto (see Chapter 12), which represented the human figure more naturalistically than medieval artists had done. In the view of Petrarch and Boccaccio, Giotto revived the art of painting, which had lain buried after the fall of Rome, and returned it to the light of day. Humanists used the metaphor of light and dark to suggest that the Classical revival brought with it a renewal of intellectual enlightenment and the creative arts.

As the humanist movement expanded in the fifteenth century, a new educational curriculum evolved, in which Classical texts were included along with Christian ones. In a few of the most enlightened humanist schools of Italy, girls as well as boys studied works on geography, history, politics, philosophy, mathematics, rhetoric (the art of persuasive argument), and the arts and music. In Italy as well as in northern Europe, Plato became a central source for humanists and gradually overshadowed the important role that Aristotle had played in medieval scholasticism.

---

plays by Plautus were located and printed. Soon the revival of Classical Roman authors extended to Greek texts, and after the fall of Constantinople (modern Istanbul) to the Turks in 1453, many Greek scholars emigrated to Italy. By 1518, every known Roman and Greek play had been published.

ARTS AND SCIENCES

The humanist emphasis on individual personality had begun to appear in the late medieval works of Dante, Chaucer, and Christine de Pisan (see Chapter 12). In the fourteenth century, Petrarch and Boccaccio wrote of a new view of man's place in the world, focusing on personality and advocating fame

through achievement as a route to immortality. In the fifteenth century, this new humanist perspective influenced the writing of history, which strove to understand human motivation and to explain the relationship of the present to the past. The fresh historical perspective was accompanied by a new grasp of the third dimension in art (see Box, p. 341) and of greater depth in music.

In theater, plays increasingly focused on everyday life. A merging of Classical subject matter and style expanded the depth of plays and of their characters. For instance, whereas the tragedy *Ecerinis* by Mussato (see Chapter 12) followed the form of Seneca's plays, its subject matter was twelfth-century Italian politics. In 1390, however, in Antonio Laschi's play *Achilles* both the style and the subject of the play were Classical. By coordinating content with style, authors began to grapple more thoroughly with the psychology of their characters, who acted and reacted in a historical context consistent with a specific dramatic form.

Farce and comedy, which had been performed on a small scale in the late Gothic period, became more popular in the fifteenth century. In around 1470, for example, a French dramatist wrote the play *Pierre Pathelin*, in which a lawyer cheats a merchant out of his cloth only to be cheated himself by a peasant. German farces, called Shrovetide plays, were derived from folk festivals and revels during Shrovetide (the period preceding Lent). Even the traditional morality plays increasingly portray human nature.

Humanism in music developed later than in the visual arts. In music, humanist tastes encouraged listener response and a move away from the sacred toward the secular. Flowing rhythms displaced the more stylized, repetitive church music of the Middle Ages, and the hierarchy of musical lines gradually altered. Where previously the tenor part was the basis of the texture and structure, now the voices tended toward equality, interweaving like threads of a tapestry and creating a sense of balance and symmetry.

These changes in the arts signaled a new naturalism emphasizing the human experience—inspired by the ancient Greek maxim, "Man is the measure of all things" (see Chapter 6). The drawing of *Vitruvian Man* (figure **13.2**) by Leonardo da Vinci (1452–1519), for example, illustrates the notion of man's centrality, which the Renaissance adopted from Classical philosophy. Vitruvius was a Roman architect under the emperor Augustus; his *De architectura* (*On Architecture*) was recovered in Italy in 1414. Like Plato, Vitruvius believed that the circle was the ideal shape, and he related human symmetry to architectural harmony. In the Middle Ages, on the other hand, theologians had conceived of the circle not in human terms but rather as symbolizing the perfection of God, the cosmos, and the universal nature of the Church.

During the Renaissance, the status of artists, who in the Middle Ages had been considered artisans (skilled or semi-skilled manual laborers) rose to that of educated gentlemen

Middle Ages). Similarly, musicians sometimes introduced themselves into the lyrics of their compositions. In a religious work, for example, a composer might ask the Virgin Mary to remember him and pray for his soul. These practices express the general interest in earthly achievement as a route to salvation.

Together with the exploration of human nature, the early Renaissance witnessed a new attitude toward science. Emphasizing observation and experiment rather than theory, science became more empirical than it had been in the Middle Ages. The Renaissance emphasis on empiricism reflected new methods of exploring the world. Artists wishing to render human form began to dissect cadavers and study anatomy. The anatomical drawings of Leonardo da Vinci, whose work marks the transition from the early to the High Renaissance (see Chapter 14), are a case in point (figure **13.4**).

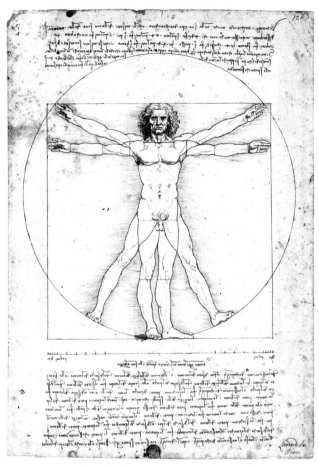

13.2 Leonardo da Vinci, *Vitruvian Man*, *c.* 1485–1490. Pen and ink, 13^1/$_2$ × 9^5/$_8$ in. (34.3 × 24.5 cm). Gallerie dell' Accademia, Venice.
In this drawing, Leonardo illustrates Vitruvius's assertion that the navel of a man standing inside a circle with arms and legs extended will be placed at the center. Man's central position in nature is thus reflected in the relation of the human navel to the Platonic notion of a geometric harmony regulating the universe. Leonardo has added the square to reinforce the Classical theory of Plato and Vitruvius.

and academicians. The notion of the academy as a place of formal art training and intellectual exchange—based on the informal academies of antiquity (see Chapter 6)—began in the late fifteenth century. Eventually, painting and sculpture (which are now considered to be art) would rise from being mere handicrafts to the higher status of the liberal arts—that is, disciplines capable of freeing or liberating the mind. The Renaissance enlarged the scope of the medieval *trivium* (grammar, rhetoric, and dialectic) and *quadrivium* (arithmetic, geometry, music, and astronomy), adding, among other disciplines, the newly invented practice of linear perspective as well as philosophy and theology.

As an expression of the new sense of authorship, Renaissance painters, sculptors, and architects practiced the ancient genres of biography and portraiture. During the Middle Ages, biography had been largely restricted to lives of saints, and portraiture was the exception rather than the rule. In contrast, Renaissance artists painted many portraits and self-portraits (figure **13.3**) and signed their works (a rare occurrence in the

13.3 Jan van Eyck, *Man in a Red Turban*, *c.* 1433. Tempera and oil on wood, 13^1/$_8$ × 10^1/$_8$ in. (33.3 × 25.8 cm). National Gallery, London.
Although there is some disagreement among scholars as to whom this represents, it is generally thought to be one of the earliest self-portraits of the Renaissance. The Netherlandish artist Jan van Eyck depicts the face in detail, along with an elaborate headpiece and fur collar. The headpiece, usually called a turban, is actually a *chaperon*—a long cloth wrapped around a padded support. As it was worn at the time, the two ends of the cloth hung down. Here, however, they do not, and this has been explained as indicating the artist's need to keep his face clear in order to paint it.

Pinpoints of reflected light in the eyes and the direct gaze animate the expression, while the gradual shading of the flesh creates a strong sense of surface texture. Van Eyck, assuming it is he, communicates with the viewer through his image as well as through the text inscribed on the frame, *Als ich kan* ("as I can"), meaning that he did the best he could, but would have done better had he been able to do so.

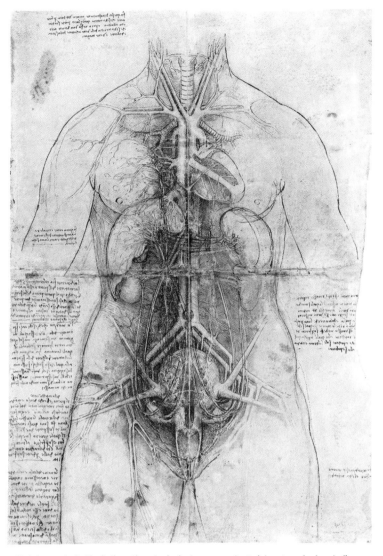

13.4 Leonardo da Vinci, dissection of principal organs and arterial system of a female figure,
***c.* 1510. 18³⁄₈ × 13 in. (46.7 × 33 cm). The Royal Collection, Windsor, U.K.**
Leonardo's notes show that he was influenced by the Greek physician Galen, with whom
he shared some misconceptions. For example, both believed that human anatomy
mirrored animal anatomy and that it was possible to reason from one species to another.
Nor did Galen or Leonardo understand the workings of the heart or the circulatory system.
Nevertheless, in the light of medieval medicine, drawings based on actual observations
were revolutionary.

Although medical training in the fifteenth century was
essentially a continuation of medieval training, certain developments required physicians to learn new techniques. With
the advent of gunpowder, for example, instruments had to
be invented for extracting bullets. This led to a new medical
specialty—the army surgeon.

EXPLORATION

A corollary to the interest in human nature and anatomy was
an exploration of the world at large. Although there had been
world travelers during the Middle Ages and even earlier, in the
fifteenth century explorations of the globe began in earnest.
Backed by Spain and sailing in ships paid for by the Medici,
Christopher Columbus (1451–1506) discovered the New

World in the last decade of the fifteenth century.
Spain tried to claim the West Indies (Hispaniola)
and, later, most of South America. The Portuguese
explorer Prince Henry the Navigator (1394–1460)
devised a better compass, built more seaworthy
ships, and learned how to use the Arabic astrolabe
to calculate latitude. In 1497 the Portuguese Vasco
da Gama (*c.* 1460–1524) sailed to India, the first
person to do so by rounding the Cape of Good
Hope on the southern tip of Africa. The Italian John
Cabot (1450–1498) sailed to Labrador, on the east
coast of Canada, and to New England, claiming
North America for England.

As European rulers vied for the potential riches
on other continents, they embraced colonialism and
planted the seeds of later turmoil. By papal decree
(the Treaty of Tordesillas) in 1494, Africa and Brazil
were awarded to Portugal; the rest of South America
remained with Spain. At the end of the fifteenth
century, the known world was larger than it had
ever been.

FLORENCE IN THE FIFTEENTH CENTURY

When the fifteenth century dawned, the
Italian peninsula was the most commercial, urbanized region of western
Europe. Enormous wealth in private hands
encouraged the notion that material success was
a virtue. More than in any other Italian city,
wealth and art converged to produce the greatest
innovations in Florence. For the mercantile Florentines, amassing wealth was something devoutly
to be wished. They not only enjoyed the benefits
of riches on a personal level, but they believed
that spending money on art to adorn their city
was a virtue. They called this *magnificentia*—the virtue of
magnificence.

Located in Tuscany, Florence was the focal point of the
Italian Renaissance. Its spoken dialect was Tuscan, the same
vernacular in which Dante, Petrarch, and Boccaccio had
written. Florence was a leader in the textile trade, especially in
the manufacture of wool, which was the original source of
Florentine wealth (see Chapter 12). The city also established
its financial influence internationally in 1252 by minting the
florin (a coin worth about one hundred dollars in today's value
and named "the flower" after Florence). This provided a stable
monetary system in the city as well as other parts of Europe.
Double-entry book-keeping, in which debits are listed with
equivalent credits, was invented in the 1300s by Florentine
businessmen and is still in general use today.

Society and Culture

The Medici Family in the Fifteenth Century

The origins of the Medici family are not known precisely. According to one legend, a distant ancestor had been a knight of Charlemagne. While traveling to Rome, this knight encountered and fought a giant whose mace dented the knight's shield. Charlemagne, impressed with the knight's bravery, awarded him a coat of arms of three gold balls (derived from the dents) on a gold field. This became the Medici coat of arms. More plausible accounts trace the coat of arms either to the pills dispensed by apothecaries (*Medici* is related to *medico*, meaning "physician") or to the triple balls of pawnbrokers (denoting the moneylending practices of the family).

What *is* known is that the Medici came from the Mugello valley outside Florence. The first wealthy member of the family, Giovanni di Bicci de' Medici (1360–1429), was notoriously ugly. He established the family fortune and the Medici bank through moneylending. Giovanni di Bicci also established the *Monte delle doti*, a bank in which fathers deposited money at high interest rates in order to build up dowries for their daughters.

Giovanni married the beautiful Piccarda de' Bueri, who belonged to an old noble family. Their sons, Cosimo (1389–1464) and Lorenzo (1395–1440), added to the family fortune, and Cosimo became the *de facto* (actual) ruler of Florence in the 1430s. He loaned money to the most important citizens and, by never calling in the loans, maintained both their dependence on him and his influence over them. Cosimo married the dutiful but boring Contessina de' Bardi, a member of the banking family that had commissioned Giotto's St. Francis cycle in Santa Croce (see Chapter 12). When Cosimo died, he was awarded the honorific *Pater patriae*, "Father of his country."

Cosimo's handsome son Piero (1416–1469), who suffered from gout, married the remarkable Lucrezia Tornabuoni. They had two sons, Giuliano and Lorenzo. Giuliano was killed in the Pazzi conspiracy, a plot organized in 1478 by the Pazzi family against Medici control of the city. Lorenzo (1449–1492), known as *Il Magnifico* (The Magnificent), continued the brilliant rule and lavish patronage of his grandfather Cosimo. His mother Lucrezia, herself a successful business entrepreneur and author of plays and musical *laude*, was his most trusted political adviser. She arranged Lorenzo's marriage to the Roman aristocrat Clarice Orsini, with a view to extending Medici influence to the highest circles in Rome.

When Lorenzo died in 1494, he left a weak son and a city that had grown tired of the family's autocratic rule. The Medici were expelled from Florence, though they returned to rule as dukes in the sixteenth century. Over the course of time there would be two Medici popes—Clement VII and Leo X—and members of the family would marry into several royal houses of Europe.

In the early fifteenth century there are estimated to have been at least seventy bankers operating in Florence. One of the leading banking families was the Medici, who had started as wool merchants and moneylenders. By the mid-fifteenth century the Medici bank had a network of branches in London, Antwerp (Belgium), Bruges (Belgium), Cologne (Germany), Geneva (Switzerland), and Lyons (France), as well as other major Italian cities, including Rome, Naples, and Venice.

Twelve trade guilds (*arti*) wielded political power in Florence. Guild members participated in the government, which was at first a republic. But Florence soon evolved into an oligarchy, controlled by a few prominent families, particularly the Medici, who dictated city policy throughout most of the fifteenth century (see Box). Nevertheless, outwardly at least, Florence was determined to maintain the image of a republic.

In the early fifteenth century, Florence was under military threat from the powerful northwestern city-state of Milan. Ruled by the Visconti family, Milan threatened the independent position of Florence and planned an invasion in 1402. The attack was thwarted when an outbreak of plague killed the Milanese leader, Giangaleazzo Visconti (1351–1402). Twenty-five years later, in 1427, Giangaleazzo's son Filippo Maria Visconti (1392–1447) again threatened Florence, though he never invaded the city. This threat prompted Florence to institute the *catasto*, a survey of the citizenry for the purpose of levying a new tax on property to provide funds for defense. Male heads of households had to list their assets, investments, family members, and other dependents. This information, which the meticulous Florentines kept with great care, has proved a rich source of information for historians.

HUMANISM AND THE STATE

At the time of the first Visconti threat, the chancellor (political head of the city) of Florence was Coluccio Salutati (1331–1406). A friend of Petrarch, Salutati was a dedicated humanist. He appointed Manuel Chrysoloras (c. 1350–1415), a Greek scholar from Constantinople, to teach Greek at the University of Florence, and in his personal correspondence he advocated reading the Classics. As chancellor, Salutati argued in favor of Florentine political freedom, and in his public speeches he compared the city to the Roman Republic.

READING SELECTION

Salutati, *Letters*, in defense of liberal studies, PWC2-153

In 1427, Leonardo Bruni (c. 1370–1444), the first official historian of Florence, became chancellor of the city. Born in Arezzo, in central Italy, Bruni was a humanist who translated Plato and Aristotle and worked as a papal secretary. He subscribed to Cicero's ideal of the philosopher-statesman, and

When Bruni died, he was honored with a new type of sculptural installation placed against the wall of a church—the so-called humanist tomb (figure **13.5**). Unlike the medieval transi tombs, which had effigies of decaying, worm-eaten bodies on their lids (see Chapter 12), Bruni's tomb idealizes the image of the deceased. It shows him fully clothed, sleeping peacefully, and holding a copy of his *History of the Florentine People*. A Roman round arch has replaced the Gothic pointed arch, and it rests on fluted Corinthian pilasters (rectangular columns), reflecting the revival of the ancient Orders of architecture. At the same time, the tomb design includes Christian elements such as the figures of Mary and Christ flanked by angels in the round frame, forming a **tondo**, inside the arch.

Humanists, who were, by and large, devout Christians, welcomed such combinations of pagan and Christian iconography as are incorporated into Bruni's tomb. At the very top, two winged nude boys (*putti*), which derive from Roman sarcophagi, display a laurel wreath, the ancient sign of triumph. Inside the wreath is the lion symbol of Florence (the *Marzocco*), which alludes to Bruni's position as the city's chancellor. A pair of eagles, suggesting the Roman Jupiter and the Greek Zeus, support his bier. On the sarcophagus two winged Victories carry an inscription announcing that the Greek and Roman Muses, even history itself, mourn the loss of Bruni's eloquence. The base of the sarcophagus is sculpted in the form of lion's paws. Below, on the plinth, reliefs of dancing *putti* carrying garlands frame another lion head. The repetition of the lion motif alludes to Bruni's name (Leo, short for *leone*, which means "lion" in Italian).

A third humanist chancellor of Florence, Poggio Bracciolini (1380–1459), was a distinguished antiquarian. Following Petrarch, Bracciolini searched for ancient texts that had lain forgotten in monastic libraries and amassed a large collection of books. His best writings, most of which were in Latin, were dialogues using the Socratic method after the manner of Plato. This marked a departure from scholastic dialectic, because Socrates sought truth in human discourse rather than through a superimposed, hierarchical system of reasoning based on faith.

THE PLATONIC ACADEMY

Inspired by Cosimo de' Medici's ambition to establish a Platonic Academy, Lorenzo did so in 1469 to encourage the study of Plato. The Academy was headed by Marsilio Ficino (1433–1499), the son of Cosimo's physician and an ordained priest who had also studied medicine, magic, and astrology. Above all, Ficino was a follower of Plato's philosophy.

Cosimo had commissioned Ficino to translate Plato's known works from Greek into Latin. Ficino's discussion of Plato's *Symposium* (the dialogue on love) distinguishes two aspects of Venus—profane and divine. He argues that physical love can lead to spiritual love.

13.5 Bernardo Rossellino, tomb of Leonardo Bruni, Santa Croce, Florence, begun 1444. Marble, 20 ft. (6 m) high.
Like many Renaissance artists, Rossellino was trained in his family's workshop, which specialized in stonecutting and sculpture. He also worked as an architect and urban designer (see figure 13.27), especially on humanist commissions.

in his *Panegyric of the City of Florence* (1401) he extolled the city's republican government and its cultural ties to Greece and Rome.

Bruni's *History of the Florentine People* (1415) exemplifies the humanist approach to recording history. Taking the Classical past as a model for the present, the *History*, which is imbued with humanist rhetoric, traces the origins of Florence to the ancient Roman Republic.

Ficino also translated Plotinus, the third-century-A.D. commentator on Plato. At the core of Ficino's philosophy, which is based on Plotinus's Neoplatonism ("new Platonism"), is the notion of a divine chain of being. In the chain of being, the lowest form of divisible matter is at the bottom, and the indivisible, perfectly unified God is at the top. At the center is the human soul, which strives toward God's perfection through reason, will, and contemplation. Ficino believed that Plato, more so than Aristotle, could be reconciled with Christianity, and he advocated the inclusion of Plato in the Christian curriculum.

Human potential similarly influenced the ideas of Ficino's student, Giovanni Pico della Mirandola (1463–1494), who came from Lombardy in northern Italy. Pico studied philosophy in Paris and advanced a system of thought that combined Greek, Arabic, and medieval Jewish philosophy with Christianity. Although Pico believed Christianity to be the highest of these, his views offended the Church; only the intervention of Lorenzo the Magnificent saved him from arrest. Pico became part of the Medici circle of Platonists, arguing for the inherent value of man. His *Oration on the Dignity of Man*

(1486) exemplifies the humanist view that man is rational, endowed with free will, and capable of determining his own destiny.

READING SELECTION

Pico, *Oration on the Dignity of Man*, the humanist view of man, PWC3-075

DECORATING THE CITY

The first generation in fifteenth-century Florence produced several artists of unusual genius. Foremost among these were Ghiberti and Donatello in sculpture, Brunelleschi in architecture, and Masaccio in painting. All received commissions that enhanced the appearance of the city and enriched its civic and religious institutions. The competition held in 1401 exemplifies the new approach to patronage and its relation to civic pride.

13.6 The cathedral, bell tower, and baptistery, Florence, Italy.
From 1294, the old cathedral of Florence was rebuilt and gradually enlarged. This building is faced with bands of green and white marble and has a dome over the crossing. The single bell tower (campanile) was designed by Giotto in the fourteenth century. The round windows in the dome's octagonal drum and the clerestory windows are the main sources of light, but surmounting the dome is a new Renaissance feature, the lantern, which is a further source of light.

13.7 Filippo Brunelleschi, *Sacrifice of Isaac*, 1401–1402. Gilt bronze, 21 × 17½ in. (53.3 × 44.4 cm). Museo Nazionale del Bargello, Florence.

13.8 Lorenzo Ghiberti, *Sacrifice of Isaac*, 1401–1402. Gilt bronze, 21 × 17½ in. (53.3 × 44.4 cm). Museo Nazionale del Bargello, Florence.
Note that Brunelleschi's relief is more powerful, as Abraham's knife is about to pierce his son's neck and the angel intervenes just in time to save Isaac. Ghiberti's relief is more graceful, and there is more attention to patterns of landscape, which reflects the influence of International Gothic style. Isaac is modeled after a Classical nude, its organic form and contrapposto indicating that Ghiberti had studied Greek sculpture.

THE COMPETITION OF 1401 At the center of Florence stood the huge Gothic cathedral, Santa Maria del Fiore (also called the Duomo), and the octagonal baptistery dedicated to John the Baptist (figure **13.6**). In 1401, the board of the cathedral held a competition for the commission of a pair of doors for the baptistery. Sculptors submitted bronze reliefs illustrating the biblical story of the Sacrifice of Isaac, in which Abraham is about to obey God's command to sacrifice his son. Judging the reliefs were clerical and lay people under the supervision of the wool refiners' guild. Only two of the submissions survive, one by Filippo Brunelleschi (1377–1446) and one by Lorenzo Ghiberti (*c.* 1378–1455) (figures **13.7** and **13.8**). Ghiberti was awarded the commission for the doors, which he completed around 1424.

BRUNELLESCHI'S DOME In 1417 the cathedral of Florence was still without a dome. The nearly 140-foot (42.6-m) diameter of space that had to be covered was the largest span since the construction of the Roman Pantheon, whose dome was 142 feet (43.28 m) in diameter (see Chapter 7). But the Pantheon was a hemisphere and rested on a round drum, whereas Florence cathedral needed a dome to cover an octagonal space.

In 1418, Brunelleschi, who had renounced sculpture and dedicated himself to architecture, submitted a model for the dome. His model was accepted and he began construction in 1420. The splendid result illustrates Brunelleschi's genius for architectural engineering and design (figure **13.9**). Ghiberti claimed to have been Brunelleschi's equal partner in constructing the dome. But Ghiberti probably exaggerated his role, given that he was dismissed from the work on the dome in 1425, after Brunelleschi objected to his participation.

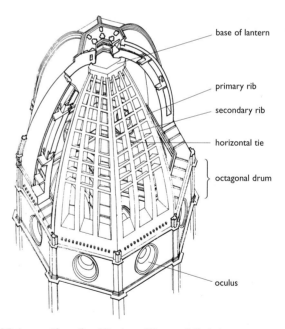

base of lantern

primary rib

secondary rib

horizontal tie

octagonal drum

oculus

13.9 Axonometric section of the dome of Florence Cathedral.
Having studied the Pantheon in Rome, Brunelleschi knew that a space of this size could be spanned, but there were no trees large enough to permit the type of centering used in the Middle Ages. Further, the octagonal drum was not as strong as the round drum of the Pantheon. Brunelleschi therefore devised a system in which eight large ribs extend from the base of the lantern to an angle of the octagon. These are visible on the exterior of the dome, but they alternate with pairs of smaller ribs, which are not visible. Reinforcing the vertical ribs are nine horizontal ties, which absorb the thrust of the ribs and prevent the wall of the dome from buckling outward. Additional support is provided by the herringbone pattern of the outer brick shell. By doubling the shell, Brunelleschi created an interior space that relieved the weight of the structure. Finally, by using brick, which is lighter than stone, he further reduced the weight borne by the skeleton.

DONATELLO'S *JOHN THE EVAN-GELIST* In 1409, the guild of manufacturers of woolen cloth commissioned seated statues of the four Evangelists for the cathedral's façade. The most innovative sculptor of his generation, Donatello di Niccolò Betto Bardi (*c.* 1386–1466), executed the statue of John the Evangelist. After the 1401 competition Donatello had accompanied Brunelleschi to Rome, where he absorbed the principles

Giotto, *Enthroned Madonna*
see figure 12.13

of ancient statuary such as naturalism and idealization evident in figure **13.10**. This commission, like the competition for the baptistery doors, reveals the influence of guilds in the artistic and political life of Florence.

MASACCIO The leading painter of the early Renaissance was Tommaso di ser Giovanni, known as Masaccio (1401–1428). Although he died at the age of twenty-seven, in a few short years he developed Giotto's approach to the picture plane and created a new pictorial style. His *Virgin and Child*, the central panel of the Pisa altarpiece of 1426, shows the enthroned Virgin and Christ according to a new system of perspective attributed to Brunelleschi (figure **13.11**) (see Box). Compared with Giotto in the *Enthroned Madonna* (see thumbnail), Masaccio has eliminated the Gothic pointed arches and delicate Gothic tracery of the throne. Instead, he has revived the

13.10 Donatello, *John the Evangelist,*
c. 1409–1411. Marble, 6 ft. 11 in. (2.1 m) high.
Museo dell'Opera del Duomo, Florence.
The elongated torso and heavy drapery folds compensate for the placement of the statue above the entrance, where it would have been seen from below. The evangelist holds his gospel and gazes upward, enrapt in a vision. Compared with medieval sculptures, this has organic form and individual character.

13.11 Masaccio, *Virgin and Child*, central panel of the Pisa altarpiece, 1426. Tempera on wood panel, 53³/₈ × 28³/₄ in. (135.5 × 73 cm). National Gallery, London.

Classical Orders of architecture (see Chapters 5 and 6), which appear on the sides and back of the throne. His use of chiaroscuro creates gradual shifts of light and dark that define the forms.

Masaccio's Christ exemplifies a new approach to depicting children, which is unlike the medieval baby-king. In the more natural form and childlike behavior of Masaccio's Christ, the figure has a miraculous nature as well as an infant's normal impulse to put things in its mouth. But this child is eating grapes, which an average infant would not be allowed to do. Masaccio's image thus conflates the reality of childhood with a symbolic allusion to the wine of the Eucharist.

In the monumental fresco of the *Trinity* (figure **13.14**), which is on the nave wall of the church of Santa Maria Novella in Florence, Masaccio again implemented Brunelleschi's perspective system. He assumed a viewer whose eye level is at

Society and Culture

Linear Perspective

Renaissance artists conceived of the picture plane as a window giving onto a view of three-dimensional space. Brunelleschi is credited as the inventor of rendering this view mathematically from the fixed position of an observer. Figure **13.12** shows Brunelleschi's conception, designed for architects, which assumes a person standing on the ground looking up at a building. Figure **13.13**, on the other hand, is designed for paintings and relief sculpture, and illustrates one-point perspective. In this system, the floor plan of the picture or relief is a grid and the sides of the squares (**orthogonals**) appear to recede toward a horizon. The squares diminish in size as they approach the horizon, creating the impression of increasing distance. When the image is symmetrical, the orthogonals meet at a single central point, known as the **vanishing point**. With this system, artists were able to replicate three-dimensional space on a flat surface and also to control the viewer's line of sight.

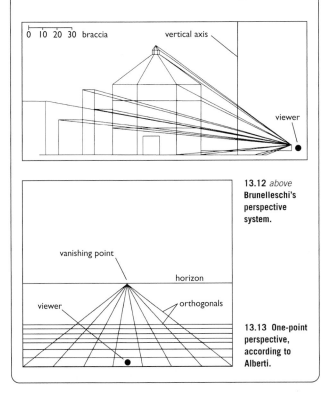

13.12 *above*
Brunelleschi's perspective system.

13.13 One-point perspective, according to Alberti.

Holy Spirit hovers above Christ's head. Mary is to the viewer's left and St. John is to the right.

Just below the steps is a foreshortened ledge supported by Corinthian columns. Between the columns, a painted sarcophagus supports an extended skeleton. The inscription over the skeleton reads: "I was once what you are, and what I am you will also be." Continuing the medieval tradition of the Quick

13.14 Masaccio, *Trinity*, 1425–1428, Santa Maria Novella, Florence. Fresco, 21 ft. 10⅝ in. × 10 ft. 4¾ in. (6.67 × 3.17 m).
The architectural rendering reflects several Renaissance developments. The round arch and barrel vault were inspired by ancient Rome, and the coffers by the Pantheon. Following the recommendations of Brunelleschi, Masaccio uses fluted pilasters and smooth-shafted columns. The capitals of the former are Corinthian, and the latter combine the Ionic volute capital with the Doric abacus.

the center of the lower step, which is also the location of the vanishing point. Looking up at the image, therefore, one sees the patrons—members of the influential Lenzi family—kneeling on the outer step. Their placement in the transitional space between the viewer and the Trinity identifies them as the donors and reflects their wish for salvation. The interior sacred space, occupied by the three persons of the Trinity, seems projected into an area beyond the wall. God stands on the back ledge, Christ hangs on the Cross, and a dove representing the

13.15 Masaccio, *Tribute Money*, Brancacci Chapel, Santa Maria del Carmine, Florence, 1420s. Fresco, 8 ft. 1¼ in. × 19 ft. 7 in. (2.47 × 5.97 m).
At the center of the fresco, Christ is surrounded by apostles as the tax collector of Capernaum, seen in rear view, demands payment. Because Christ has no money, he instructs Peter to go to the Sea of Galilee and to extract a coin from the mouth of a fish. Peter's conflicted response is shown in his ambivalent gestures: he draws back his left hand in protest, while simultaneously echoing Christ's pointing right hand. At the far left, in the distance, Peter kneels at the edge of the sea and removes the exact amount of tax due from the fish's mouth. At the right, in the foreground, he places the money in the tax collector's hand.

and the Dead (see Chapter 12), the skeleton admonishes the viewer that death and decay are the future of the human condition. Faith in Christ, the image implies, is the route to salvation.

Masaccio's next major contribution to the city of Florence was the fresco cycle in the Brancacci Chapel illustrating the life of St. Peter. The large scene entitled the *Tribute Money* is divided into three narrative events based on the Gospel of Matthew (figure **13.15**). The monumental figures, whose heads resemble ancient Roman portrait busts, dominate the landscape. Each one shows by his expression or gesture a certain astonishment at Christ's words.

ALBERTI: A RENAISSANCE MAN   Leon Battista Alberti (1404–1474) epitomizes what we today call a "Renaissance Man," a person who is highly accomplished in many fields. He was born in Florence, the illegitimate son of a wealthy merchant who was exiled from Florence for political reasons. Alberti himself studied law and classics and worked as a papal secretary in Rome. He did not return to Florence until the early 1430s.

Alberti's influential work *On Painting* (*Della pittura*), of around 1435, is the earliest Renaissance treatise on art theory. The text opens with the author's impression that the arts in Italy were in decline. After coming to Florence and seeing the work of Brunelleschi, Donatello, Masaccio, and others, however, Alberti realized that a Classical revival was taking place. He described Greco-Roman antiquity as "glorious days," when marvelous works of art and architecture were produced.

Alberti's writing is filled with Classical allusions, for he believed that Classical culture, which inspired the new generation of artists in Florence, was the ideal model. He credited Brunelleschi's system of perspective with having revived the illusion of three-dimensional space achieved by Classical Greek painters; and he credited Giotto and Masaccio with having created convincing figures to inhabit that space.

Nature, in Alberti's view, was the source of art, and art, therefore, should reflect nature. He cited the ancient myth that the first painting was made when the Greek youth Narcissus saw, and fell in love with, his own reflection in a pool of water. For Alberti, painting consists of embracing nature, just as images are reflected on the surface of water. Because the figures created by Giotto, Masaccio, and Donatello appear natural in both form and character, they conform to Alberti's ideal.

Alberti compared painting to a window. The picture plane was equivalent to the flat surface of the window, so that looking at a picture is like looking through a window. Both views, Alberti believed, should replicate what one actually sees—three-dimensional space containing figures behaving naturally and objects appearing as they would in reality.

Alberti's learning was prodigious. He wrote on many topics other than painting, including sculpture, architecture, and society. Like Ghiberti, Alberti wrote an autobiography. Published anonymously, Alberti's account describes the difficulties of being illegitimate and boasts of his physical and intellectual achievements. Most influential of all his work during the fifteenth century was the *Book of the Family* (*Della famiglia*), copies of which could be found in most of the major fifteenth-century humanist libraries. The book, which was written in the form of a dialogue, set out Alberti's ideal view of the Florentine family.

In the *Book of the Family*, Alberti uses an architectural metaphor to equate the father of the family with an architect. A father, he wrote, is responsible for guiding the development of his sons, just as an architect supervises a building. Alberti feared women's evil influence on men and recommended that they be silent and obedient. He advised husbands against sharing secrets with their wives, lest they reveal them to others. Men were to be educated and to work outside the home, Alberti wrote, but women were to tend to the servants and other household matters. When a man was selecting a wife, Alberti declared, it was better if the prospective bride had many brothers and no sisters. He also wrote a number of misogynistic short stories in which women are described in virulently negative terms.

To a considerable degree, Alberti's views were consistent with those of his time. In one respect, however, he was progressive, even by modern standards: he firmly believed that mothers should breast-feed their own infants, rather than hiring wet nurses, as was the prevailing custom. Assuming that a husband had chosen his wife well, Alberti believed that the wife's good character would thus be transferred to her children. Among the women who followed Alberti's advice was Lucrezia Tornabuoni, the wife of Piero de' Medici and mother of Lorenzo the Magnificent.

ALBERTI'S ARCHITECTURE When he was around the age of forty, Alberti became a practicing architect and embarked on an architectural treatise, *De re aedificatoria libri X* (*On Architecture in 10 Books*). This work, as well as the buildings he designed, had a lasting influence on Renaissance and later styles. From 1446 to 1451, he supervised the construction of the Rucellai Palace in Florence (figure **13.16**). This enormous palace exemplifies the virtue of *magnificentia*, for it decorated the city and

also proclaimed the wealth and status of the owner. Stylistically, the Rucellai Palace reflects Alberti's ambition to integrate Classical with Renaissance architecture. Following the principles he saw in the Colosseum in Rome (see figure 7.29), Alberti emphasized the structural logic of the building by making the ground floor appear heavier than the top two floors. The ground floor is taller, made with heavier blocks, and has smaller windows than the floors above it.

Like the Colosseum, the Rucellai Palace uses progressively lighter Orders as the building ascends. Alberti employed the heavier Tuscan Doric Order for the ground-floor pilasters, a version of the lighter Ionic Order on the second floor, and the more elaborate Corinthian Order on the third floor. In addition to adopting the Orders, which were derived from antiquity, Alberti designed a diamond pattern at the base of the ground floor. This derived from ancient Roman buildings, where a similar pattern, called *opus reticulatum*, emphasized the structural solidity of the base of a wall.

13.16 Bernardo Rossellini, after Alberti's design, Rucellai Palace, Florence, 1446–1451.
This palace was commissioned by Giovanni Rucellai, who had made a fortune manufacturing the red color (*oricello*) used in dyeing cloth. A supporter of the Medici, Rucellai's son married a sister of Lorenzo the Magnificent. In honor of their marriage, the frieze is decorated with Rucellai and Medici emblems. Medici coats of arms are visible over two of the second-story windows.

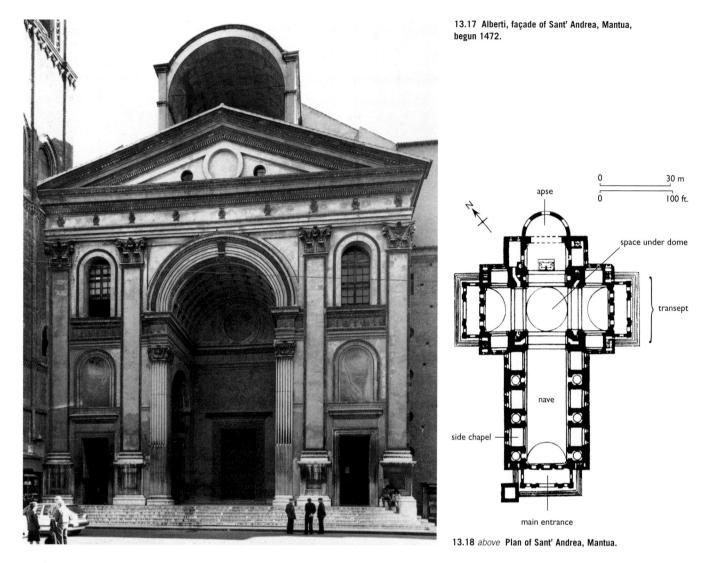

13.17 Alberti, façade of Sant' Andrea, Mantua, begun 1472.

13.18 *above* **Plan of Sant' Andrea, Mantua.**

In church architecture, too, Alberti combined Classical with Renaissance features. His late (and unfinished) church of Sant' Andrea in Mantua (figures **13.17** and **13.18**) shows the influence of Classical symmetry, harmonious proportions, and the use of the Roman round arch and barrel vault. Giant Corinthian pilasters rest on podia reminiscent of those found on Roman triumphal arches and support an entablature based on ancient Greek and Roman prototypes. Crowning the entablature is a wide pediment, also derived from ancient temples. Like a Roman temple, Sant' Andrea seems to dominate the urban space before it. Note also the symmetry and harmonious regularity of the plan (see figure 13.18).

MEDICI PATRONAGE

Not only were the Medici the *de facto* rulers of Florence for most of the fifteenth century, they were also the city's most generous patrons of the arts. They financed works for religious Orders, for churches, and for civic buildings. They commissioned book dealers to buy Classical and Christian texts and established humanist libraries. The Medici palace was both a private residence and a showcase of the family's power. Inspired by Petrarch's description of Mount Ventoux (see Chapter 12) and by the ancient Roman preference for the countryside as respite from urban tensions, the Medici commissioned several country villas. These proved particularly useful as places of refuge during outbreaks of the plague.

DONATELLO'S *DAVID* Sometime between 1420 and 1440, Cosimo de' Medici commissioned Donatello's bronze statue of *David* (figure **13.19**), which stood on a pedestal in the court-yard of the Medici palace. David was a paradigm of Florentine resistance against tyranny, which was symbolized by the Philistine giant, Goliath. David's role as an ancestor of Christ also made his victory over Goliath a symbolic triumph over the devil. As a victor, David exemplified the Renaissance notion of fame achieved through success, in this case overpowering a stronger enemy through intelligence and skill rather than by brute force.

The effeminate quality of the *David* is unusual in a male biblical hero, though it was perhaps less surprising to the humanists, who read Plato and were familiar with his argument that homosexual men make the bravest soldiers, because they fight to impress their lovers. Plato further says that republics—of which Florence was one—tolerate homosexuality, whereas tyrannies do not.

FRA ANGELICO IN SAN MARCO Cosimo de' Medici, a Christian as well as a humanist, financed the Dominican convent of San Marco in Florence and commissioned frescoes and altarpieces for the interior. Most of these were executed by Fra Angelico (*c.* 1400–1455), a pious Dominican friar, manuscript illuminator, and painter. His most monumental works are the frescoes on the walls of the friars' cells and in the corridors of San Marco (figure **13.20**). Fra Angelico's style combines the perspectival construction devised by Brunelleschi and the naturalism of Giotto and Masaccio with the intellectual and spiritual focus of the Dominican Order. In this work, the Virgin, who was the spiritual abbess of San Marco, occupies a pose of mourning, as if meditating on her son's death. The figure of St. Dominic, in contrast, reads a text, reflecting the Order's devotion to study.

INSIDE THE MEDICI PALACE As a frequent destination of visiting dignitaries, ambassadors, and other political figures, the Medici palace was decorated to enhance its image in the outside world. One series of prominently displayed paintings

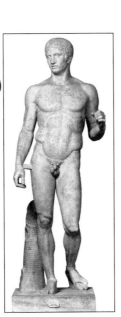

Polykleitos, *Spearbearer*
see figure 6.22

13.19 Donatello, *David*, 1420–1440. Bronze, 5 ft. 2¼ in. (1.58 m) high. Museo Nazionale del Bargello, Florence.
This is an early Renaissance nude sculpture inspired by Classical style (see thumbnail). Note the revival of contrapposto, the convincing organic quality of the body, and the relaxed pose. These characteristics of the Classical canon indicate Donatello's study of Classical sculpture. In breach of Classical style, however, Donatello gives David a distinctive personality. His smug expression signals his easy victory, as his toe plays casually with Goliath's mustache.

13.20 Fra Angelico, *Mocking of Christ with the Virgin and St. Dominic*, cell 7, San Marco, Florence, 1438–1445. Fresco, 6 ft 1⅝ in. × 4 ft. 11½ in. (1.87 × 1.51 m).
In each cell of San Marco, Fra Angelico painted an event from the life of Christ. In keeping with the Dominican Order's rigorous emphasis on asceticism, the images evoke identification with the suffering of holy figures. Here Christ is mocked and tortured by disembodied heads and hands in the background.

13.21 *above* Paolo Uccello, *Battle of San Romano*, 1440s. Tempera on wood panel, 6 ft. × 10 ft. 6 in. (1.82 × 3.20 m). National Gallery, London.

13.22 Benozzo Gozzoli, *Procession of the Magi*, east wall of the Medici chapel, Medici Palace, Florence. 1459. Fresco.

represents three scenes from the Battle of San Romano. In this battle, fought in 1432, Cosimo's ally, the **condottiere** (mercenary soldier) Niccolò da Tolentino, defeated the Sienese army. The episode in figure **13.21** was designed to show the association of the Medici family with the military triumphs of Florence. Riding the rearing white horse and brandishing his sword is Niccolò da Tolentino. The greater force of his army as compared with the Sienese is shown by the prominent lances, waving flags, and central position of the *condottiere*. Visible on the background trees are apples (despite their orange color), known as *mala medica* ("medicinal apples"), which were a symbol of the Medici family. Note the abrupt shift in perspective from the foreground to the distant landscape, where tiny figures continue the battle. The radical foreshortening of the fallen knight is characteristic of Uccello, who was known for his interest in perspective.

The frescoes by Benozzo Gozzoli (*c.* 1420–1497) that illustrate the Procession of the Magi reflect the enormous wealth of the Medici family. The scene covers an entire wall of the chapel in the Medici palace but is only one segment of a long and elaborate procession, painted as if leading toward the altar to worship before a painting in which Mary and Joseph adore the infant Jesus. The part of the procession shown in figure **13.22** contains a number of portraits of family members as well as of important political visitors to the palace. The lead Magus is the young Caspar, who has occasionally been identified as Lorenzo

the Magnificent. In fact, however, Lorenzo was only eleven in 1459 and is shown with his brother Giuliano at the center of the retinue. At the head of the group are Cosimo (in black) and his son Piero (wearing a brocade coat). Note that one figure gazes at the viewer. This is the artist, who has signed the picture in gold on his red hat—OPUS BENOTII ("the work of Benozzo"). The predominance of gold, the attention to details of costume, and the variety of figure types and animals is characteristic of International Gothic style (see Chapter 12). It is also consistent with the Medici practice of using their palace as a political center where the arts reflected their wealth and power.

BOTTICELLI'S *BIRTH OF VENUS* While collecting and translating Classical texts, humanists also revived mythological subject matter and commissioned artists to illustrate scenes from Greek and Roman mythology. Around 1470 to 1480, a cousin of Lorenzo the Magnificent commissioned Botticelli's impressive *Birth of Venus* (figure **13.23**). The goddess, in Greek myth, was

Praxiteles, *Aphrodite of Knidos*
see figure 6.33

13.23 Sandro Botticelli, *Birth of Venus, c.* 1480. Tempera on canvas, 5 ft. 9 in. × 9 ft. 2 in. (1.73 × 2.77 m). Galleria degli Uffizi, Florence.

born from the foam of the sea and is shown here drifting ashore, blown by a gentle breeze from the wind gods. She is welcomed by a personification of Spring, who carries a floral robe. Venus's languid, modest pose is reminiscent of Hellenistic statues (see thumbnail), indicating that Botticelli (1445–1510) was a humanist who studied both the form and content of ancient art.

ARCHITECTURE: GIULIANO DA SANGALLO The Medici commissioned churches as well as urban palaces and country villas. Lorenzo supported the work of Giuliano da Sangallo (*c.* 1445–1516), a leading humanist architect of the late fifteenth century (figure **13.24**). In the church of Santa Maria delle Carceri (St. Mary of the Prisons), built in the small town of Prato, near Florence, Sangallo revived the centralized Greek cross plan (figure **13.25**). Although this was a Byzantine type of plan, in the Renaissance centralized church plans were associated with the Platonic perfection of the circle and *Vitruvian Man* (see figure 13.2). The exterior view of Santa Maria delle Carceri shows the use of Greek pediments and the simple

geometric forms that had appealed to Brunelleschi. Like the Colosseum in Rome, this church uses the heavier Doric Order for the first floor and the lighter Ionic Order above. With the revival of the Greek cross plan, Sangallo introduced a new type of Renaissance church that would influence architecture in the sixteenth century (see Chapter 14).

MUSIC IN FLORENCE UNDER THE MEDICI Music and dance were popular features of Florentine festivals, pageants, and weddings (figure **13.26**). Lorenzo the Magnificent founded a music school, which, like the fifteenth-century courts, drew talent from other parts of Europe. The Flemish composer Heinrich Isaac (*c.* 1450–1517), for example, spent ten years working under Lorenzo's patronage in Florence. He was later appointed court composer to the Holy Roman Emperor Maximilian I in Innsbruck, Austria. Isaac wrote secular as well as church music, with texts in German, French, and Italian.

In Florence, the *intermedio*, which combined music with dance and poetry, became popular. Florentines also devised a

13.24 Giuliano da Sangallo, Santa Maria delle Carceri, Prato, Italy, 1485–1490.

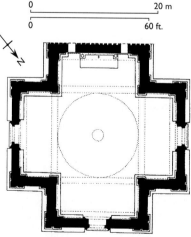

13.25 Plan of Santa Maria delle Carceri, Prato.
Note the plan's regular symmetry, which appealed to the Classical taste.

13.26 Giovanni di Ser Giovanni (lo Scheggia), Adimari wedding *cassone* panel, detail, *c.* 1450. 24¾ in. (63 cm) high. Galleria dell'Academia, Florence.
This panel from a *cassone* (wedding chest) is decorated with a scene showing the types of musical instruments that were played at such events. The setting is a tent, with a receding street and buildings in the background. Elegantly attired couples dance to the music of three shawms with fleurs-de-lis banners and a slide trumpet, as older women sit gossiping to one side. A young page and a servant carrying a wine bottle attend to the guests.

characteristic version of the **frottola**, a lighthearted, generally amorous poem for three or four voices with instrumental accompaniment. The carnival song (a type of *frottola*), or *canto carnascialesco*, was especially popular during the pre-Lenten carnival season. Some of these were written by Isaac during his stay in Florence, and Lorenzo himself composed a famous carnival song reflecting the philosophy that one should enjoy one's youth:

Quant' é bella giovanezza,
Che si fugge tuttavia!
Chi vuol esser lieto, sia:
Di doman ne c'è certezza.

How beautiful is youth,
Which quickly flies away!
Whosoever wishes for happiness, let him:
For tomorrow is never certain.

(Stanza 1)

There was also a more serious, theoretical side to music in fifteenth-century Florence. The philosopher Marsilio Ficino, for example, wrote on musical topics, referring to the practices of antiquity and in particular to Pythagoras. Contemporary accounts relate that Orpheus was an inspiration for songs Ficino performed, improvising (inventing) his own accompaniment on the "lyre." The *lira da braccio*, a bowed string instrument, was widely used by poet-musicians to accompany recitations of lyric and narrative poetry.

CONSERVATIVE BACKLASH: ANTONINUS AND SAVONAROLA

Although fifteenth-century Florence was progressive in many ways, some conservative clerics perceived humanism as a threat to the Church. They objected to the view of man's centrality in the universe and argued for greater emphasis on the power of faith. Two orthodox Dominicans took particularly strong stands on this issue. One was Antonio Pierozzi (1389–1459), a friend of Cosimo de' Medici, who was appointed San Marco's prior in 1439 and in 1446 became archbishop of Florence. A number of miracles were attributed to him, and he was canonized as St. Antoninus in 1523.

Antoninus preached fire-and-brimstone sermons, threatening Florentines with damnation if they failed to repent of their sins. Using the model of Mary Magdalene as a sinner saved through penance, he warned of a coming apocalypse and vividly described everlasting tortures in hell. The dire predictions of Antoninus took on additional force in 1448, when an outbreak of plague swept through Florence. To the populace it seemed that the apocalypse had arrived.

In 1491, another fiery, charismatic Dominican monk, Girolamo Savonarola (1452–1498), became prior of San Marco. Although he had been a friend of the Medici—Lorenzo the Magnificent had arranged for his transfer from his native Ferrara to Florence—Savonarola railed against the family. He convinced the Florentines that the Medici had abused their political power, so much so that in 1494, two years after Lorenzo's death, Savonarola managed to oust the Medici and take control of the government.

Preaching austerity, Savonarola objected to gambling, popular music (including carnival songs), and all displays of material ostentation. He banned carnival celebrations because of their burlesque eroticism. Savonarola presided over two "bonfires of the vanities," in which paintings depicting nudes and mythological subjects were publicly burned. In addition, the citizens of Florence threw into the bonfires articles of clothing, jewels, and playing cards deemed to reflect vanity. Unfortunately for Savonarola, he made the mistake of criticizing Pope Alexander VI, and he was excommunicated. In 1498, Savonarola was hanged. His body was taken down while he was still alive and burned; his ashes were scattered in the River Arno.

THE ARTS OUTSIDE FLORENCE

Although Florence was the preeminent artistic city in fifteenth-century Italy, important works of art were produced elsewhere as well. In Rome, progressive popes were influenced by humanist ideas and encouraged the revival of Classical texts and the stylistic innovations of early Renaissance artists. Nicholas V (papacy 1447–1455), for example, created the core of the Vatican library with Classical and Christian texts. Sixtus IV (papacy 1471–1484) enlarged the library and built the Sistine Chapel. Pius II (papacy 1458–1464) oversaw the development of the first Renaissance ideal city by replanning his native Corsignano (figure **13.27**). He renamed the city Pienza, after himself.

Rulers of humanist courts in Italy—the Aragon in Naples, the Este in Ferrara, the Gonzaga in Mantua, the Malatesta in Rimini, and the Montefeltro in Urbino—competed for artists and writers to convey their political images. At the humanist court of Urbino, Federico da Montefeltro (1422–1482) spent more money on the arts than any other fifteenth-century lord. He imported artists, architects, and tapestry-makers from the Netherlands and central Europe as well as from different parts of Italy. Italian courts thus became centers of humanist patronage, financing musical and theatrical performances and pageants, and staging triumphal processions in imitation of the ancient Roman emperors. A few courts also established humanist schools, where, aside from the martial arts, women were educated equally with men (see Box).

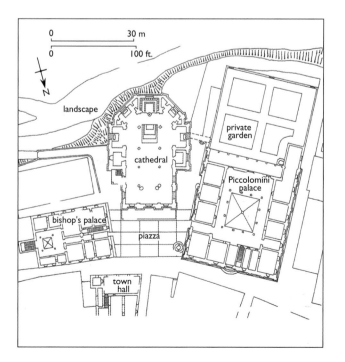

13.27 Bernardo Rossellino, plan of Pienza, Italy, 1460s.
This shows the design of the central area of Pienza. The townhall, cathedral, bishop's palace, and Piccolomini palace (the residence of the pope, named for his family) radiate from the piazza. The centralized design is related to both the Greek cross and Leonardo's *Vitruvian Man* (see figure 13.2). At the back of the Piccolomini palace, Rossellino designed a garden giving onto a landscape view inspired by Petrarch's description of Mount Ventoux (see Chapter 12).

THE STATE PORTRAIT

Like other Renaissance rulers, Federico da Montefeltro commissioned state portraits that reflected his desired political image. Around 1472, he commissioned Piero della Francesca (c. 1420–1492) to paint a pair of portraits of himself and his wife, Battista Sforza (figure **13.28**). Piero was the leading painter in central Italy in the mid-fifteenth century. He worked for a time at Federico's court and is known for his monumental style and his Latin texts on perspective and mathematics. In this **diptych** (two-paneled painting), Piero shows the couple gazing intently at each other, as if oblivious to the viewer. He captures their mutual devotion, evidenced by Federico's refusal to remarry after Battista's death.

Visible in the distance is a landscape view of the territory they ruled around Urbino. The formal posture of the figures conveys their moral uprightness. Note that despite the apparent equality of the couple, Federico appears larger and his geometric hat elevates him above Battista, reminding the viewer that the right to rule is his, even though Battista often ruled in his absence. The red color of Federico's dress, as well as his strict profile, shows his identification with ancient Rome: imperial Roman statuary typically depicted the emperor in a red porphyry garment, and on coins the emperor was similarly shown in profile.

THE EQUESTRIAN PORTRAIT

Another Roman motif revived in fifteenth-century Italy was the equestrian portrait. Inspired by the *Marcus Aurelius* (see thumbnail) in Rome, Renaissance *condottieri* such as Niccolò da Tolentino were honored with images depicting them on horseback. One of the most powerful of these portraits is the bronze *Colleoni* (figure **13.29**) by the Florentine artist Andrea del Verrocchio (1435–1488).

The monument was commissioned by the family of Bartolommeo Colleoni, who came from Bergamo, in northern Italy. He had defended the Venetian republic and is shown here as a fierce, dynamic fighter riding his powerful warhorse into battle. He sits upright in the saddle and turns abruptly, as if

13.28 Piero della Francesca, *Battista Sforza* and *Federico da Montefeltro* (after restoration), *c.* 1472. Oil and tempera on panel, each panel 18½ × 13 in. (47 × 33 cm). Galleria degli Uffizi, Florence.
Federico ran a highly organized court, which he supported by fighting as a *condottiere*. After the death of his first wife, he married Battista Sforza of

Pesaro and supervised her humanist education. Their first six children were girls. Finally, at the age of twenty-six, Battista gave birth to a son, Guidobaldo, but she died shortly thereafter. Judging from her pallor compared to Federico, it is likely that she was already dead when Piero painted the portraits.

13.29 Andrea del Verrocchio, *Colleoni*, Campo Santi Giovanni e Paolo, Venice, *c.* 1481–1496. Bronze, about 13 ft. (4 m) high.

Equestrian portrait of Marcus Aurelius see figure 7.40

catching sight of the enemy. Verrocchio has thus represented Colleoni on the alert and prepared for battle, protecting the republic against invasion.

THE STATE BEDROOM AT MANTUA

The northern Italian city of Mantua was ruled in the fifteenth century by the Gonzaga family. Andrea Mantegna (1431–1506), the court painter to three generations of Gonzaga rulers, decorated the state bedroom of the ducal palace (figure **13.30**). In this view of the fireplace wall,

Lodovico Gonzaga (at the left) turns to receive a message. He is seated on an army field-stool, indicating that he fought for Mantua as a *condottiere*. His wife, the German princess Barbara of Brandenburg, is beside him, along with family members, courtiers, a dwarf, and Lodovico's faithful dog.

The combination of painted and actual architectural surfaces merges reality with illusion, dissolving the entire wall into a painted fiction. The ceiling, only part of which is visible here, is painted as if adorned with marble busts of Roman emperors framed in laurel—an allusion to the Gonzaga family's wish to be associated with the rulers of antiquity.

13.30 Andrea Mantegna, Camera Picta (Camera degli Sposi), Ducal Palace, Mantua, 1474. Fresco, entire room about 26 ft. 6 in. (8.1 m) square.

LEONARDO IN MILAN

The northwestern city of Milan had attracted humanists, including Petrarch, since the fourteenth century. From 1287 to 1447, Milan was ruled by Visconti despots and allied with France and the Holy Roman Empire. The Visconti steered the city through a period of strife lasting to the middle of the fifteenth century. In 1443, one of the daughters of the family married the renowned *condottiere* Francesco Sforza (1401–1466), who ruled Milan until 1466. He and the subsequent Sforza dukes continued a despotic style of rule that placed Milan at odds with republican Florence. Lodovico Sforza (1452–1508), called Il Moro (The Moor) because of his dark complexion, became regent for his nephew, probably had him killed, and ordered the beheading of his own mother. He then seized power and used the arts to reinforce his political legitimacy.

Lodovico hired a number of artists, among them Leonardo da Vinci, who had written to the duke offering his services as a military engineer and describing his abilities in painting, sculpture, and architecture. Lodovico appointed Leonardo court artist and engineer in around 1482. This position entailed devising weapons, producing works of art, and designing scaffolds and other devices for theatrical pageants.

READING SELECTION

Leonardo, *Notebooks*, including his letter to Lodovico Sforza, PWC3-076

Leonardo's most famous work in Milan is the *Last Supper* (figure **13.31**). The fresco was painted opposite a Crucifixion scene on a wall of the original refectory of Santa Maria delle Grazie. Jesus was thus depicted as if facing his own death, which he foretells in the *Last Supper*. Leonardo has represented a sequence of reactions to Jesus' announcement that one of his apostles will betray him. Despite the damaged condition of the work, we can see the quick-tempered St. Peter grabbing a knife in his right hand, Thomas raising his finger in doubt, James the Less (called the Lord's brother) echoing Jesus' cruciform gesture, and the young St. John fainting on hearing Jesus' words. All the apostles gesture and converse in ways that reveal their inner distress. Judas, leaning firmly on the table to the right of Jesus, is marked as the betrayer by his sharp withdrawal and by the bag of silver he holds in his right hand.

The mathematical symmetry of the painting and its perspective is designed to focus the viewer on Jesus (see thumbnail). He is placed at the center, framed by the window, symbolically haloed by the round arch, and illuminated by the natural light of the sky. His extended arms form a triangle, alluding to the doctrine of the Trinity. Jesus is flanked by apostles arranged in four groups of three, echoing the four tapestries on the side walls and the triple window on the back wall. Like Masaccio's *Trinity* (see figure 13.14), the *Last Supper* is constructed illusionistically as if it takes place in a room beyond the actual wall. The orthogonals (see Box, p. 341) converge at a vanishing point on Jesus' eye, making him the psychological as well as the mathematical center of the fresco. The placement of the eye on the horizon can be associated with the setting sun and thus with the death of Jesus (who is traditionally associated with the sun).

Leonardo da Vinci, *Last Supper*, with superimposed orthogonals

13.31 Leonardo da Vinci, *Last Supper* (before last restoration), refectory of Santa Maria delle Grazie, Milan, *c.* 1495–1498. Fresco, oil, and tempera on plaster, 15 ft. 1⅛ in. × 28 ft. 10½ in. (4.6 × 8.6 m).
The triple arch above the painting contains the arms of Lodovico Sforza and his wife Beatrice d'Este, a member of the ruling family of Ferrara. They were married in 1491, when she was fifteen, but she died six years later. The coats of arms are thus both a memorial to Beatrice and Lodovico's statement of his patronage of the work.

THE EARLY RENAISSANCE IN THE NORTH

Like Florence, northern Europe—especially the Netherlands (Low Countries) and Germany—consisted of essentially bourgeois societies. Bankers and merchants flourished, and artistic patronage expanded beyond the Church to include wealthy individuals and civic institutions. Commerce and trade between Italy and the north were extensive, with Italian businessmen working in the Netherlands, and Netherlandish artists and musicians employed in Italy. At the same time, a few important painters were active in France, and the graphic arts, such as woodcut and engraving, were popular in Germany.

After 1415, when the English king Henry V won a decisive battle against the French at Agincourt, the French economy weakened, and France lost its important role in art patronage. Thereafter, the center of art patronage north of Italy shifted to the Netherlands.

PAINTING

Painters in the north favored the medium of oil over the fresco and tempera preferred by their Italian contemporaries in the fifteenth century. Oil paint is made by grinding **pigment** (color) in linseed oil and in this period was applied to a wood panel coated with **gesso** (chalk and plaster thickened with glue). Among the advantages of oil are rich color and a slow drying time. The medium allows the artist to build up layers of paint, to revise the work over a long period, and to depict minute details with a fine brush.

The most important Netherlandish painter in the early fifteenth century was Jan van Eyck (c. 1380/1390–1441), whose self-portrait was discussed earlier (see figure 13.3). Among his patrons were Philip the Good in Bruges and John of Bavaria in The Hague. Van Eyck's famous and much discussed *Arnolfini Portrait* (figure **13.32**) indicates that he also worked for wealthy individual patrons. This painting was commissioned by a member of the Italian Arnolfini family from Lucca, who worked for the Medici in the Netherlands.

An influential article published in the 1930s by the eminent art historian Erwin Panofsky identified the painting as a wedding document, made at a time when marriages were sealed by mutual declaration. He took the signature and the inscription to confirm that the artist had indeed been present at the marriage as a witness and that his self-portrait is among

13.32 Jan van Eyck, *Arnolfini Portrait*, 1434. Oil on wood, 32¼ × 23½ in. (81.8 × 59.7 cm). National Gallery, London.

This painting has been the subject of extensive scholarly debate, interpretation, and reinterpretation since the 1930s. It has been called a straightforward double portrait of a merchant and his wife, and a wedding document witnessed formally by the artist's signature. Van Eyck signed the picture in Latin, *Johannes de eyck fuit hic* ("Jan van Eyck was here"), just above the mirror on the back wall and dated it 1434. If the artist is among the figures reflected in the mirror, this would mean that he signaled his presence through both his image and his name.

the figures in the mirror. Later, however, in a number of studies by subsequent art historians, Panofsky's views were challenged. His primarily iconographic reading was followed by economic, social, political, feminist, and psychological interpretations, all of which attest to the complexity of this enigmatic work. Recent archival research by the British scholar Lorne Campbell has shown that the wedding in question did not take place until 1447; in his view the painting is a double portrait of Giovanni di Nicolas Arnolfini and an unidentified second wife. Whichever of the many readings of this picture is the true one, we can conclude that portraiture (and probably self-portraiture, if we accept the view that the *Man in the Red Turban* is indeed van Eyck himself) was of paramount importance to the artist and his patrons.

Van Eyck's largest and most spectacular work, filled with rich detail, is the *Altarpiece of the Lamb* (figures **13.33** and **13.34**). Also known as the Ghent altarpiece, this work reflects the Netherlandish delight in rich texture and different perspectival viewpoints. The main panels, visible when the altarpiece is closed, represent the Annunciation, the donors, and statues of John the Evangelist and John the Baptist. The small panels at the top depict Old Testament prophets and pagan sibyls, with scrolls foretelling the coming of Christ.

The New Testament figures—Mary, Gabriel, and the two Saints John—are shown in *grisaille* (imitation stone). The donors, on the other hand, are shown in flesh and blood and they wear fifteenth-century dress. Van Eyck uses this distinction between biblical figures and the contemporary donors to suggest that the message of Christianity is like stone: it will last.

When opened, the Ghent altarpiece presents a vast panorama of time and space. Beginning with the Fall of Man, it

13.33 *right* Jan van Eyck, *Altarpiece of the Lamb* (Ghent altarpiece), exterior, Cathedral of St. Bavon, Ghent, 1432. Oil on panel, closed 11 ft. 6 in. × 7 ft. 7 in. (3.5 × 2.33 m).

13.34 *below* Jan van Eyck, *Altarpiece of the Lamb* (Ghent altarpiece), interior, Cathedral of St. Bavon, Ghent, 1432. Oil on panel, open 11 ft. 6 in. × 14 ft. 5 in. (3.5 × 4.4 m).

13.35 Petrus Christus, *St. Eloy (Eligius) in His Studio*, 1449. Oil on panel, 39 × 33½ in. (99 × 85 cm). The Metropolitan Museum of Art, New York. St. Eloy is in his shop, dressed as an artisan, talking with a pair of customers. A ledge containing Eloy's wares occupies the foreground, while the shelves on the wall are filled with rings, vases, and other objects. He appears to be selling a wedding ring to the woman, a reading that is reinforced by the bridal girdle on the ledge. The rich colors and reflective light are characteristic of north European painting. The inscription on the front of the ledge reads: "Master Petrus Christus made me in 1449."

The complex iconography of *St. Eloy in His Studio* (figure **13.35**) by Petrus Christus (*c.* 1420–1475/6), who worked mainly in Bruges, has—like the *Arnolfini Portrait*—made the work the subject of several interpretations. Because the painting represents St. Eloy, a Merovingian martyr, mintmaster, and patron of goldsmiths, scholars assume that it was commissioned by the guild of goldsmiths.

Petrus Christus's style reflects the north European tendency to merge secular and religious content in a single work. For example, the coral on the shelf is both a material used in making jewelry and a Christian symbol of rebirth and resurrection. The presence of a scale and weights, used in determining the value of jewels, also alludes to the weighing of souls at the Last Judgment. The convex mirror at the right was a standard means of deterring shoplifters, but, as it is cracked, it suggests *vanitas*—a warning to those who create and wear expensive jewels that death and decay are the inevitable future.

In France, the leading court painter of the second half of the fifteenth century was Jean Fouquet (*c.* 1420–*c.* 1481). Born in Tours, in central France, Fouquet is best known for his miniature portraits. His depiction of Charles VII (figure **13.36**), with its parted curtain revealing the king, exemplifies the Renaissance notion of painting as a window.

13.36 Jean Fouquet, *Portrait of Charles VII*, after 1451. Oil on wood panel, 33⅞ × 28⅜ in. (86 × 72 cm). Louvre, Paris. Downcast and gloomy, Charles seems overwhelmed by his dark red, fur-trimmed coat, and his hat is too large for his narrow face. Nevertheless, the inscription asserts his power and his lineage: "The very victorious king of France" above, and "Charles, the seventh of the name" below. Charles owed his crown to Joan of Arc.

shows Adam and Eve occupying the upper panels at each end, with small *grisaille* scenes of Cain and Abel. Choirs of angels separate the primal couple from the three central panels, arranged hierarchically: God is in the center, flanked by the Virgin and John the Baptist. God wears a papal tiara, and a royal crown is placed at his feet.

The large central panel below depicts the Adoration of the Lamb. A sacrificial lamb, signifying Christ, stands on an altar surrounded by angels. Beyond the altar to the left is a group of confessors; to the right are virgin martyrs carrying palms (an iconographic allusion to triumph over death). In the far distance, the towers of the Heavenly Jerusalem are visible. On either side of the baptismal fountain in the foreground, groups of pilgrims arrive and kneel in adoration. The side panels show the pilgrims journeying toward the more sacred space of the center.

The Ghent altarpiece is filled with richer color and a greater abundance of minute detail than Italian paintings of the same period. Van Eyck's figures, although naturalistic, appear less Classical than those in Italian paintings. And despite the grid pattern on the floor in the upper center panels, which reflects the use of linear perspective, there are shifts in points of view from panel to panel.

13.37 Martin Schongauer, *Elephant, c.* 1485. Engraving, 4¼ × 5¾ in. (10.8 × 14.6 cm). Cleveland Museum of Art, Ohio.

GRAPHIC ART

With the introduction of illustrated books, printing became a major source of imagery. Woodcut, the earliest technique, was used for illustrating both books and playing cards. It was followed by engraving, in which lines are cut or incised into a metal plate and then inked. When a sheet of paper is pressed onto the plate, the design is transferred to the paper.

Martin Schongauer (*c.* 1450–1491), a painter who worked in Colmar, in Alsace, was also a leading printmaker. He is known for the tactile quality of his images and his ability to convey three-dimensional form through modeling. His *Elephant* (figure **13.37**) of around 1485 combines naturalism with fanciful features. Note the seashell shapes of the ear, the spiral patterns on the trunk, and the round feet.

In the north, elephants were considered exotic, and, judging from this print, one wonders whether Schongauer had ever seen one. The elephant carries a tower with figures peering out, alluding to medieval manuscripts showing warrior elephants. The derivation of this motif from India, where elephants were used in battle, reflects a migration of imagery from the East. In the West, elephants symbolized strength and long life—Schongauer's elephant is literally a "tower of strength."

MUSIC

The most innovative fifteenth-century music was composed in northern Europe. As with the visual arts, secular patronage increased and individual musicians, like artists, worked for courts and for the Church in various countries. This greatly enriched their sources of influence and their compositions.

Composers began to move away from the rigid isorhythmic structures of fourteenth-century *ars nova* (see Chapter 12),

writing music for three or four voices in a simpler polyphonic style. Of increasing concern and interest was the way the musical lines related to each other—how the notes coincided as chords and how the chords themselves fell into successions of harmonies, or **chordal progressions**. This period could thus be seen to mark the beginning of Western or "common-practice" harmony.

The trend toward secular song seen in the music of Machaut continued into the fifteenth century. The main form was the **chanson** (French for "song"). Usually written for three voices, these songs were often performed with one or two lines taken by instruments.

The greatest English composer of this period, John Dunstable (*c.* 1390–1453), wrote both French and English secular songs and was famed for his sweet style. Using the harmonious intervals of thirds and sixths rather more than his contemporaries, he became widely known as far afield as France and Italy and influenced other musicians. The major part of his output was sacred music; two complete Masses and over forty motets (polyphonic choral compositions for the Roman service) have survived. Most are written for three voices, rather than the four or five that would later become the norm. Although some of this music still uses medieval isorhythm, Dunstable unites it with lyrical melodies that prefigure the style of the High Renaissance.

GUILLAUME DUFAY   North of the Alps, the main center of music patronage was the court of Philip the Good in Burgundy—an independent region until the death of Charles the Bold in 1477. The most important early-fifteenth-century composer—Guillaume Dufay (*c.* 1400–1474) of Cambrai, in northern France—worked for Philip for several years. Dufay also studied in Italy, was employed by Italian courts, sang in the papal choir in Rome, and was choirmaster at the Savoy court. Some two hundred works by him survive, including over eighty *chansons*, eight Masses, and numerous motets.

During his lifetime, Dufay was considered the greatest composer of his day. Although the majority of his works were written for three voices, he was one of the first musicians to write skillfully for four. He was also a key figure in the development of the so-called "cyclic Mass," a musically unified setting of the Ordinary of the Mass. Unity was achieved by repeating the same tenor theme in each movement and, sometimes, by beginning sections with the same musical motif in all parts.

Most of Dufay's motets were composed to celebrate particular political or social events. One of the best-known pieces was written for the consecration of Brunelleschi's dome in 1436. In accord with the concerns of early Renaissance artists with harmony and balance, the rhythmic proportions and other elements of Dufay's motet correspond to the structural features of the dome itself.

Dufay's secular music was written for performance at banquets and other social events at the various European courts where he worked. In 1423, for example, he was employed at Pesaro in Italy, where he was required to compose a *chanson* celebrating the marriage of Carlo Malatesta, the future lord of Rimini, to the pope's niece. The song's refrain praises Dufay's patron as "Charles gentil, qu'on dit de Malateste" ("Fair Charles, called Malatesta"). Note that although it was written for an Italian audience, the French language was used. Such pieces were performed by skilled solo singers and instrumentalists. Most were for one vocalist with two accompanying players.

The influence of humanism can be seen in many of Dufay's *chansons*. "Ce moys de may" ("Ce Mois de Mai," "This Month of May") of around 1440, for instance, celebrates the coming of spring and reflects the new enthusiasm for nature. It begins:

> This month of May let us be happy and joyous
> And banish melancholy from our hearts.
> > Let us sing, dance and make merry.
> > To spite these base, envious creatures.
>
> Let each one try more than ever
> To serve his fair mistress well:
> This month of May let us be happy and joyous
> And banish melancholy from our hearts.

Another humanist element is Dufay's insertion of his name into the text of a few of his songs. In the last stanza of "This Month of May" and in the motet *Ave regina coelorum* ("Hail Queen of Heaven"), he asks the Virgin to have pity on him. This increasing presence of the author, whether by signature, self-portrait, or musical text, was part of the Classical revival and would be a feature of the Western humanities from the Renaissance forward.

JOSQUIN DESPREZ   The interest in individual genius was an aspect of Renaissance culture related to the humanist emphasis on fame. The first musician described in terms of genius by his contemporaries was Josquin Desprez (*c.* 1440–1521). Born in northern France, Josquin sang at Milan Cathedral from 1459 to 1472, and he spent one year at the Sforza court and thirteen years with the papal choir in Rome. From 1499 to 1503 he lived in France, and in April 1503 he was appointed music director at the Este court of Duke Ercole I in Ferrara. Josquin returned to France in 1504 and became canon of the collegiate church of Condé-sur-l'Escaut, where he remained until his death.

Josquin composed over a period of about sixty years, and more works by him survive than by practically any of his contemporaries. During Dufay's lifetime, the Mass had become established as a musical form with five linked movements setting the Ordinary of the Mass. Josquin's twenty Masses, all with the richer four-voice texture that was becoming the norm, consolidate this. The fact that the Italian music printer Petrucci chose to publish three volumes of Josquin's Masses and no more than one by anyone else is an indication of the esteem in which the composer was held.

Josquin's originality can be seen particularly in his motets, of which he wrote over eighty. Compared with motets of the fourteenth century, Josquin's break free from the confines of isorhythm, with flowing melodies and clearer chordal progressions. Harmony and texture are richer—in part due to the fact that at least four voices are used, and sometimes as many as six. Moreover, there is a definite attempt to express emotion in music. Josquin's *Ave Maria . . . virgo serena* ("Hail Mary . . . serene Virgin") of around 1485 is a prayer to the Virgin. Written for four voices, it uses the technique of imitation between the parts that became fundamental to later Renaissance music. The opening words, "Hail Mary," appear first in the highest voice, and are then sung by each lower part in turn to the same music. The voices overlap partially in such a way that all four singers combine only briefly to bring the phrase to a climax and conclusion. Elsewhere in the motet there are "full" sections where all four voices weave together in imitation, and lighter ones where two voices are picked out in a duet. The conclusion, "O Mother of God, remember me," is peaceful; it is also another example of an author's presence in his own work.

Josquin wrote some seventy *chansons*. In "Woodland Nymphs," he introduces a personal note again as he laments the death of the Flemish composer who may have been his teacher, Johannes Ockeghem (*c.* 1410–*c.* 1497). A loose translation of the French text reflects the inspiration of Classical myth:

> Nymphs of the woods, goddesses of fountains,
> Expert singers from every nation,
> Transform your strong voices, clear and high
> Into trenchant cries and lamentations,
> Because the ravages of Atropos [one of the three Fates of
> > Greek mythology]
> Have ensnared your Okeghem [the Fates were believed to
> > control life by a thread, which they cut to signal death]
> The real treasure and master of music
> Who no longer escapes death
> And who, to great sorrow, lies covered with earth.
>
> Clothe yourself in mourning,
> Josquin, Brumel, Pierchon, Compère [names of musicians]
> And let the tears fall from your eyes
> For you have lost a good father
> May he rest in peace [in Latin in the original].
> Amen.

The early Renaissance, affected by the Black Death of 1348, peasant rebellions, the Great Schism in the Church, and economic changes, witnessed a vast expansion in the arts. As the culture of the Middle Ages waned, a new, more questioning approach to the world developed, which extended outward to geographical exploration and inward to human character. As we will see in subsequent chapters, these developments would not be without backlash of the kind seen in fifteenth-century Florence.

Thematic Parallels

The Classical Tradition: Revival and Opposition

As we have seen, the Classical tradition that began with the culture of fifth-century-B.C. Athens was reborn during the Renaissance. Although the Italian Renaissance has proved to be the most far-reaching revival of Greek and Latin culture, such revivals have recurred intermittently in Western history, from Charlemagne to the present day. The language of Classical architecture has been particularly vital in Western history, and elements of it are still used in building design today. However, there have also been periods of conscious rejection of the Classical tradition, when artists tried to free themselves of its influence.

Each revival has adapted classicism to its own context, altering aspects of its style and thought. The ancient Romans, for example, so admired Greek sculpture that they devoted an enormous industry to making copies. Indeed, much of what we know about Greek sculpture comes from Roman copies, because many of the Greek originals have not survived. In the realm of political organization, republican Rome based its notion of elected government on Athenian democracy, in which male citizens were required to participate in self-governance. Even the Roman emperors, mindful of the tradition of republicanism, tried to maintain an impression of fair and just rule, false though that impression often was. In turn, later periods of Western history

looked to imperial Rome as a source of the "Classical tradition."

Charlemagne, crowned Holy Roman Emperor in A.D. 800, wanted to be regarded as a new Roman emperor. This, he believed, would benefit his image as the ruler of a great empire. One visual expression of this notion was his equestrian portrait, which was based on those commissioned by the emperors of Rome (see figure 10.1). Similarly, the design of his palace chapel in Aachen derived, via the centralized Greek cross plan of Byzantine churches, from the round temples of Greece and Rome. Charlemagne's educational reforms consciously emphasized Latin language and culture, as exemplified by his adoption of Roman grammar.

13.38 Charles Bulfinch, Massachusetts State House, Boston, 1795–1797.
Charles Bulfinch, the son of a wealthy merchant in Boston, studied classics at Harvard, traveled in Europe, and was an amateur architectural designer. When his family lost its fortune, Bulfinch found work as the Boston police superintendent, becoming active in politics and earning extra money as an architect.

Arch of Titus, Rome, c. A.D. 81
see figure 7.32

Arc de Triomphe, Paris, 1806–1836
see figure 18.3

the twentieth century, the modernist **avant-garde** advocated newness in place of traditional forms. Artists found new formal solutions in non-Western art—African, Oceanic, Native American, pre-Columbian, and others—which came to light as a result of colonialism, archaeological and anthropological missions, international cultural exhibitions, and increasing global travel and trade.

Despite modernist efforts to escape the Classical tradition, it persists in one form or another. Recently, Postmodernists (like the Mannerists before them) have appropriated Classical forms but have altered them in ways that defy historical meaning and structural logic. In the Piazza d'Italia, in New Orleans (see thumbnail), for example, the architects reused the grammar of Classical Orders and the round arch, accenting them with color created by neon lighting. The interest lies in the way they place them in a new context and in new relationships to each other.

In the eighteenth century the Classical tradition once again inspired democratic reform. This time, violent revolutions in America and France looked to Classical models of constitutional government to overturn the "divine right" of kings. In architecture, the Neoclassical style was introduced in France as a style of revolution; ironically, after the French Revolution it was adopted by Napoleon as a style of empire. Napoleon revived architectural expressions of Roman imperial power—such as the triumphal arch (see thumbnails) and the freestanding monumental column—as a way of proclaiming the legitimacy of his power by linking himself to ancient rulers.

In the United States, Thomas Jefferson (1743–1826) promoted the Neoclassical style, renamed the Federal style, as the type of architecture best suited to the new American republic. The effects of this can be seen today in the many Federal and public buildings—the White House, state capitols, banks, courthouses, libraries, etc.—that are inspired by the Classical Orders of architecture. A good example is the Massachusetts

State House in Boston (figure **13.38**), which was designed by Charles Bulfinch (1763–1844) in the late eighteenth century. His use of the dome, inspired by Roman and Renaissance architecture, has become characteristic of government buildings in the United States.

Despite the persistence of the Classical tradition, there have been times of outright rebellion against it. In sixteenth-century Europe, for example, as the High Renaissance evolved into Mannerism, artists subverted the Classical taste for symmetry, harmony, and an impression of stability. While using the language of classicism, they rearranged elements, creating a sense of instability, tension, and compression. Sometimes these rearrangements had a humorous quality, but more often they represented an effort to achieve new architectural solutions.

During the second half of the nineteenth century, as enthusiasm for Neoclassicism declined, European and American artists and architects began to look for alternatives to the Classical tradition. Around the turn of

Piazza d'Italia, New Orleans, 1978–1979
see figure 23.31

KEY TERMS

avant-garde newness for its own sake.

chanson (French, "song") a secular polyphonic song in the Middle Ages and Renaissance; the form includes rondeaux, ballades, and virelais.

chordal progression a sequence of chords.

condottiere in medieval and Renaissance Italy, a soldier of fortune.

diptych a two-paneled painting.

frottola a lighthearted, generally amorous poem for three or four voices sung to instrumental accompaniment, usually chordal in style.

gesso a white coating of chalk, plaster, and resin that is applied to a surface to make it more receptive to paint.

incise to cut designs or letters into wood or metal with a sharp instrument.

orthogonal consisting of, or relating to, right angles, or a line perpendicular to the plane of a relief or a picture.

pigment a substance used to give color to paints, inks, and dyes.

tondo a painting or relief sculpture having a round frame.

vanishing point in linear perspective, the point at which the orthogonals meet.

woodcut or **woodblock print** an image incised on a block of wood and printed on paper.

KEY QUESTIONS

1. Define humanism. What three characteristics would have to be included in this definition if it were to apply to the Renaissance period?
2. Cite instances of Renaissance works that contain the following:
   a. Architectural Orders derived from antiquity
   b. Linear perspective
   c. Psychological insight and motivation
   d. Emphasis on authorship
   e. Human anatomy
3. Describe Ghiberti's and Brunelleschi's submissions (figures 13.7 and 13.8) for the baptistery door of Santa Maria del Fiore. What traits of each submission show the artist's innovative approach?
4. How does Donatello's *David* illustrate the Renaissance interest in antiquity and in personality?
5. Prove or disprove the following statement: "The Medici and other rulers, including popes, used the arts to express their wealth, power, and intellectual superiority."

SUGGESTED READING

Adams, Laurie Schneider. *Italian Renaissance Art*. Boulder, CO: Westview Press, 2001.
  ▶ A well-illustrated survey of Italian Renaissance art from the thirteenth to the sixteenth century.

——. *Key Monuments of the Italian Renaissance*. Boulder, CO: Westview Press (Icon edition), 2000.
  ▶ Major monuments of the Italian Renaissance in context.

Alberti, Leon Battista. *On Painting*, trans. John R. Spencer. New Haven, CT, and London: Yale University Press, 1996.
  ▶ The first treatise on Renaissance art theory.

——. *The Family in Renaissance Florence*, trans. R. N. Watkins. Colombia, SC: University of South Carolina Press, 1989.
  ▶ A translation of Alberti's advice on family life and child-rearing.

Antal, Frederick. *Florentine Painting and its Social Background*. Boston: Boston Book and Art Shop, 1965.
  ▶ A history of Florentine painting in the Renaissance in its social context. A Marxist approach to art history, focusing on the economic forces behind the arts.

Barolsky, Paul. *Infinite Jest: Wit and Humor in Italian Renaissance Art*. Columbia, MO: University of Missouri Press, 1978.
  ▶ A witty study of humor in Italian Renaissance art.

Baron, Hans. *In Search of Florentine Civic Humanism*, 2 vols. Princeton, NJ: Princeton University Press, 1988.
  ▶ A classic study of the humanist movement.

Baxandall, Michael. *Painting and Experience in 15th-century Italy*, 2nd ed. Oxford: Oxford University Press, 1988.
  ▶ The relationship of society and money to painting.

Brown, Patricia Fortini. *Life and Art in Renaissance Venice*. New York: Harry N. Abrams, 1997.
  ▶ Venetian art in the context of its time.

Cole, Alison. *Virtue and Magnificence: Art of the Italian Renaissance Courts*. New York: Harry N. Abrams, 1995.
  ▶ A nicely illustrated study of court patronage during the Italian Renaissance.

Cuttler, Charles D. *Northern Painting from Pucelle to Bruegel*. New York: Henry Holt and Co., 1968.
  ▶ A standard survey of painting in northern Europe.

Harbison, Craig. *The Mirror of the Artist: Northern Renaissance Art in its Historical Context.* New York: Harry N. Abrams, 1995.
> ▸ North European art in context.

Herlihy, D., and C. Klapisch-Zauber. *Tuscans and Their Families.* New Haven, CT: Yale University Press, 1985.
> ▸ Life and society in fifteenth-century Italy.

Hibbert, Christopher. *The House of Medici: Its Rise and Fall.* New York: Morrow Quill, 1980.
> ▸ A study of the Medici family and its financial fortunes.

King, Margaret. *Women of the Renaissance.* Chicago and London: University of Chicago Press, 1991.
> ▸ On the roles and status of women in the Renaissance.

Lane, Barbara. *The Altar and the Altarpiece: Sacramental Themes in Early Netherlandish Painting.* New York: Grafton Books, 1984.
> ▸ A study of the role and meaning of the altar and the altarpiece in north European painting.

Panofsky, Erwin. *Early Netherlandish Painting,* 2 vols. New York: HarperCollins, 1971.
> ▸ A classic study of north European painting.

——. *Meaning in the Visual Arts.* New York: Viking Press, 1974.
> ▸ Art and meaning in the Renaissance.

Roover, Raymond de. *The Rise and Decline of the Medici Bank, 1397–1494.* Cambridge, MA: Harvard University Press, 1963.
> ▸ The history and influence of the Medici bank.

Seidel, Linda. *Jan van Eyck's Arnolfini Portrait: Stories of an Icon.* Cambridge, U.K.: Cambridge University Press, 1993.
> ▸ One of several methodological studies of van Eyck's painting.

Trexler, Richard. *Public Life in Renaissance Florence.* Ithaca, NY, and London: Academic Press, 1980.
> ▸ A study of Renaissance Florence from the point of view of society, politics, and everyday life.

SUGGESTED FILMS

1964   *The Masque of the Red Death,* dir. Roger Corman

1968   *Andrei Rublev (Andrei Rublyov),* dir. Andrei Tarkovsky

1971   *The Canterbury Tales,* dir. Pier Paolo Pasolini

1989   *Henry V,* dir. Kenneth Branagh

1992   *Christopher Columbus,* dir. John Glen

14

The High Renaissance in Italy and Early Mannerism

> *They were, while living, highly rewarded by the liberality of Princes and by the splendid ambition of States, and even after death kept alive in the eyes of the world by the testimony of statues, tombs, medals, and other memorials of that kind; none the less, it is clearly seen that the ravening maw of time has not only diminished by a great amount their own works and the honourable testimony of others, but has also blotted out and destroyed the names of all those who have been kept alive by any other means than by the right vivacious and pious pens of writers.*

(VASARI, *Lives of the Most Eminent Painters, Sculptors, and Architects*, PREFACE)

The High Renaissance in Italy lasted from around 1494, when the Medici were expelled from Florence, to around 1520, when the artist Raphael died. At the turn of the sixteenth century, the center of patronage shifted from Florence to Rome, where humanist popes and other wealthy individuals financed innovative artistic projects, although major works continued to be produced in Florence. Venice, too, was an important center of cultural innovation, not only in the visual arts but also in music and the new printing technology. In addition to Raphael (1483–1520), the great artists of the High Renaissance include Donato Bramante (1444–1514), Leonardo da Vinci (1452–1519), and Michelangelo Buonarroti (1475–1564); and the Venetian painters Giovanni Bellini (c. 1435–1516), Giorgione da Castelfranco (c. 1477–1510), and Tiziano Vecelli, known in English as Titian (c. 1487–1576).

Literary figures contributed significantly to the High Renaissance. The Prince (Il principe) by Niccolò Machiavelli (1469–1527) remains a classic work of political theory. The Courtier (Il cortegiano) by Baldassare Castiglione (1478–1529) combines philosophy and politics with manners in describing the ideal education of a gentleman. And the literary epic Orlando furioso by Lodovico Ariosto (1474–1433) reflects the persistence of chivalric and pastoral traditions. Dramatists continued to revive genres of Classical theater, often placing Greek and Roman plot structures in contemporary settings.

A few visual artists also produced important written works. Leonardo's extensive notebooks cover aspects of nature, science, technology, and the arts. They include a treatise on painting and the Paragone, in which he compares the relative merits of different art forms. Michelangelo wrote sonnets, which reveal his personal psychology and his views on art.

Around the time of Raphael's death in 1520, the High Renaissance style began to evolve into Mannerism.

Key Topics

The High Renaissance

Papal patronage

Extending the vernacular

Biography and autobiography: Vasari

Michelangelo's sonnets

Machiavelli: *The Prince*

Contrasts

Innovation and revival

Secular and sacred iconography

Painting: handicraft or liberal art

Leonardo: *Paragone*

Humanism versus conservative backlash

Cellini: *Autobiography*

Mannerism

Anti-Classical proportions

Mysticism

Saints and martyrs

Eroticism

Cellini: *Autobiography*

Music

Willaert

The Gabrielis

The madrigal

TIMELINE	HIGH RENAISSANCE c. 1494–1520	MANNERISM c. 1520–1590
HISTORY AND CULTURE	Center of patronage shifts from Florence to Rome Venice: cultural center for music Aldine Press, Venice, produces inexpensive small-scale books, from late 15th century Italy invaded by French, 1494 Magellan circumnavigates the globe, 1519–1521 Holy Roman Emperor Charles V fights French, 1522 Treaty of Cambrai, 1529, brings in period of prosperity Population of western Europe rises to nearly 90 million Antwerp and London become mercantile centers Trafficking in slaves *Conquistadores* seek silver and gold from New World, early 16th century	The Medici return to Florence, 1512 Style spreads to France, Spain, and northern Europe Political and religious turmoil
RELIGION	Humanist pope: Julius II (papacy 1503–1513) Martin Luther launches Protestant Reformation in Germany, 1517	
ART	Giovanni Bellini, *Madonna of the Meadow*, c. 1500–1505 Michelangelo, *David*, 1501–1504; Sistine Chapel ceiling, 1509–1512; *Last Judgment*, 1534–1541 Leonardo, *Mona Lisa*, c. 1503–1515; drawings Raphael, *Madonna and Child*, c. 1505; *School of Athens*, 1509–1511; *Baldassare Castiglione*, c. 1514 Giorgione, *Fête Champêtre*, c. 1510 Titian, *Assumption of the Virgin*, 1516–1518; *Venus of Urbino*, c. 1538; *Charles V Seated*, 1548	Raphael, *Fire in the Borgo*, from 1514 Pontormo, *Portrait of a Halberdier*, c. 1528–1530 Parmigianino, *Madonna of the Long Neck*, c. 1535 Cellini, saltcellar of Francis I, 1543; *Perseus*, 1545–1554 Anguissola, *Self-portrait at a Spinet*, after 1550
ARCHITECTURE	Bramante, Tempietto, Rome, c. 1502 Plans of New St. Peter's, Rome: Bramante, Antonio da Sangallo, Michelangelo	Romano, Palazzo del Tè, Mantua, 1527–1534 Palladio, San Giorgio Maggiore, Venice, begun 1565; *The Four Books of Architecture*, 1570
LITERATURE	Machiavelli, *The Prince*, 1513 Ariosto, *Orlando furioso*, 1516 Castiglione, *The Courtier*, 1528	Vasari, *Lives of the Most Eminent Painters, Sculptors, and Architects*, 1550; autobiography added 1568 Cellini, *Autobiography*, 1558
THEATER	Court patronage Increased use of the vernacular Ariosto, *The Casket*, 1508 Machiavelli, *The Mandrake*, 1513–1520 Trissino, *Sofonisba*, 1515	
MUSIC	Venice in the forefront of music printing Musical instruments developed Organ used in liturgy Split choir Adrian Willaert (c. 1490–1562) chapel master of St. Mark's Cathedral, Venice The Gabrielis: grand choral works New Renaissance form: madrigal Music for instrumental ensembles	

This refers both to an artistic style that continued to the end of the century and to a worldview that rejected the humanist classicism, symmetry, and use of linear perspective that characterize Renaissance style. Michelangelo and Titian lived well into the Mannerist period, and there are discernible elements of Mannerism in their late styles. In the case of Michelangelo, his late work reflects his sense of spiritual conflict which, in turn, conformed to political and religious tensions in the sixteenth century.

The quotation that opens this chapter is taken from the Preface to the Lives of the Most Eminent Painters, Sculptors, and Architects *by Giorgio Vasari (1511–1574). First published in 1550 and revised and expanded in 1568, the* Lives *reflects the Renaissance preoccupation with fame and individual genius. Vasari reports that Renaissance artists were well paid by ambitious rulers and remembered through their works, but he notes that time destroys or diminishes the reputation of those not kept alive by the written word. Vasari thus takes as his mission the preservation of the memory of Renaissance artists by writing about them. He also included an autobiography in the revised edition of 1568.*

Although there is much to be learned from Vasari, his Lives *often contains misinformation, either because he is mistaken about certain facts and events or because he wishes to embellish them. For example, Vasari describes Leonardo's death as if the French king, Francis I, rushed to the artist's bedside, when in fact he was not there at all. We may know (or discover through further research) that such stories are not literally true. Nevertheless, Vasari's distortions often contain an implied truth—in this case, Vasari conveys Francis I's devotion to Leonardo and his work.*

Beginning with Cimabue (see Chapter 12) and concluding with Vasari's autobiography, the Lives *provides a framework of Italian art from the late thirteenth to the mid-sixteenth century. It contains a wealth of source material on artists, descriptions of works of art, gossip, and anecdotes that bring the social context of the Renaissance to life. Throughout the* Lives, *Vasari makes clear his opinions of art and artists—their characters and their talent. Above all he admires Michelangelo, who was his personal friend. For Vasari, Michelangelo is* Il divino *("The divine one"), a reflection of the Renaissance view that genius is an inborn, God-given gift.*

POLITICAL AND ECONOMIC DEVELOPMENTS

By the late Middle Ages, the modern nation-state, defined by national boundaries, had begun to evolve more or less into its present form. France and England had been ruled by single kings for centuries. Spain had been divided into different kingdoms until the marriage of Isabella of Castile (ruled 1474–1504) and Ferdinand of Aragon (ruled 1479–1516), who reigned jointly from 1479. In a show of Christian unity and political might, they expelled the Muslims, whom they defeated in Granada in 1492, and the Jews. In addition, they solidified their power through the Spanish Inquisition, which persecuted anyone suspected of disloyalty to the Church or the Crown.

The Holy Roman Empire—which encompassed most of modern Austria and Germany, the Netherlands, the southern half of Italy, and Sicily—continued to be a force in Europe and remained so through the High Renaissance. By 1500, the dominant European powers were England, France, Spain, and the Holy Roman Empire. The rest of Europe also had more or less established national boundaries.

The High Renaissance was a period fraught with continual political turmoil. Repeated invasions of the Italian peninsula disrupted the power of the Church. In 1494, the armies of the French king, Charles VIII (ruled 1483–1498), invaded Italy on the grounds that France had long-standing claims to Milan and Naples through marriage. Italy's defense depended on support from Venice, the pope, the Holy Roman Empire, and Spain. In 1499 the French under Louis XII (ruled 1499–1515) invaded Milan—continuing to attack Italy despite, and perhaps because of, their admiration for Italian culture. The Valois king Francis I (ruled 1515–1547), for example, hired Leonardo to work at the French court in 1516.

In addition to trying to secure Milan and Naples for himself, Francis I wanted to obtain the Holy Roman Empire. His failure to do so led to years of war against Charles V (of the House of Habsburg) (figure **14.1**), whose reign as emperor lasted from 1519 to 1556 (map **14.1**, p. 369).

Charles V was born in 1500 to Philip I, king of Castile, and Queen Joanna, who went insane. When he was fifteen, Charles was named regent of Castile in central Spain, and in 1516, when his maternal grandfather, Ferdinand II, died, he became Charles I of Spain. In 1519 his paternal grandfather, the Habsburg Holy Roman Emperor Maximilian I, died, and Charles was elected Holy Roman Emperor as Charles V. By the age of nineteen Charles was on his way to leading the world's largest empire.

Charles was unable to control his kingdom as tightly as he wished, and his ambition to rule a unified Christian empire was never realized. In 1522 he fought the French in Italy, and he sacked Rome five years later. This led to a decline in papal patronage and weakened the papacy itself. In 1529, the Treaty

14.1 Titian, *Charles V Seated*, 1548. Oil, 6 ft. 8¾ in. × 4 ft. (2.05 × 1.22 m). Alte Pinakothek, Munich.
This portrait reflecting Charles V's imperial status also suggests the burdens of the cares of state. A genius in conveying character and aware of the importance of flattering his imperial patrons, Titian manages to make the emperor's unattractive jutting jaw contribute to a pensive expression. The silhouetting of the black stockings and shoes against the red carpet gives the emperor an appearance of strength, while the red color and the imposing column indicate that Charles wished to be linked with the Roman emperors.

Despite warfare and religious conflict, the early decades of the sixteenth century were a time of relative prosperity in western Europe. The population rose to nearly 90 million in the course of the century, and cities such as Antwerp and London became large centers of commerce. Raw materials from the New World—including South American gold and silver (see Box)—increased trade and manufacturing. Prosperity brought more people to the cities in search of work.

Another development that benefited commerce was the entry of several European countries into the already existing West African slave trade. The Portuguese had begun importing African slaves in the mid-fifteenth century, and for over a hundred years they monopolized the European end of such trafficking. Meanwhile Arab traders were shipping central African slaves to the Middle East and India. During the sixteenth century the Portuguese began to supply slaves to the Spanish colonies in the Americas to work on plantations.

of Cambrai brought about a period of relative peace after thirty-five years of hostilities. But threats to Charles's power came from France in the west, the Ottoman Empire in the east, and North Africa in the south.

Charles also faced unrest within the Holy Roman Empire as princes of the principalities vied for power during Charles's frequent absences. Compared with the tight organization of France under Francis I, the Holy Roman Empire remained bogged down in disarray. Charles was further frustrated by protests within the Roman Catholic Church (see Chapter 15), which would become a source of major upheaval. He abdicated in 1556 and spent the remainder of his life in a monastery.

Then England entered the slave trade, followed by France, Holland, and Denmark. The practice brought profit but inevitably sowed seeds of future conflict over the morality of owning human beings and forcing them to work without pay.

By the middle of the sixteenth century, Europe's prosperity began to decline. Inflation rose and poverty and begging became serious social problems. Spain depended on gold and silver from the New World and launched religious wars before financing was actually available. Thus, in the 1570s, when the Spanish king Philip II (ruled 1556–1598) was unable to pay his soldiers, they rebelled and destroyed Antwerp. Nevertheless Philip II was able to fight wars against England and France and was successful against the Ottomans.

Map 14.1 The Holy Roman Empire under Charles V, 1526.

border of Holy Roman Empire, 1526

Habsburg possessions

Danish possessions

Venetian possessions

Cross-cultural Influences

Exploration and Colonialism

The sea voyages that had begun late in the fifteenth century increased during the sixteenth, resulting in a global expansion of exploration and trade. The Spanish explorer Vasco Nuñez da Balboa (1475–1517) discovered the Pacific in 1513, and the Portuguese explorer Ferdinand Magellan (c. 1480–1521) departed to circumnavigate the globe in 1519. Magellan was killed in the Philippines in 1521, but his ships sailed on and returned to Spain the following year. The French explorers Jacques Cartier (1491–1557) and Samuel de Champlain (c. 1567–1635) secured France's claim to territory in North America. Spain and Portugal were the first to control the seas, but the English and French soon rivaled them.

Expanding exploration resulted in conquest and colonialism. In the first half of the sixteenth century, Hernando Cortés (1485–1547) and Francisco Pizarro (c. 1475–1541), two Spaniards known as conquistadores (foreign conquerors), unleashed their troops on two New World empires. Seeking gold, silver, and other raw materials for the king of Spain, Cortés and Pizarro decimated the Aztec Mexica and the Inka civilizations, respectively. And most of those who escaped immediate death soon succumbed to measles and other diseases brought to the Americas by the invaders.

The Aztec Mexica had flourished from the middle of the fourteenth century; by the sixteenth they were a powerful empire. Their capital, Tenochtitlán, with a population of around 100,000, was located at what is now Mexico City. Extensive building programs had transformed the capital into a thriving city, with temples, palaces, schools, and gardens. A network of roads and bridges tied the empire together. The Aztec were literate and had a rich tradition of art and poetry. Their religion was polytheistic and they practiced human sacrifice, believing that the gods demanded human blood.

Despite being a warrior culture (figure **14.2**), the Aztecs found that their spears and slings were no match for Spanish pistols. In 1519, Cortés arrived in Tenochtitlán with an army of six hundred men and was welcomed as the Aztec god-king, Quetzalcoatl. But fearing that the Aztecs would attack him, Cortés captured the king, Montezuma II (ruled 1502–1520). Cortés razed the city and destroyed Aztec religious texts. In an effort to impose Christianity on the native population, the Spanish conqueror built churches and a cathedral on the sites of ruined Aztec temples.

The Inka—which is both the designation of the people and their term for "king"— rose to imperial power around the same time as the Aztec Mexica. The Inka capital was at Cuzco, a highland city in the Andes Mountains of present-day Peru. Comprising an empire of several million people inhabiting a 2000-mile (3220-km) stretch of territory, the Inkas built some 20,000 miles (32,200 km) of roads. The empire controlled all agriculture, which used irrigation and was the basis of the economy. The Inka ruler was an absolute monarch, venerated as a god. An elite priesthood controlled the temples, but, unlike the Aztecs, the Inka had no writing system and therefore no religious texts.

When Pizarro arrived in 1531 with 168 men, he, like Cortés, was dazzled by the abundance of gold and silver. Lacking iron tools, the wheel, and modern weapons, the Inka were annihilated by the *conquistadores*. In 1532, Pizarro destroyed the empire using brutal tactics, including torture. One of the few sites to escape destruction was the secluded mountaintop city of Machu Picchu (figure **14.3**). Probably the royal enclave of an Inka king, Machu Picchu is built of huge blocks of stone without mortar.

Despite the devastation of the Aztec Mexica and the Inka civilizations by the Spanish *conquistadores*, there were positive results from contacts between Europe and the New World. The two regions exchanged aspects of their culture, food, and technology. In the future these contacts would broaden the outlook of both Europe and the Americas.

14.2 *Eagle Warrior*, **from Tenochtitlán, Aztec culture, 15th century. Terra-cotta, 67 × 46½ × 21½ in. (170 × 118 × 55 cm). Museo del Templo Mayor, Mexico City.**
The eagle warriors were an elite, aristocratic military group, dedicated to capturing their enemies alive so they could offer their blood to the gods. Eagle imagery characterizes the costume: a beak functions as a helmet, wings spread out at the arms, and claws project from the knees.

14.3 Machu Picchu, near Cuzco, Peru, Inka culture, 15th–16th century.

FLORENCE IN THE HIGH RENAISSANCE

In 1492, when Lorenzo the Magnificent died, his weak son, Piero di Lorenzo (1471–1503), called Piero the Unfortunate, became head of the Medici family. Piero made several poor political decisions, including granting concessions to Charles VIII of France. In 1495, under the influence of Savonarola (see Chapter 13), the citizens of Florence forced the Medici from the city. After Savonarola's execution four years later, a brief period of turmoil ensued.

At the turn of the century, Florence was in political disarray. In 1502, in an attempt to restore order and stability, the Florentines elected Piero Soderini (1452–1522), a member of a patrician family with political influence, to the lifetime mayoral position of *gonfaloniere* (literally "standard-bearer"). But he was forced into exile in 1512, and the grandson of Lorenzo the Magnificent, also called Lorenzo, was installed as *gonfaloniere*.

Expelled from Florence in 1527 by citizens who wanted to preserve a republic, the Medici returned again in 1530 when the Holy Roman Emperor Charles V installed Alessandro de' Medici, Lorenzo's illegitimate son, as hereditary ruler of Florence. Alessandro dismantled all traces of republicanism and ruled as duke until 1537, when he was assassinated by a cousin. Alessandro was succeeded by Cosimo I de' Medici (1519–1574), a ruthless but effective ruler and, like the earlier Medici, an important patron of the arts. He was crowned grand duke of Tuscany by the Dominican pope, Pius V (papacy 1566–1572), and his descendants ruled Florence until nearly the middle of the eighteenth century.

MACHIAVELLI

The political intrigues of Renaissance Italy inspired the best known political theorist of the period, Niccolò Machiavelli (1469–1527). Machiavelli had had a long political career, but he was accused of plotting against the Medici and exiled from Florence in 1513. Machiavelli was a political realist. He studied the Roman histories of Livy in the belief that it was possible to learn how to function politically in the present from knowing about past political events. In his classic work *The Prince* (1513), Machiavelli describes a shrewd statesman as one who follows the dictates of strategy and tactics. He also advocates the appearance, if not the practice, of morality. The modern word "Machiavellian" connotes ruthless deceit purely for the pursuit of power, but that is a distortion of the author's point of view and does not convey the nuances of his thinking. In addition to *The Prince*, Machiavelli wrote *Discourses on the First Decade of Livy* (c. 1516), *The Art of War* (1519–1520), and *The History of Florence* (1520–1525).

READING SELECTION
Machiavelli, *The Prince*: how to hold onto power by understanding and manipulating the desires of the nobility and the people, PWC3-085; whether it is better to be loved than feared, PWC3-088-B

MICHELANGELO'S *DAVID*

By the turn of the century, Michelangelo had already made his name as an emerging genius in sculpture. In 1502, at the age of twenty-six, he was commissioned by the guild of cloth manufacturers to produce a statue of David for the exterior of Florence Cathedral (figure **14.4**). For three years the artist worked on the enormous

14.4 Michelangelo, *David*, **1501–1504. Marble, 17 ft. 1½ in. (5.22 m) high. Gallerie dell' Accademia, Florence.**
According to Vasari, Michelangelo wanted to become a sculptor from an early age. His father, a minor bureaucrat, opposed his son's aspirations because he considered sculpture a low-class occupation. But when Michelangelo was around fourteen, his father apprenticed him to the Florentine painter Domenico Ghirlandaio (on the grounds that painting was superior to sculpture). By the age of sixteen, Vasari tells us, Michelangelo had been invited to join the Medici circle of artists and philosophers and went to live in the household of Lorenzo the Magnificent.

Donatello, *David* see figure 13.19

sculpture, which he carved from a single block of marble from the quarry in Carrara, near Lucca, that had supplied ancient Roman builders. Michelangelo's marble block, which had been abandoned by a previous sculptor because of a flaw, was nick-named "the Giant." A surviving preliminary sketch of the *David* depicts the figure and a detail of an arm. Written on the sketch is the phrase "David with his sling and I with my bow," referring to the hand-drill used by sculptors. In 1504, when the *David* was completed, city leaders persuaded the guild to place the statue at the entrance to the Palazzo Vecchio, Florence's town hall, instead of outside the cathedral.

This decision reflected Florence's identification with the David and Goliath story. Like Donatello's *David* (see thumbnail), Michelangelo's figure symbolized the republican spirit of the city. In this case, however, there is no Goliath, and David, at 17 feet (5.22 m) tall, has become the giant. Michelangelo's *David* "stands guard" over Florence, tensely alert, watching out for the safety of the city and ever ready to defend it from tyranny.

Stylistically, the *David* shows the influence of Hellenistic sculpture (see Chapter 6). The figure is posed in the relaxed contrapposto stance of Classical figures, but the torso is tense, which is more characteristic of Hellenistic than Classical style. The proportions, notably the large right hand and the slightly awkward youthfulness, are also more Hellenistic than Classical. In addition to being a structural reinforcement, the little tree trunk support behind the figure alludes to Roman marble copies of Greek sculpture.

In his *Lives*, Vasari says that the *gonfaloniere* Piero Soderini asked Michelangelo to reduce the size of the *David*'s nose, which he found offensively large. Accordingly, Michelangelo climbed the scaffold with a handful of marble dust. Pretending to chip away at the nose, he dropped some dust to the ground. Soderini, believing that the artist had complied with his wishes, was satisfied.

In this story (which may or may not be true), the humanist Vasari conveys two aspects of art and artists. On the one hand, he shows that art is illusion and that the artist, like a magician, can make viewers believe a fiction. On the other hand, he reminds his readers that the viewer's suspension of reality and willingness to believe the fiction is a necessary component of art appreciation.

LEONARDO'S *MONA LISA*

In 1508, after working for several years for the duke of Milan, Leonardo returned to Florence, where he painted an enigmatic portrait that has intrigued viewers for centuries. According to Vasari, the *Mona Lisa* (figure **14.5**) depicts the wife of the Florentine aristocrat Francesco del Giocondo. As a result, the woman in the painting is sometimes called "La Gioconda," or "the smiling one." Although she is famous for her smile, it is not clear that she actually is smiling. The impression that her

14.5 Leonardo da Vinci, *Mona Lisa*, c. 1503–1515. Oil on wood, 30¼ × 21 in. (76.7 × 53.3 cm). Louvre, Paris.

lips curve upward is created by the artist's subtle use of chiaroscuro and soft, smoky lighting, or *sfumato*, which define the features as well as the expression.

As a portrait, the *Mona Lisa* is innovative. The figure's three-quarter view and length—from the head to below the waist—were new. Previous portraits tended to be either frontal or profile views like Piero della Francesca's diptych of the Urbino rulers (see figure 13.28). Leonardo's Mona Lisa sits on a balcony overlooking an imaginary landscape in the distance; our view of her is head on, whereas we have a bird's eye view of the background.

This portrait identifies the figure with the landscape through a series of formal parallels. Her pyramidal form echoes the rock formations; her veil filters light as does the misty horizon; the aqueduct at the right curves into the fold over her left shoulder; and the spiral road at her right repeats the folds of the sleeves. These parallels correspond to Leonardo's famous metaphor comparing the earth to the human body: the rocks, he wrote, are the bones, the waterways are the veins and arteries, and the soil is the flesh.

Little is known of the *Mona Lisa*'s patron, but he apparently never received the portrait. Even less is known of the sitter. However, it is clear that the painting was of great importance to Leonardo. He took it with him when he went to the court

Society and Culture

Technology and the Inventions of Leonardo da Vinci

The greatest inventive genius of the High Renaissance was Leonardo da Vinci. Besides painting, sculpture, and architecture, his fields of study included geology, physics, alchemy, botany, geology, anatomy, optics, astronomy, and music. He worked as an engineer for Lodovico Sforza of Milan, for whom he devised tanks, catapults, multiple-barrel guns, and cannons. Leonardo drew up plans for draining marshes, designed underwater machines for attacking boats, and proposed the use of the Screw of Archimedes (see Chapter 6) for raising the level of water.

In his drawing of a helicopter-like flying machine, Leonardo envisioned the principle of a screw rising in the air (figure **14.6**). According to the drawing, the machine was powered by the pedaling man at the center. Although Leonardo never succeeded in creating a machine that could actually fly, he was intensely interested in flight and wrote extensively on the physics of flight and the movement of bird wings.

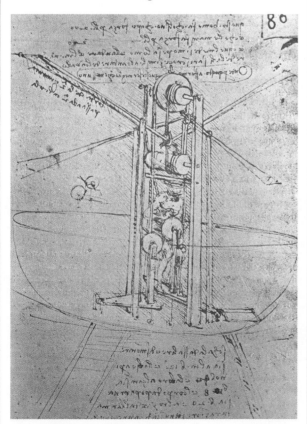

14.6 Leonardo da Vinci, drawing study for a flying machine, *c.* **1490. Pen and ink. Institut de France, Paris.**
Leonardo's notebook drawings are accompanied by detailed texts in mirror writing—that is, they have to be read in a mirror. To date, there is no explanation for this unusual practice; it is not due to left-handedness. In addition to machines, Leonardo designed a number of musical instruments and was an accomplished musician.

of Francis I and kept it until his death. From the French court, the painting entered the French national art collection that is housed today in the Louvre, in Paris.

LEONARDO ON THE ART OF PAINTING VERSUS SCULPTURE AND POETRY

The *Mona Lisa* exemplifies Leonardo's genius for visual metaphor. In his writings, he also uses metaphor to convey his artistic, philosophical, and scientific theories (see Box). His passion for imagery pervades the *Paragone*, in which he compares the art of painting with sculpture and poetry. Leonardo personifies Nature, which he believes to be the inspiration for art. Art itself he considers a "science." In Leonardo's view, painting is the most noble of the arts, because it is closest to nature.

> The divinity of the science of painting considers works both human and divine, which are bounded by surfaces, that is to say the boundary lines of bodies, with which she [Nature] dictates to the sculptor the way to perfect his statues. Through her principle, that is to say, draughtsmanship, she teaches the architect how to make his buildings convey pleasure to the eye; she teaches the potters about the varieties of vases, and also the goldsmiths, the weavers and the embroiderers. She has invented the characters in which the various languages are expressed; she has given numerals to the mathematicians; she has taught the drawing of figures to the geometrician; she has taught the students of optics, the technicians and the engineers.
>
> *(On Painting)*

Leonardo notes that poets use words to praise poetry. But the impact of painting, he says, is more direct and immediately understood by the viewer because it is an image. He says that "painting does not speak, but is self-evident through its finished product." Engaging in the ongoing quarrel over the merits of poetry, which was considered a liberal art, and painting, which was still considered a manual craft, Leonardo strove to raise the social position of painting and to elevate artists to the status of gentlemen. "With justified complaints," Leonardo concludes:

> painting laments that it has been excluded from the number of the liberal arts, since she is the true daughter of nature and acts through the noblest sense. Therefore it was wrong, O writers, to have left her outside the number of the liberal arts, since she embraces not only the works of nature but also an infinite number that nature never created.
>
> *(On Painting)*

RAPHAEL

Raphael (Raffaello Sanzio) was born at the court of Urbino, then ruled by Guidobaldo da Montefeltro, the son of Federico da Montefeltro and Battista Sforza (see Chapter 13). Raphael's own father, Giovanni Santi, was Urbino's court poet and painter and the author of an epic poem praising Federico.

14.7 Raphael, *Madonna and Child* (*The Small Cowper Madonna*), c. 1505.
Oil on wood panel, 23⅜ × 17⅜ in. (59.5 × 44 cm). National Gallery of Art,
Washington, D.C.

Santi apprenticed Raphael to Pietro Perugino (*c.* 1450–1523), the leading Umbrian painter, when his son was eleven years old. Raphael went on to become a prolific artist, known for his charm, political skill, and classically harmonious style. His brilliant career, however, was cut short by his death at the age of thirty-seven.

From 1504 to 1508, Raphael worked in Florence, painting mainly Madonnas and portraits. The *Madonna and Child* (figure **14.7**), known as the *Small Cowper Madonna* after the family that once owned it, is typical of his numerous early Madonnas. Raphael's Mary is a simple, everyday mother supporting a squirming infant. The only indications that the figures are sacred are the faint, translucent haloes and the distant church building. Like most of Raphael's Madonnas, this one has delicate features and a downcast expression—the latter a convention of Christian art alluding to her foreknowledge of her son's Crucifixion.

Raphael's reputation for personal grace seems reflected in his painted figures, especially the Madonna and Christ. At the Urbino court, Raphael had been exposed to the Classical texts in Federico's vast library and to the artists, writers, scientists, and philosophers who lived and worked there. His own enthusiasm for humanist thought and the revival of antiquity became an important force in his future career in Rome.

HIGH RENAISSANCE PATRONAGE IN ROME

The High Renaissance in Rome is linked with the patronage of a few wealthy bankers and humanist popes and with the artists who worked for them. The most extensive patronage was that of Giuliano della Rovere, who chose the name Julius II (papacy 1503–1513) because he admired Julius Caesar. Julius II was a warrior pope—a skilled military strategist who led the armies of the Papal States and was admired by Machiavelli for his political acumen. Despite his career in the Church, Julius II was a man of the world who had fathered three illegitimate children while still a cardinal. As pope, he hired the greatest artists of the age. His acquisition of Classical and Christian manuscripts enriched what later became the Vatican library, and his passion for collecting launched the vast papal collection of Greek and Roman sculpture.

A NEW ST. PETER'S

One of Julius II's first decisions as pope was to replace the Early Christian basilica of Old St. Peter's (see Chapter 8), which had been built near the Vatican Hill under Constantine in the fourth century. Julius entrusted the commission to Donato Bramante, who had worked in Milan and been in contact with Leonardo. In Rome, Bramante achieved fame with the Tempietto (figure **14.8**).

14.8 **Bramante, Tempietto, San Pietro in Montorio, Rome,** *c.* **1502.**
This little round *martyrium* (a building over the tomb or relics of a martyr) was commissioned by Ferdinand and Isabella of Spain. The cella, which contained an altar, was placed over the traditional site of St. Peter's martyrdom. The peristyle columns are Doric, as is the frieze with alternating triglyphs and metopes. Bramante has combined Classical with Christian features and has surrounded the drum with a balustrade.

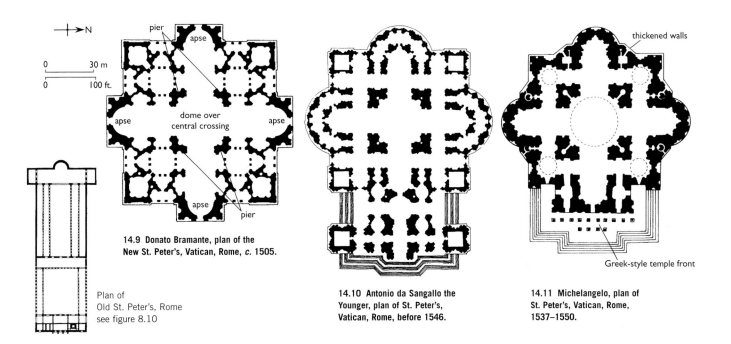

14.9 Donato Bramante, plan of the New St. Peter's, Vatican, Rome, c. 1505.

Plan of Old St. Peter's, Rome see figure 8.10

14.10 Antonio da Sangallo the Younger, plan of St. Peter's, Vatican, Rome, before 1546.

14.11 Michelangelo, plan of St. Peter's, Vatican, Rome, 1537–1550.

Bramante's interest in humanism is reflected in his plan for the New St. Peter's (figure **14.9**). Whereas the old basilica had a longitudinal Latin cross plan (see thumbnail), Bramante envisioned a perfectly symmetrical, centralized Greek cross plan of the type preferred by Leonardo, Alberti, and Vitruvius (see Chapter 13). Bramante designed a central nave surmounted by an enormous dome and surrounded by four apses connected by piers. The pier vaults would carry the weight of the dome.

The project was cut short by Bramante's death in 1514, but the foundations were in place, and the dimensions and general shape of the church were fixed before he died. Other architects worked on the New St. Peter's for over a century. Raphael was the first to succeed Bramante, but his plan did not progress very far. Leo X (papacy 1513–1521), a member of the Medici family, commissioned the nephew of Giuliano da Sangallo (see Chapter 13), Antonio da Sangallo the Younger (1485–1546), to continue the project. Sangallo's plan (figure **14.10**) extended the nave, but little else was achieved before his death in 1546.

A year after Antonio's death, Paul III (papacy 1534–1549) appointed Michelangelo architect of St. Peter's, and he devised a simplified version of Bramante's Greek cross plan (figure **14.11**). Michelangelo increased the dome's support, thickened the walls, and added a Greek temple front to the façade. The exterior view from the south (figure **14.12**) shows the giant, two-story Corinthian pilasters, the pedimented windows, and the dome

that Michelangelo planned as a hemisphere but that was slightly elongated after his death. The entire structure was not completed until the seventeenth century, when a new style and new religious requirements would call for further alterations (see Chapter 16).

14.12 Michelangelo, St. Peter's from the south, Vatican, Rome, 1546–1593.

RAPHAEL'S *SCHOOL OF ATHENS*

From around 1509 until 1511, Raphael worked for Pope Julius II decorating the Stanza della Segnatura (Room of the Seal) in the Vatican. A huge chamber containing the papal library and used for signing official documents, the Stanza, like the Medici palace in Florence and the ducal palace in Milan, was both a public and a private space. Raphael designed a program consisting of four lunettes, one on each wall; two depicted Christian subjects (the *Dispute over the Eucharist*—the *Disputà*—and the *Three Cardinal Virtues*) and two contained pre-Christian and mythological iconography (*Parnassus*, home of Apollo and the Muses, and the *School of Athens*).

The *School of Athens* (figure **14.13**) is a summation of High Renaissance Classical humanism. It combines Renaissance perspective and architecture with Classical subject matter and is imbued with the Renaissance admiration for Greek philosophy. The setting is a barrel-vaulted, symmetrical space, which recedes, like the grid pattern on the floor, according to the laws of linear perspective. The central dome, inspired by Roman and Renaissance buildings, is indicated by the architectural curve behind the foreground vault. Statues of Greek and Roman gods occupy wall niches—at the left is Apollo with his lyre and at the right, Minerva with her Gorgon shield.

Occupying the central space of the fresco is an assembly of philosophers whose texts had been recovered, collected, translated, and studied throughout the Renaissance. Plato and Aristotle are the central figures on the top step. Plato points upward toward the realm of ideas and carries the *Timaeus*, the

14.13 Raphael, *School of Athens* (after restoration), Stanza della Segnatura, Vatican, Rome, 1509–1511. Fresco, 16 × 18 ft. (7.92 × 5.49 m).

dialogue in which he discusses the cosmos. Aristotle holds his *Ethics* and points toward the space of this world, a gesture consistent with his empiricism.

A few other philosophers can also be identified; they appear to be arranged more or less with the idealists on Plato's side and the empiricists on Aristotle's. On the left is Pythagoras outlining his proportional system. Peering over his shoulder is Averroës, the turbaned Arabic scholar. Behind Averroës are Zeno, the Stoic philosopher, and Epicurus, the founder of Epicureanism. Diogenes, the Cynic who roamed the streets of Athens with a lantern in search of an honest man, sprawls across the steps. On the right, a group of scholars includes Euclid drawing a circle with a compass, the Persian astronomer Zoroaster with a celestial globe, and the Greek philosopher Ptolemy with an earthly globe.

Raphael's fresco blends portraits of his contemporaries with those of the ancient philosophers. Plato resembles a self-portrait by Leonardo da Vinci, his questioning gesture reflecting the artist's passion for inquiry and investigation. The bald-headed Euclid is a portrait of Bramante, Raphael's mentor and the first architect appointed to design the New St. Peter's. He is shown drawing a circle with a compass, reflecting his preference for centralized church plans and echoing his own domed head. At the far right, wearing a black hat and peering at the viewer, is Raphael himself. Brooding in the central foreground is the portrait of Raphael's rival in Rome, Michelangelo. His stonecutter's boots show that he is a carver of marble, and his detached, inner contemplation conforms to his depiction as the Greek philosopher Heraclitus. Raphael's Michelangelo is writing and thinking at the same time, a visual metaphor for the obscure, "either-or" philosophy of Heraclitus (see Chapter 5).

In these and other portraits, Raphael follows Alberti's principle that images keep a person alive in the cultural memory. The artist has "memorialized" ancient philosophers and famous contemporary figures, including himself, with his brush. Raphael's inclusion of written texts in the *School of Athens* shows that they were a cornerstone of the humanist revival of Classical antiquity.

MICHELANGELO ON ART

As a humanist and member of the Medici intellectual circle in Florence, Michelangelo held views that were influenced by Plato's notion of a pre-existing realm of ideas. He believed that the raw material of art, such as stone or wood, contained an inherent form that the artist reveals. For Michelangelo, the artist's mind, which has access to the realm of ideas, guides his hand.

He left a sizable body of poetry, in particular sonnets inspired by Dante and Petrarch (see Chapters 11 and 12). These sonnets, many of them autobiographical, cover a range of subjects, including love, death, and the nature of art.

Michelangelo believed that art mediates the human struggle with love and death. He observed that artistic creations are fixed, outlast nature, and do not age. Art, therefore, resists time:

Not even the best of artists has any conception
that a single marble block does not contain
within its excess, and *that* [the conception] is only attained
by the hand that obeys the intellect.
    The pain I flee from and the joy I hope for
are similarly hidden in you, lovely lady,
lofty and divine; but, to my mortal harm,
my art gives results the reverse of what I wish.
    Love, therefore, cannot be blamed for my pain,
nor can your beauty, your hardness, or your scorn,
nor fortune, not my destiny, nor chance,
    if you hold both death and mercy in your heart
at the same time, and my lowly wits, though burning,
cannot draw from it anything but death.

(Sonnet 51)

Note the comparison of the image inherent in the marble block with emotions hidden in a "lovely lady," which relates the passion of art with the passion of love.

THE SISTINE CHAPEL

Both Raphael and Michelangelo worked for Julius II. Michelangelo designed Julius's monumental tomb and much of the New St. Peter's, and he was commissioned to paint the interior of the Sistine Chapel. The chapel had been built from 1473 by Pope Sixtus IV, the uncle of Julius II. In accordance with Sixtus IV's wishes, its proportions match those of Solomon's Temple (see Chapter 8)—the length is double the height and triple its width. The pope commissioned frescoes to decorate the side walls with Old Testament scenes on the left and New Testament scenes on the right. These were in place when Michelangelo began his work, decorating the rest of the chapel from the level of the windows upward. The view of the ceiling in figure **14.14** gives some idea of the complexity of the artist's conception (see Box, p. 380). He has filled the space with figures, each engaged in its own narrative. Aside from the spandrels (curved triangles) over the window lunettes, the architectural sections dividing the scenes are painted illusions.

The diagram in figure **14.15** shows the disposition of the paintings. The best-known scene on the ceiling is the *Creation of Adam* (figure **14.16**), the first man and the typological ancestor of Christ. Michelangelo shows Adam as a monumental nude inspired by Hellenistic naturalism. Adam has been formed but not yet brought to life: between God's energetic forefinger and Adam's more relaxed finger there is a space. Michelangelo has thus painted the moment before Adam comes to life, fixing an image of tension between the creator God and his creation. God himself is a powerful patriarchal figure, whose flowing hair and drapery indicate his swift movement through space.

14.14 Michelangelo, Sistine Chapel ceiling frescoes, Vatican, Rome, 1509–1512.

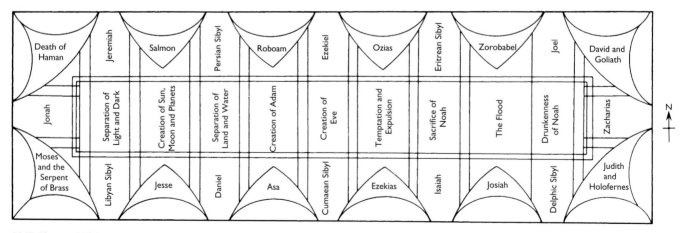

14.15 Diagram of Michelangelo's scenes in the Sistine Chapel, Vatican, Rome.

Dynamic monumentality also characterizes the *Libyan Sibyl* (see Box, p. 380, and figure 14.17). Her twisting pose, robust muscularity, and sculpturesque drapery create a sense of massive energy and power. The rich orange color accentuates her vigor. She holds up an enormous open book, which alludes to her oracles foretelling the coming of Christ. She, like the other sibyls and prophets, is framed by illusionistic *putti* who support an entablature that seems to project from the ceiling.

14.16 Michelangelo, *Creation of Adam*, Sistine Chapel, Vatican, Rome, 1510. Fresco.

Defining Moment

The Sistine Chapel Ceiling: Imagery for the Ages

On May 10, 1506, Michelangelo received an advance payment from Pope Julius II to paint frescoes on the ceiling of the Sistine Chapel. This would prove to be one of the great defining moments in the history of Christian art. Michelangelo built his own scaffold for the project, but he complained bitterly about the physical discomfort of painting a ceiling. Vasari, in his *Lives*, describes how difficult it was:

> He executed the frescoes in great discomfort, having to work with his face looking upwards, which impaired his sight so badly that he could not read or look at drawings save with his head turned backwards; and this lasted for several months afterwards. I can talk from personal experience about this, since when I painted five rooms in the great apartments of Duke Cosimo's palace if I had not made a chair where I could rest my head and relax from time to time I would never have finished; even so this work so ruined my sight and injured my head that I still feel the effects, and I am astonished that Michelangelo bore all that discomfort so well. In fact, every day the work moved him to greater enthusiasm, and he was so spurred on by his own progress and improvements that he felt no fatigue and ignored all the discomforts.

(Vasari, *Lives*)

The frescoes, blackened and dulled by centuries of incense and candles, were recently cleaned—a restoration that has provoked intense controversy. Those in favor admire the bright colors that have been revealed. Those who opposed the cleaning regarded the materials used as too abrasive. They have shown that much of the chiaroscuro has been removed, flattening the artist's powerful, muscular three-dimensionality. Nevertheless, today the Sistine Chapel is one of the world's most visited sites.

When Michelangelo arrived in Rome in 1508, the pope suggested that he paint the Twelve Apostles and a few customary ornaments on the ceiling. But Michelangelo envisioned a larger project. He created a grand view of the beginning of time, the creation of the world and the human race, and God's wrath in destroying what he had made. The window lunettes and the spandrels depict the ancestors of Christ listed in the "begats" at the beginning of the Gospel of Matthew. In the spaces between the windows, twelve Old Testament prophets alternate with twelve pagan sibyls—women of Classical antiquity said to possess prophetic powers. Four Old Testament scenes fill the corner spandrels. Nine scenes from Genesis—three depicting the Creation, three showing the life of Adam and Eve, and three telling the story of Noah—occupy the central area of the barrel-vault ceiling. Although Christ himself does not appear, Michelangelo's iconography alludes to his birth through prophecy and figures such as Adam, Noah, and Jonah, who were seen as his typological precursors. By the end of October

1512, the artist had painted more than three hundred lifesize or overlifesize figures on the Sistine Chapel ceiling.

Michelangelo began slowly, not having painted frescoes before. The work suffered numerous setbacks, such as mold and damp weather that interfered with the drying of the plaster and its bonding with the paint. In addition to having to learn the medium, Michelangelo had the challenge of making his figures look "correct" on curved surfaces, viewed from nearly 60 feet (18 m) below (figure **14.17**).

The project was frequently in jeopardy while Julius was at war or near death. It was also risky for Michelangelo perched high above the floor on scaffolding while he worked. The scaffolding itself was difficult to secure because Michelangelo did not want to leave holes in the ceiling. But once the ceiling was painted, in Vasari's opinion, other painters could lay down their brushes and renounce their art, for no one would ever equal the genius of Michelangelo's Sistine Chapel frescoes.

Critical Question Is the purpose of art to provide viewers with concrete images or abstract ideas? What are other functions of art? What "use" is the Sistine Chapel ceiling?

14.17 Michelangelo, *Libyan Sibyl*, Sistine Chapel, Vatican, Rome, 1509. Fresco.

14.18 Michelangelo, *Last Judgment* (after restoration), Sistine Chapel, Vatican, Rome, 1534–1541. Fresco, 48 × 44 ft. (14.6 × 13.4 m).
Michelangelo focuses on the attributes of martyrs in heaven with the instruments of their torture and death. St. Sebastian, for example, kneels at the far right and holds a set of arrows. Next to him, St. Catherine carries a broken wheel, while an angry St. Peter faces Christ and brandishes the keys to the gate of heaven. Seated on a cloud below and to the right of Christ, St. Bartholomew displays the knife with which he was flayed alive. The flayed skin drooping from his other hand contains Michelangelo's distorted self-portrait.

More than twenty years after completing the frescoes, Michelangelo was commissioned by Pope Paul III to paint a huge *Last Judgment* on the altar wall of the Sistine Chapel (figure **14.18**). This is the artist's vision of Christ's Second Coming. Compared with Giotto's vision in the Arena Chapel (see figure 12.15), Michelangelo's image is agitated, filled with nude figures, and pervaded by terror. Michelangelo's *Last Judgment* reflects the political and religious uncertainties of the times and the artist's own spiritual conflicts. He envisions a cataclysm at the end of time, filled with souls either straining to reach heaven or struggling against eternal damnation.

The hell to which the souls descend is the Greek Hades. The boatman of Greek myth, Charon, ferries the damned across the River Styx and then swings his oar to beat them from his boat. Presiding over Michelangelo's hellfire and darkness is a horned creature entwined by a serpent, a monstrous combination of Minos (see Chapter 4) and Satan. Here again Michelangelo combines Classical myth and Christianity—a hallmark of Renaissance humanism.

VENICE IN THE HIGH RENAISSANCE

The port city of Venice, on Italy's northeast coast, is built on a network of canals flowing into the sea. At the dawn of the High Renaissance, Venice had been an independent republic for some eight hundred years. It was ruled by an oligarchy consisting of an elected doge (senator), a patrician Council of Ten, and the Great Council (also composed of patricians). But its independent status was threatened in 1509 by the League of Cambrai, in which the pope, the Holy Roman Emperor, Milan, France, and Spain united to strip Venice of all its territory outside the city. Not until the Treaty of Cambrai was signed in 1529 was Venice allowed to keep most of its possessions.

As a result of this reprieve, a myth evolved in Venice celebrating its steadfastness in the face of external danger. Venice depicted itself as a tolerant republic, ruled by just leaders, free of social unrest, and protected by its patron, St. Mark. This self-image was not restricted to the political and social arenas. The city's waterways produce an atmosphere of shimmering light and luxurious color, and are often enveloped by mist from the sea. These qualities are reflected in Venetian painting, especially oil painting. Artists used canvas sooner in Venice than elsewhere in Italy as a support for oil paint. The medium of oil had long been known in Italy. It was used on panel paintings in Florence, admired in the imported works of van Eyck and other north European painters (see Chapter 13), and was a favorite in Venice. Oil paint was particularly suited to the depiction of subtle atmospheric effects as it enabled artists to build up layers of paint to enrich color and light.

THE ALDINE PRESS

Venice was a publishing center, the home of the Aldine Press, which printed practical, pocket-size books for a growing readership. The owner of the press, Aldus Manutius (1450–1515), was a humanist who had learned Greek from scholars emigrating to Venice after the fall of Constantinople in 1453. He arranged for Greek manuscripts to be edited and then printed them in the original, for which he commissioned a Greek typeface. From 1494 onward, Manutius printed all the existing manuscripts of Greek dramatists, poets, philosophers, and historians. He also published revised editions of Latin and Italian authors, including Dante and Petrarch. Manutius's introduction of italic type (slanted, thinned lettering) in 1500 was important in the production of inexpensive, small-scale books that were affordable for students.

The advent of printing in fifteenth-century Europe had made books more widely available (see Chapter 13). This, combined with increasing literacy among the general population, led to a demand for reading material. With the establishment of Gutenberg's press in Mainz, Caxton's printing concern in London, and the Aldine Press in Venice, several million books had been printed by 1500.

VENETIAN PAINTING

Venice's connections with the East meant that the Byzantine style persisted longer in that city than elsewhere in Italy. Venice also retained the medieval tradition of family workshops, in which artists were thought of as artisans rather than as intellectuals. The leading artist-family was the Bellini family; the career of Giovanni Bellini (c. 1430–1516) embodies the transition from early to High Renaissance.

Little is known of Giovanni's personal life. At first influenced by the linear style of his brother-in-law Andrea Mantegna (see Chapter 13), he soon turned to more textured surfaces and richer colors. His landscape backgrounds became vehicles for studying the atmospheric effects of light and shade.

Giovanni's *Madonna of the Meadow* (figure **14.19**), which was painted at the turn of the sixteenth century, shows Mary humbly seated on the ground, praying over the sleeping infant Jesus. Her large scale and the arch formed by her hands allude to her symbolic role as the church building—the "House of God." In Venice, the association of sleep and death (twins in ancient Greek mythology) was often used by artists to foreshadow the future of Jesus. Here, the sleeping infant (like the dead trees and the crow at the upper left) refers forward in time to his death, and his mother's melancholy expression suggests mourning. The landscape extends to the blue hills of the horizon, and rolling clouds form leisurely curves across the sky. Soft lighting bathes the scene, emphasizing the subtle modeling of the figures.

In the following decades, the two most important High Renaissance painters in Venice were Giorgione da Castelfranco (c. 1477–1510), a student of Giovanni Bellini who died young of the plague, and his pupil Titian (c. 1487–1576), who had a long and prolific career. Both Giorgione and Titian used oil paint and **glazes** (coats of translucent paint) to produce the rich colors and textures characteristic of Venetian style.

According to Vasari, Giorgione was sociable and musical and frequented a humanist circle in Venice. His interest in music and the pastoral tradition of antiquity is evident in his *Fête Champêtre*, or *Pastoral Concert* (figure **14.20**). This work conveys the sense of a dream unfolding in an idyllic, atmospheric landscape. There is no apparent explanation for the nudity of the two women, whose soft flesh and voluptuous proportions are no longer strictly Classical. Nor is their interaction with the clothed men made clear. The men seem to be conversing as one woman pours water into a well and the other holds a flute. In the distance, a shepherd tends his flock.

The lack of a readily identifiable narrative and the unanswered iconographic questions are typical of Giorgione. Softened contours, velvet textures, and muted lighting create a

14.19 Giovanni Bellini, *Madonna of the Meadow*, *c.* 1500–1505. Oil and tempera on wood panel, 26¹/₂ × 34 in. (67.3 × 86.4 cm). National Gallery, London.

dream-like quality and, as with dreams, much of the artist's imagery has remained a mystery.

The work of Titian is no less complex than Giorgione's and includes a wide range of subject matter—mythological and Christian scenes, portraits, and allegories. At the age of nine, Titian left his native town of Pieve da Cadore and went to Venice to study painting. Later in life, he numbered among his patrons the leading churches of Venice, Paul III (papacy 1534–1549), and Charles V. Charles's son, Philip II of Spain (ruled 1556–1598), commissioned Titian to paint several pictures based on Greek mythology. Also famous for his portraits, Titian produced several of the Holy Roman Emperor Charles V (see figure 14.1), who knighted him in 1533.

Some sense of Titian's artistic range can be gleaned from a comparison of his colossal *Assumption of the Virgin* (figure **14.21**) with his *Venus of Urbino* (figure **14.22**). The *Assumption* is a religious, Christian painting, whereas the *Venus* is erotic and inspired by Classical mythology (see thumbnail). The *Assumption*

was commissioned for the altar of Santa Maria Gloriosa dei Frari, in Venice, to be viewed publicly, whereas the *Venus* was a private commission from a duke of Urbino.

The minimal setting of the *Assumption* focuses attention on the miracle of Mary's Assumption into heaven and on the

14.20 Giorgione, *Fête Champêtre*, *c.* 1510. Oil on canvas, approx. 3 ft. 7¹/₄ in. × 4 ft. 6¹/₈ in. (1.05 × 1.38 m). Louvre, Paris.

14.21 Titian, *Assumption of the Virgin*, Santa Maria Gloriosa dei Frari, Venice, 1516–1518. Oil on panel, 22 ft. 7½ in. × 11 ft. 9¾ in. (6.9 × 3.6 m). The apostles occupy the lower, darkened area of the picture, forming a transition from the earthly space of the viewer to the dazzling light of heaven. Their agitated poses and gestures are accentuated by the intense reds of the draperies. A radically foreshortened God the Father, surrounded by angels, sweeps across the top of the picture. The divine connection between the gazes of God and the Virgin bridges the yellow light of heaven. Unveiled in 1518, this picture established Titian's reputation as the greatest painter in sixteenth-century Venice.

astonishment of the apostles who witness the event. The woman in the *Venus of Urbino*, on the other hand, occupies the carefully depicted room of an aristocratic Venetian palace. In contrast to the *Assumption*, the *Venus of Urbino* is languid and calm. It reflects the influence of Giovanni Bellini and Giorgione in the voluptuousness of the nude, the textural variations, and the filtered light of the sky.

MUSIC IN HIGH RENAISSANCE VENICE

Music in High Renaissance Venice was more innovative than elsewhere in Italy. In addition to housing the Aldine Press, Venice was in the forefront of the printing of music. The first chant books had been published in 1473, and polyphonic music became available from 1501. The violin was invented and other types of musical instruments developed. The violin was derived from the Arabic rebec (a bowed instrument with a pear-shaped body and three strings based on the lute-like medieval Arabic *rebab*) and from the Western fiddle used in the Middle Ages. The viola da gamba (a bowed string instrument with frets) was played widely, and **consorts** (families of instruments) were developed. The string and wind instruments of this period would eventually led to the instrumental groupings of modern orchestras.

In liturgical music, the **split choir**—in which groups of singers sing against, or in response to, each other—increased musical variation and complexity. Venice spearheaded the use of the organ in the liturgy, which led to new genres of composition. Among the types of organ work that became standard before a church service are the *intonazione* (which sounds improvised, or invented on the spur of the moment) and the *toccata* (which displays the instrumental potential of the organ and the dextrous "touch" of the performer—the Italian word meaning "to touch" is *toccare*).

The leading musician in Venice was Adrian Willaert (*c.* 1490–1562). He had been a student of Josquin Desprez (see Chapter 13) and was Netherlandish by birth. He visited Rome in 1515, and then worked at the Este court and in Milan. His success in Venice, where he was chapel master of St. Mark's (San Marco) from 1527, exemplifies the international flavor of the city.

Using the two organs in St. Mark's and writing for split choirs, Willaert took advantage of the layout of St. Mark's to create music that echoed back and forth across the cathedral. His basic polyphonic style uses a four-voice texture, but sometimes he wrote more sumptuous works using up to seven voices. Willaert composed over 170 motets, and in the later ones he abandons the *cantus firmus* structure that had been the foundation of polyphony throughout the medieval period. Now the voices are treated equally when they are woven together in polyphony, and there are contrasting chordal sections using the **triadic** harmony that became the basic language of Western music. Rhythms are less intricate than in medieval music, and where all the voices coincide, there can be an almost declamatory feeling. For the Church, Willaert also composed Masses, hymns, and psalms; his collection of psalms for double chorus published in 1550 was to foster a tradition of such psalms for the next fifty years.

14.22 *above* **Titian, *Venus of Urbino*, c. 1538. Oil on canvas, 3 ft. 11 in. × 5 ft. 5 in. (1.19 × 1.65 m). Galleria degli Uffizi, Florence.**
There are several interpretations of this painting, but none is definitive. They range from considering the woman a high-class courtesan to a bride awaiting her husband. The roses and myrtle are attributes of Venus. The dog symbolizing marital fidelity and the two maidservants removing clothes from a *cassone* (marriage chest) would seem to reinforce the latter interpretation. But the mood of the painting is decidedly erotic, as the gaze of the nude, her slightly parted lips, and the placement of her left hand are designed to entice a male viewer.

Botticelli, *Birth of Venus*
see figure 13.23

Willaert's secular music includes pieces for instrumental ensembles, *chansons*, and the Italian equivalent, **madrigals**. Unlike the *chanson*, which had a history dating back to the minstrels of the twelfth and thirteenth centuries, the madrigal was a new form in the Renaissance. Originating in Italy, it later spread across Europe, in particular to England. One of its characteristics was **word painting**—the musical illustration of the meaning of a word. Thus, a text about ascending a hill would be set to a rising scale, the words "running down" would be sung to fast, descending notes, all the voices but one would drop out for a phrase such as "all alone," and so forth. Such techniques brought into the musical arena the concept that art imitates nature; composers strove to express the ideas and emotions contained in their texts.

THE GABRIELIS The Gabrielis were the most prominent family of musicians in sixteenth-century Venice. Andrea Gabrieli (*c.* 1510–1586), a native of the city, worked for a time at the court of Bavaria. He returned to Venice in 1566 and was hired as one of the two organists at St. Mark's. His compositions, especially light madrigals, were extremely popular. They move away from polyphony toward homophony, and the setting of words is often virtually syllabic. Andrea's most monumental work was the ceremonial sacred music he composed for St. Mark's. By using the upper galleries of the cathedral as spaces for choirs accompanied by instruments, Andrea created music that flowed expansively from different directions, creating a new depth of sound.

Andrea's developments in sacred music were elaborated by

his nephew, Giovanni Gabrieli (*c.* 1554–1612), who became the greatest composer of his generation in Venice. Like his uncle, Giovanni had been a court organist in Bavaria before settling in 1585 in Venice as one of the organists of St. Mark's. His output includes a greater proportion of instrumental music than was usual at the time, both solos for organ and ensemble music for instruments. Venice had a particularly rich pool of players from which he could draw, with a nucleus of six instrumentalists employed at St. Mark's, and up to about twenty being engaged for grand festivals to perform with a choir of about thirty. Giovanni innovatively transferred the methods of writing for split choirs to instruments. Some of the music has elaborate solo writing, particularly for cornetts (a form of trumpet) and violins.

Giovanni is most famous for his sacred choral music. Like Willaert and Andrea Gabrieli, Giovanni composed a large number of grand motets for split choirs accompanied by a range of instruments. Increasingly, he contrasted different groups, for example, alternating choirs of high and low voices in dialogue. This produced a new formal coherence. In developing the practice of contrasting and opposing different sonorities, Giovanni is considered a forerunner of seventeenth-century Baroque music (see Chapter 16). Interestingly, he was always more admired by contemporaries in Germany than in Italy.

LITERATURE AND THEATER

Italian literature in the High Renaissance continued to expand the use of the vernacular and reflect the influence of humanism. Although not generally ranked among the greatest Western drama, Italian theater was enormously influential. The introduction of vernacular dialogue and the revival of Classical genres brought about a total break with medieval theater.

CASTIGLIONE'S *BOOK OF THE COURTIER*

Baldassare Castiglione (1478–1529) (figure **14.23**) wrote the classic High Renaissance treatise on manners. Born near Mantua to a family of small landowners and administrators at the Gonzaga court, Castiglione had a humanist education. He traveled to various courts as an ambassador and was known for his gentlemanly demeanor. From 1504 to 1517, he was at the Montefeltro court in Urbino.

In 1528, Castiglione published *The Courtier* (*Il cortegiano*), which is imbued with humanist ideas and meant for courtly audiences. Plato's influence is evident in the author's use of the dialogue form. *The Courtier* takes place during four evenings at the court of Urbino, which was so vast that Castiglione compares it to a small city. Actual historical characters engage in imaginary conversations on subjects ranging from the formation of an ideal courtier and the relative merits of

monarchies and republics, to the meaning of love. Discussions of contemporary controversies include arguments over whether texts should be written in the vernacular or in Latin and whether the ideal education of a gentleman should emphasize the arts and humanities or physical training for war. Castiglione concluded that, as in the humanist curriculum of Mantua's Gioiosa (see Chapter 13), both should be included. The courtier should be skilled in horsemanship and sword play, and in all things his demeanor should be elegant and appear effortless.

The Courtier also had something to say about the formation of the ideal lady. Castiglione attributes to women the ability to civilize men. His ideal lady is attractive and well educated and a witty hostess, endowed with grace and charm. As for relationships between men and women, Castiglione preferred that they be Platonic, which was consistent with the medieval tradition of courtly love.

As regards the visual arts, *The Courtier* remarks that in ancient Greece aristocratic children were trained in drawing and painting. He notes that drawings of military installations

14.23 Raphael, *Baldassare Castiglione, c.* 1514. Oil on canvas, 32¼ × 16½ in. (81.9 × 67.3 cm). Louvre, Paris.
Raphael's genius for incorporating the innovations of important artists in his work is apparent in the influence of *Mona Lisa*. Note the three-quarter view, the seated pose, the folded hands, and the soft lighting. Castiglione exudes an air of understated sophistication. The rich black of the velvet hat, the voluminous fur sleeves, and the white silk shirt reflect courtly style. At the same time, the minimal background and crisp edges have the direct clarity for which Raphael is famous. Castiglione's slightly cocked head and penetrating gaze suggest the careful social observation that informs his descriptions of courtly life.

and of potential military targets, such as bridges and fortresses, serve practical political purposes. In accord with Leonardo, Castiglione says that since the art of painting both represents and is inspired by nature, it should be ranked among the highest human achievements.

The ideal outcome of the courtier's education, in Castiglione's view, is the creation of a *uomo universale* ("universal man"). In 1561, *The Courtier* was translated into English. It was considered the paradigm of elite courtly behavior and of the qualities of the Renaissance *uomo universale*. The treatise influenced Shakespeare (see Chapter 15) and by 1600 had been translated into most European languages.

READING SELECTION

Castiglione, *The Courtier*: the ideal courtier and the ideal court, PWC3-001; what women want from their lovers, PWC3-010

ARIOSTO'S *ORLANDO FURIOSO*

Lodovico Ariosto (1474–1533) came from an aristocratic family in Reggio Emilia and moved to Ferrara when he was ten. He received a humanist education, studying law, Latin, and Greek, and in 1503 became a courtier at the Este court. Fifteen years later, he went to work for the duke of Ferrara. While at the court of Ferrara, Ariosto wrote his classic epic *Orlando furioso* (published in 1516, 1521, and 1532), a long poem in octaves (stanzas of eight lines).

Written in the tradition of medieval legend, the work also has elements inspired by Roman poets, as well as by Dante, Petrarch, and Boccaccio. While focusing on Charlemagne, *Orlando furioso* alludes to contemporary figures as it interweaves two distinct narratives. In one, Orlando falls passionately in love with a princess and descends into madness (*furioso*) when she fails to return his affections. In the other, a pagan prince becomes a Christian, marries a virgin warrior, and founds the Este line of Ferrara, under whose patronage the poem was written. *Orlando furioso* is remarkable for its versatile style, combining different literary genres with various time periods, plots and subplots, and widely divergent characters.

Like the musicians and artists of the Renaissance who included references to themselves in their work (see Chapter 13), Ariosto fills *Orlando furioso* with autobiographical allusions. He makes his identification with its hero explicit, particularly in the maddening effects of unrequited love. The poem was an immediate success and came to exemplify one side of a new aesthetic quarrel, for advocates of the type of Classical unity recommended by Aristotle (see Chapter 6) objected to the discursive variety of Ariosto's style.

THEATER IN HIGH RENAISSANCE ITALY: FROM LATIN TO THE VERNACULAR

Most fifteenth-century plays were written in Latin, but in the early sixteenth century this began to change. With court patronage, vernacular theater was aimed at aristocratic audiences. Plays were often performed as segments of festivals, pageants, and courtly entertainments.

While he was at the Este court, Ariosto staged comedies by the Roman dramatists Terence and Plautus (see Chapter 7). Ariosto himself wrote the first vernacular play of the Renaissance, *The Casket* (*La cassaria*), which was produced in 1508. He used a standard Roman comic plot, in which a pair of servants arrange marriages for their masters, but the setting is sixteenth-century Italy. This combination of Classical and contemporary features, common today, was at the time a new idea—and one that quickly caught on.

Between 1513 and 1520, Machiavelli wrote *The Mandrake* (*La mandragola*). In this case, the plot was original, but the form was based on Roman comedy. *The Mandrake* is a farce, in which a foolish, doting husband is cuckolded by his young wife. By 1540, Italian comedy in the vernacular had become an established genre, and Italian theater was soon influencing dramatists in France and England.

Italy's first important tragedy in the vernacular was written by the humanist Giangiorgio Trissino (1478–1550). Entitled *Sofonisba* and published in 1515, it is the story of the beautiful and virtuous queen of Carthage who chooses suicide over defeat during the Punic Wars (see Chapter 7). Her history was first recorded by the Roman author Livy and then taken up in fourteenth-century Italy in Petrarch's *Africa* (see Chapter 12).

Trissino added another layer to the Latin-versus-vernacular controversy (see Chapters 12 and 13). He preferred Greek to Roman drama, the latter mainly known by way of Seneca. By using the Greek chorus and obeying Aristotle's rules of tragedy, Trissino's work led to arguments over whether Greek or Roman drama provided the better model for contemporary theater.

EARLY MANNERISM

In the visual arts, High Renaissance style was supplanted by Mannerism, which rejected Classical proportions, symmetry, and linear perspective, although mythological subjects were often represented. Mannerist artists preferred odd, agitated poses (especially the *serpentinata*, a sharply twisted, serpentine pose), spatial exaggeration, and jarring, incongruous color schemes. Although very much a style of the courts, Mannerism also appealed to Church patrons. The style first appeared in Florence after the return of the Medici in 1512 and eventually spread to France, Spain, and northern Europe. In architecture, Mannerists self-consciously tried to subvert the Classical Orders that had been revived during the Renaissance.

Paintings for private or court patrons tended to have erotic, even perverse overtones, often exhibited with considerable humor. And sculptures emphasized open space, an impression of instability, and spiraling motion. To what degree the Mannerist style reflected political and religious turmoil is a matter of debate. But that Mannerism and the turmoil of the time coincided is certain, which argues for some cause-and-effect relationship between what artists were doing and broader contemporary developments.

PAINTING

In Rome, early manifestations of Mannerism appear in the late work of Raphael (figure **14.24**). This is one of a series of frescoes that he completed under the Medici pope, Leo X (papacy

14.25 *right* Jacopo Pontormo, *Portrait of a Halberdier*, c. 1528–1530. Oil (or oil and tempera) on panel transferred to canvas, 36¼ × 28⅜ in. (92.1 × 72.1 cm). **The J. Paul Getty Museum, Los Angeles.**
Note the bulky arms and ballooning upper torso, which seem mismatched with the slim hips. Despite the large halberd and prominent sword hilt, the boy seems too refined for his profession. The slim red hat and light feather, the gold chain, and ruffled sleeves convey an air of delicacy. The slightly parted lips curve downward, creating a wistful expression that contradicts the self-assured pose.

14.24 Raphael, *Fire in the Borgo*, Stanza dell'Incendio, Vatican, Rome, from 1514. Fresco, 22 ft. 1 in. (6.7 m) wide at base.
Note the young man at the left carrying an old man on his shoulders with a young boy beside him. This detail quotes the ancient Roman sculpture group depicting Aeneas escaping from the burning city of Troy with Anchises and Ascanius (see figure 7.1).

1513–1521). It alludes to a ninth-century event in the life of Pope Leo IV (papacy 847–855), whose gesture of blessing miraculously extinguished a fire raging in Old St. Peter's. Compared to the restrained *School of Athens* (see figure 14.13), this fresco is filled with animated, muscular figures in a state of panic. The contorted poses, frantic gestures, and agitated draperies are keynotes of Mannerist style.

The early Mannerist painter Jacopo Pontormo (1494–1557) was born two years after the death of Lorenzo the Magnificent. An outstanding draftsman and painter of altarpieces and fresco cycles, he was also in demand as a portraitist. The odd proportions of his *Portrait of a Halberdier* (figure **14.25**), the varied surface textures, and the ambiguous characterization of the figure are typical of Mannerist style.

Madonna and Christ with Angels, also called *The Madonna of the Long Neck* (figure **14.26**), by Parmigianino (1503–1540), was commissioned for a private chapel. It juxtaposes large foreground figures with an illogically small prophet at

14.27 Sofonisba Anguissola, *Self-portrait at a Spinet,* **after 1550. Oil. Museo di Capodimonte, Naples.**
Sofonisba, named after the Carthaginian queen, was one of six sisters from a noble family in Cremona. All six were encouraged by their father to become painters. While Sofonisba worked at the court of Philip II of Spain, she was commissioned by Pope Pius IV to paint a portrait of the Spanish queen. In 1570, the artist married a Sicilian and went to live in Palermo. Widowed four years later, Sofonisba next married a sea captain and settled in Genoa. The self-portrait conveys the sense of a serious, introspective young woman.

14.26 Parmigianino (Francesco Mazzola), *Madonna of the Long Neck,* **c. 1535. Oil on panel, approx. 7 ft. 1 in. × 4 ft. 4 in. (2.16 × 1.32 m). Uffizi, Florence.**

the lower right. A truncated column without a capital was probably a reference to the Virgin as a metaphor for church buildings; in hymns her neck is sometimes compared to a column. In that metaphor, Mary is not only the sacred building, she is also its supporting member. Parmigianino's Mary and Christ defy Classical proportions: she is elongated from her waist down, and Christ is unnaturally contorted. His sleeping state alludes to his death and especially to *pietà* scenes, where Mary supports his dead body. Observing Christ at the left is a group of leering angels, who imbue the picture with a perverse cast.

The *Self-portrait at a Spinet* (figure **14.27**) by Sofonisba Anguissola (1527–1625) reveals Mannerist tendencies in the fussiness of the lace collar and cuffs, as well as in the details of the spinet. Sofonisba was one of the first women to have a successful international career as a painter. She was admired by Vasari, and her success was unusual for a woman at the time. Traditionally excluded from artistic training, women were at a disadvantage unless they came from artist families and could study at home. However, in the sixteenth century women gradually began to be taken seriously as professional artists.

SCULPTURE: BENVENUTO CELLINI

One of the most elegant examples of Mannerist sculpture is the gold and enamel saltcellar in figure **14.28**, made by Benvenuto Cellini (1500–1571). Trained as a goldsmith and sculptor, Cellini worked in Florence for the grand duke of Tuscany, Cosimo I de' Medici, and in France for Francis I. The saltcellar, which was made for the French king, exemplifies the complex iconography, unstable poses, and erotic overtones of Mannerist court art. In this case, the mythological figures probably allude to the king and his amours. The sea god Poseidon holds a trident and leans so far backward that he seems about to topple over. The same is true of the woman, an earth goddess, who tweaks her breast and seductively extends her leg toward Poseidon.

14.28 Benvenuto Cellini, saltcellar of Francis I, finished 1543. Gold and enamel, 10¼ × 13⅛ in. (26 × 33.3 cm). Stolen from the Kunsthistorisches Museum, Vienna.

When he was fifty-eight and under house arrest, Cellini wrote an autobiography. He describes a life of art, crime, and sexual experimentation. On the run from the law, he racked up debts, committed acts of violence, and was accused of murder. He was bisexual and an occasional transvestite. Having studied for the priesthood, Cellini finally married the mother of two of his children.

Cellini's major large-scale bronze sculpture is the *Perseus* in Florence (figure **14.29**). Commissioned by Cosimo I de' Medici, the 18-foot (5.48-m) high statue portrays the Greek hero Perseus displaying the severed head of Medusa. The statue is located in front of the town hall, thereby associating Cosimo with the heroism of Perseus. Perseus extends his sword and carefully looks down to avoid being turned to stone by gazing at the head. The self-conscious pose, animated surface patterns, and elaborate winged cap are typical of Mannerism. Similarly, the depiction of Medusa's blood dripping downward in waves of bronze from the head and sideways from the neck exemplifies the Mannerist taste for disturbing imagery (see Box).

14.29 Benvenuto Cellini, *Perseus*, Loggia dei Lanzi, Piazza della Signoria, Florence, 1545–1554. Bronze, 18 ft. (5.48 m) high.

Society and Culture

Cellini on the Casting of the *Perseus*

In his autobiography, Cellini describes casting the bronze *Perseus* as an exciting and harrowing process that could have been accomplished only by a genius such as himself. While preparing his chisels for the job, he tells us, a splinter flew into his eye and was removed when a surgeon spilled pigeon blood over the eye. In gratitude Cellini thanked St. Lucy, who had gouged out her own eyes on discovering that a Roman taken with her beauty could not help looking at her with desire.

After casting the Medusa, Cellini covered the model of Perseus in wax in preparation for making a mold of it. Thereupon his patron Cosimo de' Medici said that he did not believe it could be made in bronze. In Cosimo's view, it would not be possible to cast the head at a height of 18 feet (5.48 m). Cellini replied that Cosimo, being a patron rather than an artist, could not possibly understand the extent of his genius. He reminded Cosimo of his remarkable saltcellar for Francis I (see figure 14.28) and of the king's generosity. He did acknowledge, however, that the foot of the sculpture would be a problem.

When Cosimo left the artist's house, Cellini set to work, creating the mold, drawing off the wax, using pulleys and ropes to lift sections of the sculpture, and forcing himself to continue despite a raging fever. He soon took to his bed, leaving instructions for his assistants to finish the work. But they were unable to do so and declared the task impossible. Newly propelled into action, Cellini overcame fires, furnace explosions, and curdling metal until the finished bronze was unveiled. At that point, every feature except the toes was perfect, and Cellini completed them with a little more work. When the duke came to view the statue, he was impressed with the result—even more so because, as Cellini had predicted, the foot was not quite right and had to be redone.

ARCHITECTURE: GIULIO ROMANO AND ANDREA PALLADIO

Mannerist architecture used the Classical Orders, but it changed the relationships between their individual parts. This is evident, for example, in the work of Raphael's pupil Giulio Romano (*c.* 1499–1546). From 1527, Romano was in the employ of the Mantua court, designing the villa known as the Palazzo del Tè, which served as both the court's horse farm and a place for royal entertainments. The view of the courtyard façade (figure **14.30**) illustrates the Mannerist disruption and reconfiguration of the Classical tradition and Renaissance style. The pediment above the round-arched entrance is no longer supported by columns and an entablature. Instead, it rests on scroll-shaped brackets above an open wall space. The pediments over the blind niches lack horizontal bases and also rest on brackets.

Although the columns of the façade support a Doric entablature, some of the triglyphs dip below the narrow architrave as if falling from the wall. The columns stand on narrow podia (projecting bases) formed by rectangular blocks repeated on the entire surface of the wall. This heavy **rustication** (rough masonry blocks having beveled, or sloping, edges and recessed joints), alternating with the opened architectural spaces, dominates the wall surface. Compared with the canonical Classical Orders, those at the Palazzo del Tè create an impression of instability by increasing spatial movement, opening space, and altering the expected arrangement of forms. There is a playful quality in these forms that conforms to the purpose of the Palazzo as a place of entertainment.

In the churches of Andrea di Pietro (1508–1580), known as Palladio, the Classical Orders of the façade are rearranged in order to unify the tall nave with the shorter side aisles. This is the case with San Giorgio Maggiore in Venice (figure **14.31**), where the façade is composed of a double portico. The taller

14.30 Giulio Romano, courtyard façade, Palazzo del Tè, Mantua, 1527–1534.

14.31 Andrea Palladio, San Giorgio Maggiore, Venice, begun 1565.

portico, consisting of four Corinthian columns on podia supporting an entablature and a pediment, corresponds to the nave. The wider portico behind it is framed by pilasters, and the wall surface is animated by pediments and round-arched niches containing statues. As in Romano's Palazzo del Tè courtyard, Palladio has used elements of the Classical Orders but juxtaposed them in new ways.

Palladio was the author of an important architectural treatise, the *Quattro libri dell' archittetura* (*The Four Books of Architecture*), which would influence architects in eighteenth-century Britain and the United States. In particular, the buildings designed by Thomas Jefferson (see Chapter 17), who was himself a student of Classical architecture, show evidence of Palladio's style.

As the High Renaissance and then Mannerism were developing in Italy, cultural changes were unfolding elsewhere in Europe. The Renaissance arrived north of the Alps, where it took on a different shape than in Italy. In northern Europe, where Christian humanism dominated progressive thinking, one of the most significant events in the history of the West came as a protest to corruption in the Roman Church. In the next chapter we focus on northern Europe and consider the northern Renaissance and the movements known as the Protestant Reformation and the Catholic Counter-Reformation.

KEY TERMS

consort a set of musical instruments of the same family for playing music composed before about 1700.

glaze a translucent paint layer that enriches colors.

madrigal a secular contrapuntal song for several voices, from the Renaissance.

rusticate to give a rustic appearance to masonry blocks by roughening their surface and beveling their edges.

split choir a choir in which groups of singers sing against, or in response to, each other.

triadic based on the three notes of the "common" chord in Western music, using notes 1, 3, and 5 of the scale.

word painting in a vocal work, the musical illustration of the meaning of a word.

KEY QUESTIONS

1. What was the result of the exploration and colonization of the New World for those living in the conquered lands?

2. Portraits were a popular subject in an age of patronage and a source of commissions for artists. Name three other genres or subjects found in the High Renaissance period and explain their particular relevance in this era.

3. Why is the *School of Athens* called "a summation of High Renaissance humanism"? Explain how Raphael creates the illusion of a real space containing historically significant figures—what techniques were used?

4. In what ways did music and literature "extend the vernacular" and include humanist interests? Does *The Courtier* illustrate these concerns? What two other works show extensions of the vernacular and humanism?

5. What are the characteristics of Mannerism? What stylistic features would a person who had never seen a Mannerist work look for?

SUGGESTED READING

Ariosto, Ludovico. *Orlando furioso*, trans. Barbara Reynolds. London: Penguin Classics, Vol. 1 1975, Vol. 2 1977.
▸ Ariosto's classic tale in translation.

Barolsky, Paul. *Michelangelo's Nose: A Myth and its Maker*. University Park, PA: Pennsylvania State University Press, 1990.
▸ Based on Vasari's account of Michelangelo reducing the size of the nose on the *David*.

——. *Why Mona Lisa Smiles and Other Tales by Vasari*. University Park, PA: Pennsylvania State University Press, 1991.
▸ A discussion of the meaning of the smile in words and images.

Castiglione, Baldassare. *The Book of the Courtier*, trans. G. Bull. New York and London: Penguin Books, 1967.
▸ A study of manners and society in the Renaissance.

Cellini, Benvenuto. *Autobiography*, trans. J. A. Symonds, ed. John Pope-Hennessy. New York: Modern Library, 1985.
▸ Cellini's lively autobiography, through which a picture of his life and times emerges.

Cole, Bruce. *Titian and Venetian Painting: 1450–1590*. Boulder, CO: Westview Press, 1999.
▸ A brief account of Titian and the High Renaissance Venetian painters.

Hall, Marcia (ed.). *Raphael's School of Athens*. Cambridge, U.K.: Cambridge University Press, 1998.
▸ A collection of essays on the painting from different viewpoints.

Hauser, Arnold. *Mannerism: The Crisis of the Renaissance and the Origin of Modern Art*. Cambridge, MA: Harvard University Press, 1986.
▸ A Marxist history of art that looks at works in their economic context.

Kemp, Martin (ed.). *Leonardo on Painting*, trans. Martin Kemp and Margaret Walker. New Haven, CT: Yale University Press, 1989.
▸ An edition of Leonardo's writings on the art of painting.

Machiavelli, Niccolò. *The Prince*, trans. George Bull. London: Penguin Classics, 2003.
▸ A classic view of Renaissance politics.

Meilman, Patricia (ed.). *The Cambridge Companion to Titian*. New York: Cambridge University Press, 2004.
▸ Essays on Titian.

Ruggiero, Guido. *The Boundaries of Eros: Sex, Crime, and Sexuality in Renaissance Venice*. New York: Oxford University Press, 1985.
▸ A study of sexual crime and punishment in Venice.

——. *Binding Passions: Tales of Magic, Marriage, and Power at the End of the Renaissance*. New York: Oxford University Press, 1993.
▸ A social and psychological account of the late Renaissance.

Saslow, James M. *The Poetry of Michelangelo*. New Haven, CT, and London: Yale University Press, 1991.
▸ A translation of the artist's poetry.

Shearman, John K. G. *Mannerism*. Baltimore: Pelican Books, 1967.
▸ A survey of the style and the ideas behind it.

Vasari, Giorgio. *The Lives of the Most Eminent Painters, Sculptors, and Architects*, trans. Gaston du C. de Vere. New York: Random House, 1979.
▸ Biographies of Italian Renaissance artists from Cimabue to Vasari; concludes with Vasari's autobiography.

SUGGESTED FILMS

1950   *The Story of Michelangelo*, dir. Robert J. Flaherty and Richard Lyford

1965   *The Agony and the Ecstasy*, dir. Carol Reed

1969   *The Royal Hunt of the Sun*, dir. Irving Lerner

1990   *Cabeza de Vaca*, dir. Nicolás Echevarria

GLOSSARY

abacus the square element of the Doric capital.

agora an open public space in a city.

Althing in medieval Iceland, a general assembly governed according to a law code.

ambulatory in a church, the curved passageway that surrounds an apse.

antechamber a room before, and leading into, another room.

anthropomorphic human in form.

antiphon in music, a liturgical chant with a Latin text sung with a psalm.

antiphonal in music, a style of composition using two or more groups of performers to create effects of echo or contrast.

antipope the name given to a rival pope, often resident in Avignon, but not legitimized by the Roman Church.

apse the curved section at the end of a nave.

aqueduct a structure designed to transport water.

architrave the lowest long horizontal part of the entablature, which rests directly on the capital of a column.

archivolts the attached arches around the tympanum.

Ark of the Covenant the original container for the Tablets containing the Ten Commandments.

ashlar rectangular blocks of stone.

aulos (plural **auloi**) a double-reed pipe.

autocracy absolute rule by one person.

avant-garde newness for its own sake.

baptistery a building in which baptisms are performed.

barrel vault a vault made by extending a round arch through space.

bay a space in a building defined by piers.

Beghards in medieval northern Europe, a group of lay men dedicated to leading a spiritual life and working for the community.

Beguines in medieval northern Europe, a group of lay women who established spiritual centers.

benefice originally land granted for services, the word later included ecclesiastical offices.

bipedal able to walk upright on two feet.

burin a sharp instrument used for incising.

bust a sculpture or picture showing a figure from the head to just below the shoulders.

caliph a Muslim ruler or leader.

canonical authorized; used with reference to a collection of writings or works applying to a particular religion or author.

canopic jar a container for organs removed during mummification.

cantor in Jewish worship, the singer who chants Bible readings, prayers, or parts of the liturgy.

capital the decorated top of a column.

cartouche a rectangle with curved ends framing the name of a king.

caryatid a supporting column carved to represent a woman; the male equivalent is an *atlantis* (plural *atlantes*).

catacomb an underground burial place or cemetery, held sacred by the Romans.

catharsis "cleansing"; a term used by Aristotle to describe the emotional effect of a tragic drama on the audience.

centering a means of holding stones in place during the construction of an arch.

ceramics pottery made by firing (heating) clay.

chanson (French, "song") a secular polyphonic song in the Middle Ages and Renaissance; the form includes rondeaux, ballades, and virelais.

chivalry a code of values in which knights promised service and loyalty to a lord in return for protection.

chordal progression a sequence of chords.

chthonic relating to underground aspects of the earth.

citadel a fortified elevated area or city.

clerestory in a church or temple, an upper story of the nave, above the aisle, that is pierced with windows to admit light.

coffer a recessed geometric panel in a ceiling.

colonnade a row of columns.

column cluster a group of attached columns.

condottiere in medieval and Renaissance Italy, a soldier of fortune.

consort a set of musical instruments of the same family for playing music composed before about 1700.

contrapposto a type of pose characterized by a twist at the waist.

convention an accepted practice.

corbel brick or masonry courses arranged to form an arch or dome.

cornice the topmost horizontal part of an entablature.

courses layers of stone.

covenant a formal agreement; the conditional promises made between God and his people in the Bible.

creed a formal statement of the beliefs of a particular religion or philosophy.

cromlech a circle of stones, characteristic of the Neolithic period in western Europe.

cross-vault (or **groin vault**) a vault made by the intersection of two barrel vaults.

cuneiform a form of writing used in Mesopotamia and consisting of wedge-shaped characters.

cursive handwriting in flowing strokes with the letters joined together.

curvilinear having curved forms.

cyclopaean masonry huge stone blocks used to construct walls, especially in the Mycenaean citadels.

deme a unit of local government.

diptych a two-paneled painting.

discant in medieval music, a style in which the lower, tenor voice sings in a steady rhythm, while one or more higher voices sing slightly faster melodies above.

dithyramb a type of lyric poem sung and accompanied by flute music.

dome a hemispherical roof or ceiling; made by rotating a round arch.

dromos a roadway.

drum the circular support of a dome.

dynasty a family of kings.

echinus (Greek, "hedgehog") part of the Greek Orders above the abacus.

edda a type of Icelandic poetry that recounts myths and legends.

encaustic a type of paint in which beeswax is mixed with pigment.

engaged column a column that is attached to a wall.

entablature the portion above the capital on a column; it includes the architrave, the frieze, and the cornice.

entasis (Greek, "stretching") the bulge in the shaft of a Greek column.

epithet an identifying adjective or phrase.

equestrian monument a portrait of a ruler on horseback.

Exodus the forty-year journey made by the Israelites, led by Moses, out of Egypt to freedom; also, the second book of the Hebrew Bible.

falling action the means by which a complication in a literary work is unraveled and resolved.

fealty an oath of allegiance sworn by a vassal to a lord.

feudalism in medieval Europe, a fluid political, military, and social organization based on mutual obligations between lords and their vassals, who swore allegiance to them.

finial a decorative feature at the top of an object or building.

foliate leaf-shaped.

foreshortened shown in perspective.

forum the public center of an ancient Roman city.

freeman a property-owning peasant, who turned the property over to a lord in return for protection and certain economic and legal rights.

fresco a technique of applying water-based paint to a damp plaster surface, usually a wall or ceiling.

friar a member of a mendicant ("begging") Order.

frieze the central section of an entablature, often containing relief sculpture.

frontal facing front.

frottola a lighthearted, generally amorous poem for three or four voices sung to instrumental accompaniment, usually chordal in style.

gallery a row of figures.

gesso a white coating of chalk, plaster, and resin that is applied to a surface to make it more receptive to paint.

ghazal a Middle Eastern poem in couplets having strict meter and a double rhyme scheme.

glaze a translucent paint layer that enriches colors.

gorgoneion the severed head of the Gorgon Medusa.

guild an organization of workers within a particular craft.

helot a member of the native population enslaved by the Spartans.

heresy a belief or practice that is contrary to established Church teaching.

hierarchical proportion a convention in ancient art in which size is equated with status.

hieratic a cursive script derived from hieroglyphs.

hieroglyphs a writing system using pictorial representations as characters.

hoplite a heavily armed ancient Greek foot-soldier who fought in close formation (phalanx).

hoplon a shield carried by a hoplite.

hubris arrogant grandiosity, often characterizing Greek tragic heroes.

humanism an intellectual and artistic trend, beginning in the late thirteenth century and based on a renewed interest in the Classical tradition.

hymn a song praising a god.

hypostyle a hall with a roof supported by rows of columns; the center columns are taller than those at the sides.

icon a sacred image.

iconoclasm the destruction of religious images.

iconography the apparent meaning of an image and its underlying symbolism.

iconophile someone who supports religious imagery.

ideogram a pictorial representation of an idea.

idyll a short descriptive poem describing rural life.

illumination the decoration of biblical and other sacred manuscript texts with painted images.

illusionistic a type of representation in which objects appear real.

impost the support of an arch attached to a wall.

incise to cut designs or letters into wood or metal with a sharp instrument.

Inquisitors officials appointed by the Roman Church to combat heresy.

intaglio a process in which lines or images are incised in a surface.

interval in music, a difference in pitch between two notes.

irony a literary device in which the implication of the words is the opposite of their literal meaning.

isocephaly the horizontal alignment of heads in a painting or sculpture.

isorhythm in fourteenth-century music, the use of a repeated rhythmic scheme, usually applied to a plainsong melody.

kennings concrete, compound words used to enrich a narrative.

keystone in a round arch, the top center stone holding the voussoirs in place.

knight in the Middle Ages, a man who carried out military service in return for the right to hold land.

krater an ancient Greek vessel in which wine and water are mixed.

lancet a tall, narrow arched window.

lapis lazuli a semi-precious, light blue stone.

Lares and Penates Roman household gods.

lay a short poem, sung to the accompaniment of a harp.

libation the pouring of a drink as an offering to a god.

Linear A undeciphered Minoan writing used for record-keeping and religious dedications.

Linear B readable Mycenaean script; an early form of Greek.

lintel a horizontal cross-beam.

litany a type of prayer in which a leader and a congregation speak alternately.

liturgy rites of worship.

lunette a half-moon shaped wall section.

maat the Egyptian concept of cosmic order, truth, and justice; also (when capitalized) the name of the goddess embodying those qualities.

madrigal a secular contrapuntal song for several voices, from the Renaissance.

mandorla an oval of light around the entire body.

manor in the Middle Ages, a group of farms and villages.

manorialism in medieval Europe, a social system organized around a manor in which a landlord allowed peasants to live and work on the land in exchange for a percentage of their produce and other obligations.

maqam in Arabic music, a specific scale having certain phrases and patterns.

martyr a person who dies for his or her beliefs (the meaning of the Greek word is "witness").

martyrium (plural **martyria**) a structure built over the tomb of a martyr.

master-builder one who supervises the building of a cathedral.

mausoleum (plural **mausolea**) a large, elaborate round tomb.

mayor of the palace in Merovingian France, the king's major-domo (prime minister) and often the real ruler.

megalithic a Neolithic structure made of large stones.

megaron the main building in the Mycenaean citadel.

melismatic music in which several notes are sung to one syllable.

mendicant a member of a religious Order who wandered from town to town begging.

menhir a single upright stone.

menorah a candelabrum with seven candlesticks, three on each side and one in the center.

metaphor a comparison without using "like" or "as" in which one thing stands for another.

meter in music, regular division into set numbers of rhythmic beats.

metope the square area between the triglyphs of a Doric frieze, often containing relief sculpture.

minaret a thin tower on the exterior of a mosque.

minstrel a wandering performer who sang secular songs in medieval courts.

minuscule a small cursive script.

miracle play a medieval religious play dramatizing miracles.

misogynist someone who dislikes and distrusts women.

mode in ancient music, an arrangement of notes forming a scale; Dorian mode: strong and military; Phrygian mode: passionate; Lydian mode: mournful; Mixolydian mode: elegiac.

monophonic consisting of a single line of music.

monotheism a religion whose adherents believe in a single god.

morality play a medieval religious play that gives dramatic form to the human struggle between good and evil.

mosaic an image on a wall, ceiling, or floor created from small pieces of colored tile, glass, or stone.

motet a polyphonic choral work, generally written in Latin for church performance; some early motets were secular and multilingual.

muezzin in Islam, a crier who calls the faithful to prayer from a minaret.

mummification in ancient Egypt, a process taking seventy-two days in which bodies were embalmed and organs were removed.

mystery (or **mystery cult**) cultish religion, based on ancient myths, of a type that was common in Greece and throughout the Roman Empire.

mystery play a medieval religious play based on a Bible story.

narrative sequence a story that follows chronologically.

narthex a vestibule or porch across the west end of a church.

natural selection Darwin's theory of the survival of species best adapted to their environment.

naturalistic representing objects as they actually appear in nature.

nave in basilicas, a wide central aisle separated from the side aisles by rows of columns.

necking the lowest of three elements comprising the capital of a Greek column.

necropolis (plural **necropoleis**) a city of the dead.

neume in plainsong, a diagonal mark indicating a note or group of notes over the word to be sung.

nominalism in philosophy, the belief that universals (general ideas, abstract concepts) are nothing more than names; the opposite of realism.

obelisk a tall, pointed, square pillar.

obverse the front of a coin.

Ockham's razor the principle of reducing—shaving—an assumption to its simplest form.

octave in music, the interval between two notes of the same name, twelve semitones apart; in poetry, a stanza of eight lines.

oculus a round opening in a wall or ceiling.

ode a lyric poem.

oligarchy a form of government by a few people.

onomatopoeic the use of words that sound like the objects to which they refer.

oracle the revelation of a god, the person who utters the revelation, or the place the revelation is spoken.

Order one of the architectural systems—Doric, Ionic, Corinthian—used by the Greeks to build their temples.

organum a form of plainsong in which two or more melodic lines are sung at once; a type of polyphony.

orthogonal consisting of, or relating to, right angles, or a line perpendicular to the plane of a relief or a picture.

oxymoron a figure of speech using an apparent contradiction.

pagoda in Buddhist architecture, a multi-tiered tower that contains relics.

paradox a statement that seems to contradict common sense.

parchment the treated and dyed skin of a sheep or calf used for manuscripts.

pastoral a poem dealing with the life and loves of shepherds.

pediment the triangular section at the end of a gable-roof, often decorated with sculpture.

pendentive an architectural feature resembling a curved triangle between the lunettes of a dome.

peristyle the freestanding columns surrounding a building.

personify embody as a person.

phalanx an ancient Greek military formation in which heavily armed soldiers lined up close together in deep ranks, defended by a wall of shields.

pharaoh a king of ancient Egypt.

phonogram an image denoting sounds.

pictographic based on pictures.

pier a vertical support, usually rectangular.

pigment a substance used to give color to paints, inks, and dyes.

pilaster a square column.

pitch in music, height or depth of a tone.

plainsong (sometimes called **plainchant** or **Gregorian chant**) unaccompanied monophonic music sung to Latin texts as part of a church service.

plaque a small, decorated slab.

podium (plural **podia**) the masonry forming the base (usually rectangular) of a temple, arch, or other building.

polis (plural **poleis**) a city-state in ancient Greece.

polyphony a form of music in which two or more melodic lines are sung at once.

polytheism belief in many gods.

Poor Clares nuns who belong to the Order of Abbess Clare.

post-and-lintel an elevation system in which two upright posts support a horizontal lintel; also called a trilithon.

precinct a sacred area.

prehistory a period of history before the development of writing systems.

profile the side view of a figure or object.

program in art, a series of related images.

proportion the relation of one part to another and of parts to the whole in terms of scale.

prothesis the lying-in-state of the dead.

psalter a psalm book.

pylon in ancient Egypt, a massive trapezoidal gateway.

pyramid an Egyptian tomb.

Pythagorean theorem a theory developed by Pythagoras: the square of the hypotenuse of a right-angled triangle equals the sum of the squares of the other two sides.

qawwâli a genre of Muslim devotional song, generally with lyrics in Urdu, popular in north India and Pakistan, typically sung by two to four vocalists, with hand-clapping, harmonium, and barrel-drum accompaniment.

radiating chapels chapels placed around an ambulatory.

rayonnant a style in Gothic rose windows in which shapes of glass radiate from the small circle at the center.

realism in philosophy, the belief that universals (general ideas, abstract concepts) have an objective existence; the opposite of nominalism.

relics the physical remains of saints and martyrs or objects associated with them.

relief a sculpture that is not completely carved away from its original material.

relieving triangle in architecture, a space that reduces the weight on the lintel below it.

reliquary a container housing a sacred relic.

resolution the outcome of a literary narrative.

responsorial a style of music in which a soloist alternates with congregational or choral responses.

reverse the back of a coin.

rhetoric the art of eloquent argument.

rhyton a drinking cup.

rib vault a vault made by the intersection of pointed arches.

romance a medieval tale in a Romance language depicting heroic deeds.

rose window a large, round window in Gothic cathedrals.

round a musical form in which each voice enters in turn with the same music after the previous one has sung several measures.

rule in monasteries, a systematic regimen.

rune-stone a large, upright memorial stone engraved with runic text.

rusticate to give a rustic appearance to masonry blocks by roughening their surface and beveling their edges.

saga an Icelandic story that mixes history, legend, myth, and folk tradition.

scaldic a type of Norse poetry that recounts tales of kings and heroes.

scholasticism a system of thought developed in the Gothic period that addressed the apparent contradiction of faith and reason.

scop a type of German performer who sang tales of Germanic heroes in the fifth to seventh centuries.

scribe in ancient Egypt, a professional record-keeper, usually a member of the court.

scriptorium (plural **scriptoria**) a room for writing, usually in a monastery.

serf a peasant worker unable to leave the land.

shaman a religious figure believed to have supernatural powers, including the ability of self-transformation from human to animal.

simile a comparison using "like" or "as."

simony the selling of spiritual benefices.

sistrum a type of rattle.

spandrel in architecture, the triangular area between (1) two adjacent arches or (2) the side of an arch and the right angle that encloses it.

sphinx a human-headed lion.

split choir a choir in which groups of singers sing against, or in response to, each other.

springing the upward thrust of an arch.

stained glass pieces of colored glass held in place in windows by strips of lead.

stele a vertical stone marker or pillar.

stigmata marks resembling Christ's wounds on the Cross.

stupa in Buddhist architecture, a round structure derived from the Buddha's burial mound.

stylization a technique in art in which forms are rendered as surface patterns rather than naturalistically

stylobate the top step from which a Doric column rises.

syllogism a logical system of deductive reasoning, in which a conclusion follows from a major and a minor premise.

symmetry a type of balance in which two sides of an object or picture are mirror images of each other.

symposium a type of Greek banquet.

syncretism a process through which differing belief systems are assimilated.

synoptic referring to three books of the New Testament, the Gospels of Matthew, Mark, and Luke, which are considered to form a group.

Tablets (**Tables**) **of the Law** the stones on which were inscribed the laws given to Moses on Mount Sinai.

taqsim in Arabic music, an improvised elaboration of *maqams* in a free-rhythmic style.

template a diagram of an architectural section used by master-builders.

tenor in medieval music, the low voice singing long held notes of plainchant in polyphonic pieces.

tetrachord a series of four notes, with the first and last separated by the interval of a perfect fourth.

tetrarchy a form of government by four co-rulers.

thalassocracy rule through the control of the sea.

theocracy rule by priests or other religious leaders.

tholos (plural **tholoi**) a circular tomb of beehive shape.

tondo a painting or relief sculpture having a round frame.

tragic flaw in theater, a characteristic of a hero that causes his or her downfall.

transept in a church, the cross-section corresponding to the arms of the Cross.

transi tomb a tomb with an effigy of the deceased in a state of decay.

translate in religion, to transfer or remove to another place.

transubstantiation in the Mass, a process in which bread and wine are believed to be transformed literally into Christ's body and blood.

transverse arch in a church or cathedral, an arch that spans the nave.

travertine a type of pale limestone, used in Roman building, that turns yellow as it ages.

triadic based on the three notes of the "common" chord in Western music, using notes 1, 3, and 5 of the scale.

triglyphs in a Doric frieze, the three verticals between the metopes.

trilithon a single post-and-lintel.

trilogy a set of three related works of literature.

trireme an ancient Greek warship with an iron-covered prow.

trope a passage, with or without words, inserted in Gregorian chant.

trumeau the central vertical support of a lintel or tympanum above a wide doorway.

tufa soft, easily workable, volcanic rock, used in Etruscan building.

Tuscan column a form of Doric style, used by the Etruscans.

tympanum in Christian architecture, the curved triangular area between an arch and the lintel below it.

tyranny a form of rule in which power is concentrated in a single person.

tyrant an illegitimate leader who exercises absolute power, often oppressively.

vanishing point in linear perspective, the point at which the orthogonals meet.

vassal in the Middle Ages, a man who held land in return for duties of allegiance to a lord.

vignette a small section of decoration or a literary sketch.

villa in ancient Rome, a country estate.

voussoir a wedge-shaped stone used in round arches.

whirling dervish a Sufi ascetic who seeks divine ecstasy through whirling to music.

woodcut or **woodblock print** an image incised on a block of wood and printed on paper.

word painting in a vocal work, the musical illustration of the meaning of a word.

ziggurat in Mesopotamia, a monumental stepped building signifying a mountain.

LITERARY CREDITS

Laurence King Publishing, the author, and the literary permissions researcher wish to thank the publishers and individuals who have kindly allowed their copyright material to be reproduced in this book, as listed below. Every effort has been made to contact copyright holders, but should there be any errors or omissions, Laurence King Publishing would be pleased to insert the appropriate acknowledgment in any subsequent edition of this publication.

Starter Kit

p. xxi From "Happy Birthday to You" by Mildred J. Hill, © 1935 by Jessica Hill, administered by International Music Publications Ltd., U.K., on behalf of Warner Chappell Music, reprinted by permission of International Music Publications, London. All Rights Reserved.

p. xxii From Derek Walcott, *Omeros* (New York: Farrar, Straus and Giroux, 1990).

Chapter 2

pp. 16, 24, 25, 27 From *Gilgamesh*, translated by John Gardner and John Maier (New York: Alfred A. Knopf, 1984), © 1984 by Estate of John Gardner and John Maier.

Chapter 3

p. 40 From *Ancient Egyptian Literature: An Anthology*, translated by John L. Foster (Austin, TX: University of Texas Press, 2001), © 2001.

p. 46 From *The British Museum Book of Ancient Egypt*, edited by Stephen Quirke and Jeffrey Spencer (London: British Museum Press, 1992).

pp. 46–47, 49, 53–54 *Ancient Egyptian Literature: An Anthology*, op. cit.

p. 55 From T. G. H. James, *An Introduction to Ancient Egypt* (New York: Farrar, Straus and Giroux, 1979).

p. 61 *Ancient Egyptian Literature: An Anthology*, op. cit.

Chapter 4

pp. 74, 75 From Homer, *The Iliad*, translated by Robert Fagles (New York: Viking Penguin, 1990), © 1990 by Robert Fagles.

p. 77 From *Aeschylus: Volume II, LCL 146*, translated by Herbert Weir Smyth, Cambridge, MA: Harvard University Press, © 1926 by the President and Fellows of Harvard College. The Loeb Classical Library ® is a registered trademark of the President and Fellows of Harvard College.

Chapter 5

pp. 102–103 From *Anacreon: Volume II, LCL 143*, translated by David A. Campbell, Cambridge, MA: Harvard University Press, © 1988 by the President and Fellows of Harvard College. The Loeb Classical Library ® is a registered trademark of the President and Fellows of Harvard College.

Chapter 6

pp. 129–130 From *Euripides: Volume III, LCL 11*, translated by A. S. Way, Cambridge, MA: Harvard University Press, 1912. The Loeb Classical Library ® is a registered trademark of the President and Fellows of Harvard College.

p. 130 From *Aristophanes: Volume II, LCL 488*, translated by Jeffrey Henderson, Cambridge, MA: Harvard University Press, © 1998 by the President and Fellows of Harvard College. The Loeb Classical Library ® is a registered trademark of the President and Fellows of Harvard College.

p. 130 From *Thucydides: Volume 1, LCL 108*, translated by C. F. Smith, Cambridge, MA: Harvard University Press, 1919, © 1928 by the President and Fellows of Harvard College. The Loeb Classical Library ® is a registered trademark of the President and Fellows of Harvard College.

p. 131 From *Aristophanes: Volume III, LCL 180*, translated by B. B. Rogers, Cambridge, MA: Harvard University Press, © 1924 by the President and Fellows of Harvard College. The Loeb Classical Library ® is a registered trademark of the President and Fellows of Harvard College.

p. 138 From *Greek Bucolic Poets [Theocritus], LCL 28*, translated by J. M. Edmonds, Cambridge, MA: Harvard University Press, 1912. The Loeb Classical Library ® is a registered trademark of the President and Fellows of Harvard College.

Chapter 7

p. 161 From *Plautus: Four Comedies*, edited by Erich Segal (translator) (Oxford: Oxford University Press, 1996).

p. 162 From *The Poems of Catullus*, edited by Arthur Guy Lee (translator) (Oxford: Oxford University Press, 1990).

pp. 162–163 From *Horace: The Complete Odes and Epodes*, edited by David West (translator) (Oxford: Oxford University Press, 2000).

p. 175 From Suetonius, *The Twelve Caesars*, translated by Robert Graves (London: Penguin Classics, 1957).

p. 176 From Petronius, *The Satyricon*, translated by J. P. Sullivan (London: Penguin, 1965, 1977), © J. P. Sullivan, 1965, 1969, 1974, 1977, 1986.

Chapter 9

p. 233 From *The Arabian Nights: The Thousand and One Nights*, translated by Husain Haddawy (New York: W. W. Norton, 1990), © 1990 by W. W. Norton and Company, Inc.

p. 233 From Coleman Barks and John Mayne, *The Essential Rumi* (New York: HarperCollins, 1997).

p. 234 From *Drunk on the Wine of the Beloved: 100 Poems of Hafiz*, translated by Thomas Rain Crowe (Boston, MA: Shambhala Publications, 2001), © 2001.

Chapter 10

pp. 251, 252 From *Everyman and Medieval Miracle Plays*, edited by A. C. Cawley (London: Phoenix Editions, 1993).

pp. 254, 255 From *Beowulf: A New Verse Translation* by Seamus Heaney (New York: W. W. Norton, 2001), © 2000 by Seamus Heaney.

p. 259 From *The Poetic Edda*, translated by Lee M. Hollander, 2nd edition, revised (Austin, TX: University of Texas Press, 1990), © 1962, renewed 1990.

Chapter 11

p. 276 From BULL *Summis desiderantes*, published by Pope Innocent VIII (December 5, 1484), from *Translations and Reprints from the Original Sources of European History*, published by the Department of History of the University of Pennsylvania, Philadelphia, University of Pennsylvania Press (1897?–1907?), Volume III: 4, pp. 7–10. Fordham University Center for Medieval Studies, Internet History Sourcebooks Project, edited by Paul Halsall. Online at www.fordham.edu/halsall/sources/witches1.html.

p. 279 From *Abbot Suger on the Abbey Church of St.-Denis and Its Treasures* by Erwin Panofsky (Princeton, NJ: Princeton University Press, 1979).

pp. 293–294 From *The Divine Comedy, Volume 1: The Inferno* by Dante Alighieri, translated by Mark Musa (Bloomington: Indiana University Press, 1997).

pp. 295, 296 From *The Divine Comedy* by Dante Alighieri, translated by John Ciardi (New York: W. W. Norton, 1980), © 1954, 1957, 1959, 1960, 1961, 1965, 1967, 1970 by the Ciardi Family Publishing Trust.

Chapter 12

p. 298 From Petrarch, *Canzoniere and Other Writings*, edited by Mark Musa (translator) (New York: Oxford University Press, 1999).

p. 313 From Geoffrey Chaucer, *The Canterbury Tales*, translated by Nevill Coghill (London: Penguin Classics, 1951, fourth revised edition 1977), © 1951 by Nevill Coghill, © the Estate of Nevill Coghill, 1958, 1960, 1975, 1977.

p. 316 *Canzoniere and Other Writings*, op. cit.

p. 316 From *Petrarch's Africa*, translated by Thomas G. Bergin and Alice S. Wilson (New Haven, CT: Yale University Press, 1977).

Chapter 13

p. 359 From *The Cambridge Music Guide*, edited by Stanley Sadie with Alison Latham (New York: Cambridge University Press, 1990).

PICTURE CREDITS

Laurence King Publishing, the author, and the picture researcher wish to thank the institutions and individuals that have kindly provided photographic material for use in this book. Museum, gallery, and library locations are given in the captions; further details and other sources are listed below.

Abbreviations
AKG: Archiv für Kunst und Geschichte, London
BPK: Bildarchiv Preussischer Kulturbesitz, Berlin
Maeyaert: © Paul M. R. Maeyaert, El Tossal, Spain
Mauzy: Craig and Marie Mauzy, Athens. mauzy@otenet.gr
MET: The Metropolitan Museum of Art, New York
MFA: The Museum of Fine Arts, Boston
NGA: The National Gallery of Art, Washington, D.C.
Pirozzi: © Vincenzo Pirozzi, Rome. fotopirozzi@inwind.it
RMN: Réunion des Musées Nationaux, Paris
SMB: Scala, Florence—courtesy of the Ministero Beni e Att. Culturali

Chapter 1
Chapter opener (Stonehenge) A. F. Kersting, London
1.1, 1.4 Colorphoto Hans Hinz, Switzerland
1.2a, 1.2b, 1.7 AKG
1.5 Photo Yanik Le Guillou
1.6 Reproduced by permission of Prentice Hall, Inc., from Stokstad, Art History, 2nd edition (2001). © Pearson Education
1.8 © English Heritage Photo Library. Photographer Sky Eye Aerial Photography
1.10 © G. Chaloupka, Australia
1.11 Rock Art Research Unit, University of Witwatersrand, South Africa
1.12 Photo Monika Heidermann

Chapter 2
2.2, 2.7, 2.9, 2.17, 2.18, 2.19 © Hirmer Archive, Munich
2.4a, 2.4b RMN/Hervé Lewandowski
2.5 John Hay Library, Brown University, Rhode Island
2.6 © Ashmolean Museum, Oxford
2.8 BPK. Photo Gudrun Stenzel
2.10 © British Museum, London
2.12, 2.13, 2.14 © Photo Josse, Paris
2.15 Ancient Art and Architecture Collection, Harrow, U.K.
2.16 Robert Harding World Imagery, London
2.20 BPK
2.21 Werner Forman Archive
2.22 Courtesy of the Oriental Institute of the University of Chicago
2.23 © Danny Lehman/CORBIS
2.24 Bridgeman Art Library, London
2.25 Pirozzi
2.26 Photo Jerry L. Thompson
2.27 MA.36.21.62, Musée de l'Homme, Paris

Chapter 3
3.1 SMB
3.2a, 3.2b © Jurgen Liepe, Berlin
3.3, 3.4, 3.6, 3.7, 3.11, 3.12, 3.20 © British Museum, London
3.5a, 3.5b, 3.5c MFA. Gift of the Egypt Exploration Fund. 95.1407a
3.8 Maeyaert
3.9 Werner Forman Archive/Dr. E. Strouhal
3.13 AKG/Andrea Jemolo
3.15, 3.16, 3.22, 3.31 © 1997 Photo Scala, Florence
3.17 Courtesy of the Oriental Institute of the University of Chicago
3.18 Reproduced by permission, from Robins, Women in Ancient Egypt, British Museum Press (1993)
3.19 MET. Purchase: Edward S. Harkness Gift 1926. 26.7.1450. Photograph © 1997 The Metropolitan Museum of Art
3.21 MET. Rogers Fund and Edward S. Harkness Gift, 1929
3.24 Brooklyn Museum, New York. Charles Edwin Wilbour Fund 39.602
3.25 © Araldo de Luca, Rome

3.26 Drawing by Philip Winton, from Richard H. Wilkinson, The Complete Temples of Ancient Egypt, Thames and Hudson, Inc., New York (2000)
3.27 Robert Harding World Imagery, London
3.28 Klaus-Peter Kuhlmann
3.30a, 3.30b BPK. Photo Margaret Büsing
3.32 AKG/Erich Lessing

Chapter 4
4.1, 4.4, 4.5, 4.6a, 4.6b, 4.8, 4.10, 4.12, 4.13, 4.16, 4.17 Mauzy
4.2 R. A. Higgins, The Archaeology of Minoan Crete, Henry Z. Walck (1973). © Random House, Inc.
4.3 Studio Kontos Photography
4.7 Courtesy John G. Younger
4.9 © Thera Foundation
4.14 Fondazione Giorgio Cini, Istituto di Storia dell'Arte, Venice
4.15 Courtesy of Ekdotike Athenon, S.A.

Chapter 5
5.1 Reproduced by permission of Thames and Hudson, Ltd., from Boardman, Greek Art (1985)
5.2 Reproduced by permission of Phaidon Press, from Richter, Handbook of Greek Art (1959)
5.3 © 1990 Photo Scala, Florence
5.4, 5.15a, 5.15b, 5.20 Mauzy
5.6 MET. Rogers Fund, 1921. Photograph © 1996 The Metropolitan Museum of Art
5.7, 5.23, 5.24, 5.25 Staatliche Antikensammlungen und Glyptothek, Munich
5.8, 5.12, 5.26 © British Museum, London
5.9 Pirozzi
5.11 Photo Devos, Boulogne
5.13a, 5.13b MFA. Henry Lillie Pierce Fund, 99.538. Photo © 2004 Museum of Fine Arts, Boston
5.17, 5.22 Reproduced by permission of Thames and Hudson, Ltd., from Boardman, Greek Sculpture: The Archaic Period (1978)
5.18 Reproduced by permission of Thomson Learning, from Cunningham and Reich, Culture and Values, 5th edition (2002)
5.27 Robert Harding World Imagery, London

Chapter 6
6.1a, 6.5, 6.8, 6.19, 6.38 Mauzy
6.1b, 6.18 Studio Kontos/Photostock, Athens, Greece
6.2, 6.27, 6.29, 6.32, 6.37 © Fotografica Foglia, Naples
6.3 Pirozzi
6.4 Alinari/Art Resource, New York
6.6, 6.9, 6.24 AKG/Peter Connolly
6.11 By permission of the Royal Ontario Museum. © ROM
6.12 Professor Ernst Berger, Antikenmuseum Basle und Sammlung Ludwig. Drawing by Miriam Cahn
6.13, 6.14, 6.15, 6.16, 6.17, 6.20a, 6.20b, 6.23 © British Museum, London
6.21, 6.34 Staatliche Antikensammlungen und Glyptothek, Munich
6.22, 6.33 © Hirmer Archive, Munich
6.26 Vatican Museums, Rome. Photo M. Sarri
6.28 SMB
6.30, 6.31 Photograph by John C. Huntingdon, Courtesy of the Huntingdon Archive, Ohio State University
6.35 © Photo Josse, Paris
6.36 © Araldo de Luca, Rome

Chapter 7
7.1 © 2003 Photo Scala, Florence/Fotografica Foglia
7.2 © Quattrone, Florence
7.3, 7.7, 7.8, 7.10, 7.14, 7.24, 7.25, 7.29, 7.30, 7.37, 7.41 Pirozzi
7.4a MET. Rogers Fund, 1909
7.5, 7.32, 7.33, 7.34 SMB
7.6, 7.13, 7.31 © Araldo de Luca, Rome
7.11 Maeyaert
7.12 AKG/Pirozzi

INDEX